D1317380

JAMES B. DUKE MEMORIAL LIBRARY
JOHNSON C. SMITH UNIVERSITY
CHARLOTTE, N. C. 28216

COMPUTERS AND COMPUTER LANGUAGES

McGraw-Hill Publications in Electronic Computer Technology

Gordon Silverman, Project Editor

Books in This Series:

SMALL COMPUTER THEORY AND APPLICATIONS by Denton J. Dailey
MATHEMATICS FOR COMPUTERS by Arthur D. Kramer
INTEGRATED CIRCUITS FOR COMPUTERS: PRINCIPLES AND APPLICATIONS by William L. Schweber
COMPUTERS AND COMPUTER LANGUAGES by Gordon Silverman and David Turkiew
DIGITAL TECHNOLOGY WITH MOS INTEGRATED CIRCUITS by Ronald J. Webb

COMPUTERS AND COMPUTER LANGUAGES

GORDON SILVERMAN
Fairleigh Dickinson University

DAVID TURKIEW
New York City Technical College

McGRAW-HILL BOOK COMPANY

New York Atlanta Dallas St. Louis San Francisco Auckland Bogotá Guatemala Hamburg Lisbon London Madrid Mexico Milan Montreal New Delhi Panama Paris San Juan São Paulo Singapore Sydney Tokyo Toronto

Dedicated to our wives, Rosyln and Rachel

Sponsoring Editor: John J. Beck
Associate Editor: Paul Sobel
Editing Supervisor: Melonie Parnes
Design Supervisor/Cover Designer: Nancy Axelrod
Production Supervisor: Catherine Bokman

Cover Photo: James Nazz

Library of Congress Cataloging-in-Publication Data

Silverman, Gordon.
Computers and computer languages.

Includes index.
1. Electronic digital computers. 2. Programming languages (Electronic computers). I. Turkiew, David. II. Title.
QA76.5.S5524 1987 004 86-21070
ISBN 0-07-057523-1

Computers and Computer Languages

1 2 3 4 5 6 7 8 9 0 DOCDOC 8 9 4 3 2 1 0 9 8 7

ISBN 0-07-057523-1

CONTENTS

PREFACE

Computers and Computer Languages is written for students preparing for careers in computers, electronics, and electricity, and their related technical fields. Technically trained individuals need to be both conversant about computers and able to speak with computers. This text provides the students with an accurate, up-to-date introduction to computers and the two most widely taught and used languages, BASIC and Pascal. Upon completing this text, students can say that they *know* computers and how to *speak* to them.

The text requires very few prerequisites on the part of the students. We assume that the students have not had any extensive preparation in electronics or mathematics beyond high school algebra. This text is intended to satisfy curricular needs of explaining computer organization and operation in a basic way.

We have made an effort to use language that is familiar to the students, including the computer terminology that students and instructors use in the classroom, and some of the popular phrases and jargon associated with technical environments. Overall, our goal is to present a comprehensive survey of computers, while also giving the student firsthand experience in computer programming.

The organization of the book is flexible so that either BASIC or Pascal can be studied following the general introduction to computers. The functional approach that we have taken requires very little preparation on the part of the student. Thus, *Computers and Computer Languages* can accommodate a variety of curricular alternatives.

In principle, the text has two focal points—the computer itself, and the languages, BASIC and Pascal. The first ten chapters contain a functional description of the computer. This includes the architecture of the principal parts of the machines: the CPU, the memory, and input/output. A discussion of the data that the computer processes follows this material. Once the hardware and the data, are described, the student is ready to explore the nature of computer languages.

Chapters 11 to 23 describe the rules for the two computer languages, BASIC and Pascal. These are among the most widely used and most frequently implemented languages presently found in the technical, industrial, commercial, and business environments, areas where students are likely to choose their career opportunities.

Wherever possible, we have used the elements of each language that are found in the most popular language versions in use today. This enhances the ability of the student to transfer skills and understand programs that are written in other dialects of the languages.

Concerning our approach to teaching computer programming, we know that there are many ways to teach students the skills needed to understand and use these computer languages. One such method explains the rules of syntax. The student can study these rules, but may still not understand the way in which the language and the computer interact. The student may not comprehend what occurs within the computer for a command phrase such as "C = A + B" beyond the fact that such a statement will cause two numbers to be added together. With the evolution of so many new languages, a simple change in the format of such a statement to "C := A + B" is not understood by the student. Rote learning can therefore hinder the transfer of skills to new linguistic situations. The approach taken in this text avoids knowledge obsolescence by incorporating material that describes how control phrases are constructed. We call this a *generic* approach, in contrast to the rote learning method.

The text explains the rules of syntax of the two computer languages, but with a significant difference: The languages are discussed within the context of the machine itself. Thus, when a student OPENs a file within the secondary storage system of the machine, the instructor does not require that he or she simply copy such statements in the program without question. The student will have a grasp of the input/output operations of the machine, and file opening will become a natural, functional part of the computer control sequence. We think that instructors will welcome this fresh, active learning approach, which reinforces theory with hands-on experience.

In addition to the generic approach used in this text, the examples and problems, which are used to reinforce learning, are taken from "real-life" industrial stituations. These learning devices reflect the kinds of experiences that computer technologists are likely to encounter.

Whenever possible, the examples are kept short and easy to read and understand. Each example is designed to illustrate a point relating to either the computer or the computer language. We have made a concerted attempt to keep extraneous details to a minimum. In this way students can readily absorb the pertinent information. In many cases, however, we felt that extra detail would aid the students in finding their way through more intricate program assignments. In either case, by providing students with step-by-step programming aids and suggestions, we are hopeful that they will not become lost in the syntactical details. In this way students will understand the important information regarding the way computers and their languages are used as tools to solve technical problems.

In this text, a given industrial problem, such as process control, is addressed from different points of view in the various examples. The students retain a clear goal without losing sight of the important facts and rules.

To maintain students motivation, this textbook includes numerous illustrations that will help students focus on key basic concepts. Problems are given at the end of each major topic within a chapter to help reinforce student understanding before the next chapter is begun. The problems are generally organized in increasing order of difficulty, and they vary from ones that reinforce basic principles to ones that challenge a student's programming creativity.

We would like to acknowledge the help of the many instructors who responded to the preliminary research survey and made this book possible. Special thanks are in order to Frank T. Gergelyi, Robert T. Campbell, Nelda Cuppy, Richard A. Pointer, Dr. Norman H. Sprankle, Robert C. Blanchard, and Frank T. Duda for their thorough review of the manuscript, which helped produce a pedagogically sound and timely textbook.

Gordon Silverman
David Turkiew

1 INTRODUCING COMPUTER PURPOSES

Computers have an important impact on our daily work and leisure activities. The food that we eat, for example, might have been produced as a result of decisions aided by a computer; factors such as crop rotation, acreage, and type of fertilizer are commonly computer-analyzed by modern farmers. This text, for example, was written with the help of a computer. Word processing software makes the composition and editing involved a far less time-consuming effort. In an increasing number of situations, the computer is a visible component of engineering, manufacturing, scientific, business, and other activities.

This chapter briefly describes the history of the computer. It also discusses the elements of a modern computer and the roles they play in making the computer a useful tool for solving problems.

1-1 HISTORY

Commerce and war—these two human endeavors have had the greatest effect on the development of the computer. A merchant intent on trading goods in distant places needs to ship those goods over long distances. Until recent times, navigation was based upon the position of the moon during the year. Such information was presented in the form of tables. Many calculations are necessary to produce such tables, introducing the possibility of error when those calculations are performed by human beings.

During the eighteenth century many machines were invented to free human beings from the dull but simple tasks of addition, subtraction, multiplication, and division. Such machines carried out arithmetic calculations automatically and could be used as aids or tools in computing the navigation tables. They were the forerunners of today's computing machines, mechanical versions of the electronic pocket calculators which many students carry today.

The most dramatic period in the development of computing machines occurred during World War II, especially in the United States. Ironically, the motivation for such machines was again based on the need to send a product—in this case, an artillery shell or bomb—over a relatively long distance and have it arrive accurately at its intended destination. The path that such missiles follow is based on many factors, including the firing angle, the type of propellant used, the temperature and density of the air, and the aerodynamic qualities of the projectile. Such information exists in the form of tables, called *ordnance tables*. To produce such tables requires many calculations. If these are performed on a machine, they are accomplished swiftly and usually without error.

Many people have contributed to the evolution of the computer. Changes in the design—or *architecture,* in the jargon of computer technology—occur all the time. Table 1-1 lists a few of the many outstanding contri-

TABLE 1-1 IMPORTANT PEOPLE AND EVENTS IN EARLY COMPUTER HISTORY

1580	Francis Vieta: Uses letters for unknowns
1614	John Napier: Logarithms
1632	William Oughtred, Richard Delamain: Slide rule
1637	René Descartes: Analytic geometry
1642	Blaise Pascal: Mechanical adding machine
1660	Isaac Newton, Gottfried Leibniz: Calculus
1670	Gottfried Leibniz: Adds multiplication and division to Pascal machine
1805	Joseph Jacquard: Automatic loom
1820	Charles Babbage: Difference engine
1823	Charles Babbage: Analytic engine
1854	George Boole: Algebraic formulation of mathematical logic
1890	Herman Hollerith, John Billings: Automatic census tabulation
1907	Lee De Forest: Electron vacuum tube
1927	Vannevar Bush: Differential analyzer, electromechanical integration
1936	Alan Turing: Theory of automatic machines
1940	John Atanasoff: Proposes special-purpose electronic machine to solve systems of simultaneous equations; suggests memory refresh and shifting to produce the operation of division
1943	George Stibitz: Relay interpolator—orders for a digital machine stored in numerical form on tape
1946	John Mauchly, John Eckert, Jr.: ENIAC (Moore School of Electrical Engineering)—first electronic digital computer
1948	William Shockley, John Bardeen, Walter Brattain: The transistor
1949	M. V. Wilkes: EDSAC (Cambridge University)—Electronic delay storage automatic computer, first delay-line computer
1950	Moore School of Electrical Engineering staff (J. von Neumann): EDVAC
1952	John von Neumann [Institute of Advanced Study (IAS), Princeton]: First computer to operate on principles of today's computers
1952	Heinz Rutihauser: First problem-oriented language (first compiler)
1953	Jay Forrester, Andrew Booth (1947): Core memory
1954	J. H. Laning, W. Zierler: Interpretive language for Whirlwind I (MIT)
1957	John Backus: FORTRAN language
1959	ACM-GAMM report (John Backus): ALGOL language

butions to early computer technology. Table 1-1 goes only to 1959; to extend the table beyond 1959 would fill many pages. A few of the most important developments include very large scale integrated (VLSI) circuits, multiprocessor-based machines, multiprogrammed operating systems, structured languages, and computer networks.

For the past 30 years, computer architecture and principles have followed concepts developed by John von Neumann. He recognized that the computer performed logical operations. His greatest contribution was to design the machine so that it inspected and then executed one instruction at a time in a strict, serial manner. (In recent years some people have studied machines which operate in a different way. These machines perform computations in parallel, but this technology is still in its infancy.)

Throughout the 1940s and 1950s revolutionary changes took place in the design of hardware for automatic computing machines. Developers were faced with nonmachine problems as well. Early machines required that the instructions which specified the operations to be performed be entered, not in written form, but in wired form using removable plug boards. Many people were needed to put the instructions into the correct form, and entering information into the machine was a time-consuming operation. It was thus natural that a good deal of effort was devoted to ways of simplifying and speeding up this part of the computing operation. Written, rather than wired, methods of programming were developed. An outstanding feature of the written programming languages which came out of this period was the use of English-like statements for each instruction. These programming tools were greatly advanced by the work of John Backus. In 1959 Backus contributed along with others to the development of the ALGOL language. A cousin of the ALGOL language is Pascal. The Pascal language grew out of the efforts of Niklaus Wirth to devise a simple way of teaching students about computers. Another language which has gained popularity is the language BASIC. This also grew out of a need to quickly teach students about computers. It was developed at Dartmouth College.

Today, the greatest changes in computer technology come from the reduction in size, power consumption, and cost; increased speed of operation; and increased reliability of computer components. These trends will undoubtedly continue. In fact, these changes can be expected to become more rapid. The underlying principles, however, remain valid, and an understanding of these principles will support a foundation of computer knowledge that will help in understanding the many changes in design that will come along in the future.

1-2 EXAMPLES OF COMPUTER USAGE

Three examples of computer usage can help to pinpoint what functions a computer carries out.

Example 1-1 A Telephone Directory: An Example of Comparing Objects

The local telephone company normally provides subscribers with assistance in finding an unknown telephone number. To do so, it keeps a list of customer names and telephone numbers in a directory. To further identify subscribers, the list usually includes an address which is useful when there are two or more people with the same name. In this example we will ignore both the potential difficulties of repeated names and no address. The list will be considered to be in no particular order.

A computer is normally employed to locate the desired number. The sequence of steps in the assistance process is shown in Fig. 1-1. The

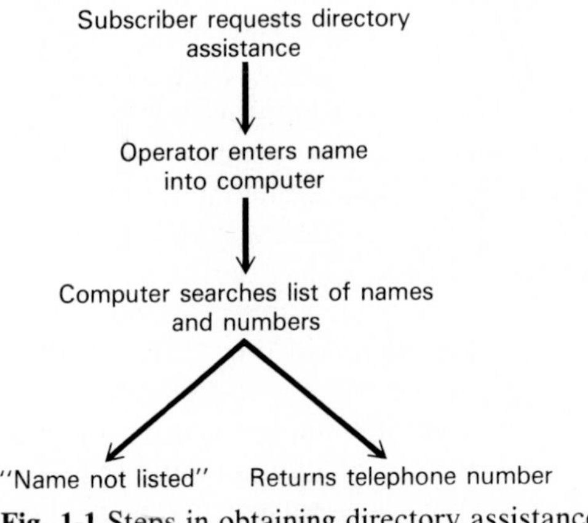

Fig. 1-1 Steps in obtaining directory assistance.

operator enters the name on a keyboard similar to one you might find on a typewriter. The telephone number, if it exists, will be shown on a screen very similar to a television screen, located close to the operator's keyboard. The combination of keyboard and screen forms part of a *computer terminal*. It is often the way in which the computer communicates with a user.

The computer searches the directory for the name entered by the operator. One of the things that a computer does rapidly is compare items. It can determine if two names are the same. The names appear to the computer as a series, or string, of letters called *character strings*. The character strings in the directory are compared with the character string that the operator has entered for the name. Two things can happen. The computer may find the name, in which case it sends the corresponding telephone number to the screen (monitor) of the terminal. However, it may also search the entire list of names in the directory without finding a match. If so, it would send an appropriate message, such as "Name not listed," to the monitor.

Let us examine in more detail the way in which the computer searches the list. The search method is shown in Fig. 1-2. To explain the search

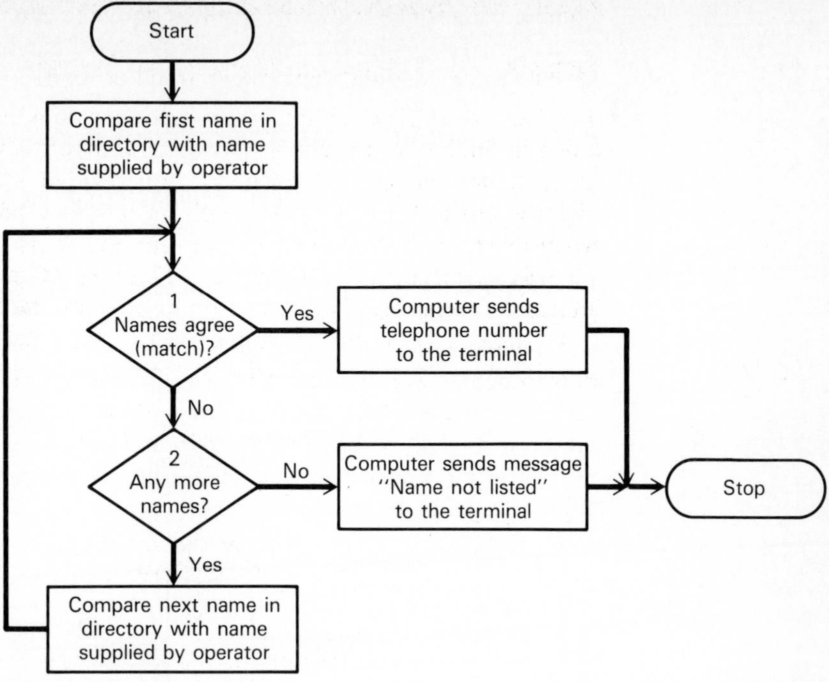

Fig. 1-2 Search sequence in obtaining directory assistance.

procedure more easily, a diagram has been drawn using arrows, ovals, rectangles, and diamond shapes. Such a diagram is called a *flow diagram*. Often used to depict what happens in a program, it saves a lot of confusing explanations. Start at the begining (at the oval marked "Start") and follow the arrows. When following the arrows, we may come to a rectangle. The computer carries out whatever instructions are enclosed by the rectangle. Sometimes we come to a fork in the road which has a diamond as its symbol. This fork, called a *decision block*, has two arrows leaving the symbol. To follow the diagram at this point, leave either on the branch marked "Yes," indicating that the condition in the diamond is true, or the branch marked "No," indicating that the specified condition is false. Eventually the arrows lead to the end, which appears in an oval and may be marked "End" or "Stop."

There are many other problems similar to this one. Good solutions to the problems associated with the telephone directory may be applicable to other problems. An electronic parts inventory, for example, is a list of items and their corresponding storage locations. Keeping track of a company's inventory is very similar to keeping track of the telephone company's list of subscribers. Another example of a list similar to that of a telephone directory can be found in a bank. In this case the bank wishes to keep track of the names of its depositors and their account information. If we think of the depositor's account information in place of the telephone number, then once we know how a computer can be used to help in the case of the telephone company's directory, we can immediately apply such knowledge to helping a bank keep track of its depositors.

Example 1-2 Computer-Aided Manufacturing: An Example of Repeated Operations

In Example 1-1 we saw that a computer can be helpful when we wish to compare names (or numbers). A computer is also a powerful machine when we have to repeat a series of operations over and over again. When human beings are asked to perform tedious operations, they often make mistakes. A computer can perform a series of operations repeatedly with very few mistakes. When we wish to mass-produce products—say, cars—we can often reduce such manufacturing to a sequence of repeated operations. One important example is shown in Fig. 1-3. Here a computer is

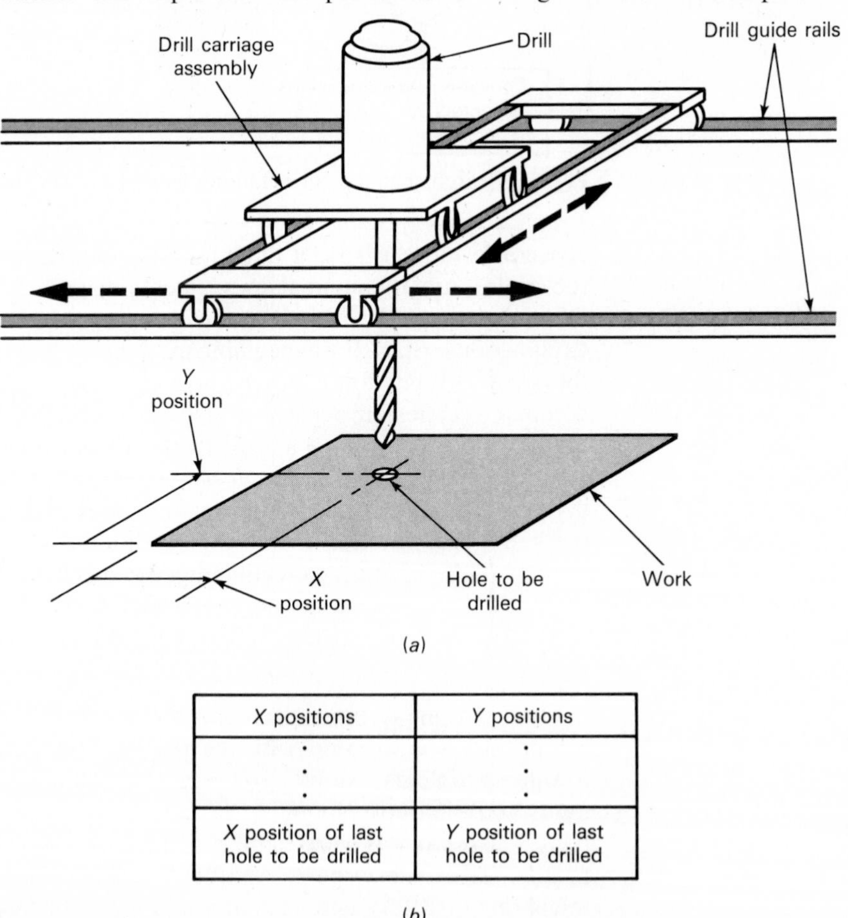

X positions	Y positions
⋮	⋮
X position of last hole to be drilled	Y position of last hole to be drilled

Fig. 1-3 Automatic drilling machine. (*a*) Sketch of the drill assembly. (*b*) List of drilling positions used by the computer to direct the drill.

combined with a drill press, creating an automatic drilling machine. These machines can be used to automatically drill printed-circuit boards or gear plates for mechanical assemblies.

In this case, the drill is attached to a drill carriage assembly which is free to move on a set of drill guide rails. This permits the drill to be driven by suitable power sources such as motors. The drill carriage can move left to right and forward and backward. The computer which controls the drill has a list of numbers which specifies the places on a work piece—the printed-circuit board or gear plate—where holes are to be drilled. For each hole to be drilled, the computer has an *X* and *Y* number, or value. This list is shown in Fig. 1-3*b*. Figure 1-4 is a flow diagram which describes the

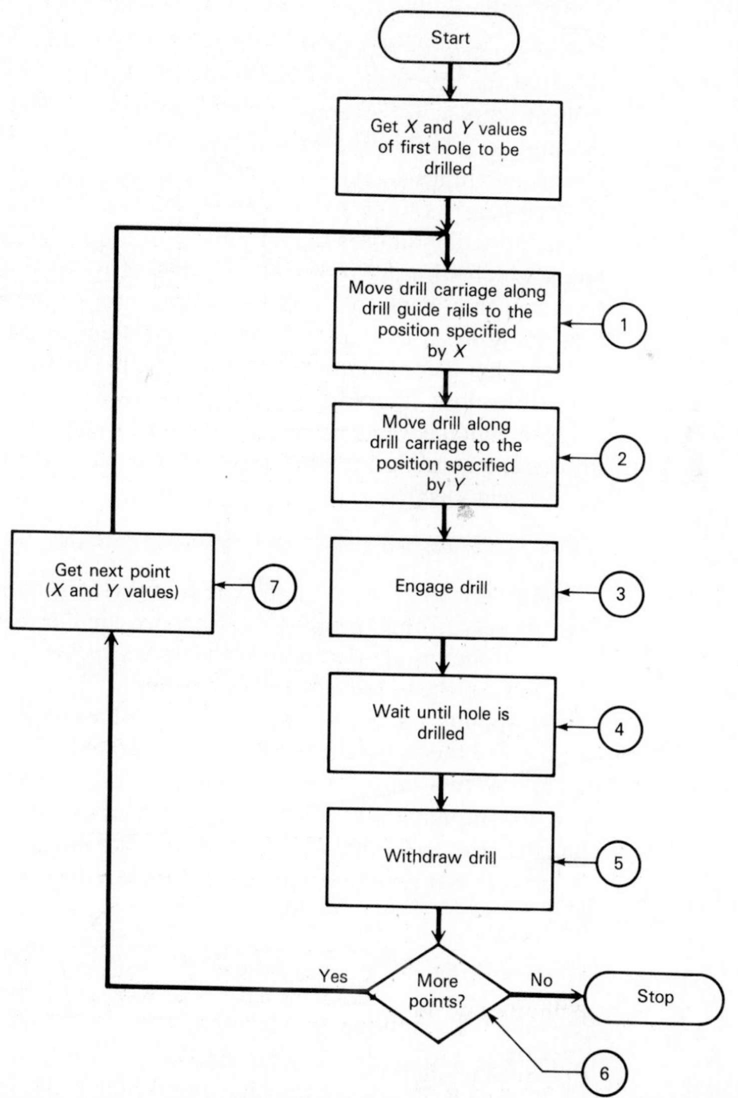

Fig. 1-4 Flow diagram for the automatic drilling machine of Example 1-2.

sequences of operations which the computer carries out to drill a series of holes. As with the flow diagram for the directory example, the sequence of operations begins at the box marked "Start" and continues until operations terminate at the stop point.

The following list summarizes the sequence of operations:

1. Position X
2. Position Y
3. Drill engage work
4. Wait
5. Withdraw drill
6. Check for more points
7. Get next point

This sequence is repeated until the list is exhausted. Notice how every detail of the operation has to be clearly stated. If we do not withdraw the drill at step 5, for example, the work will be badly damaged when we attempt to position the drill at the next point to be drilled. One of the important things to remember when using a computer is that every step the computer is to perform must be explicitly stated.

The flow diagram for the automatic drilling machine includes a series of steps which form a *loop* in the picture. This loop consists of the steps 1 to 7, and then back to 1. (The numbers refer to the steps of Fig. 1-4.) The loop identifies the steps which are repeatedly performed. It emphasizes the fact that a computer can carry out steps over and over again. The loop pattern in flow diagrams will be encountered often. It is one of the basic ways in which computers are used, namely, to repeat a series of operations until some condition is reached (such as "no more holes to be drilled" in the present case).

Again, the solution to the problem of the automatic drilling machine can help to solve other problems which are similar. For example, the same series of operations can be used to move two leads of an ohmmeter. We can replace the "engage drill" step with "lower the leads so that they contact points on the wiring assembly." Now we can use the ohmmeter to measure the resistance between two points. If the resistance is zero, it means the two points are connected. In this way the computer could be used to automatically check a wiring harness or assembly. With a few changes, the machine could be made into an automatic wiring device, connecting a terminal at one XY coordinate to one at another XY coordinate.

Example 1-3 Solutions of Simultaneous Algebraic Equations: An Example in Arithmetic Computation

This example shows us the way in which we can use the computer to help us in science, engineering, and other activities involving numerical analysis. In these branches of human activity we may be called upon to solve a set of simultaneous algebraic equations. While the example here involves only two equations and two unknowns, it is possible to deal with many equations and unknowns. We would ordinarily use pencil and paper to solve this example because there are only two equations. When there are 100 equations and 100 unknowns (not at all uncommon), a computer can solve the equations much faster and more efficiently than we can. Because of the large number of calculations required for such a large number of equations, the method outlined here would take a long time on a digital computer. However, the solution is still far speedier than if the same calculations were performed manually.

The flow diagram appears in Fig. 1-5. Also shown are the results at each step of the computation. The equations to be solved are

$$2X + 3Y = 8 \tag{1}$$
$$4X - Y = 2 \tag{2}$$

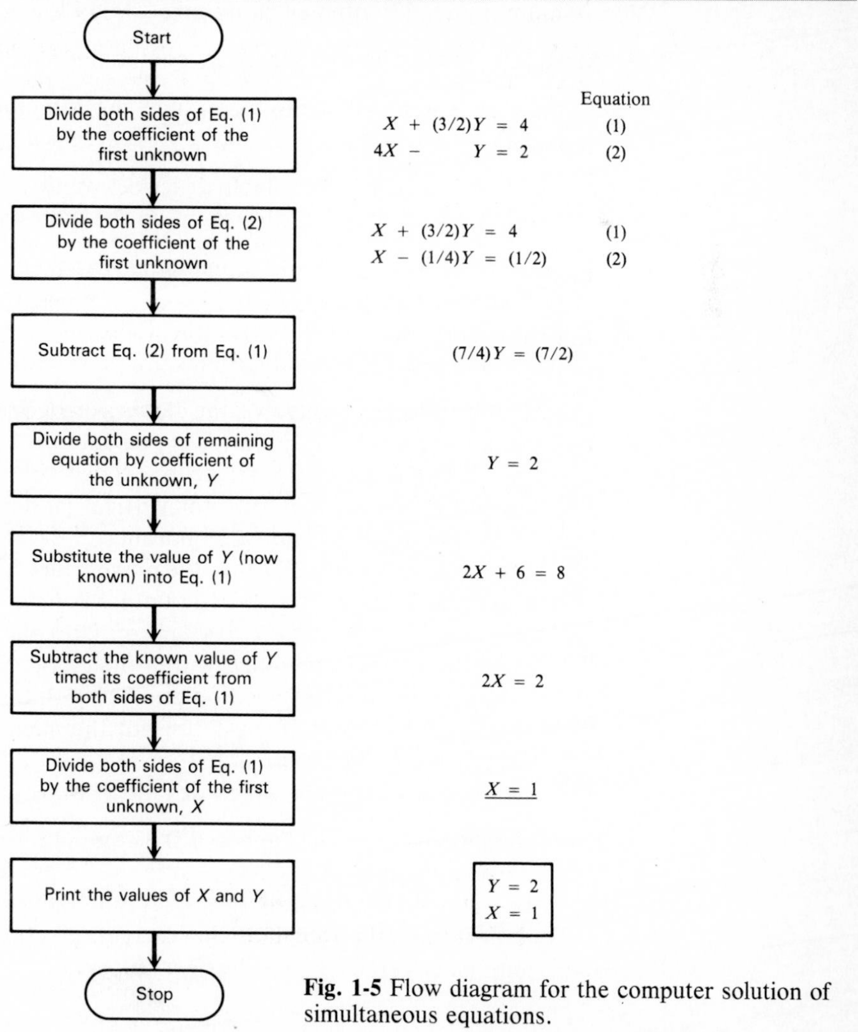

Fig. 1-5 Flow diagram for the computer solution of simultaneous equations.

This kind of computation is just one way in which the computer helps us to deal with large amounts of information. Other examples include helping us to find statistical associations between our actions and their consequences. For example, the computer helped to find out that smoking and certain forms of disease seem to be associated with each other. The computer was instructed to perform comparisons between many human activities and possible consequences (such as various diseases). Not too long ago such computations using pencil and paper would not (or could not) be done because of the possibility of human error, as well as the economic cost and the time needed to complete the calculations.

PROBLEMS FOR SECTION 1-2

1. It takes an average of 50×10^{-6} seconds for the computer to decide if the name supplied by the operator agrees with any one of the names in the list. The directory contains 1 million names. What is the maximum time the computer could take to find a name?
2. Repeat Prob. 1 with a directory containing 5 million names.
3. Why is it more efficient to arrange the directory list in alphabetical order?
4. Draw a flow diagram which describes how a name entered by the operator is compared with a name in the directory.
5. Assume that you have a computer-controlled, printed-circuit board drilling machine similar to the one described in Example 1-2. In order to position the drill carriage, the following steps are executed (this could be used for both horizontal (X) or vertical (Y) positioning):

   a. If the numerical value of the target, or desired, position is greater than the present position (as represented by a number in the computer), then move the carriage in a "positive" direction—say, "east" for horizontal and "north" for vertical motions.
   b. If the condition in part (a) is not met, the computer must command the carriage to move in the "negative" direction.
   c. Continue to move the carriage until a contact closure is detected.
   d. Increment or decrement (as appropriate) the value of the present position number contained within the computer.
   e. Compare the present position number with the number representing the target position. If these are not the same, go back to step (a). Stop if the numbers are equal.

   Draw a flow diagram which describes steps (a) to (e).
6. a. Indicate what might happen if the computer fails to detect a contact closure as required in Prob. 5, or if the computer accidentally detects two contact closures when in fact only one is correct.
   b. Suggest a method for detecting carriage position which reduces problems uncovered by your answer to part (a).

7. In Example 1-2 the computer (program) wastes time until a hole is drilled. The computer does not have information about the actual state of the hole being drilled—is the job complete? Such methods are called *open loop* designs. They can lead to errors. Describe some potential problems with the open loop design. Devise a method for drilling holes which avoids these problems.

1-3 WHAT THE COMPUTER DOES

Each example described in Sec. 1-2 reveals important things about computers. Each case specified a series of steps which could be carried out by the computer. When something is specified for the computer to do, it must be possible for the computer to perform such an operation. At present, for example, we cannot instruct the computer to simply "solve the problem" without telling it *how* the problem is to be solved. The series of steps to be performed (considered all together) is called an *algorithm* (or method of solution). Within the computer, the steps for carrying out such algorithms (or solutions) form *programs*. The program itself consists of a series of commands which the computer can perform. These commands are called *instructions*.

Instructions are simple commands. One example might be "Add A and B" (or in shorthand form "$A + B$"). Sequences of such instructions are combined to form programs. Programs can be combined to form algorithms. For example, a program for drawing electronic symbols (resistors, capacitors, etc.) can be combined with a wire list program to carry out the algorithm for drawing electrical schematics. In spacecraft, individual programs to activate rockets, calculate current position, and determine trajectories can be combined to guide the spaceship.

In a program, operations may be performed on numbers which are supplied by the user. The automatic drilling machine moved the drill to X and Y positions. The X and Y positions were supplied by the user in the form of numbers. The user must identify every hole that is to be drilled. The operation may also be carried out on nonnumeric data, as in the telephone directory system. Here we manipulated alphanumeric information. Programs can thus be considered as a sequence of operations acting on numbers or letters to produce a new set of numbers or letters. However, there are times when we shall have occasion to supply a program not simply with numbers or letters but with another program. This is very important, as we shall see in subsequent chapters. We now define *data* to be either numbers, alphanumeric characters, or programs. *A computer program accepts data, operates on this data according to the program instructions, and produces new data as a result.* As a program completes each instruction, the numbers or alphanumeric characters which are generated are called *results*; when the instruction has been complete, the computer is said to have *executed* the instruction. A program is executed when it has been completed.

1-4 HOW THE COMPUTER DOES ITS WORK

Part of the computer system includes the instructions that the user wishes to execute. These instructions can be changed if necessary; this part of the system is called the *software*. The software includes all the programs needed to carry out intended algorithms.

The second part of the computer consists of the equipment and circuits that have the capability of executing the processes detailed in the software. The components in which those capabilities are embodied form the computer *hardware*.

1-4-1 The CPU

In Examples 1-1 to 1-3, three separate kinds of instructions had to be performed by the computer. These functions are summarized in Fig. 1-6,

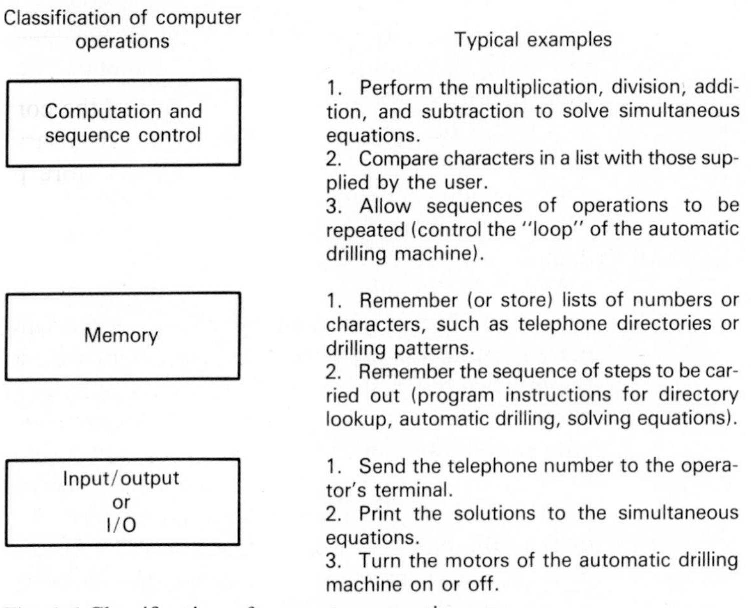

Classification of computer operations
Typical examples
Computation and sequence control
1. Perform the multiplication, division, addition, and subtraction to solve simultaneous equations.
2. Compare characters in a list with those supplied by the user.
3. Allow sequences of operations to be repeated (control the "loop" of the automatic drilling machine).
Memory
1. Remember (or store) lists of numbers or characters, such as telephone directories or drilling patterns.
2. Remember the sequence of steps to be carried out (program instructions for directory lookup, automatic drilling, solving equations).
Input/output or I/O
1. Send the telephone number to the operator's terminal.
2. Print the solutions to the simultaneous equations.
3. Turn the motors of the automatic drilling machine on or off.

Fig. 1-6 Classification of computer operations.

together with detailed examples from the cases that we discussed. The computation and sequence control is usually called the *central processing unit*, or *CPU*. The CPU carries out:

- Instruction acquisition, or "fetching"
- Instruction execution: arithmetic operations (add, subtract, etc.), logical operations (comparison), sequencing

Instruction execution includes the details for carrying out a particular instruction. For example, the instruction "add *B* to *A*" (where *A* and *B* are two numbers) may itself include many detailed steps. A computer user may not need to know exactly how B is added to A. When a user does not need to know how something happens, such details are called *transparent* (or invisible).

Instruction sequencing involves the order in which instructions are executed. Simply stated, it means *which instruction is executed next.* Recall from the automatic drilling machine example that the computer checks to see if the list is exhausted (or completed). If it is, the machine halts. If it is not, the machine gets the next drill point. This is the fork in the road that was mentioned earlier. At this point in the program, the computer executes either a "stop" or the instruction to "get the next point." The CPU is the part of the computer which determines which of these two instructions is the next one to be executed.

Part of the CPU includes hardware for performing arithmetic. This is called *arithmetic and logic unit,* or *ALU.*

1-4-2 The Memory

The *memory* is a very important part of the computer. The name itself (memory) is very descriptive. This part of the computer *remembers* data. Recall, we include numbers, alphanumeric characters, and programs in the term "data." Thus, the memory can store programs or data which programs process.

1-4-3 Input and Output

Finally, we need to be able to transmit information from the user to the computer and results from the computer to the user. This is performed by the *input/output*, or *I/O*, portion of the computer. The term "user" needs some clarification. There are times when the source or destination of the data is not a human operator but another machine. Such was the case for the automatic drilling machine. Signals to operate the drive motors and those needed to find the drill position are also classified as part of the I/O of the computer. The drill can be considered a "user" in this case. In general, a *user* is the *source* or *destination* of the computer data or results.

In summary, three main parts of the computer include the following.

- CPU: Arithmetic operations and control of instructions.
- Memory: Storage of data, including numbers, alphanumeric data, and instructions.
- I/O: Transmission of data from user to computer, and transmission of results from computer to user.

1-4-4 The Computer Bus

The communication links between the various parts of a computer comprise the computer **bus**. The particular interconnection scheme for a given computer is described by its bus architecture. There are a number of popular bus architectures. One of these is shown in Fig. 1-7. The line

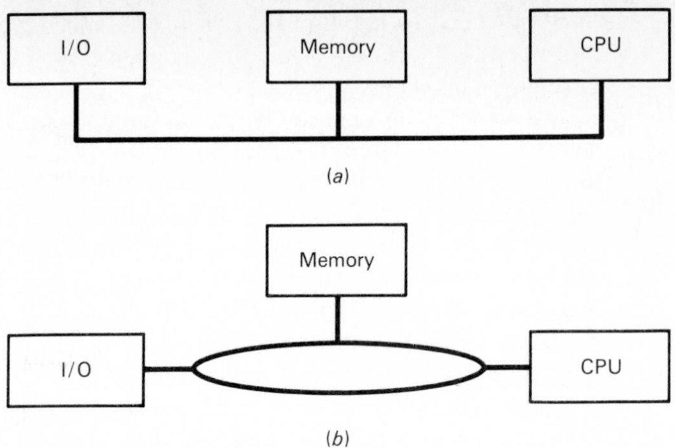

Fig. 1-7 (*a*) Common bus and (*b*) loop interconnection architecture with CPU, memory, and I/O joined in order to transmit data between these parts of a computer.

connecting the computer elements carries data between the various parts of the computer. This bus architecture is called the *common-bus*, or *single-bus*, architecture: CPU, memory, and I/O are all connected to one common bus. As shown in Figure 1-7*b*, a bus may also have a *loop* architecture. Most important is the fact that the bus architecture describes the communication path between internal parts of the computer. The bus is like a highway which allows cars to travel between cities.

Let us examine what information must be present and how it must be transmitted for proper communication to take place. From the examples we saw, information might pass from memory to CPU on some occasions and from CPU to I/O at other times. The bus must therefore include provision for:

- The actual data to be transmitted, and
- Identification of the data destination within the computer

Destinations within the computer are called *addresses*. This is very similar to a postal system. The destination of a letter is designated by the address on the envelope. The message contained in the letter is the data to be transmitted between parts of the computer. As the parts of the computer are connected by a common bus, we must be careful that two elements do not try to transmit data at the same time. The CPU should not try to send results to memory at the same time that a user's I/O device (terminal) is trying to send data to the CPU. This would result in confusion similar to that which arises when two people talk into the telephone at the same time. The bus must provide the means for cooperation between parts of the computer. The bus therefore includes the following:

- Lines on which data is to be transmitted
- Lines for destination identification (address)
- Lines for cooperative communication (called *bus control*)

Figure 1-8 shows a flow diagram that explains what happens when data is to be transmitted between parts of a computer. A *read* operation is said to occur when data is *received* from a component of the computer. A *write* operation consists of *transmitting* data from one part of the machine to

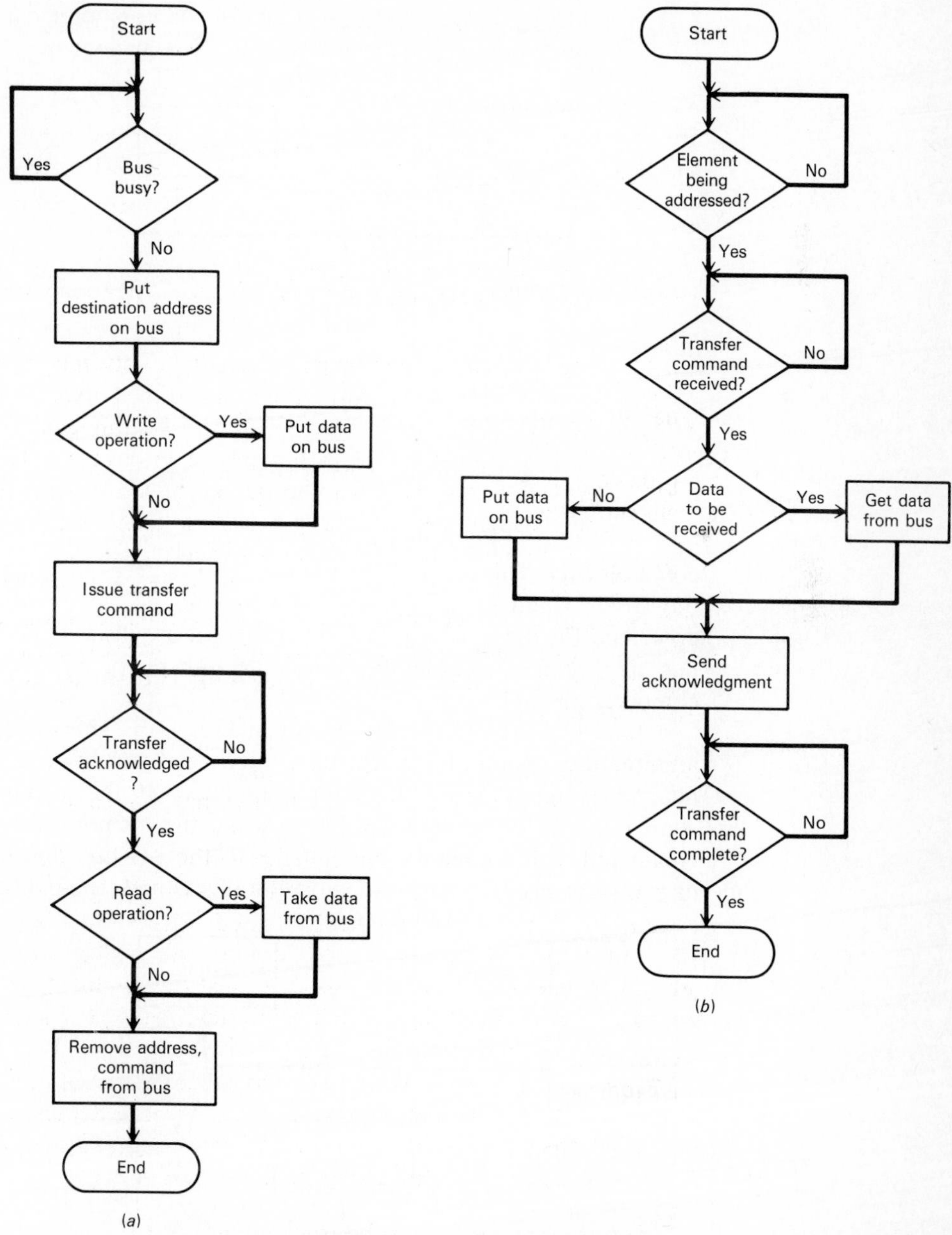

Fig. 1-8 Flow diagram for the transfer of information or data between parts of the computer on a computer bus. (*a*) Typical flow diagram for a control component (or master). (*b*) Typical flow diagram for a "passive" part of the computer.

another. The sequence of events associated with transfer of information is called a *protocol*. This protocol is a composite of protocols which can be found on a number of different computer buses.

Within the computer, this sequence (the command being placed on the bus, followed by acknowledgment of the command, followed in turn by removal of these signals from the bus) is referred to as *handshaking*.

A second way in which the elements of the computer can be arranged for communication is shown in Fig. 1-9. This arrangement includes two

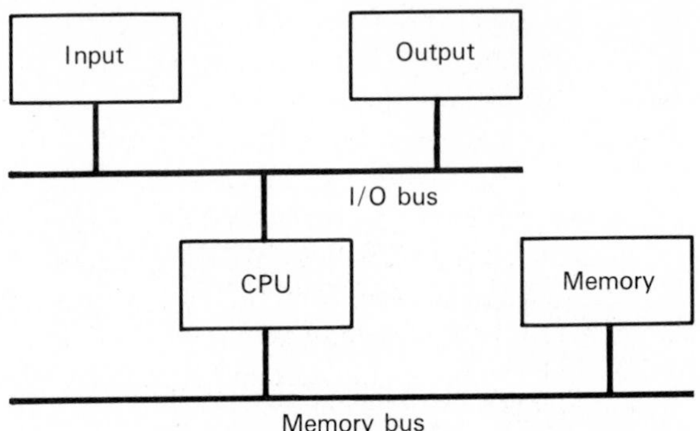

Fig. 1-9 Another kind of computer bus architecture.

buses. The first bus, called the *memory bus*, allows CPU and memory to communicate. The second, the *I/O bus*, allows users to communicate with the CPU. Handshaking signals, similar (but not identical) to the ones described for the common-bus arrangement, are also needed for the two-bus arrangement in order to coordinate transfer of information between computer elements.

A final bus architecture is shown in Fig. 1-10. This is also a two-bus architecture. Notice the slight difference between this one and the two-bus arrangement shown in Fig. 1-9. In Fig. 1-10 the memory element is shown connected to both the I/O bus and the memory bus. The CPU is connected to the memory bus but not to the I/O bus. I/O data is placed directly into predetermined memory; the CPU finds the data there and can

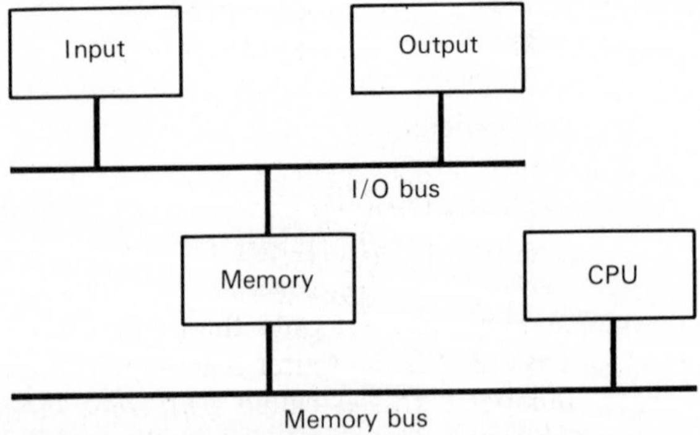

Fig. 1-10 The traditional or historic computer bus architecture.

then operate on it. This arrangement is the traditional computer communication arrangement. As before, bus control or handshaking is needed to coordinate information transfer.

1-5 NUMBERS, THE LIFEBLOOD OF COMPUTERS

We have used the term "data" many times in this chapter. What may not be apparent is that, ultimately, all data within a computer *must* be reduced to some numerical form. A computer does not recognize the letter "A." Indeed, we cannot physically place an A into the computer. How then do we inform the computer that an A is intended? The answer is to replace or represent A by a number. When the computer encounters the number for A, it will treat this number as if it were an A. Thus, *all data within the computer is represented by numbers*. If we were to look inside the memory element, we would find only numbers. In fact, if we pick a number from the memory at random, we have no way of knowing whether that number really has a numeric value or if it is a substitute for an alphanumeric character. It might also be part of a program and represent an instruction code.

How does the computer deal with all these different kinds of numbers? One way is to assume that the first number encountered is an instruction (part of a program). The instruction implies the nature and number of data elements that follow. A given instruction might require 0, 1, 2, or more data items; thus the next 0 (none), 1, 2, or more data items are interpreted correctly. The computer regards the item which follows the data as another instruction, repeating the process until some kind of instruction that halts the machine is encountered.

One of the unfortunate ways in which a program can fail occurs when the number of elements following an instruction is inconsistent with the expected number—e.g., one number follows when two are expected. As a result, an alphanumeric character may be taken for an instruction, an instruction may be interpreted as a numeric item, etc. From that point on, the interpretation of data is incorrect. Usually, such problems are the result of a poorly defined program or typographical error (both examples of human error) rather than an actual computer error.

In summary, information or data in the computer is always in the form of numbers. This includes destination addresses, data, commands, transfer acknowledgments, etc. We may think of numbers as the lifeblood of computers, the circulation of these numbers allowing the actual computation.

The fact that numbers are the lifeblood of the computer creates a very big problem for a person who wants to use a computer. Programmers must find a way to translate all intentions (programs) into numerical form since numbers are the only things that computers can act upon. One way to program the computer is to supply the instructions directly in the form of numbers. This is called a *machine language* method of programming. In general, such a method is tedious, time-consuming, and prone to error. A second method uses mnemonics (symbols) for the instructions. An example of this would be to use the symbol ADD when we want to instruct the computer to perform addition. In reality we have simply substituted a word—ADD in the example just cited—for the machine language number that the computer would interpret as arithmetic addition. This is an improvement over the machine language method, for it is much easier to program the computer using these symbols instead of numbers. Since the machine must have numbers, translation of the mnemonics into numbers is still needed. This is a straightforward but tedious task. It is just the kind of operation that a computer can do so well. Why not use the computer itself to translate these symbols into machine language? Translation programs of this kind exist for all modern computers. Of course, someone must have written a machine language program (using only numbers) at some point. However, once this is done, all new programs can be written using the mnemonics or symbols. This method of programming (using symbols) is called *assembly language* programming. The mnemonics, taken together, form the assembly language. The program that converts assembly language into machine language is called an *assembler*.

Assembly language programs, although easier for a programmer to create than machine language programs, are far from ideal. They often hide or mask the simple intentions of the programmer, since assembly language commands are closely related to machine language commands and are burdened with required information. The assembly language program to divide one number by another and to store the result might require thirty or more commands.

To overcome this difficulty, *symbolic languages* such as Pascal, and BASIC have been developed. Using a symbolic language, a programmer uses English-like statements to signify complex commands to the computer. For example, the division problem described above might be written as

C = A/B

Translation of programs written in symbolic languages into machine language—remember, this must be done or the computer will not function properly—is more complicated than translating assembly language programs. In this book, we shall study symbolic languages and elements of the computer needed to use these languages effectively.

SUMMARY

The computer is a powerful machine that can carry out repeated, tedious tasks rapidly and without error. These tasks include computation, control, and management of large quantities of data. A computer has three functional elements: the CPU (central processing unit) for arithmetic operations and instruction control; the memory for storage of data, results, and programs; and the I/O (input/output components) for communication between user and computer. A typical computer installation is shown in Fig. 1-11.

Computer elements communicate with each other via a computer bus. Use of the bus is controlled by commands and handshaking signals.

To solve problems, algorithms (methods of solution) have to be developed and programs (instruction sequences) written to implement the solutions. Symbolic languages can be used to write programs.

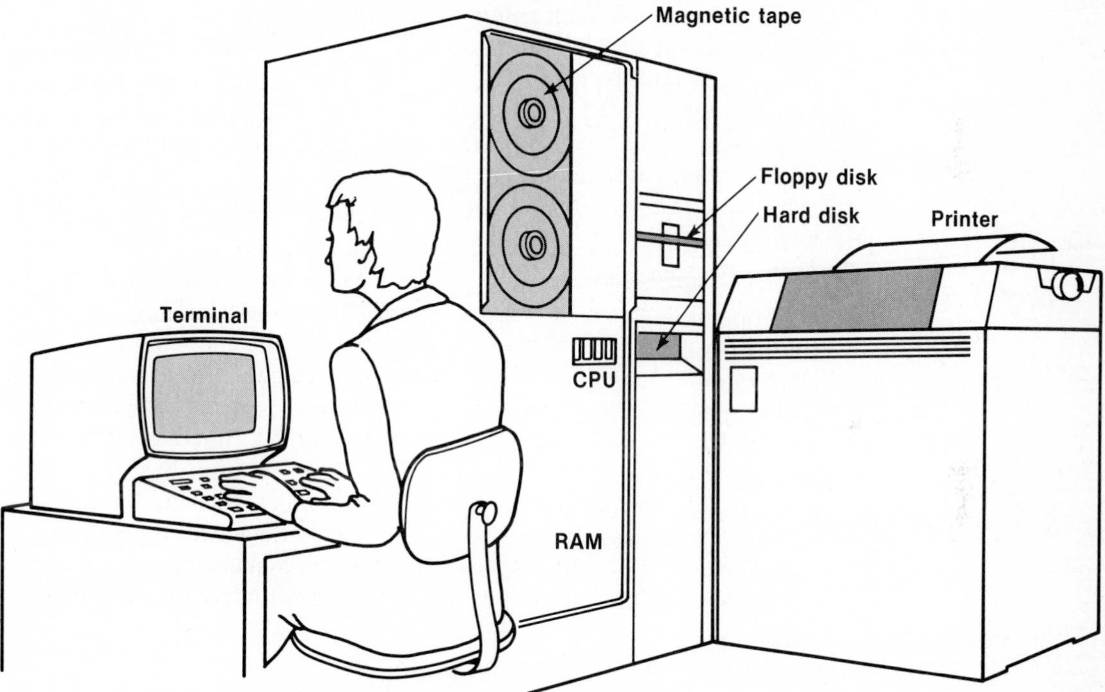

Fig. 1-11 Sketch of a typical computer installation.

REVIEW PROBLEMS

1. An elevator is used to transport astronauts from the ground to the top of the spaceship. Draw a flow diagram which could be used as the basis for a computer program to control such an elevator. The following facts should be considered:

- There are only two stops; ground and spaceship.
- There are two call panels outside the elevator, one at the spaceship and one on the ground. Each call panel has a single call button. (Why is only one button needed at each station?)
- Within the elevator is a single button.

In your flow diagram make provisions for control of the elevator door and for simple up-and-down operations of the lift mechanism.

REVIEW QUESTIONS

1. What are the three main functional elements of a computer?
2. Briefly describe the purpose of each functional element of the computer. Describe what job each component performs.
3. How do elements of a computer communicate with each other?
4. Describe what information is necessary for successful communication between elements of a computer.
5. Name three ways (languages) to write programs for a computer. Cite an important characteristic of each method.
6. What kind of operations or calculations are particularly well suited for a computer?
7. Define the following:

   read operation
   write operation
   instruction
   program
   algorithm
   machine language
   assembly language
   symbolic language
   architecture
   software
   hardware
   terminal

8. What is an ALU? What is its function in a computer?
9. What important roles did the following people play in the development of the computer?

   Blaise Pascal
   Joseph Jacquard
   Charles Babbage
   George Boole
   Herman Hollerith
   John Mauchly and John Eckert, Jr.
   William Shockley, John Bardeen, and Walter Brattain
   John von Neumann
   John Backus

COMPUTER ARCHITECTURE: THE MEMORY

We now know that the computer includes the means to perform arithmetic, store the sequence of operations (program) to be performed as well as the data and results of these operations, and communicate results to a user or accept data from a user. This raises very important how questions about the computer:

- How does the computer store data, programs, and results?
- How does the computer carry out arithmetic and control?
- How does the computer accomplish input and output?

In the next few chapters we will answer these questions. This chapter will describe the way in which the computer stores data, programs, and results.

2-1 THE MEMORY

The *memory* is perhaps the most important part of the computer. Understanding how this element works and how it is organized is an important part of knowing the way in which the computer as a whole operates. The organization (structure or architecture) of the memory is one factor which controls the speed at which a computer carries out (executes) a program. In fact, if the memory is not well organized, the computer itself may function so slowly that the results are unsatisfactory. For example, consider a way in which computers are often used today. Because computing machines are often very expensive, it may be necessary to share the cost among many users. They all must be able to use the computer at the same time. Since each active user needs memory to store data and programs, we are immediately faced with a problem: How do we keep one user from interfering with another user? If we assign each user a fixed segment of memory, the program seems to be solved. But, in fact, this is a poor solution, as memory requirements vary—a user may have a wastefully large segment. Even worse is the situation of having a segment that is too small. The program may not run at all. In addition, we might have to put restrictions on a user's ability to access memory not assigned to him or her. The control or management of memory is important to prevent this from happening.

2-1-1 What Is a Memory?

A memory is an element which stores numbers. Remember, in a computer, numbers, alphanumeric characters, or instructions are represented, internally, as numbers. We can think of a memory as a set of cells in which to keep numbers. To be able to store numbers in such places we must have ways to put numbers into the cells and we must be able to examine the numbers. A memory cell would be of no value if we could not examine the numbers stored within. Figure 2-1 shows how we can picture a memory cell. The cell contents are words. Storing numbers in memory is called *writing* into memory. Examining the contents of memory is called *reading* memory.

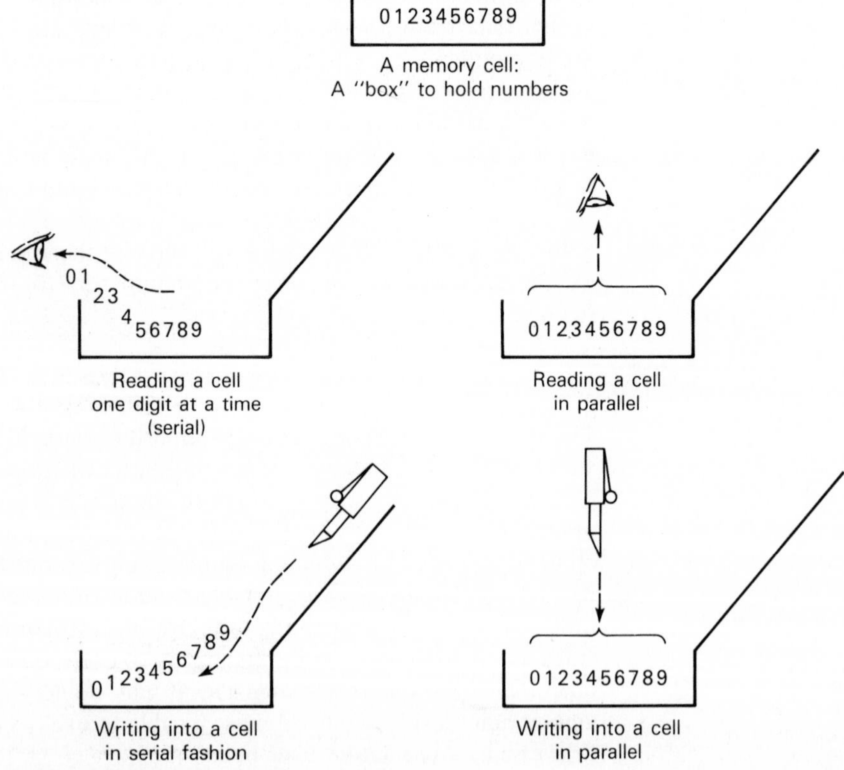

Fig. 2-1 A memory location or cell and its uses.

2-1-2 How to Classify Memory

When a number with many digits is stored into a memory cell, it may be stored one digit at a time or all at once. How it is stored depends on the kind of memory. When a number is read out of a memory cell, one digit at a time may be read or the whole number (all digits) may be read simultaneously. The term "serial" applies to memory transfers (reading or writing) which occur one digit at a time. The term "parallel" applies to memory transfers in which all digits of the number are written or read simultaneously. Let us point out several characteristics that such memory cells may have.

In general, when writing into a cell, whatever number was there before will be lost. The old number is said to be written over, or erased. For some memories, just reading a cell will destroy its contents. For such cases the number must be immediately rewritten into the cell to save the contents.

An important characteristic of the memory cell is the maximum size of the number that it can store. We need to know how many digits we can store in a memory cell. The number which tells us this information is called *word size*. This usually limits the size of numbers a computer can handle in its arithmetic computations and other operations.

While we shall restrict ourselves to decimal numbers in this text (whenever possible), we must understand that the numbers stored in a computer memory cell do not look like decimal numbers. Instead, a coded form of the decimal number will be found in a computer memory cell. The memory cell itself cannot store decimal numbers. In fact, the electronic elements of a memory are either on or off; the numbers they can store must be formed using 1s (ones—on) and 0s (zeroes—off). Using only 0s and 1s, it is possible to make codes which are equivalent to decimal numbers. For example, here is a code using only 1s and 0s for the decimal numbers 0 to 9.

Decimal Number	0, 1 Code
0	0000
1	0001
2	0010
3	0011
4	0100
5	0101
6	0110
7	0111
8	1000
9	1001

Using this code we can represent a 5 by 0101 without causing any confusion. No other number in the list has 0101 as its code. We can continue our code beyond 9 to store numbers greater than 9. The 0, 1 code shown could be used by the computer to store decimal numbers within a memory cell. For this reason, these 0, 1 numbers are called the *internal* representation of the number. Most computers translate decimal numbers into numbers with a 0, 1 code. This translation occurs when a user enters decimal numbers into the computer. A reverse translation occurs before the computer transmits results back to the user. The internal numbers (in 0, 1 code) are then translated into decimal numbers or characters for external representation. Think of this as follows: Find the 0, 1 code in the list; send the corresponding decimal digit or character to the user. For example, if the internal number is 0100, send information which the user can identify as the decimal number 4. To review: External representation of numbers uses decimal form; internal representation of numbers in the computer memory cell uses a 0, 1 code.

The 0, 1 numbers have a special name. They are called *binary numbers* to emphasize the fact that only 0s or 1s appear in the number. (The word "binary" means having two states.) The size of numbers which can be stored in a memory cell depends on the number of 1s and 0s that the cell can hold. Since internal representation of numbers is binary, the maximum size of numbers within a memory cell is specified by the number of binary digits (0s and 1s) it can hold. If the first two letters of *bi*nary and the last two letters of digi*ts* are combined, the word "bits" is formed. The unit of measurement of the maximum number size in a memory cell is a *bit*. Typical cell sizes include 4, 8, 12, 16, 32, 48, and 60 bits. A very popular cell size at present is 16 bits, but 32-bit (and greater) sizes will become more popular as technology changes. Since our concern is the external representation of numbers, Table 2-1 shows the maximum decimal number that a memory cell can hold for each of the more popular cell sizes. A computer may also treat several contiguous memory cells as a group so that even larger quantities can be processed.

TABLE 2-1

Internal Bit Size	External Decimal Equivalent
4	15
8	255
16	65,535
32	4,294,967,295
48	281,474,976,710,655

Another property of the memory cell refers to its ability to maintain the number stored within the cell without power. Some types of cells do not need power to maintain their contents. Power, of course, is needed to write into or read from such cells. Once the number has been written, these cells retain their contents without the need for power. Memory cells like these are called *nonvolatile* memory cells. Cells which need power to retain their contents are called *volatile* cells (or volatile memory). Turning power off causes loss of cell contents. Computers usually have some of both types of cells installed. Nonvolatile memory might be used to store startup information so that it is not lost each time the computer is turned off.

Some volatile cells retain their contents indefinitely once a number has been written (and power is maintained). Such cells are called *static* cells. Alternatively some volatile cells lose their contents spontaneously even with power applied unless the computer periodically renews the cell's contents. The computer has to *refresh* the contents of the cell. This re-writing process must take place faster than the speed at which these cells naturally lose their data. Such memory is called *dynamic* because of the need to periodically refresh the cell contents.

One last difference between types of cells should be noted. Some nonvolatile memory cells are manufactured with numbers already in the cells. The computer cannot write (store) new numbers into these cells, but it can read the numbers which were entered at the factory. These cells are called *read-only memory* cells, or *ROMs* for short. A ROM is a very useful way to store unchanging data and is one of the ways in which such memories are used.

Table 2-2 summarizes the characteristics that can be associated with a computer memory cell.

TABLE 2-2 SUMMARY OF MEMORY CELL DESCRIPTION

Word size	Number of bits (or largest decimal number) that a cell can hold
Volatile, nonvolatile	Loses or retains contents when power is turned off
ROM, read/write	Cell contents can be read only or be read and changed
Static, dynamic	No need to refresh or memory needs to be re-freshed to retain contents

PROBLEMS FOR SECTION 2-1

1. Compare serial and parallel memory systems with respect to the speed of reading and writing.
2. Using the binary (0, 1) code, suggest two different methods for extending the internal representation of decimal numbers beyond 9—from 10 to 99.
3. A computer treats two contiguous (adjacent) 8-bit cells as a single word. What is the largest decimal number which can be represented with such an organization?
4. A computer has a 20-bit word size. What is the largest decimal number which can be represented? If both positive and negative numbers are to be represented by such a scheme, what is the range of possible numbers?

2-2 ADDRESSING MEMORY

A memory cell provides us with a way to store a number. Many cells are needed to store all the numbers associated with a computer program. One of the facts about a computer which is important to users is the number of memory cells that the computer contains. Small computers may have only 128 cells or less. Very large computers may often contain millions of cells.

To read from and write into such cells, we must be able to distinguish one cell from another. If we want to write a number into a cell, we have to know two things: *the value to be written and the specific cell in which the number is to be stored.* When we want to read the contents of a cell, we have to know which cell is to be examined. To tell one cell from another, we assign a number, or *address*, to each cell. Since each cell has a different address, we can find any cell within the memory of the computer. Figure 2-2 shows a bank of cells together with their cell addresses. In this case the cell address is a number, such as 1, 2, or 3, which uniquely identifies each of the 16 cells.

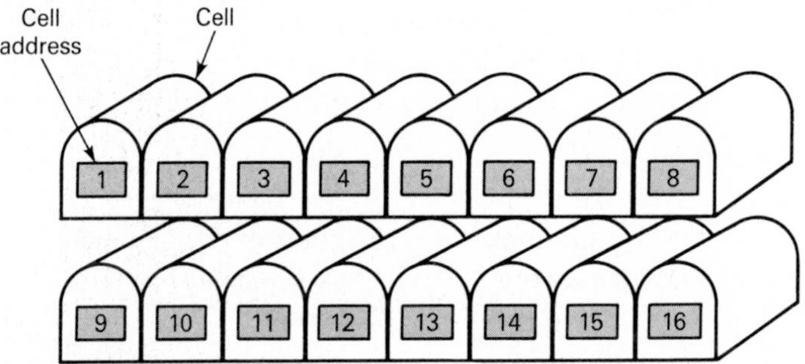

Fig. 2-2 A bank of memory cells with cell addresses, which can be thought of as mailboxes.

We have a very good way to think about banks of memory cells. Figure 2-2 appears to look like the mailboxes of a building or post office. The letters to be put into (or taken from) the boxes are exactly like the numbers to be stored (or examined) in the memory cell. The names on the mailboxes are exactly like the addresses of our cell. In fact, while we said that numbers were assigned to distinguish one cell from another, it is also possible to *associate names with each cell.* We could assign the name CELL1 to the memory cell labeled 1 in Fig. 2-2. In the same way CELL2, CELL3, etc., could be used for the names of the other cells.

In Fig. 2-2 all the memory cells are equally accessible. It would take about the same time to read the contents of CELL5 as it would to read the contents of CELL16. When the memory cells are arranged so that it takes the same time to access any one of the cells, the memory is called *random-access memory,* or *RAM*.

2-2-1 Memory Size Problems

The size of the cell bank, or number of individual cells, determines how large a program or how much data can be stored in the computer at any given instant. Memory size is specified in bytes. A *byte* is equivalent to 8 bits and is often the smallest amount of memory which can be directly addressed. While the computer may be able to manipulate groups which are larger than 1 byte, it usually cannot address less than 1 byte at a time. (On rare occasions the computer addresses the upper or lower 4 bits of a byte. Such segments of a byte are called *nibbles*.)

Typical memory sizes are 1, 2, 4, 8, 16, 32, 64, 128, and 512 KB, and 1, 2, and 4 MB. The "KB" stands for *kilobyte*, which you might expect to represent 1000 bytes, and the "MB" stands for *megabyte*, which you would similarly expect to be 1 million bytes. However, since we are dealing with machines that use binary for internal representation, we generally deal with quantities that are exact powers of 2. Thus, 1 KB really represents 1024 bytes of memory, close enough to 1000 for general approximations; 64 KB of memory is really 65,536 bytes; 512 KB is 524,288 bytes. The term "megabyte" also represents an approximation; 1 MB is really 1024 × 1024 bytes, or 1,048,576 bytes of memory. Table 2-3 shows the relationship between the common memory size designations and the exact number of bytes they represent. (The abbreviation KB is sometimes shown as K alone.)

TABLE 2-3

Approximate RAM Size	Actual RAM Size, Bytes
4 K	4,096
8 K	8,192
16 K	16,384
32 K	32,768
64 K	65,536
128 K	131,072
256 K	262,144
512 K	524,288
1 MB	1,048,576
2 MB	2,097,152
4 MB	4,194,304

The greater the RAM size (number of cells), the greater the number of addresses needed to identify all cells. A 4K RAM needs 4096 different addresses to identify all the cells. While computers are usually built so that additional RAM can be added, the amount of RAM which a machine can contain cannot be greater than the number of different addresses which the machine can generate.

Unlike RAM, some types of memory are arranged with their cells in a sequential, or serial, order. Figure 2-3 shows such an arrangement. For

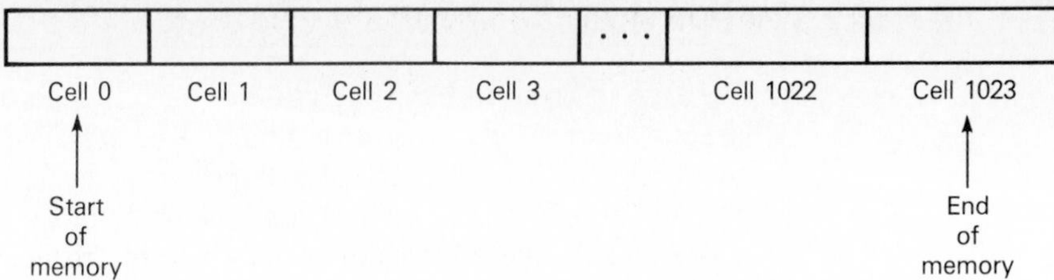

Fig. 2-3 The arrangement of sequential memory cells.

this kind of arrangement the time it takes to locate (access) a cell to read or write a number depends on the cell position. It does not take much time to access a cell near the beginning. If the cell is near the middle, it takes more time to access the data. In serial arrangements we do not see all cells at the same time. To gain access to a cell in such a memory, we must start at the beginning of the memory and compare each cell address with the desired cell address. When the actual cell address and the desired cell address agree, we have reached the correct memory location.

Serial memories are often much larger than RAMs, and they can store more data than RAMs. A memory of this type might contain 100 million or more cells. RAMs rarely exceed 10 million cells. Another factor is cost; serial memory is often much less expensive than RAM when cost is calculated as cost per number of cells. One common example of a serial memory is a magnetic tape. Figure 2-4 shows the way magnetic tape, or *mag tape*, memory is arranged. The data or numbers are stored as magnetic impulses on a flexible plastic tape which has a coating of magnetic material.

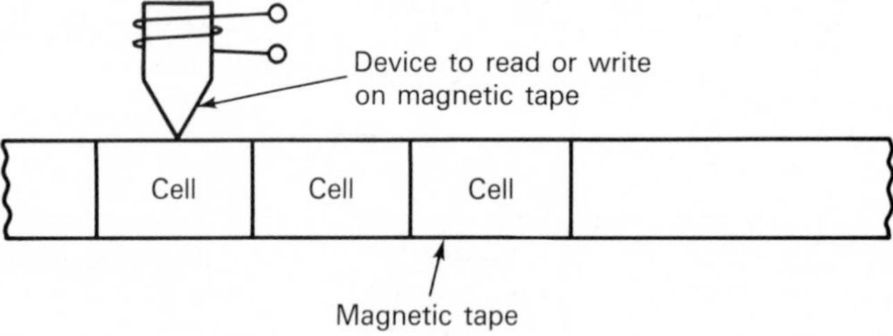

Fig. 2-4 Magnetic tape memory cells.

PROBLEMS FOR SECTION 2-2-1

1. Within a computer, the binary (or 0, 1) code is used to represent the address of a memory cell. How many binary digits (bits) are needed to address 131,072 RAM cells?

2. Create a table of values with one column containing the number of bits in a RAM address and the second column containing the maximum number of cells which can be addressed. Complete the table to 20 address bits.

3. Given the following RAM data:

Address	Contents
2000	−25
4095	2,356
3102	31,807

a. What is the address of the cell whose contents are negative?
b. How many bits are needed to address all the locations in the table?
c. How many bits are needed to represent all possible data (cell contents) shown in the table?

4. Indicate a limitation for a computer which uses 16 bits for RAM addresses and 8 bits for cell contents.

2-2-2 Blocks and Pages

In some computers memory locations are grouped together. A number of cells may be grouped into a unit of memory called a *block* or *page*. The memory cells which form the block or page must have consecutive addresses. If 4K cells make up a page, the 4096 cells must have sequential addresses. An illustration of one such arrangement is shown in Fig. 2-5. Different computers have different numbers of cells for each page or block. Page sizes of 256 (.25K), 512 (0.5K), 1024 (1K), or 4096 (4K) cells, are widely used. Block size is determined by the memory organization which is most convenient for the programmer.

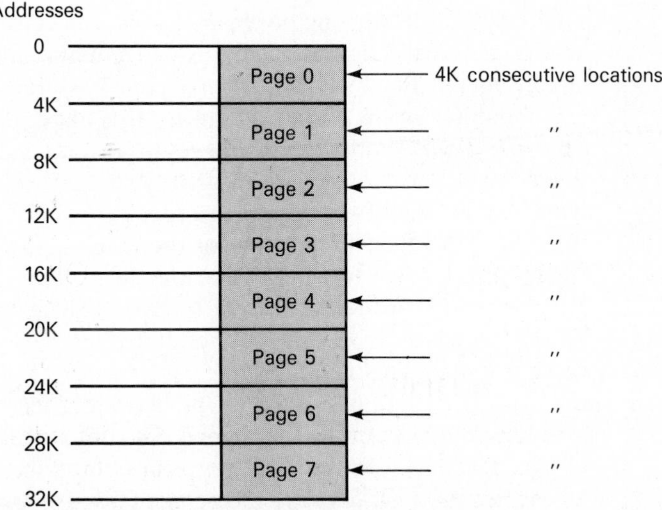

Fig. 2-5 Block or page arrangements of memory.

2-2-3 RAM Organizations

We have shown one way in which we can think of a RAM. Other ways are possible. For example, instead of the post office arrangement of Fig. 2-2, we can imagine a RAM as a *stack* of memory cells. This is shown in Fig. 2-6. Aside from the fact that we think of these cells as stacked on top of each other, they still form a RAM. The main feature of a RAM is that it takes the same time to locate any one of the cells. In most computers, part of the computer's RAM is set aside; this portion is called the *stack*. More than one stack can be set aside in a RAM.

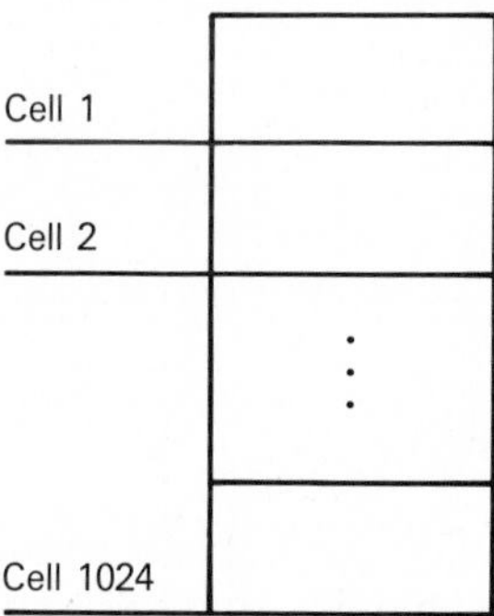

Fig. 2-6 Stack arrangement of memory cells.

Why is the stack arrangement useful? We defined the digital computer as a machine which imitates human calculation methods. When we use pencil and paper to carry out calculations, we sometimes perform our operations in a *stacklike* manner. This will become clear after we have described how the stack works.

Figure 2-7 shows a stack and helps to explain how it works. Before the computer starts carrying out instructions, the cells of the stack are empty. In Fig. 2-7, we have 1024 cells which initially are all empty. (''Empty'' simply means that we *do not care* what is stored in the cell.) Each time the computer needs to store data on the stack, it simply puts such data into one of the empty cells. However, it does not put the data into *any* empty cell. It puts the data into the *first available* (empty) cell, starting from the bottom of the stack. In order for a stack to work, the computer must keep track of the bottom of the stack and the top of the stack. By ''keep track of,'' we mean ''know the address of.'' The computer remembers or points to the address of the first cell of the stack—cell 1, called *bottom of stack* (BOS). It also points to the address of the first available or empty cell. This is called the *top of stack* (TOS). To start, the top of the stack is the same location as the bottom of the stack. Storing a number is called a *push* operation (or pushing data onto the stack). The flow diagram of Fig. 2-8 shows the steps for a push operation. Data is stored in a cell whose location or address is specified by the top of stack. Each push operation proceeds in the same way. An empty cell is filled and the top of

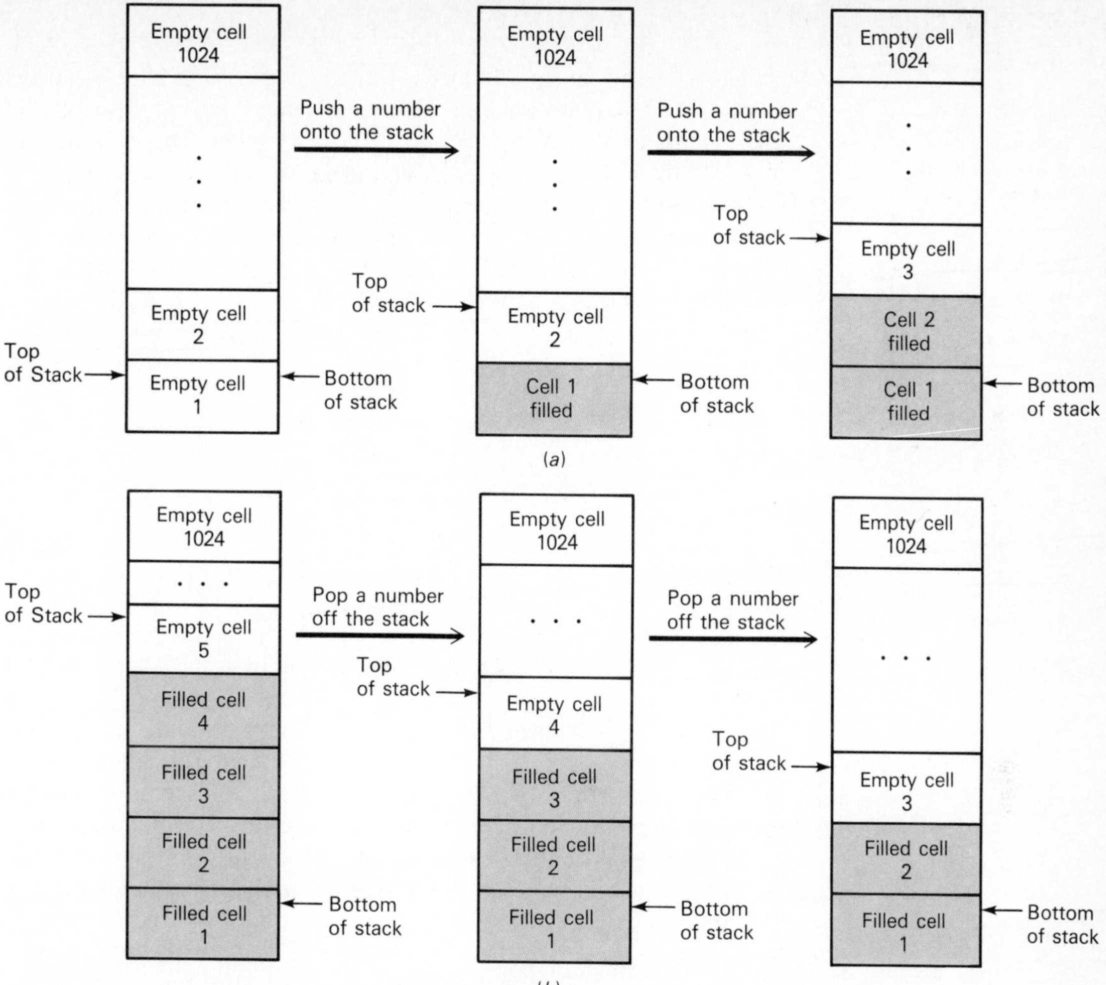

Fig. 2-7 Operations which can be performed using stacks. (*a*) Filling a stack with data. (*b*) Removing data from the stack.

the stack is set to the next empty cell. Figure 2-7*a* shows what happens for two push operations. This is summarized as follows:

First push	Cell 1 is filled	Top of stack is cell 2
Second push	Cell 2 is filled	Top of stack is cell 3

If necessary, the computer could continue to perform push operations. However, there is a limit. The computer cannot fill cells beyond cell 1024 (in this example). The flow diagram of Fig. 2-8 contains a decision block. If the top of the stack is higher than cell 1024, the computer must stop what it is doing and take some corrective action. Usually, the user receives a message (called an *error message*) which describes the problem and also stops the user's program. If the stack does not overflow, the successful push operation is complete.

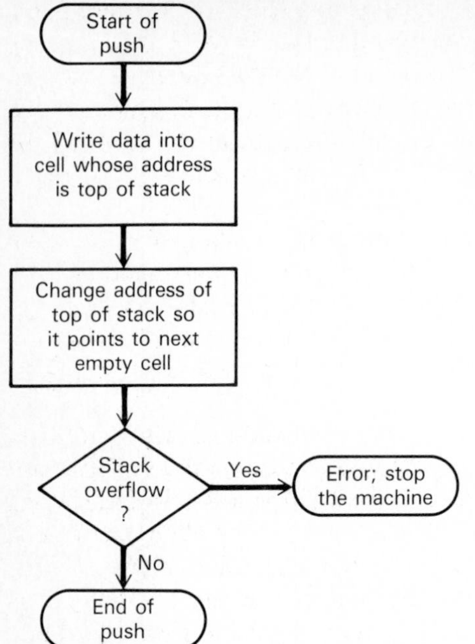

Fig. 2-8 Flow diagram for a stack push operation.

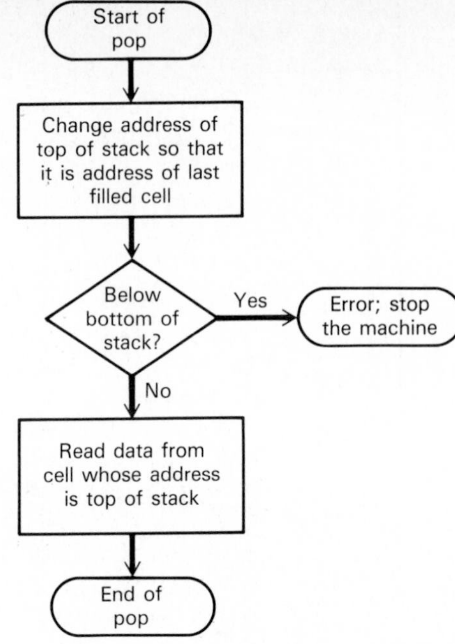

Fig. 2-9 Flow diagram for a stack pop operation.

We also wish to retrieve or remove numbers from the stack. This operation is called a *pop* operation. A flow diagram for the sequence of steps needed to pop a stack is shown in Fig. 2-9. The flow diagram for a pop is different from the flow diagram for a push. Before a pop operation is started, we know that the top-of-stack pointer indicates an address which must be the first available empty cell. This is true for either of the two possible conditions:

1. No operations (push or pop) have occurred, and all cells are empty.
2. One or more push operations have occurred, leaving the top-of-stack address at the first available empty cell.

First we must adjust the address of the top-of-stack pointer so that it contains the address of the last-filled cell. If the addresses of the cells of the stack are numbered in order, subtracting 1 from the top-of-stack pointer causes it to contain the address of the last-filled cell. Again we come to a decision block. We cannot perform pop operations indefinitely. If we did, we would eventually point to a location below the bottom of the stack. Therefore, during a pop operation we must always check to see that the top-of-stack pointer is not less than the address of the first cell of the stack. When this happens, the user will get a message such as "stack underflow," and the machine will be stopped so that some corrective action is possible.

If no errors have been introduced, the top-of-stack pointer now contains the address of the last-filled cell. The data from this cell can now be read or examined. Even though the reading process does not destroy the data in this cell, we now consider this to be an empty cell. We must not pop a number from the stack unless we can afford to lose it. We only use a pop operation when we do not care about the data after we have used it. Although the cell is not physically empty, it is said to be *logically* empty. If a push operation were to be performed, the data in this cell will be replaced by new data. Figure 2-7*b* shows a stack sequence for two successive pop operations.

Numbers at the top of the stack are new data. Numbers at the bottom of the stack have been there for a while. These are older numbers. The numbers which are popped from the stack are the newest or most recent numbers. The last numbers put on a stack are the first numbers taken from a stack. This data arrangement is called a *l*ast-*i*n, *f*irst-*o*ut, or *LIFO*, arrangement.

Figure 2-10 shows a cell whose contents are an address. The number in cell 1 tells the computer where to go (location) to get the information it may need. In the case of a stack, the pointer cell stores the top-of-stack address. When the computer wants to push data, the address of the cell where the data is to be stored is found in the pointer cell. When the data has been deposited at that address, the number in the pointer cell is increased by 1. The cell then points to the next available stack location.

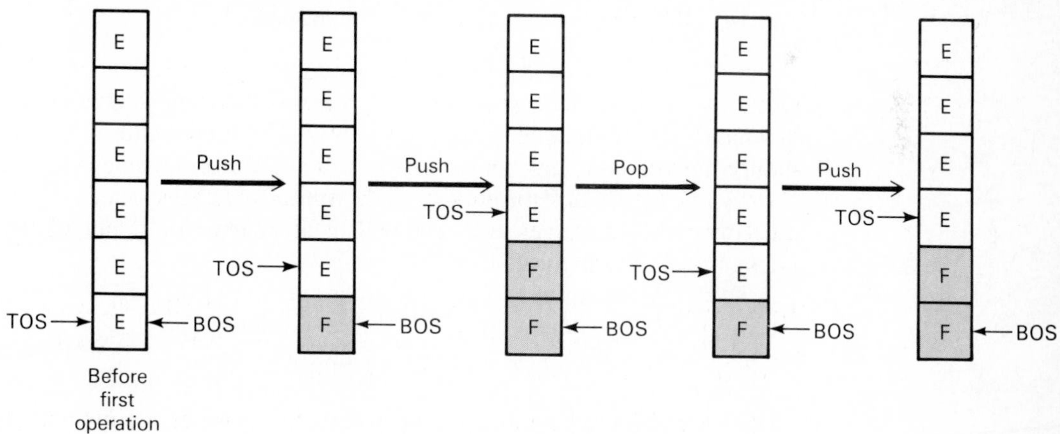

Fig. 2-10 A pointer and how it works.

Sometimes a stack in RAM is not the best arrangement for data. The RAM may need to include other arrangements in addition to stacks. Let us cite some reasons. Computers may be very expensive. Therefore, it is economically sound if they can be shared among a number of users. Each user maintains programs in the computer's memory. Think of the users as customers in a bank. Each customer arrives and waits in line to carry out some business transaction. If the bank teller decided to service the last customer in line, all the other customers would be upset. A very similar problem exists for the computer. Figure 2-11 shows how the users' programs might appear in memory. As each user comes along to be serviced by the computer, a program is placed in the memory on top of the last one. The computer now executes the users' programs. If the computer treats the memory as a stack, user 5's program will be executed first.

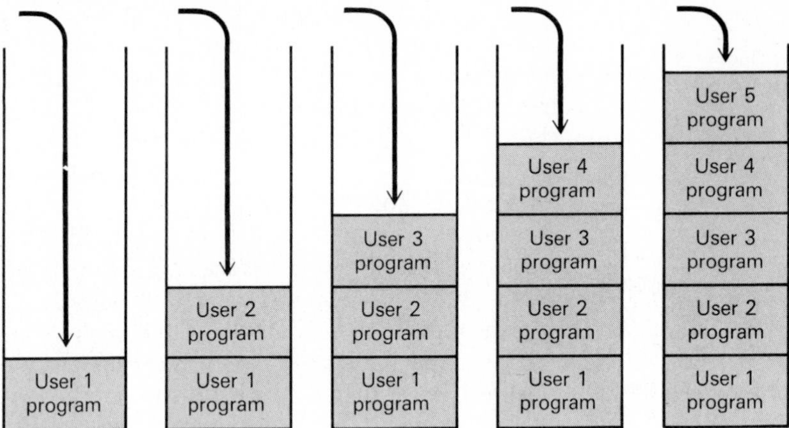

Fig. 2-11 How users' programs are stored in memory.

Other users might be upset. What is needed is an arrangement in memory in which user 1 would be the first program that the computer services even though user 1 is at the bottom of memory. This arrangement means the first in line is the first to be serviced. We call such a list a *first-in, first-out*, or *FIFO*, arrangement. The FIFO arrangement is called a *queue* (pronounced like the letter "Q").

A flow diagram for managing a queue is shown in Fig. 2-12. Two pointers are used: *head of queue* (*HOQ*) and *tail of queue* (*TOQ*). The HOQ tells us the address of the first memory location of our queue and that it is the starting point of the queue. The TOQ tells us the address of the last memory location of the queue and that it is the end of the queue.

The number of items (memory locations) in a queue can be calculated using the formula

$$\text{TOQ} - \text{HOQ} + 1$$

This formula takes the number found in the cell where TOQ is stored, then subtracts the number found in the cell which stores HOQ and adds 1 to the result.

Figure 2-13 is a flow diagram which shows how items are removed from a queue.

Another arrangement is called a *circular queue*. When (during item additions) we reach the end of the RAM set aside for our queue, we check the top of the queue (circle back). If the top of the queue is empty, we

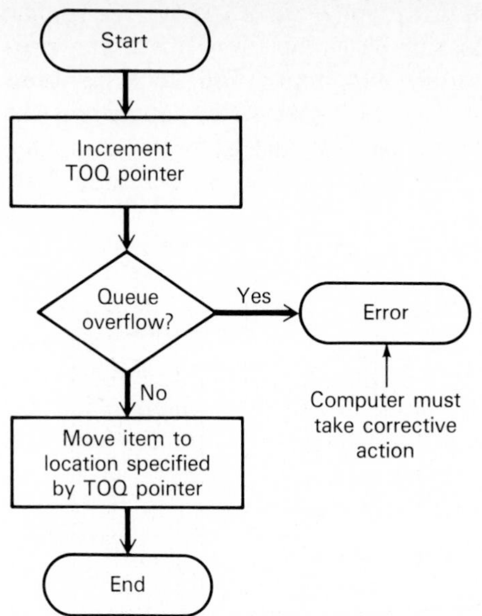

Fig. 2-12 Flow diagram showing how to add an item of data to a queue.

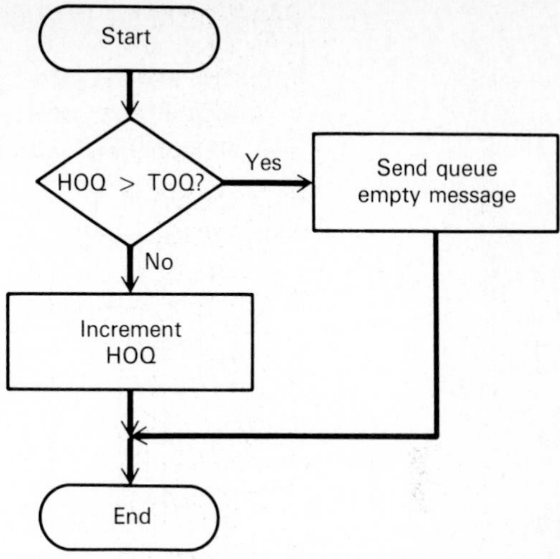

Fig. 2-13 Flow diagram showing how to get an item of data from the queue.

can add our item(s) there. Figure 2-14 represents additions and deletions using the idea of circling back to the head of the queue when we reach the bottom. Another way to think of this circular queue is shown in Fig. 2-14*b*. Imagine that the bottom of the RAM space which has been set aside for the queue is picked up and bent around to the top of the RAM space set aside for the queue. The circular shape of Fig. 2-14*b* is the result. The dark line indicates where the two ends have been "joined." They are not physically connected, but we can think of them in this way as far as the queue is concerned.

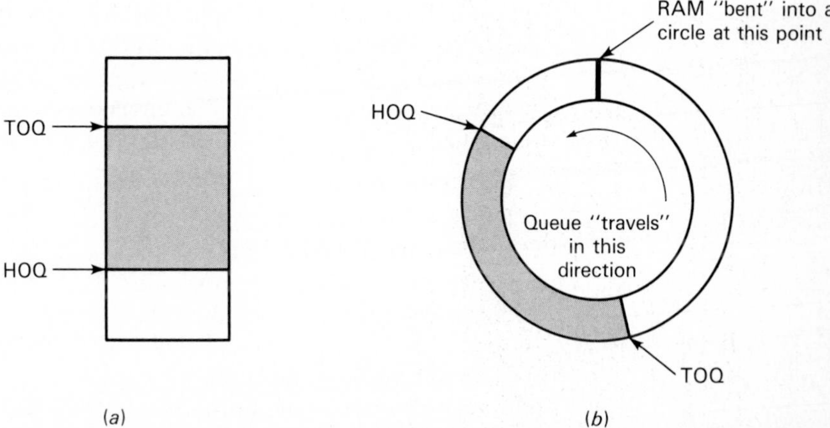

Fig. 2-14 The way to avoid queue problems. (*a*) The queue after additions of data to the top of an ordinary queue. (*b*) A new way of looking at a queue.

PROBLEMS FOR SECTION 2-2-3

1. Draw a diagram of a stack with all cells empty. The stack has been allocated five locations. For each sequence given below, show how the cells are filled and emptied. Indicate the TOS and BOS.

   a. Push, push, pop, push
   b. Push, push, pop, pop, pop
   c. Push, push, push, push, push, push
   d. Push, pop, push, push, pop

2. A stack begins at address 3000 in a computer's RAM. It contains 128 locations. The first two locations have already been filled. What are the values of the TOS pointer and the BOS pointer after the following additional stack operations: pop, push, push, push, pop?

3. a. A stack contains the following data:

   TOS A code number for the letter "A"
   A code number for a space or blank
   A code number for the letter "M"
   A code number for the letter "E"
   A code number for the letter "S"
   A code number for the letter "S"
   A code number for the letter "A"
   A code number for the letter "G"
   BOS A code number for the letter "E"

   Nine pops are performed and the data is transmitted to the terminal of a computer. What appears on the terminal?

   b. On the basis of the example shown in Prob. 3*a*, suggest one use for a stack.

4. Stacks are helpful in calculating formulas. Suppose you are given two stacks, one containing a list of operations to be performed and another containing the numbers (operands) to be used in the calculations. (This architecture is similar to the one envisioned by Charles Babbage.) The following rules describe the way these stacks are used:

   a. Pop an operation to be performed from the operations stack.
   b. Pop an operand from the number stack and call it N1. Pop a second operand from the number stack and call this one N2.
   c. Perform the indicated operation on the two numbers. Use N1 as the first number in the operation and N2 as the second number in the operation.
   d. Push the result on the operand stack.
   e. Repeat the sequence until the operations stack is empty.

   Follow these rules for the following stacks:

Operations stack	Number (operand)
TOS −	25 TOS
*	20
BOS +	−8
	5 BOS

* Indicates multiplication.

e. What formula is being calculated?
f. What is the result of the calculations? Carry this out by following the rules indicated above.

5. Cite another example (in addition) to the one described in this section) where a queue might be a useful structure to solve the problem.

6. Draw a flow diagram which shows how to make additions to a circular queue.

7. Draw a flow diagram which shows how to take items from a circular queue.

8. Compute the number of items in a queue when TOQ = 125 and HOQ = 38.

9. You are supervisor of a computer-controlled automated railroad switching yard. Freight cars are lined up as shown in Fig. 2-15. Cars can be shunted from the "in" track to the stack using a Push command. Cars can be shunted from the stack track to the "out" track using a pop command. What sequence of pushes and pops will rearrange the cars as shown in the diagram?

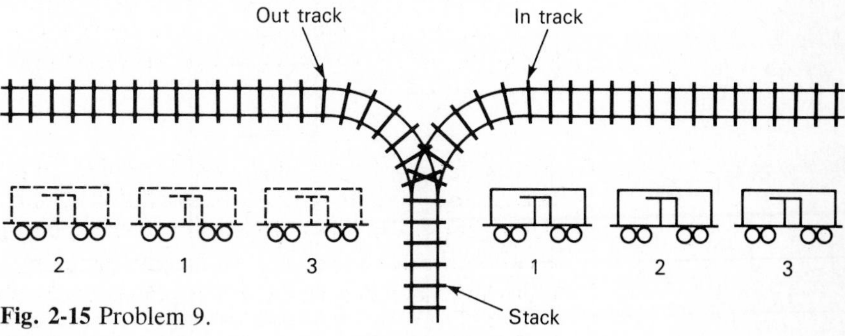

Fig. 2-15 Problem 9.

2-3 SECONDARY MEMORY AND THE COMPUTER FILE SYSTEM

Some computers are built to serve many users at the same time. For this reason they include a large main memory in the form of RAM. They may also include one or more small, high-speed memory areas called *caches*. Such an arrangement can increase the speed of operation of the main memory. However, RAM memory is costly. Therefore, computers rarely contain enough main memory to store all the potential data and programs of the many users. Instead, the computer is equipped with very high data capacity memory devices called *secondary memories*. These are much less expensive than the main memory components. (The cost may be computed by taking the ratio of total cost to number of items stored.) The secondary memory is also much slower than main memory. It takes longer to retrieve a number from a secondary storage device. Usually, secondary storage is nonvolatile. When the computer is turned off, information in secondary memory will not be lost. This is important because a user completing a program may want to save the data, results, or program itself in some kind of record. A secondary storage device allows a user to store such information.

When the computer is executing users' programs, only the necessary instructions and data are kept in main memory. The remainder of the program and data are kept in secondary memory, to be transferred into main memory only when they are needed. In this way the limited amount of main memory may be shared among many users. The relationship between the various parts of the computer's memory is shown in Fig. 2-16. The blocks marked "User 1," "User 2," etc., are the programs and data of the various people and other computers which are using the machine. Yes, one computer can be thought of as a user on another computer. For the example shown in the figure, the cache may currently contain part of the programs and data of user 1, user 2, and user 3. A RAM is shown containing a portion of the programs of user 1 to user 5. The secondary memory contains the complete programs of user 1 to user 8. Each user is

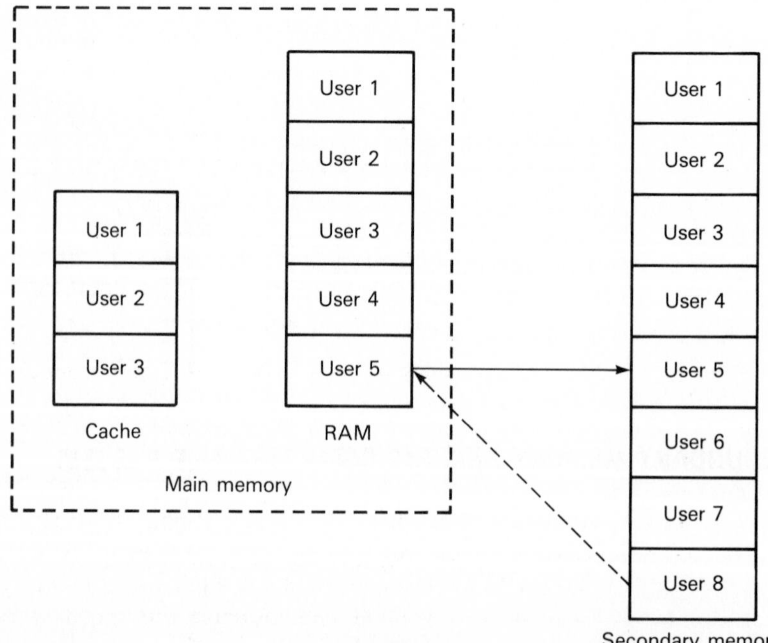

Fig. 2-16 The various parts of the computer memory and how they are shared among users.

allowed a small amount of time (called a *time slice*) in which to execute part of a program in the computer's central processing unit (CPU). When the time comes to give user 8 a chance on the computer, the program of user 8 is moved from secondary storage into main memory. One of the programs in main memory must be removed. The computer may decide to remove the program of user 5. Such an operation is called a *swap*.

2-3-1 Secondary Storage Systems

Secondary storage devices usually use magnetic material. Portions of this material can be magnetized. A magnetic code may be created for each number to be stored on the device. The numbers are placed on the magnetic surface in a sequential manner by a device which magnetizes the surface according to the coded form of the number to be stored. The device which lays down (writes) the magnetic pattern can also detect (read) the magnetic code. The device is called the *read/write head,* or simply *head*. Various kinds of magnetic arrangements are shown in Fig. 2-17.

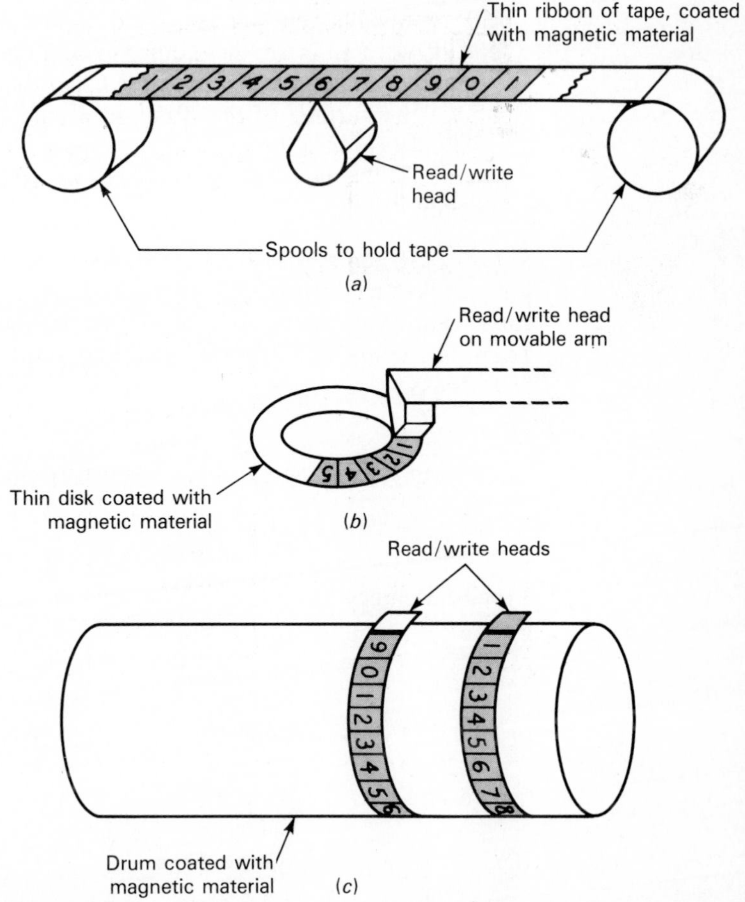

Fig. 2-17 Secondary storage devices. (*a*) Magnetic tape. (*b*) Magnetic disk. (*c*) Magnetic drum.

These include magnetic surfaces in the form of a ribbon called a *tape,* or mag tape, a *disk,* or a *drum.*

One type of secondary storage not shown in the figure is *bubble storage.* Its great advantage is that it has no moving parts. Operation of this is quite complicated, and we shall not discuss it here.

There are two general classes of magnetic disk drives:

1. *Flexible disk (floppy disk)* - A system in which the medium is not rigid. The disk is made of a thin sheet of plastic coated with magnetic material and is contained in a protective envelope. The floppy disk can be removed from its drive, thus making transportation of a program or data file a simple matter. The head or heads in a floppy disk drive come into actual contact with the rotating magnetic material of the disk. Any contamination of the disk surface with dirt, grease, or other foreign substances may make the disk unreadable.
2. *Rigid disk (hard disk)* - A system in which the medium is rigid. The disk is made of an aluminum platter coated with the magnetic material. This type of disk is usually housed in a hard plastic cartridge if it is of the removable type, or is contained within an airtight housing within the drive if it is of the nonremovable type. In a hard disk system (sometimes called a *Winchester drive*) the head or heads ride slightly above the surface of the disk, on a cushion of air. However, since a hard disk rotates at a much higher speed than a floppy disk, any foreign matter on the disk will generally cause severe damage to the disk, head, or both.

Table 2-4 compares several secondary storage methods, including the time it takes to retrieve data from the device. The numbers for speed and capacity indicate ranges of many systems; they are not strict boundaries. There are many different devices, and some include small capacity and fast access.

TABLE 2-4 COMPARISON OF SECONDARY STORAGE DEVICES AND RAM

Type of Memory	Capacity (Number of Characters)	Average Time to Access Data*
RAM	To 4 million	50–100 ns (0.05–0.01 ms)
Drum	2 million to 9 million	8–50 ms
Disk (floppy)	125,000 to 1 million	100–800 ms
Disk (hard)	0.5 to 300 million	25–500 ms
Tape	Many billions	15 s to 30 min

* The abbreviation "ms" stands for milliseconds, or 0.001 s; "ns" stands for nanoseconds, or 10^{-9}s.

PROBLEM FOR SECTION 2-3-1

1. Draw a graph which has capacity (number of characters) on the Y axis and average access time on the X axis. On the graph outline the regions occupied by RAM storage, floppy disk, hard disk, and mag tape.

2-3-2 Computer File Systems

Proper cell identification is needed to read or write data. In the secondary storage device identification is aided by prerecorded magnetic coding called its *format*. Figure 2-18*a* illustrates the physical arrangement or format of a floppy disk, while Fig. 2-18*b* shows what information is con-

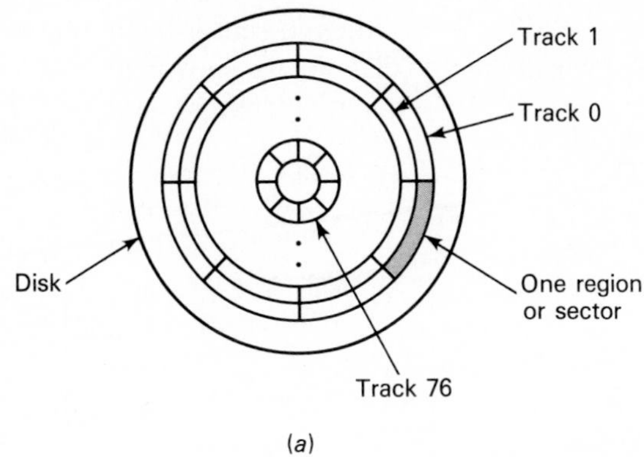

(*a*)

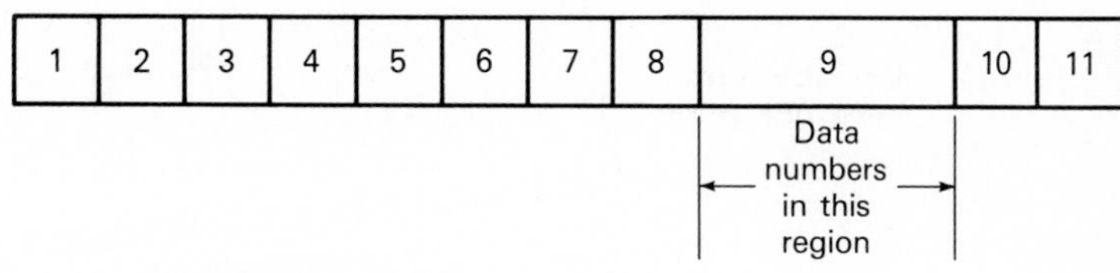

Subregion	Purpose
1	Marks start of the sector
2	Track number
3	Head number
4	Sector number
5	Length of sector
6	Used to find read/write errors made by device
7	Space or gap on disk before start of data
8	Marks start of data region
9	128, 256, 384, 512, or more cells of secondary memory
10	Used to find read/write errors made by device
11	Space before start of next sector

(*b*)

Fig. 2-18 Format for IBM soft-sectored single-density flexible diskette. (*a*) Physical arrangement. (*b*) Information (signs) found on the diskette.

tained within a single sector of the floppy disk. This is the format known as the IBM soft-sectored, single-density, flexible diskette format. The disk is divided into regions just like floors in a building. The regions include 77 *tracks*. There are 26 *sectors* within each track. In addition to storing a user's data, a sector may also include information which positively identifies the location of each sector within the disk. Since the drive can always determine the position of the head by reading any sector's location information, a very reliable secondary storage system is realized.

The number of bytes stored within each sector can be varied but is often a multiple of 128 bytes. There might be 128, 256, 384, 512, or more bytes stored in each sector. Data sets larger than one sector in length are stored in multiple sectors. A program which includes 129 bytes and which is stored on a disk with 128-byte sectors would be allocated two sectors, with 127 bytes of the second sector being unused.

A typical floppy diskette is shown in Fig. 2-19. Floppy disk sectors occur in strictly sequential manner. Sector 1 is followed physically by

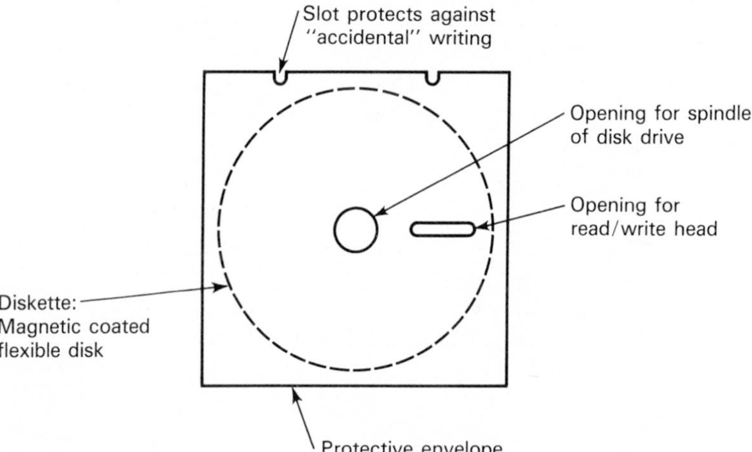

Fig. 2-19 What floppy (flexible) diskettes look like.

sector 2. This continues for all 26 sectors on each of the tracks of the diskette. Imagine the sectors passing under the reading head. The computer might require the disk device to read (or write) sectors 1 and 2. Normally, the floppy disk reads one sector at a time and sends the data to the computer before reading another sector. Transmission of the data in sector 1 takes time. During this time sector 2 passes under the head. The floppy disk cannot read this data yet because it has not completed its transmission for sector 1. It has missed sector 2. The computer must wait until sector 2 again passes under the head before reading the data in this sector to complete the required operation. The time it takes for the diskette to make a rotation can be as much as 0.8 s. For computers this is a very long time. The lost time may severely slow operation of the machine.

To avoid this lost time, a different scheme is used to store the data. Sector 2 is still physically next to sector 1, but sector 2 is not written after sector 1. A file needing two sectors could use sector 1 for the first sector and sector 14 for the second logical sector. This would give the drive time to access the data in sector 1 and be ready to access the next portion of the file before the sector in which it is contained (sector 14) comes into position under the head. If additional sectors were needed to contain the file, sector 2 could be used, followed by sector 15, followed by sector 3, etc. This is called *interleaving*.

If the drive is capable of high-speed communications with the computer, the sectors may be interleaved in two, three, four or more parts. In this manner, as many as three or four sectors could be read and transmitted within the time of a single revolution of the disk.

The disk's format locates places within the secondary memory. However, the format does not help to identify data within each sector. Does the information belong to user 1 or user 2? Some data in the computer's secondary storage may be shared by many users. One common example of this is an airline reservation system. All information about a particular flight is maintained in the secondary memory. This could include flight numbers, departure and arrival times, destinations, passenger list, number of seats, and other items of importance. Each airline reservation agent needs to be able to access the data. Thus, the data does not belong to any one user. It must be available to many people. We need a way to identify such data.

The computer's file system manages the details of file storage on the disk. We have established that a given program might be stored on a number of sectors. This collection of sectors forms a *file*. A file may also contain data. If so, it consists of a collection of data *records*. Again, this file may include one or more sectors.

This relationship is shown in Fig. 2-20. In the example depicted, sectors 1, 2, and 4 contain the data which make up record 1. Sectors 6, 7, and 9

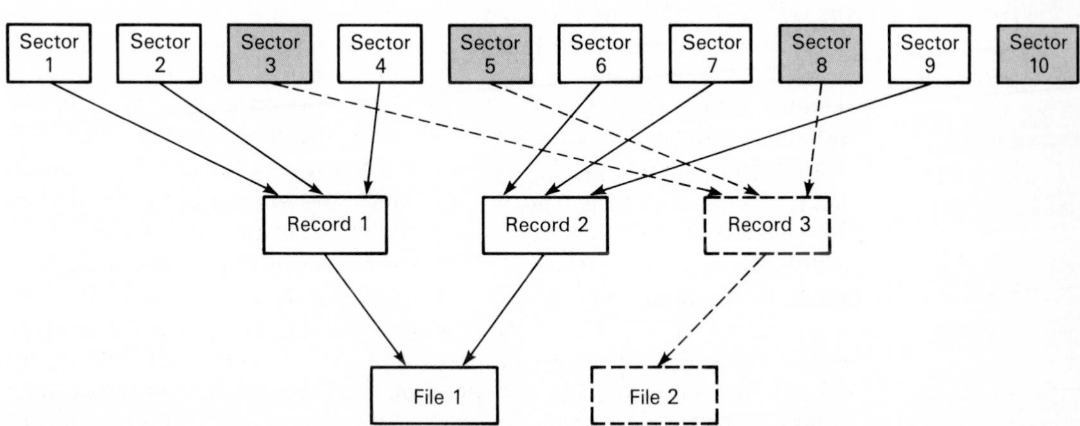

Fig. 2-20 How sectors form records and then files in the secondary memory.

contain the data which make up record 2. Together, records 1 and 2 make up the complete data file, namely, file 1.

Sectors might not be associated with any file at a given moment. The sectors are unallocated and may be used for storing new data. For example, a user might need to store a program once it is completed. The user would instruct the computer to save the program on the disk. The computer determines how many sectors are needed to store the program. If three sectors are needed, it might allocate sectors 3, 5, and 8 to form this new file (file 2).

The file system must keep track of the files. This is accomplished in a way which is very similar to systems employed by libraries to keep track of its books. We can think of each sector as a page within a book even though they are not contiguous as they would be in a real book. Sectors (pages) are collected into files (books). In a library, a book must be put on a shelf. In a similar way each file must be located somewhere in the secondary memory. The library uses an index and index cards to locate books in the library. The file system uses a *directory* to tell us where to find each file.

What kind of information does a file system keep in its directory for each file? The following list includes some of the information which might be found in a directory entry:

File name
Owner or creator
Size of file
Sector locations
Type of file (attributes of the file)
Date and time created
Date and time last used
Other miscellaneous information

Each item deserves a brief explanation. The *file name* identifies the file so that it can be accessed by the computer when necessary.

The *owner* entry specifies who has control of the file. In general, only the owner has the right to alter (modify or delete) a file. There may be other considerations, such as additional users who might be allowed access privileges. Security may dictate that only certain persons have access to the information in the file and that no one but the file's owner may change the data in the file.

The *file size* helps the file system keep track of how many sectors are needed to retain the file. This in turn helps to manage the pool of available sectors.

The file sector *locations* can be handled in several ways. Two such methods are shown in Fig. 2-21. One method uses *pointer sectors*. The entry for "location" (Fig. 2-21*a*) contains 15. This is sector number 15. In sector 15 we see the numbers 100, 101, and 102. These numbers tell us the numbers of all the sectors which make up the file. A second method is shown in Fig. 2-21*b*. This uses a *linked list*. It works as follows. In the

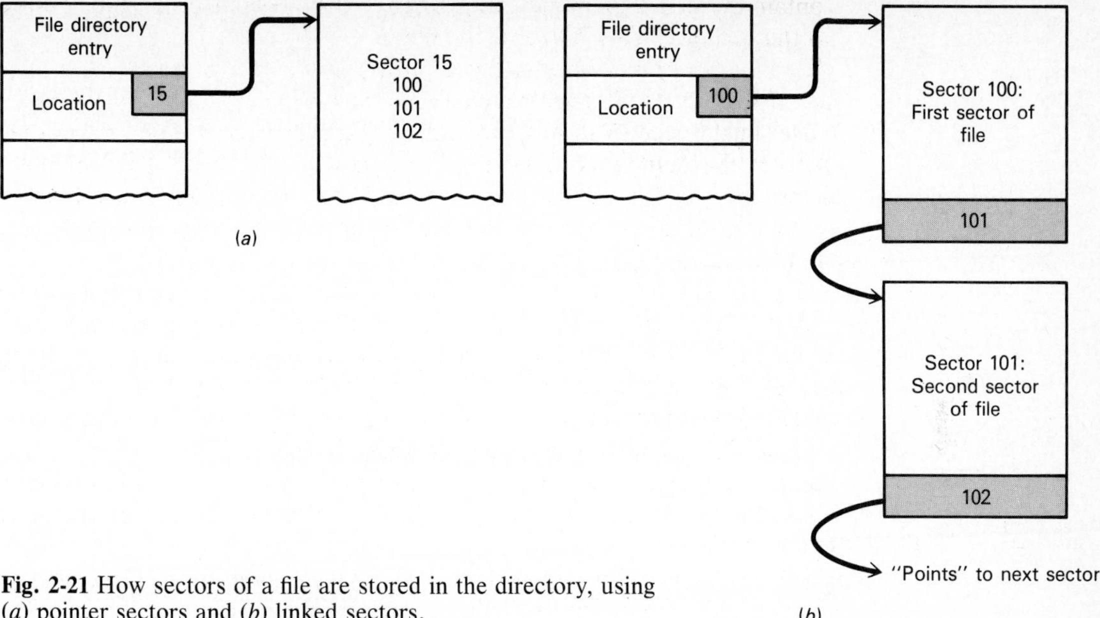

Fig. 2-21 How sectors of a file are stored in the directory, using (*a*) pointer sectors and (*b*) linked sectors.

location entry of the directory, the number of the first sector of the file can be found. In the example shown the number 100 indicates that sector 100 is the first sector of the file. The last number in sector 100 tells us where to find the next sector of the file. In this case it is sector 101. The last number in each sector tells us where to find the next sector in the file. Each sector contains a link to the next sector. The last sector of a file might contain the number 0 (as its last number). This tells us that there are no more sectors in the file. It is called the *null pointer.*

The *attributes* in the directory tell the computer what kinds of operations are permitted with the file. If the file contains data, it cannot be executed; it contains no instructions. Similarly, we would not usually want to read a file which contains a program as if it were a data file. The attributes entry tells the computer what operations may be performed with the file. In some systems the attributes may further specify whether a file may be deleted by any user, read by any user, or changed by any user.

PROBLEMS FOR SECTION 2-3-2

1. The same data is written at several different places on a floppy diskette. Describe a purpose (and advantage) for this. Name a disadvantage.

2. The number of physical sectors between logical sectors is called the *interleave factor.* For example, the physical sector sequence

   1, 4, 7, 10, 13, 16, 19, 22, 25, 2, 5, 8, 11, 14, 17, 20, 23, 26, 3, 6, 9, 12, 15, 18, 21, 24 corresponds to an interleave factor of 3. Write the sector sequence for an interleave factor of 5.

3. There are 2002 possible sectors (77 tracks and 26 sectors per track) on a diskette. These are assigned logical numbers from 1 to 2002. The diskette uses an interleave factor of 3. What is the track number and physical sector number on that track which corresponds to logical sector 1308?

4. A file system uses a linked list to locate sectors in a given file.

   a. Describe the steps which can be used to insert a new sector in the middle of the list.
   b. Describe the steps which can be used to delete a sector from the middle of the list.

   You may use flow diagrams to simplify explanations.

SUMMARY

The computer's memory consists of cells which can store or remember numbers. Numbers may be data or instructions (commands) which make up the program that the computer executes. There are different kinds of memory. Nonvolatile memory can retain data even without power. If the memory forgets or loses data when power is turned off, it is called volatile memory. Even when power is applied, dynamic memories need to be refreshed or they will lose data. Examining memory locations or cells is called reading the memory. Putting new numbers into a memory cell is called writing. RAM memory cells can be read or changed (written over). ROM memory can only have read operations performed on its cells.

If all cells of a memory are equally accessible, the memory is called random-access memory. Sometimes the cells appear in a sequential arrangement. This kind of memory is slow because we must always start at the first cell when we want to access any particular location. However, sequential memories can store a lot of data.

Memory cells can appear like cafeteria trays—on top of one another. Cells organized like this form a stack. Stacks are useful arrangements in the performance of arithmetic calculations. They are called last-in first-out arrangements, or LIFOs. In order to keep track of all computer users and maintain order, the first-in first-out memory organization is preferable. Such an arrangement is called a FIFO.

To increase memory capacity, data and programs can be kept on a large but slow secondary storage device and can be swapped into faster RAMs when needed. To keep track of all the data in the secondary storage system, a file system—similar to that found in a library—is used to organize the data into convenient groups.

REVIEW QUESTIONS

1. What is a memory?
2. Define what is meant by a write operation.
3. Define what is meant by a read operation.
4. Name four attributes (characteristics) which can be applied to a computer's memory.
5. Describe the four characteristics named in Question 4.
6. Name three possible interpretations for the number stored in a memory cell.
7. What is the binary code (0, 1) form of the decimal numbers 0 to 9?
8. What is a bit?
9. How many bits are needed to represent all decimal numbers from 0 to 3250?
10. What is the address of a memory cell?
11. What is an important characteristic of RAM?
12. What is a block of memory?
13. What is another name which is sometimes used to describe a block of memory?
14. Describe a memory stack.
15. Describe what happens during a push operation.
16. Describe what happens during a pop operation.
17. What is another name for a stack structure?
18. What is a queue?
19. What is another name for a queue structure?
20. Define and explain the meaning of the terms TOQ and HOQ.
21. Using TOQ and HOQ, write a formula which can be used to calculate the number of items in a queue.
22. What are the characteristics of a computer's secondary memory compared with its main memory?
23. What is meant by the format of the secondary storage device?
24. How many tracks and sectors are there in the IBM soft-sectored, single-density, flexible diskette format?
25. What is meant by interleaving?

26. Why is interleaving useful?

27. What is a file?

28. What is a record?

29. What data may be found in a file directory entry?

30. Describe two methods for keeping track of all the sectors associated with a given file.

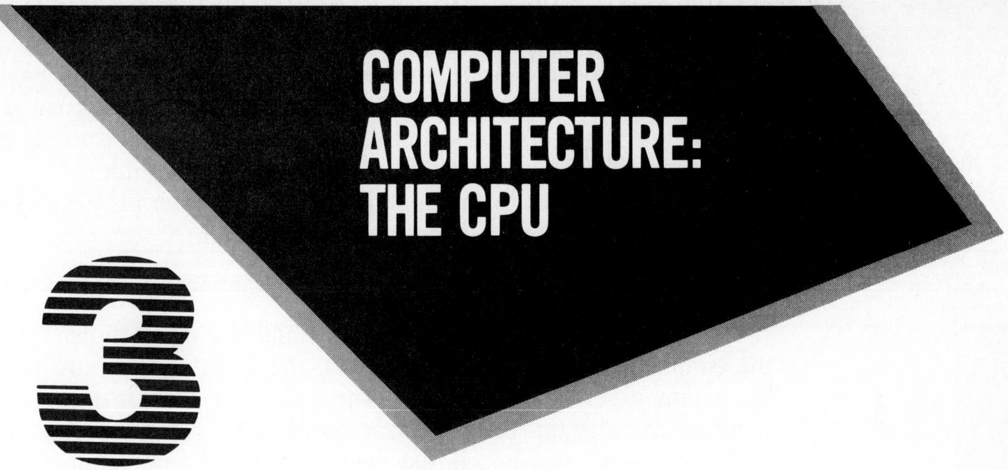

The central processing unit, or *CPU,* is another main element of the computer. The CPU controls the operation of the machine through the series of instructions contained within the user's program. This chapter will discuss the CPU and its functions.

3-1 WHAT THE CPU DOES

As a sample of what the CPU does, consider the following example.

Example 3-1. The Nature of Instructions

The computer is to be programmed to calculate the sum of two numbers. This can be stated in the form of sentences which describe the calculation to be performed:

> Calculate the sum of two numbers. The first number is designated "A" and the second number is designated "B." The result is to be called "C." When they are needed, the user will supply the values for A and B from the keyboard of the machine. The result is to be displayed on a suitable device such as a printer or visual monitor.

The following sequence of commands using a *symbolic* language might be used to describe the simple addition problem:

```
INPUT A, B
LET C = A + B
PRINT C
END
```

The first command instructs the computer to accept the two numbers, A and B, from the device normally used to enter numbers (the keyboard). The second command describes the calculation (addition) to be performed, with the sum (result) being called C as required by the original problem. Finally, the value of C is displayed, or printed, on the device used for human communication—usually a printer or visual monitor. The final statement (END) signifies to the computer that this is the physical end of the sequence of operations to be performed (program).

The computer cannot directly understand the instructions specified in the commands just described. Instead, these instructions are first *translated* into a series of numbers. The computer then uses the resultant numbers to carry out the necessary operations.

Computer instructions, in the form of numbers, are retained or stored in the memory section of the machine. The purpose of the CPU is to examine and interpret these numbers. The numbers control a sequence of operations within the machine, and this sequence of operations is controlled by the CPU. This chapter describes the CPU and the elements which are needed to perform this control function.

Perhaps you can see some of the operations which a CPU must perform from Example 3-1. If you examine how the computer executes a program you will see that it carries out a sequence of repetitive steps. These include:

1. Get an instruction from the memory. This operation is called a *fetch*.
2. The instruction may require data to be supplied from one or more memory locations. Data within such locations are called *operands*. If an operand is required, it must be read from the memory as well.
3. Next, carry out the instruction. For example, if the instruction requires addition, then the machine is required to perform the addition at this point.
4. It may be necessary to store the results of the calculation in the memory. If this is required, then the computer writes this information into the memory.
5. The sequence of operations, starting at step 1, is repeated. On occasion, the instruction which is executed (step 3) causes the computer to stop. If this is the case, then the sequence will halt.

On the basis of the steps just described, the CPU has two well-defined tasks to perform. The first is to be sure that the instructions are carried out. If the instruction is an addition instruction, then the CPU must have circuitry which carries out this operation. Second, instructions and data must be obtained (fetched) from the memory. The CPU is responsible for accessing memory in order to read or write data. This might be called *managing the memory*. In short, the CPU must be able to execute instructions and to interact (interface) with the memory of the computer. (The word "memory" implies a location within the computer. For example, data which comes from the keyboard may be said to be stored in a location which has been set aside for the exclusive use of the keyboard.) These functions can be included in a simple block diagram which describes the CPU. This is shown in Fig. 3-1.

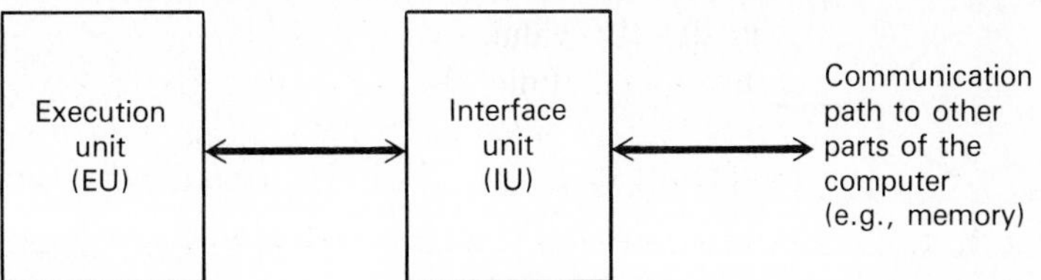

Fig. 3-1 The modern CPU consists of two components: an execution unit for calculations and an interface unit for memory accesses.

Problems for Section 3-1

1. Modify the instructions in Example 3-1 so that the difference of A and B is computed.
2. Modify the instructions in Example 3-1 so that the product of A and B is calculated. Use an asterisk (*) for the multiplication sign.

3-2 HOW THE CPU WORKS

In the past there have been many different kinds of CPUs. The CPU organization described in Fig. 3-1 is the kind of device that may be found in a modern computer. In particular, it is a simplified picture of a processor known as the 8086. The 8086 is a very popular processor found in many computer systems.

Early computers (CPUs) carried out memory accesses and instruction execution in a strictly serial way. The five steps outlined above were performed just as they appear in the list. Very large scale integrated circuit (VLSI) fabrication techniques have provided a way in which to perform these steps more rapidly. The modern CPU actually contains two distinct components. The first one carries out the instructions which are stored in the memory. This part is called the *execution unit,* or EU. The second part of the CPU fetches instructions and data from the memory of the computer. This section is called the *interface unit,* or *IU*. Because these are separate units, the two operations (fetching and executing) can take place *simultaneously.* The IU can fetch new instructions while the EU carries out those which have already been fetched. The CPU does not have to wait to receive the next instruction from the memory. This greatly speeds the operation of the computer and execution of the program. This results in two orders of magnitude (100 to 1) improvement in the speed of operation over the older computer systems.

Figure 3-2 shows a flow diagram which outlines how instructions may be fetched and executed simultaneously. This diagram consists of two parts. One part describes the tasks performed by the EU, while the second part describes the steps carried out by the IU.

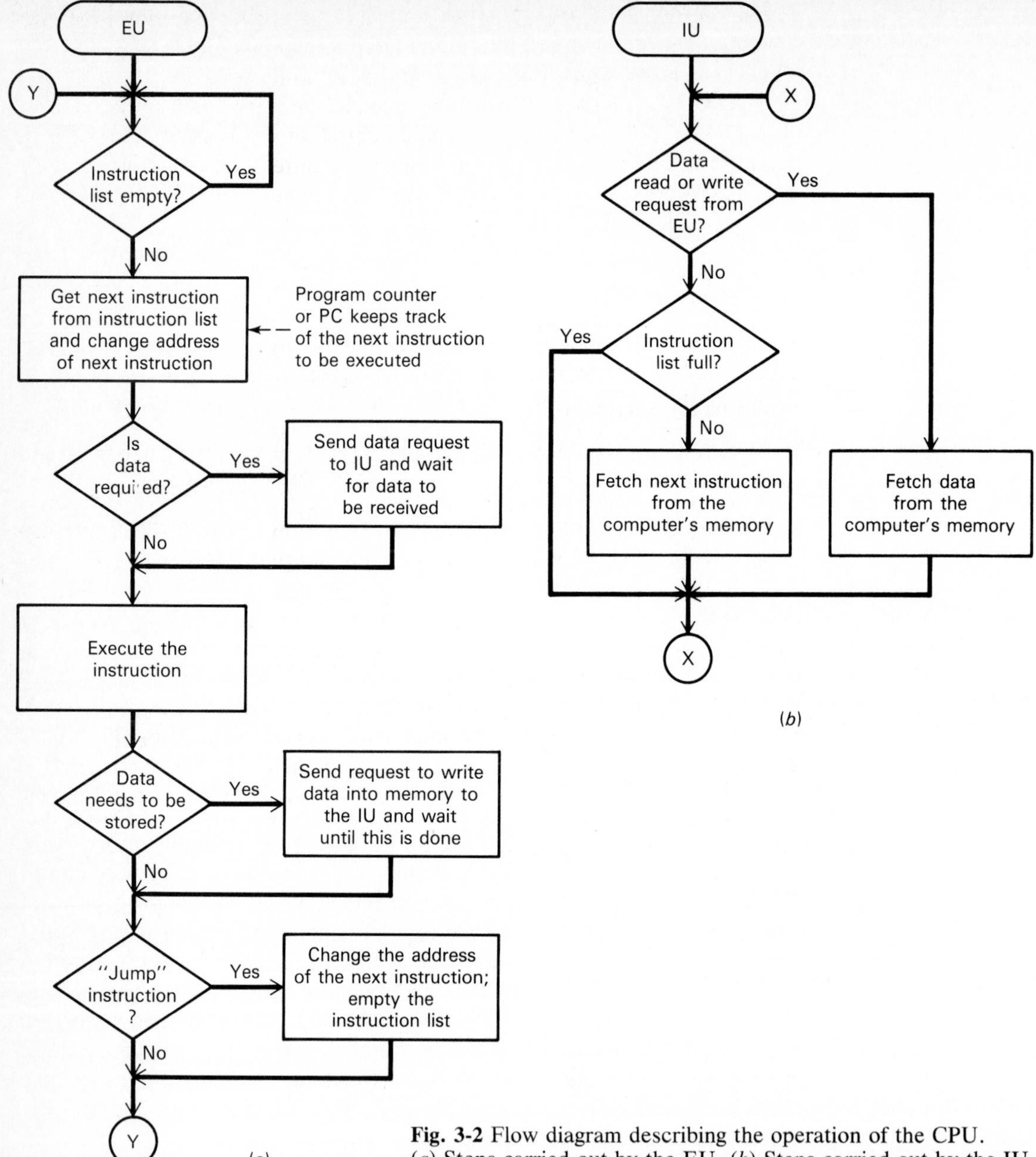

Fig. 3-2 Flow diagram describing the operation of the CPU. (*a*) Steps carried out by the EU. (*b*) Steps carried out by the IU.

The key to the operation of the modern CPU is the instruction list, or queue. This is a list of the next several instructions which are to be carried out. The IU fills this list and the EU empties the list. The IU tries to keep the list filled all the time. The EU empties the list one instruction at a time as it executes the instruction. This can be compared to a bucket of water with a hole at the bottom of the bucket. The IU fills the bucket with water; water leaks from the hole, imitating the operation of the EU. If the bucket is filled to the top, the IU does not add any water; overflow does not occur.

There are a variety of instructions or operations which the EU may carry out. One class of instruction is called the *jump,* or *branch,* instruction. When this instruction is encountered in a program, the CPU is required to fetch the next instruction from a different part of the memory. The simple sequence shown in the accompanying table will help to explain the uses and value of the jump instruction.

Address	Instruction
Address X	Get the number at location Y in the memory
Address X + 1	Add the number found at location Z to this number
Address X + 2	Jump to address X + 10 if the result is positive (or zero)
Address X + 3	Continue here if the answer is negative

Suppose that during the course of executing such a sequence of instructions, the result of the addition of the two numbers is positive. In that case, instead of continuing the program at address X + 3, the program will continue at address X + 10. The next instruction must be fetched from this address. However, the results of the addition cannot be known in advance because you cannot predict the numbers stored at addresses Y and Z. The program must jump to address X + 10, but the IU has been filling the instruction queue in strict sequence. The IU cannot anticipate that there will be a skip in the instruction sequence. The instructions in the queue are therefore invalid. When a jump or branch instruction is encountered, the EU changes the address of the next instruction, and empties, or *flushes,* the remaining instructions in the queue. The IU fetches this new instruction (at address X + 10), but the EU must now wait until this is done before it can proceed.

At this point the IU has brought one instruction into the instruction list. While the EU is executing this instruction, the IU is free to fetch additional instructions. The queue is refilled. In general, the IU can fetch instructions faster than the EU executes instructions, and, in time, the queue will be full again. Jump or branch instructions are a small percentage of most programs, and the instruction queue thus speeds the overall operation of the modern computer.

Example 3-2 Timing Diagram for the CPU

A very simple program consists of three instructions. While the exact instructions are not important, the first instruction must store its result in the computer's memory, the second instruction does not require data and does not need to store results, and the third instruction needs data from the memory. These conditions are summarized as follows:

Instruction 1: Execute and write results
Instruction 2: Execute
Instruction 3: Read data from the memory and execute

Figure 3-3 is a timing diagram showing the sequence of operation for two kinds of CPUs. Figure 3-3*a* shows what happens in a traditional CPU where the machine can only carry out the instruction-fetch, instruction-execute sequence in a purely sequential manner. Figure 3-3*b* shows the fetch-execute sequence for a modern CPU in which both operations can be carried out concurrently. This diagram clearly shows how the modern CPU decreases the time required to execute a computer program. In both cases the time needed to execute the individual instructions is the same. In both cases it is assumed that the first instruction has already been fetched and is waiting to be executed.

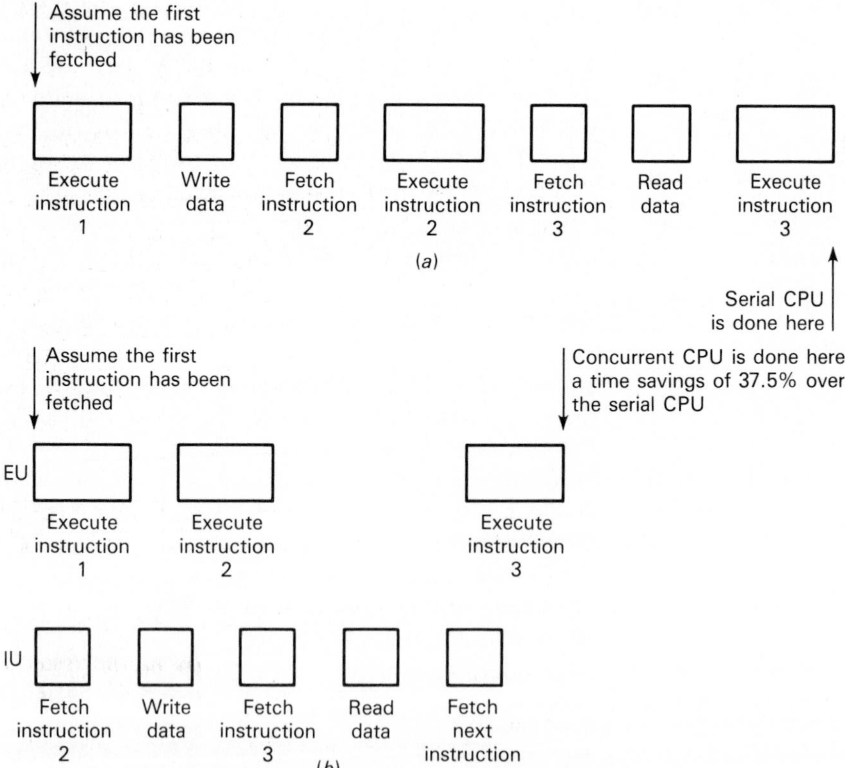

Fig. 3-3 Timing diagrams for two types of computer CPUs. Sequence of fetch-execute operations for (*a*) a strictly serial CPU, and (*b*) a CPU which consists of separate execution (EU) and memory interface (IU) units operating concurrently.

PROBLEMS FOR SECTION 3-2

1. Draw CPU timing diagrams similar to those shown in Fig. 3-3 for the following sequence of instructions:

Instruction 1: Read data, execute
Instruction 2: Read data, execute
Instruction 3: Execute, write data to the memory

Assume the following: the first instruction has already been fetched; execution of the instruction takes the same amount of time in each case; instruction fetches all require the same time; memory accesses (read or write) also take the same time. For this case compute the amount of time which is saved for a CPU which can carry out the fetch-execute sequence in a concurrent manner.

2. Repeat Prob. 1 for the following instruction sequence:

Instruction 1: Execute data
Instruction 2: Read data and execute
Instruction 3: Execute and store (write) the results

3-3 THE EU AND HOW IT WORKS

The EU is like a computer in miniature; that is, it contains a program of its own. However, instead of having instructions which can be changed (programmed), its commands are fixed. The kinds of operations that the EU can carry out are permanently embedded into this part of the machine. The EU contains a list of instructions and a sequence of operations to be performed for each instruction in the list. These operations describe how the data within the EU is to be moved from one part of the EU to another. Figure 3-4 summarizes the table of instructions which the EU can execute,

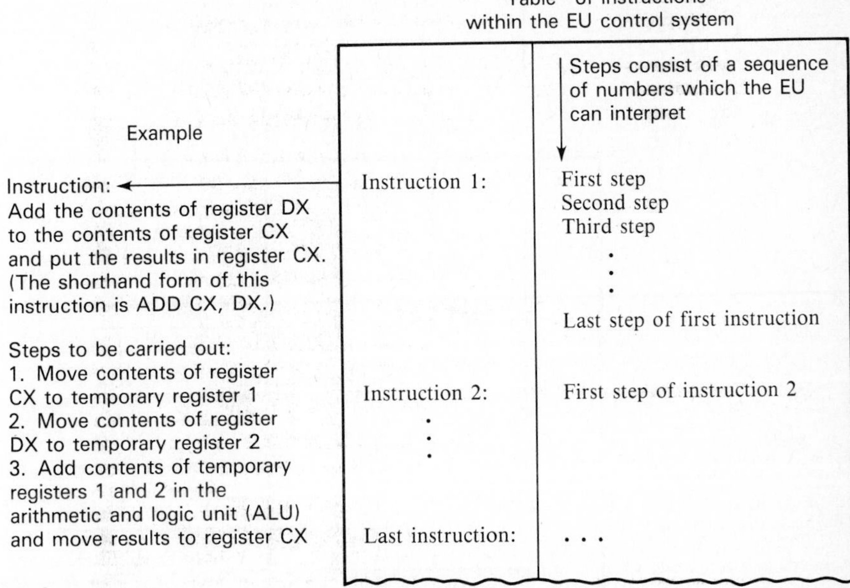

Fig. 3-4 Operations which the EU can perform are contained in a *microprogram* which forms a permanent part of this portion of a CPU. It consists of a table of instructions and the steps to be carried out for each entry in the table.

including the instruction itself and a very detailed sequence of steps to be followed when the instruction itself is invoked or called into action.

Whenever the EU gets an instruction from the queue, it carries out the following steps:

1. Find the instruction in the look-up table.
2. Carry out the sequence of operations specified by that instruction.

The detailed steps are sometimes referred to as the processor's *microprogram*.

3-3-1 A Block Diagram of the EU

Figure 3-5 is a simplified block diagram of the EU portion of the CPU and its main elements. They include:

1. General registers. These registers are very similar to ordinary RAM cells within the computer's main memory. They can be used to store

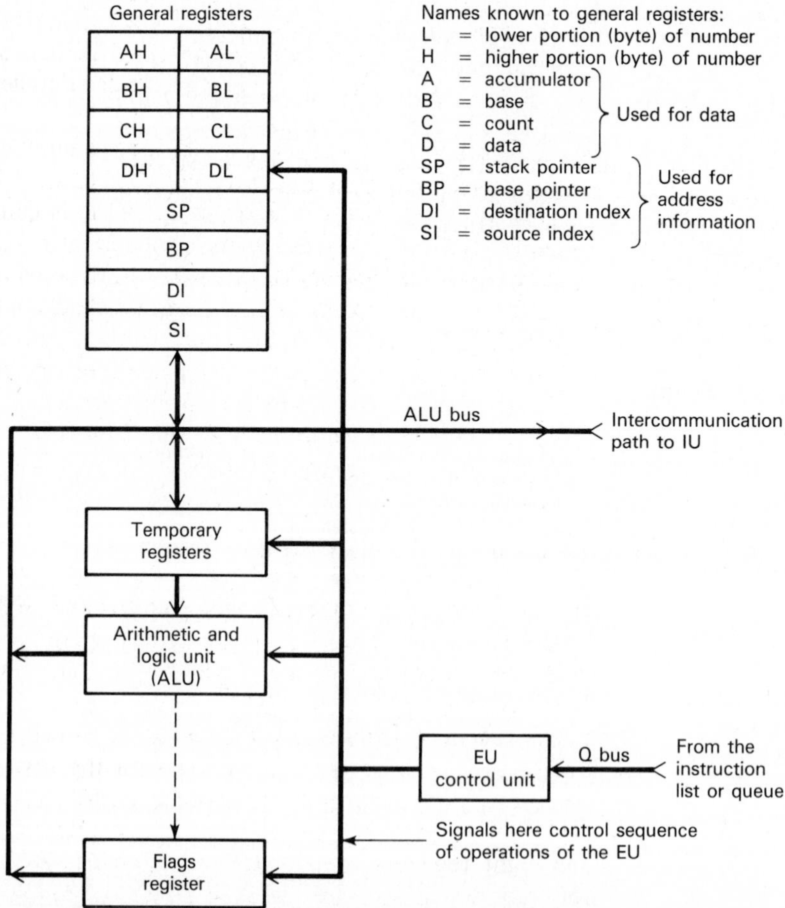

Fig. 3-5 Block diagram of the EU portion of a CPU.

data or intermediate computational results. They can also be used to store memory address information.

2. Temporary registers. These registers are used exclusively to store data on a temporary basis. The data which is stored will be used by the arithmetic and logic component.
3. The arithmetic and logic unit, or *ALU*. The ALU part of the EU carries out arithmetic and logical operations. Arithmetic operations can include adding, subtracting, multiplying, and dividing. Logical operations combine two operands according to the rules of AND, OR, NOT, and exclusive-or (XOR) operations.
4. The condition-code flags register. This register contains information about the results produced by the ALU. For example, one of the elements of this register indicates if the result of the most recent ALU operation was 0. Other flags signal sign information, certain numerical overflow conditions, data which is useful in detecting errors during communication with other parts of the computer (parity), and the state of the CPU regarding the interruption of its normal sequence of operations.
5. The EU control system. This system generates a series of control signals based on the steps specified by the instruction being executed. These control signals are derived from the detailed operations (for each instruction) as shown in Fig. 3-4.
6. Communication buses. The bus includes a number of wires which carry such information as address, data, and control (handshaking) signals. There are two buses within the EU. One is called the *ALU bus,* and the second is the *Q bus*. The Q bus transfers instructions, one at a time, from the instruction queue to the EU control system. The ALU bus transmits information from the EU back to the IU. For example, the IU gets memory address information from the EU via the Q bus when it is to access the computer's memory to read or write data. These two buses are separate from the bus or buses external to the CPU which provide for communications between the CPU and other resources of the computer, such as the memory and secondary storage system.

3-3-2 A Brief Description of the EU Registers

The EU contains a number of registers previously referred to as the *general registers*. Refer to Fig. 3-5 for a moment—there you will find that names have been assigned to these registers. If names have been assigned to these registers, why are they designated as general-purpose registers? The names are used to describe the functions which such registers perform when they are used in conjunction with the instructions that the CPU executes. Eight general-purpose registers are shown; this is the case for the 8086 CPU. Other computers may have a different number of registers. The eight registers are divided into two groups of four. One group is normally associated with data, and the second group is usually used for address information.

The data registers are designated as A, B, C, and D, with each register further subdivided into halves, identified by the suffixes "H" and "L." The L stands for lower and the H stands for higher, indicating that the numbers which can be stored in the register can be divided into lower and upper portions. Data can be directed to the lower portion of the register, the upper portion of the register, or both portions at the same time. This provides greater flexibility in the kinds of instructions which can be executed.

One of the more frequently used general-purpose registers is the A register. This is referred to as the *accumulator*. For many instructions, the final destination of the operand or the operational results is the accumulator.

Moving data from one part of the computer to another is an important operation performed by the CPU. In such cases the C, or *count,* register can play an important role. When large amounts of data are to be moved, it is possible to do this most efficiently if three pieces of information are available: the address of the first piece of information to be moved (the source), the address of the data destination, and the number of data elements to be moved. The C register is often used to keep track of the number of data elements to be moved. The computer does not need a separate instruction to move each piece of data. Instead, it continues to move data until it has completed N operations, where N is the number stored in the C register.

Other registers in the EU normally provide address information to the IU. The SP register is the *stack pointer*. Recall that the stack is a special portion of the computer's memory section. The SP register contains the value of addresses in this portion of the RAM.

3-3-3 Hold on There a Moment—Computer Interrupts

Suppose you are seated in front of the computer terminal and a momentary drop in the line voltage occurs. In some cases such surges can disrupt your program or destroy or alter data. If you are using a well-designed computer system, it is likely that damage will be held to a minimum. This is because the computer may have a component which senses the drop in line voltage and alerts the processor to the imminent danger. The processor can be directed to take emergency action and save all the information which is essential to your program. When power returns to its normal level, the program may be resumed in a graceful manner. In order for the CPU to carry out the emergency procedures, it must *interrupt* the program that it is currently executing and undertake a new emergency program. The modern CPU has the ability to interrupt its normal sequence, save important information, and jump to a new location where it begins executing instructions. The ability to do this is referred to as the *interrupt* capability. The program which is executed as a result of an interrupt is usually called the interrupt service routine, or *ISR*. In the case of the power "glitch," the computer may have as little as 0.001 s (1 ms) before the power falls to a level which causes errors to occur in the circuitry. Because of the speed of the modern CPU, it is possible for a thousand or more instructions to be executed in this time. An appropriate ISR program can be designed to provide a "soft landing" for the computer instead of a damaging *crash*.

Figure 3-6 shows a simplified flow diagram for the sequence of steps carried out by the 8086 CPU when an interrupt occurs. This CPU can identify up to 256 different types of interrupt. Every interrupt has a code

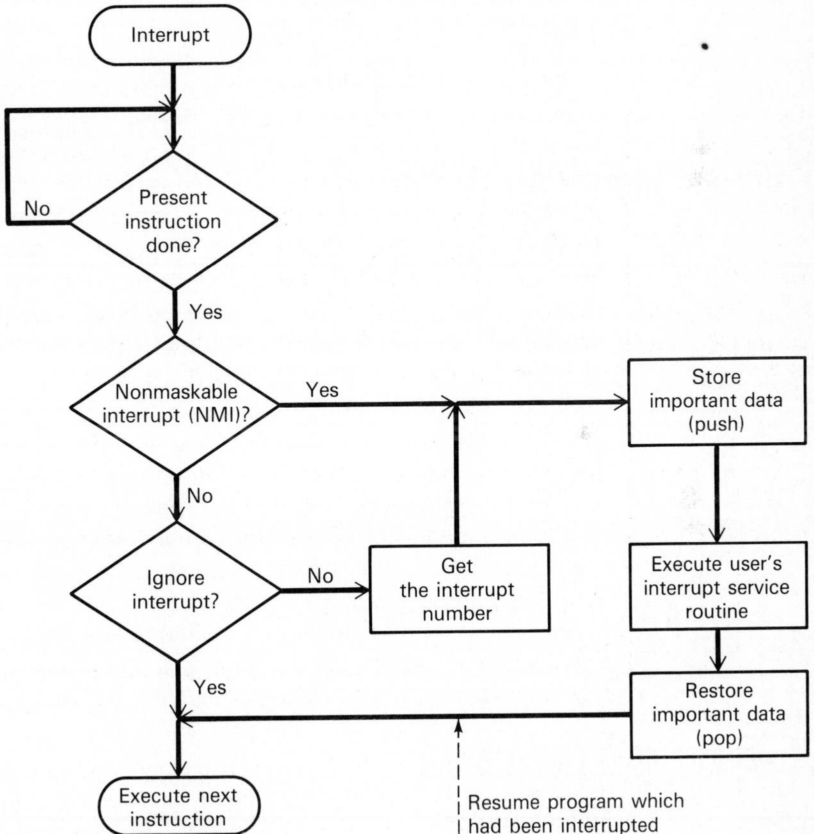

Fig. 3-6 Flow diagram describing the important operations which take place in the EU when an interrupt occurs.

which identifies it to the CPU. The CPU may then carry out an ISR appropriate for that interrupt. Interrupts may be initiated by devices outside the CPU. They may also be started by certain kinds of software interrupt instructions. One example of this latter interrupt class results when the computer detects division of a number by 0. If the CPU is in the middle of an instruction when the interrupt occurs, the instruction is completed before any other action is started.

Figure 3-6 describes two classes of interrupt. One is called the *non-*

maskable interrupt, or *NMI,* and the other is the normal, or *maskable,* interrupt. As the name implies, the NMI cannot be ignored by the computer. Ordinary, maskable interrupts can be ignored by the computer if the programmer has included an instruction which disables such interrupts.

PROBLEMS FOR SECTION 3-3-3

1. Name at least three sources of computer interrupts.
2. Describe what may happen when an interrupt is received while a prior interrupt is being serviced by the computer.
3. Can you think of any limitations on the number of interrupts which can be serviced by a computer?
4. Why is it desirable to include an NMI capability in a computer?

3-4 THE INSTRUCTION SET OF THE CPU

To this point we have described how the CPU is divided into two parts, one which executes instructions and one which fetches instructions and data from the memory. We have not said too much about the instructions themselves. In this section we will briefly discuss the kinds of instructions that you are likely to find supported within the modern CPU.

Recall that the computer can act only on numbers. The computer and the CPU do not understand words. Computer users are much better equipped to deal with words than numbers when faced with the problem of writing a program. As a compromise, special programs have been created which accept words from a user and translate these into numbers that the computer can use. To simplify matters we shall refer to words or mnemonics for the various instructions which will be discussed.

The instructions which are available may be grouped into several classes: *data transfer* instructions, *arithmetic* instructions, *bit manipulation* instructions, and *program transfer* instructions.

3-4-1 Data Transfer Instructions

Data transfer instructions are designed to move information between memory and registers, or between registers (in particular, the accumulator) and the I/O ports. A list of such instructions and their meanings is shown in Table 3-1. The list is by no means complete. However, it is representative of instructions which can be found in many CPUs.

3-4-2 Arithmetic Instructions

Just as the name implies, arithmetic instructions include addition, subtraction, multiplication, and division. Not every CPU can perform all these operations directly. Those that cannot, use software to provide the operation. Multiplication may be performed by repeated additions; division by repeated subtractions. However, if the multiplication operation is carried

TABLE 3-1 TYPICAL DATA TRANSFER INSTRUCTIONS IN MODERN CPUs

Instruction (Keyword)	Meaning
MOV	Move data between registers and memory
PUSH	Move data from registers to the stack portion of the memory
POP	Move data from the memory stack to the registers
XCHG	Exchange data (two-way move)
IN	Input data from a port (into the acccumulator)
OUT	Output data to a port (from the accumulator)

out using software (a program) rather than hardware, the speed of the operation will be greatly reduced. Indeed, the speed penalty is so great that some computers have special high-speed arithmetic processors, aside from the ALU in the CPU, to perform complex arithmetic operations. Table 3-2 contains sample arithmetic instructions which are often found in the modern CPU.

TABLE 3-2 ARITHMETIC OPERATIONS IN THE MODERN CPU

Instruction (Keyword)	Meaning
ADD	Add two operands together and store the result in one of the operand locations
ADC	Same as the ADD instruction but also add the "carry" (from a previous operation) if there is one
INC	A special kind of ADD which increments a location by 1
SUB	Subtract two operands and store the result in one of the operand locations
SBB	Same as SUB but include the "borrow" from the previous operation
DEC	A special kind of SUB which decrements contents of the operand address by 1
NEG	Change the contents of the operand address to a negative number
CMP	Compare the two operands by subtracting the two target operands; this leaves the original values unchanged but can be used to find out how they compare with each other
MUL	Multiply the two target operands together
IMUL	A special multiplication instruction that is useful when the two target operands are integers
DIV	Divide the target operands and store the result in one of the target operand locations
IDIV	A special division instruction which is useful when the target operands are integers

3-4-3 Logic Operations (Bit Manipulations)

Suppose you are asked to write a computer program which will monitor and control the operation of a chemical processing plant. One of the operations that you are monitoring requires emergency action if the pressure or temperature exceeds certain limits. The computer program would have to include instructions to take the correct action should this occur. In plain English, it would need to support a statement such as "If the temperature exceeds *X* degrees *or* the pressure exceeds *Y* pounds per square inch, then take emergency action." The key word in this case is "or." This word implies that a logical test must be performed to determine if either the temperature or the pressure, or both, exceed safe limits. The group of instructions described in this section can be used to perform the logical operations implied by the example just cited. Table 3-3 contains a group of such instructions.

TABLE 3-3 TYPICAL LOGIC INSTRUCTIONS IN THE MODERN CPU

Instruction (Keyword)	Meaning
NOT	Logically invert the target operand
AND	Combine the target operands with a logical AND operation. Replace one of the original operands with the result
OR	Combine two target operands with a logical OR operation. Replace one of the original operands with the result
XOR	A special OR operation which is called the *exclusive-OR*. One of the original target operands is replaced with the results
TEST	An AND operation: The original operands are left intact; the results are reflected in the flag register
SHL, ROL	The keywords stand for "shift" and "rotate" left. There are some technical differences but a simple example explains what often occurs. Left-shifting the binary number 0111 produces the result 1110. The original leftmost bit is lost. In a rotation, the original leftmost bit is placed in the rightmost position: 1110 → 1101
SHR, ROR	Similar to SHL, ROL. However, the shift takes place to the right: 1011 → 0101 or 1011 → 1101

3-4-4 Program Transfer Instructions

Program transfer instructions permit a programmer to control the order in which instructions are executed. This is essential if one is to be able to write useful programs. The list shown in Table 3-4 indicates some of the instructions which fall into the category of program control.

TABLE 3-4 PROGRAM TRANSFER INSTRUCTIONS

Instruction (Keyword)	Meaning
CALL	Can be used to arbitrarily execute a predefined block of instructions and then return to the point in the program at which the transfer was made
RET	This stands for "return"; it can be used in conjunction with the CALL to indicate at which point to return to the calling program
JE/JZ	There are a number of "jump" instructions. These transfer control of the program to a new place if certain tests on the flags turn out to be true. The flags are set by the prior instruction. This instruction is interpreted as "Jump if the zero flag indicates that prior results were zero"
JG/JNLE	Jump if greater/not less or equal
JGE/JNL	Jump if greater or equal/not less
JL/JNGE	Jump if less/not greater or equal
JLE/JNG	Jump if less or equal/not greater
JNE/JNZ	Jump if not equal/not zero
JO	Jump if overflow occurred
JNO	Jump if no overflow occurred
JP/JPE	Jump if even parity occurred
JNP/JPO	Jump if odd parity occurred
INT	This is a "software" interrupt. If this instruction is encountered, the ISR previously described will be executed
INTO	Also a software interrupt. An interrupt will occur if an overflow was detected (overflow bit in the flags register is set)
IRET	Return to the point in the program at which an interrupt occurred

3-4-5 Symbolic Language Programs and the CPU

Programs written in *high-level languages (HLLs)* will have a *symbolic* appearance. The HLL statement which adds two quantities and saves the result might look like

$$C = A + B$$

The quantities to be added are identified as A and B. The result is denoted as C. The instructions which actually perform the operations in the CPU will be those contained in Tables 3-1 to 3-4. The following example shows how the symbolic statement ($C = A + B$) and its corresponding CPU instructions are related.

Example 3-3 Decomposing an HLL statement

Shown below is one way to translate the HLL statement C = A + B into a series of CPU instructions of the kind just described:

CPU Instructions	Explanation
MOV AX, A	Get the first quantity to be added (A) and store it in register A (accumulator)
ADD AX, B	Add the second quantity (B) to the quantity already stored in the accumulator
MOV C, AX	Store the result of the addition into the location which has been set aside for the result, C

In both the data-moving (MOV) and addition (ADD) instructions, the first operand is the data destination and the second operand is the data source. The result of the addition operation is retained in the destination location.

The HLL statement has been decomposed into three CPU instructions. This HLL statement translation has been greatly simplified. In practice, many more CPU instructions are needed. The addition operation used in this example applies to the binary number system.

PROBLEMS FOR SECTION 3-4-5

1. Translate the HLL statement C = A * B into a series of CPU instructions. Treat A and B as binary numbers.
2. Write a program using CPU instructions which will calculate the sum of 10 resistors. (This is the same as finding the equivalent value of 10 resistors connected in series.) Write a program which uses fewer than 12 instructions.

SUMMARY

The CPU executes the instructions which are included in a computer program. To do so requires two basic steps:

1. Fetch an instruction from the memory.
2. Execute (carry out) the instruction.

The modern CPU performs the fetch-execute sequence in a concurrent manner. This means that new instructions are fetched while old ones are being executed. The execution unit, or EU portion of the CPU, executes instructions, while the interface unit, or IU portion of the CPU, fetches instructions and data from the computer's memory when they are needed.

The instruction queue contains a list of instructions to be executed. This queue is filled by the IU and emptied by the EU. Usually, the CPU does not have to wait for new instructions. On occasion the computer must jump to instructions which are out of sequence. When this happens, the instructions in the queue are no longer valid. The IU fills the queue with instructions beginning with the one at the new destination.

Information transfer between parts of the CPU takes place on a bus. Buses contain address, data, and handshaking (control) signals. A modern CPU may have two buses. One bus transfers instructions between the IU and the EU, while a second bus transmits information from the EU to the IU (e.g., operand address information).

The CPU includes many registers, or special-purpose memory locations, to help carry out its tasks. These registers can store data or address information.

The instructions which the CPU can carry out fall into three main categories: data moving, arithmetic and logic operations, and program transfer instructions.

REVIEW QUESTIONS

1. What are the two main tasks which the CPU performs?
2. What is the form of the instructions which the CPU executes?
3. What are the main elements of the EU?
4. Describe what happens when the normal fetch-execute sequence is disrupted by a CPU interrupt.
5. Name two kinds of CPU interrupts.
6. Name four possible operand sources or destinations within the computer.
7. What are three classes of CPU instructions found in the modern computer?
8. Name six data transfer instructions which may be found in a CPU.
9. Name at least 10 useful arithmetic CPU instructions.
10. Name three logical operations in addition to NOT, AND, OR, and XOR which can be found in a CPU.
11. Explain what happens when the CPU executes a CALL instruction.
12. What instruction can you use to return control to a program which originally contained a CALL instruction?

COMPUTER ARCHITECTURE: PERIPHERALS

This chapter deals with the hardware that is external to the computer itself. This collection of hardware is known as *peripherals;* quite literally, it is hardware that is on the periphery, or outside, of the main computer system.

Peripherals give the computer important capabilities:

- The ability to receive information from the outside, in machine-readable form. One example would be a keyboard.
- The ability to transmit information in machine-readable form to human-readable form. An example would be a printer producing a report.
- The ability to store in machine-readable form, external from the computer itself and in a nonvolatile environment, data, programs, and results.

These three areas are generally referred to as *input* devices, *output* devices, and *storage* devices. Some equipment can combine two or even three of these functions. A computer terminal will usually contain both a keyboard and a display of some type; thus it is an *input/output,* or *I/O,* device. Sometimes microcomputers are programmed to behave as terminals; since most microcomputers include (at least) floppy disk drives as external storage, a microcomputer used as a terminal would be an *input/output/storage* peripheral to the larger computer.

The distinction between whether a device is external, and thus a peripheral, or is internal, and is thus a part of the computer proper, is not always clear. Since many computers contain an input device, output device, and storage device, all in the same physical case, we can no longer use internal or external as the measure. We will therefore define peripherals as that hardware that is *other than* the main CPU, memory, bus structure, and support that these items require directly.

This chapter will deal with input and output devices.

4-1 INPUT DEVICES

Input devices can be broken down into two general categories:

- Text entry devices: Includes straight text and numeric values
- Nontext devices: For entry of values that must be first measured and then translated into machine-readable form

4-1-1 Text Entry Devices

The most common text entry device is the *keyboard*. Most keyboards are for general purposes and are alphanumeric in nature; that is, they contain all the letters of the alphabet, all the numerals, and the punctuation that is commonly used in normal text.

It is important to realize that the keyboard does *not* transmit the actual character selected to the computer. What is transmitted is a numeric code (usually ASCII, or American Standard Code for Information Interchange) that represents the particular key pressed. It is up to the software controlling the computer to interpret that code and act accordingly.

There are many variations on the layout of keyboards. The standard "QWERTY" keyboard is so named because of the arrangement of the first six alphabetic characters on the keyboard.

While the arrangements of the alphabetic and numeric keys is somewhat standardized, the arrangement of punctuation marks and special keys that are often found on keyboards designed for computer use is not. There is much controversy as to how these keys are best arranged, with different users claiming their own preferences.

In addition to general-purpose keyboards, there are special-purpose keyboards. These keyboards may have fewer keys than a general-purpose keyboard. Each key might represent a particular function that can be performed or a given value to be entered. An example would be an automated teller machine (ATM). Banks use these devices to allow customers to access their accounts. Such a keyboard would commonly be combined with some kind of display device.

PROBLEM FOR SECTION 4-1-1

1. Suggest an application, other than the ATM example cited in the text, where a special-purpose keyboard is useful.

4-1-2 Optical Character Recognition

Much of the work that computers perform consists of entry of text, processing of that text, and generation of a response. One example might be a typical billing cycle. The selling company prepares an invoice and mails it to the buying company. The buying company enters the data from the invoice into its computer, which generates a check in response. The buying company mails this check and a copy of the invoice back to the selling company. The selling company enters the receiving of the check into its computer, thus updating its files. All the data entry has typically been done via keyboard entry of the text. However, if the data could be read from the paper by a machine and transmitted to the computer directly, much data entry time could be saved.

Optical character recognition (OCR) units do just that. They are special-purpose devices which can scan a sheet of paper and recognize typewritten or printed data. Some of these devices can even read some styles of handwriting. This results in the printed text being translated into the computer codes representing the characters printed.

Most such systems are limited to one or several *fonts,* or type styles, and may be unable to read other styles. Further, these systems tend to make errors in recognition when the page is dirty, creased, or otherwise imperfect. Those systems that can interpret handwriting require that the written material be produced according to very restricted letter and numeral shapes.

Even so, the reduction of the amount of text that needs to be entered into the computer via the keyboard makes OCR a popular system for data entry, one which will undoubtedly be improved as technology advances.

Example 4-1 A Simple OCR

Figure 4-1 shows one scheme for transforming textual material into computer-readable form. On one side of the medium (paper) are a series of

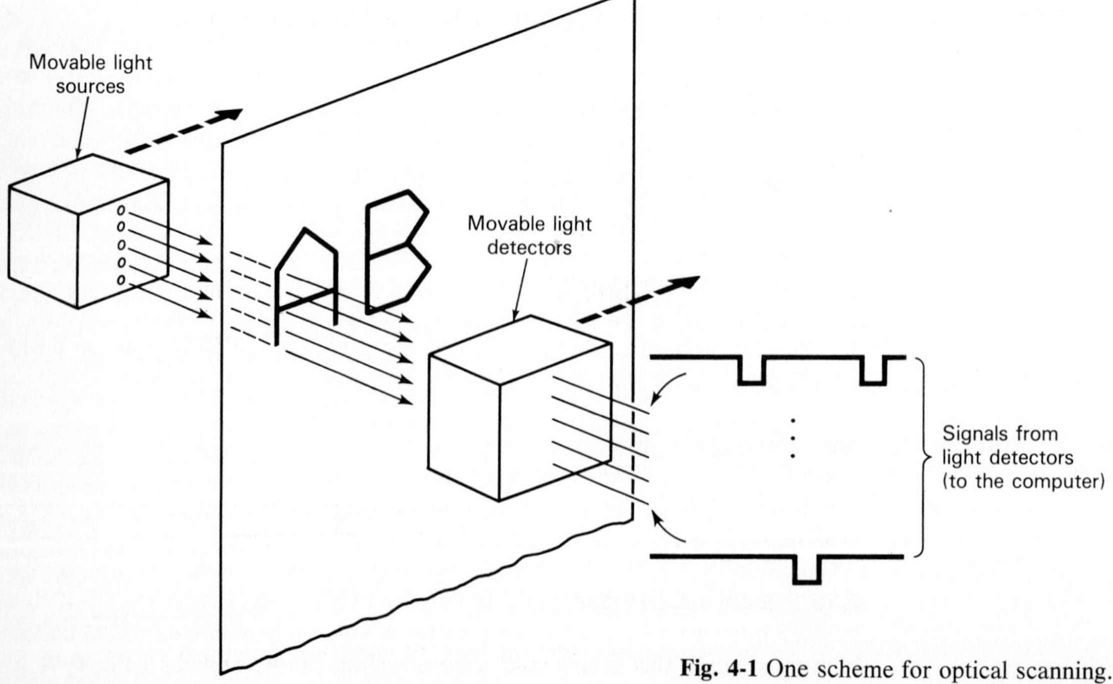

Fig. 4-1 One scheme for optical scanning.

light sources, perhaps infrared. On the other side are a series of compatible light detectors. Textual material on the page tends to block transmission of light. Each detector "sees" a pattern of light and dark images. These are converted into on-off signals which are in turn transmitted to the computer. Within the computer the patterns are matched against a set of patterns which have been previously stored. In this way the letters on the page can be identified. The light sources and detectors move across the page, and such scanning results in entry of the character strings.

PROBLEMS FOR SECTION 4-1-2

1. Indicate some disadvantages of the scheme shown in Fig. 4-1.
2. Suggest another way to implement an OCR.

4-1-3 Magnetic-Ink Character Recognition

Before OCR devices became available, magnetic-ink character recognition (MICR) was being used by the banking industry for encoding account numbers on the bottom of checks so that this data could automatically be read into the computers processing the transfer of funds. The ink that is used can be sensed magnetically and is read by a scanning device which is sensitive to magnetic field variations. The characters are specially shaped so that they are readily differentiated by the reader. See Fig. 4-2 for an example of the MICR typeface. Since this is not an optical process, it is less sensitive to slight disturbances in the appearance of the paper. It is a highly reliable, fast system that is used by many banks.

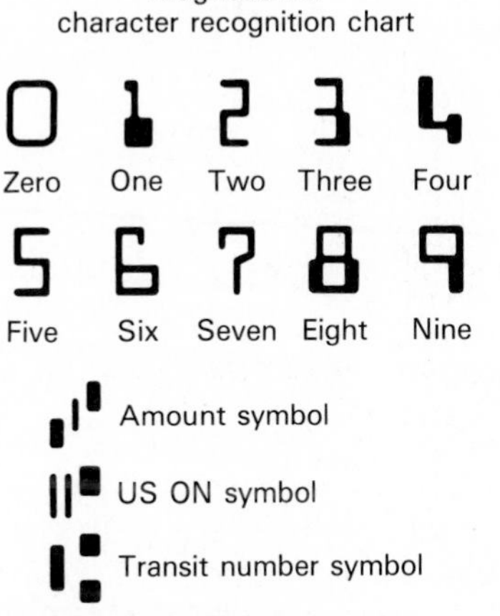

Fig. 4-2 Magnetic-ink character recognition typeface and examples.

PROBLEM FOR SECTION 4-1-3

1. Cite some possible problems with MICR reading devices.

4-1-4 Punched-Card Readers

A once very popular means of entering data into the computer is the punched card. Also known as the *Hollerith* card, 80-column card, or IBM card, this system involves the punching of holes in a paper card using a device called a *keypunch*. Each card contains up to 80 columns of data (80 characters). Each column contains one or more holes in it, the combination of holes uniquely denoting the character represented. See Fig. 4-3 for a listing of the various codes and how they are placed on the card.

The main advantages to this system are as follows:

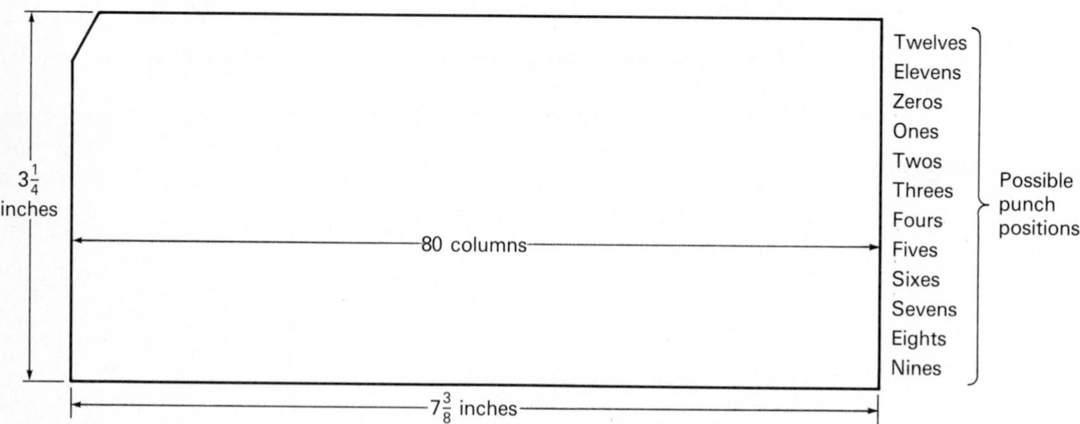

	Alone	In combination with a punch in column 12	11	0
0	0	Left brace	Right brace	—
1	1	A	J	(Illegal code)
2	2	B	K	S
3	3	C	L	T
4	4	D	M	U
5	5	E	N	V
6	6	F	O	W
7	7	G	P	X
8	8	H	Q	Y
9	9	I	R	Z

Fig. 4-3 Hollerith code and 80-column card layout.

- Hollerith cards are fairly inexpensive.
- Data entry using Hollerith cards is relatively fast; modern card readers can easily read 600 cards per minute.
- The generation of the punched cards is done *off-line*. This means that you may have many operators on keypunch machines, none of which are connected to the computer. The cards are then combined and carried to the card reader. It is the card reader that transmits the data to the computer.

- Hollerith cards may be stored and reread if the need arises.
- Errors found in cards cannot be corrected, but the card containing the error can be replaced without affecting the rest of the deck.

The main disadvantages are as follows:

- Punched cards are large in comparison to the amount of data they can contain; storage requires a great deal of space.
- Since the creation of punched cards is done off-line, the computer cannot assist in the screening for errors in data entry. These errors must be caught manually or corrected after the data has been fed to the computer.
- The system still involves a form of keyboard entry; the keypunch machine is merely a method of converting keypresses to holes punched in the card.
- If the order in which the cards are to be read is important, very careful attention must be paid to maintaining that order, since the deck of cards can easily become shuffled out of order. If the order is *critical,* a sequence number may be placed in each card (as part of the data) which the computer must verify as being in the correct order.
- Punched-card readers, particularly high-speed models, are sensitive to wrinkled or bent cards. A bad card can jam the machine so badly that the machine must be taken apart to remove the jam. This problem becomes more serious as the cards wear with usage and age.
- Anything that might make additional holes in the card must be avoided. Any additional holes may be read as data or may corrupt other data.

When punched cards are used for input, they usually originate from keypunch machines. Another computer peripheral, the *card punch,* can be connected to a computer to receive data from the computer and punch appropriate holes into the cards. These cards can be read back into the computer at a later time, as they might represent data that the computer needs the next time a given application is run. An example might be a payroll system that keeps track of year-to-date earnings of its employees. The next time the payroll system is run, the totals must be updated and made available for the following run. A new set of output cards would need to be punched to use as input for the subsequent weekly run.

4-1-5 Punched Paper Tape

A close relation to punched cards, punched paper tape uses a paper tape approximately $1\frac{1}{2}$ inches wide, and as long as needed, to store data and programs in the form of punched holes. Also not nearly so popular as it once was, paper tape has many of the inherent problems of punched cards. The exceptions are that the tape cannot be read out of order and that the tape must be cut and spliced to replace areas that contain errors.

While relatively inexpensive, paper tape has been replaced by faster, quieter (paper tape readers and punches are often quite noisy), more efficient devices.

4-1-6 Bar Code Readers: Universal Product Code (UPC) Scanners

If you examine almost any packaged item you purchase in a supermarket, you will find a small zebra-striped patch. This series of stripes encodes information about the product (manufacturer and item) in a form that can be read by a device at the checkout counter. This device may take the form of a wand that is passed over the stripes (as if it were a pen and you were crossing the stripes out), or the device may read the stripes without any contact with the item at all—a scanning laser locates and reads the pattern. This information is passed to a computer, which then looks up the item code and determines the item's cost. The cost and identification information is sent back to the cash register, where it is totaled and printed on the receipt. In addition, the computer keeps track of each item sold and can generate reorder lists, so that the item is always in stock. Those items that do not sell well can also be listed and ultimately removed from the grocer's shelves.

There are several different bar code systems in use. Some are capable of transmitting only numeric information; some permit the complete ASCII character set to be represented. Bar codes are used in many different industrial and commercial applications, as they allow an item to be uniquely identified and tracked throughout the manufacturing or sales process. The computer can keep a perpetual inventory of items in stock by scanning the codes of items entering and leaving the plant.

PROBLEMS FOR SECTION 4-1-6

1. Suggest several applications in addition to the one cited in Sec. 4-1-6 in which a UPC scanning system would be useful.

2. Cite ways in which a bar code system could be used in a factory.

4-1-7 Magnetic Strip Readers

On the backs of many credit cards is a dark brown or black stripe, about $\frac{1}{4}$ inch wide, running the length of the card. This stripe is used for a variety of purposes, but most frequently contains an account number in a machine-readable form. This allows the number to be entered without a keyboard. Some cards also contain a password which must agree with one entered from a keyboard, before a transaction is completed.

PROBLEM FOR SECTION 4-1-7

1. Suggest a way in which a magnetic strip reader could be used to improve security in a computer center.

4-1-8 Optical Mark Sensing

Examine Fig. 4-4. The optical mark reader sees the black pencil marks and translates these marks in much the same way as a Hollerith card reader does. The main advantage of this system is that the data encoding device, that is, the device needed to mark the card, is as simple as a pencil. For this reason, this method of data entry is often used for test taking or for collecting data such as a marketing survey.

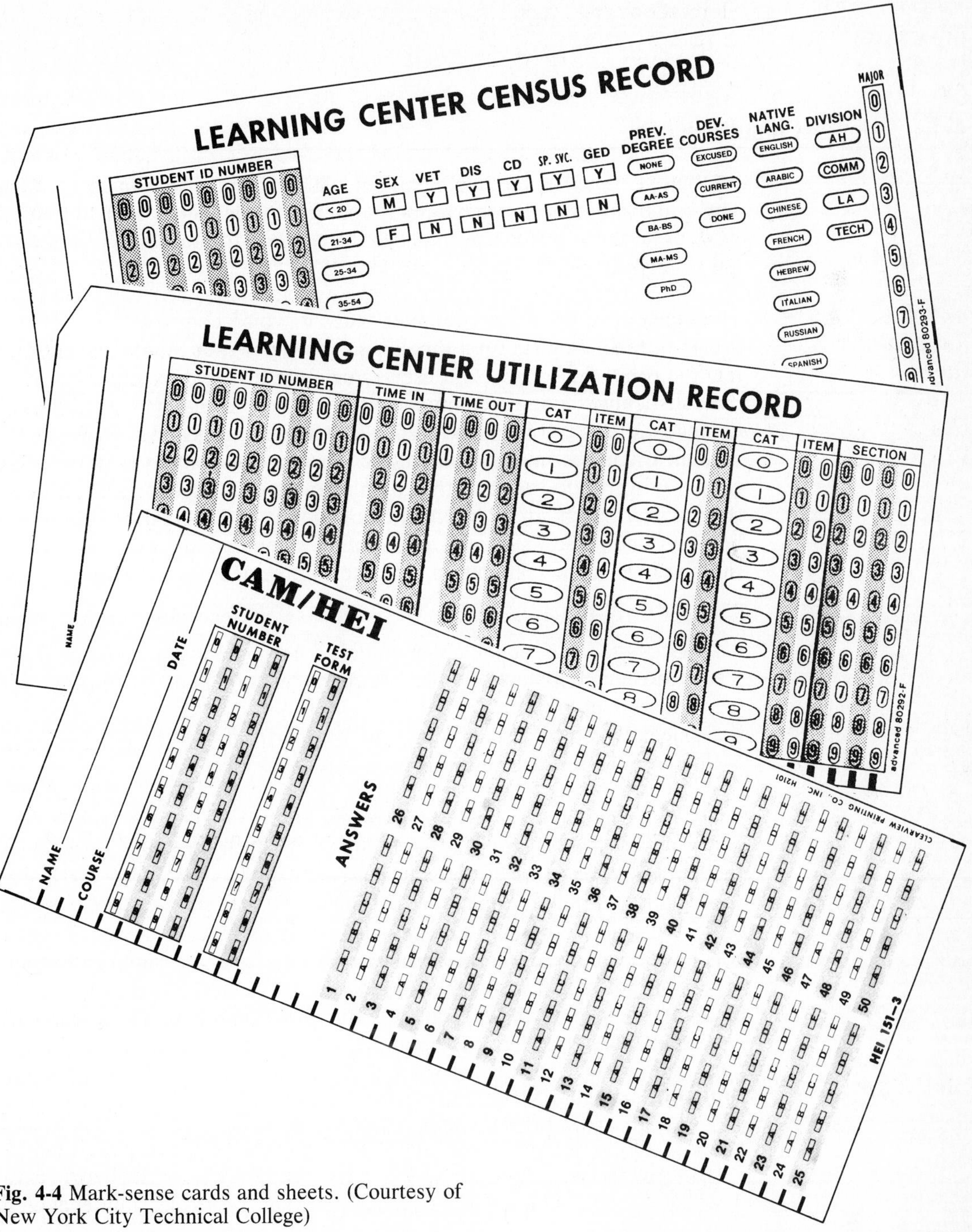

Fig. 4-4 Mark-sense cards and sheets. (Courtesy of New York City Technical College)

PROBLEMS FOR SECTION 4-1-8

1. Suggest a simple method for automatically tracking (marking) answers to multiple-choice test questions where a pencil has been used to indicate the answers.

2. Describe two problems with mark-sense cards which could lead to errors.

4-1-9 Nontext Input Devices

A nontext input device handles input which is not in the form of alphanumeric characters. It often employs some type of energy transformation, such as sound to electrical impulses. A number of nontext input devices are described in the following sections.

a. Voice Recognition Units

The concept of having a computer react to voice commands has been a dream of technologists for a long time. The typewriter that takes dictation and the robot that reacts to a user's voice are just two examples.

Realistically, having a computer obey voiced commands is fraught with complications. For the same reasons that a computer cannot be instructed in plain English from a keyboard, a computer cannot (yet) be made sufficiently powerful to interpret the complex syntactic and idiomatic structure of spoken English. In addition, the complexity introduced by differences between one person's speech and another's compounds the problem.

However, voice recognition has been implemented and exists in two general forms:

- Devices that analyze the components of the incoming speech and translate those components into ASCII characters which are then processed in the normal manner
- Devices which have been "trained" to perform a given function each time a given series of utterances is received

The first class of devices is the more complex. The device is programmed with rules regarding how the words of the English language are spoken. Incoming speech is electronically dissected into its phonetic parts. The combination of these phonetic parts is analyzed, and the results are passed on to the main computer. The advantage of this type of device is that it will react to many different speakers, as long as the pronunciation and syntax of the spoken words are reasonably standard (the range of standard being determined by the recognition unit's programming). The vocabulary of recognized words depends upon the power of the recognition unit: how large and fast its CPU and memory are, and how flexible its programming is. The translation task may be performed entirely by the recognition unit, or it may be shared by the main computer, depending on how the system has been constructed.

The second class of units has certain advantages over the first. The device typically requires its operator to speak each of the words or phrases the unit is to decode, followed by keyboard entry of the function the computer is to perform when that word or phrase is detected. In this manner, a translation table is generated. By comparing future speech to those sounds stored in the unit's memory, the matching response can be found and the translation, in text, can be transmitted to the host computer. Since this unit "learns" the voice of its operator, the accuracy of translation is quite high. By the same token, if the operator's voice should change (a cold or other illness would sufficiently change a voice), the unit may no longer be able to perform translations accurately. Other operators could not use this person's machine without retraining it to recognize their voices. This may not be a disadvantage; it may be used as a security feature, preventing intruders from accessing a computer system.

Clearly, the value of voice recognition is so high that the technology it requires will be continually advanced. Accurate, wide-range translation devices would make the computer's power available to many who are now excluded because they are unable to use keyboards owing to physical inability or lack of training.

b. Transducers and Other Sensors

Often the computer is used to control a mechanical process. Many of today's automobiles have pollution and performance controls that are regulated by an on-board computer. This computer monitors such factors as road speed, air temperature, exhaust oxygen content, engine rotational speed (revolutions per minute), throttle position, engine vacuum, water temperature, and combustion temperature. The combination of these readings is used to control engine timing, carburetion, transmission operation, and pollution controls. The devices that do the transformations from the physical (i.e., temperature) to an electrical signal that the computer can use are called *transducers.* A *thermistor* is commonly used to convert temperature to an electrical signal. An electromechanical device, called a *tachometer,* produces an output signal (voltage) which is proportional to the rotational speed of its shaft. It can be used to measure engine revolutions per minute and road speed. Special chemical sensors can measure oxygen or carbon monoxide content and produce a proportional electrical signal. Together, these sensors allow the computer to change the automobile's operating conditions very rapidly in response to changing road and environmental conditions.

Each industry has requirements for different types of sensors. Sometimes weight must be measured. When a package is sufficiently filled, the filling operation stops. A *photocell* may be used to sense the absence or presence of an item on an assembly line. When the object is properly positioned, the item breaks the beam of light and the computer responds appropriately.

Alarm systems may use *ultrasonic* detectors to sense an intruder's presence. An ultrasonic tone is broadcast in a room; it is received and the reflections are analyzed. Any movement in the room causes the reflections to be distorted due to the *Doppler effect.* This distortion is detected and the alarm procedure is initiated. Other sensors may be used to detect smoke, fire, flood, and other emergency conditions, and cause the computer to react appropriately.

Computerized scales find uses where automated packaging of products is expected. Such scales not only weigh each item to be packaged but also compute a price where necessary.

Finally, as one more example of the use of sensors, consider the U.S. Weather Bureau. Temperature, humidity, wind speed and direction, rainfall, and other factors are measured and entered into the computer directly by a myriad of sensors. Satellite photographs may be converted to computer-readable form and fed to the computer as well.

PROBLEM FOR SECTION 4-1-9

1. The following is a list of other computer input devices. Explain how each of these work. (You may have to do some research to answer this question.)

   ultrasonic tablet
   light pen
   mouse
   joystick
   touch screen

4-2 OUTPUT DEVICES

Output devices perform the operation of taking information in the form of the computer's internal electrical signals and putting them in a form that is of use to us. Again, there are two general categories of output devices:

- Text output devices—possibly in the form of printed material or an optical display device such as a cathode-ray tube (CRT) monitor
- Nontext output devices—usually in computer-readable or electrical actuator form

4-2-1 Text Output Devices

There are many ways to categorize a printer. It can be categorized by the method used to make the character on the paper, by the style of the characters produced, by the speed of output, or by whether it prints a character at a time or a line at a time. The distinctions are mostly comparative in nature—useful when we are comparing two types of printers—but otherwise we may conduct a study of the various types of printers without concern as to the various categories into which a particular printer type falls.

a. Fully Formed Character Printers

Fully formed character printers print one character at a time in a manner similar to a typewriter. A hammer or other mechanism forces a metal or plastic model of the letter to be printed against a ribbon, which in turn presses against the paper. It makes little difference in the final printed product whether the model of the letter was carried on a ball-shaped device, a thimble-shaped device, or a print wheel where the characters look like the petals of a daisy; the concept is the same (see Fig. 4-5).

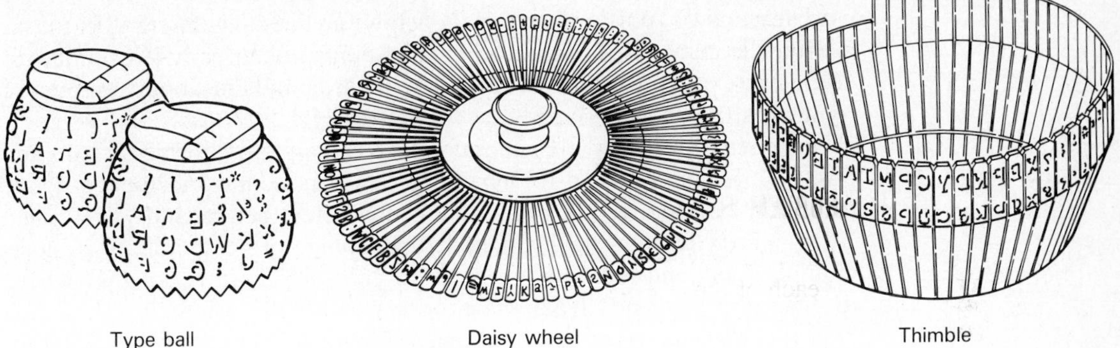

Fig. 4-5 Type ball, daisy wheel, and thimble.

These printers are relatively slow; they range from 10 to 100 characters per second. While even the slowest of these printers is faster than the average typist, long documents can take uncomfortable amounts of time to print; a 50-character-per-second printer takes roughly 1.2 s per line of text, on the average. A standard letterhead may contain 40 printed lines, so a printed page would take approximately 48 s to complete. A 20-page document would require approximately 960 s (20 × 48), or 16 min.

Another restriction is that you are limited to the type fonts (styles) available in the type balls, wheels, or thimbles made for your machine. While it is possible to change type wheels in the middle of a document, this is generally time-consuming.

b. Dot-Matrix Printers

Examine Fig. 4-6 carefully. It shows how the letter "A" can be made from a series of properly positioned dots. In a similar manner, all the letters, numerals, and symbols commonly used can be made from the correct sequence of dots.

The minimum-size matrix that can generate all the numbers and capital letters is a 5 by 7 matrix. This means that in a field of dots 5 dots wide and 7 dots high, we can select patterns that uniquely identify all the

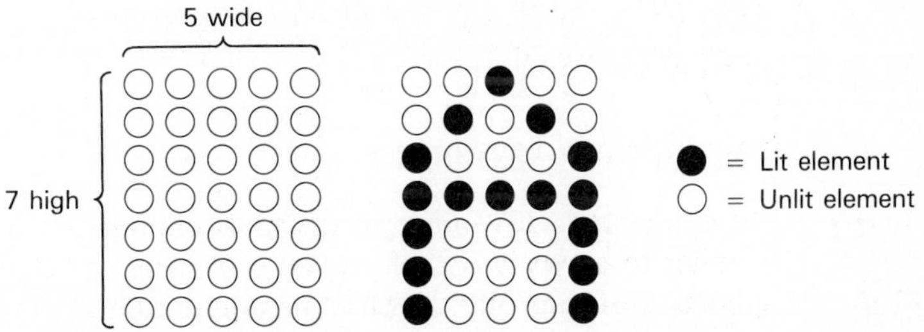

Fig. 4-6 A 5 by 7 dot-matrix display of the letter "A."

numbers and capitals. Unfortunately, lowercase letters (small letters) cannot be accurately produced. Those letters that extend below the line (that is, g, j, p, q, and y) are not produced correctly.

To correct this problem, many printer manufacturers increase the size of the matrix to 7 dots wide by 9 dots high. This provides for the letters with descenders (portions extending below the line). The more dots in the matrix, the more filled in the character. So manufacturers use even larger dot matrixes to form their letters. The main complaint about dot-matrix printers is the unattractiveness of the output.

Dot-matrix printers are generally faster than fully formed character printers, ranging from 80 to 300 characters per second. A 20-page document may be produced in 240 s (at 200 characters per second), or 4 min.

Dot-matrix printers have the added advantage of being able to print in multiple fonts and sizes under software control. There is no print wheel to change; commands from the program cause the printer to shift into italics, condensed type, or other styles. Figure 4-7 shows a representative sampling.

Dot-matrix printers can also be used to create graphics. Since each of the wires in the print head is controllable, intricate designs can be produced. Resolutions of 80 dots per inch are not uncommon. Again, this can be controlled by software, so a document might automatically combine text and charts or other graphics.

Given these two methods of printing individual characters on a line, we can now discuss some of the options available for making the actual marks on the paper. One popular method is using an inked ribbon between the character-creating mechanism and the paper. When the device forces the ribbon into contact with the paper, the image of the device is transferred to the sheet. This is called *impact printing*.

It is also possible to create letter images on the paper without a ribbon and without the impact process. These methods, as a group, are known as *nonimpact printing*.

c. Thermal Printing

Commonly implemented on dot-matrix printers is a process known as *thermal imaging*. A special, heat-sensitive paper must be used. As the print head passes over the paper, minute areas of the head, corresponding to the wires in a conventional dot-matrix print head, heat and cool very rapidly. The area immediately under the print head at the moment of heating darkens. This pattern of darkened areas forms characters or graphics, using the dot-matrix process.

By using a special plastic material in place of paper in this type of printer, a projectable transparency can be created directly.

PROBLEM FOR SECTION 4-2-1*c*

1. Cite one disadvantage of thermal printing.

d. Electrostatic Printing

Instead of using heat, an electrostatic printer, a type of dot-matrix printer, uses a high-voltage power supply to induce carefully controlled sparks

COMPUTERS FOR LESS

************* PRESENTS THE *************

**** PANASONIC KX-P1090 ****

** MATRIX PRINTER **

THIS HIGH QUALITY, LOW COST PRINTER IS THE MOST VERSATILE PRINTER IN ITS CLASS.
IT OFFERS FEATURES FOUND ONLY ON MORE EXPENSIVE DOT MATRIX PRINTERS
FEATURES INCLUDE:

- -BOTH FRICTION AND TRACTOR FEED STANDARD!
- <u>-ONE FULL YEAR WARRANTY</u>
- -TOTAL GRAPHICS CAPABILITIES
- -TWELVE DIFFERENT CHARACTER FONTS.

1) PICA PITCH, 80 CHARACTERS PER LINE. THIS IS THE NORMAL FONT UTILIZED.

2) ELITE PITCH, 96 CHARACTERS PER LINE. THIS IS AN OPTIONAL PRINT FONT.

3) DOUBLE WIDTH ELONGATED, TWICE NORMAL WIDTH.

4) **EMPHASIZED AND DOUBLE WIDTH.**

5) DOUBLE PRINTED CHARACTERS.

6) **DOUBLE PRINTED & EMPHASIZED.**

7) **EMPHASIZED.**

8) COMPRESSED, SMALLER SPACES BETWEEN LETTERS

9) COMPRESSED SUBSCRIPT

<u>10) UNDERLINED SUBSCRIPT.</u>

<u>11) UNDERLINED SUPERSCRIPT</u>

COMPUTERS FOR LESS &

PANASONIC

WE'RE JUST SLIGHTLY AHEAD OF OUR TIME!

PROGRAMS BY CFL INC.

Fig. 4-7 Variety of dot-matrix typefaces.

from the print head wires to an aluminum-coated paper. Wherever such a spark is generated, the aluminum coating is vaporized, leaving the black surface underneath.

This method was popular at one time with very inexpensive printers designed for home use. While the cost of the printer itself was fairly low, the continuing cost and unusual appearance of the aluminized paper made the system inappropriate for business use, and the method is rarely used.

e. Laser-Xerographic Printing

A laser, controlled by output from a computer, illuminates the sensitized drum of a photocopier. Then, in the same way that an image is produced in a photocopier, the image is transferred to paper. While the process is technologically complicated, this type of printer is among the fastest of any type available, printing hundreds of pages per minute!

In addition, this type of printer has great flexibility. Because of its high speed and ability to create graphic representations, the printer can print the form as well as the data on the form; since fewer forms need to be stocked, costs go down. In addition, should a form need to be changed, there is no waste; the printing routine is changed and all future forms are printed using the new format.

These printers can enlarge or reduce the graphic output (optical *scaling*); two-sided printing is also possible. While paper jamming may sometimes be a problem, this technology is rapidly becoming very popular and its reliability should be improved.

4-2-2 Line and Other Types of Printers

All the printers we have described so far print one character at a time. It is possible to print multiple characters at a stroke instead of just one. This kind of printer is known as a *line printer,* since it appears to print an entire line at a time.

These printers are almost universally of the fully formed character, impact type. They are high-speed, high-capacity devices, with output speed of between 200 and 1500 lines per minute. A 20-page document could be produced in approximately 1.2 min, assuming a printer running at 600 lines per minute.

This type of printer has a band or chain of character dies (metal or plastic parts that have the shape of the letter they are to produce) circulating in a track (see Fig. 4-8). A series of hammers, one for each possible printing position on a page (typically 132 print positions on a $14\frac{7}{8}$-inch-wide page) strikes the chain when circuitry within the printer signals that the correct character die lies under the hammer. The die is pressed into a ribbon and a character impression is thus formed. Since each of the hammers is independently controlled, and since the common characters are represented a number of times in the character dies, many print positions can be struck at the same instant.

Most such printers allow for the print chains or bands to be changed, thus providing a variety of typefaces. However, in most cases, the choices

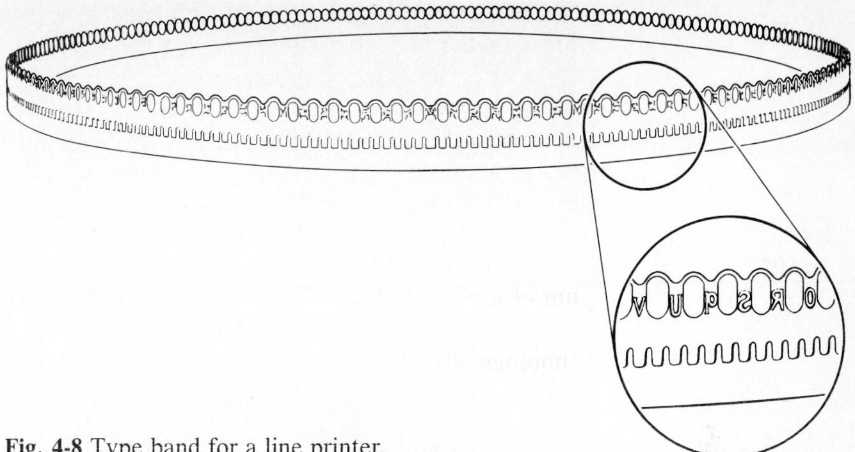

Fig. 4-8 Type band for a line printer.

are limited to a chain containing upper- and lowercase characters (plus numerals and punctuation) or one that contains only uppercase characters, numerals, and special data processing symbols. Graphics are generally not produced on this type of printer, although a primitive picture can be produced using fully formed characters.

4-2-3 Other Types of Output Devices

a. Cathode-Ray Tube (CRT) Displays

Most computers are equipped with at least one CRT display. This device, resembling a television monitor, generates an electronic display of text or graphics. Figure 4-9*a* is a photograph of a typical CRT display.

Images on this device are produced by projecting an electron beam onto a phosphor coating. Whenever the activated electron beam strikes the coating, the coating glows. If the beam is not active, the phosphor remains unstimulated and dark. The beam is scanned across the face of the tube continuously, from left to right and from top to bottom, and is brought back to the top of the display at the end of each trip. Figure 4-9*b* depicts one electron-beam scanning pattern for such devices.

Most character-oriented CRT displays create characters using a dot-matrix format, in the same way characters are produced in a dot-matrix printer. The dots are formed by pulsing the electron beam on and off as it traverses the screen. This is by far the most popular method of character generation. In the same way that a dot-matrix printer can draw graphics, so too can many CRT displays.

Standard units display 24 or 25 lines of 80 characters, although there are units that display as many as 132 characters per line or as many as 60 lines per screen.

As text is presented on this type of display, it is placed on the screen sequentially. When the text fills the screen, the top line of the display is erased, all the existing text on the screen is moved up by one line, and subsequent text fills the bottommost, now empty, line. This process is called *scrolling* and repeats, as necessary, automatically.

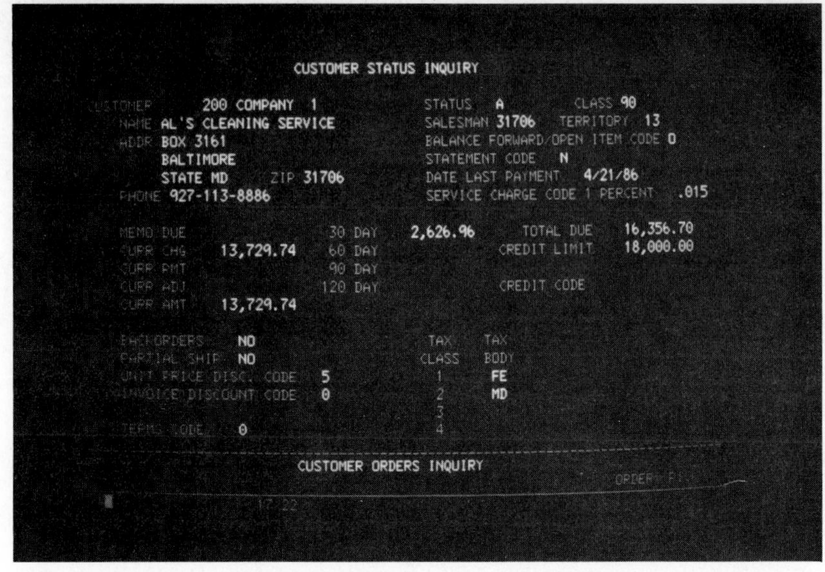

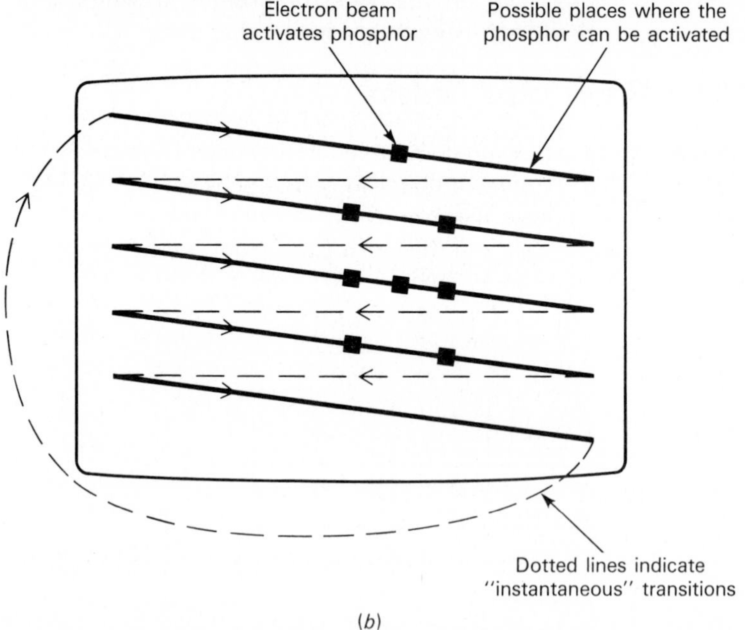

(*b*)

Fig. 4-9 (*a*) CRT monitor display. (Courtesy of IBM Corp.) (*b*) CRT monitor raster.

Many CRT displays also react to a variety of screen formatting commands that permit erasing the entire screen, printing at specific screen coordinates (e.g., line 14, character 56), erasing selected parts of the screen, and reversing scrolling (adding lines at the top instead of at the bottom). Some CRTs permit text to be highlighted; it may blink or be displayed in reverse (dark characters on a light background). Some displays use color CRTs; in these cases each character can be displayed in a different color.

By using these screen attributes carefully, program designers are able to generate applications that help prevent operators from entering incorrect or inappropriate information. Colors or highlighting can be used to call an operator's attention to data which is outside a normal range of values, allowing the operator to correct or verify such entries before they are processed.

There is a second class of CRT displays, called *graphics displays,* that are specifically designed for presenting information in pictorial form. Rather than generate images by using dot-matrix techniques, these units may use a technique known as *vector scanning*. Images on this type of display are created in much the same way that an oscilloscope image is formed, in a continuous sweep of the electron beam rather than in a pulsed manner. Lines formed in this manner are continuous; lines appearing at angles are not stepped. Circles and other curves are smooth, without jagged edges. This type of display unit is found on systems that are graphically oriented: those used for computer-assisted drafting (CAD) and computer-assisted manufacturing (CAM).

PROBLEM FOR SECTION 4-2-3*a*

1. A dot-matrix CRT is arranged to display 80 characters per line. Each character to be displayed consists of an array of 7 by 9 dots. If a single scan line must be completed in 64.2 microseconds (μs), how much time is allotted for each dot or picture element (also called *pixel*)?

b. Plotters

Similar in function to the vector-scanned CRT display is the *plotter.* This special-purpose printer literally draws pictures, usually using a variety of pens or special markers. A plotter may have a carousel carrying four to eight pens. Under software control, the plotter selects and uses the pen required, then draws the shapes desired. The different pens may have varying line widths or may contain different color inks, allowing a multicolored drawing to be produced.

These plotters are usually connected to computers supporting systems that produce diagrams, charts, or blueprints. Programs used to design electronic circuits, draw floor plans for houses, convert tabular business data into charts and graphs, and draw geometric designs are all candidates for a plotter.

Two types of plotters are common:

- Flatbed plotters, where the entire sheet of paper is laid out and the pens can travel anywhere over its surface
- Moving-paper plotters, where the paper is moved under the pen for one axis of movement and the pen rides a rail across the width of the paper for movement along the other axis

A flatbed plotter must be as large as the largest diagram it is to draw. If drawings as large as 48 by 60 inches are to be created, that is the size of the bed. Smaller diagrams are plotted on a portion of this field. All movement is in the pen mechanism and is very precise, since the dynamic attributes of the pen (inertia and momentum factors) are constant no matter where on the diagram the pens are working.

A moving-paper plotter need only be as *wide* as the widest diagram to be produced. If the paper is fed from a roll, the plotter can produce a drawing of *any* (reasonable) length. If we consider the length of the paper to be the *X* axis and the width to be the *Y* axis, movements along the *Y* axis are performed by the pen mechanism and movements along the *X* axis are performed by shifting the paper. Since characteristics of the paper, such as small changes in the speed, change as it shifts from one end to the other, the positioning is not quite as precise as on a flatbed plotter. In most cases, this is more than offset by the small size and relatively lower costs of the moving-paper plotter.

Figure 4-10 shows a typical flatbed and moving-paper plotter.

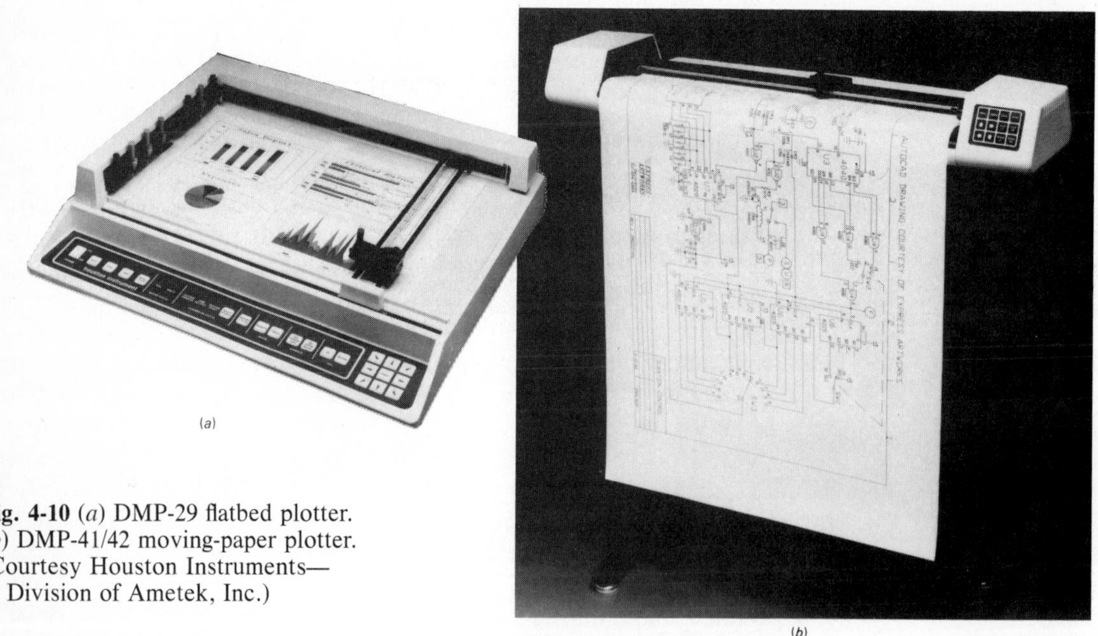

Fig. 4-10 (*a*) DMP-29 flatbed plotter. (*b*) DMP-41/42 moving-paper plotter. (Courtesy Houston Instruments—A Division of Ametek, Inc.)

c. Electronic Displays

Many times, a display as sophisticated as the CRT display is not needed. It might be that only numbers are to be displayed, or that a warning light is to be lit if a given condition exists or ceases to exist. Or the display may need to be so large that a CRT that size does not exist. In these cases, and others, various types of electronic displays may be used, as described in the following sections.

Seven-Segment Displays

A seven-segment display is a very common type of display and is described in Fig. 4-11. It shows how the digits can be produced by selectively lighting combinations of seven lights arranged in the pattern of an 8. Also shown are some of the numbers that can be produced by lighting other combinations of segments.

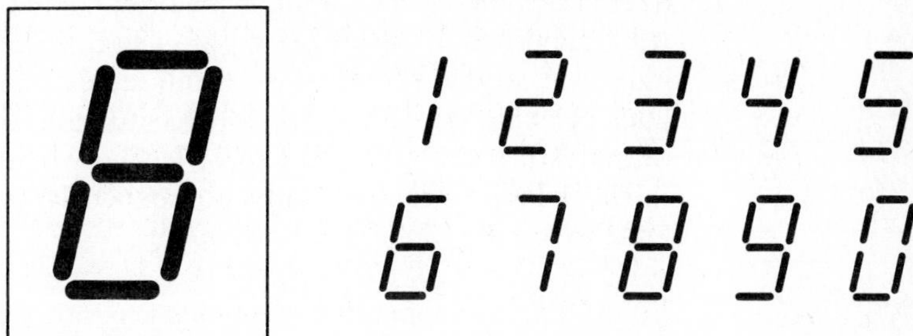

Fig. 4-11 Seven-segment display and examples of digits 0 to 9.

This kind of display appears in many forms. The segments can be made very large and lit by multiple lamps, producing displays suitable for large sporting events or clocks on buildings. Or, the segments can be made very small, and powered by light-emitting diodes (LEDs), thus requiring little power. This type of display was very popular on early digital wristwatches. More modern watches use liquid-crystal diode (LCD) displays, whose main advantage is that they require even less power (in the microwatt range) to operate than the LED displays (several milliwatts per segment).

The main disadvantage of a seven-segment display is its limited ability to display alphanumeric characters.

Dot-Matrix Displays

As the name implies, by creating an array of lights in a dot-matrix pattern, a message can be displayed, creating characters in the same manner as a dot-matrix printer. This is another common display type since the size of the display can be varied according to the intended application.

Displays of this type can be rather expensive. Each character position requires at least 35 lamps (for a 5 by 7 array). If we wanted a display that could show 10 lines of 20 characters each, we would have to mount, wire, and control 7000 lamps. Just replacing burned-out light bulbs on an array that size is a monumental task.

However, in applications where a small display is required, LCD arrays are being produced by integrated-circuit techniques that allow display of 24 lines of 80 characters in a 5 by 7 matrix—a total of over 48,000 controlled points.

Indicator Displays

At times, a computer system monitors an industrial process and must indicate when certain parameters fall outside an acceptance range. For example, pressure readings in a nuclear power generating station may grow too high or too low, or the voltage at a given test point in a circuit may be excessive.

The computer can then simply control a labeled indicator light. If the light is lit, the condition is normal. If the indicator is unlit, or lit in an alternate color, the condition is abnormal, and the legend tells the operator what condition is out of the norm. The lit indicator is used as the normal indicator, so that a burned-out lamp indicates an abnormal condition that must be explored. Usually in critical situations there are multiple indicators or indicators that change color or legend when conditions change.

These indicators are relatively inexpensive and can be designed to operate in a wide range of environments.

d. Voice Synthesis

If you dial a telephone number that has not yet been assigned, you get a recording telling you so. In many areas of the country, that recording is a computer-synthesized voice.

There are two general methods used in voice and sound synthesis:

- Record a real sound, convert it in such a manner that it can be stored in a computer's memory as a series of values, and then reassemble the sounds as required and feed them to a device that recreates the sound.
- Analyze the way in which vocal sounds are made (i.e., the speech mechanisms such as the lips, tongue, and teeth) and create the electronic waveform that, when reproduced, will resemble the desired words and phrasing.

The first method creates a more realistic sounding synthesized voice, since its origin is human speech. However, any sound that is desired must be recorded or created from existing stored sounds. For instance, by storing the names of each of the numerals (''one'' ''two,'' etc.), common multiples (''twenty,'' ''thirty,'' ''hundred,'' ''thousand,'' etc.), some common prefixes (''milli-'', ''micro-,'' etc.), and names of units (''volts,'' ''ohms,'' etc.), the synthesizer can assemble such phrases as ''six thousand five hundred thirty-seven microvolts.''

The second method, at the moment, does not create as natural a sound, but it has the potential for greater use. The sound is actually synthesized; it has never existed as a sound before, only as an algorithm for creating a given sound. As the algorithms are further refined and machines become more powerful, this type of true speech and sound synthesis will become more prevalent.

SUMMARY

Peripherals give the computer important capabilities. They can be used to channel information into the computer from the outside world as well as transmit data to the outside world. They are generally referred to as input/output, or I/O, devices.

Input devices can be text-oriented as well as nontext-oriented machines. The computer's keyboard is the most common form of a text-oriented input device. Optical character recognition (OCR) units can scan a sheet of paper, convert the information to electrical signals, and transmit the result to the computer. A traditional input device is the punched-card reader. One of the newer input devices associated with the computer is the bar code reader. Some nontext input devices include voice recognition units, thermistors, tachometers, photocells, and ultrasonic detectors.

Output from the computer can be displayed on the computer's monitor as well as a printer where a hard, or printed, copy of the information can be made available to the user. Printers include dot-matrix units which form characters using an array of dots. They can also be used to create graphic images. Other forms of printing devices include thermal printers, which use heat-sensitive paper and a thermal printing head; electrostatic printers, in which a high-voltage discharge creates an image of the character; and xerographic machines, which employ laser beams. Plotters can produce diagrams (graphics) as well as textual information. Nontext output can be generated by a voice synthesizer.

REVIEW QUESTIONS

1. What is the purpose of an input device?
2. What is the purpose of an output device?
3. What is the difference between text-type data and nontext-type data? Give three examples of each type of data.
4. What are the two general types of keyboards? Give at least two examples of each type.
5. Why is the keyboard such a universally found device? What kinds of devices might replace the keyboard in the future?
6. What industries are most likely to benefit from optical character recognition? Why?
7. What industry has made MICR equipment popular? What are the relative advantages and disadvantages of MICR?
8. Why were punched cards once the most frequently used method of entering data? Why is this no longer so?
9. What are the roles of the card reader, card punch, and punched card?
10. Where are magnetic stripes commonly found? What kind of data is often included on such devices?

11. What is the difference between mark-sense cards and punched cards? What are the similarities?

12. Under what conditions might the use of mark-sense cards be a highly efficient method of gathering data?

13. What are the two general types of voice recognition systems?

14. What is meant by "training" such a system?

15. What is a transducer? Name five physical properties that are commonly measured by transducers.

16. What is the purpose of a printer?

17. Why are fully formed character printers so popular? What are their relative advantages and disadvantages?

18. Describe the method used by a dot-matrix printer to form characters.

19. What is thermal printing?

20. What is electrostatic printing? What is its main disadvantage?

21. Describe the process of laser-xerographic printing. What are the advantages and disadvantages of this form of printing?

22. What is the difference between a line printer and a character printer?

23. Describe the purpose of plotters and the two general types of plotters available.

24. When would a cathode-ray tube display be unsuitable? Under what conditions would it be ideal?

25. Describe the action of scrolling.

26. What is a vector-scanned display?

27. What are three common types of electronic displays? What are their relative advantages? Why would such a display be used instead of a CRT display?

28. Name two methods of voice synthesis. How do they differ?

29. Which method of voice synthesis produces a more natural sound? Why?

30. Which method of voice synthesis is more flexible? Why?

31. If you were designing a system that was to use voice synthesis for output, what criteria would you examine to determine which method of synthesis to employ?

5 HIGH-LEVEL LANGUAGE AND DATA

Human languages contain a good deal of redundancy. A person can break off a thought in midsentence and the listener is still able to complete the idea. You cannot do this when transmitting needs or intentions to a computer. If you saw the word "qick" in a sentence, you would have little difficulty knowing that the word should be "quick." At present, computer programs cannot make such distinctions within a program.

A program, written in English-like phrases, is an efficient way to transmit intentions to a computer. To write such a program you need to specify

- What is to be done, and
- The order in which it is to be done.

High-level language (HLL) is the name applied to the English-like phrases used to meet these needs. To learn an HLL, one must study the rules of the language. These permit the computer user to write the steps to be executed. All HLLs have such rules. While they differ in detail, their purposes remain the same. After one has studied the purpose of such rules, learning an HLL is greatly simplified.

There are many computer languages available, hundreds by one recent survey. If all languages have similar goals, why should there be so many? Studying these languages shows that each is designed to have advantages for certain kinds of programs. One may be more efficient (execute programs more rapidly) for engineering problems, while another may be better suited for managing large amounts of data (such as keeping medical records for many patients). Yet another might be better suited for generating drawings such as one finds in drafting.

In the next few chapters the important parts of HLLs will be discussed. Since programs have to accept data and produce results (information), a discussion of data types will be one of the important topics covered. When studying these chapters, keep in mind these categories of HLL statements:

- Data types
- Input/output (I/O); directing data to the external world
- Processing or computation
- Control

5-1 DATA IN COMPUTERS: THE RANGE OF NUMBERS

All HLLs deal with numbers. It is therefore important to describe numbers as they might be encountered in an HLL. Two kinds of numbers are commonly used in programming. Some numbers contain a decimal point, while others do not. Numbers without a decimal point are *integers*. Numbers which contain a decimal point are *real numbers*.

Example 5-1 Number Classification

See the accompanying table for representative numbers and how they are classified.

Number	Classification
0	Integer
1.5	Real
−4	Integer
3.14159	Real
−64.	Real

Notice that the last number in the table is a real number. Even though −64 is a whole number, which would normally make it an integer, the presence of the decimal point makes it real. In some cases a minus sign appears in the number. Integers and real numbers can be either positive or negative.

All computers are limited in the size of numbers which they can handle. In addition, the maximum size of the numbers is different for integers and reals. Figure 5-1 shows a typical range for integers in a computer. The horizontal line is called the *number line;* it represents all possible integers. Notice that the range is not symmetric. This lack of symmetry exists in some machines. For positive numbers the range extends to +32,767, while for negative numbers the limit is −32,768.

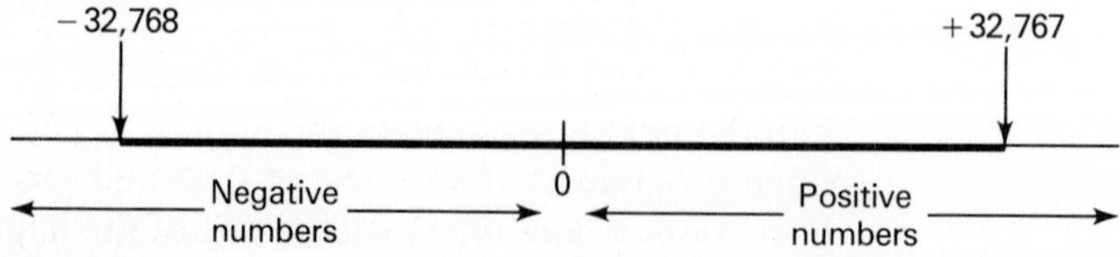

Fig. 5-1 Typical range of integers within a computer.

You can find two kinds of real numbers in HLLs. Both contain a decimal point, but the placement of the decimal point and the numerical arrangement (format) differ. The first kind is called a *fixed-point* number. For these numbers the decimal point appears in a fixed, specified position. The computer and the HLL expect these numbers to have the decimal point in the same position. The following example shows some possibilities.

Example 5-2 Fixed-Point Numbers

Number of Digits after Decimal	Typical Examples
2	125.12, 15.01, −16053.86
3	0.001, −8.325, 162.529
4	0.1562, 25.6815, −10.8914

When dealing with fixed-point numbers, one must specify how many digits appear after the decimal point. The allowed range of such numbers depends on the number of digits after the decimal point and the total number of digits which the computer can handle for each number.

Example 5-3 Fixed-Point Number Ranges

If a certain computer can handle seven-digit numbers, then here are some fixed-point number ranges you might encounter.

Number of Digits after Decimal Point	Range		
1	+99,999.9	to	−999,999.9
2	+99,999.99	to	−99,999.99
3	+9999.999	to	−9999.999
4	+999.9999	to	−999.9999
5	+99.9999	to	−99.9999
6	+9.999999	to	−9.999999
7	+0.9999999	to	−0.9999999

There are many problems that do not lend themselves to the fixed-point arrangement. In electronic technology you can find voltages which range from 1 microvolt (0.000001 or 1×10^{-6} volt) to 10,000 (or more) volts. Using fixed-point real numbers forces the computer (and HLL) to handle numbers with the format

nnnnn.nnnnnn

In this case each *n* is a decimal digit and the decimal point is followed by six places. The machine must be able to handle numbers containing 11 digits in total. Many machines cannot do this. Is it possible to take care of such situations?

Floating-point numbers are used to solve problems with a broad range of real numbers. Two pieces of information are needed to specify a floating-point number: the sequence of digits of the number and where to put the decimal point. The following rules set out the way in which to write floating-point numbers:

1. First indicate the sign of the number, plus (+) or minus (−). If you do not indicate a sign, a plus sign is assumed.
2. Write a decimal point.
3. Write down all the digits of the real number.
4. Write the letter "E." This letter precedes the digits which determine where to move the decimal point.
5. Follow the E with a sign. If a − appears, it means that the decimal point is moved to the left in order to establish the value of the real number. If a + appears, or if the sign is omitted altogether, it signifies that the decimal point should be moved to the right to identify the value of the real number.
6. The number which follows the sign indicates the number of places to move the decimal point in order to establish the value of the real number.

Example 5-4 Writing a Decimal Number in Floating-Point Notation

To write a current of +5.689 amperes in floating-point notation, follow steps 1 to 6 shown in the accompanying table.

Step Number	Meaning	Result
1	Number is positive	+
2		+.
3	"5689" are the digits of the values	+.5689
4		+.5689E
5	Decimal point must be moved right to get the true value of the real number	+.5689E+
6	Move decimal point one place to produce floating-point equivalent number	+.5689E+01

The floating-point result is +.5689E+01. This is equivalent to 5.689.

The general form of a floating-point number is

$$(\text{sign}).\underbrace{fxxx\cdots}_{\text{mantissa}}\ \text{E}(\text{sign})\underbrace{yy\cdots}_{\text{exponent}}$$

A few more observations about such numbers are in order.

1. If the first digit after the decimal point—*f* in this case—is not zero, the number is said to be *normalized*.
2. Most computer HLLs restrict the number following the E to two digits.
3. The number following the E is called the *exponent*. The numbers following the decimal point make up the *mantissa*.

Figure 5-2 shows a typical range for floating-point numbers in a computer. Notice that the number 0 cannot be represented as a floating-point number. The smallest floating-point number which can be written is +.0000E−50. This is a very small real number because it consists of a decimal point followed by 54 zeros! However, it is *not* exactly 0. Since +.0000E−50 is very small, it can usually be used in place of real zero without making an error. If, in the course of a calculation, the computer obtains a result such as +.6055E−70, it will force the result to +.0000E−50, which is the smallest floating-point number available to the computer.

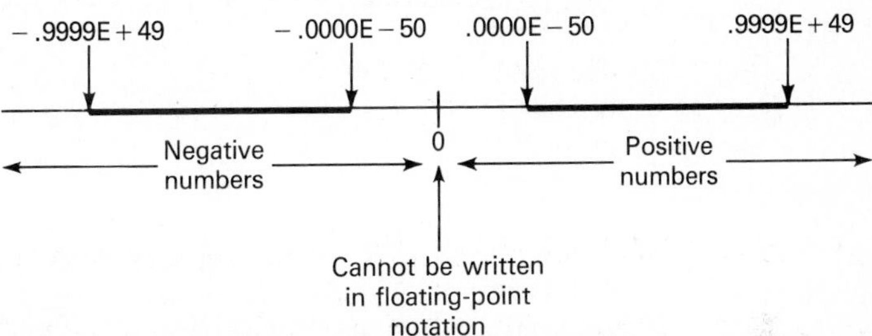

Fig. 5-2 Typical range of floating-point numbers in a digital computer.

Example 5-5 Examples of Floating-Point Numbers

Real Number	Floating-Point Forms	Normalized
25.	.25E+02	Yes
	.25E+2	Yes
	.25E2	Yes
−0.0563	−.5630E−01	Yes
	−.5630E−1	Yes
	−.0563E0	No
10500	.1050E+5	Yes
	.10500E5	Yes
	.0105E6	No

Comparing the fixed-point and floating-point methods for writing real numbers, one can see that, for a fixed number of significant digits, the floating-point method results in a greater range of allowed numbers. Figure 5-3 shows one such case.

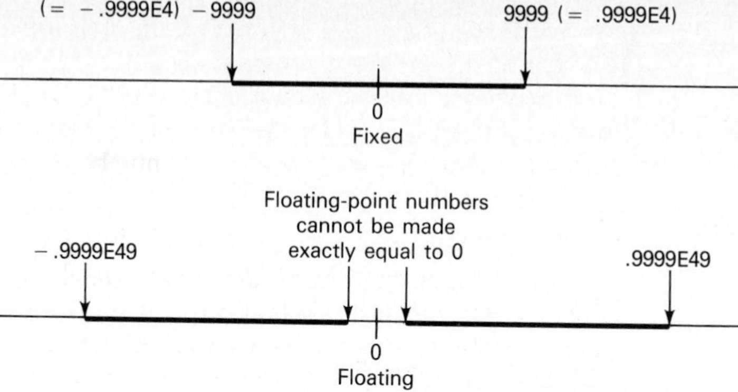

Fig. 5-3 Comparing the ranges of fixed-point and floating-point numbers with each one having four significant digits.

PROBLEMS FOR SECTION 5-1

1. Write the following as floating-point numbers.

a. 25
b. 3.14159
c. −2.25
d. 0.0001

2. Some computer systems use only positive numbers for the exponents of floating-point numbers. Suppose the computer recognizes exponents from 00 to 99.

a. Suggest a way in which such a scheme could be used to represent exponents from −50 to +49.
b. Using the method derived in part (a), write the following floating-point numbers as they should appear in the computer:

−.215E−5
21.6
1000000

3. A digital computer can handle eight-digit numbers. What is the largest possible range (including both negative and positive numbers) of fixed-point numbers?

4. Which of the following are normalized?

a. −0.01E2
b. .105E0
c. 1.25E−3

5-2 INTEGER AND FLOATING-POINT ARITHMETIC

Two kinds of numbers have been described: integers and real numbers. HLLs usually include ways of writing a series of arithmetic calculations using such numbers. For example, each of the sequences $A + B$, $A - B$, $A * B$, and A/B have similar meanings in the HLLs included in this book. They would produce addition, subtraction, multiplication, and division, respectively, of the numbers represented by A and B. However, the actual calculations vary for integer and real number operations.

5-2-1 Integer Arithmetic

Adding, subtracting, multiplying, or dividing two integer quantities produces an integer result. The range of values which an integer quantity may attain, assuming that 2 bytes are used to represent an integer quantity, is −32,768 to +32,767. As a result, arithmetic operations which produce results outside this range produce errors. (The number sequence for such computers is 0 to 32,767, followed by −32,768 after the largest positive number. Conversely, negative numbers proceed from 0 to −32,768 and then jump to +32,767.)

Some computers will detect and report these errors. For instance, if you were to try to add 8655 and 28,681, the result should be 37,336. However, since this is larger than 32,767 (the largest integer permitted), we have an error condition. Most computers would report this occurrence as an *integer overflow* error. However, in some cases, it is possible that no error would be reported. In such cases, because of the way that negative integers are represented inside the computer's memory, a result of −28,200 might be reported, clearly an error.

A similar condition could occur if a subtraction produces a result less than −32,768. Trying to subtract 19,256 from −29,999 would result in −49,255, a value too small for the allowable range. This might be reported as an *integer underflow* error. If the machine is set up so that no error is reported, it might return a value of 16,280.

A different condition may occur during division. Suppose we want to divide the integer 33 by the integer 4. The true result is 8.25. However, since we are performing integer operations, there may be no decimal portion in the result. Most machines will simply *truncate,* or shorten, the decimal portion of the answer and return the integer portion, in this case, 8. This may produce errors if the results of this division were used later on. If the integer 4 was divided by 5, the result 0.8 would be truncated to 0. If this result were used as the divisor of another operation, we would be attempting to divide by zero! This may cause the machine to go into an infinite computing loop, which can be broken by externally halting the program.

In any case, it is important to realize that, while various combinations of HLLs and computers may not produce identical results when error conditions arise, it is the programmer's responsibility to know how the particular system reacts, and to take appropriate steps to detect and correct such errors and prevent them from upsetting other aspects of the program.

You can see from these examples that HLL integer arithmetic may introduce errors into computer calculations if the results fall outside the integer storage limitations. Then, why use integer arithmetic? Even with the limited range of integers within many computers, many practical applications using integer arithmetic are possible. While these may also be accomplished using floating-point numbers, it is more efficient (i.e., it requires less time and storage space within the CPU) to use integers. (In addition, floating-point arithmetic may introduce subtle errors when used to represent integer quantities.)

The problems encountered in integer arithmetic may be minimized. Errors occurred because of the limited integer range. Why not extend the range? If instead of one word of memory, two words are used, the integer is said to be a *double-precision* integer. Double precision allows the integer range to be extended: −2,147,483,648 to +2,147,483,647. Compare this to the single-precision integer range of −32,768 to +32,767. The range has been increased by a factor of 65,536.

PROBLEMS FOR SECTION 5-2-1

1. The range of integers in a certain computer is −32,768 to +32,767. The computer does not flag (signal) underflow or overflow errors. What are the internal results (values of C) for each of the following:

a. $A = -8655$; $B = 28{,}681$; $C = A - B$
b. $A = 15{,}210$; $B = 17{,}895$; $C = A + B$
c. $A = 18$; $B = 3106$; $C = A * B$ (* = multiply)
d. $A = 20$; $B = 7$; $C = A/B$ (/ = divide)

2. A computer has an integer range of +127 to −128. What is the range of such a machine for double-precision integers?

5-2-2 Floating-Point Arithmetic

A second form of calculation is required to handle floating-point numbers. To begin a calculation, each floating-point number must be in normalized form. This means that the first digit after the decimal point is *not* a zero.

Example 5-6 Adding Floating-Point Numbers

Two floating-point numbers are to be added. They are given as follows:

Number	Floating-Point Form	Decimal Value
A	0.0525E4	525.
B	0.6185E+01	6.185
		531.185

The following steps are used to add two floating-point numbers:

1. Normalize the numbers to be added. If one or more digits after the decimal point are zero, move the decimal point to the right one digit at a time, and reduce the exponent by 1 for each move until the first digit

after the decimal point is not zero. If there are digits ahead of the decimal point, move the decimal point one digit to the left and increase the exponent by 1 for each move. Continue to do this until the decimal point appears just in front of the first digit.
2. If the exponents of the two numbers are different, adjust the position of the decimal point of the number with the larger exponent. This adjustment is performed by moving the decimal point to the right and reducing the exponent one digit at a time. Repeat this operation until the exponents of the two numbers are the same.
3. Add the mantissas of the two numbers.
4. Normalize the result.

Carrying out these steps for the example produces the accompanying table.

Step	A	B	Result
Given	0.0525E4	0.6185E1	
1. Normalize *A*	0.525E3	0.6185E1	
2. Adjust *A*	05.25E2		
	052.5E1	0.6185E1	
3. Add	052.5E1	0.6185E1	53.1185E1
4. Normalize the result	—	—	5.31185E2 .531185E3 (= 531.185)

The answer is not the answer found in the computer's memory. If the computer can store only four digits for the mantissa (the fractional number after the decimal point), then the result in the computer would be 0.5311E3. The computer would throw away the numbers 8 and 5 in the result. Because the computer cannot store these extra numbers, it has introduced a small error. If the true answer is 531.185 and the computer uses 531.1 for the answer, the error is only 0.016 percent. In some computers the answer is rounded off to 531.2.

Example 5-7 Multiplying Floating-Point Numbers

The rules for multiplying floating-point numbers are not difficult. Assume that the numbers to be multiplied have already been normalized. The four rules for multiplication are:

1. If the signs of the two numbers to be multiplied are different, the sign of the result is negative; otherwise the sign is positive.
2. Multiply the mantissas together. Adjust the result by truncation or rounding. This gives the mantissa of the result.
3. Add the exponents together. This gives the exponent of the result.
4. Normalize the result.

These rules are applied to the following floating-point problem:

Number 1 = .8541E − 1
Number 2 = − .3152E + 02

Multiply number 1 times number 2. In the accompanying table, M_1 is the mantissa of the first number and E_1 is its exponent; corresponding designations are made for the second number and for the result.

					RESULT		
Step	**M_1**	**E_1**	**M_2**	**E_2**	**Sign**	**M_R**	**E_R**
1	.8541	−1	.3152	2	−	x	x
2	.8541	−1	.3152	2	−	.2692	x
3	.8541	−1	.3152	2	−	.2692	1
4					Already normalized		

The result is − .2692E01. M_1 and M_2 are multiplied in step 2. The result is really .26921232. When you multiply two four-digit numbers, you get an eight-digit result. If the computer can store only four-digit mantissas, the answer must be reduced to four digits. One method throws away the last four digits. This is called *truncation*. Alternatively, if the leftmost digit to be thrown away is 5 or more, add 1 to the rightmost digit, which is saved. This method is called *rounding off*. In this example both methods give the same answer.

Example 5-8 Dividing Floating-Point Numbers

The rules for division are similar to the rules for multiplication. Once again assume that the numbers are already normalized. The four rules for division are:

1. If the signs of the numbers to be divided are different, the sign of the result is negative; otherwise the sign is positive.
2. Divide the mantissas. Adjust the result by truncation or rounding. This yields the mantissa of the result.
3. Subtract the exponent of the denominator from the exponent of the numerator. The answer becomes the exponent of the result.
4. Normalize the result.

These rules are applied to the following floating-point problem:

Number 1 = .2180E02
Number 2 = .1900E02

Divide number 1 by number 2. Follow the steps shown in the accompanying table.

Step	M_1	E_1	M_2	E_2	RESULT Sign	M_R	E_R
1	.2180	2	.1900	2	+	x	x
2	.2180	2	.1900	2	+	1.147 (1.147368)	x
3	.2180	2	.1900	2	+	1.147	0
4	.2180	2	.1900	2	+	.1147	1

The result is +.1147E01.

PROBLEMS FOR SECTION 5-2-2

1. Draw a flow diagram which describes floating-point multiplication.
2. Following the procedures outlined in Example 5-6, perform the following addition:

$$A + B \quad \text{where} \quad A = -.2183\text{E}2 \text{ and } B = .15\text{E}-1$$

3. Assume that a computer can store only four significant figures. What percentage error is introduced in your answer to Prob. 2?
4. How can you implement floating-point subtraction if your computer can only carry out floating-point addition?
5. Multiply the floating-point numbers shown below. The computer can handle four significant digits in the mantissa.

$$A = .5193\text{E}1 \qquad B = -.81\text{E}0$$

5-2-3 Mixing Integer and Floating-Point Calculations

Integer and floating-point arithmetic calculations use different rules. The computer cannot perform arithmetic in which one number is an integer and the other a floating-point value. There are times in a computer program when this cannot be avoided. There are ways to solve this dilemma. These include:

- Instruct the computer to convert floating-point values to integers; then perform integer arithmetic.
- Convert integer values to floating-point numbers; then perform floating-point arithmetic.

An HLL might include a statement which directs the computer to convert a number from a floating-point value to an integer.

A typical statement is:

INT (A)

which will calculate the largest integer which is less than or equal to the floating-point number represented by A.

If keeping track of the number type is left to the user, the computer may not permit mixed number calculations. In such cases the computer will send the user an error message. This happens when mixed number calculations are detected in the program. For example, the error message might say "MIXED VARIABLE ERROR."

Instead of leaving the task of keeping track of the number type to the user, the computer can solve this problem automatically. In some cases the computer converts integers into floating-point numbers when a user unintentionally specifies a mixed calculation. The arithmetic calculations are then performed using floating-point operations. The result, however, may be left in floating-point form.

PROBLEMS FOR SECTION 5-2-3

1. Convert the following numbers into floating-point notation:

a. −25
b. 0
c. 21,835

2. Draw a flow diagram which can be used to convert floating-point (FP) numbers into integers. Truncate fractional parts of the result. Assume exponents from −50 to +50, and four significant digits. The integer range is −32,768 to +32,767. If the FP number is too large, issue an error message.

5-3 MORE THOUGHTS ON DATA

The kinds of operations which can be performed on numbers stored in the computer depends on the type of number. You have seen that addition is performed differently when the numbers to be added are integers or floating-point values. This means that different types of numbers (or data) may coexist in the computer. For each type, a set of rules or operations can be defined. These tell what can be done with the data types. For example, it is possible to consider some of the numbers within the computer to be letters (actually a coded form). You could then instruct the computer to find or *locate,* a letter (or group of letters). The *locating* operation is new. It has a set of rules different from integer or floating-point addition. Computers have many different types of data in addition to integer and floating-point numbers. Some of the various data types which are found in HLLs are discussed in this section.

5-3-1 Data Types in HLLs

Someone who is writing a program should specify the various kinds or types of data which the HLL can expect to find. This is called *data typing.* The English-like statements that one uses are called *declarations* (or *type declarations*).

For example a data item might be specified as an integer by employing a declaration of the form.

INTEGER {the data item}

a. Numerical Data

Type declarations vary from one HLL to another. However, all HLLs have some way of specifying data types. In some cases you can let the HLL specify the type. When this happens you have *defaulted* (or deferred) to the HLL. The HLL program will examine the data item and specify a type according to certain rules. These rules vary from one HLL to another. In some HLLs, if you fail to declare a data item, an error message will be sent to you.

Four data types have already been discussed. They are:

1. Integer
2. Floating-point numbers
3. Double-precision integers
4. Double-precision floating-point numbers

Double-precision numbers are very similar to their single-precision cousins. However, they have greater range. Also, a slightly different set of rules is needed to perform arithmetic calculations on such data types.

In many HLLs you will find words used to specify these types. Here are some examples:

	HLL	
Type	**Pascal**	**BASIC**
Integer	INTEGER	%
Floating-point	REAL	!
Double-precision integer	†	*
Double-precision floating-point	†	#

† Not available in many implementations.

In many engineering and mathematical problems it is helpful to be able to use complex numbers. In electrical technology, for example, the impedance of an ac network may be written as

$$R + jX \qquad \text{or} \qquad R + iX$$

where R is the resistance and X is the reactance of the network. Such numbers have special rules for addition, subtraction, multiplication, and division.

PROBLEM FOR SECTION 5-3-1*a*

1. Suggest a format for storing complex numbers in the computer's memory.

b. Logical Data

When a computer is called upon to make decisons, numerical results may not be important. The answer that is needed is simply a "yes" or a "no." In HLLs the words TRUE and FALSE are sometimes used to mean yes and no. This is a new type of data. It is called *logical* or *boolean* data in many HLLs.

Example 5-9 Examples of Logical Data

(a) Switches on the front panels of appliances, test instruments, or communication equipment can be on or off (a "start" switch, an AGC switch on a communication receiver, etc.). In an HLL program, to control equipment of this kind, you can use the LOGICAL data type to keep track of the condition of the switch (on or off). The data for the switch is set equal to TRUE if the switch is on and FALSE if the switch is off.

(b) An HLL program might be designed to control operation of a chemical plant. In such a program the condition of the inlet valve (open or closed), and the waste valve (open or closed) could be logical data. Open could be made equivalent to TRUE and closed could be equivalent to FALSE.

Only numbers are allowed inside a computer. Words such as "true" or "false" have no meaning. In the computer, a true condition is usually set equal to the number 1 and a false condition is usually set equal to the number 0. This does not mean that a 0 in the computer always means false (or that a 1 always means true). Only if a memory location is known to contain logical data does a 1 in that memory location mean true and a 0 mean false.

In the performance of operations on logical data, the results are logical quantities. Results can only take the values true (1) or false (0). There are three operations which are commonly performed on a LOGICAL data type. These are the AND operation, the OR operation, and the NOT operation. Tables 5-1 and 5-2 show what happens when an AND or OR calculation (operation) is performed on two logical values. The first logical value involved in the operation is called "FIRST." The second logical value involved in the operation is called "SECOND."

TABLE 5-1 THE AND OPERATION

If FIRST Is	While SECOND Is	Then RESULT Is
True	True	True
True	False	False
False	True	False
False	False	False

TABLE 5-2 THE OR OPERATION

If FIRST Is	While SECOND Is	Then RESULT Is
True	True	True
True	False	True
False	True	True
False	False	False

The NOT operation involves only one value; it returns the inverse of that value (see Table 5-3).

TABLE 5-3 THE NOT OPERATION

If FIRST Is	Then RESULT Is
True	False
False	True

Addition, subtraction, and usually multiplication and division form part of the hardware of the computer. In a similar way, the logical rules are built into the computer. In an HLL program, suppose you write

C = A AND B

The computer uses the binary representation of the number it has been keeping for A and combines it with the binary representation of B, according to the rules in Table 5-1. The combination is performed on each of the binary digits making up the numbers. The resultant binary pattern is assigned (stored) to the location allocated for C.

Example 5-10 Compound Logical Calculations

An HLL program used to control operation of a chemical processing plant should include some instructions to detect malfunctions or errors in the operation of the factory. One kind of malfunction occurs when either a waste container is overfilled (possibly detected by a photocell) or a mixing operation is in progress while an inlet valve is open. We can write out these conditions in a shorthand form. To do so, make note of the following:

W is logical data. This is the condition of the waste container. If W = true, the container is said to be overfilled. If W = false, the waste container is normal.

M is logical data. M = true means that mixing of chemicals is in progress. M = false means no mixing is in progress.

I is logical data. If I = true, then the inlet valve is open and chemicals are entering the mixing vat. If I = false, then the inlet valve is shut off.

The error condition can now be written using shorthand. This error condition is

(I AND M) OR W

The parentheses help us to keep the inlet valve and mixing operations together. (Parentheses in logical operations perform the same role as in numeric operations; they alter or clarify the order in which operations are to occur.) To check that this is the calculation which correctly describes the malfunction, use Tables 5-1 and 5-2. These show the rules for two LOGICAL data types. How do you handle the compound calculations (three LOGICAL data types)? To obtain results, perform two calculations:

1. Using Table 5-1, calculate I AND M. This produces partial results. Call these results R′.
2. Using the partial results of step 1, use Table 5-2 to calculate R′ OR W. The result is the answer to the complete calculation.

The calculations are summarized as shown in the accompanying table.

I	M	(R′) I AND M	W	R = R′ OR W
True	True	True	True	True
True	True	True	False	True
True	False	False	True	True
True	False	False	False	False
False	True	False	True	True
False	True	False	False	False
False	False	False	True	True
False	False	False	False	False

Notice that R is true (a malfunction exists) when the waste container is overfilled or when the inlet valve is open and mixing is taking place (R′ is true). Therefore, the calculation (I AND M) OR W is the shorthand form of the error condition stated at the beginning of the example.

PROBLEMS FOR SECTION 5-3-1*b*

1. Can a computer use arithmetic addition to implement the logical OR operation? Explain your answer.

2. Can a computer use arithmetic multiplication to implement the logical AND operation? Explain your answer.

3. Following the procedure outlined in Example 5-10, produce a table of true and false logical values which can be used to describe the results of the following compound logical operation.

(A AND B) OR (C AND D)

4. Fluid in a tank is to be kept at a safe level (not too much and not too little). Fluid detectors are placed at the low-level and high-level positions on the tank. If fluid is above a detector, it produces a logical value equivalent to true, otherwise it reports a logical false result. Call the detectors L (for low-level) and H (for high-level). Write the logical calculation which must be performed to test for a safe fluid level.

c. Some POINTER Remarks

The next type of data which can be found in some HLLs is the *pointer*. The numerical value of a POINTER data type is the address of a memory location. Example 5-11 describes one way in which a POINTER data type may be used.

Example 5-11 Using a POINTER Data Type

A computer is used to control an automatic wiring machine. A pointer value keeps track of which connection is being made. The flow diagram of Fig. 5-4 describes the HLL program which controls the automatic wiring

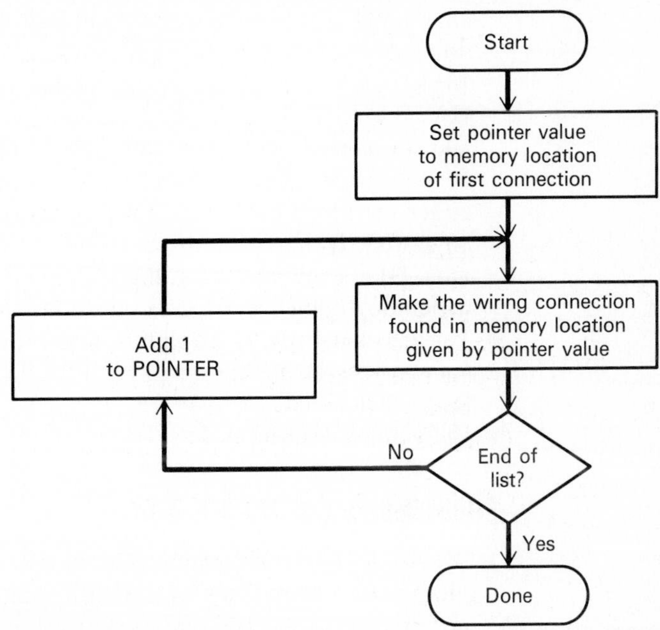

Fig. 5-4 Flow diagram for an automatic wiring machine using a POINTER data type to keep track of the wiring list.

machine. A POINTER data type is an integer because it is the address of a memory location. Memory addresses are integers. There are no special calculations which can be performed on pointers as there are on logical data.

d. Character Data

A very useful and important type of data is the character. This usually consists of alphanumeric characters such as:

1. Letters A to Z and the lowercase counterparts a to z
2. Numbers 0 to 9
3. "Special" characters that you might see on a typewriter keyboard such as $, =, (,), "blank" or "space," ., /, +, -, and *

Within the computer, a number or code is used for each character. Different computers use different codes. A popular code is *ASCII* (American Standard Code for Information Interchange) (see Appendix A). ASCII codes are 7 or 8 bits long, and thus one ASCII character fits in a single byte.

A CHARACTER data type may also refer to a *sequence* of individual characters. This is called a *character string*. HLLs allow variations in CHARACTER type data. These will be described, as well as the way in which they are stored in memory.

- **Fixed declared length:** The number of characters permitted in the string is fixed. You cannot do anything to change the length. If, by mistake, you attempt to store more characters than you have specified, some characters are lost. The string will be truncated. For example, suppose you specify that a fixed-length character string called "MESSAGE" has 10 characters. The character string that you would like to store is "YOU HAVE MADE A MISTAKE.", which has 24 characters including spaces and the period. The character string "MESSAGE" has room for only 10 characters. Different HLLs would produce different results, but either the first 10 characters will be stored or the last 10 characters will be stored. If the string to be stored is shorter than the declared length, most HLLs will pad the string with blanks, either on the left or the right depending upon the HLL in question, to make up the specified length.
- **Variable length** with maximum limit: Here, the character strings may vary in length, but they will be truncated if they exceed the maximum length permitted.
- **Unbounded length:** A few HLLs allow character strings of unlimited length.

PROBLEMS FOR SECTION 5-3-1*d*

1. Devise a character string format of unbounded length for which you do not need to keep track of the string length.
2. How many different characters are possible using a 6-bit ASCII code? How many are possible with a 7-bit code?

3. Given the following message:

A SAMPLE MESSAGE

a. What is stored in the computer if a declaration allocates 10 memory locations (one character per location) for this message, and only the last characters are retained?
b. What is stored in the computer if a declaration allocates 12 memory locations (one character per location) for this message and only the first characters are retained?

e. Stringing Data Along

What kind of operation or calculations can be performed on characters and character strings? Unfortunately, character operations vary greatly from one computer to another. A survey of character operations which can be found in HLLs includes:

- Concatenate
- Locate characters
- Locate substrings
- Extract part of a string

Concatenate means to join together. This operation joins characters or character strings together. This could be useful when composing messages. The remaining operations (locating or extracting) depend on being able to compare letters. In order to do this each computer may have a *collating* sequence. This means, for example, that the letter "A" has a smaller "value" (or binary representation) than the letter "B." B in turn is smaller than C, etc.

Example 5-12 A Case of Character Manipulation

An HLL program keeps track of wiring lists for a commercial television receiver. The program keeps several forms of lists. One form might be a list of connections. An example of a typical entry might be

```
source Q1-8:destination Q3-10
```

The term "Q1-8" means "integrated circuit 1, pin 8." Another form of list includes an alphabetized listing of all signal wires. Each signal might have a name like VERTSYNC. For each signal, a number of facts could be gathered. These facts could include such things as source (the electrical circuit which generates the signal), electrical load (how many circuits it must drive), all connections to that signal, and perhaps locations on electrical schematics where this signal appears. How do you add a new signal

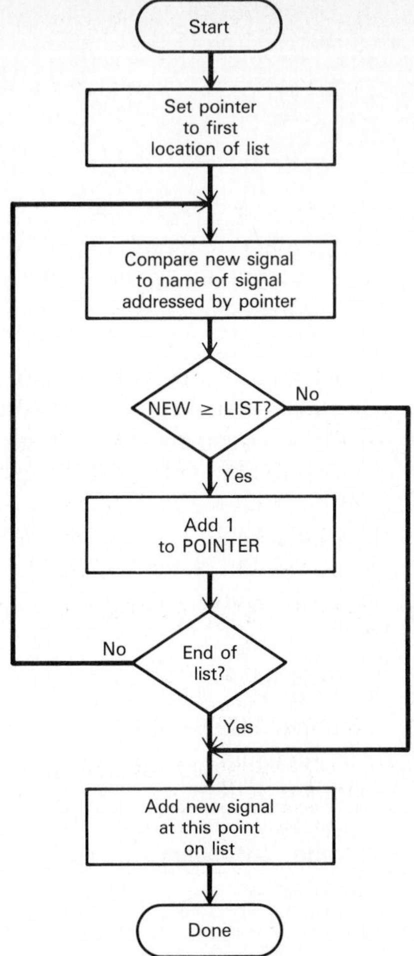

Fig. 5-5 Flow diagram for servicing an electrical wiring list.

to this alphabetized list? Figure 5-5 shows a flow diagram for doing this. This flow diagram depicts the sequence of steps which an HLL program would follow in order to carry out a new signal insertion. A POINTER data type is used to keep track of the position in the list. To add a new element, a decision block is used to compare the name of the new signal to the names on the existing list. Suppose that it is necessary to add the signal VERTBLANK to the list. Before adding the new signal, the list (partial) contains the following:

```
        •
ON-OFF SWITCH
        •
        •
        •
VERTSYNC
        •
```

The name or character string "VERTBLANK   "will be compared with each name on the list. At some point in the program it will be compared with the character string (signal name) "ON-OFF SWITCH". Imagine that the collating sequence for the computer is:

$$A < B < C < D \cdots < Z$$

Comparison begins. The letter "V" (of "VERTBLANK   ") is compared with the letter "O" (of "ON-OFF SWITCH"). In the collating sequence, V > O. Without going further the computer decides that "VERTBLANK   " is "greater" than "ON-OFF SWITCH". Following the flow diagram (Fig. 5-5), the computer passes to the next signal on the list. Some time later the pointer reaches the location containing the data for "VERTSYNC   ". "VERTBLANK   " is compared with "VERTSYNC   ". The first four letters are the same. For the fifth letter, a "B" is compared with an "S." From the collating sequence notice that B comes before (is less than) S. Therefore the computer decides that "VERTBLANK   " is "less than" "VERTSYNC   ". The new signal is inserted at this point in the list.

Problems for Section 5-3-1*e*

1. Examine the ASCII code in Appendix A.
   a. What are the equivalent decimal numbers for the letters A to Z? What is the collating sequence for these letters?
   b. What are the equivalent decimal numbers for the letters a to z? What is the collating sequence for these letters?
   c. What is the collating sequence for the coded form of the decimal digits 0 to 9?
2. The signal names in Example 5-12 are stored as a string of ASCII characters. Can you use arithmetic operations to carry out the comparisons required by the flow diagram of Fig. 5-5? Be sure to explain your answer.

5-3-2 Arrays

The data types that we have discussed to this point are called *simple variables*. For simple variables, one symbolic name represents one value, a single numeric quantity or single alphanumeric string. We will now discuss a method of using a single name to represent a group of data values rather than a single value. Such a group is called an *array.*

Example 5-13 Grouping Data

It is sometimes more convenient to group common data elements together. Suppose that a computer is to keep track of ocean conditions in order to improve navigation. To do so, it might need to store seawater temperatures. Figure 5-6 shows two lists in the computer memory. The first list (Fig. 5-6*a*) shows how the list would appear if it contained a floating-point number for each 24-h temperature record. If you choose to store the temperatures as 24 separate floating-point numbers, an additional list of 24 addresses is required in order to relate variable names with the actual location of the hourly temperatures.

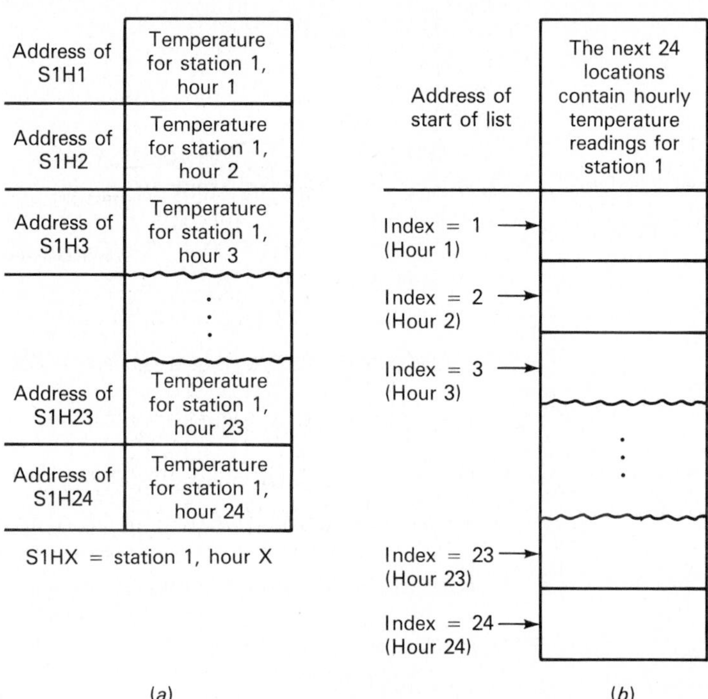

Fig. 5-6 Data records for a temperature monitoring station. (*a*) Using floating-point (or real) data. (*b*) Using an indexed method.

If the temperature list is arranged according to the format shown in Fig. 5-6*b*, the computer needs to store only (1) a single name and starting address of the list, and (2) the total number of items in the list. This last piece of information helps to avoid errors such as trying to find the temperature at hour 25, which obviously does not exist.

Using this indexed method of storing data saves a lot of memory space. The first case needs a second list of 24 addresses to know where each data item is to be found. The second case needs only two addresses to do the same job.

Notice that if the array were made larger, that is, if we now wanted to store 100 values instead of 24, additional space is required for the data only. Using individual simple variables, we would need space not only for the values, but for the list of 76 additional variable names and addresses as well. Consider the savings in space for arrays of 1000, 10,000, and 100,000 items!

The entire list is known by a single name. We might choose the name TEMPERATURES. The list, in this case, contains 24 items or members, each of which has a numeric value. To differentiate between the different members of the list, we specify an *index,* or *subscript*. This subscript tells the computer which member of the list TEMPERATURES we want to reference. Thus TEMPERATURES (1) refers to the first member in the list; TEMPERATURES (10) refers to the tenth member in the list, etc.

The portion of the array which contains the information about the array is called the *descriptor*. It contains the information which the HLL needs to locate each item in the array. The array's descriptor and data may be stored in separate parts of the computer's memory. Figure 5-7 shows such an arrangement.

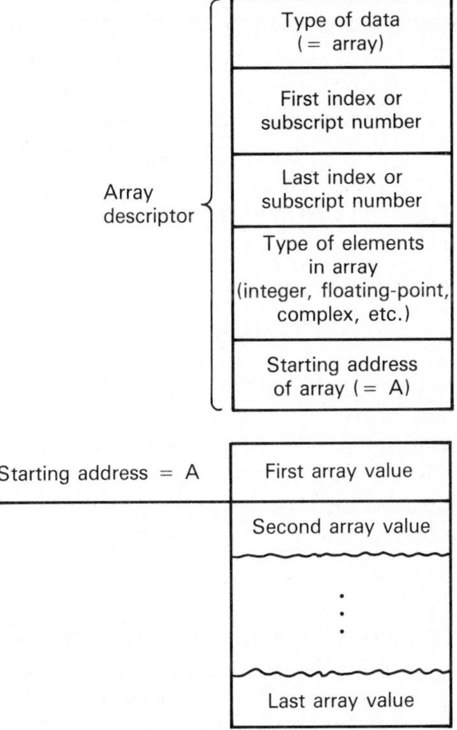

Fig. 5-7 Storing arrays in the computer memory.

This descriptor contains additional information about the way the array is structured. Some HLLs permit array subscripts to begin with numbers other than 1; any integer value may denote the beginning and end of the subscript range. This is useful if we want to store annual data in an array (we might have subscripts of 1986 to 1996), or number of students scoring within 10 points of the median score (we might have subscripts running from -10 to $+10$, including the member whose subscript is 0, for a total of 21 items). No matter what subscript range we select, the physical arrangement of the array is the same, and the HLL must make the transformation between the subscript range we select and the actual physical location (address) of the data within the computer's memory. Happily, this transformation is transparent to the computer user.

An array can store a group of numeric values, as in the example we have just discussed, or an array can be used to store a group of alphanumeric values. In either case, just as a simple variable can store either a numeric value or an alphanumeric value, all the values stored in an array must be of the same type. They may all be numeric or they may all be alphanumeric, but a single array may only contain values of one type of data. Most HLLs permit many arrays to be in use at the same time, so we might have some arrays containing numeric values and others containing alphanumeric values. The array's descriptor includes information about the type of data the array may contain (i.e., integer, floating-point, character, etc.).

Finally, the descriptor contains the location of the start of the actual data associated with the array. The computer assumes that as much memory as necessary to contain the array follows this starting location, and that the members are located in this contiguous block of memory in a sequential manner: The second member follows the first, the third member follows the second, etc.

Example 5-14 Higher-Dimensional Arrays

A wiring list, which can be used by an automatic wiring maching or by a technician, can be treated as a list with a wire *source* and a wire *destination*. Suppose someone writes an HLL program which includes this wiring list. The program might be for control of the machine, and the wiring list would be the data for the automatic wiring machine. If the list were written out, it might look as follows:

Wire Source: Chip Number, Pin Number	**Wire Destination: Chip Number, Pin Number**
01 01	0508
Chip Pin	
0102	1921
0103	0305
.	.
.	.
.	.

One way to arrange the data is to separate the list into two simple arrays of the kind already discussed. The computer could access one of the wires from the array of wire sources and a corresponding wire from the array of wire destinations. However, it is less confusing if there is a single list of wires made up as follows:

	Column 1: Source Numbers	Column 2: Destination Numbers
Row 1 = wire 1	0101	0508
Row 2 = wire 2	0102	1921
.	.	.
.	.	.
.	.	.
Row 100 = wire 100	6516	6016

In HLLs this table can also be considered an array. It is very similar to a simple array. Now, however, it has both rows and columns. It is called a *two-dimensional array* (for rows and columns). In a computer memory the array has a data descriptor and a table of values similar to the one shown in Fig. 5-8. The first entry in the data descriptor specifies a two-dimensional array—i.e., one having rows and columns—or a *matrix*.

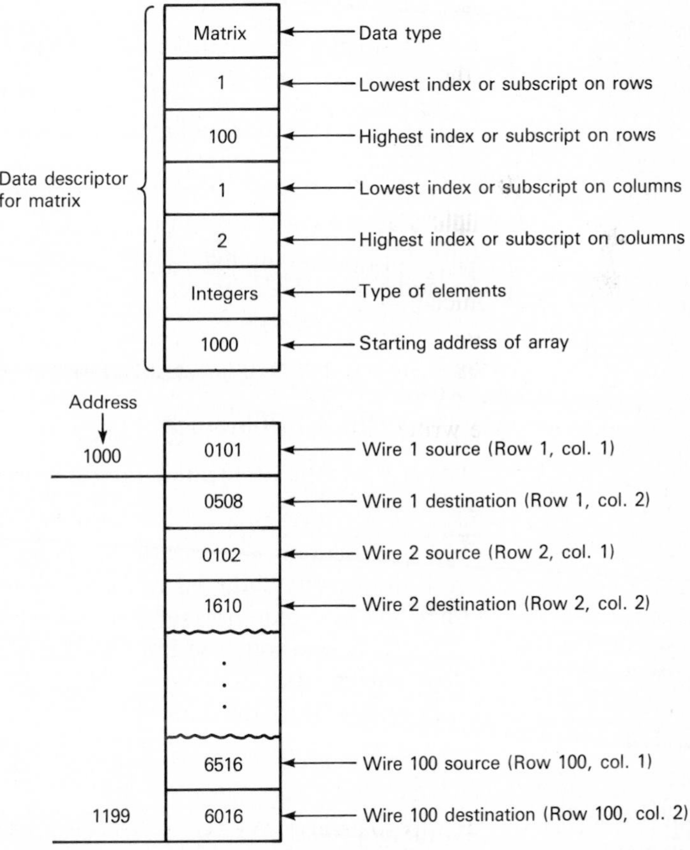

Fig. 5-8 A compound array for the wire list composed of a two-dimension array within the computer memory. The name "matrix" is sometimes used to describe such arrangements.

Within HLLs, arrays can be extended to matrices with more than two dimensions. The HLL may place limits on the number of dimensions.

Example 5-15 Higher-Order Arrays

Suppose that a certain computer is used to study the relationship between behavior and disease. This study is to be carried out over a period of time, say 10 years. For each year of the study there are records which look as follows:

	Smokes	Diet Type 1	Diet Type 2	Income Bracket 1	Etc.
Diabetes	X				
Heart disease					
Cancer					
Etc.					

Each entry in the table includes the number of people in the study who fit that category. For example, X would be the number of people who have diabetes and who smoke. One such table would be needed for each year of the study. We could use a three-dimensional array to store such information within the computer. Each dimension relates to one of the factors in the study. The three factors are type of disease, type of behavior, and time (year of the study).

PROBLEMS FOR SECTION 5-3-2

1. Devise a formula for locating the Ith item in an array. Use the following definitions:

   I = ith item in the array (to be found)
   A = the starting address of the array (from the data descriptor)
   LB = the first index or subscript number of the array (lower bound) (It is also found in the data descriptor.)
   E = the number of memory locations needed for each item in the array (from the data descriptor)

2. Suppose the array descriptor shown in Fig. 5-7 contains the following information:

   Array data type
   5
   15
   Floating point (E = 2)
   1000

Using the formula from Prob. 1, find the address of item number 10.

3. Using the format shown in Fig. 5-8 for a two-dimensional array, devise a formula for the address of an item whose index is (I, J), where I stands for the row and J stands for the column of the matrix.

4. Give two examples where a three-dimensional array structure would be used to store the data.

5-3-3 Records and Building New Data Types

Up to now, all the values within the arrays have been the same type. They might all be integers, or floating-point numbers, or other types of values—but all are the same type. Sometimes this can be awkward. Example 5-16 shows a case in which an array with mixed types of data is useful.

Example 5-16 The Need for Mixed-Data-Type Arrays

A manufacturer wants to keep track of a parts inventory. Such an inventory might appear in the form of a list as follows:

Part	Value	Tolerance	Stock Number	Count
Resistor	2200.	5	382546	1500
Resistor	2700.	5	382553	250
Capacitor	0.001	10	256820	1000
Etc.				

Notice that it would be convenient for the part (name) to be a character type, the value of the part to be a floating-point number, the tolerance to be an integer, the stock number to be a double-precision integer (because stock numbers are larger than single-precision numbers can support), and the count (number of parts of the given type) to be an integer value. In the present case this structure is referred to as a *record*.

It is possible to declare such structures in some HLLs. Within the computer's memory, the data in a structure looks similar to data in arrays with nonmixed data types. It has a data descriptor and locations for the data itself. Figure 5-9 shows what this array might look like for the inventory example.

There are many variations of arrays in HLLs. Those which have been mentioned are the most important. However, there is one more variation which can be very useful—one in which a user could make up new data types as needed.

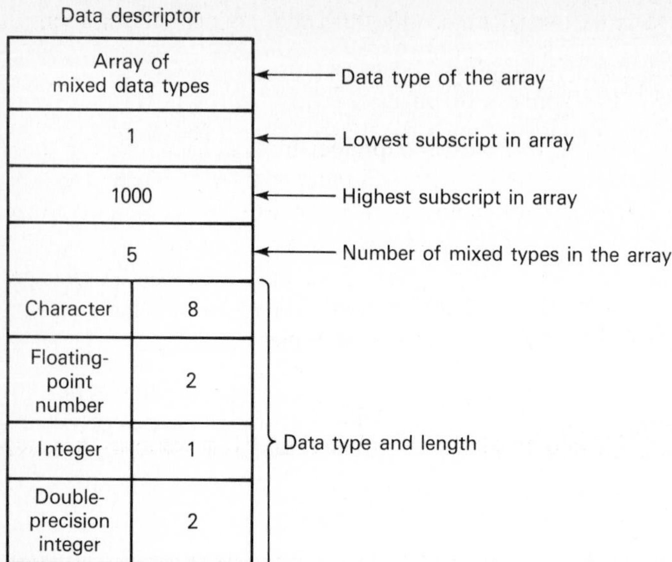

Fig. 5-9 An array of mixed data types—a record.

Example 5-17 Making Up New Data Types

An HLL program is required to automatically package (sort) resistors according to their values. Assuming that a machine can read the colors on the resistors, then it is possible to write such a program. The data which the program receives is the color on the resistor body. The colors might consist of brown, red, orange, yellow, green, blue, violet, white, and black. One way to think of this is to treat the colors as CHARACTER data types. Another method which is more convenient is to define a new data type which consists of all the colors just mentioned. For example, a DECLARATION statement which defines this new data type looks as follows:

```
type color = (black, brown, red, orange, yellow,
green, blue, violet, white);
```

Within the program, using the words "black," "brown," etc., will correctly identify the data type "color."

This method of declaring a new kind of data is called *enumeration*. This means that each member of the group is specified or explicitly enumerated. For example, you could define the alphabet by specifying all the letters, A to Z.

The ability to define new data types is of little value unless you can perform calculations using such data. HLLs which include the capability to define new data types also permit a programmer to use such data in calculations. Usually such calculations take the form of logical comparisons such as (written as an English-like statement):

Is the first resistor color brown?

PROBLEMS FOR SECTION 5-3-3

1. Using enumeration, devise a new data type consisting of the days of the week.
2. The collation sequence of an enumerated data type is embodied in the order in which the items are written. Explain how this could be useful for the color data defined in Example 5-17.
3. Name two examples (in addition to those described in Example 5-16) where a record structure is useful. For each case describe the format of the record.
4. Using a data descriptor similar to the one shown in Fig. 5-9, explain how the computer could locate an item and any of its parameters. Use a flow diagram for simplicity. Assume you are given an entry number (i.e., the fifteenth part on the list).

SUMMARY

Computers perform operations on numbers. HLL programs deal with these numbers in a systematic way. These numbers or data are treated in categories. Simple data types consist of numbers without decimal points. These are called integers. Putting a decimal point in the number causes it to be classified as a floating-point or real number. When programs use large numbers, the computer can be instructed (through the HLL) to set aside more memory locations for integers or floating-point numbers. Such instructions are given by specifying those numbers to be double-precision. For some applications it is useful to be able to work with complex numbers. If you only need to know if data is true or false, then declare such data to be boolean or logical. To be able to communicate with a user through messages it is best to use character data.

Grouping data which are related to each other is accomplished using an array. In order to deal with individual items in the array an index is used. When the data in the array contains mixed data types such as characters and integers, the array becomes a record. Some HLLs have ways to create new data types. This is done by defining or declaring the new type and then naming or enumerating all the data to be included in the new type.

REVIEW QUESTIONS

1. Define an integer.
2. Define a real number.
3. What is meant by a fixed-point number?
4. What is meant by a floating-point number?
5. What is meant by the allowed range of a number?
6. What is the general form of a floating-point number?
7. When is a floating-point number said to be normalized?
8. Can floating-point numbers always be normalized?
9. What is the exponent of a floating-point number?
10. What is the mantissa of a floating-point number?
11. What is meant by overflow?
12. What is meant by underflow?
13. Name eight different data types which can be found in modern HLLs.
14. Describe the logical OR operation and its results.
15. Describe the logical AND operation and its results.
16. Describe the logical NOT operation and its results.
17. What is significant about the POINTER data type?
18. What is meant by the term "collation sequence"?
19. What is an array?
20. What is a record data structure?
21. Can you mix arrays and records within a single data structure? Explain your answer.
22. Describe a way in which to define new data types.

The raw material of HLL programs, namely, the data, was discussed in Chap. 5. Some of the data types that one is likely to encounter were described. In this chapter study of the important elements of HLLs continues. We begin with a discussion of how to carry out calculations using the English-like statements of HLLs. The fundamental idea of an expression is introduced. This will be extended to assignment statements. Finally, the order or sequence in which operations are carried out is considered.

6-1 HLL EXPRESSIONS

In order to direct a computer to carry out calculations using English-like phrases, three important elements must be present:

- Which data is involved in the calculations
- The operations to be carried out
- The order in which the operations are to be carried out

An expression is a series of symbols which specifies operations to be performed on data and the order in which to carry out the operations. A very simple example of an expression is the English-like phrase A + B. This instructs the computer to add the numbers representing *A* and *B*.

6-1-1 Specifying Data Within Expressions

Recall that data within the computer is stored in memory. To add two numbers, you have to specify which numbers are to be added. This means that the memory locations containing these numbers must be identified. Because computers are likely to have millions of memory locations, this could become a tedious, error-prone, and time-consuming task for computer users. Fortunately, HLLs are designed so that the computer keeps track of this information. In the course of writing an HLL program you will direct the computer to set aside memory locations needed to store the necessary data. You do not have to specify which memory locations to set aside. Once the data type is specified (see Chap. 5), the computer automatically allocates the proper number of locations and makes a notation of their addresses. However, you still need to identify such data. To do so, a symbolic name is assigned to each data item to be used in the program. If an array is used, one name is assigned to all the array elements collectively and an index or subscript is used to pick out the data item of interest.

Expressions are written using the names of the data items involved in the calculations. When such a name appears within an expression, the computer automatically replaces that name with the data item taken from the memory location which corresponds to that name.

Such data is referred to as a *variable* since its use suggests that it is likely to change. Examples of such data abound throughout HLL programs. A brief list of examples includes the following:

- Names and telephone numbers in a telephone directory
- Parts (names, values, number of items) within a manufacturer's inventory
- Wire sources or destinations in a wire list (which sometimes undergoes engineering changes)

Sometimes, data within an HLL program does not change during the time that the program runs. Such data is called *constant* data. For example, you may need to compute the radian frequency of a sine wave. This is done by multiplying the frequency (in hertz) of the sine wave by 2π (pi). The value of π remains the same throughout such a program, as does the value of 2. They are both constants. If the constant is an integer, then the data is considered to be an integer constant. If the constant appears as a floating-point number, then it is considered to be a real constant.

Example 6-1 Data Within an Expression

An expression within an HLL has an English-like form which expresses a series of calculations to be performed on data stored within the computer. The following is a list of data which might be found within such expressions. Alongside each example is an important characteristic of that data. Notice that the data may appear as a *named* quantity.

SAMPL	A variable quantity.
3.14159	A real constant, perhaps the value for π in a certain calculation.
ANSWER1	A variable quantity. In some HLLs this would not be permitted because it contains too many alphanumeric

characters in the name. Each language has its own rules regarding assignment of names.

cursor$position	A variable. Some HLLs allow special symbols like "$" in variable names. If an HLL includes special symbols, and allows one to use as many characters as needed when naming variables, then the program will be easier to read and understand. It is not always necessary to use capital letters when specifying a name.
10	An integer constant.
ITEM(25)	A variable such as this usually refers to the twenty-fifth item in an array.

However, a variable such as "2ND" would not appear in an expression because it starts with a number. How could the computer distinguish numbers from variables if "2ND" were permitted?

PROBLEM FOR SECTION 6-1-1

1. Identify the following data types. Specify as many characteristics of the data as you can. Use Example 6-1 as a guide.

   2.75
   −3
   ARRAY (6, 1)
   MATRIX (I, J)
   2.1415
   hit
   miss

6-1-2 Operations Within Expressions

To perform an *operation,* two things must be present. The computer must be able to carry out the *rules* which govern the operation. It must also know on which *data* to perform the operation.

Consider an operation familiar to everyone: addition. If the rules of addition and the numbers to be added are known, then addition can be performed. The rules for addition may be in the form of tables, such as addition tables. These tables are built into the computer's hardware. Most modern computers have certain operational rules included within its hardware. These may include rules for addition, subtraction, multiplication, and division. The operations to be considered fall into three categories: (1) arithmetic, (2) relational, and (3) boolean, or logical.

a. Arithmetic Operations

Some arithmetic operations were considered in Chap. 5. All HLLs have certain simple arithmetic operations built into the language. A sampling of these includes addition, subtraction, multiplication, division, and exponentiation, or raising a number to a power. Some HLLs designed for scientific computing contain an extended set of arithmetic operations which further includes square root and trigonometric operations such as finding the tangent of an angle.

Example 6-2 Examples of HLL Arithmetic Operations and Their Symbols

Arithmetic Operations	SYMBOL IN VARIOUS LANGUAGES	
	BASIC†	Pascal‡
Addition	+	+
Subtraction	–	–
Multiplication	*	*
Division	/	/, DIV§
Raising a number to a power	↑	

† Microsoft BASIC (MBASIC).
‡ ANSI (American National Standards Institute) Pascal.
§ "/" is used for division of real numbers; DIV is used for division of integers, and the answer is truncated.

Example 6-3 Examples of Arithmetic Functions and Their Symbols

In addition to the important operations shown in Example 6-2, most HLLs include additional arithmetic operations. These are usually in the form of mathematical functions. Although these examples represent standard functions which can be found in such languages, a given language executing on a given computer may include other functions. The name dialect is applied to nonstandard forms of an HLL. The absence of a symbol implies that the function is not to be found in the HLL.

Other Arithmetic Operations (Functions)	SYMBOL IN VARIOUS LANGUAGES	
	BASIC	Pascal
Squaring a number	. . . .	SQR
Square root of a number	SQR	SQRT
Absolute value	ABS	ABS
Sine of an angle	SIN	SIN
Cosine of an angle	COS	COS
Tangent of an angle	TAN	. . .
Cotangent of an angle	COT	. . .
Arctangent of an angle	ATN	ARCTAN
Exponential (e^x)	EXP	EXP
Natural logarithm	LOG	LN
Produce a random number	RND	. . .
Find the sign of a number	SGN	. . .
Convert a real number to an integer (truncate)	. . . .	TRUNC
Convert a real number to an integer (largest integer which is less than or equal to the real)	INT	
Convert a real number to an integer by rounding off	. . . .	ROUND
Find remainder after dividing two numbers (real or integer)	MOD	. . .

b. Relational Operators

One kind of operation which a computer is well suited to perform is the comparison of two numbers. Within an expression, the programmer must specify the comparison to be made. Table 6-1 lists all the *relational* or *comparison* operations that are possible between two numbers.

TABLE 6-1 RELATIONAL OPERATIONS

Symbol	Definition of Operation
=	Are two quantities equal?
≠	Are two quantities unequal?
<	Is one quantity less than another?
>	Is one quantity greater than another?
⩽	Is one quantity less than or equal to another?
⩾	Is one quantity greater than or equal to another?

6-1-3 Writing Simple Expressions

An expression consists of a sequence of symbols which defines the calculations to be performed by the computer. The sequence must include:

- The data involved in the calculations
- The operations to be performed
- The order in which to perform the calculations

In HLLs, the way in which the words or symbols are put together to form expressions is called the *syntax*. Each dialect or language has its own syntax. The syntax includes the rules by which expressions or other phrases may be formed.

6-2 OPERATIONAL ORDER OR SEQUENCE

It is possible to write all expressions in HLLs using only two operands, but this is often not convenient because such programs will be difficult to read. If more than two operands are to be added, a single expression indicating such a calculation is desirable. To add the operands X, Y, and Z together, the expression $X + Y + Z$ represents a direct way to do so. The operands X and Y will be added to each other, and the result of this operation will be added to Z to obtain the final answer. The sequence of operations is from left to right, just as you would perform such a calculation, manually.

For many expressions, combining operators and operands in this straightforward manner is perfectly satisfactory. Unfortunately it does not work in all cases (see Example 6-4).

Example 6-4 A Confusing Expression

Suppose you are told that

$$A = 8$$
$$B = 5$$
$$C = 12$$

It is necessary to calculate the product of B and C and then to subtract this result from A. For the given numbers, $B \times C = 60$. When this is subtracted from A, the result is -52. Can you write an expression in an HLL to perform this calculation? One answer which comes to mind is A − B * C. If you substitute values for A, B, and C and carry out the calculations in the ordinary manner, you will get the correct answer. You evaluate the expression A − B * C by first performing the operation B * C. Call this partial result D. Next, you compute A − D. This sequence of operations is shown in Fig. 6-1. In this figure, the squares represent operands and the circles are operations carried out on the operands. Operands B and C are combined using the "*" operation. The result of this operation is then combined with the A operand using the "−" operator.

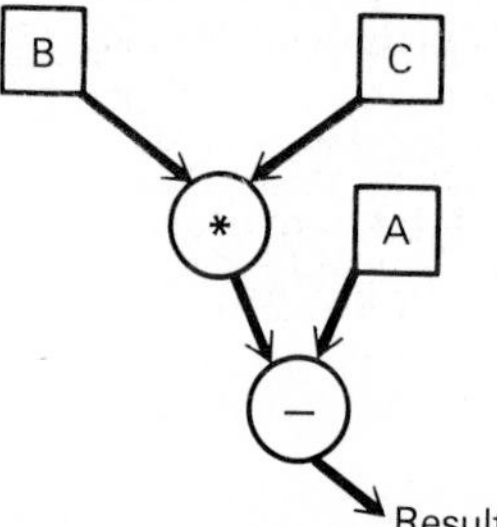

Fig. 6-1 Steps in calculating A - B * C.

Unless the HLL has rules specifying the order in which operations are carried out, the expression A − B * C may be evaluated incorrectly. Another interpretation of the expression might be:

Subtract B from A; then multiply the result by C.

This is not the intended sequence. For this reason, all operations within HLL expressions are carried out in a predetermined sequence. This sequence is called the *hierarchy of operations*. While many HLLs have the same hierarchy of operations, it is by no means universal.

Example 6-5 Hierarchy or Sequence of Operations

Table 6-2 shows the order in which operations are carried out in several representative HLLs. The operations are listed in order of priority. Priority 1 is the highest priority. These operations will be carried out first. In general, expressions are evaluated from left to right. That is, the expression is examined from left to right and any operations with priority 1 are

TABLE 6-2 OPERATIONAL HIERARCHY IN POPULAR HLLs

Priority	BASIC	Pascal
1 (Done first)	Expressions within parentheses and functions	
2	↑	unary minus
3	unary minus	not
4	*, /	*, /, DIV, MOD, AND
5	MOD	+, −, or
6	+, −	<, >, <=, >=, =, <>
7	=, <>, <, >, <=, >	
8	NOT	
9	AND	
10	OR	
11	XOR	
12	EQV	

completed. The expression is again examined from left to right, and any operations with priority 2 are executed. This process of examination and execution from left to right is repeated until there are no more calculations to be performed. Figure 6-2 is a flow diagram showing how the expressions

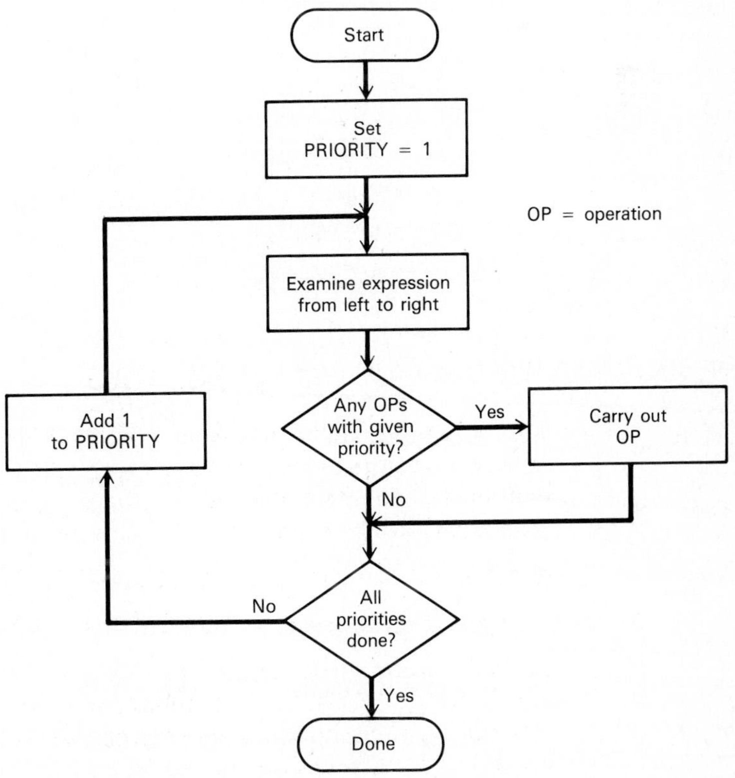

Fig. 6-2 Flow diagram for evaluating HLL expressions.

are evaluated. Some operations have the same priority. Such operations are performed as they are encountered in the expression. For example, if "*" and "/" operations are both present in a Pascal expression, each * and / operation is performed in order from left to right. You will notice an operation called "unary minus." This operation multiplies or negates a value. A simple example of this is "– A." This is an operation performed on only one data value (as is the "not" operation).

PROBLEMS FOR SECTION 6-2

1. Write expressions in the HLLs BASIC and Pascal for each of the following algebraic formulas.

a. $\dfrac{a - b}{c} + d$

b. $-a + b^c d$

c. $-a - b$

d. $\ln (a - b)$

e. $a^2 + b^2$

2. Write algebraic formulas for each of the following. In each case indicate if such expressions might appear in a BASIC or Pascal program.

a. A + B * C

b. ABS (–2 ↑ 3)

c. SUM/N

d. ARRAY (6) — (SUM/N) ↑ 2

3. Give the value of each of these Pascal expressions.

a. 5 * 4/2

b. –3 * (–5) + (–8)

6-3 READING AND WRITING COMPOUND EXPRESSIONS

If you combine all the information discussed to this point, you will be able to read and write expressions in a variety of HLLs. A number of examples will illustrate important facts. In particular, the sequence or hierarchy of operations will be emphasized. With a little practice you can read or write expressions in any HLL. Figure 6-2 should be used as a guide.

Example 6-6 Sample BASIC Expressions

Find the sequence of operations for the BASIC expression

(2 * X ↑ 3 + 3 * Y ↑ 3)/A/B

Figure 6-3 shows you how a computer executing a BASIC program would carry out this calculation.

The resultant algebraic expression which has been calculated is

$$\frac{2X^3 + 3Y^3}{AB}$$

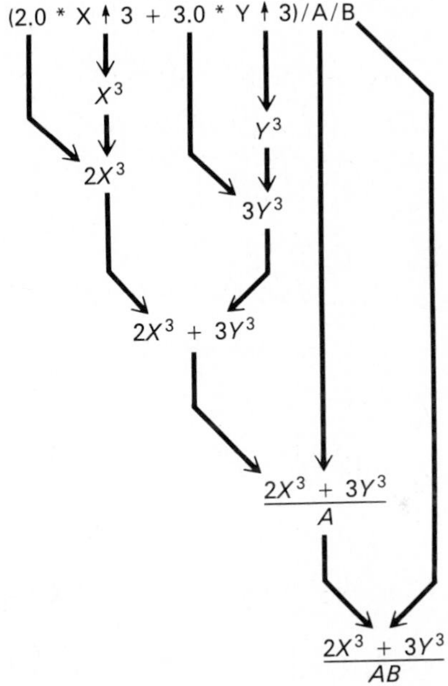

Fig. 6-3 The sequence of operations for evaluating (2.0 * X ↑ 3 + 3.0 * Y ↑ 3)/A/B.

Example 6-7 Pascal Expressions

The HLL Pascal has a slightly different hierarchy or sequence of operations from BASIC.

Draw a picture of the sequence of operations which would occur when a computer calculates the Pascal expression

1.0 − SQR(X)/2.0 + SQR(X) * SQR(X)/24.0

This formula computes an approximate value for the cosine of the angle X. Figure 6-4 shows the order in which the operations are performed.

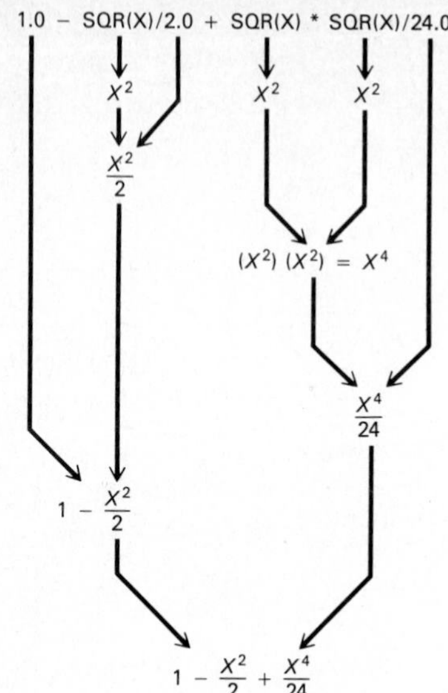

Fig. 6-4 Sequence of calculations for a Pascal expression.

PROBLEMS FOR SECTION 6-3

1. Write BASIC and Pascal expressions for each of the following formulas.

a. Area A of a regular polygon:

$$A = nr^2 \tan\left(\frac{180°}{n}\right)$$

where n = number of sides in the figure

r = distance from center of polygon to center of a side.

b. Radiated power P from an antenna in free space.

$$P = \frac{P_t}{4\pi R^2}$$

where R = distance from the antenna, meters

P_t = transmitted power, watts

c. Input resistance R (approximate) for a grounded-base transistor amplifier:

$$R = Re + Rb(1 - a)$$

where Re, Rb, and a are all characteristics of the transistor.

d. Capacitor discharge D:

$$D = I_o e^{-t/RC}$$

where I_o = initial current

t = time at which expression is evaluated starting from $t = 0$

R = resistance in the circuit

C = capacitance in the circuit

2. Write algebraic expressions for each of the following.

a. BASIC

p ↑ 2 + q ↑ 2

X ↑ Y ↑ Z

X ↑ (Y ↑ Z)

DEGREES * 3.141593/180

b. Pascal

SQRT (S * (S − A) * (S − B) * (S − C))

EXP(x) − EXP(−x)

(x − 1)/(x + 1)

2 * 3.14159 * SQRT (L/g)

3. The HLL Pascal does not have an exponentiation operation—raising a number to a power. Devise a way in which this can be done. That is, find a Pascal expression for

$$A^x$$

(Hint: $A^x = e^{x \ln A}$.)

6-4 THE ASSIGNMENT STATEMENT

All HLLs have an *assignment* statement. Sometimes such statements are called *replacement* statements. Figure 6-5 shows you how the assignment

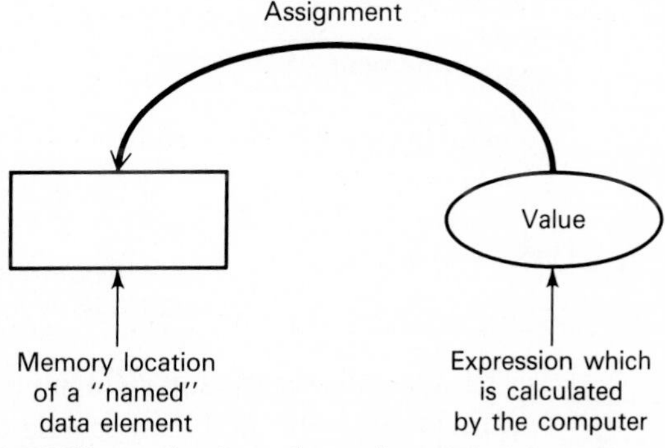

Fig. 6-5 Illustrating how the assignment statement works.

statement works. An expression, similar to those discussed above, is evaluated within the computer. The resultant value is *assigned* to a memory located which is specified in the statement itself. The value is stored into the memory element which has the name specified in the assignment statement. The new value *replaces* the old value. The old value is lost and cannot be recovered. In the course of a program, the computer often executes the same assignment statement many times. Each time that it does so, a new value is stored in the indicated memory location. Remember, memory locations are assigned symbolic names in HLLs. The general form of such assignment statements is:

$$\begin{bmatrix}\text{Named memory}\\ \text{location to}\\ \text{be replaced}\end{bmatrix} \quad \{\text{assignment operator}\} \quad \begin{bmatrix}\text{expression}\\ \text{evaluated}\\ \text{by the computer}\end{bmatrix}$$

The symbol representing the assignment operator varies from one HLL to another. Several use the = symbol. A list of the assignment symbols for several well-known languages is shown in Table 6-3.

TABLE 6-3 THE ASSIGNMENT SYMBOL OR OPERATOR FOR SEVERAL POPULAR HLLs

HLL	Assignment Statement Symbol
FORTRAN	=
BASIC	=
Pascal	: =
PL/1	=
LISP 1.5	SETQ
SNOBOL4	=
APL	← (“back arrow”)

Example 6-8 Basic Assignment Statements

Some typical assignment statements used in the language BASIC include the following.

Statement	Comment
C = A + B	
LET PI = 3.14159	Makes statement which follows easier to read; in effect, an approximation for π has been replaced by a word
TX = SIN(X)/COS(X)	Another way to create a calculation for the tangent of an angle.

The second assignment statement is a little different from the general form which has been shown to you. The word LET appears on the left-hand side of the statement along with the name of the variable, PI. The language BASIC varies from one computer to another. Some versions (dialects) require the word LET to appear in an assignment statement. Some dialects do not require the word LET. Usually the word LET is optional. The assignment statements PI = 3.14159 and LET PI = 3.14159 may both be correct. You must consult the programmer's manual for the BASIC dialect you are using in order to find out what is required in an assignment statement.

Example 6-9 Assignment Statements in Pascal

The standard version of the HLL Pascal permits you to use any number of letters when naming variables and functions. Not every Pascal dialect follows this rule, and you should check the language reference manual for your machine to be sure. Sometimes only the first eight characters are used by the machine even though your name may contain more. Names such as "resistor1" and "resistor2" would be considered the same. Each has nine characters, but the first eight are the same. Programs become easier to understand when names are close to their purpose. Sample Pascal assignment statements are:

```
noofenrolledstudents := noofenrolledstudents +
newstudents
onethird := 0.33333
toll := noofaxles * 0.50
timedelay := 2.2 * resistor * capacitor
transconductance := 2.0 * idss * (1 - vgs/vp)/vp
```

Notice the use of := as the assignment operator in Pascal.

PROBLEMS FOR SECTION 6-4

1. Write assignment statements in BASIC and Pascal for the following:
   a. The equivalent resistance for two resistors, R_1 and R_2, which are wired in parallel.
   b. Volume of a sphere:

$$V = \frac{4\pi r^3}{3}$$

   c. An equation which can be used to calculate voltages in a network containing a resistor and a capacitor while the capacitor is charging up:

$$v = E_f - (E_f - E_{\text{in}})e^{-t/T}$$

   where v = voltage at time t (variable)

E_f = final voltage to be reached (constant)

E_{in} = initial or starting voltage (constant)

t = time (variable)

T = time constant (= RC) (constant)

d. Reactance x of a parallel-tuned circuit:

$$x = \frac{2\pi fL}{1 - (2\pi f)^2 LC}$$

where f = frequency (variable)

L = inductance in the circuit (constant)

C = capacitance in the circuit (constant)

6-5 MIXING DATA TYPES IN ASSIGNMENT STATEMENTS

Recall that storage of data values within the computer depends on the data type. Integers and real values are stored differently. In assignment statements this sometimes leads to problems. This happens when the expression portion of the assignment statement (the right-hand side) is calculated with one data type and the variable (the left-hand side) has a different data type. For example, the expression might have an integer result and at the same time the variable requires a real quantity. Alternatively, the expression can be real and the variable might be an integer. As a general rule it is a good idea to keep the same data types on both sides of an assignment statement. Example 6-10 indicates how some popular HLLs treat such problems.

Example 6-10 Mixing Data Types in Assignment Statements

(a) BASIC includes numeric variables, string variables (characters), and subscripted variables. You may not directly assign string values to numeric variables or numeric values to string variables. If "*A$*" is a string variable, and *A* is a numeric variable, then

$$A\$ = A + 5$$

will very likely produce the error message "Type mismatch error." The program halts and the error must be corrected before execution can proceed. However, BASIC will automatically interconvert integer and floating-point values, and these may therefore be mixed.

(b) The HLL Pascal is called a *strongly typed* language. This means that each data item must have a type. These types must be defined before the program is executed. Pascal treats assignment statements with differing expressions and variable types in a manner which is different from methods used in other HLLs.

If the expression yields an integer result, it may be assigned to either an INTEGER variable or a REAL variable. As a simple example, if "timer" is specified as a REAL variable and "count" as an INTEGER quantity, then

Timer := count + 1

will be calculated as follows. The value of count (at the time this assignment statement is executed) is increased by 1. Since the number 1 is an integer and count is an INTEGER quantity, the result of the calculation will be an integer. An implicit conversion from an integer quantity to a real quantity is performed. The resultant real quantity replaces whatever is stored at the memory location reserved for timer, which is a REAL quantity.

This last discussion might lead one to believe that an assignment statement of the form

INTEGER variable := REAL expression

would produce an integer result.

This is not the case with Pascal. In many versions of Pascal, *assignment statements with REAL expressions and INTEGER variables are not permitted.*

Example 6-10 demonstrates that there are different ways to deal with assignment statements having different data types. This requires the user to remember special rules for each case. The best way to avoid having to remember such rules is to *use the same data types on both sides of an assignment statement*. In this way, you will avoid possible errors which can either halt your program or, worse, accidentally assign undesirable values to variables. While results may appear correct, subtle errors may have been introduced.

SUMMARY

Expressions form a fundamental part of HLL programs. These English-like phrases instruct the computer to make calculations. An expression includes: symbols that specify operations, the data on which to perform the calculations, and the order in which the operations are performed.

Operations performed in computers that execute HLL programs include:

Arithmetic: Addition, subtraction, multiplication, division, and sometimes exponentiation; trigonometric functions and square root operations are less universal

Relational: Comparisons between data in order to determine equality, nonequality, and relative magnitude or order

Boolean: AND, OR, and NOT.

Character: Concatenation, location of strings or substrings, extraction, and transformation of numbers into characters (ASCII), or the reverse

Simple expressions are formed with an operation (the operator) and two data items (or operands).

The order in which operations are performed is fixed by a hierarchy, precedence, or priority. Each HLL has its own hierarchy.

An assignment statement includes an English-like phrase containing a variable, followed by a symbol (e.g., an equals = sign), followed by an expression. The sign can be thought of as an assignment operator. The expression is calculated and the result stored in the memory location set aside for the named variable. The variable is said to be assigned a value. Any time this statement is executed, a new value replaces the existing value of the variable.

Different data types are sometimes possible on both sides of an assignment statement. To avoid accidental errors it is best to make sure both sides of an assignment statement have similar data types.

REVIEW QUESTIONS

1. Name three important elements required by an HLL in order to carry out calculations using English-like phrases.
2. Define the term "constant data."
3. Define the term "variable data."
4. What are real and integer constants?
5. What are real and integer variables?
6. What arithmetic operations are common to BASIC and Pascal?
7. Name two kinds of arithmetic division operations which are found in Pascal. Explain their different functions.
8. What arithmetic operation is found in BASIC but not in Pascal?
9. What seven common functions are found in BASIC and Pascal?
10. Why is the SQR function found in Pascal unnecessary in BASIC?
11. The function TAN is found in BASIC but not in Pascal. How can you create such a function in Pascal?
12. How can you create a function in BASIC and Pascal which returns the log (in the base 10) of a real variable?
13. For each of the following functions, state the HLL in which they may be found, and explain what operation is performed.

    RND SGN TRUNC ROUND MOD
14. What is meant by the term "relational operator"?
15. State six relational operators.

7 BUILDING HLL PROGRAMS

An HLL program may contain a great many statements. These fall into several categories:

- Information to the computer regarding the kinds of data to expect for each variable, i.e., data types
- The calculations to perform, in the form of assignment statements
- The order in which to perform the calculations
- The form and location of data which is used by the program and the form and destination of the results of the calculations, i.e., the input/output, or I/O

The types of data encountered by HLLs have been discussed in Chap. 5. Expressions and assignment statements were discussed in Chap. 6. In this chapter you will see how to control the order in which statements are carried out or executed. The statements which determine the sequence of calculations or program flow are called *control statements*. Input/output (I/O) statements will be discussed in the next chapter.

7-1 PROGRAM BUILDING BLOCKS

Following the sequence of steps carried out by a program is not always easy when simply reading the HLL statements. In part this can be due to the length of a program. Describing the sequence of instructions which a computer executes can be simplified by a picture of what is happening. These pictures can be drawn using flow diagrams (see Chap. 1).

Many HLL programs can be reduced to a simple set of basic components or control sequences. These components, or *modules,* once described, can be used to *build* a program. This is akin to constructing a building. If one puts enough bricks together in the proper sequence, it is possible to construct a building. This building relies on the bricks for structure, but the ultimate purpose of the building far exceeds the capabilities of individual bricks.

Only two kinds of components are needed to completely describe the sequence of instructions carried out by an HLL program. Alternatively, the same two components can be used to build a program. These components are:

- **Process block**
- **Decision block**

7-1-1 The Process Block

Unless otherwise instructed, HLL programs are thought of as executing one statement at a time in the exact order in which they are encountered. Figure 7-1 shows a series of simple assignment statements. The computer

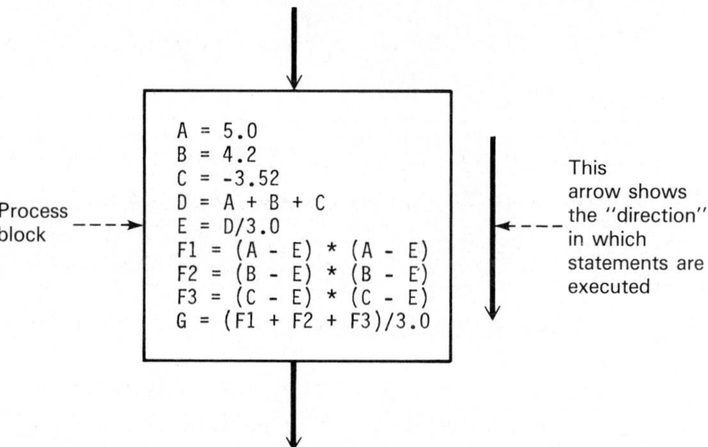
A = 5.0
B = 4.2
C = -3.52
D = A + B + C
E = D/3.0
F1 = (A - E) * (A - E)
F2 = (B - E) * (B - E)
F3 = (C - E) * (C - E)
G = (F1 + F2 + F3)/3.0
Process block
This arrow shows the "direction" in which statements are executed

Fig. 7-1 A simple sequence of assignment statements which are executed in strict order.

executes these one at a time. Except for the symbol used for the assignment statement ("="), these statements would be acceptable in a number of HLLs. These statements could be used to compute the *average* (*E*) of the numbers *A*, *B*, and *C*, and the *standard error* (*G*) of these numbers. While there are far better ways to write such a simple program, the statements shown here avoid operations which may not be found in some popular HLLs. That is why, for example, exponentiation is not used. (It would be better to write F1 = (A − E) ↑ 2, but the HLL Pascal does not permit the exponentiation operation.) The operations are enclosed in a box. Sometimes there is only one statement within the box; sometimes, many statements are enclosed. In either case, the sequence of instructions has a single starting or entry point and a single exit or ending point. Such an arrangement is called a *process block*.

Figure 7-2 shows the general form of a process block. The word "process" need not appear in the block. The rectangular shape of the box is enough to identify this as a process block. The single entry point, shown as an arrow entering the rectangle, indicates the point at which execution of this process starts. The single exit point, indicated by an arrow leaving the rectangle, indicates the last statement to be executed. Computation or statement execution continues at the point where the arrow at the exit terminates. This can be read and understood just as if it appears in a flow diagram.

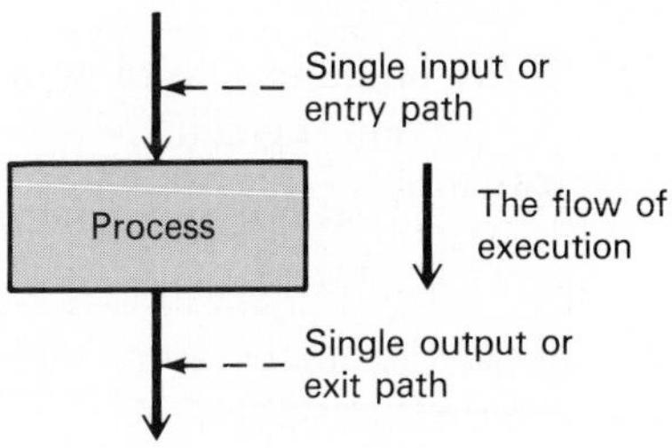

Fig. 7-2 A process block.

7-1-2 The Decision Block

The *decision block* is the second basic building block. This is what gives computers and HLLs their power and flexibility; it provides the ability to *change the path* taken by the program on the basis of the value of some data element or expression. For example, you already know that a computer can compare two numbers. A test for equality can be used to decide which of two program paths to follow as a result of the test. Figure 7-3 shows the decision block. Such a block has a single entry path. However, in contrast to the process block with its single exit, the decision block contains *two* possible exit paths. Each path is given a different name. One path is variously called the *true, yes,* or *then* path. The other path may have names like *false, no,* or *else*. You will find many languages with the path names built into the language itself. These names appear in the statements which are the HLL equivalents of the decision block.

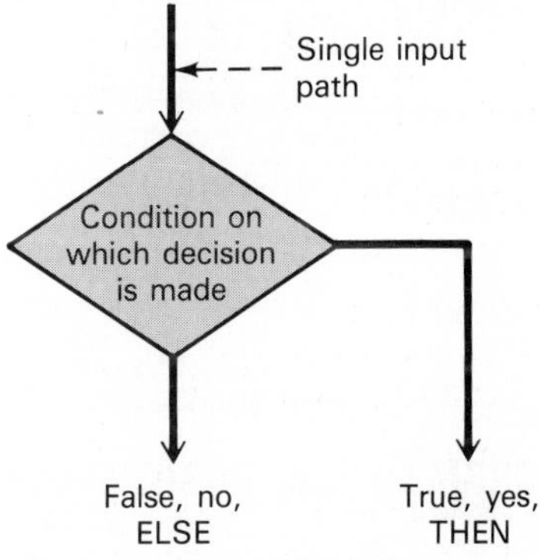

Fig. 7-3 A decision block.

PROBLEMS FOR SECTION 7-1

1. The following English-like statements describe programs to be executed by a computer. For each statement, indicate if it will be implemented by a process block or a decision block.

   a. A partial program for control of the automatic filling machines in a bottling plant:

   Read the status of the photocell used to detect liquid level in a container.
   If the liquid is sensed at or above the photocell, stop filling, and go on to the next operation.
   If the liquid is sensed below the photocell, go back to the start of this program segment.

   b. A partial program for automatic error checking in the control room of an energy generating plant:

   Read the temperature within the energy conversion vessel. Read the pressure within the energy conversion vessel.
   If the temperature is too high, sound the high-temperature alarm.
   If the temperature is too low, sound the low-temperature alarm.
   If the pressure is too high, sound the high-pressure alarm.
   If the pressure is too low, sound the low-pressure alarm.
   Otherwise, go back to the beginning of this segment.

2. You are required to design a computer program which automatically checks wiring connections for a product that your employer manufactures. The problem that you face is as follows:

   > There are *n* wires in the product. Each wire starts at some point which you may call the *source* and terminates at a second point which you may call the *destination*. Because there are so many wires, you cannot visually inspect the connections between sources and destinations. Moreover, visual inspections are not sufficient for ensuring electrical continuity (connection). You have a meter which can be used to measure continuity between two points; the meter has two inputs. For convenience, you may call the inputs source and destination. In order to check the wiring, you must verify (a) that no wire is missing and that all wires are connected correctly, and (b) that extra wires have not been added where they do not belong.

   Outline the program to be followed using English-like statements similar to those in Prob. 1. To make your program simpler to write and follow, use words like IF, WHILE, REPEAT, THEN, OTHERWISE, and GOTO to help you.

7-2 BUILDING PROGRAMS FROM BASIC BLOCKS

Using the fundamental building blocks just described, it is possible to develop complete programs. Starting with the process and decision blocks, a series of *fundamental program structures* can be made. These, in turn, can be used to make complete programs. These steps are shown in Fig. 7-4. Process blocks and decision blocks can be combined into a series of

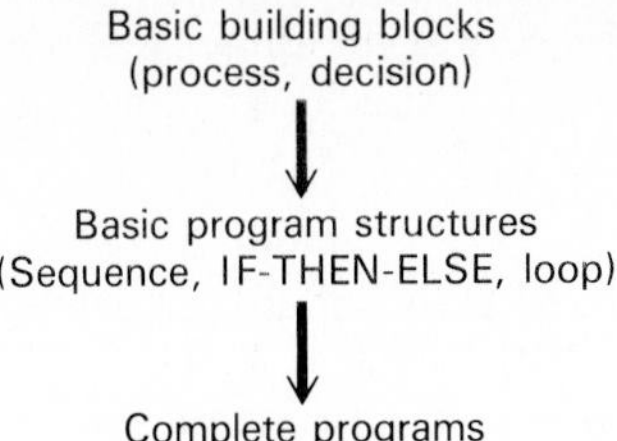

Fig. 7-4 How to build a program from basic building blocks and program structures.

larger standard components called *program structures*. The names of these principal program structures are *sequence structure, IF-THEN-ELSE* structure, and *loop* structure (of which there are two types). These statements allow you to control the order in which assignment statements are executed.

These program building blocks often have corresponding statements within HLLs. They are written equivalents of the flow diagrams which describe their operation. Pictorial equivalents of the control structures are described in the following sections.

7-2-1 Sequence Control Statements

The simplest sequence of statement execution is obtained when two or more process blocks are executed in an ordered or serial manner. The flow diagram for such a sequence is shown in Fig. 7-5. This program control

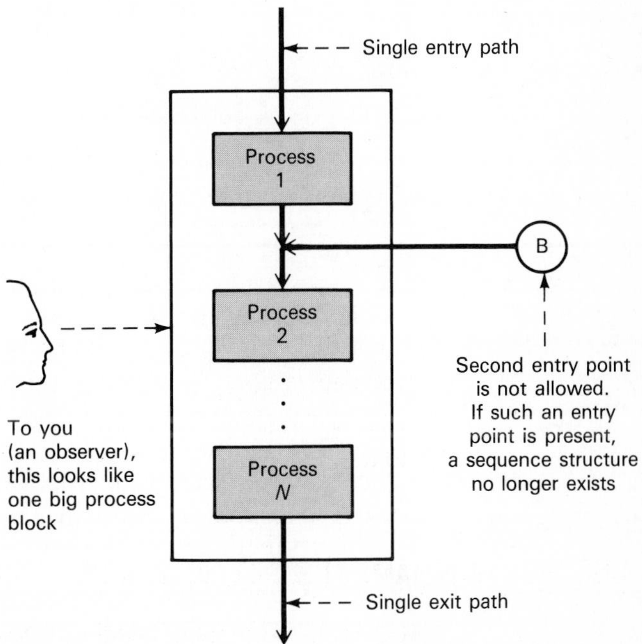

Fig. 7-5 Flow diagram of a sequence structure.

sequence has a single entry point. This is the first statement of process 1. It has a single exit point. The exit point is the last statement of process N. If there are two entry points, such as the case where it is possible to enter process 2 from either process 1 or control path B from somewhere else in the program, the picture is no longer a sequence structure. Multiple entry or exit points are not permitted. If a large box is placed around all the processes, it looks like one big process block.

If sequence structures look like a single process block, why create such a control structure in the first place? In contrast to a complete program made up of a single process block, it is often better to break up such a program into a series of separate process blocks. Reasons for this include:

- Efficiency of program writing. Different people can be put in charge of separate processes.
- Ease of program testing. Each process block can be tried separately. To do so, results from another process which may be needed can be "faked" until the process in question is completely tested. Program testing for the purpose of eliminating errors is called *debugging*.
- Ease of program modification. There are times when programs have to be modified. For example, a new piece of equipment such as a new printer might require portions of a program to be changed. This is easier to do when everything related to such equipment is found in one process block.
- Modularity. If programs are composed of separate process blocks, it is often possible to use one process block in more than one program.

Example 7-1 A Sequence Structure

A certain program helps you to design circuits which can be used as timers. Such timers require a resistor and a capacitor to work properly. The combination of the resistor and the capacitor sets the duration of the timing period. Without showing you any assignment statements which may be needed, Fig. 7-6 shows how such a program might be composed of a simple sequence structure.

Breaking up this component selection program into three process blocks which control input (timing interval), component calculation, and output (return resistor and capacitor values) makes such a program easier to understand and easier to write. While the component calculation process block does not contain detailed program statements, it should take into account such things as restricting resistors and capacitors to standard values, limits (both large and small) on the component values, and tolerance of the parts to be used.

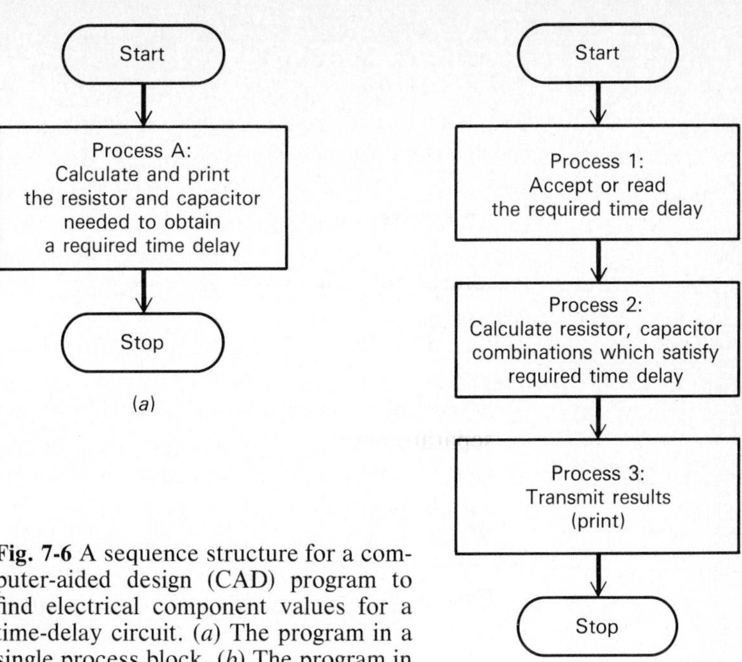

Fig. 7-6 A sequence structure for a computer-aided design (CAD) program to find electrical component values for a time-delay circuit. (*a*) The program in a single process block. (*b*) The program in modular form.

7-2-2 IF-THEN-ELSE Structure

Combining a single decision block with two process blocks creates a control structure in which a program path can be altered. The resultant structure is called the IF-THEN-ELSE structure. It is a second fundamental program structure. The IF-THEN-ELSE control structure is shown in Fig. 7-7.

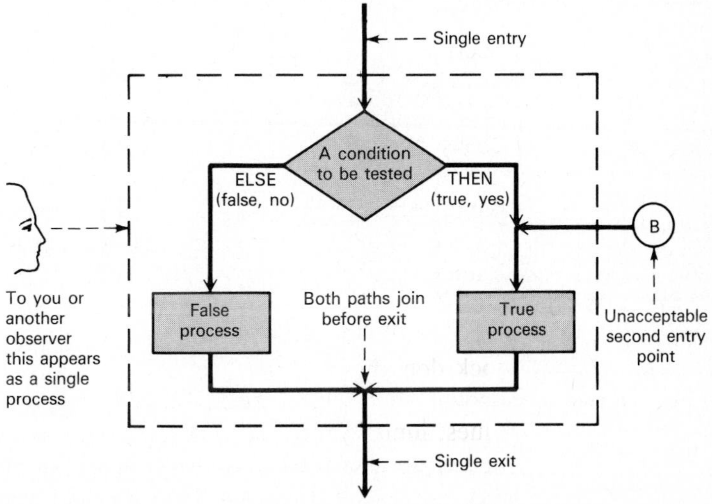

Fig. 7-7 Flow diagram of the IF-THEN-ELSE basic program control structure.

The IF-THEN-ELSE program sequence has a single entry point and a single exit point. This feature makes it appear like a process block if you enclose the entire structure in one box. A second entry point such as point B (in Fig. 7-7) violates the rules for this structure.

The IF-THEN-ELSE structure includes some condition which is tested. If the condition is satisfied, then a "true process" block is executed. If the condition is not satisfied (or is false), then a "false process" block is executed. When the true process or the false process is completed, the control paths are joined before the IF-THEN-ELSE control structure is completed.

The condition to be tested appears in the form of an expression. The expression can have only one of two outcomes, *true* or *false*. The only kind of expressions which can have such outcomes are *logical* or *boolean* expressions. Therefore, the condition to be tested will appear as a boolean expression (see Chap. 6 for a complete description and examples of boolean expressions).

Sometimes the true process or the false process may not require any action. In such cases one of these process blocks may not be present. At least one such true or false process must be present. If not, the IF-THEN-ELSE structure makes no sense. Figure 7-8 shows a modified IF-THEN-ELSE control sequence in which either the true process or the false process is not required.

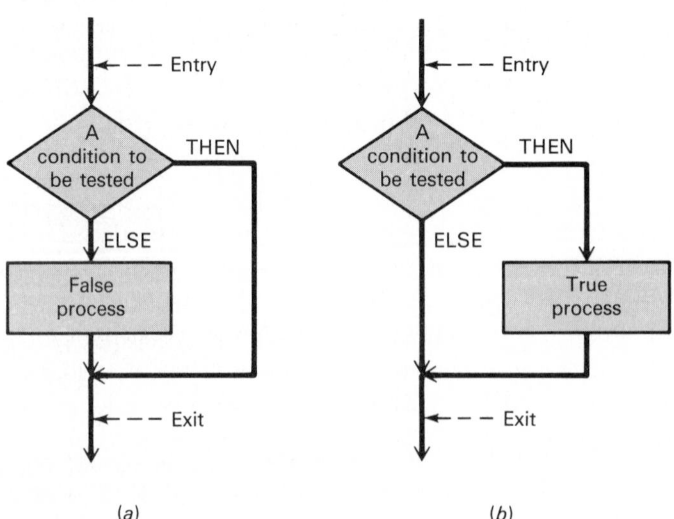

Fig. 7-8 Some special cases of the IF-THEN-ELSE program control sequence. (*a*) The true process block is absent in this case. If the condition is satisfied, then nothing needs to be done. (*b*) Here, the false process block is not needed. If the condition is not satisfied, control passes to the exit point.

Example 7-2 IF-THEN-ELSE Statement in HLLs

A typical IF-THEN-ELSE statement in an HLL has the following form:

```
IF   {condition on which decision is made}
THEN {specifies what to do when condition is true}
ELSE {specifies what to do when condition is false}
```

The words IF, THEN, and ELSE are used by the HLL to indicate that this statement is to be associated with an IF-THEN-ELSE structure. In HLLs such words are called *reserved* words. You cannot use such words as names of variables or for any other purpose. You will encounter more reserved words as you study a particular HLL.

Example 7-3 Examples of IF-THEN-ELSE Statements from Pascal and BASIC

(a) A typical Pascal statement might be:

```
IF fowarddrop > 0.5
THEN diodecurrent := fowarddrop/fowardresistance
```

(b) A BASIC statement (without ELSE) might be:

```
IF V > HI OR V < LO THEN PRINT "SUPPLY MALFUNCTION"
```

(Not every BASIC dialect recognizes the IF-THEN-ELSE structure.)

PROBLEMS FOR SECTION 7-2-2

1. a. Figure 7-9 illustrates two tanks for storing chemicals. Variables are defined as follows:

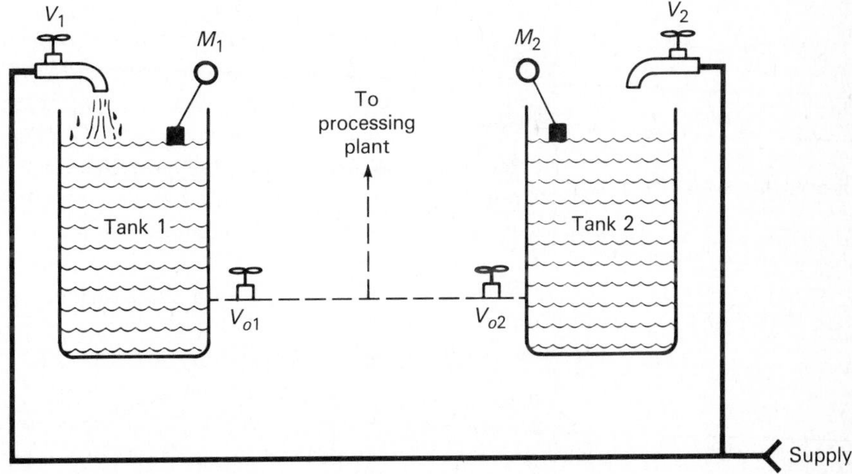

Fig. 7-9 Problem 1.

V_1 = valve to fill tank 1.
V_2 = valve to fill tank 2.
M_1 = Meter for tank 1. When tank 1 is filled to the top, M_1 indicates full, and when there is no liquid in tank 1, M_1 indicates empty.
M_2 = Meter for tank 2. When tank 2 is filled to the top, M_2 indicates full, and when there is no liquid in tank 2, M_2 indicates empty.

To start, assume that both tanks are empty. Write out the series of tasks necessary to fill both tanks and to refill a tank should it become empty.

b. Translate the tasks specified in part (a) into a series of English-like statements using IF-THEN-ELSE constructions to control valve operations.
c. Draw a flow diagram for the algorithm developed in part (b).

2. a. Two additional valves, Vo_1 and Vo_2, are added to the system. These control the supply of chemicals to the processing plant. Write out the tasks needed to ensure a smooth supply of chemicals to the plant. Wait until both tanks are filled initially. Assume that a tank can be filled before the other is drained off. If both tanks become empty, sound an alarm.
b. Translate the tasks outlined in part (a) into a series of processes and IF-THEN-ELSE control sequences.

7-2-3 Loop Structures

The IF-THEN-ELSE program structure allows you to skip over instructions. Either the true process or the false process is executed but never both. The next set of program control structures combines a single decision block and one or more process blocks. This combination allows you to *repeat* a number of statements as many times as needed. The statements which are to be repeated are found in the process blocks. The number of times these statements are to be executed is determined by the decision block. The flow diagram which results from these structures has the shape of a loop, and the name *loop structure* (or simply *loop*) is used to describe them. There are two structures like this. One is called a *DO-UNTIL* structure. The second is called a *DO-WHILE* structure. HLLs sometimes have these names built right into the language itself just like the IF-THEN-ELSE structure. If not, the action can be simulated using other statements.

a. The DO-UNTIL Loop Structure

Figure 7-10 shows a flow diagram for the DO-UNTIL structure. Like other program structures, it has a single entry and a single exit. For this reason it can be made to appear like one big process block to an observer.

Upon entry, the statements of the process block are executed. In this structure the process block is executed at least once. Next, a condition is checked to see if the process block should be repeated. If the condition has been satisfied, the result of the boolean condition will be true. Under

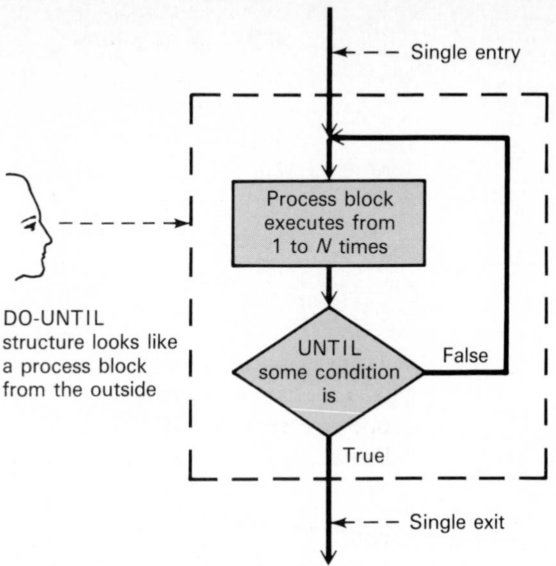

Fig. 7-10 Flow diagram for a DO-UNTIL loop structure.

these circumstances, control passes out of the structure. If the logical condition is not satisfied, control passes back to the process block. The statements of this block are executed once again.

Execution of the process block followed by checking of the condition is repeated until the logical condition becomes true. The loop is then complete and program control passes out of the DO-UNTIL structure via the exit path. The next statement or program structure element becomes the instruction to be executed.

Example 7-4 Sample DO-UNTIL Program Structures in HLLs

a. The DO-UNTIL structure in the HLL Pascal has the following form:

```
REPEAT
{statement of process block}
UNTIL {condition}
```

b. In BASIC you can use the IF statement to mimic the DO-UNTIL loop shown in Fig. 7-10. A part of a BASIC program which illustrates this follows.

```
n1      {First statement in loop structure}
n2       .
         .  {Other statements in loop structure}
         .
```

```
nk      {Last statement in loop structure}
nk + 1  IF {condition} THEN nk + 3
nk + 2  GOTO n1
nk + 3  {First statement of next program structure}
```

Here are some rules which you need to understand to see how this loop works.

- In BASIC, statements usually require a number (label) for identification. These numbers are designated n1, . . ., nk + 3. They might be numbers like 10, 20, . . ., 100. BASIC sorts these numbers and their associated statements in ascending order. They will be executed in this order unless instructed to do otherwise.
- The "IF {condition} THEN nk + 3" statement works as follows. When the condition within the braces is true, the statement number after the keyword THEN is executed. For a false result, the statement following the IF is executed.
- Understanding what the statement GOTO n1 does is not difficult. If this statement is executed, control next passes to statement number nl.

b. The DO-WHILE Program Structure

If you interchange the positions of the process block and the decision block in Fig. 7-10, you get a program structure called a DO-WHILE arrangement. This is shown in Fig. 7-11.

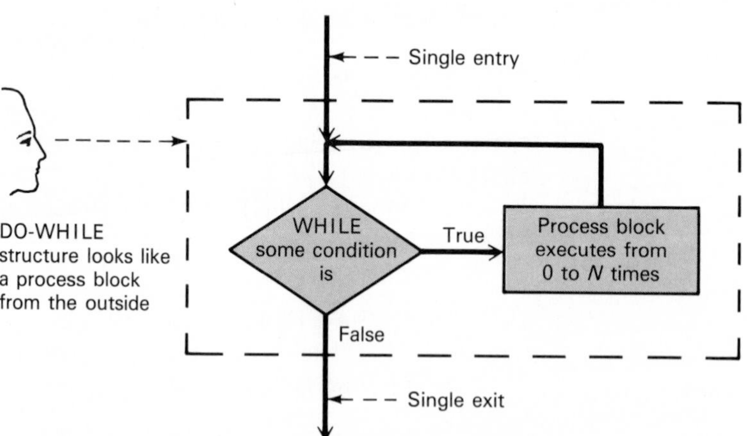

Fig. 7-11 Flow diagram of the HLL program control sequence for a DO-WHILE structure.

A significant change has occurred:

> The logical condition within the decision block is tested *before* the statements of the process block are executed.

If the logical condition is false, the process block statements are not executed. The process block statements will be executed if the logical condition is true. These statements can have any number of repetitions from none to some number N.

If the condition within the decision block never becomes false, the process block statements will be executed *forever.* This is sometimes a desirable goal. If a program is designed to control a power station, it is important to run the program as long as the computer is turned on and the program started.

Example 7-5 Sample DO-WHILE Program Structures in HLLs

(a) The HLL Pascal is one of the languages which has the DO-WHILE structure included directly in its syntax and vocabulary. A DO-WHILE program structure in Pascal takes the following form:

```
WHILE    {condition}    DO
   BEGIN
      {statements of process block}
   END
```

Some things to note:

- The positions of the keywords WHILE and DO are reversed compared with their positions in the title of the structure (DO-WHILE).
- In order to identify all the statements which belong to the process block, the keywords BEGIN and END are used. The keyword BEGIN marks the start of the process block. It appears before the first process block statement. The word END follows the last statement. One exception to this rule occurs when the process block contains a single statement. When that happens, BEGIN and END are not necessary. To avoid having to remember many special cases, it may be easier to include BEGIN and END all the time.

(b) A DO-WHILE program written in the HLL BASIC would look like this:

```
n1       IF {condition} THEN n3<--loop entry (decision process)
n2       GOTO nK + 2
n3      {Process block starts here.}
         . . .
nK      {Process block ends here.}
nK + 1   GOTO n1<--loop repeat
nK + 2  {First statement of next program structure.}
         (Loop exit).
```

The BASIC keywords IF, THEN, and GOTO must be written just as you see them. The symbols n1, n2, etc., are all integers. They identify statements in a BASIC program.

PROBLEMS FOR SECTION 7-2-3

1. The IF-THEN-ELSE structure was used to skip over instructions, and the DO-UNTIL and DO-WHILE structures describe ways to repeat instructions. It is also possible to use the IF-THEN-ELSE structure to repeat instructions. Draw a flow diagram which uses the IF-THEN-ELSE structure to repeat a group of instructions. Show the group of instructions to be repeated as a single process block. In the flow diagram show the process block being executed at least one time.

2. A data array contains the daily low temperatures outside your employer's factory for the past year (365 data points). You must write a program which will find all the temperatures below 0° Celsius (0°C). Your program must print all days on which the temperature was below this limit and must also print the total number of such days. Draw a flow diagram in the form of a loop which will solve this problem. Use English phrases or expressions to describe the operations needed at each step of the solution.

3. Given the following program, which uses English-like expressions to describe the operations, analyze the program by breaking it into a series of control structures. *Hint:* Use a flow diagram to analyze the program.

```
        turn on motor drive.
REPEAT  read actual position of motor shaft.
        calculate error between actual position and
          desired position.
UNTIL   [error < 0.1%]
        turn off motor drive.
```

   This symbolic program could be used to control the mechanical motion of an industrial robot.

7-2-4 Other HLL Control Structures

All computer programs can be built using IF-THEN-ELSE, DO-UNTIL, and DO-WHILE structures. Several additional control structures are found in HLLs. Such structures include *indexed DO loops* and *n-way branches*. These will be described in this section.

a. Indexed DO Loops

In the DO-UNTIL and DO-WHILE structures of Sec. 7-2-3, the loop repeats until or while a given condition exists. In both structures a decision block is needed to decide when to exit the loop.

Within HLLs another possibility exists for program loops. If we know how many times the loop is to repeat, we can let the computer keep track of the number of times that the loop has been repeated. The counter which keeps track of the repetitions is called an *index*. A flow diagram of such a loop is shown in Fig. 7-12. Such loops may be called *DO loops*. The diagram looks very much like a DO-UNTIL structure. Indexed loops are similar to DO-UNTIL structures. There are two differences:

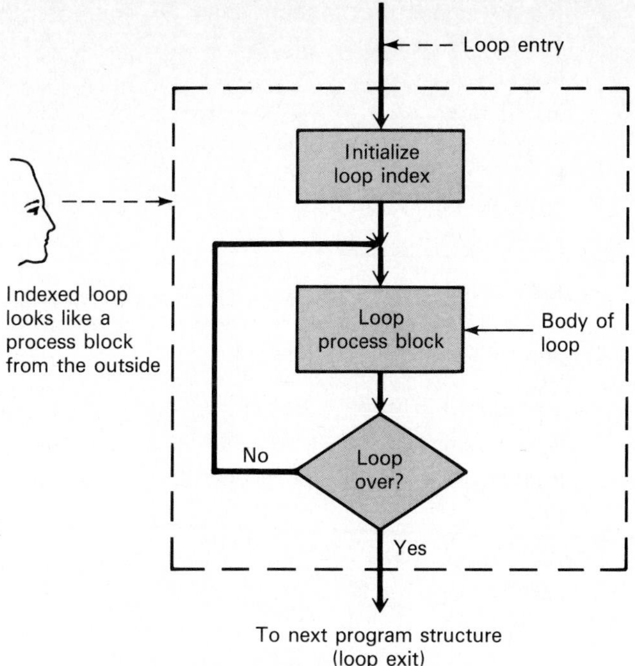

Fig. 7-12 Flow diagram of the HLL control sequence for an indexed loop structure sometimes called a DO loop.

- For indexed loops the programmer must indicate how many times the loop is to be repeated.
- The computer manages the incrementing of the index variable and calculates when the indexed or DO loop terminates. The decision block shown in Fig. 7-12 is carried out by the computer. No IF statements are required.

The programmer is required to provide initial or starting values for the loop index. To describe the loop index, *three pieces of information* are needed:

1. The value at which the index is to begin.
2. The index value at which the loop should terminate.
3. How much to change the index or loop counter each time the loop process block is executed.

Statements within the loop process block make up the *body* of the loop. The start and end of the body must either be marked or known.

The index or counter may be used in expressions within the body of the loop. This is particularly valuable. Although some HLLs permit it, it is not a good idea to allow the index variable's value to change as a result of appearing on the left side of an assignment statement within the body of the loop. If I is an index, an assignment statement such as

I = I + 1

should not appear in the loop, since the statement changes the value of *I*. Statements such as

J = 2 * I

or LIST(I) = LIST(I) + 1

are permissible, since the value of I is not changed.

Example 7-6 DO Loops in HLLs

While all HLLs require the information just described, each HLL has a somewhat different set of rules for specifying this data.

(a) Examples from BASIC

Sample 1

```
 10 FOR I = 1 TO 10 STEP .5
  .
  .
  .
100 NEXT I
```

Sample 2

```
 20 FOR J = .1 TO 10.1
  .
  .
  .
999 NEXT J
```

Sample 3

```
20 FOR K = 20 TO 1 STEP 2
 .
 .
 .
99 NEXT K
```

(b) Examples from Pascal

Sample 1

```
FOR numbers := 1 to finalvalue DO
BEGIN
.
.
.
END
```

Sample 2

```
FOR index := 100 DOWNTO 1 DO
BEGIN
.
.
.
END
```

Exiting the DO loop via the single path shown in Fig. 7-12 is called a *normal exit*. That is, if the number of repetitions of the loop is completely determined by the index, its initial value, its final value, and increments, the loop is said to operate in a normal way.

It is possible that within the loop process block there will be a decision block. This decision block could cause the loop to terminate before the index has reached it final value. Loop termination of this kind is called a *nonnormal exit*. Figure 7-13 shows the flow diagram for loops with multiple exits. This structure can no longer be viewed as a process block from the outside. While there is a single entry point, there are two possible exits.

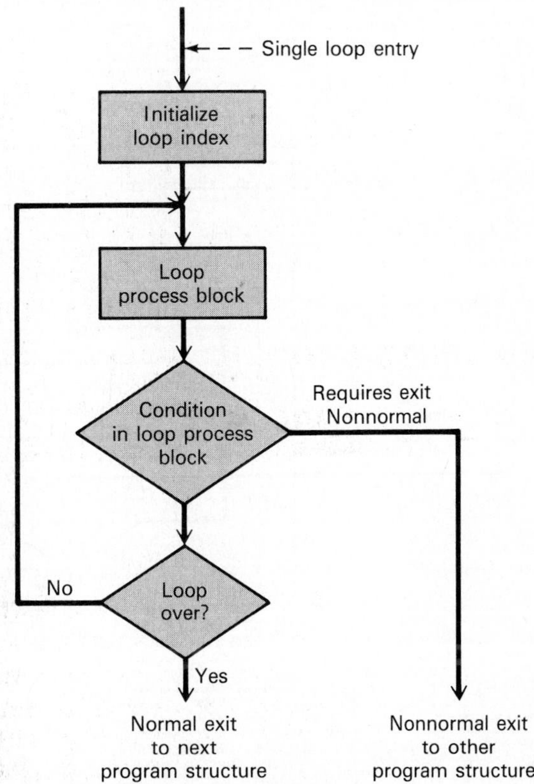

Fig. 7-13 Flow diagram for indexed loops with more than one exit point. If the index takes all its values during a loop repetition, the exit is said to be normal. Premature exit from the loop is called a nonnormal exit.

If there is more than one decision block within the loop, it is possible to have several nonnormal exit paths. Such nonnormal exits are often included in order to take care of *exceptions*. These exits will be included to provide action when data or partial results are tested and found to be in error. An *error message* or warning message may be sent to the user in such circumstances. While loops with nonnormal exits are sometimes found in HLL programs, in general, they are to be avoided. Programs with such structures are usually more difficult to follow, debug, and understand than programs whose DO loops contain only normal exits.

The process block within the DO loop shown in Fig. 7-12 may contain a DO loop. Arrangements and programs which contain DO loops within DO loops are called *nested DO loops*. A flow diagram showing how nested DO loops work is shown in Fig. 7-14.

There is a single entry point. The loop index is defined. As there are two loops, the first loop is called the *outer loop*. The process block of the outer loop contains another DO loop. This is called the *inner loop*. The index of the inner loop specifies its starting, final, and incremental values. The process block of the inner loop is executed. This process block is

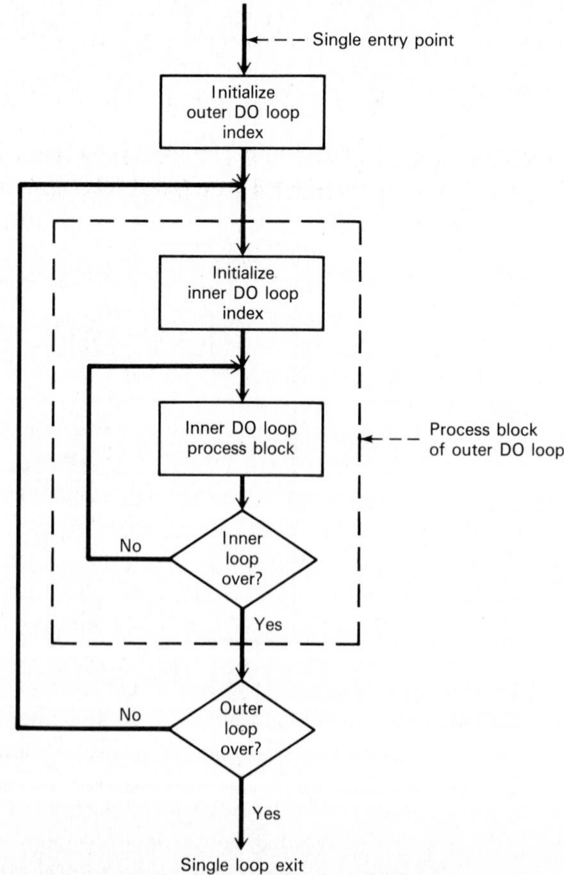

Fig. 7-14 HLL control sequence which contains nested DO loops.

repeated as many times as necessary to satisfy the inner loop index. The inner DO loop is completed first. When that is done, the outer loop index is checked to see if it should be repeated. If it requires repetition, then its process block is executed once again. Since its process block contains the inner DO loop, the entire inner loop is repeated from the beginning. The index of the inner loop is set to its initial value and the inner process block executed as required.

The inner DO loop process block may itself contain a DO loop. This introduces another *level of nesting*. Execution of such nesting is carried out in a way similar to that shown in Fig. 7-14. The innermost loop is completely executed first. The loop which contains this innermost loop is completed next. Finally, the outer loop is completed. Most HLLs have limits on the number of nesting levels which are permitted.

PROBLEMS FOR SECTION 7-2-4*a*

1. Indicate two cases where it is convenient to decrement the loop index after each iteration.

2. Consider the following problem in Pascal. You want the effective index value to increment by 2 at each iteration. However, the rules for this HLL only allow the index to be incremented by +1 (or decremented by −1). How can you create an effective index which increments by 2 without interfering with the value of the nominal index?

3. This problem will demonstrate how a simple structure can lead to very long execution time requirements. Figure 7-15 shows a nested DO loop

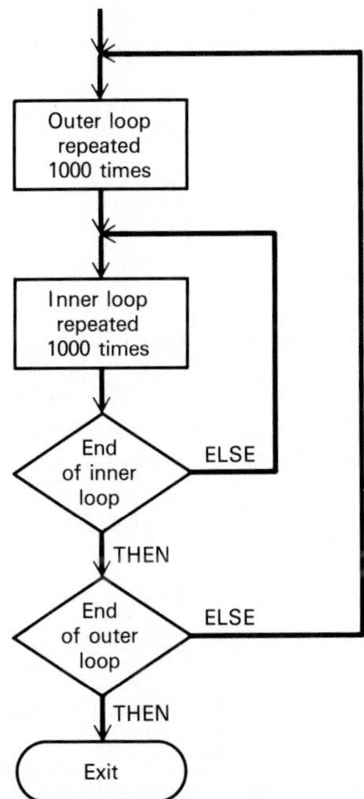

Fig. 7-15 Problem 3.

structure. Each iteration of the inner loop takes 0.001 s. Each iteration of the outer loop takes an additional 0.002 s. How long does it take to complete the nested combination?

4. Suppose you are given the partial BASIC program shown below. There are no syntax errors in this fragment, but there is a mistake which can cause a serious error which goes undetected. Find and correct the error.

```
10 DIM A(10)
20 S = 0
30 FOR I = 1 TO 10
40 S = S + A(I)
50 NEXT I
60 PRINT I
70 END
```

b. *n*-Way Branch

Up to this point all the control sequences have included a single entry point and a single exit point. (One exception to this was the case of nonnormal loop exits.) Another kind of control sequence found in HLLs has a single entry and a number of separate exits. As a result of the execution of a single HLL statement, any one of a number of paths can be followed. Figure 7-16 shows a picture of this type of statement. It is

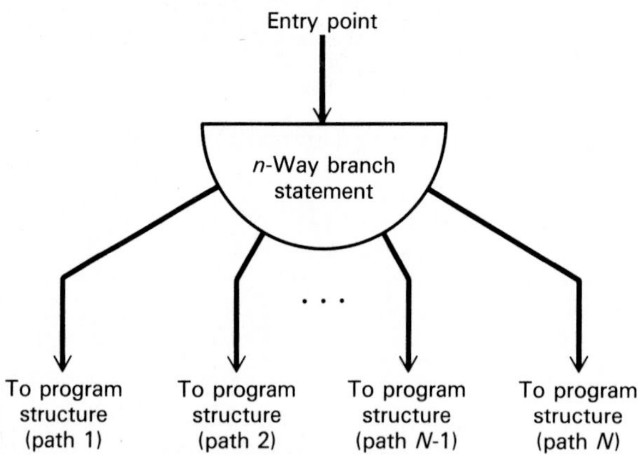

Fig. 7-16 The *n*-way branch, another control structure found in HLLs.

not a flow diagram because it is not made up of process blocks and decision blocks. One way to think of this is to consider a *switch* to be enclosed within the box. This switch connects the input path to one of the output paths. Usually, the value of an integer variable determines the switch position.

BASIC has an *n*-way branch of the following form (syntax):

{BASIC statement number} `ON` {variable} `GOTO` {list of line numbers}

A sample of this is:

```
10   ON   A1   GOTO   50,100,150
```

This BASIC statement has the following effect:

Value of Al	Next Statement Executed
1	50
2	100
3	150

If Al is less than 1 or greater than 3, the next sequential statement is executed.

In Pascal the *n*-way branch is called a *CASE statement*. There are a wide variety of examples of the CASE statement.

The form of this statement is

```
CASE {expression or variable} OF
  constant list :
                        statement;
  constant list :
                        statement;
                     .
                     .
                     .
END
```

For example,

```
CASE switch OF
  1:
     answer := first;
  2:
     answer := second;
  3:
     answer := third;
END
```

The accompanying table explains how the Pascal CASE statement works.

If Switch Has the Value	Then
1	The variable answer is assigned the value of variable first
2	The variable answer is assigned the value of variable second
3	The variable answer is assigned the value of variable third

The *n*-way branch can be accomplished using control sequences previously described. These sequences have a single entry and a single exit. Many programmers consider such structures to be more desirable than the *n*-way branch.

PROBLEM FOR SECTION 7-2-4*b*

1. Devise a structure which is equivalent to an *n*-way branch but has a single entry point and a single exit point. *Hint:* Draw a flow diagram of the structure as a series of decision blocks.

7-3 BUILDING A PROGRAM

Starting with a process block and a decision block, it has been possible to build fundamental program structures. The process block includes HLL statements which were executed in strict sequential order. A decision block permits one of two paths to be followed. With these building blocks several more useful structures, called *program structures,* were devised. These include:

- Sequence structure—a serial arrangement of process blocks
- IF-THEN-ELSE structure—a switch between one of two different process blocks
- Loop structure—a repetition of a process block; includes DO-UNTIL and DO-WHILE forms

By nesting or enclosing these basic program structures within each other, an HLL program of any size or complexity can be constructed. To do this, certain rules must be observed:

1. A program should have only one input or entry path and one output or exit path.
2. The structures within the program may be nested, but each structure must be totally enclosed or contained inside the structure in which it is being nested. No overlap construction is permitted.
3. No arbitrary branching may be used; there must be no multiple exits from a structure and only one structure entry point. A slight relaxation of this rule will be permitted in some cases. For example, branching will be allowed if the control sequence remains entirely within the structure. (GOTO statements in BASIC should be used with care.)

The program shown in Fig. 7-17 is an example of one which is built up using the primitive program structures. They are enclosed within dotted boxes to show which structures are used. The boxes also emphasize the nesting of one structure within another.

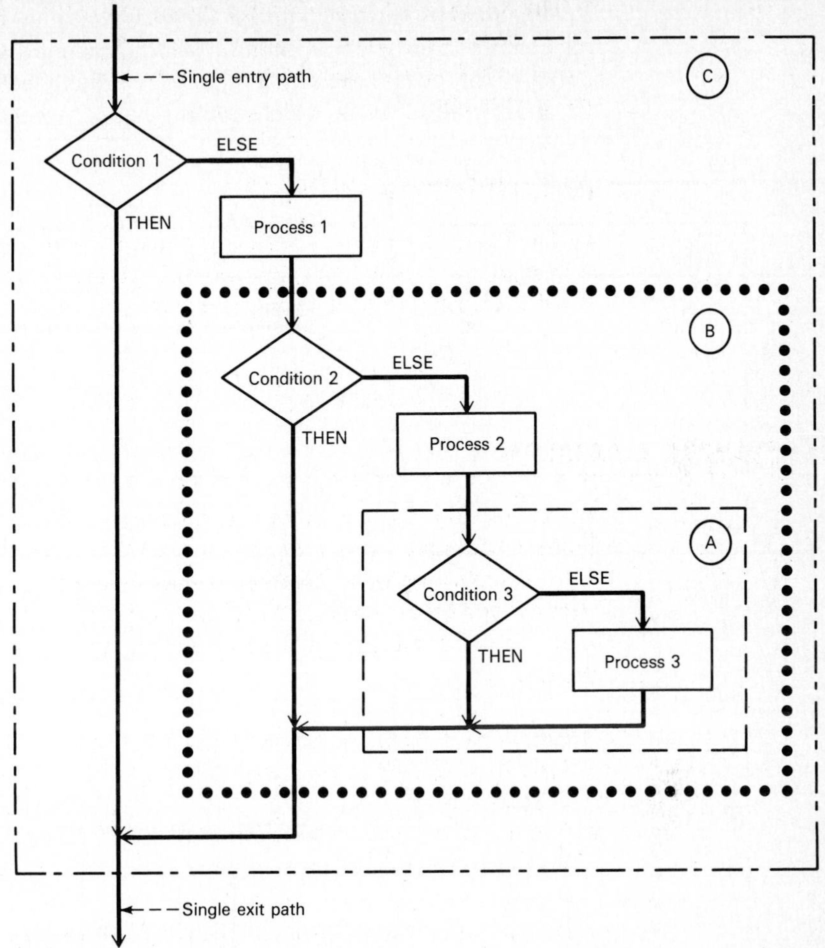

Fig. 7-17 For modularity, ease of development, ease of debugging, and readability, programs should be constructed by nesting basic program structures. Here is one program which builds a program from IF-THEN-ELSE structures.

Example 7-7 Automobile Safety Control System

Many modern automobiles are equipped with a buzzer (or speech synthesizer in more expensive models) which reminds the driver of certain irregular conditions. Two of these conditions are:

- Leaving the key in the ignition, but the engine not running, and the driver's door open
- Leaving the headlights on with the ignition (engine) off

Figure 7-18 illustrates a flow diagram that may be used as the basis for a computer program to monitor the automobile safety features outlined above. A process block for a time delay is included. This simply introduces a short time delay in which nothing happens before rechecking the con-

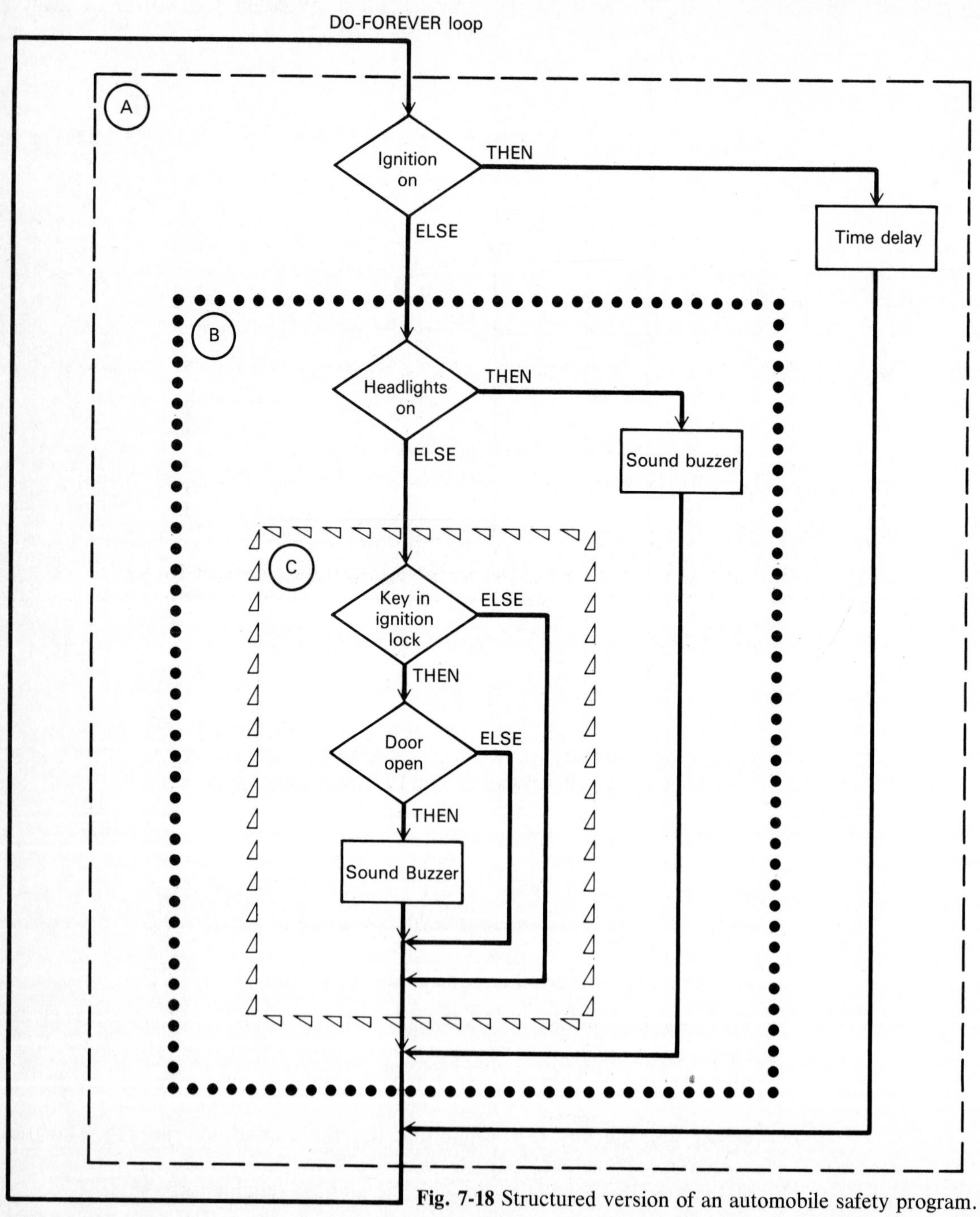

Fig. 7-18 Structured version of an automobile safety program.

ditions. The computer marks (or wastes) time. This program conforms to the rules set down for structured programming.

Note that the instruction "sound buzzer" is repeated. You might think that it makes sense to save instructions by combining certain paths. For example, the modification shown in Fig. 7-19 could be incorporated into

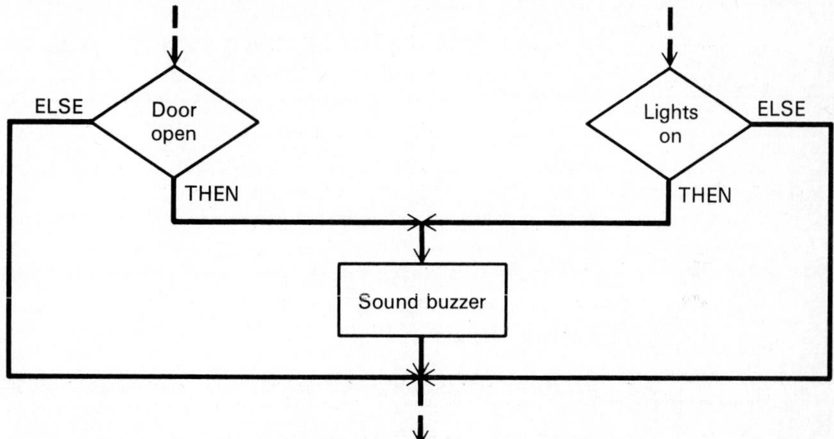

Fig. 7-19 A programmer might be tempted to make a modification in the structured version of the program. This would reduce the space taken up by the program in the computer's memory.

the program. If this is done, then the instruction "Sound buzzer" will have two entry points. The rules for structuring will be violated. By retaining one extra process, structuring is preserved. Readability and simplicity of program checking (debugging) are maintained.

Figure 7-20 shows a BASIC program which will accomplish the tasks

```
10   IF I1 = 1 THEN  FOR X = 1 TO 5000: NEXT X: GOTO 70
20   REM --IGNITION OFF, CHECK LIGHTS--
30     IF L1 = 1 THEN {sound buzzer} : GOTO 60
40     REM --LIGHTS OFF, CHECK KEY AND DOOR--
50         IF K1 = 1 AND D1 = 1 THEN {sound buzzer}
60     REM --BOTTOM OF BLOCK "B"
70   REM --BOTTOM OF BLOCK "A"
80   REM GO TO BEGINNING OF DO-FOREVER LOOP
90   GOTO 10
```

Fig. 7-20 Structured program written in the HLL BASIC showing how to translate the picture (flow diagram) into words for the auto safety and convenience problem.

required by the flow diagram of Fig. 7-18. Within this program, the variables and their meanings are as follows.

Variables	Meaning
I1	State of ignition (on or off): ON = 1, OFF = 0
K1	State of the key (in ignition lock or out of ignition lock): ON = 1, OFF = 0
L1	State of headlights (on or off): ON = 1, OFF = 0
D1	State of the door (open or closed): ON = 1, OFF = 0

The boxes surrounding the various portions of the BASIC program are meant to emphasize the nesting of operations, and correspond to the nesting shown in Fig. 7-18.

PROBLEMS FOR SECTION 7-3

1. Figure 7-21 illustrates the flow diagram for a nonstructured program. It is nonstructured because it is not composed of fundamental program structures such as IF-THEN-ELSE structures or DO loops. Rearrange the flow diagram so that it performs the same function but does so using structured methods.

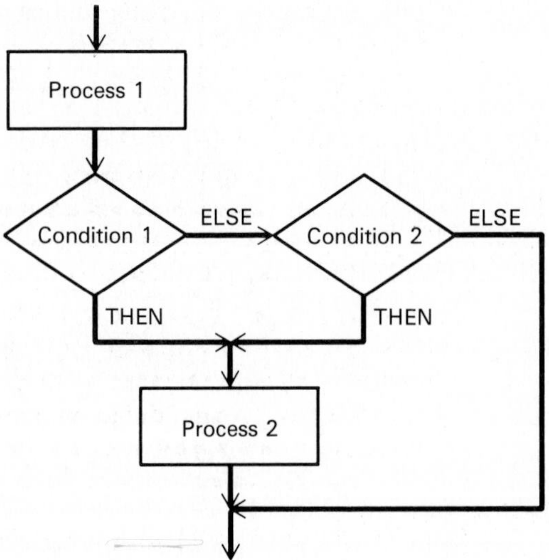

Fig. 7-21 Problem 1.

2. (a) Draw a (structured) flow diagram for the following English-like program fragment. This algorithm shows a way to calculate the square root of a number when such an operation is not provided by an HLL.

```
read (unknown)
IF unknown < 0
  THEN write ('square root of negative number not allowed!')
ELSE IF unknown = 0
  THEN write ('square root = 0')
ELSE
  BEGIN
      root = 1;
      DO
        root = (unknown/root + root)/2
        UNTIL (absolute value of (unknown/root² - 1) < 1E-6)
      write ('square root =', root)
  END
```

(b) Following the procedure indicated in the flow diagram, find the square root of 6. Use a calculator if necessary. Compare your result with the square root function on the calculator if it has such an operation.

3. You work for the highway department of your state as a computer technologist. You are testing auto utilization of 10 exits on one of the limited-access state highways. You are to keep track of the number of cars which leave each exit every hour. The flow diagram of Fig. 7-22 describes this part of the program. Write out a program using English-like, structured statements, that represents the diagram.

7-4 SUBROUTINES AND PROCEDURES

In Example 7-7 you saw the need to write exactly the same set of instructions more than once within a program. The instructions for "Sound buzzer" appeared twice in the program. HLLs provide a way to save space in a program by allowing the user to write the instructions for operations and functions that will be repeated in various parts of the program only once, and make them available throughout the program. Each time that you want to use this set of instructions you *invoke,* or *call,* them. The computer locates the group of instructions that you invoke and executes them. When finished, the computer resumes executing the program at the point following the invocation. Figure 7-23 shows how this transfer of execution occurs. The group of instructions which are executed have different names, depending upon the HLL: typically they are called *subroutines* or *procedures*.

7-4-1 The Calling Program

The program which is being executed when such a subroutine or procedure is called is referred to as the *calling program;* sometimes it is the *main program*. In Example 7-7, the operation "Sound buzzer" could be replaced by

GOSUB n1

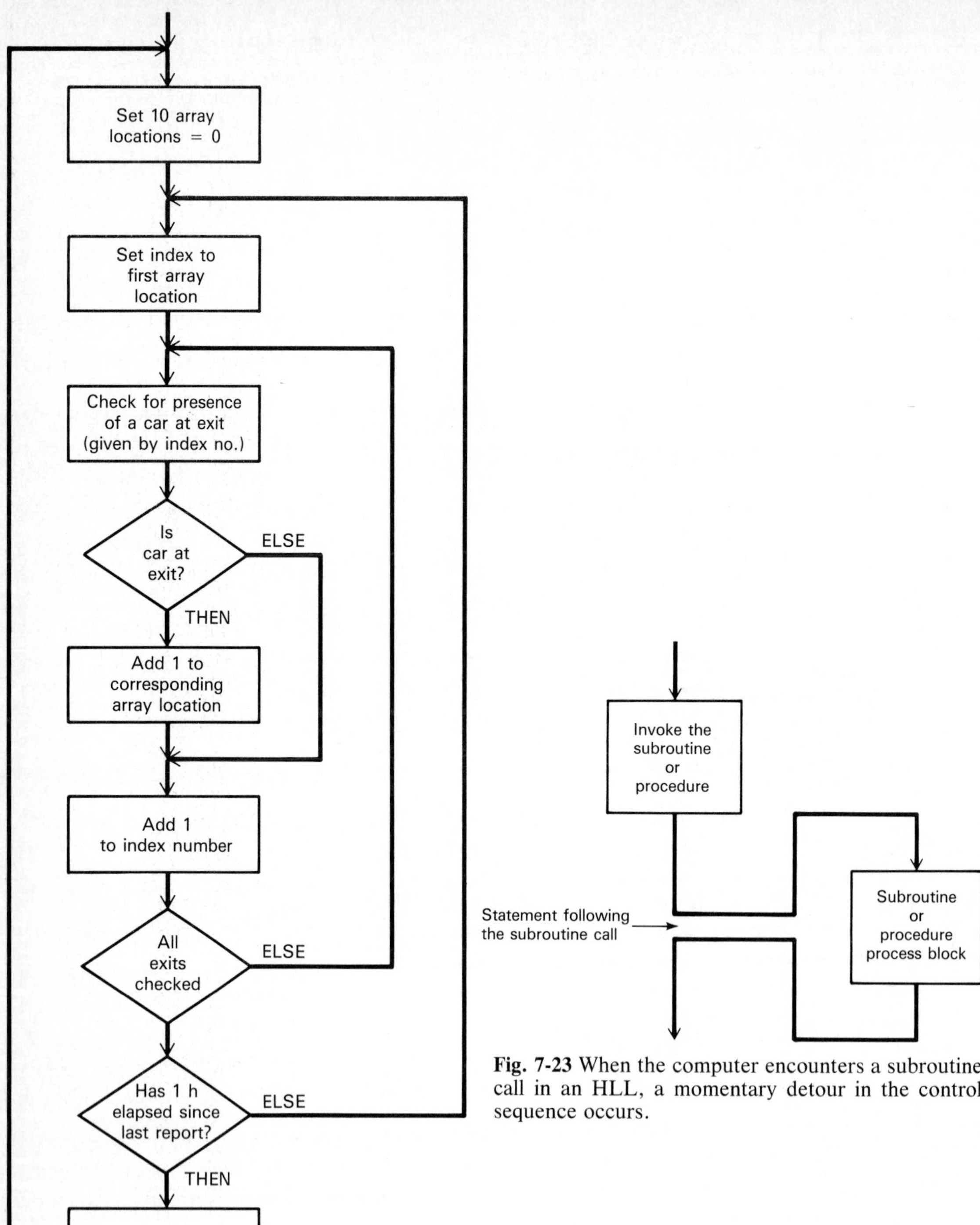

Fig. 7-23 When the computer encounters a subroutine call in an HLL, a momentary detour in the control sequence occurs.

Fig. 7-22 Problem 3.

In this BASIC statement, n1 is one of the BASIC statement numbers. At line n1, you would find the first line of the subroutine.

```
n1   {First instruction line of subroutine}
      .
      .  {Other subroutine statements}
      .
nk   RETURN
```

At the end of the subroutine you will find the BASIC statement RETURN. This causes the *automatic* return to the point at which the subroutine was invoked or called, i.e., to the instruction following the CALL statement.

PROBLEMS FOR SECTION 7-4-1

1. a. Given the English-like program which follows, indicate those parts of the program which are good candidates for inclusion as subroutines. This program will periodically sample the voltage output from each of 100 power supplies undergoing a *burn-in test* and report results, including those supplies which have failed.

```
start timer;
DO
  DO
    nothing
  UNTIL (elapsed time = time to test);
  reset timer;
  i = 1;
  DO
    testresult (i) = voltage from power supply i
    i = i + 1
  UNTIL (i = 101);
  i = 1
  DO
    print testresult (i);
    IF (testresult (i) > highlimit OR testresult (i) < lowlimit)
    print ('power supply failed', i, testresult (i))
    ELSE
    print (i, testresult (i));
    ENDIF
    i = i + 1
  UNTIL (i = 101);
UNTIL (user enters stop signal)
```

b. Rewrite the program in a way which reflects inclusion of the subprograms (subroutines).

2. Programs in HLLs can be structured as a sequence of subroutines to be executed. A program is to be written to automate the testing of integrated circuits (ICs). You are told that the subroutine procedures shown in the accompanying table exist. (Each procedure has a brief explanation.)

Procedure	Explanation
getfile(ic)	Reads a file from the secondary storage with correct test voltages for each pin of the IC whose number is specified by "ic". When completed, the values exist in a data structure in RAM. The last value in the structure is the number of pins to be tested. It is called "lastpin."
compare(i)	Compares a measured voltage against correct test voltage for pin *i,* and returns a boolean (logical) value—true if there is a match, else false.
readpin(i)	Tests the signal on pin *i* of the IC under test and returns a measured value.
askforic	Gets the number of the IC to be tested from a user via the standard input (keyboard). Returns an IC number.

Using English-like statements and the procedures outlined in the table, write a program which can be used for automated testing of ICs.

3. State a disadvantage of using a subprogram.

7-4-2 Varieties of Subroutines

There are a number of different kinds of subroutines in HLLs. The type described in Sec. 7-4 is a simple CALL-RETURN type. Two topics are important with regard to subroutines:

- What types of subroutines can you expect to find in HLLs and how do they work?
- How is data supplied to these subprograms and how are results treated?

In this section some important types of subroutines and their HLL control structures are discussed. In the next section, transmission of data to and from such programs is described.

a. CALL-RETURN Subroutines

In an HLL program it is possible to invoke a set of statements, transfer control to such statements, and, when these are completed, return to the point in the program where they were first invoked (see Fig. 7-23). Another name for invoking such a group is *calling*. The group of statements form a subprogram. Each subprogram—programs may use many such subprograms—usually has a name. To call such programs one of two methods is used:

- Use a GOSUB statement
- Use the name of the subroutine

Example 7-8 Invoking a Subroutine

Table 7-1 summarizes statements in BASIC and Pascal which invoke a subroutine.

TABLE 7-1 SUMMARY OF CALL-RETURN SUBROUTINE CALLING STATEMENTS

HLL	Statement	Comment
Pascal	name;	"name" identifies the subroutine which is called a *procedure*, e.g., average
BASIC	GOSUB n1	n1 is a BASIC statement number where the subroutine begins

Subroutines may be *nested* as shown in Fig. 7-24.

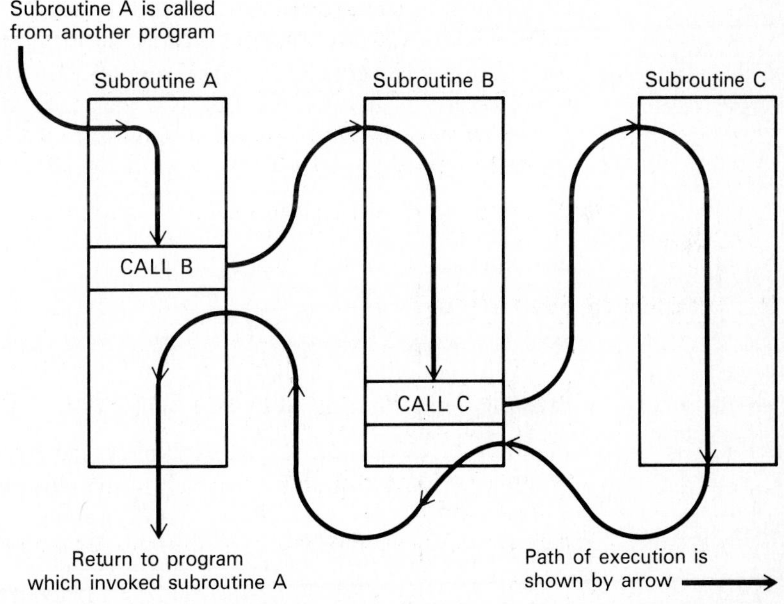

Fig. 7-24 Nesting of subroutines. The arrows show the control path through a series of nested subroutines.

b. Recursive Subprograms

It is sometimes useful for a subroutine to be able to call itself. Such subroutines are called *recursive* subroutines. The CALL-RETURN subroutines previously discussed cannot call themselves. If they tried to do so, they would destroy (*overwrite*) the place at which to resume the program which originally called them. The problem which must be solved in order to allow subroutines to call themselves is to be able to *save all resume addresses*. One way to do this is by using a memory stack. Each time a call to a subprogram is executed in a program, the address following that instruction (RESUME) is *pushed* onto the stack. If program A is a subroutine, it can still call itself because the RESUME address is saved on the stack. When a subroutine completes its instructions, the computer returns to the program which invoked the subroutine.

Recursive control sequences similar to those described are useful in certain nonnumeric applications:

1. Translating HLL programs into computer instructions by compilation
2. Processing English as in record keeping, robotics, or artificial intelligence
3. Solving problems in mathematics where numbers do not play a role (such as proving theorems in geometry)

7-4-3 Data in Subroutines

Up to now only the control sequences for subroutines have been discussed. Subroutines, like all programs, receive data and produce results. How is data transmitted from a calling program to a subroutine? How are results returned from subroutines to calling programs?

Data is not *always* transmitted to a subroutine. When subroutines are used in this way, they are called *parameterless* (without parameters). When a subroutine is invoked in BASIC, the statement is always GOSUB n (where *n* is a BASIC statement number). No data is specified in this statement.

A subroutine may need to work on different data at different times. How then does it receive the data to work on if none is specified? A simple example will show how this is done.

Example 7-9 Passing Data to a Subroutine in BASIC

Figure 7-25 shows the way data is accessed by subroutines of a BASIC program. A very simple BASIC subroutine appears at statement 200. This

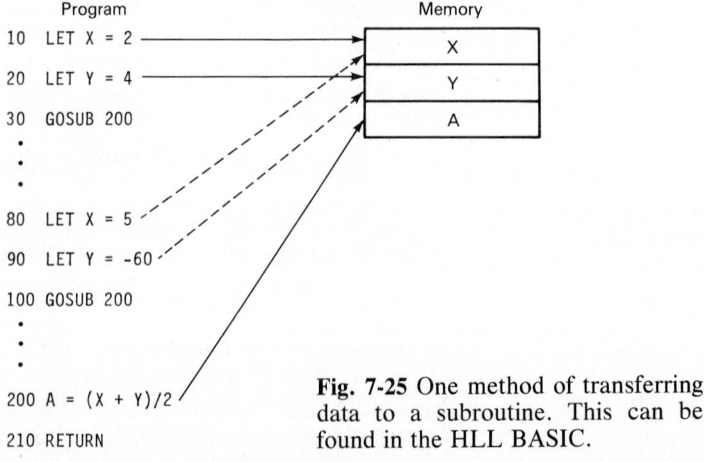

Fig. 7-25 One method of transferring data to a subroutine. This can be found in the HLL BASIC.

averages two variables, X and Y. The subroutine is called at 30 and again at 100. Before the subroutine is called, values for X and Y are assigned. The computer's memory contains locations for X and Y.

When a subroutine is to be given different data to work with each time it is called, a different method of communication can be useful. Subroutine actions for this second method are summarized in Fig. 7-26. Whenever a

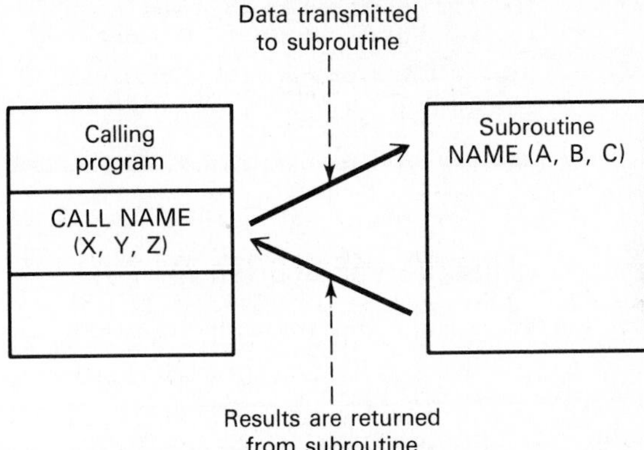

Fig. 7-26 Flow of data between subroutines and the programs which invoke them.

program invokes a subroutine, the data needed for the subroutine must be specified. These data are contained as part of a *parameter* list. Another part of the parameter list contains the names of the variables which are returned as results. The parameters in the calling program are *actual* parameters. The subroutine also has a list of parameters. These parameters are called the *formal* parameters. These are *dummy* names given to the parameter list. They "hold a place" for the actual parameters which are substituted for these dummy variables when the subroutine is involved.

Example 7-10 Sample HLL Subroutine CALLs

Pascal. In this HLL subroutines are called PROCEDUREs. A sample which includes the important parts follows.

```
PROCEDURE marie (VAR y:real);
    body of procedure
END; (*marie*)
    .
    .
    .
marie (x)
    .
    .
    .
```

The PROCEDURE (subroutine) is named "marie". A list of parameters (formal variables) follows. In Pascal the formal variables are preceded by the word VAR. This simply means that this is going to represent an actual parameter. Following the parameter is a colon (:). This in turn is followed by the word "real". This tells the computer that the parameter y is a real data type.

When you invoke the PROCEDURE, only the name is required. Thus the statement "marie (x)" will cause the PROCEDURE to be executed. The value of x, at the time the statement "marie (x)" is executed, is substituted for y wherever it appears in the body of the PROCEDURE.

PROBLEMS FOR SECTION 7-4-3

1. Assume the following statement appears in a calling program:

```
SUB (8 + 3, 2 * 7, Z)
```

The following statements appear in the subroutine.

```
SUB (X, Y, Z)
Z = 3 * X + Y
```

What is the value of Z after program control passes back to the main program?

2. For the following statements, list the actual and formal parameters.

```
(INVOKE) SMART (JOHN, MARY, LEE)
SUBROUTINE SMART (MALE, FEMALE, UNKNOWN)
```

Summary

HLLs include a number of statements or language phrases that control the sequence in which calculations are performed. Starting with two simple building blocks, it is possible to construct complex programs. The simple control sequence consists of the process block and the decision block. Using these, fundamental program structures can be constructed. These include sequences, IF-THEN-ELSE structures, and loops. Loops are further divided into DO-WHILE, DO-UNTIL, and indexed DO loops. Loops may contain other loops. Such an arrangement is called nesting. In order to make use of these program structures, some HLLs use statements such as GOTO or *n*-way branches. Complete programs can be built with these program structures. When portions of a program can be used over and over, it is best to create a separate program component. This is the subroutine. Instead of copying all the statements included in the subroutine, the programmer invokes the subroutine by calling or using its name.

REVIEW QUESTIONS

1. What kind of HLL statements determine the sequence of calculations to be performed?
2. Two kinds of program components are needed to completely describe the sequence of instructions carried out within a computer. Name these components.
3. Draw flow diagrams for the components named in Question 2.
4. What are two important facts relating to fundamental program structures?
5. Name the principal program structures.
6. Draw flow diagrams for the principal program structures.
7. What is the most important difference between DO-WHILE and DO-UNTIL structures?
8. Name the differences between DO (indexed) loops and DO-UNTIL structures.
9. Name four reasons for decomposing a program into a series of separate blocks.
10. Write out the syntax of an IF-THEN-ELSE statement using English-like expressions.
11. What are reserved words?
12. What is the purpose of the IF-THEN-ELSE statement with regard to the control of which instructions of a program are to be executed?
13. What statement allows you to repeat a group of instructions?
14. What information is needed to completely specify the way in which an indexed DO loop is to be executed?
15. What is an n-way branch?
16. What is the symbol that is used for the Pascal assignment operator?
17. What are the symbols which are used for the assignment operators in BASIC?
18. What is a nested DO loop?
19. How is an n-way branch implemented in Pascal?
20. What is a subprogram?
21. Describe two ways in which data can be passed between a program and a subroutine.

8 DATA INPUT/OUTPUT IN HLL

This chapter deals with those HLL statements which move data from one part of the computer to another part of the computer. Because a good many of these statements involve data movement from the user to the computer and vice versa, and because the user is considered to be outside, or external to, the machine, these statements are called *input/output,* or *I/O,* statements. This chapter describes the operation of such HLL statements.

8-1 THE NATURE OF I/O STATEMENTS

HLL I/O statements require *four* pieces of information in order to properly move data from one part of the computer to another:

- The *source* of the data
- The data *destination*
- The *amount* and *type* of data to be moved
- The *form* (or *format*) that the data is to take

Data sources can include such things as the keyboard of the terminal device, the secondary storage system, another computer, or a special device such as a machine which stores data on paper in the form of a series of punched holes. Data can be moved from the computer to different destinations, such as a printer, the screen of a monitor, the secondary storage system of the computer, or a special device such as a machine which punches holes in paper or cards.

You have already learned that there are several different types of data. The computer must know which type of data is to be moved. Is the data an integer, a real number, a logical expression, or some other form?

Perhaps the data includes a mixture of data types. The computer must also know or be able to figure out how much data is to be moved. Otherwise, it will not be able to determine when all the data has been moved.

The last important part of an I/O statement includes the form or arrangement of the data. This is referred to as the *format*. If the format information does not agree with the actual data, serious errors may result. The user may not be aware of these errors. In some cases, the HLL and/or the computer will signal the user that something is wrong. For example, if the data to be printed in the summary requires more positions than the program has indicated, a series of asterisks (*******) may be printed in place of the actual data. This lets the programmer or user know that the results calculated do not agree with the description (format) of the expected results.

A programmer should include statements which check the data received from the user. If these values do not agree with expectations, actions should be taken to alert the user to this fact. Such actions are called *error escapes*. A reliable program includes steps which are followed when an error is encountered.

This chapter describes some of the statements that you will find in HLLs that can be used to:

- Accept data from the computer's resources or peripheral equipment, or
- Transmit data to such devices

The data format, or the way in which data is arranged, is important. Data formats are important in order to:

- Make programs easier to use (*user-friendly*)
- Make computer results easier to read and interpret
- Promote efficient use of the computer's resources and peripheral components

PROBLEMS FOR SECTION 8-1

The following shorthand notation should be used for Probs. 1 and 2 below:

CHAR (L): Character data with L characters expected
INT (L): Integer data with L digits (including sign) expected
REAL (L, F): Real data with L positions (including sign and decimal point) and F places after the decimal point
_: Indicates space or blank

1. Indicate one format that will describe the sequence of program input data shown below. In your format specify the type of data to expect, the number of positions occupied by each piece of data, and such details as the number of places needed for fractional parts of real numbers. Be sure your format provides for all possible cases of the data to be

received. The input data is needed for a program that is to keep records and make statistical calculations on power supplies manufactured by your employer. A typical entry looks as follows:

Serial Number	Load	Output	Temperature	Isolation Option (True/False)
BX235A	+ 150.0	+ 4.983	20	T

2. Show how the following data should appear on a monitor when the computer expects it with the indicated format. Assume 80 positions on one line of the monitor.

   a. Format: CHAR (12), INT (5), CHAR (7), REAL (5, 2)
      Data: FREQUENCY _ = _100, GAIN _ = _ −.107E+2
   b. Format INT (5)
      Data: 655321
   c. Format: REAL (8, 3)
      Data: 502.100

3. Suppose you are given the following heading, which forms part of a computer program (listing) for generating an electronic subassembly parts list:

   _ _ _ _ _ Part Number _ _ _ _ _ Type _ _ _ _ _ Value _ _ _ _ _ Tolerance

   The underscoring indicates blank spaces which are to be included in the title. The first blank corresponds to column 1 of the printout. Assume that the output device has enough printing positions to accommodate this title.

   a. Provide a verbal description of this format using keywords such as BLANK, CHARACTER STRING, and WIDTH.
   b. Repeat part (a), but use a different description in which the keyword TAB is used instead of BLANK.

4. Design a listing format for a program which will print information regarding a wire list. The information should include name of the wire (signal name), origin (chip and pin number), destination (chip and pin number), and electrical load on the wire.

8-2 PHYSICAL COMMUNICATION WITH A COMPUTER

A computer sends and receives information in the form of electrical signals. These signals are usually sent over wires between the computer and the originating or terminating device. In Chap. 2 you learned that data in the real world (letters and numbers) are translated into binary codes (using 1 and 0) before this information can be used within the computer. Similarly, binary numbers within the machine are normally translated into letters and numbers before being presented to a user. It is easier for one to understand

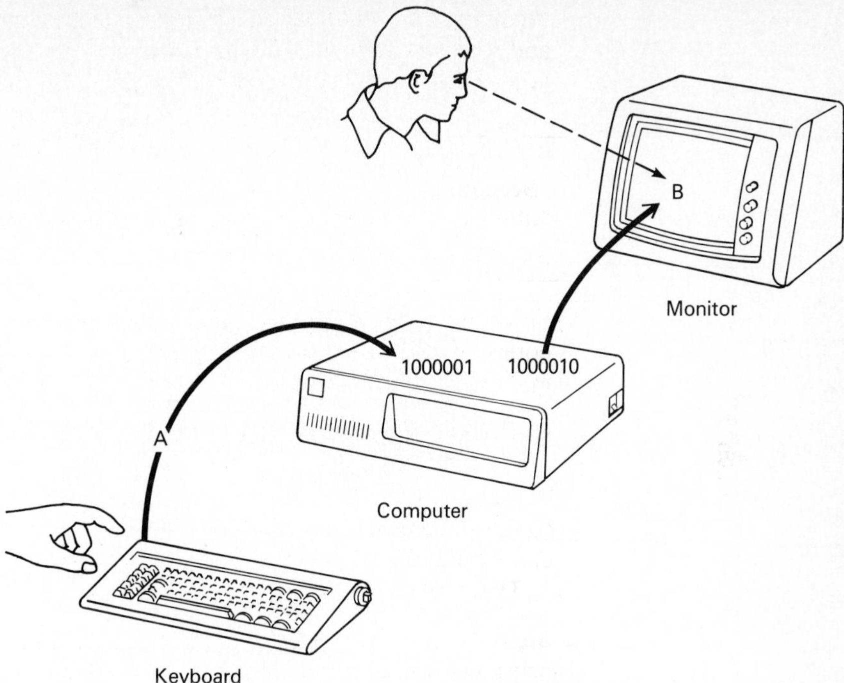

Fig. 8-1 How data appears inside and outside the computer.

the letter "B" than to have to read and interpret the binary code for the letter. These conversions are represented in Fig. 8-1.

The information which is transferred between a computer and its resources is in binary coded form. There are two methods for doing this, as shown in Fig. 8-2. The individual parts of the code (the bits) can be sent one at a time over a single wire. Such a method is called *bit-serial* (or simply *serial*) and is shown in Fig. 8-2*a*. The code bits may also be sent all at the same time, as shown in Fig. 8-2*b*. This requires as many wires as there are bits in the code. Even though all bits are sent at the same time, the code represents only one character (such as a letter or a number). This method is called *byte-parallel* and is usually referred to as *parallel* communication. Parallel transmission is faster than serial, but it is also more expensive, as it requires many more wires and may use more expensive connectors.

Sometimes data passes from a peripheral to a computer. At other times data is transmitted from the computer to the peripheral. Figure 8-3 shows some of the ways in which this happens. The case in which data can flow from computer to peripheral and from peripheral to computer over different paths is called *full-duplex* communication (Fig. 8-3*a*). If a single communications channel is used, the direction of data flow on this channel must be reversible if two-way communication is to occur. This is called *half-duplex* communication and is illustrated in Fig. 8-3*b*. Full-duplex communication is faster and more expensive; yet it may give rise to subtle problems when data is passed between components, similar to what might

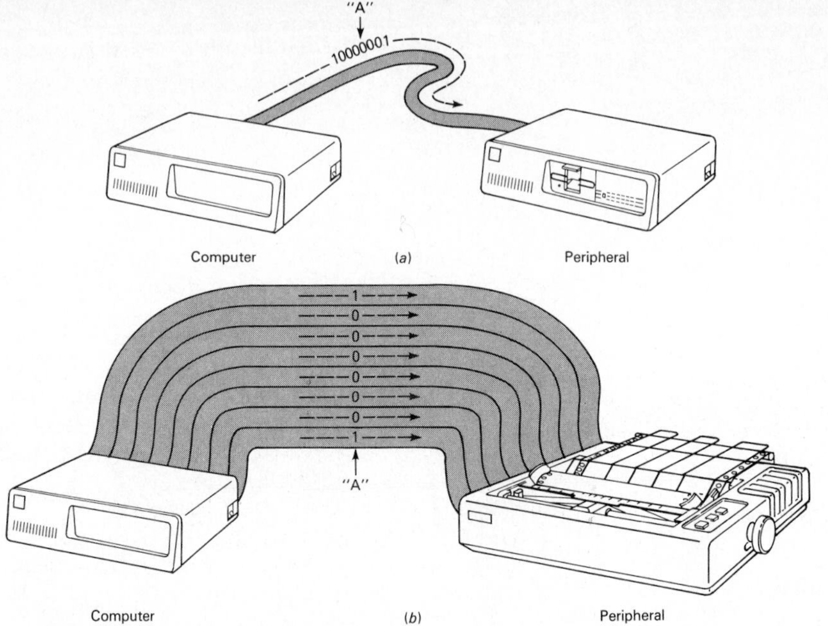

Fig. 8-2 Two methods by which data is transmitted between a computer and its peripheral devices. (*a*) Bit-serial transmissions. (*b*) Byte-serial transmission: transmitting all bits of the data at once.

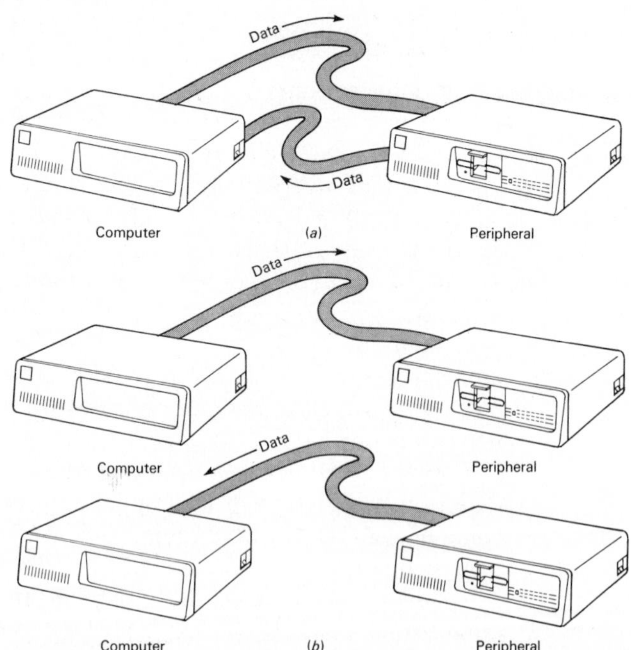

Fig. 8-3 Two kinds of physical connections between the computer and its peripherals. (*a*) Two sets of wires between devices leads to full-duplex communication. (*b*) When data flow is made to alternate on a single wire, the connection is half-duplex communication.

happen when two people are trying to talk into a telephone at the same time. Bidirectional communications using half-duplex systems are slow, as the data direction of the channel must be reversed and this takes time. The parts needed for such reversal tend to be complicated and expensive.

PROBLEMS FOR SECTION 8-2

1. Draw a flow diagram which describes the steps necessary to ensure successful communication in a half-duplex system.
2. A computer transmits information to a printer in a serial fashion (sequentially). How does the printer "know" when it has received a digit or character? To help you to answer this question, assume that transmission can occur using two separate signal wires. Is such transmission possible using one signal wire? If so, can you think of a way to do this?
3. One important way to measure the quality of physical communication is to calculate the information capacity of the connection. This is done by computing the rate of transmission in bits per second.
   a. A serial communication line can transmit 110 characters in 1 s. Each character consists of 10 bits. What is the information rate?
   b. A parallel communication line can send a bit over each line in 100 microseconds (μs). A character contains 8 bits of information. Compute the information rate.

8-3 HOW A PROGRAMMER VIEWS I/O

While parts of the computer may be physically connected with wires, these communication paths remain inactive until the computer enables them to transmit data. The data often passes over these connections one character at a time (either serial or parallel). The sequence of data can be referred to as a *stream* of data. It resembles a stream of flowing water. In a similar way the channel over which the data flows can be considered to be a *pipe*.

Figure 8-4 shows the computer and its *potential* connections to various components and peripherals. The communications channels, or pipes, are shown as dashed lines. The computer will activate these channels at the appropriate time. If an HLL program contains statements which include data transfer instructions before a proper connection is established, an error will result. The program may halt and corrective action may be required.

The programmer is responsible for instructing the computer to *enable*, or make ready, any connections which may be needed before data transfer begins. Statements within the HLL program cause this to happen. When data transfer is complete, other instructions in the program will deactivate the communication path. The sequence of operations is shown in Fig. 8-5.

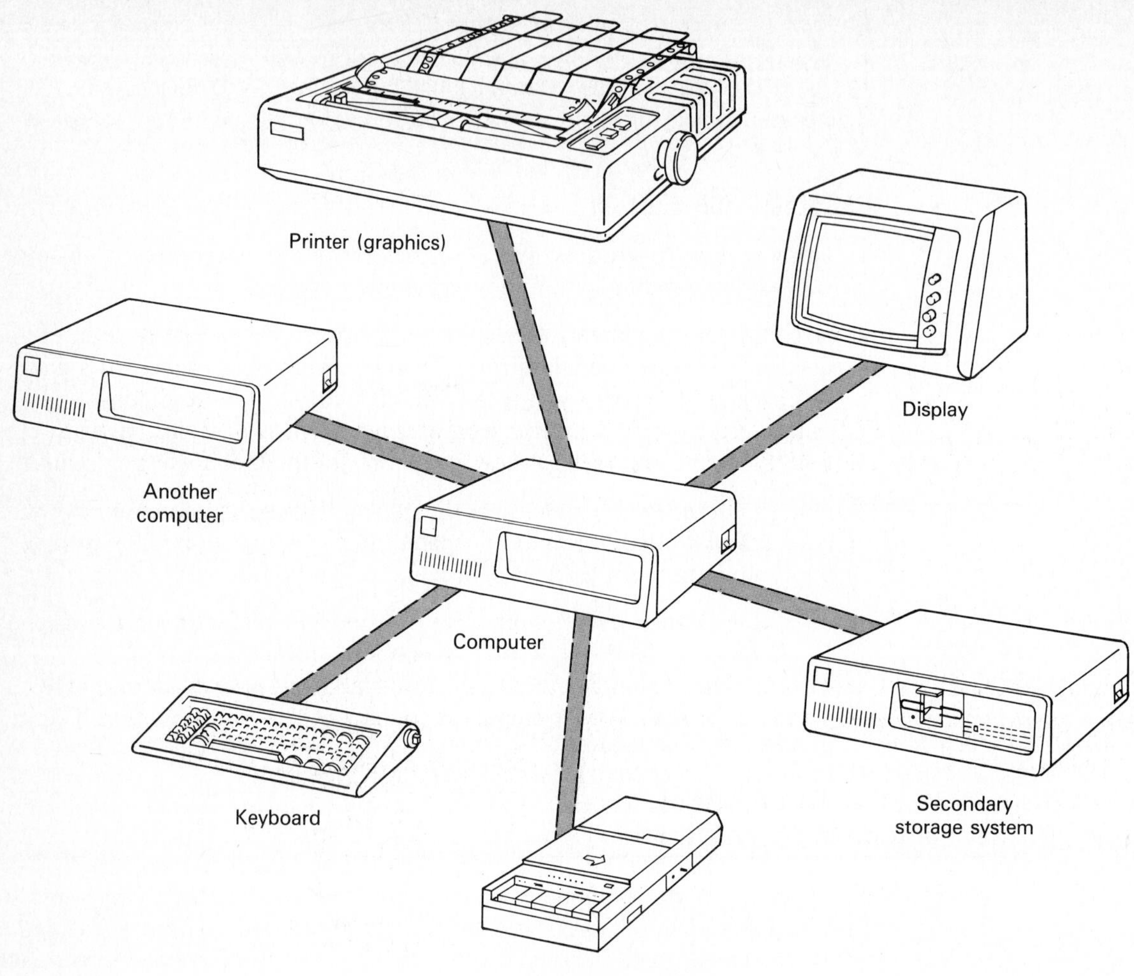

Fig. 8-4 Potential connections between the computer and its peripherals.

In Fig. 8-5*a* a statement within the HLL program has enabled a connection between the computer and one of the peripheral components, in this case a disk. The solid lines joining these devices indicates that the connection is enabled. Dashed connections to other peripherals imply that these connections have not been enabled or readied for data transmission.

8-3-1 Making Connections

When the connection has been made ready, the computer is considered to have *opened a connection*. The HLL statement which causes this to happen is called an *OPEN* statement. Another way of referring to this is to say, "A pipe has been opened." This statement does not move the data. It only readies the computer-peripheral link for data transfer.

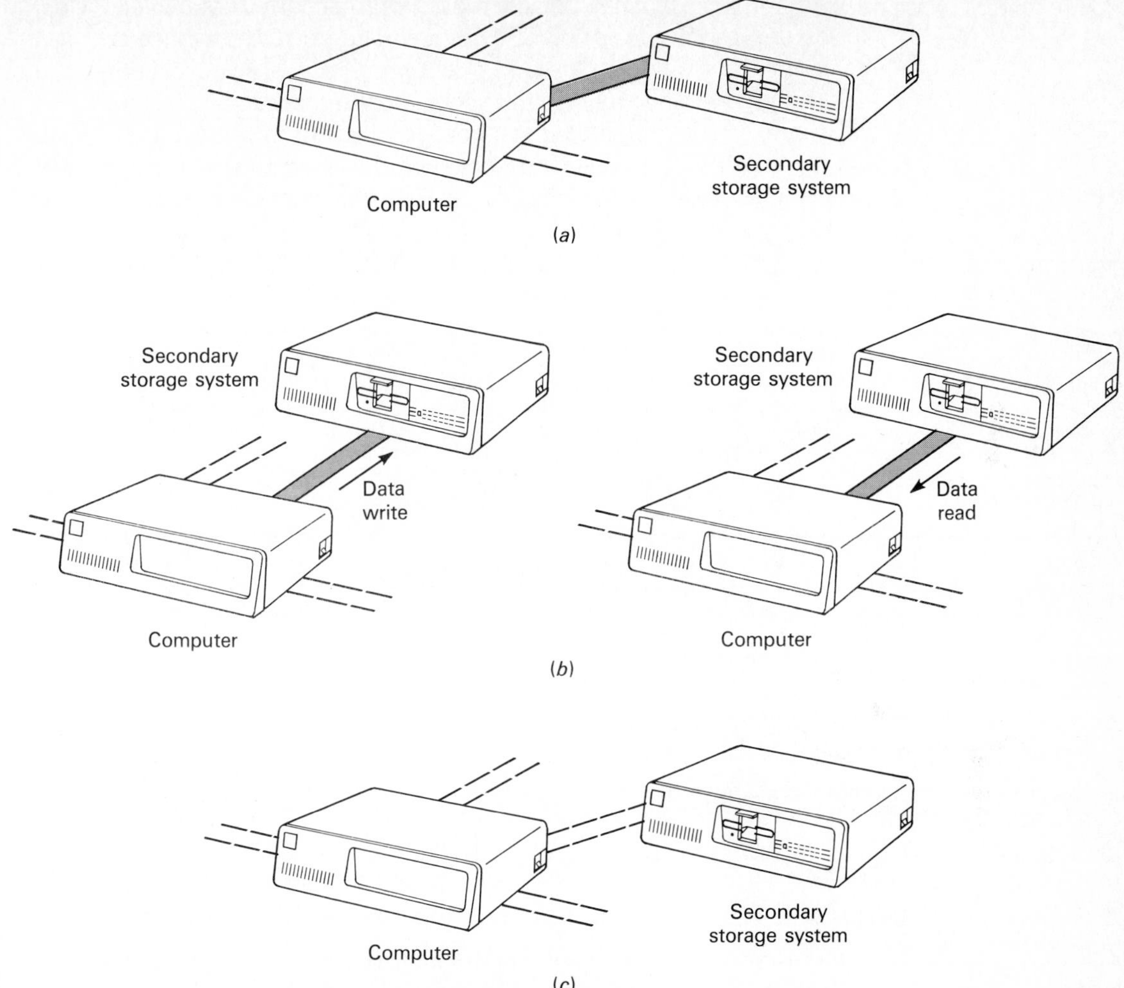

Fig. 8-5 The connection between the computer and a peripheral changes during the course of data transfers. (*a*) A connection is established or opened between the computer and one of its peripherals. (*b*) Data is transferred over the connection from the peripheral to the computer (a read operation), or from the computer to the peripheral (a write operation). (*c*) Data transfer is complete and the connection (pipe) is deactivated.

Figure 8-5*b* shows data flowing from the peripheral (disk) to the computer. This will happen only when an HLL program statement is executed which instructs the computer to obtain data from, or *read* from, the disk. Alternatively, the program can contain statements which will transfer data from the computer to the peripheral. In this case data flows within the pipe from the computer to the peripheral. When this happens the computer is carrying out a *write* operation. For some peripherals only a read operation or a write operation (not both) is possible. You can only read data from a keyboard, and you can only write data to a printer.

When the data transfer is complete, the communication path, or pipe, must be deactivated, or disabled. This is the case in Fig. 8-5*c*. The connection, or pipe, can be considered *closed*. The HLL statement which causes this to happen is a *CLOSE* statement. All OPEN connections to the computer should be closed before a program finishes executing.

Some pipe connections to the computer are needed at all times. In particular, it is important to have connections between the computer and the keyboard, and a connection between the computer and the monitor. These connections are shown in Fig. 8-6. If such connections did not exist,

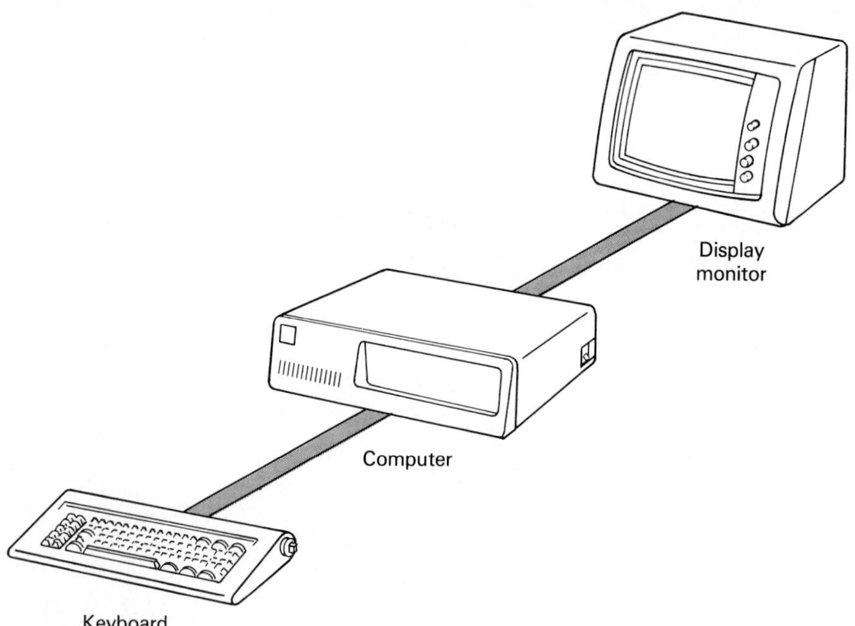

Fig. 8-6 Standard computer connections: those which are activated automatically and are permanent.

it would be difficult (perhaps impossible) to open them. There would be no way to enter the instructions that could open them, allowing entry of other commands. Such connections are referred to as *standard connections*.

In some HLLs you do not have to explicitly open a connection. The statement which transfers data automatically opens the connection. There is considerable variation in the OPEN and CLOSE statements from one HLL to another. Indeed, there is much variablity in such statements within different versions of a single HLL. You must check the programmer's manual for the exact form of such statements. Some examples from various HLLs will explain opening and closing of connections.

Example 8-1 The OPEN Statement in HLLs

a. The OPEN statement in BASIC. There are several versions of the OPEN statement in BASIC because it varies according to dialect:

OPEN ⟨logical connection number⟩, ⟨device number⟩, ⟨secondary address⟩, "⟨filename⟩"

OPEN ⟨name of data and device⟩ FOR ⟨data direction⟩ AS ⟨logical connection number⟩ LEN = ⟨record length for random files⟩

OPEN ⟨data direction⟩, ⟨logical connection number⟩, ⟨name of data and device⟩, ⟨record length for random files⟩

Notes:

1. The file name consists of drive number, name of file, type of access, and data direction. An example is B:RESULTS,S,W.
2. Reserved words include OPEN, FOR, AS, LEN.
3. A *logical* connection number is assigned to the connection between the computer and the peripheral.
4. The peripheral has a *physical device number.*
5. Secondary address is optional. It often represents commands such as those to a printer. For example, 0 = use graphic characters; 7 = use upper- and lowercase characters; 5 = change number of characters per inch. It may also refer to one of the separate channels within a disk system.
6. Data may have a name, such as PARTSLIST.
7. Type of access: SEQ or S = sequential (serial) files; REL or R = relative files.
8. Data direction: W = write data; R = read data.
9. LEN =: sets the length of records within the file (optional).

b. Pascal does not provide an OPEN statement; establishing connections is automatic.

PROBLEMS FOR SECTION 8-3-1

1. Using the syntax of the first version of BASIC shown in Example 8-1, open connections to the following files:

   a. Physical unit 4; no secondary address. The logical connection is being opened to a printer. Do you need to include the name of a file? Do you have to specify a data direction?
   b. The physical device number for a cassette is given as 1. A secondary address of 0 means read access. The name of the file is DATA. Do you need to specify a sequential access file?

2. Using the syntax of Prob. 1 explain the connection which is created by the following:

```
50 OPEN 1, 8, 7 "1:MAIL, SEQ, WRITE"
```

Unit 8 is a dual disk drive.

3. One type of error message which you can get when opening a disk file in BASIC is

```
FILE TYPE MISMATCH
```

Can you explain under what circumstances this occurs?

4. Using the syntax of Microsoft (MS) BASIC (see Example 8-1), write OPEN statements for each of the following using two methods:

   a. A file named MYFILE on the computer's default device (say, the cassette). Information is to be written to this device.
   b. A file named OURFILE on the diskette in drive B; random input and output; record length is 256.

8-3-2 Disconnecting Pipes

While moving data between the computer and the external world, it may become necessary to:

- Connect a unit to different data at different times, or
- Connect your data to different units.

In addition, when a program is completed, the programmer should make sure that all devices have been disconnected. Pascal does not require a connection statement and therefore does not have any CLOSE statements.

Example 8-2 Closing Statements in HLLs

a. The CLOSE statement in BASIC. The details of the exact form vary with the dialect being used. A general form is:

CLOSE ({connection numbers to be terminated})

Samples

```
CLOSE #1, #5, #4
CLOSE 1, 5, 4
CLOSE                 {all connections terminated}
```

An important warning: It is a good idea to close all connections in BASIC before the end of a program.

b. No CLOSE is used in Pascal.

8-4 MORE ON FILES

Combining or grouping information is a good way to keep track of large amounts of data. In your own work you are likely to use separate envelopes for each job or subject. These may then be combined still further. You may use a cabinet to house a group of such folders. The cabinet can be thought of as a *volume,* and the individual folders of the cabinet are *files.* Each folder may contain various related documents or *records.* A direct comparison can be made with the data which is moved between the computer and external devices. Figure 8-7 shows a familiar example of how people store data.

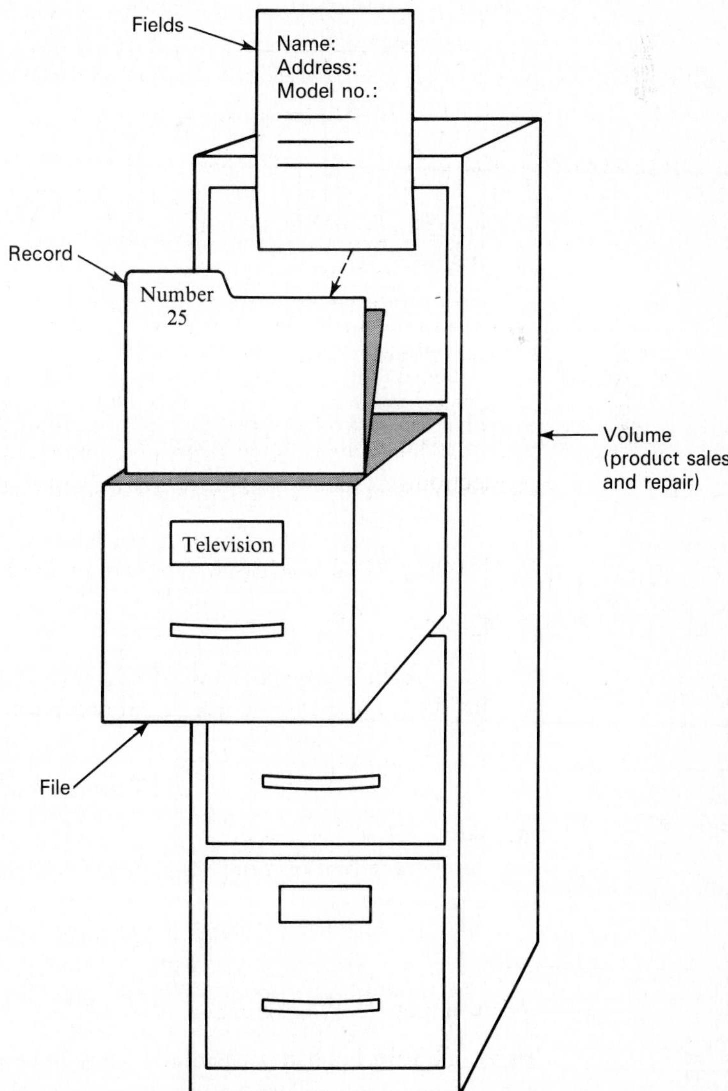

Fig. 8-7 A pictorial review of files.

When opening a pipe connection between the computer and a peripheral device, the data to be moved is often given a name. Even in those HLLs which do not have OPEN statements, the data to be moved may have a name. This *name identifies a file* similar to one with which you are familiar. The data within this file is further subdivided into smaller units called *records*. A *record number* can be used to distinguish each one. Just as your file folder can contain individual pieces of paper, HLL files can contain smaller groups of data (records). A picture of an HLL file is shown in Fig. 8-8.

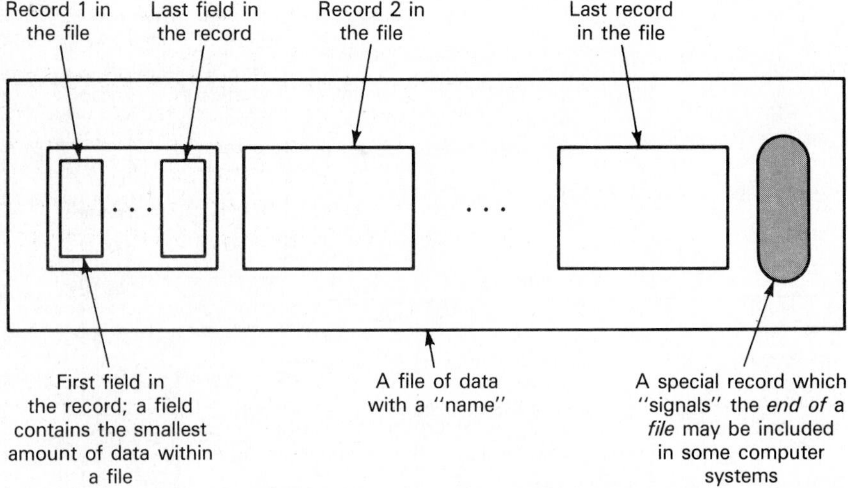

Fig. 8-8 Diagram of a file, describing those parts which are often encountered in HLLs.

8-4-1 Makeup of a File

The file is usually given a name. When you read the programmer's language manual for your particular HLL and computer you will find the following:

<filename>

This appears in that part of a statement where the programmer must supply the name of the file.

A file contains records which are large subdivisions within a file. For example, you may be responsible for keeping track of all the customer sales and experience (repairs, etc.) for each product manufactured by your company. A separate file could be created for each type of product. A manufacturer of consumer products may have files for electric irons, washers, dryers, televisions, etc. A record within each of these files might contain information such as the following:

Customer name
Address
Model number
Date purchased } A record
Where purchased
How learned of product
Repairs

Each of the individual parts of the record is called a *field*. In the above example, customer name, address, etc., are fields of the record. A field is the smallest subdivision of a file. Each field may contain different data types. The customer name could consist of a CHARACTER data type. The model number might be INTEGER data. Usually, each record consists of identical fields. As an example, each record in the case above contains a field for customer name, address, etc. Clearly, the data in the fields (e.g., customer name field) will vary from one record to the next.

8-4-2 SA and DA Files

Files depend on the type of device on which they are stored. When moving files between the computer and peripherals, the programmer must be aware of how the file appears to the device. Two kinds of files are possible: sequential-access (SA) or direct-access (DA) files. These names are applied to the way in which the records are accessed for reading or writing.

SA files are read or written in strict sequential order. You cannot ''jump over'' records when going from one record to the next. This restriction is due to the fact that the read/write mechanism (head) cannot be moved. Because of the strict order of such files, they are called *sequential-access (SA)* or simply *sequential files*.

For some files the reading or writing point can be selected as needed. This ability to read or write anywhere is due in part to the fact that the read/write mechanism can be readily moved to any file. Because files and records can be located (accessed) in a random way, such files are called *direct-access (DA)* or *random-access files*. (In some circumstances these may be called *relative files*.)

8-4-3 Computer HLL Operations on Files

Various operations which can be performed on sequential files are shown in Fig. 8-9. The reading or writing position within the file is shown by the arrow (↑). Some commands may access the first record component (OPEN, or REWIND or RESET).

Example 8-3 HLL Sequential File Commands

Table 8-1 shows the operations that are permitted on SA files. In addition, the table includes the HLL statements that can be used for these operations

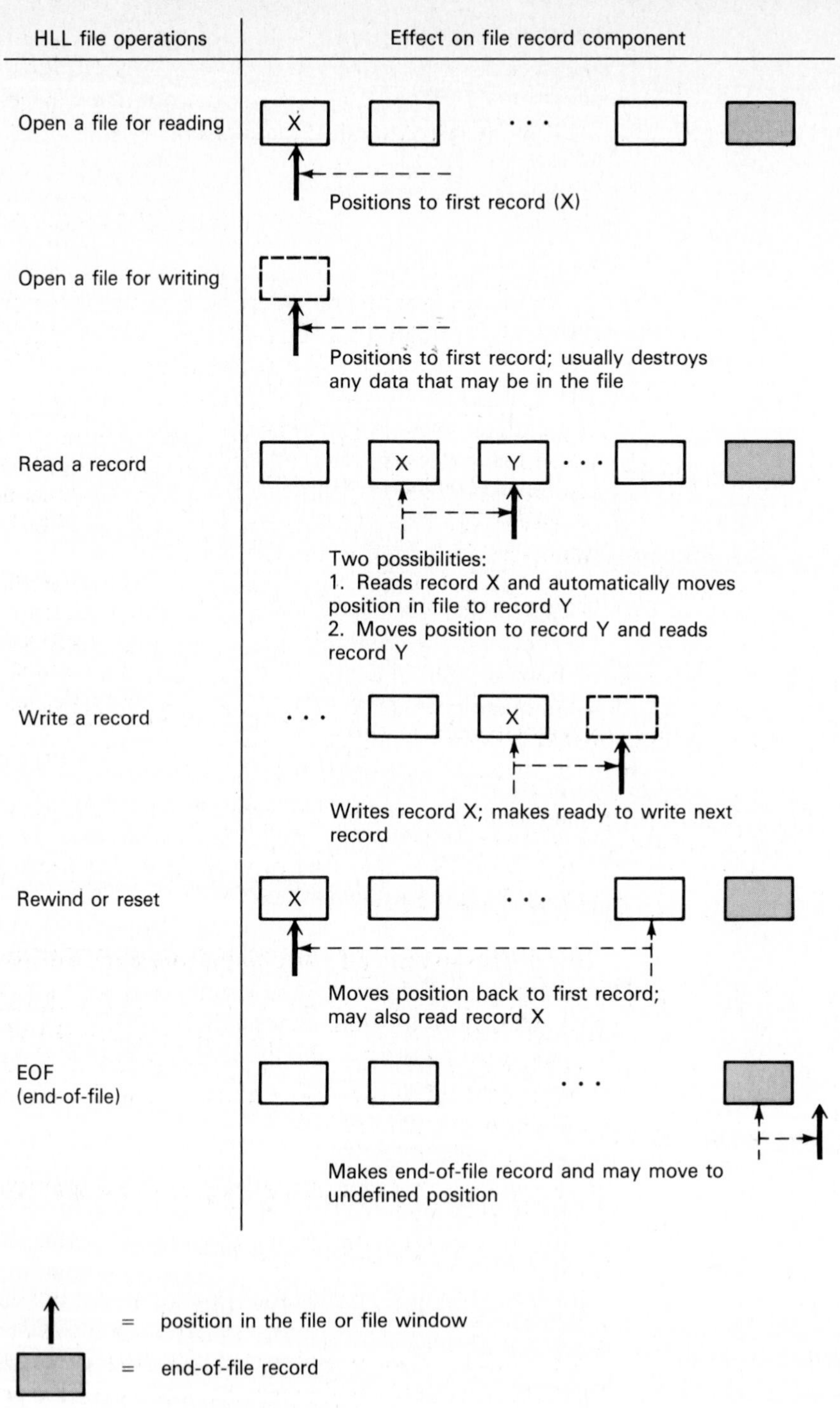

HLL file operations
Effect on file record component
Open a file for reading
X
Positions to first record (X)
Open a file for writing
Positions to first record; usually destroys any data that may be in the file
Read a record
X
Y
Two possibilities:
1. Reads record X and automatically moves position in file to record Y
2. Moves position to record Y and reads record Y
Write a record
X
Writes record X; makes ready to write next record
Rewind or reset
X
Moves position back to first record; may also read record X
EOF (end-of-file)
Makes end-of-file record and may move to undefined position
= position in the file or file window
= end-of-file record

Fig. 8-9 The operations which HLLs might control on sequential-access (SA) files.

in two popular languages. HLL keywords are shown using capital letters. Lowercase letters imply that information will have to be supplied by the programmer. The details of the information can be found in the chapters devoted to the individual languages.

TABLE 8-1 HLL SA FILE OPERATIONS

Operation	Pascal	BASIC†
Open for read		OPEN <SA file information>
Open for write	REWRITE <SA file information>	OPEN <SA file information>
Read a record component	GET <file record> READ <file record>**	INPUT# <SA file information> LINEINPUT# <SA file information>
Write a record component	PUT <file record> WRITE <file record>**	PRINT# <SA file information> WRITE# <SA file information> PRINT# <n>, USING <SA file information>
Rewind or reset	RESET <SA file>	CLOSE, then REOPEN file
Test for end-of-file	EOF <file>§	EOF <SA file information>

† Microsoft BASIC version 2.0.
** May not be used with some versions of Pascal for SA files.
§ Can be used to check for EOF but will not write such a record. This is done automatically in Pascal.

Direct-access, or DA, files differ from SA files. The programmer must specify a record number when referring to a DA file because each record can be addressed or accessed independently. Since a record number is supplied with DA files, operations such as REWIND or RESET or ENDFILE are normally not valid.

Example 8-4 HLL DA File Commands

Table 8-2 shows the operations that are permitted on DA files. In addition, the table includes the related HLL statements in Pascal and BASIC. Only important HLL keywords are shown using capital letters. Lowercase letters show information that is to be supplied by the programmer. The details of this information can be found in the chapters devoted to the individual languages.

TABLE 8-2 HLL DA FILE OPERATIONS

Operation	Pascal*	BASIC**
Open for read	RESET ⟨DA file information⟩	OPEN ⟨DA file information⟩
Open for write	REWRITE ⟨DA file information⟩	OPEN ⟨DA file information⟩
Read a record component	GET ⟨DA file information⟩ READ ⟨DA file information⟩	GET ⟨DA file information⟩
Write a record component	PUT ⟨DA file information⟩ WRITE ⟨DA file information⟩	PUT ⟨DA file information⟩
Locate a DA component	SEEK ⟨DA file information⟩	
Terminate a connection	CLOSE ⟨DA file information⟩	CLOSE ⟨DA file information⟩

* Some versions of Pascal do *not* have DA statements. This version is OMSI (Oregon Minicomputer Software, Inc.) Pascal-1 version 1.2 for use with the Digital Equipment Corporations RT-11 operating system. Read carefully the Pascal language programmer's manual for the computer being used to be sure DA files are permitted and to learn what must be done to create such files.
** Microsoft BASIC version 2.0.

PROBLEMS FOR SECTION 8-4

1. What SA file operations are not provided in the HLL Pascal?
2. What happens to the data in the SA file named "myfile" after the following Pascal procedure is executed?

```
REWRITE (myfile);
```

3. Using Microsoft BASIC, write a statement which reads the next record from a random file into the computer. Assume that the file has been previously opened as connection 1.
4. Using Microsoft BASIC, write a record to a DA file which has already been opened as 2. The record number is 25.
5. For the OMSI version of Pascal, what statement will position the file window to record 16 of the DA file named "success"?

8-5 MOVING THE DATA

To move the data between the computer and the outside world (or the reverse), it is usually necessary to specify how much data is to be moved and the nature of this data. Are these characters? Are these integers? If so, how many integers should the computer transfer or how many integers should the computer expect to receive? Description of the data is called the *format* or *arrangement* of the data. Data format requirements vary widely in HLLs. (Formats and specific data-moving statements can be found in the chapters on the individual languages.)

Example 8-5 Data-Moving Key Words in Various HLLs

Table 8-3 shows the reserved words which control the movement of data into or out of the computer.

TABLE 8-3 SUMMARY OF DATA-MOVING KEYWORDS IN HLL

Purpose of Operation	BASIC	Pascal
Moves data into the computer from a device or file	GET INPUT INPUT# INP LINE INPUT LINE INPUT#	GET READ READLN
Moves data from the computer to a device or file	PRINT PRINT USING PRINT# LPRINT LPRINT USING WRITE WRITE# OUT PUT	PUT WRITELN WRITE PAGE (a data format control; does not actually move data)

8-6 COMPLETE I/O OPERATIONS

A program is a fixed set of operations on the data which the computer receives or uses to generate results. It is clear that the computer would not be very helpful if it could not receive data from the external world or send results to the outside world. Moving data can be thought of as a series of steps:

1. Open a communication channel or pipe between the computer and the source or destination of the data.
2. Organize (format or arrange) the data to be moved.
3. Move (read or write) the data.
4. Close the channel when the data has been moved.

In some languages one or more of these steps may be invisible or combined into a single statement. The programmer does not have to include separate statements to carry out such steps. These steps are performed even if they are transparent. The steps describe a sensible (logical) way to think of the job of moving data between the computer and the world outside the machine.

SUMMARY

Input/output (I/O) operations which are found in HLLs and computers move data between the computer itself and other devices. These devices are part of the external world and are called peripherals. These operations allow a user to enter the programs to be run by the computer and the data to be used by the programs. Finally, I/O operations move the results of the program to the outside world. The I/O operations implemented depend a great deal on the HLL being used; they vary from one machine to another. I/O operations are the most individual parts of the computer and the HLLs which can be run on these machines. When you use an HLL for a particular computer, consult the guide for your particular machine. These guides or manuals will have titles such as

<HLL> Programmer's Manual
<HLL> User's Manual
<HLL> User's Guide
<HLL> Programmer's Guide

where <HLL> will be the language that you are using.

The difference between machines can be troublesome when you attempt to run a program on your computer which was designed for another machine. This can be the case even if you are using the same HLL. However, even though I/O operations vary, they can be divided into a series of common logical steps.

Collecting or organizing the data to be moved can be thought of as a series of smaller jobs or tasks (subtasks). HLL statements will specify:

- How much data
- The meaning of the data:

  Does it form a message?
  Is it to be assigned or associated with variables in the program?

- The physical arrangement of the data:

  How many letters in the message?
  How many digits in the data numbers?
  Are there decimal points in the numbers?
  If so, where are they?

All these answers taken together make up the format of the data to be moved.

Data is usually treated in groups, known as files. There are two main types of files. If any component in the file can be retrieved as readily as any other, then the file is called a direct-access, or DA file. It may also be called a relative or random-access file. If a given file component (a particular record) can be located only by examining all records from the beginning of the file, the file is called a sequential-access, or SA file.

Keywords such as READ, WRITE, PRINT, INPUT, OUT, GET, or PUT can be found in HLLs. These keywords translate into "move the data." READ, INPUT, or GET moves data from a peripheral to the computer. WRITE, PRINT, OUT, or PUT moves data from the computer to a peripheral.

Finally, the computer must be programmed to close the channel which was established in the beginning. These channels will now be available for a new I/O operation. While some computers or HLLs will close channels when a programmer forgets to do so, it is good practice to close communication channels in the program itself.

REVIEW QUESTIONS

1. What kind of HLL statements control movement of data between the computer and a user?
2. Name four pieces of information which are required to move data from one part of the computer to another.
3. Name four possible sources of data.
4. Name five possible data destinations.
5. What describes the arrangement of data which is moved between different parts of the computer?
6. What often happens when data to be printed requires more positions than indicated in a program?
7. In what form does the computer send and receive information?
8. Name two methods for transferring data between the computer and the external world.
9. Describe serial transmission of data.
10. Name two kinds of serial transmission schemes.
11. Define the term "data stream."
12. Name three logical parts or steps of a communication process.
13. What is a standard connection?
14. Name an HLL which does not require an explicit OPEN operation.
15. Describe two variations of the OPEN statement in BASIC.
16. Name two purposes for a secondary address.
17. What is a file?
18. Name and describe two methods for accessing file data.
19. What kind of statement disconnects a file from the computer?

GETTING STARTED ON A COMPUTER

The computer is a tool which can assist us in our daily activities. As with all tools, the intelligence needed to use the computer ultimately comes from the human user. Computers are useful and powerful because we have been able to devise methods to command and control them. These methods rely on English-like statements which specify the operations which the computer is to carry out. The computer cannot act directly on such commands. Instead, the statements must be converted or translated into a series of numbers that the computer can use. Because modern computers are very sophisticated machines, the translation can, and usually is, performed by the computer itself. This chapter will explain what steps the programmer can expect to take to perform the translation, and then execute the program once the translation is complete.

9-1 HARDWARE AND SOFTWARE OVERVIEW

One useful way to think of a computer system is shown in Fig. 9-1. The system starts with hardware, which includes elements described in pre-

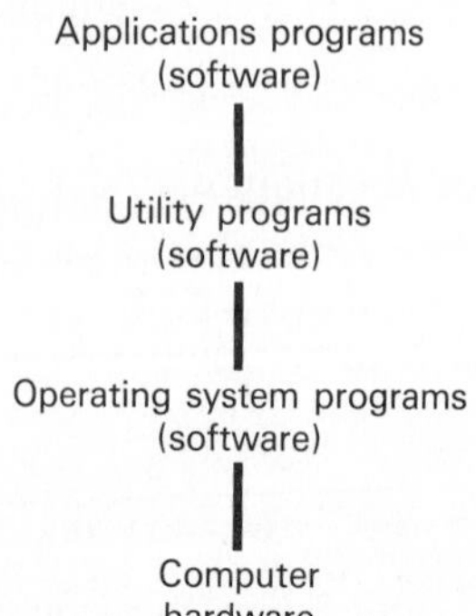

Fig. 9-1 A useful way to think of computers: as a combination (hierarchy) of hardware and software.

vious chapters: the CPU, the main memory, the secondary storage system, the terminal, and peripheral devices such as printers or other special-purpose machines. By itself, the hardware is not particularly useful because it can be very cumbersome to use. For this reason computers usually come equipped with a series of programs that greatly simplify use of the hardware. These programs, taken together, are referred to as the *operating system* (*OS*).

The operating system provides the series of instructions that the computer needs to perform such primitive functions as displaying a character on the screen, accepting a keystroke from the keyboard, opening a file and creating a directory listing on the secondary storage system, and keeping track of the allocation of memory. Such operations are typically required by other programs. One can think of these programs as *building blocks*, provided by the manufacturer of the computer system, to simplify and standardize the way these universal tasks are performed.

Utility programs consist of software that provides functions which supplement the operating system and provide higher-level functions. Examples of such software include the very important HLL translating programs that convert statements written in an HLL to a form which can be executed by the computer. These utility programs are closely related to the operating system. Consider a translation program that must convert the BASIC PRINT statement. This statement would call upon the portions of the operating system that cause characters to be displayed on the console device (usually a screen monitor). The translator makes use of the routines provided in the operating system to perform this function. The design of the translation program is simplified since it need not know how to communicate with the screen directly; it need only know how to get the operating system to perform that function.

Finally, *applications software* is the series of commands or programs which instruct the computer to perform the specific tasks that the programmer has in mind: calculate a payroll, design an electronic circuit, control operation of a steel smelting plant, or process words. It is the specific combination of hardware, operating system, and application software that makes the computer such a valuable and versatile tool.

PROBLEMS FOR SECTION 9-1

1. Name five application programs in addition to the translation programs cited above.

2. Name at least three programs that you think should be included in a computer operating system.

9-2 HLL Translation

The process of writing and executing a program on a computer, assuming it has been equipped with a suitable operating system, can be broken down into a series of logical steps or operations. These steps will be detailed later but can be broadly summarized as follows:

1. Carefully specify the problem to be solved and the method of solution (algorithm).
2. Following the logical and syntactical rules of a selected HLL, write out the program which is to be used to implement the solution, and enter this program into the computer. This is done with the aid of a program called an *editor.* Many operating systems include an editor, or a commercially available editor program may be used. The process of entering the program, or making changes in the program stored in the computer, is called *editing*.
3. Translate the HLL commands to machine-executable form and execute this program on the computer. These operations are performed with the help of utility programs available to the machine.

While these steps describe the overall process, they differ in detail from one computer installation to another. One reason for this rests on the fact that there are several ways in which to translate HLL programs. The two most important ways are shown in Fig. 9-2.

Figure 9-2*a* shows how HLL translation is performed using *compilation*. The original set of program statements, written in the HLL, is called the *source program* or *source code*. To successfully translate this program, the computer must be supplied with a program called a *compiler.* Such

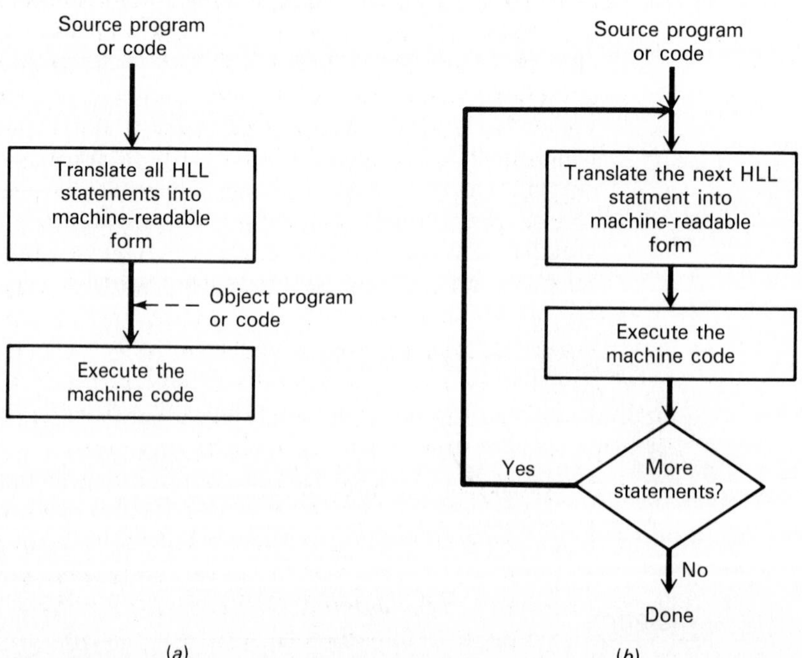

Fig. 9-2 Two kinds of HLL translation schemes, (*a*) Compiled method. (*b*) Interpretive version.

programs are not usually part of the operating system. In most cases they must be purchased from a company which manufactures such software.

The compiler accepts source code as its input and produces code in a machine-executable form (machine language code) as a result. The code produced by a compiler is called the *object program* or *object code*. Next, the object code is loaded from the secondary storage device on which it has been stored into the main memory of the computer, where it can be executed. The program which performs the loading operation is called a *loader*.

To summarize, translation of an HLL program by compilation is a two-step process comprised of compiling followed by loading. Only then can the program be executed.

One additional detail should be mentioned: the object code may include references to programs which are stored in a *library* of programs (functions or utilities). These program segments must be loaded into the computer together with the object code. This process is called *linking*. (The object program is linked to all required software routines.) A program which performs this operations is called a *linker,* or *linkage editor.* The linking and loading operations may be performed concurrently on many computer systems, in which case the program is often called a *linking loader.*

Figure 9-2*b* describes a second method of translation and execution, called *interpretive*. Each statement of the HLL source program is translated into machine-executable form as it is encountered in the program sequence. The resultant machine code is then executed by the computer. This process (translate-execute) is continued until there are no more HLL statements left to execute. Interpretive languages take longer to execute than compiled languages because they must be translated each time they are executed, and because they do not include pretranslated source code. However, interpretive programs are quicker to modify because they do not have to be recompiled after each program modification. One simply makes the necessary changes and executes (runs) the program again. There is no need to repeat compilation, linking, and loading.

Most languages operate in only one form, as either compiled or interpretive languages. However, some HLLs include a combination of compilation and interpretation. For such languages the source code is first compiled. The resultant object code is not in a machine-executable form. Instead, it exists in a second symbolic form. This intermediate language code becomes the input to another program which performs the interpret-execute sequence characteristic of interpretive programs. Such languages are slower to execute than compiled languages but faster than pure interpretive languages. They have one advantage: they are easier to transport from one type of computer to another. The intermediate code can be distributed to users. Then, only the interpreter program needs to be custom-designed for different CPUs or operating systems.

Finally, it is important to note that a given HLL may be available in two or more translation forms. For example, there are both compiled and interpretive versions of BASIC and Pascal.

PROBLEMS FOR SECTION 9-2

1. Draw a diagram similar to the ones shown in Fig. 9-2 which describes the translation process for combined compiled-interpretive languages.

2. During compilation, interpretation, or execution of an HLL program, the computer may detect errors. These errors include syntactical mistakes (HLL rule violation) and execution errors, such as trying to divide a number by zero. Modify the diagrams shown in Fig. 9-2 to include changes in the translation processes due to error detection.

9-3 DEVELOPING APPLICATIONS PROGRAMS

The step-by-step process for developing applications programs is presented in Fig. 9-3 in the form of a flow diagram and in the following steps (note that Fig. 9-3*a* shows the case for compiled languages and Fig. 9-3*b* depicts the circumstances for interpretive languages):

- Developing software using a compiled HLL starts with a complete specification of the problem to be solved. This must be done carefully, as it forms the basis for all the work that follows. Once the problem has been defined, a solution (algorithm) can be outlined. The algorithm may first be outlined using a symbolic notation such as a flow diagram.
- The logic represented in the flow diagram is then converted into the HLL statements which will actually perform the desired function. These statements are entered into the computer using an editor which permits the programmer to enter and modify HLL programs in a convenient manner.
- The source code which now resides within the computer's secondary storage system is translated. If the translation process is successful, then an object program is produced. If, during the translation, syntactical errors or rule violations are detected, the compiler program informs the user of such errors. These errors must be corrected before the compiler can produce a satisfactory object code. Syntactical errors are eliminated by editing the source program. The edit-compile sequence is repeated until all the syntactical errors have been removed. However, this does not imply that the program is error-free. The program may still contain errors in logic even though the syntax is correct.

Once an object code module exists, it can be linked to other programs within the computer which may be needed to carry out the desired operations. (Such programs may exist within a library.) The linked version of the program can now be loaded from the secondary storage system into the main memory and executed. Some logical errors, such as attempted division by zero, may cause the program to *crash*, or cease executing. However, even if no logical errors are detected, you must examine the results of the program carefully to determine if they make sense. A statement specifying addition when subtraction is desired may be syntactically

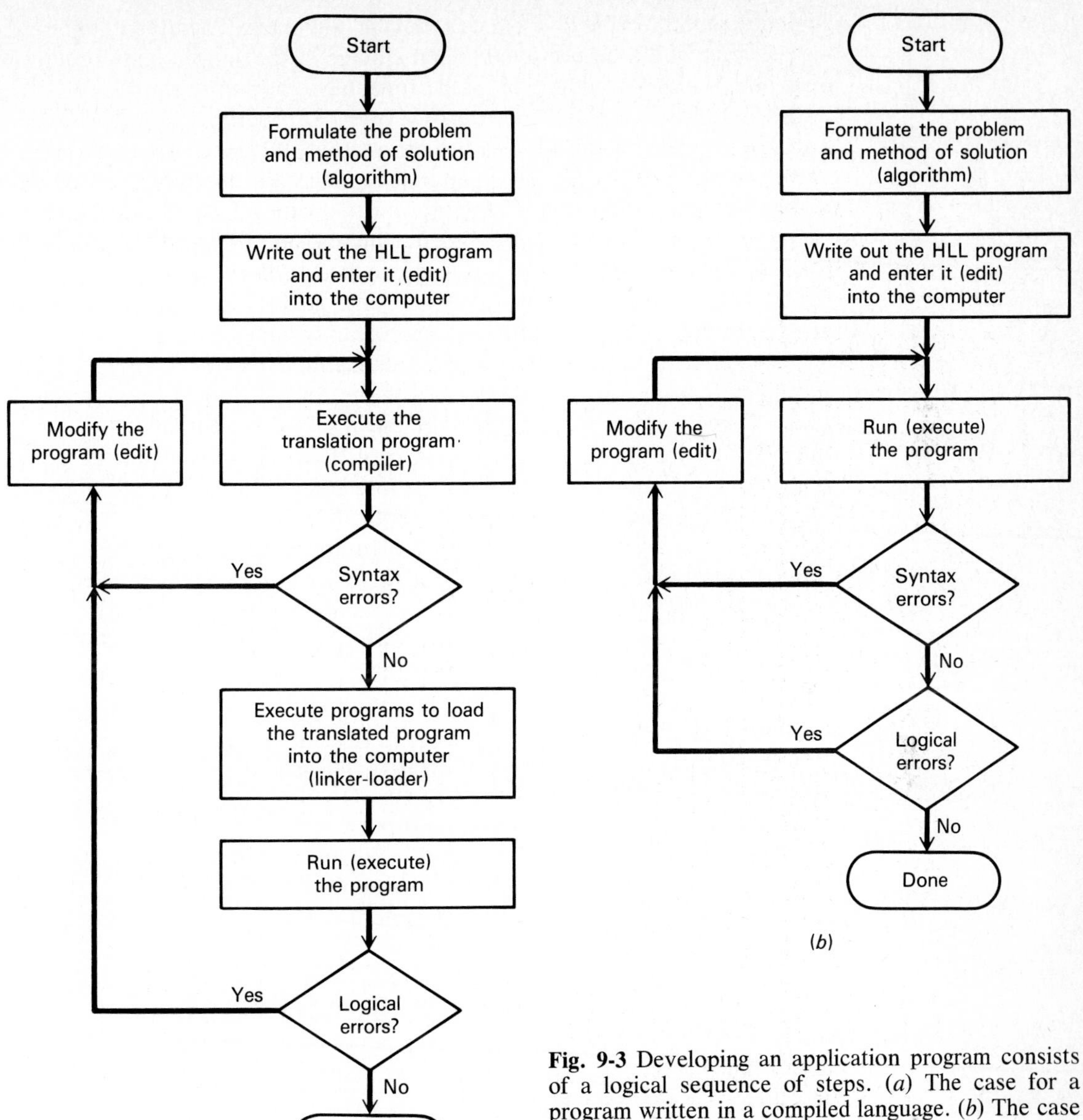

Fig. 9-3 Developing an application program consists of a logical sequence of steps. (*a*) The case for a program written in a compiled language. (*b*) The case for a program to be developed using an interpretive language.

correct but will produce incorrect results. A good way to test the program is to consider some typical cases or values for the data. Using the values of the test case, "walk through" (manually perform) the intended calculations to determine if the results agree with those produced by the computer. If the results do not match, the programmer must track down the source of the discrepancy through the process of *debugging*.

One way to do this is to temporarily insert HLL commands (in the source code) to report intermediate results. These intermediate results help to locate the errors, which can then be corrected. Then the temporary instructions would be removed. Each change in the source code requires that the edit-compile link process be repeated.

Successful development of interpretive HLL programs (Fig. 9-3*b*) also starts out with an accurate and precise statement of the problem and its intended solution. The algorithm intended to meet the needs of the problem is then designed, and the HLL program is written and entered into the computer. Again, this occurs under the supervision of an editor program. Now, however, program development proceeds differently.

The source program which has been entered into the computer exists as a file in the secondary storage system or may have been left in memory by the editor. If stored, the file is loaded into the main memory of the computer, possibly with a command of the form "LOAD myprogram," where "myprogram" is the name of the file which contains the source code. When this has been performed (or if the program was left in memory), one may issue a command to the interpreter which actually initiates the translation and execution of the application program now resident in main memory. To do so might require a command such as RUN.

Recall that interpretive systems function by translating each instruction as it is encoutered in the program into machine code and then executing the resultant code. This can be particularly inefficient and slow. An HLL statement must be translated each time it is encountered; if a given HLL statement is in a loop which executes 100 times, then that statement must be translated 100 times.

Now, all errors, syntactical or otherwise, are detected at *run* (execution) time. If a run-time error is detected, the computer will halt with an error message on the standard (or normal) output device—usually the terminal—indicating the nature of the problem. The offending statement may be examined and altered as necessary. The program may then be executed again without resort to the edit-compile-link-load sequence needed for compiled languages.

The need for checking results with test values is the same as for compiled languages. Temporary statements can help locate logically incorrect operations. When this debugging process is complete, an error-free version of the interpretive program resides in the main memory. This program can be stored on the secondary storage system with a command such as "SAVE myprogram." The old version of the program will then be replaced with the newer, corrected version.

PROBLEMS FOR SECTION 9-3

1. What are some other run-time errors, in addition to the divide-by-zero example cited above? List as many as you can.
2. An error message "Device timeout" appears on your terminal and the computer halts. What do you think this means?

9-4 THE COMPUTER OPERATING SYSTEM AND WHAT IT DOES

The key to all the operations outlined in the preceding sections is the computer's operating system. To understand just what an OS does, consider what everyday activities would be like without any organization or order. For the student this would mean attending a school which consists of the physical plant—classrooms, chairs, etc.—without assigned lecture hours or laboratory hours. The laboratory might include equipment but no user rules. A similar situation would exist in the workplace if there were no organization of the tasks associated with work activities. People would not know their assigned tasks, when to use the machines or business equipment, or how to coordinate their activities with other workers. (There would be no indication of the time or duration of coffee breaks.)

The computer's hardware is a combination of electronic and electromechanical parts. It is the computer's OS which transforms this bare machine into a useful tool. The OS consists of a program, or rather a series of programs, which can be used to control the computer hardware in an efficient, flexible, and easy (user-friendly) manner. There are many OSs; in fact, you can often execute a number of different OSs on the same computer hardware—not at the same time, of course. These OSs differ in their capabilities, in the amount of computer (main) memory, secondary storage, and other resources which they require, as well as in the speed with which they complete various operations. Some OSs are designed to execute on large computer systems which service many users, while others are intended for use on small computers involving one user at a time (*single user*).

No matter what the size or complexity of the OS, its programs have several well-defined jobs to do. These include:

1. Schedule the work or programs to be executed by the CPU. This part of the OS can be referred to as the *scheduler*.
2. Provide a standard interface to the computer's peripherals (particularly those involved with input/output) and to other programs so that these programs need not concern themselves with specific details regarding the nature of the devices connected to the computer. For example, a program need not specify how a file is to be stored on a secondary storage device but only that this operation is to occur. The OS will contain the software specific to the particular model of disk drive installed (which may vary from one computer to another) and will perform the program's requested operation.
3. Organize and keep track of the user's programs and data on the secondary storage system. This is a special subset of task 2, and is referred to as the file system (see Sec. 9-5).

PROBLEMS FOR SECTION 9-4

1. Suppose you were asked to design a scheduler. Suggest some topics (scheduling problems) you would have to consider in your design.

2. A file system for a computer is to be shared among a number of users (a *time-shared system*). As one of the users, what would you consider important features and capabilities of such a file system? (You may consider both hardware and software features in your answer.)

9-5 THE FILE SYSTEM

The main memory of the computer normally stores small amounts of programs and data. To overcome the limitations of main memory, the OS makes use of the relatively large, but slower, *secondary storage system*. Because the secondary storage system can retain large amounts of information, it must be organized in an efficient manner. If not, it will take an unreasonable amount of time to find a given piece of data, greatly slowing the operation of the OS. The organization of the secondary storage system is often referred to as the *file system*.

An important principle in the organization of any file system is to minimize the time it takes to locate a given piece of information.

Example 9-1 Arranging Data Efficiently

Figure 9-4 shows two ways to arrange wiring data for all the products

wiring X-band radar subass1	wiring radar V-band subass2
wiring sonar subass1	wiring VHF receiver subass1
parts sonar subass2	wiring VHF receiver subass2
wiring UHF receiver subass1	wiring navigation Loran subass2
wiring navigation Loran subass1	wiring UHF transmitter subass1
parts radar X-band subass1	wiring UHF transmitter subass2
wiring radar X-band subass2	wiring navigation Shoran subass1
wiring sonar subass2	wiring navigation Shoran subass2
wiring sonar subass3	wiring ULF transmitter subass1
wiring radar V-band subass1	wiring ULF transmitter subass2

(a)

wiring

radars	sonars	transmitters	receivers	navigation
X-band	subass1	UHF	UHF	Loran
subass1	subass2	subass1	subass1	subass1
subass2	subass3	subass2	VHF	subass2
V-band		ULF	subass1	Shoran
subass1		subass1	subass2	subass1
subass2		subass2		subass2

(b)

Fig. 9-4 Methods for organizing data. *(a)* A strictly serial method. *(b)* A hierarchical breakdown.

manufactured by one company. In the first arrangement (Fig. 9-4*a*) the data is arranged in a strictly serial fashion without regard to the type of product or subassembly within the product. Figure 9-4*b* shows a more efficient way to organize such data. The wiring lists for the various products are divided into logical groups. Within each group the lists are further divided into the product itself and the subassemblies which are used in that product.

To see why the second arrangement is more efficient, consider the following problem. Using the arrangement shown in Fig. 9-4*a*, locating the wiring list for subassembly 1 (subass1) of the Shoran navigation system requires 17 names to be examined starting with "Wiring X-band radar subass1." On the average, 10 accesses are needed to locate any given item. If one can access the groups directly, the organization shown in Fig. 9-4*b* requires only five steps.

On average, one needs three accesses to locate an item in the arrangement shown in Fig. 9-4*b*. If searching for the wiring list were being carried out by the computer, the second data arrangement would have a speed advantage of 3.3 to 1 over the first method.

The efficient data arrangement described in Example 9-1 uses a *hierarchical* arrangement for the data; it is found repeatedly throughout computer technology. In such an arrangement, data is combined into collections of items. This collection is called a *file*. The names of files are then grouped together and are listed in *directories*. A picture of this type of organization is shown in Fig. 9-5. One form of the hierarchical arrangement is shown

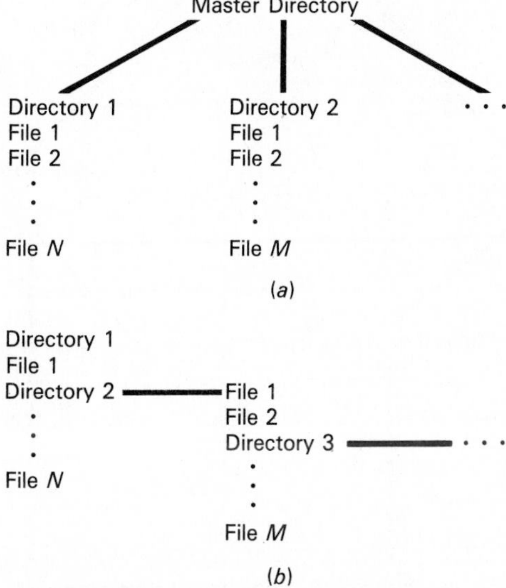

Fig. 9-5 Data is grouped into files, and such files may be organized as (*a*) a master directory system, or (*b*) a nested directory system.

in Fig. 9-5*a*. This consists of a master directory that contains a list of all other directories. Each of the *subdirectories* contains the names of files of data items. An alternative arrangement is shown in Fig. 9-5*b*. This form permits a directory (name) to be included within another directory—this may lead to a *nested* file structure.

Example 9-2 The Tree-Structured File System of PC-DOS (IBM)

A typical example of the hierarchical arrangement of user information on the secondary storage system is found in the OS known as PC-DOS—the letters "DOS" stand for *disk operating system*. The hierarchical organization can be referred to as a *tree structure*. One example of a file system in DOS is shown in Fig. 9-6. The figure contains a picture of the tree. It could be part of a larger directory system which includes other departments of the company such as accounting and personnel. The *master directory*,

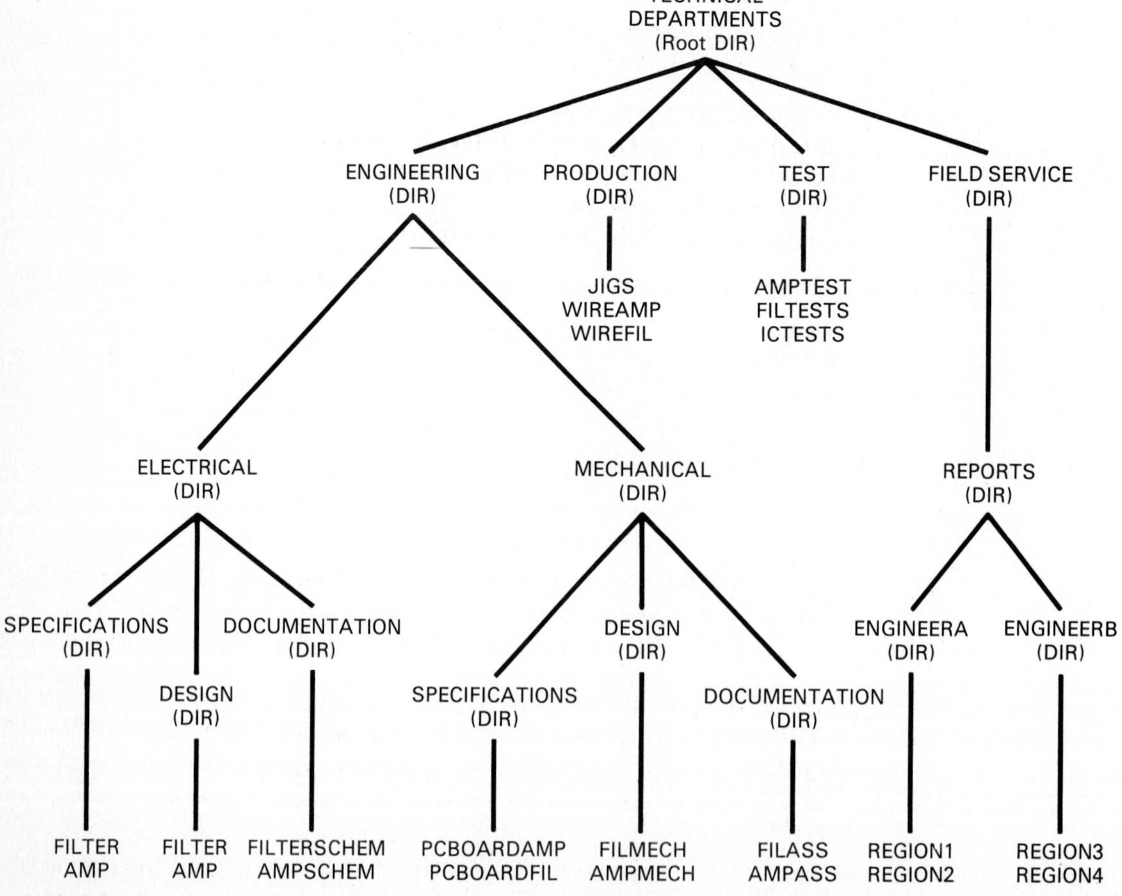

Fig. 9-6 A tree-structured file system under the PC-DOS operating system.

which may correspond to the *root directory*, is named TECHNICAL DEPARTMENTS. Four subdirectories are named within the root directory. The subdirectories may contain either names of files or other subdirectories.

Example 9-3 Displaying the Contents of a Directory

The directories in Fig. 9-6 are deliberately shown in pictorial form. The computer does not retain such a description of the directories and files. A common representation of a directory on a computer which executes PC-DOS is shown in Fig. 9-7. Figure 9-7*a* shows what a computer might report

```
                 Volume in drive B has no label
                 Directory of B:\

ENGNRNG          <DIR>          6-30-87     9:30a
PRDCTION         <DIR>          3-04-87    13:45p
TEST             <DIR>          3-08-87    10:52a
FIELDSRV         <DIR>          3-10-87    15:09p
               4 File(s)     5899 bytes free
```

(*a*)

```
                 Volume in drive B has no label
                 Directory of B:\prdction

                 <DIR>          3-04-87    13:45p
..               <DIR>          3-04-87    13:45p
JIGS              3968          4-01-87    11:54a
WIREAMP          25267          4-23-87    15:00p
WIREFIL          10822          5-11-87     9:15a
               5 File(s)     5899 bytes free
```

(*b*)

Fig. 9-7 (*a*) A sample of the way the computer reports a directory to the user. (*b*) A subdirectory looks slightly different from a directory.

for the TECHNICAL DEPARTMENTS directory, while Fig. 9-7*b* shows a similar listing for the subdirectory PRDCTION. The TECHNICAL DEPARTMENTS directory contains four entries. These are each followed by the designation "<DIR>," which indicates that the entry is itself a directory.

Following the DIR designation are the date and time at which the directory was first created. At the bottom of the listing is a summary which indicates that the current directory contains four files. In addition, PC-DOS indicates that there are 5899 free bytes in this particular secondary storage system.

The computer which is executing PC-DOS may have a number of secondary storage devices. Each has a logical designation consisting of a letter followed by a colon. "B:" designates one of the flexible disk drives of the computer.

Figure 9-7*b* shows the listing for the PRDCTION directory. It is slightly different from the directory shown in Fig. 9-7*a*. In particular, note the files entitled JIGS, WIREAMP, and WIREFIL. These are followed by the number of bytes occupied by each file on the disk. Again, the date and time that the file was created are also listed. Two additional entries appear in this subdirectory. These are indicated by a period (".") and a double period (".."). Both are important to the OS, but they serve primarily as a signal to the user that this listing represents a subdirectory.

To get listings of the kind shown in Fig. 9-7, the user must request the listing from the computer. For PC-DOS this is accomplished by the command

```
DIR > PRN:
```

This instructs the computer to list on the printer, which is designated by "PRN:," all the items in the directory. In order to list the PRDCTION directory, two commands are used. The first causes the computer to locate the PRDCTION directory, and the second produces a listing of the directory on the printer as before.

```
CHDIR \PRDCTION
DIR >PRN:
```

PROBLEMS FOR SECTION 9-5

1. Using the data organization shown in Fig. 9-4*b*, indicate the sequence of steps needed to locate the file containing the wiring list for subass1 of the Shoran navigation system. This should require no more than five steps.
2. Show how the data in Fig. 9-4*b* can be described as consisting of files and directories.
3. Using the commands available in PC-DOS, show how all the files in the directory TEST (Fig. 9-7*a*) can be printed.

9-6 THE PROGRAM DEVELOPMENT CYCLE FOR COMPILED LANGUAGES

Five distinct steps are necessary for successful development of a compiled computer program:

1. Initiating interactive communication with the computer (*log-on*)
2. Creating the source code for the program using the statements of the HLL, accomplished by *editing*
3. Translating the source code by use of a *compiler* program
4. Integrating routines or programs with the compiled program by linking such programs to the code (called variously, *linking* or *linking and locating*)

5. Testing the program and correcting logical errors through the process of debugging

These steps are shown in Fig. 9-8. Figure 9-8*b* shows a flow diagram which

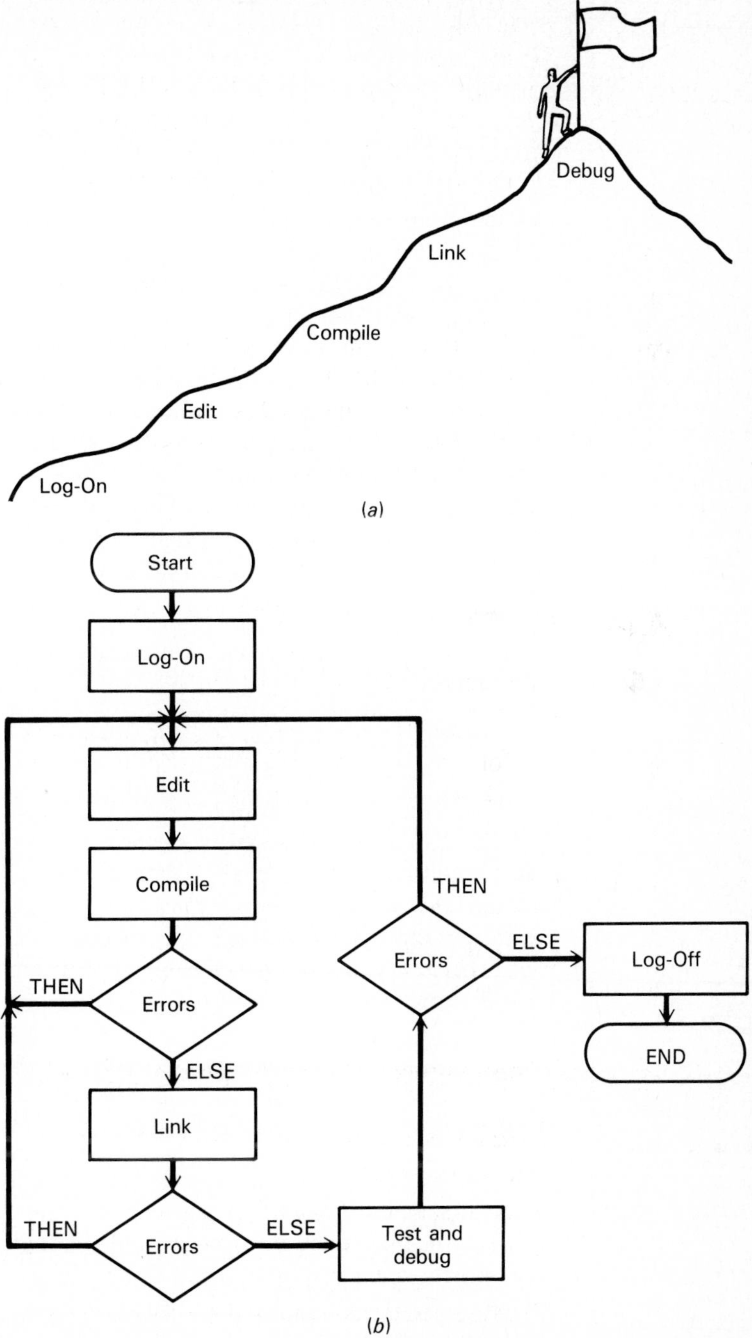

Fig. 9-8 (*a*) Successful development of an applications program written in a compiled language includes several plateaus, or milestones. (*b*) Flow diagram showing the sequence for developing successful applications programs.

indicates the relationships between the different steps. For each step of the complete process the computer or the user may detect errors. When this happens, the errors must be corrected; this is usually accomplished by returning to the editing process. This, in turn, is followed by compilation and linking. Each of the steps outlined above will be examined.

9-6-1 Initiating a Dialogue with the Computer: Logging On

There are several ways in which the overall operation of a computer and its resources may be organized. These broad categories include:

1. **Batch operation:** Individuals submit their programs to computer operators who run each job and return results to the users. (This is a more traditional way to arrange computer use and is rarely found in modern computer centers.)
2. **Multiuser operation:** A number of individuals can communicate interactively with the computer. They normally enter commands or data into the computer via a terminal which may be connected to the computer by a telephone line or local area network. The computer returns results to the monitor of the terminal. Sometimes the user has a printer located near the terminal, and printed results may appear on this device.
3. **Single-user operation:** A single individual controls all aspects of the operation of the computer. This mode of operation is common on small (personal) computers.

Each of these systems uses different procedures for starting a session on the computer.

In batch operation the computer operator performs all tasks associated with the process of running programs. Users must submit their programs and remember to collect results.

Where many users share the use of the computer and its resources, the OS must provide for security for a user's programs and data, protection from unauthorized use of the computer, and apportioning charges (billing or accounting) among the various users. To accomplish these tasks, a user initiates communication with the computer by a procedure called *logging-on*. The next example describes a typical log-on process for a multiuser installation.

Example 9-4 Logging-in Under UNIX

The UNIX OS is found on a great many computers and is representative of an OS which supports a great many users concurrently. Once a user has completed the log-on process under UNIX, the computer knows how much time each uses, what files belong to the user, and the type of terminal being used, as well as other information.

Before a user can log-on to a UNIX-based computer the administrator of the system must assign an account to that person. Once this has been done, a user may log-on at any time—as long as the computer is operational (on-line). The computer provides a prompt which indicates that log-on can proceed. A typical cue is

```
login:
```

At this point a user would enter the name of the account which has been previously established. For example, after the user types the name of the account, the terminal might show

```
login: gorsil <CR>
```

(The symbol <CR> means strike the *carriage return* key.) If this is an active account, the computer will prompt a user for the password. The password is a key which permits a user to gain access to his or her files. The prompt message might be

```
password:
```

The actual password that a user types is not echoed (visually displayed) on the monitor. This is an added safety precaution so that others cannot readily learn a user's password. If the password is correct, the computer issues a prompt or cue which notifies the user that further commands can be issued. The prompt varies from one computer to another, but "$" and "%" symbols can be found on many installations. With the symbol

```
$
```

displayed on the terminal, the user is free to issue commands to the computer such as:

```
$ vi myprog <CR>
```

This command runs a program ("vi") which permits a user to edit a file called "myprog." The file (myprog) might contain the source statements for an HLL program.

Example 9-5 A Single-User Configuration

The OS PC-DOS can be found on many small computers where only one person at a time is using the machine. In such circumstances, accounting for the use of the machine is not very important. In addition, all those who use the machine (at different times) must cooperate with regard to file security and access. The steps for initiating a working session on machines which can execute PC-DOS are typically the following:

1. Insert the disk which contains the OS program into the disk drive.
2. Turn on the computer.
3. A message such as

```
Current date is Tue 1-01-1986
Enter new date:
```

   appears on the terminal.
4. The user enters the current date (e.g., 6-20-88 <CR>).
5. The computer provides a second message:

```
Current time is 0:00:33:08
Enter new time:
```

6. The user responds with the current time (e.g., 10:36 <CR>).
7. If the user has not violated the format rules for the time or date, the computer responds with the prompt which indicates that it is ready to receive commands:

```
A>
```

   This prompt indicates that the user is logged into the secondary storage unit designated "A."

9-6-2 Creating a Source File: Editing

Each program starts out as a series of HLL statements which represent the algorithm. Such statements are collectively called the *source code*. These statements must be entered into the computer using the editing process. The editing process is under the control of another program, the editor. This program may be part of the OS, or it may be a program which has been purchased separately and has been designed to operate within the computer's OS. An editing session may consist of either creation of a new source file or modification of an existing source file.

Once the source code has been created, it will normally be saved in a file. The file also provides a record of the original program; copies can readily be made for reports or other documents.

In general there are two kinds of editors: *line editors* and *full-screen editors*.

The name "line editor" is very descriptive because such editing programs operate on lines of text. The HLL source code is treated as a group of lines of text because the statements themselves consist of alphanumeric characters terminated by a carriage return character (<CR>). Operations are carried out by specifying the line on which the editor is to act, and then specifying the action that the editor is to perform.

Screen editors provide a *window* into the text file. A full screen of text (approximately 24 lines, depending on the particular editor) is displayed and can be altered by issuing a command that operates on the text at the cursor position. Such editors are very powerful, and many operators find them easier to use than a line editor. However, when the terminal is linked to the computer via telephone lines, the transfer of information—remember, changes on the screen require transmission of 24 lines of text—can be very slow. A trade-off must be considered between speed of response and power and ease of use of the editor. Example 9-6 provides a sample session using a typical line editor, named EDLIN, which operates on machines supported by the OS PC-DOS.

Example 9-6 A Typical Line Editor—EDLIN

Table 9-1 summarizes the commands and operations which can be performed using the EDLIN program. These commands are representative of the kinds of operations which can be found in other line editors.

TABLE 9-1 SUMMARY OF LINE EDITING OPERATIONS

Command	Explanation
Append Lines	Adds lines from the file being edited to the end of text in the main memory; useful when the file must be edited in pieces because the entire file cannot fit in memory
Copy Lines	Copies one or more lines from one part of the text being edited to another part of the text
Delete Lines	Erases one or more lines
Edit Line	Specifies the line of text to be edited—accomplished by indicating its line number
Insert Lines	Inserts text; this command is used to enter text for a new file
List Lines	Displays one or more lines of the text being edited in the main memory
Move Lines	Moves a block of text data
Page	Lists 23 lines (a page) at a time
Replace Text	Replaces one string of characters with another string at each occurrence of the test string
Search Text	Locates a specified (test) string of characters
Transfer Lines	Merges the contents of a specified file into the text currently being edited
Write Lines	Writes one or more lines from main memory to a secondary storage device; permits large files to be edited in segments when combined with the Append command
End Session	Saves the text file and stops the EDLIN program
Quit Session	Ends a session without saving any changes in the text

PROBLEM FOR SECTION 9-6-2

1. Describe an important difference between the results produced by the EDLIN Move Lines command and the Copy Lines command.

9-6-3 Troubleshooting Software with a Debugging Program

Compiling (translating) an HLL program does not always disclose all errors. The compilation process may reveal the syntactical (grammatical) errors, but since compilers differ in their characteristics, some syntactical errors may go undetected until one tries to execute the program. In addition, the program's logical errors are not revealed until the program is executed.

During the last phase of program development, all errors should be eliminated. Some programs are so complex that some logical errors may go undetected for long periods of time, in some instances, years! Manufacturers and developers of software spend more time on refining and "fixing" programs than on any other aspect of program development. This part of the development cycle is called *software maintenance*.

Most often, debugging of an HLL program takes place at the source code level, that is, correcting, adding, or deleting HLL statements. However, sometimes the error that is introduced is very subtle and stems from an error that the compiler made in translating the source program into executable form. This may occur because of a previously unknown bug in the compiler that is only exhibited when an unusual combination of events occurs. Additionally, the program may use a feature of the HLL in a manner which was not supported and for which no error message was designed. As a result, the statement is not translated properly and the program does not execute correctly.

One way to locate and correct errors is by using a utility program known as a *debugger.* The purpose of the debugger is to allow the controlled execution of an object code program in an environment that allows one to examine what is happening inside the computer's memory and registers as the program executes.

A debugger may have one or more of the following capabilities:

- Permit a user to monitor and control the execution of a program to be debugged
- Fix problems in the program and then execute the modified software to determine if the problem has been corrected (retranslation should not be necessary to find out if changes work)
- Permit a user to load, alter, or display any file
- Execute programs in machine language format (object files)

The debugger displays memory contents and the object code representation of the program. Therefore, to make use of the debugger, one must have an understanding of the machine language of the computer being used, as well as binary and hexadecimal data representation. A full description of the operation of a typical debugger is beyond the scope of this text.

9-7 THE PROGRAM DEVELOPMENT CYCLE FOR INTERPRETIVE HLLS

Figure 9-9 pictures the paths available for successful development of programs written in interpretive languages. (Many HLLs now have interpretive versions.)

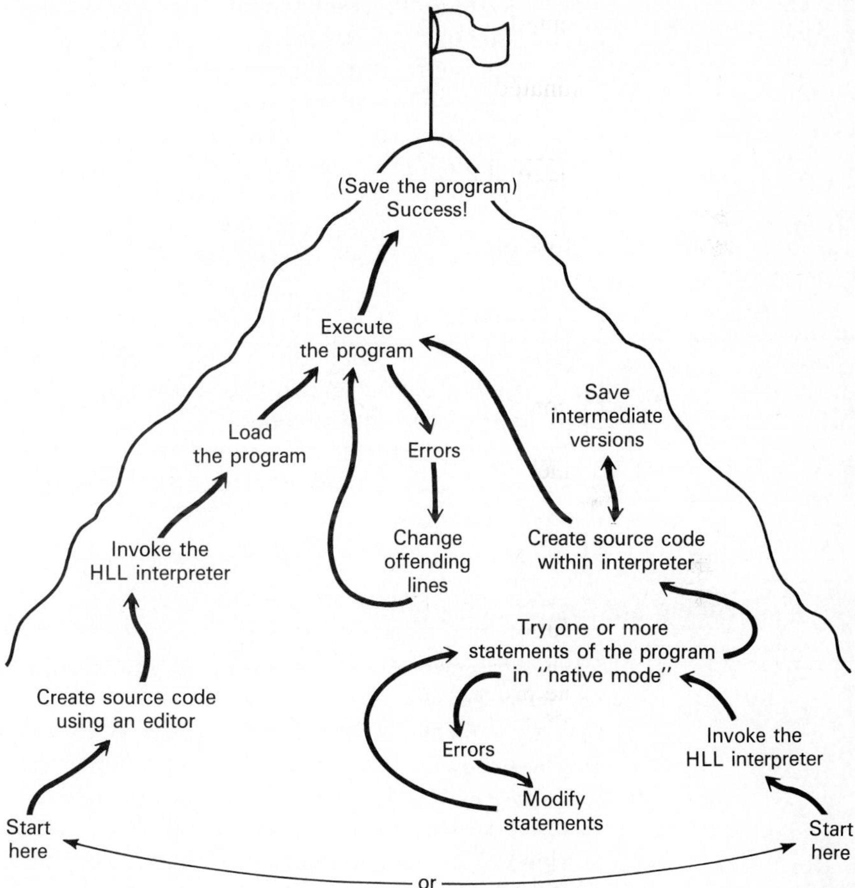

Fig. 9-9 The paths to successful development of an interpretive language applications program.

One path starts by using an editor program to create the program source code (left path of Fig. 9-9). This code is saved in a file in the secondary storage system, using the commands available within the editor. When this operation is complete, the user will usually return to the OS. The OS can then be used to invoke the program which translates and executes the source code. The program which is invoked is called an *interpreter.*

Once the interpreter resides within the main memory, it can be used to load a program from the secondary storage system, such as the one just created using the editor. Once the source code has been loaded, the interpreter is commanded to run.

During execution of the program two types of errors may occur. The programmer may have violated the syntactical rules of the HLL, or the program may contain logical errors, that is, steps which produce incorrect results. When this happens, the offending statements must be corrected and the program rerun. Eventually, all errors will be eliminated. When this occurs, the final (correct) form must be replaced on the secondary storage system. Successful (operational) programs may be executed more directly: invoke the interpreter (from the OS), load the operational program, then run (execute) the program to completion.

Some interpreters allow a user to perform two other useful operations once the interpreter is invoked; this provides a second path to developing successful programs. The interpreter often provides a way to enter source programs: it acts like an editor program.

In addition, the interpreter may include the ability to execute a single HLL statement in isolation, that is, one which is not part of a complete program. This is called *immediate mode* execution. Such statements may be tested (and debugged) before inclusion in the complete program. While the interpreter is testing or executing such individual statements, the other parts of the program remain undisturbed. Thus a program may be developed statement by statement.

Since editor programs have already been discussed, they will not be described in the sections that follow. However, some characteristics of interpreters which a user is likely to encounter will be examined, and methods for debugging interpretive language programs will be described.

9-7-1 Invoking and Using Interpreters

Language interpreters are separate programs within a computer. They may reside in the secondary storage system of the computer, in which case they are used like other programs which are executed from the computer's OS. Some interpreters reside within a portion of the computer's nonvolatile memory—in ROM. When power is first applied to the computer, the computer automatically transfers control of its operation to the resident interpreter. Some computers will transfer control to the ROM interpreter only if an OS disk is not available.

When computers are specifically designed to execute the statements of a particular HLL in an efficient and speedy manner, they may be referred to as an *engine* (e.g., a BASIC engine or a Pascal engine). While this limits the usefulness of such a computer, it does serve to optimize its performance.

Example 9-7 Calling an Interpreter from the OS

Consider the case of the BASIC interpreter which is invoked from within the PC-DOS OS. While PC-DOS is awaiting a user's instructions, a prompt appears on the monitor. The prompt symbol is usually ">," and is preceded by a designation for the secondary storage system where the programs to be invoked are assumed to be located. Thus,

A>

may appear on the monitor, indicating that the computer assumes that files will be located on the part of the secondary storage system which has the designation "A" (generally one of the disk drives), and indicating that the OS is awaiting a command. To invoke the BASIC interpreter, the user types

basic {or basica for a more powerful interpreter}

followed by <CR>. The complete line looks like,

A> basic <CR>

After the interpreter has itself been loaded, the computer prompts the user that it is ready to accept commands. Figure 9-10 shows how the monitor may appear. (There are other details regarding the way BASIC is invoked, but these vary from one computer installation to another and they have been omitted for clarity and ease of understanding.)

The phrase "OK" is the prompt that this interpreter uses to indicate that it is ready to accept commands. The bottom of the monitor contains

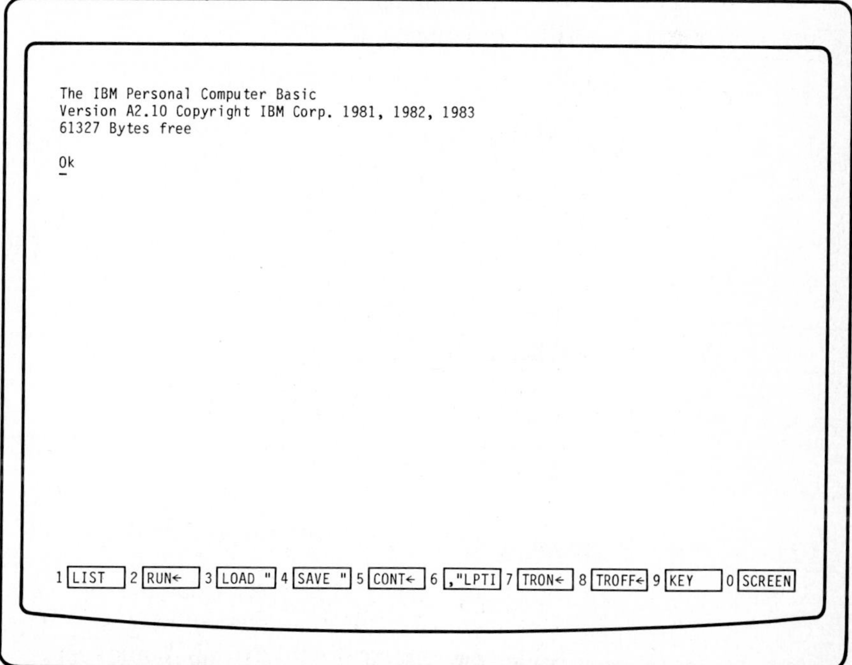

Fig. 9-10 The monitor of an IBM-PC after the BASICA interpreter has been invoked under the PC-DOS OS.

some visual aids for the user. A series of keys (called *function keys*) may be used to invoke certain commands rapidly. These keys have numbers (F1 to F10), and the legend spells out the purpose of each key. For example, the F2 key can be used to run a BASIC program resident in main memory.

To be useful, an interpreter has several commands available to the user. Such commands may also be available to be used within an HLL program, but, in general, they provide a convenient method for controlling the movement of programs and data into and out of the main memory in addition to providing debugging aids. We shall differentiate between commands that control the interpreter and statements which appear inside an HLL program.

Example 9-8 Using the PC BASIC Interpreter

A number of typical interpreter commands are found in IBM PC BASIC. For manipulating programs and data, the following commands are useful:

LIST
RUN
LOAD "programname"
SAVE "programname"

Each command is discussed below.

- LIST. There are a number of forms of the LIST command. For explanatory purposes, only the simplest form is presented. If the user types LIST, the interpreter displays, on the monitor, the statements which comprise the program currently in memory. If the program is too long to be displayed in one screenful of text, the lowest-numbered statements will scroll off the top of the screen as new lines are added at the bottom. It is also possible to display the program in segments; if the user types LIST 1,10 then all program statements with line numbers from 1 to 10, inclusive, will be displayed.
- RUN. Typing RUN causes the program to start execution at the lowest-numbered line and proceed to its conclusion. Typing RUN 25 causes the program to start with the statement which is numbered 25. This form is useful when debugging or testing part of a program.
- LOAD "programname." Typing LOAD "MYPROG" will load the file (program) named MYPROG from the secondary storage device into main memory. This is necessary before attempting to run a program. An alternative form of the RUN command is RUN "programname," where the file "programname" is loaded and then automatically executed.
- SAVE "programname." Once the HLL program in memory has been

debugged, it is essential to save it in the secondary storage system. The SAVE command allows a user to perform this operation. Typing SAVE "B:MYPROG" will save the BASIC program presently in memory on the secondary storage device which is designated "B:" with the name MYPROG.

PROBLEMS FOR SECTION 9-7-1

To solve the following problems refer to Example 9-8.

1. Write a BASIC command which will save a program named WIRELIST on drive A of the computer.
2. Specify the command which lists all lines of a program from 1 to 100.
3. What command will run a BASIC program stored in main memory, starting at line number 100?
4. What command will load a BASIC program whose name is TIMER from secondary storage device B?

9-7-2 Debugging Interpretive Language Programs

There are two techniques which can be used when testing or debugging interpretive language programs. The first is to insert test statements at various points in the program. These statements are temporary, and once the program has been debugged, they are removed. Such statements are often simply PRINT statements, which, when executed, will instruct the computer to display results up to that point in the program. They serve two useful purposes: the results which are reported (displayed on the monitor or printed out) can be checked for consistency with the algorithm, and second, this serves as a check that the program sequence has reached the designated place in the program.

The second debugging technique makes use of the resources and functions which may be available to the user in the interpreter. The following example demonstrates one interpreter with useful debugging aids.

Example 9-9 Some Debugging Aids

The IBM PC BASIC interpreter contains the following useful user controls (commands):

Control-break key (Ctrl-Break)
CONT <CR>
TRON <CR>
TROFF <CR>

- Crtl-Break. On a typical keyboard, striking the key marked "Ctrl" and simultaneously striking the key labeled "Break" causes a BASIC program to be unconditionally interrupted with control returning to the interpreter. At this point the user can instruct the computer to display the value of any of the variables in the program by issuing an immediate or native mode PRINT command. (Statements without line numbers are executed immediately after a carriage return.)

- CONT <CR>. This command can be used to resume execution of a program after a Ctrl-Break, or a STOP statement within the program. CONT is usually used in conjunction with STOP for debugging. After examination of all relevant variables, CONT <CR> resumes the program where it left off. A user will also find a GOTO statement in the immediate mode useful for resuming at important places in the program.
- TRON <CR>. This command is shorthand for "trace on." When this command is encountered (it may be used in a program or issued as an immediate mode command), the line number of the currently executed program line is displayed as it is executed. While this slows the execution of the program, it is very powerful for determining the sequence of steps or operations carried out by the program.
- TROFF <CR>. This command cancels the TRON command. It too may be used in immediate mode or be included in a program.

PROBLEMS FOR SECTION 9-7-2

Use the information provided in Example 9-9 to solve the following problems.

1. Consider the following simple BASIC program.

```
10  K = 1
20  PRINT K
30  K = K + 1
40  IF K = 11 THEN STOP
    ELSE GOTO 20
50  END
```

What sequence of line numbers is displayed if this program is executed after TRON has been involved?

2. Given the following simple fragment of a BASIC program:

```
10  J= 10
20  K = J * 2
30  PRINT K
40  J = J - 1
50  K = K + 15
60  . . .
```

Ctrl-Break is depressed just after line 50 has been executed. What is displayed for the following immediate mode commands?

```
PRINT J
PRINT K
```

SUMMARY

To enhance the usefulness of the computer, a series of programs is often supplied with the hardware. These programs comprise the operating system. The OS supports all other software, primarily in the area of I/O.

Other tasks of the OS include:

- Scheduling the work performed by the CPU
- Managing the computer's resources
- Keeping track of users' programs and data—the file system, including system security

Tree-structured file system organizations provide efficient ways to keep track of programs and data for individual users as well as groups of users.

Writing and executing programs can be broken into a series of tasks:

- Specify the problem and its solution.
- Create the source code for an HLL program using a program called an editor. The editor program is used to enter, modify, or delete data.
- Translate the HLL program into machine-readable form.
- Execute the program.

A compiler translates all the HLL statements (of a compiled language) into machine code prior to execution of any of the instructions. An interpreter translates each statement of the HLL program and then executes it. Some translation programs use a combination of compilation and interpretation.

A complete program development cycle includes log-on, creation of source code, HLL translation, integration of library routines, and program testing and debugging. The OS and the log-on process provides security for a user's program and data, protection from unauthorized use of the computer, and charging (billing) users for the use of the machine.

To assist with debugging, some OSs have utility programs called debuggers. These permit the user to control and monitor the execution of an application program in order to verify the algorithm and its results and correct any errors which may be present.

REVIEW QUESTIONS

1. What is a compiler?
2. What is an interpreter?
3. What is the main difference between an interpretive language and a compiled language?

4. When translating an HLL program by compilation, what two steps are required?
5. What function does a linker program perform?
6. What is the function of an editor program?
7. Define a run-time error.
8. Define a syntactical error.
9. What is meant by a logical program error?
10. What is an operating system (OS)?
11. Name three important tasks that an OS should perform.
12. What is a scheduler?
13. What is the purpose of a file system?
14. What principle is important for the organization of a file system?
15. What is meant by a hierarchical arrangement of data, and what is an advantage of such an arrangement?
16. What is a directory? What is a subdirectory?
17. Describe a tree-structured directory system.
18. Name five steps which are needed for succcessful development of a computer program written in a compiled HLL.
19. What is meant by logging-on?
20. Describe batch operation of a computer installation.
21. Describe multi-user operation of a computer installation.
22. Describe single-user operation of a computer installation.
23. Name at least 10 operations (commands) which are likely to be found in an editor program.
24. What is meant by source code?
25. What code is produced by a compiler?
26. Name at least five options that are desirable when executing a compiler.
27. What is the process of debugging a program?
28. What is a debugger program?
29. Name four capabilities that a debugger program might support.
30. Name four commands which are useful for manipulating programs and data with an interpreter.

''c,'' through ''z.'' A ''picture'' for selecting a letter is shown in Fig. 10-2. The word ''letter'' is the starting point which leads to an acceptable letter from the English alphabet. From this starting point, simply follow any of the indicated paths. You will notice that a path can lead you to either a, b, c, . . . , or A, B, C, . . . , Z. If you choose the first path, it will lead you to a circle containing the letter ''a.'' Copy the symbol exactly as it appears: ''a.'' The path exits at the right. You have completed your choice of the English letter ''a.'' If you choose the second path, you will encounter the ''b'' symbol inside a circle. Writing this symbol exactly as it appears produces ''b'' as a result. Again the path exits at the right. The diagram in Fig. 10-2 shows how it is possible for you to specify any letter in the English alphabet.

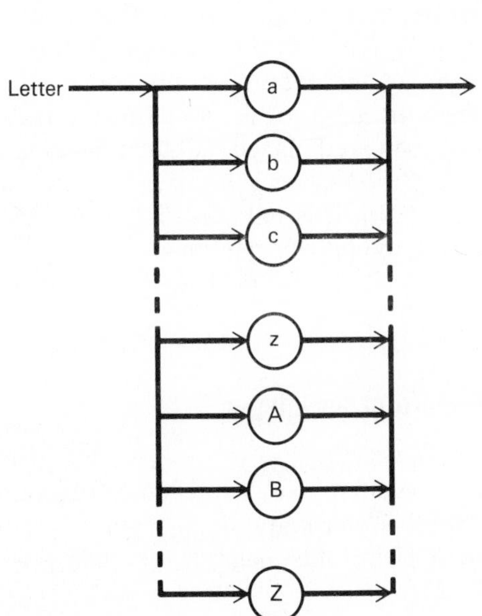

Fig. 10-2 Diagram showing how to define a letter in the English language.

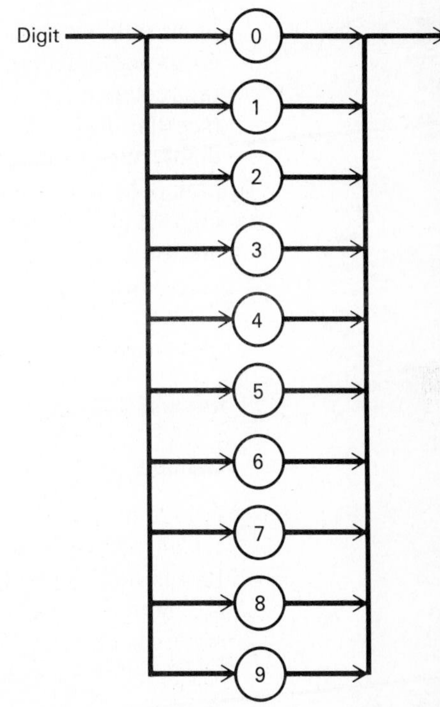

Fig. 10-3 Diagram describing how to specify a digit.

Example 10-2 A Language Picture for a Digit

In much the same way, a diagram can be devised to produce all possible digits. Figure 10-3 represents such a diagram. Once again, start at the word which describes the element to be produced, in this case, ''Digit.'' You will see 10 possible paths. Follow any one of them. Each path leads to a circle containing the symbol for a digit. Write that symbol exactly as it appears in the circle. Each path then exits to the right. All possible paths from ''Digit'' to the exit at the right will produce any and all possible digit elements. If you follow these rules, you will reproduce either 0, 1, 2, 3, 4, 5, 6, 7, 8, or 9—all the possible digits in decimal notation.

Example 10-3 A Language Picture for an Integer

Look at Fig. 10-4. This figure shows you how to write any integer. Start at the word "Integer" and follow the only path available until you encounter a rectangle. This is something new. Up to now you have encoun-

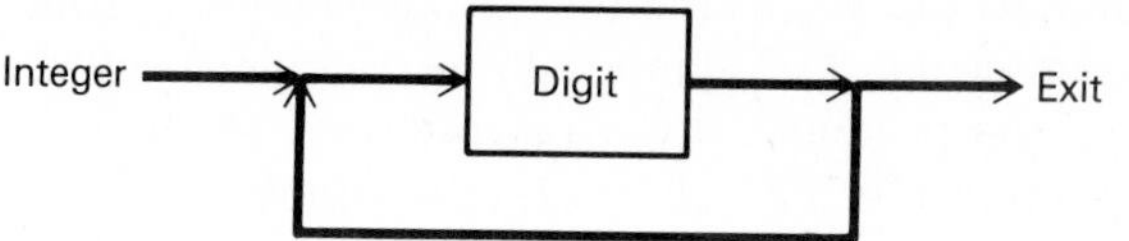

Fig. 10-4 A picture of an integer.

tered only circles. Whenever you see a rectangle, it means that you must go to another diagram to find out what is allowed for the element within the rectangle, in this case, "Digit." Example 10-2 supplies this information (see the diagram in Fig. 10-3, which indicates 0, 1, 2, 3, 4, . . . , 9 for a digit). Write one of the allowable forms of the digit. Continue along the path. The path now offers two choices: exit, or go back and write another digit. If at any point you choose to exit, you are finished. All the following are integers: 0, 25, 43862172.

Is 32a621 an integer? If not, why not? No, it is not: "a" is located in the letter diagram. You have not followed the integer road map which tells you to go to the digit diagram.

Example 10-4 A Better Language Picture of an Integer

Is −25 an integer? Yes, it is.

Can you write such an integer using Fig. 10-4? No, you cannot. Figure 10-4 is not the right diagram for integers as you know them. Figure 10-5 is a better diagram for writing integers. Using this diagram, you can get results such as −100, 25682, −10823625.

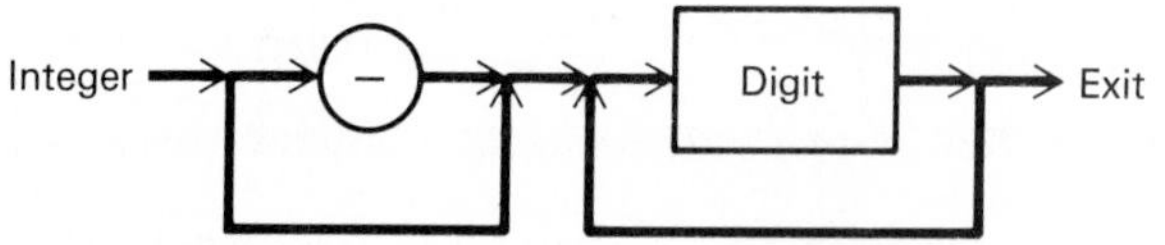

Fig. 10-5 A better picture of an integer.

Is 10,800 an integer? No, because the symbol "," is not found in the diagram for digit. HLLs do not permit commas in integers.

Example 10-5 Picture of a Real Number

So far, the examples presented have been very simple. A somewhat more complicated diagram is shown in Fig. 10-6. This is a diagram for a real

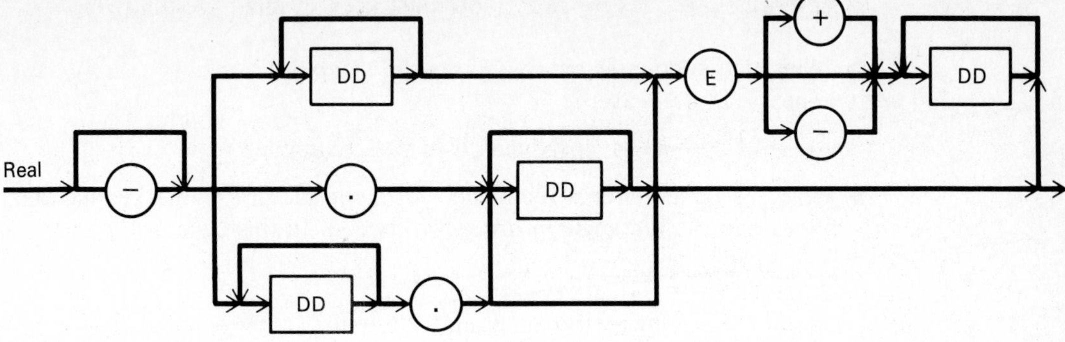

Fig. 10-6 A picture of a real number.

number. All the following are possible results for a real number: −100., 0.25, 0.25E25, −6.E−1, 5.1E+2. This is not the only possible picture for a real number. In this form, a digit must appear in front of the decimal point. Some HLLs only permit real numbers in the form "*.xxx.*" If you make it a habit to always place a digit in front of the decimal point, you will be using a *safer* form of the real quantity. If you take a path which leads to a circle containing the letter "E," copy this letter just as you find it.

Is 0.8E+12083256218 a real number? Yes, it is.

Is this number permitted in an HLL? Theoretically, it is. However, computers cannot deal with numbers that large.

While the picture forms tell you about the kinds of numbers that are allowed (i.e., the elements they may contain), they do not tell you anything about the acceptable size of these numbers. Usually, only your computer manual provides such information.

Pictures of the type presented in Figs. 10-2 to 10-6 can be used to help explain HLL rules. These pictures are called *syntax diagrams*. They will contain three kinds of symbols. These are summarized in Fig. 10-7.

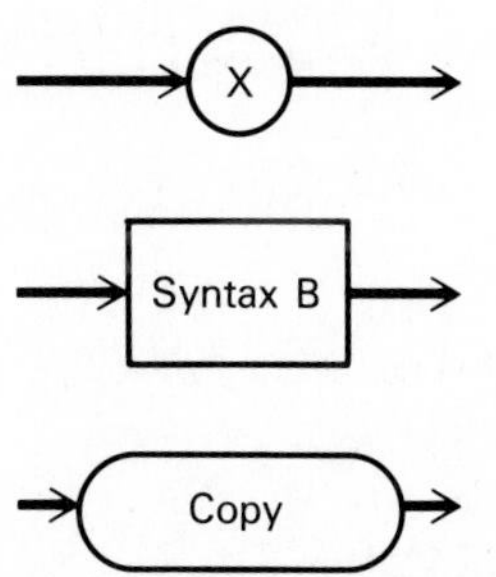

Fig. 10-7 Syntax elements.

To follow the rules properly, you must keep in mind the following:

- When you encounter a circle, copy the symbol it contains exactly as it appears. In this case,

  ——→(E)——→ produces E in your example

- When you encounter a rectangle, go to the picture of the syntax that appears in the rectangle in order to proceed. In this case,

  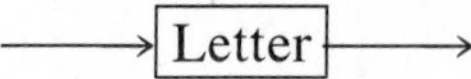

  directs you to the syntax diagram for a letter.

- When you encounter a box with rounded ends, copy what is contained in it exactly as it appears. In this case,

  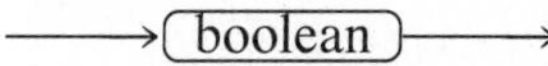

  would produce the word "boolean" in your example.

PROBLEMS FOR SECTION 10-2

1. Follow the diagram in Fig. 10-5. Which of the following is an integer? If it is not an integer, state which rule is violated.

   23867
   291468213
   2.1
   −67
   cat
   2,152
   $21.52
   $32
   −4210
   −6.

2. Follow the diagram in Fig. 10-6. Indicate which of the following are real numbers. If there are errors, correct the mistakes.

   2,352.1
   −6.0E−25.
   4.1
   −5000
   25A
   6.2835E2
   −1
   3.14159
   2.0E−1
   0.0

10-3 GOOD PROGRAMMING

This text will concentrate on teaching good HLL programming habits, as well as on teaching how to recognize such habits. In general, there are three *guiding principles* of *good programming:*

- Extensive documentation
- Modularity
- Clarity

Each of these will be discussed briefly.

10-3-1 Documentation

Program documentation is required to:

- define the problem being solved
- describe the solution (algorithm)

All HLLs make provision for descriptive comments in programs. These comments are ignored by the computer since they are not executable HLL statements. They are written in natural language and explain the author's intent. They appear in the typed or printed copy of the program. The importance of these explanatory comments can be seen further in the case of a programmer who leaves an employer. There could be problems for others unless the programs were well documented (had adequate explanatory comments).

10-3-2 Modularity

The most efficient way to complete a task is to break it down into a sequence of easier subtasks. This is especially true in programming. When using an HLL, it will be possible to divide the program into a series of modules. These may be executed in sequence. This sequence is shown in Fig. 10-8. Some HLLs are more powerful in this respect than others. Modularity leads to a programming method called *structured programming*.

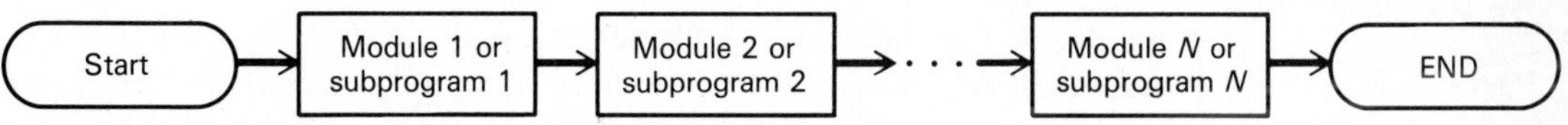

Fig. 10-8 A good program contains a sequence of simple subprograms or modules. They are usually executed in sequence.

10-3-3 Clarity

When writing programs, *do not be "fancy"*! Use the simplest, most direct HLL statements. If you encounter a program that contains clever tricks, you may find it both difficult to read and follow (with respect to the solution algorithm), and error-prone. The use of simple HLL statements as opposed to fancy ones may sometimes produce programs that are less efficient (in terms of the time it takes the computer to execute them). However, when you consider the labor hours that could be lost in attempting to follow a tricky program, the simpler approach may be less time-consuming.

10-4 DEBUGGING AND PROGRAM TESTING

A program may fall into one of two categories:

- **Utility**—A program written to help you write other programs. Programs of this kind are sometimes called *system programs*.
- **Application**—A program designed to be used over and over again, each time with new data. (Obviously, if the program is not changed and the data is not changed, the results will always be the same.)

A programmer's goal is to create a program that operates correctly each time it is run. When working with programs, you are likely to be faced with any one of the following situations at one time or another:

- The program works correctly each time it is run, no matter what data is used (assuming the data is reasonable).
- The program always fails, no matter what data is used.
- The program works correctly sometimes and fails sometimes.

10-4-1 Program Testing

The first possibility described above is, of course, the aim of all programming efforts. It may be difficult to determine that a program works with all possible data. A simple example will demonstrate this: Suppose the HLL statement

$$Y = X/(A - C)$$

appears in a program. Even if you know nothing about HLLs, you can figure out what is to be done. If A = C, this program will fail because you will be asking the computer to divide by 0. The computer will *flag* this error. However, you may never be aware of this potential for program failure since the data for A may never equal the data for C. Application programs have been known to fail after years of trouble-free testing. The failure can occur when data not previously used causes the kind of error just described.

Although you can never be 100 percent certain that your program will work under all circumstances, you can build your confidence in it by trying out different sets of data. An important part of program development is just such *program testing*. In fact, by some estimates, it may cost more to test a program (*program verification*) and debug it than to design it. To test your program, you will need to use a number of test cases. First, supply the program with data which will produce known results. It is sometimes helpful to include data whose values are the largest or smallest values expected. It is usually unrealistic to try every possible data combination, as this is a very time-consuming procedure.

Using samples to test a program is not totally satisfactory, as you have just seen. Some day it will be possible for the computer itself to verify that a program is correct in all respects. In fact, such a possibility is already being seriously studied. Until it becomes a reality, however, the use of samples for program testing remains an important alternative.

10-4-2 Program Debugging

The second possibility noted above is that your program fails all the time. It is usually easy to find the problem. In fact, the computer may find it for you. It may be that you have violated one of the rules of the HLL. These are generally syntactical errors. If the computer does not find the error(s), then the problem solution (algorithm) of your program may contain faulty reasoning (known as *logical errors*). The procedure for finding logical errors when a program always fails, or fails occasionally (the last possibility noted above), is called *debugging*. The error itself is called a *bug*.

Debugging a program is similar to finding a problem in an electric circuit. In an electric circuit the current flows around the circuit. By placing a meter at various important points, you can locate the problem. In a program, results are similar to the electric current. In order to measure such intermediate results, you need a testing device similar to the electric meter. In HLL programming, one such device is the PRINT statement (or other I/O statement) which is part of the language. Figure 10-9 shows a program in modular form. At each *critical* point in the sequence of operations,

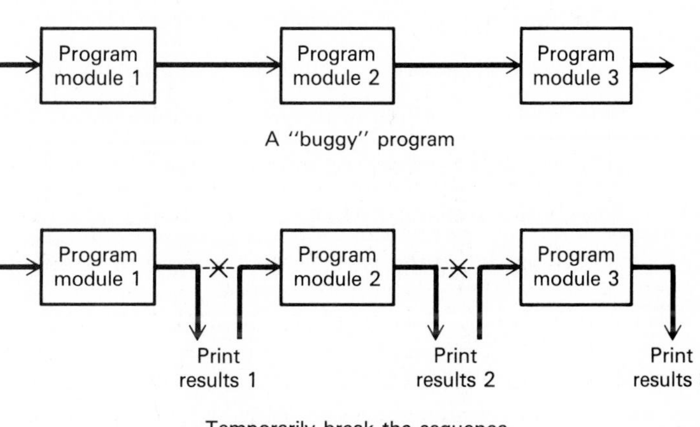

Fig. 10-9 Debugging using the PRINT or other I/O statements.

temporarily insert a PRINT statement which will report the values of important results at that point. This should help to tell you where your program has gone astray.

SUMMARY

HLLs are used to exchange information between people and computers. These languages have rules. Pictures can be used to help explain these rules.

In the study of the HLL rules presented in the following chapters, good programming habits should be developed. Remember to:

- Document programs
- Write modular programs
- Write programs which are simple and easy to read and understand

Program testing and debugging can be accomplished by:

- Trying test cases for the data expected by the program
- Using temporary PRINT or other I/O statements which report intermediate results and comparing these with expected results
- After debugging the program, removing the PRINT statements

REVIEW QUESTIONS

1. State the purpose of natural languages.
2. State the role of computer languages (HLLs).
3. What is meant by redundancy in a language?
4. Name two kinds of programs which you may find in a computer.
5. Name the good programming habits.
6. What is meant by bug?
7. What is a good way to troubleshoot or debug a program?

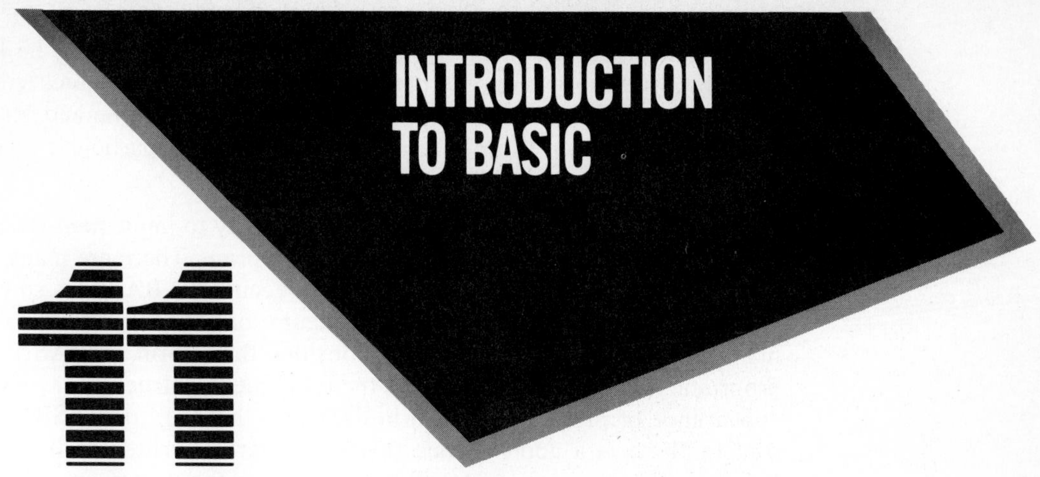

11 INTRODUCTION TO BASIC

The next several chapters deal with the rudiments of programming in the BASIC programming language. You will learn how statements are written to be syntactically correct. You will also see how programs are constructed from the building blocks that the BASIC language provides.

11-1 OVERVIEW

BASIC stands for beginner's all-purpose symbolic instruction code. It was developed at Dartmouth College to train students who were unfamiliar with computers.

BASIC is frequently the first language a future computer programmer will learn. BASIC is available on more machines than any other language. There are several good reasons for BASIC's popularity:

1. BASIC is an easy-to-learn language. Designed as a language for beginners, BASIC has a syntax that is fairly free of format restrictions. Some languages require that commands must begin and end in a certain column, or that spaces must appear in certain places but may not appear in others.
2. Despite its simplicity, BASIC is a language sufficiently powerful to allow even sophisticated applications to be programmed.
3. BASIC is often implemented as an interpretive language. This makes program debugging a relatively easy task as execution continues up to the point of the actual error; editing and rerunning a program are simple, since recompiling is not necessary.
4. The BASIC language is relatively easy to modify to take advantage of the special hardware capabilities found on a variety of systems. Color displays, graphics, music, and external control commands are found on those machines capable of supporting these hardware additions.
5. Almost all forms of BASIC have a mechanism for branching to subroutines written in machine language. This permits functions that either

cannot be written in BASIC or that run too poorly in BASIC to be performed efficiently. Thus, while the bulk of a program may be written in BASIC, those sections that must be executed most quickly or that require operations not supported by the BASIC command structure can be written in the native machine code of the particular computer in question.

This flexibility and ease of learning, and ability to implement BASIC on a variety of machines do not come without a price. There are many, many different *dialects* of BASIC in existence, because (1) BASIC is so easy to implement, (2) different hardware configurations require additional commands, and (3) software creators consider their form of BASIC to be proprietary. This means that while the fundamental structure, syntax, and appearance of programs written in different "brands" of BASIC may be similar, there is a good chance that the program written in the form of BASIC native to machine A will not operate, without some modifications, on machine B.

Since there are so many different dialects of BASIC, the teaching of BASIC becomes a difficult task. Differences in dialects can make perfectly correct statements from one dialect totally incomprehensible (to the computer) in another dialect.

You will see the superscript "DD" from time to time. This means that the command or explanation just given is often *dialectically dependent*. In other words, the particular item under discussion often varies widely, depending upon the particular form of BASIC you are using. You should ask your instructor for the correct form of the command to use.

11-2 STATEMENTS AND COMMANDS

A BASIC program consists of a series of *statements* which specify the calculations or operations to be performed. Each statement must meet two requirements:

1. The statement must be syntactically correct; that is, it must be written according to the rules applying to that particular statement. This takes into account such things as correct spelling of the command, correct positional placement of the parameters, and compliance with the rules regarding the use of variables.
2. The statement must be logically correct; that is, it must represent the operation that you actually wanted to perform. A statement may be syntactically correct but still not perform the operation you had in mind.

Furthermore, in order for the program to accurately reflect the requirements of the algorithm, the statements must not only reflect the above two requirements, they must also, as a group, appear in the correct order. In most cases, if the order in which the steps of the program are carried out is not correct, the program will fail to perform properly, even though each statement is syntactically and logically correct.

BASIC has two general classes of operations: *statements,* which are operations that are normally performed as part of a program, and *commands,* which usually perform "housekeeping" operations. Some forms of BASIC are very strict about a command never appearing inside a program and a statement only appearing inside a program; some forms of BASIC allow almost all commands and statements to be used in either environment.

Figure 11-1 shows some common examples of both statements and commands.

Commands:

LIST	Causes the display of the program currently in memory
FILES[DD]	Causes the display of the programs and data files on the currently active diskette
LOAD	Causes a program to be read from the diskette and placed into memory, erasing any program that was in memory before
SAVE	Causes the program currently in the computer's memory to be written on the diskette so that it may later be recovered by the LOAD command
NEW	Causes the program currently in memory to be erased (used in preparation of receiving a new program)
CLS[DD]	Causes the information on the screen to be erased (assuming that a CRT display is in use); the program currently in memory is not affected

Statements:

PRINT	Causes the display of information on the CRT screen during the execution of the program
LET	Causes a value to be assigned to a variable
IF	Causes a condition to be tested and an action to be performed if the condition is true
INPUT	Causes data to be solicited from the keyboard (usually) during the execution of a program, and assigns that data to a selected variable

Fig. 11-1 Some common BASIC commands and statements.

11-3 PROGRAM FORMAT

Examine the simple BASIC program shown below:

```
100  REM COMPUTE THE VOLTAGE ACROSS A CIRCUIT WHEN R AND I ARE KNOWN
110  LET R = 120
120  LET I = 0.05
130  LET V = I * R
140  PRINT "VOLTAGE ACROSS THE CIRCUIT (IN VOLTS) = "; V
150  END
```

This program calculates the voltage across a circuit when the current through the circuit and the resistance of the circuit are known (according to Ohm's Law).

The first statement is a REM statement, or *remark*. It is simply a note the programmer leaves as part of the program. REMs are used frequently within a program to explain the function of parts of a program, the usage of a particular name, or for other notations. The text that appears after the REM statement will never be executed; it can only be seen if the program text itself is examined.

The REM statement is preceded by the number 100. *Every BASIC statement must be preceded by a line number.* The line number performs two important functions:

1. It shows the order in which the statements are meant to be organized, *and the order* in which they will be executed unless that order is explicitly changed by the action of another statement.
2. It provides a means of labeling statements so that a particular statement may be added, deleted, or edited. This labeling also provides a way of specifying that a given statement is to be executed next, even though it is not the next sequential statement.

The rules for line numbers are as follows:

1. Statement numbers must be positive integers (whole numbers).
2. Statement numbers must fall between 0 and 65,000+. (The highest line number varies from BASIC to BASIC^{DD}.)
3. Line numbers may be issued with any integer increment; 10 is commonly used so that additional statements can be inserted at a later time.
4. Any convenient starting line number may be used; 100 is commonly used so that additional statements can be added at the beginning of the program later.
5. Lines may be created in any order; however, they will always be sorted and listed in ascending numerical order, and will be executed in this order unless additional statements specify to do otherwise.

Following the REM statement at line 100 are four LET statements (lines 110 to 140). A LET statement assigns a value to a variable. A *variable* is a symbolic name, of our choosing, for a location in the computer's memory where BASIC will store a value. This value may be assigned directly, as in the LET statements at lines 110, 120, and 130, or the value may be the result of a computation, as in line 140. The asterisk (*) between the I and R in line 130 is the symbol used in BASIC to indicate that multiplication is to occur. The operation of the assignment statement and the naming of variables, and the use of the computer for mathematical computations, will be covered in detail in the next chapter, but for now, the action of the LET statement should be clear from its use. (Some versions of BASIC do *not* require the keyword LET; line 110 may be written as R = 120.)

Line 140 contains a PRINT statement. The PRINT statement causes the computer to display results, usually on the CRT screen. In this particular

PRINT statement we have instructed the computer to display the words "VOLTAGE ACROSS THE CIRCUIT (IN VOLTS) = " followed by the current value of the variable "*V*." (Remember, the value for this variable was calculated and assigned as a result of line 130 being executed.) We specify the words "VOLTAGE ACROSS THE CIRCUIT (IN VOLTS) = " to be printed by the presence of *double quotes*. The variable name "*V*" does *not* appear in quotes in the PRINT statement, and therefore its *value* is displayed.

Finally, line 150 contains an END statement. The purpose of this statement is to mark the end of the program for the computer. While the use of this statement is optional in many BASIC dialects, *we encourage you to use it*. Good programming practice requires that the beginning and end of a program be clearly discernible, and the END statement provides such a mechanism for marking the end.

11-4 STATEMENT SYNTAX

Earlier we mentioned that program statements must be syntactically correct. This means that for every allowable BASIC statement or command there are very definite rules about how that statement or command must appear, what additional information must appear along with the statement or command, what additional information is optional, and under what conditions the statement may be used. We will use the following notation for indicating the syntax or structure of a BASIC statement (or command):

1. The statement or command name will always appear in all capital letters, e.g., PRINT, REM, or LIST.
2. Parameters of the statement or command that are variable will be enclosed within braces { }. (Parameters are the information on which the statement or command is to act; in line 140 of the example, "VOLTAGE . . . =" and "V" are the specific parameters of the PRINT statement.)
3. Where a choice of parameters exists, each of the possibilities will be shown within the braces, separated by the word "or."
4. Where multiple parameters are permitted, additional sets of parameters will be shown as {. . .}, where the options of the previous parameters apply.
5. Where the use of a parameter is optional, the entire optional clause will be enclosed within brackets [ ]. (Within the brackets, the previous rules apply.)
6. The following abbreviations will be used:

nvar (numeric variable): The name of a variable (storage location) that contains a numeric value. This will be described in detail in the next section.

nlit (numeric literal): An actual numeric value, e.g., 6, 27.34, 1.287E−9 (scientific notation, the same as 1.287×10^{-9}).

avar (alphanumeric variable): The name of a variable (storage location) that may contain alphanumeric data (that is, one with which we do not intend to do arithmetic). This will be described in detail in the section dealing with character data.

alit (alphanumeric literal): An actual alphanumeric value, e.g., "VOLTAGE . . . =" (as in line 140). An alphanumeric literal always appears between two sets of double quotation marks.

nexpr (numeric expression): A formula conforming to the rules for BASIC arithmetic calculations, which may contain any of the legal operations for manipulating numeric data. Anywhere an nexpr is permitted, numeric literals or numeric variables are also permitted. *Therefore, {nexpr} is the same as {nlit or nvar or nexpr}.*

aexpr (alphanumeric expression): A formula conforming to the rules for BASIC string calculations, which may contain any of the legal operations for manipulating alphanumeric data. Anywhere an aexpr is permitted, an alphanumeric literal or alphanumeric variable is permitted. *Therefore, {aexpr} is the same as {alit or avar or aexpr}.*

expr: May be used where either an nexpr *or* an aexpr may be used.

7. Punctuation that is shown is required. If choices regarding the selection of punctuation exist, the choices will be shown as {, or ;}.
8. Since the line number is a required part of every program statement, it is omitted from the syntactical description, unless it is a parameter, in which case it is abbreviated as *lnum*.
9. Where there is more than one common form of a statement or command, each form will be shown.

11-5 GETTING INFORMATION OUT OF THE COMPUTER

In the program example you just examined, the PRINT statement was introduced. We will now explore this statement more thoroughly.

Syntax

Syntax *a*: PRINT
Syntax *b*: PRINT {nvar or nlit or avar or alit or nexpr or aexpr}
Syntax *c*: PRINT {expr} {, or ;}
Syntax *d*: PRINT {exprl} {, or ;} {expr2} {, or ;} {. . .}

Description:

Syntax a: Syntax *a* is the simplest form of the PRINT statement. The PRINT statement with no parameters or punctuation following causes the printing of a single blank line.

Syntax b: Syntax *b* is the PRINT statement with a single parameter and no trailing punctuation; it causes the parameter's value to be printed. If the parameter is an expression, the expression is first evaluated and the result is displayed. If the parameter is a variable, the value of the variable is displayed. Finally, if the parameter is a literal, the literal itself is displayed. In the case of an alphanumeric literal, the literal must appear between double quotation marks, but the quotation marks themselves are not printed as part of the value of the literal. Following the PRINT operation, the cursor is positioned at the beginning of the next line.

Example 11-1 Samples of BASIC PRINT Statements

PRINT A	Prints the current value of the numeric variable A.
PRINT NAMES$	Prints the current value of the alphanumeric variable NAME$.
PRINT 12	Prints the numeric literal 12. (This is not a terribly useful form of the PRINT statement, but it is syntactically correct.)
PRINT "THE VOLTAGE IS: "	Prints the alphanumeric literal "THE VOLTAGE IS: ". Remember, the *value* of this literal is everything *between* the double quotation marks, but not including the double quotation marks. What will actually be displayed is everything from the T of THE up to and including the space following the colon (:).
PRINT A * 2 + 6	Calculates the value of the arithmetic expression, then displays the result.

Syntax c: Syntax *c* is almost the same as syntax *b,* with the exception that there is trailing punctuation (a comma or semicolon) at the end of the line. Note also that the shorter notational form {expr} is used instead of {nvar or nlit or avar or alit or expr}. Again, the two notations are interchangeable.

The punctuation at the end of the statement line supresses the normal advance to the next line at the end of the PRINT operation. A PRINT statement without trailing punctuation will display the parameters as instructed, then advance to the beginning of the next line. If another PRINT operation were to follow, it would begin printing its parameters at the beginning of the new line. However, if a PRINT statement has trailing punctuation, it will *not* advance to the new line when it has completed its operation. Thus, the *next* PRINT operation will take place on the *same* line as did the previous end-punctuated PRINT operation.

If the PRINT statement is ended with a semicolon (;), the following PRINT operation will take place in the next available printing *position*. If the PRINT statement is terminated with a comma (,), the following PRINT operation will take place in the next available print *column*. BASICs operating on a machine that displays 40 print positions on a line usually divide the screen up into three or four columns. Versions of BASIC which are designed for machines using an 80-position display may have as many as 10 such columns.[DD] This is highly machine-dependent, and the actual size of each column may vary not only from one version to the next but even from column to column (the columns may not all be the same width). (Refer to the documentation that supports the machine you are using to get the exact column width and starting point.)

Example 11-2 Some additional PRINT Statements

PRINT VALUE;	Displays the current value of the numeric variable VALUE. The *next* PRINT operation would appear on the same line, in the next available printing *position*.
PRINT 3 * 4,	Calculates the result (12) and displays it. The *next* PRINT operation would appear in the next available printing *column*.[DD]

Syntax d: Syntax *d* demonstrates that a single PRINT statement may be used to display more than one value. Each value to be displayed is separated from the next by a comma (to display the next item in the following printing *column*) or by a semicolon (to display the next item in the following printing *position*). The last item may be followed by punctuation, which would have the same effect as in syntax *c*.

Example 11-3 Printing More than One Value

PRINT A, B, C	Displays the current value of the variable A in the first display column, the value of the variable B in the second display column, and the value of the variable C in the third display column.
PRINT "THE SUM IS "; 2 + 9	Displays the alphanumeric literal "THE SUM IS ", followed immediately, in the next display position, by the result of the computation 2 + 9. Notice that a space was included as the last character of the alphanumeric literal. This was done to ensure that a space would be displayed between the literal and the result of the computation.
PRINT "THE SUM IS "; 2 + 9,	Displays exactly as above, but does not advance to the next line when finished. Instead, the computer prepares to display the next item (that is, the first item appearing in the next

PRINT statement to be executed) in the following display column (trailing *comma*).

SUMMARY

BASIC is an easy HLL to learn. Because it is an interpretive HLL (there are some compiled dialects), program debugging is a relatively easy task. A BASIC program consists of a series of statements which reflect the operations that the programmer wants to perform. Each statement is preceded by a line number which specifies the order in which to execute statements. Numbered statements make it easy to add, delete, or change (edit) such statements. An important element of the language is the variable which symbolically identifies a location in the computer's memory where data may be stored. The PRINT statement commands the computer to display results to the user. The syntax of a BASIC statement consists of the rules governing the appearance, the data to be included, and under what conditions the statement may be used.

REVIEW PROBLEM

1. Write PRINT statements that will do the following:

a. Display the value of the variable *ABC*.
b. Display the value of the following expression: 6 times the value of the variable ONECELL.
c. Display the value of the string variable FIRSTNAME$.
d. Display the string literal "THE VALUE IS " followed immediately by the value contained in the variable RTOT.
e. Display the values of the variables A, B, and C, spaced in the first three printing columns.
f. After skipping a line, display the value of the variable X, five spaces from the left edge of the screen, using an alphanumeric literal to achieve the spacing. (This is two statements.)
g. Display the string literal "NAME: " in the third printing column.
h. Display the literal "TOTAL CAPACITANCE = ". Then, on the same screen line, but using a second PRINT statement, display the value of the sum of variables C1, C2, and C3 in a logical position. (This is two statements.)
i. Display the value of the variable CAPREACTANCE, preceded by a suitable caption.
j. Display the value of the result of the calculation ETOT/ITOT, surrounded by appropriate captions.

REVIEW QUESTIONS

1. Discuss five reasons for the popularity of BASIC.
2. What is meant by a dialect of BASIC?
3. What is meant by syntax?
4. What is the difference between statements and commands?
5. Describe the actions of the following commands:

   SAVE
   LIST
   CLS

6. Describe the action of the following statements:

   INPUT
   PRINT
   REM

7. What is the difference between a numeric and an alphanumeric quantity?
8. What is a variable?
9. What is a literal?
10. How is an alphanumeric literal shown?

12 MATHEMATICAL OPERATIONS

One of the primary functions of the computer is to perform mathematical calculations. These calculations may be in a variety of fields—e.g., business (payroll, profits); calculations that determine the proper trajectory for a landing on the moon (velocity, rate of descent, rate of deceleration); those involved in the design of a complex electrical network (calculation of impedances, inductances, bandwidths). This chapter describes the fundamental mathematical operations which make it possible to perform such calculations and which are supported in all dialects of BASIC.

12-1 BASIC DATA

Certain HLLs have been designed to be particularly powerful in their ability to perform mathematical computations. They are equipped with built-in functions that can perform a variety of mathematical operations, using a variety of data types. However, quite often, these languages are rather poor or inefficient in their ability to process alphanumeric data. If the application is one in which significant amounts of both arithmetic operations and alphanumeric operations are performed these super "number-crunching" languages may not be suitable.

All general-purpose HLLs have, as a minimum, the ability to perform the four basic mathematical operations: addition, subtraction, multiplication, and division. Most HLLs also include a number of built-in mathematical functions. These generally include functions to perform such operations as calculating square roots, absolute values, sines and tangents of angles, logarithms, and integer truncation. More advanced dialects include functions to perform modular arithmetic, calculate other trigonometric values, and allow the use of hexadecimal or octal constants.

BASIC is a general-purpose HLL. Most dialects are reasonably powerful in their ability to perform arithmetic operations and contain most of, if not all, the functions listed above.

12-1-1 Data Types

Numerical values in BASIC fall into one of four categories:

1. Integer: Whole numbers
2. Real: Single-precision numbers (those with fractional parts, expressed as a decimal)
3. Real: Double-precision numbers (same as single-precision numbers, but with the ability to store more significant digits)
4. String: Alphanumeric characters, discussed in a later chapter

Integers are stored in a very straightforward manner. The decimal value is converted to binary and is then stored in 2 bytes of memory. If we only had to deal with positive numbers, we could store values of from zero ($00000000\ 00000000_2$) to 65,535 ($11111111\ 11111111_2$). However, most systems are designed with the ability to deal with both positive and negative integers. The leftmost bit is used to indicate the sign: a 0 indicates a positive value; a 1 indicates a negative value. What this does is split the range in half and allows the storage of values from $-32{,}768$ to $+32{,}767$.

Almost all forms of BASIC support single-precision floating-point values. Typically, single-precision values are stored in 4 bytes of memory, in a binary exponential format which provides 23 bits for the mantissa, 1 bit for the mantissa's sign, 7 bits for the exponent, and 1 bit for the exponent's sign. Thus the largest positive or negative value that can be contained is

$$.11111111111111111111111_2 \times 2^{+127} = 1.7014 \cdots \times 10^{38}$$

The smallest normalized positive or negative value that can be contained in a single-precision value is

$$.10000000000000000000000_2 \times 2^{-127} = 5.8775 \cdots \times 10^{-39}$$

Double-precision values allocate an additional 4 bytes to the mantissa. *This allows a value to be specified more precisely, but does not provide for larger values to be stored.* While you might think that because more digits of precision are available, smaller numbers could be specified, this is not the case. Even though there are more digits available, all values are normalized before storage; that is, before the number is stored, it is adjusted so that the first digit appears immediately to the right of the binary point. Some examples of how single- and double-precision values are stored are shown in the accompanying table.

Note that even as the value to be stored gets smaller, the first digit (of the binary fraction) must fall into the first position to the right of the radix point. Since the largest negative exponent that can be stored is -127, values of less than 2^{-127} would cause normalization to generate an exponent of -128, which is not valid.

While this description is valid for the manner in which numbers may be

Decimal Value	Stored As (Binary)	Precision
36	$.10010000000000000000000 \times 2^{+6}$	Single
36	$.10010000000000000000000000000000000000000000000000000000 \times 2^{+6}$	Double
189	$.10111101000000000000000 \times 2^{+8}$	Single
189	$.10111101000000000000000000000000000000000000000000000000 \times 2^{+8}$	Double
0.140625	$.10010000000000000000000 \times 2^{-2}$	Single
0.140625	$.10010000000000000000000000000000000000000000000000000000 \times 2^{-2}$	Double

stored, there are some dialects that store numeric values in a different manner. Rather than converting the decimal value to a binary value and then storing that, the decimal value is converted to a binary-coded decimal (BCD), which is a digit-by-digit translation of the decimal number into a binary representation. Since each decimal digit may attain a value of 0 to 9, a digit's value can be represented in 4 bits. Therefore, an 8-bit byte can contain two decimal digits. Additional bytes are allocated depending on the length of the original number. An exponent may also be stored. In addition to providing for very large or small numbers, there are no errors caused through the rounding off in the decimal-to-binary conversion process. While this also changes the manner in which arithmetic and other arithmetic functions are performed, these considerations are taken care of by the HLL.

12-1-2 Variables and Constants

We have been discussing the manner in which most forms of BASIC go about the business of storing values. We will now discuss the manner in which BASIC makes it easy to refer to these stored values.

Low-level languages make it the programmer's responsibility to remember the addresses in memory where values have been stored. High-level languages usually remove this responsibility from the programmer and allow the language to take care of such housekeeping details. Rather than require the programmer to state the actual address in memory where a value is stored in order to use it, HLLs allow a programmer to assign a name to a set of memory locations and then use that symbolic name in all future references to those storage locations. The program takes care of such details as allocation of space, remembering which space has been assigned which symbolic name, and location of the actual data required at the appropriate time.

BASIC is particularly easy to use in this respect. When BASIC recognizes that a variable is being used, it first searches its list of variables already in use. If BASIC finds the variable referenced in its list, it provides the address of the variable to whatever portion of the program that requires it. If the variable is not found, BASIC creates the variable, *assigns an initial value of zero to that variable,* and then returns the *address* of the newly created variable to the program. The programmer need not know where in memory the values actually lie.

12-1-3 Naming Variables

There are two sets of rules for the naming of variables, depending on whether or not your form of BASIC supports *extended variable names*. If not, the rules are as shown in Table 12-1. If your form of BASIC does support extended variable names, the rules are as shown in Table 12-2.

TABLE 12-1 RULES FOR NAMING BASIC VARIABLES WITHOUT EXTENDED VARIABLE NAMES

1. The first character of the variable's name *must* be a letter of the alphabet (A to Z).
2. A second character *may* be used but is optional. If used, it *must* be a single digit from 0 to 9.
3. The rightmost character (the second or third character, depending on whether or not the optional digit is used) indicates the *type* of variable used:

   % for integer variables
   # for double-precision variables
   $ for string variables
   ! for single-precision variables

Note: If none of these suffixes appears, the default is!, or single-precision.

LEGAL VARIABLE NAMES

Name	Attributes
A	Single-precision (default)
X	Single-precision (default)
L!	Single-precision (explicit indication)
D#	Double-precision
K6#	Double-precision
J1%	Integer
P9%	Integer
X$	String
B2$	String

ILLEGAL VARIABLE NAMES

Name	Illegal Because
7	Does not begin with an alphabetic character
LONG	Variable name too long
X?	Illegal suffix character
B 4	Includes spaces not permitted
PP	Second character not a digit

TABLE 12-2 RULES FOR NAMING BASIC VARIABLES WITH EXTENDED VARIABLE NAMES

1. The first character of the variable's name *must* be alphabetic (A to Z).
2. The remaining characters may consist of the letters of the alphabet (A to Z), or the numerals (0 to 9). Some forms of BASIC permit certain symbols to be used, such as "@," "#," and the period. *The number of additional characters permitted varies from* one version of BASIC to another; typically ranges extend from 16 to 30 additional characters.
3. The suffix characters remain the same:

   % For integer variables
   # For double-precision variables
   $ For string variables
   ! For single-precision variables

Note: If none of these suffixes appears, the default is!, or single-precision.

LEGAL **EXTENDED VARIABLE NAMES**

Name	Attributes
REACTANCE	Single-precision (default—no suffix)
STARTVALUE%	Integer
PRECISE#	Double-precision
CIRCUITNAME$	String

ILLEGAL **VARIABLE NAMES**

Name	Illegal Because
6THVALUE	Does not begin with a number (use VALUE6)
ANSWER?	Illegal character ("?")
FIRST VAL	Contains a blank; would be treated as two separate variables—FIRST and VAL (use FIRSTVAL)
#WHOLENUM	Number sign (#) must be the rightmost character to indicate that this is a double-precision variable

If the version of your BASIC being used supports extended variable names, there is one more thing to watch out for—*reserved words*. These are words that BASIC uses for its commands and instructions, and if they were allowed to appear as variables, the computer could not determine whether you were referring to the value of a variable or wanted a command to be performed. In general, this problem is avoidable, since the choice of valid variable names is so great.

12-2 MATHEMATICAL OPERATIONS

The manner in which you express mathematical operations that BASIC is to perform is called *notation*. This is simply the set of characters that BASIC recognizes as representing the mathematical operations of addition, subtraction, multiplication, division, or exponentiation. While most of these symbols are the same as those you are accustomed to using [such as + (plus for addition) or − (minus for subtraction)], there are some differences that need to be taken into account.

12-2-1 Addition

The operation of addition is shown with the plus sign (+) between the two operands you wish to add. In the event that more than two operands are being added, the additions are performed between pairs of operands, taking pairs of operands from left to right. Examples of the operation of addition are as follows:

6 + 10	Takes the value 6 and adds it to the value 10
A + B6	Takes the current value of the single-precision variable A and adds it to the current value of the single-precision variable B6
8 + 3 + 12	Takes the value 8 and adds it to the value 3; then takes the value 12 and adds that to the partial result (11) of the previous addition

12-2-2 Subtraction

The operation of subtraction is shown with the minus sign (−) appearing between the two operands that need to be subtracted. The operand to the right of the minus sign is subtracted from the operand to the left of the minus sign. In the event of multiple subtractions, partial results are computed between pairs of operands, taking pairs of operands from left to right. Examples of the operation of subtraction follow:

12 − 7	Takes the value 7 and subtracts it from the value 12
K8 − 4	Takes the value 4 and subtracts it from the current value of the single-precision variable K8
B5# − 8 − A2	Takes the value 8 and subtracts it from the current value of the double-precision variable B5#; then takes the current value of the single-precision variable A2 and subtracts that from the result of the previous subtraction

12-2-3 Multiplication

The operation of multiplication is shown with the asterisk (*) appearing between the two operands. If multiple multiplications are to be performed, the operands are taken in pairs from left to right. Examples of the multiplication process follow:

19 * 3	Takes the value 19 and multiplies it by the value 3
3 * D4	Takes the value 3 and multiplies it by the current value of the single-precision variable D4

B# * 8 * P! Takes the current value of the double-precision variable B# and multiplies that by the value 8; then takes the result of that multiplication and multiplies it by the current value of the single-precision variable P!

12-2-4 Division

The operation of division is shown with the slash (/) symbol, the dividend appearing to the left of the symbol and the divisor appearing to the right. In the event of a series of divisions, the divisions are performed by taking pairs of operands (dividend first, then divisor) from left to right. Examples of the division operation follow:

16/3.8 Takes the value 16 and divides it by the value 3.8

B9/K2 Takes the current value of the single-precision variable B9 and divides it by the current value of the single-precision variable K2

T3#/6/L Takes the value of the double-precision variable T3# and divides it by the value 6; then the result of this division is divided by the current value of the single-precision variable L

12-2-5 Exponentiation

The operation of exponentiation (raising to a power) has three common notations—the up arrow (↑), caret (^), or double asterisk (**)—which separate the value to be exponentiated (to the left of the symbol) and the power to which the number should be raised (to the right of the symbol). While the symbol indicating exponentiation varies from one dialect of BASIC to another, in general, a single form of BASIC will support only one of the above notations.

In the event of multiple exponentiations, the operands are taken in pairs from left to right, so that the last exponentiation to be performed is the rightmost. This order of operations in exponentiation is not universal. The dialect of BASIC being used should be checked to determine whether this left-to-right order is correct. If PRINT 3 ^ 2 ^ 3 produces a result of 729, it means that exponentiation was performed as described, from left to right. However, if the result 6561 is obtained, it means that exponentiations were performed from right to left, with the leftmost exponentiation occurring last; i.e., $[3^{2^3}] = 3^8 = 6561$. For the following examples of the operation of exponentiation note that the caret (^) is used to indicate exponentiation, though the BASIC utilized may use the caret, up arrow (↑), or double asterisk (**) to denote exponentiation:

4 ^ 6 Takes the value 4 and raises it to the sixth power

F% ^ D Takes the current value of the integer variable F% and raises that value to the power indicated by the current value of the single-precision variable D

A ^ B ^ C Takes the current value of the single-precision variable A and raises it to the B power: then takes this partial result and raises it to the C power *if the BASIC used performs exponentiations from left to right*. Otherwise, takes the current value of the single-precision variable B and raises this value to the C power; then takes this partial value as the exponent in computing A to the B ^ C power (computes exponentiations from right to left)

12-3 THE ORDER OF OPERATIONS

To make use of the mathematical computational abilities of BASIC, you must know in what order mathematical operations are performed (*hierarchy*). The order is as follows:

1. Exponentiations
2. Multiplications or divisions (same priority)
3. Additions or subtractions (same priority)

When items have the same priority, they are performed as they appear, from left to right.

Thus, in the accompanying table the expressions are evaluated as shown.

Expression	Result
5 + 8 * 3	8 times 3 equals 24, plus 5 equals 29
9 ^ 2 * 3	9 raised to the second power equals 81, times 3 equals 243
3 * 9 ^ 2	Same as above; despite the apparently different order, the exponentiation is performed first, then the multiplication
250 − 4 * 6/2 ^ 2	1. Exponentiation: 2 ^ 2 = 4
	2. Multiplication: 4 * 6 = 24
	3. Division: 24/4 = 6
	4. Subtraction: 250 − 6 = 244

12-3-1 Changing the Order of Operations

It is often useful to be able to change the order of operations. For instance, suppose you had to compute the average of five voltage measurements. The voltages are contained in the variables V_1, V_2, V_3, V_4, and V_5. To compute the average you might write

V1 + V2 + V3 + V4 + V5/5

However, this would not be correct. Applying the rules you have just been shown, you know that the division of V_5 by the value 5 would occur *first,* followed then by the addition of the remaining voltages. So, if all the measurements had been 85s, the result would have been

$$85 + 85 + 85 + 85 + 85/5 = 340 + 17 = 357$$

hardly the average to expect.

The order of operations may be altered by placing expressions in *parentheses*. If the expression above were written as

(V1 + V2 + V3 + V4 + V5)/5

BASIC is being instructed to *perform the operations in parentheses first,* then to continue with the remaining operations in the normal order. Therefore, the sum of the five voltages is computed first, and then this sum is divided by 5, giving the expected and correct average of 85.

Before summarizing the rules for the order of operations, there is another modification to be made. So far, we have been talking about *dyadic* operations, that is, those in which there are two operands. There are also commonly used *monadic* operations, or operations in which there is only one operand. One such operation is the operation of *negation.* This operation, also called *unary minus,* is symbolized by placing the minus sign before the value to be negated. The operation is the same as if we multiplied the operand by −1.

There are other monadic operations available through BASIC. Earlier, we mentioned that most dialects of BASIC are equipped with a number of mathematical functions that can calculate such values as the square root of a number, the sine, cosine, or tangent of an angle, and the absolute value of a quantity. These numeric function calls are also monadic operations, since we are sending a single value to the function and receiving a single value in return.

Taking parentheses into account as well as monadic operations, the order of operations becomes:

1. Parenthesized expressions (within a parenthesized expression, the order of operations is the same as that outside the parentheses; that is, parenthesized expressions may contain other parenthesized expressions, which may contain other parenthesized expressions, etc.)
2. Monadic operations: unary minus and function calls (some dialects supporting the MOD function place this function in a different priority than the rest of the functions)
3. Exponentiation
4. Multiplication or division (some dialects supporting integer division place this operation at a different level of priority)
5. Addition or subtraction

Some examples of the use of order of operations can be examined in Table 12-3.

TABLE 12-3 HOW THE OVERALL ORDER OF OPERATIONS AFFECTS THE EVALUATION OF EXPRESSIONS

Expression	Result
6 * (3 + 4)	1. Add 3 + 4 = 7
	2. Multiply 6 by the result (7)
	3. Final result = 42

TABLE 12-3 *(continued)*

Expression	Result
3 ^ (2 + 2 * 4) * 2	1. Parenthesized expression first: multiply 4 by 2; then add 2 = 10 2. Raise 3 to the tenth power = 59,049 3. Multiply by 2 4. Final result = 118,098
10/.5/((2 + 2 ^ 3) + 6)	1. Parenthesized expression first a. Inner parentheses first b. Exponentiation: 2 ^ 3 = 8 c. Plus 2 = 10 d. Outer parentheses: add 6 = 16 2. Divisions from left to right a. 10/.5 = 20 b. 20/16 = 1.25 3. Final result = 1.25
−5 * −(3 + 6/2)	1. Unary negation −5 and −( ) (value not yet computed) 2. Parenthesized expression a. Division: 6/2 = 3 b. Addition: + 3 = 6 3. Multiplication: −5 * −6 = 30

12-4 THE ASSIGNMENT STATEMENT

So far we have been talking about computing values as a result of executing a mathematical expression. We have also talked about how BASIC allocates memory space to the variables in use. What we have not yet dealt with is how the values that we may compute get assigned to the variables we choose to use.

BASIC uses the LET statement to assign a value to a variable.

Purpose: The purpose of the LET statement is to provide a mechanism for assigning a numeric or alphanumeric value to a memory location which will henceforth be referenced by a symbolic name of our choosing.

Syntax:

Syntax *a*: LET {nvar} = {nlit, nvar, or nexpr}
Syntax *b*: LET {avar} = {alit, avar, or aexpr}

Syntaxes *a* and *b* are alike except that they show that only numeric values may be assigned to numeric variables and only alphanumeric values may be assigned to alphanumeric variables.

Examine the following examples. They show the LET statement being used in a variety of ways.

LET VAL1 = 0	Assigns the value of 0 to variable VAL1
LET ANSWER = ANSWERKEY	Assigns the current value of the variable ANSWERKEY to the variable ANSWER
LET X = 3 * 5 + V1	Computes the value of the numeric expression (3 * 5 + V1) and assigns that computed value to the variable X
LET NAME$ = "HAROLD"	Assigns the alphanumeric literal value "HAROLD" to the alphanumeric variable NAME$
LET A$ = K3$	Takes the current value of the variable K3$ and assigns that value to the variable A$

It is important to realize that the assignment statement is not the same as an algebraic equation. When a LET statement such as

LET A = 6 * 4/2

is written, the statement is commanding BASIC to calculate the value of the expression on the right side of the equals sign and assign that calculated value to the variable A. Because of this, it is perfectly valid to have a statement such as

LET B = B + 1

meaning take the current value of the variable B, add 1 to it, and then assign this new calculated value to the variable B. So, while algebraically the statement cannot be valid, it is perfectly valid when taken in the correct context of the LET statement.

SUMMARY

Computers are particularly useful when used to perform mathematical calculations. The numerical values used in such calculations include integers, real numbers, and character sequences in the form of strings. These values are stored in the computer's memory and are referenced or accessed by using symbolic values. The fundamental mathematical operations which can be performed in BASIC include addition (+), subtraction (−), multiplication (*), division (/), and exponentiation (^). In a given mathematical expression these operations are carried out in the following order:

1. Exponentiations
2. Multiplications or divisions (as encountered from left to right)
3. Additions or subtractions (as encountered from left to right)

The order of operations may be altered by placing expressions within parentheses. The assignment statement is a fundamental way in which variables are assigned values.

REVIEW PROBLEMS—MATHEMATICAL OPERATIONS

1. Assuming a BASIC that permits extended variable names up to 16 characters long, which of the following variable names would be invalid and why:

   a. NEW VALUE
   b. OKSUM45
   c. TWOTYPE$%
   d. X
   e. 7
   f. Q6$
   g. A12345%
   h. LONGVARIABLENAME
   i. SHORTERVARIABLENAME
   j. GOODNAME*

2. What are the type and precision attributes of each of the following variables:

   a. A3
   b. K$
   c. CIRCUIT$
   d. VALUE%
   e. RESISTANCE!
   f. P#
   g. HENRIES
   h. REALTHING$
   i. MMMM
   j. STUFF$

3. Assuming a BASIC that permits extended variable names up to 16 characters in length, write descriptive variable names having attributes suitable for the kind of data the variable is to contain:

   a. A variable which will contain an employee's first name.
   b. A variable which will contain the speed of light in millimeters per second.
   c. A variable which will contain a count of the number of TTL integrated circuits passing inspection.
   d. A variable which will contain a circuit's power dissipation.
   e. A variable which will contain a transistor number such as 2N3055.
   f. A variable which will contain the weight of a PC board to be sent through the mail.

g. A variable which will contain the percentage of parts failing to pass quality control.
h. A variable which will contain the switch-on time for an SCR.
i. A variable which will contain the computed output voltage of a full-wave rectifier.
j. A variable which will contain a telephone number, including area code.

4. Evaluate the following numeric expressions according to the rules of a BASIC. Assume that exponentiations are performed from right to left.

a. 3 * 4 + 5
b. 24/3 + 3
c. 4 + 6 * 2
d. 48/4/2
e. 6 ^ 2 + 2
f. 2 + 2 ^ 3
g. 2 ^4/2 ^ 2
h. 2 + 3 + (−28/2 + 2)/2
i. 3 * 3 ^ 2 + 2
j. (3 * (2 + 2)) ^ (2 + 2/2 − 1)

5. The following formulas are written in standard algebraic notation. Convert them as necessary so that they will be correctly evaluated according to the rules of BASIC.

a. $\dfrac{125 \times 34 + 16}{6(3)}$

b. $\dfrac{12(42) + 16}{19^2 + 9}$

c. $\dfrac{X^{3+2}}{2Z}$

d. $\dfrac{1}{2\pi f C}$

e. $\dfrac{X_2 - X_1}{Y_2 - Y_1}$

f. $\dfrac{C_1 C_2}{C_1 + C_2}$

g. $\dfrac{Q_1 Q_2}{KD}$

h. $\dfrac{c^2 \times h}{4\pi}$

i. Degrees $\times$ 1.745 $\times$ 10^{-2}

13 GETTING DATA INTO THE COMPUTER

This chapter describes methods of providing the data on which a program performs its functions.

13-1 DATA INPUT NEEDS

The benefit of using a computer to perform a given task usually begins to accrue when the same task is performed over and over again.

Example 13-1 A Case Where Program Data Is Changed.

Consider a CAD (computer-assisted design) program designed to convert a schematic diagram into a printed-circuit board layout. Such a program usually contains a set of rules regarding how wide a printed circuit trace must be to carry a given current, how close together traces may be for a given voltage, or how far apart components that dissipate heat must be. These rules are generally considered to be a constant for a given type of printed circuit.

This type of program would also contain a collection of data regarding the nature of certain components—the electrical and physical specifications of many popular integrated circuits, semiconductors, and passive components. The nature of this data would vary widely depending upon the types of circuits being designed. There might be different data for designing audio circuits, RF circuits, or logic circuits. This data changes when manufacturers announce new devices or new electrical or physical specifications for existing devices.

Finally, the system's operator would enter data representing the interconnection of the components. The actual mechanism of how this data is entered is not of importance at this point; what is important to realize is that each time the program is used, new data (or modifications of previously entered data) is being provided.

This program makes use of three different kinds of data:

1. Data that rarely (if ever) changes
2. Data that changes occasionally
3. Data that changes each time the program is executed

How are these three different forms of data handled?

Data that is considered to be substantially unchanging can be made an integral part of the program. We might incorporate such data into LET statements (such as LET MINTRACE = .016) or be incorporated directly into formulae wherever the values are needed (such as LET RSPACING = Power * .8). Changing these values would require modification of the program. As the data may be located anywhere within the program, making such changes is difficult and likely to introduce error. That is why we usually reserve building data directly into the program for that data which is not likely to require change.

Data that will require changes on a somewhat more frequent basis might be built into the program using READ and DATA statements. In addition to being a more efficient method of making assignments, use of the READ and DATA statements allows all the data to be grouped in one physical area of the program. As a result, data is more likely to be updated completely and without introducing errors into the program. Another approach that a programmer might take is to totally isolate the data from the program's structure by placing all the data in a file external to the actual program and then reading the contents of the file using a mechanism similar to that of the READ and DATA statements. This will be discussed further in Chapter 18.

Data that changes with each *iteration* of the program (an iteration can be thought of as a cycle—for example, each time a new layout procedure is begun) is usually entered during program *execution*. As the program runs, the required information is solicited by the program and supplied by the operator. In actuality a CAD program would generally accept data from a keyboard, pointing device (such as a mouse or graphics tablet), or from other on-line sources. In this section we will deal with information that is entered through the keyboard. The technique of entering data during program execution, particularly from the keyboard, uses the *INPUT* statement.

13-2 THE INPUT STATEMENT

Purpose: The purpose of the INPUT statement is to allow data to be entered during program execution.

Syntax. There are several forms of the statement, including:

Syntax *a*: INPUT [;] {avar or nvar}
Syntax *b*: INPUT [;] [“prompt string”] {, or ;} {avar or nvar}
Syntax *c*: INPUT [;] {avar1 or nvar1} [{,} {avar2 or nvar2} {· · ·}]
Syntax *d*: INPUT [;] [“prompt string”] {, or ;} {avar1 or nvar1} [{,} {avar2 or nvar2} {· · ·}]

Syntax a: Execution of this form of the INPUT statement causes the computer to print a question mark (?) on the screen and then wait for the operator to enter data. If a numeric variable is named in the INPUT statement, this data may be a single number (consisting of a series of digits) with (optionally) a single sign (+ or −; if the sign is omitted, positive is assumed), containing (optionally) a single decimal point; *or* a single number (consisting of a series of digits) with (optionally) a single sign (+ or −; if the sign is omitted, positive is assumed), containing (optionally) a single decimal point, followed by the letter “E” for single-precision or “D” for double-precision, followed by another sign (optional) and another number representing the exponent of the value, in scientific notation. If an alphanumeric variable is named in the INPUT statement, the data may consist of the letters of the alphabet, the numerals, and most of the symbols, including the space, but *excluding the comma (,) the semicolon (;) and the double quotation marks* (”). These characters act as *delimiters,* or characters that BASIC uses to differentiate one item in a group from the next, and may not appear in the response to this form of the INPUT statement. Some BASIC dialects have additional characters which may not appear in the input.

Completion of the keyboard entry is signaled by pressing the carriage return key (<CR>). This tells the computer that you have entered all the characters of the number or alphanumeric data you had intended.

BASIC then resumes execution. It checks the value that was entered to make sure that a number was entered if a numeric variable was named. If there is no error in the type of data that was entered (BASIC has no way of knowing if the correct *value* was entered; it can only determine *type* of data), the value that was typed in will be assigned to the variable that was named in the statement. At this point, the named variable will contain the entered value just as if it had been assigned by a LET statement.

The punctuation that appears immediately after the INPUT keyword is optional, and if included will prevent the carriage return that signals the end of entry from being seen on the screen. Thus, the cursor remains in the next available print position. This is the same as the action of a semicolon at the end of a PRINT statement.

See Table 13-1 for some examples of the INPUT statement in this form.

Syntax b: The operation of this form of the INPUT statement is identical to syntax *a,* except that a *prompt string* appears on the screen. This prompt is a message that the programmer wishes to have displayed when this statement executes and usually contains text such as “ENTER EMPLOY-

TABLE 13-1 THE INPUT STATEMENT ACCORDING TO SYNTAX *A*

Statement	Result
INPUT K1	Displays a question mark, then waits for a keyboard entry to be made. When the carriage return key is pressed (signaling the end of the entry), the entry is checked for validity as a numeric value. If the entry is valid, the value is assigned to the numeric variable K1.
INPUT B$	Displays a question mark, then waits for a keyboard entry to be made. When the carriage return key is pressed (signaling the end of the entry), the value is assigned to the alphanumeric variable B$.

EE'S NAME: " or "HOW MANY HOURS WERE WORKED THIS PERIOD? ", or something similar that tells the person entering the data exactly what data is being requested at this point.

The punctuation that follows the prompt determines whether or not the question mark that would normally be printed will appear. Usually, if your prompt ends with a colon (:), you would not want the question mark to appear. Alternatively, if your prompt is in the form of a question (e.g., "DO YOU WISH TO CONTINUE (YES OR NO)", you can take advantage of the automatic printing of the question mark. In any case, the comma in this position inhibits the printing of the question mark; the semicolon causes the question mark to be printed. One or the other must appear.

Table 13-2 shows examples of the INPUT statement in the form of syntax *b*.

TABLE 13-2 THE INPUT STATEMENT ACCORDING TO SYNTAX *B*

Statement	Result
INPUT "WHAT IS YOUR NAME"; NAME$	Displays "WHAT IS YOUR NAME" followed by a question mark, then accepts a value from the keyboard. BASIC assigns the value entered to the alphanumeric variable NAME$.
INPUT "ENTER TODAY'S DATE: ", DATE$	Displays "ENTER TODAY'S DATE: ", does *not* display the question mark (comma suppresses the question mark), then accepts a value from the keyboard. BASIC assigns the value entered to the alphanumeric variable DATE$.
INPUT "ENTER THE VOLTAGE: ",V1	Display "ENTER THE VOLTAGE: ", does not display a question mark, then accepts a value from the keyboard. If what was typed was a valid numeric value, BASIC assigns that numeric value to the variable V1.

TABLE 13-2 *(continued)*

Statement	Result
INPUT; "IC TYPE NUMBER:" ICNUM$	Displays "IC TYPE NUMBER: ", does not display a question mark, then accepts an alphanumeric value. The entered value is assigned to variable ICNUM$. The carriage return that is typed after the entry is not echoed to the screen, and the cursor remains positioned in the print space immediately following the last character of the part name that was entered.

Syntax c: This syntax is identical in operation to syntax *a,* with the added ability to accept more than one value at a time. Several different variables may be named in this form of the INPUT statement, separated from each other by commas. The variables need not be of the same type; they may be any mixture of single-precision, double-precision, integer, or string variables. When the statement is executed, BASIC will print a question mark on the screen and then wait for values to be entered. A value must be entered for each variable named, because the values that are entered are assigned *sequentially* to the variable named. The first value entered is assigned to the first variable named, the second value to the second variable, and so on, until values have been assigned to each variable named. Values are separated by *commas*. (This is the reason that commas were not allowed as part of actual data.) If an insufficient number of values is entered (less than the number of variables named), most forms of BASIC will prompt again, sometimes with a double question mark (??), indicating that more information is required. Some other forms of BASIC will force you to reenter all the values, until the number of values entered equals the number of values expected. If you accidentally enter too many values, most dialects of BASIC will give you a message such as "EXCESS IGNORED"—i.e., the extra values were simply thrown away.

The same kind of type screening that occurs with the other forms of the INPUT statement occurs with this form, and data types must agree with variable types. The (optional) punctuation following the INPUT keyword has the same action as in previous forms of the statement.

Table 13-3 contains examples of this form of the INPUT statement.

TABLE 13-3 THE INPUT STATEMENT ACCORDING TO SYNTAX *C*

Statement	Result
INPUT R1,R2,R3	Displays a question mark on the screen, then waits while values are entered, with items separated from each other by commas, until

TABLE 13-3 *(continued)*

Statement	Result
	the <CR> key is pressed. BASIC then checks that three valid numeric items were entered, and if so, assigns the first value entered to the variable R1, the second value entered to the variable R2, and the third value entered to the variable R3. If too few items were entered BASIC, prints a double question mark (??) and awaits further entry. If too many values were entered BASIC, prints a message such as "EXCESS IGNORED" on the screen, and throws the surplus values away.
INPUT PARTDESC$, QUANT	Displays a question mark on the screen, then waits while two values are entered. The first value is expected to be alphanumeric, and the second value is expected to be numeric. The two values are expected to be separated by a comma. If both items are of the correct type, the first value entered will be assigned to the variable PARTDESC$ and the second value will be assigned to the variable QUANT. The error conditions of too many or too few values being entered are handled as above.
INPUT; PARTDESC$, QUANT	Exactly the same as the preceding example, except that when the <CR> key is pressed, signaling the end of the entry, the cursor will *not* advance to the beginning of the next line. This would allow a subsequent PRINT or INPUT statement to display information on the same line in which the entry appeared.

Syntax d: This form of the INPUT statement provides for the display of a prompt message before expecting data entry from the keyboard. As in the previous form, multiple variables may be assigned values in one statement. As in syntax b, the optional punctuation between the prompt string and the list of variables causes the printing (semicolon) or suppression (comma) of the question mark following the displaying of the prompt string. Table 13-4 demonstrates this syntax.

TABLE 13-4 THE INPUT STATEMENT ACCORDING TO SYNTAX *D*

Statement
INPUT "ENTER PART DESCRIPTION AND QUANTITY NEEDED", PARTDESC$, QUANT

Result
Displays the indicated prompt (question mark suppressed), then waits for keyboard entry of an alphanumeric value followed by a comma, followed by a valid numeric value. When entry is completed, the two valid values will be assigned to the variables PARTDESC$ and QUANT.

Statement
INPUT "ENTER INDUCTANCE, RESISTANCE, AND CURRENT CAPACITY OF THE COIL ", L,I,R.

Result
Displays the prompt string on the screen, then waits for three numeric values to be entered (separated by commas and ended with the <CR> key). If three valid answers are entered, they will be assigned to the variables R, L, and I. *Note: This is an error!* Analyzing the structure of the INPUT statement, we see that we expected the values to be entered in the following order: Inductance (L), then Resistance (R), then Current (I). If this were done correctly, however, the first entered value would be assigned to the variable L, *but the second entered value would be assigned to the variable I and the third entered value would be assigned to the variable R. This is not what was intended.* So, while the statement is syntactically correct, it is logically incorrect and should be written as INPUT "ENTER THE INDUCTANCE, RESISTANCE, AND CURRENT CAPACITY OF THE COIL: ", L,R,I.

13-3 USING THE INPUT STATEMENT

An example will help clarify important ways in which the INPUT statement is used.

Example 13-2 Exercising the INPUT Statement

Task: Write a program that someone could use to calculate the reactance of a capacitor, given the capacitor's value (in microfarads) and the frequency of operation (in hertz). The program should display the capacitor's value, the frequency of operation, and the capacitive reactance.

Algorithmic Analysis: Since this program may be used any number of times, but with different component and frequency values, these pieces of data should be obtained for the program through INPUT statements. When these two values have been entered, the capacitive reactance can be calculated. The formula for capacitive reactance is:

$$\frac{10^6}{2 \times \text{pi} \times f \times c}$$

where: f is the frequency in hertz
c is the capacitance in microfarads

Figure 13-1 illustrates the flowchart for the operations to be performed.

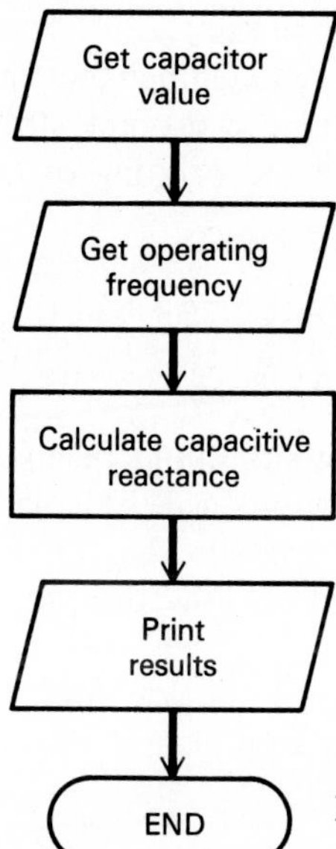

Fig. 13-1 Flowchart for the algorithm for calculating capacitive reactance.

Program Development: We are now ready to start constructing the program in BASIC. First, write a series of REM statements to identify the program and the variable names used in the program. Remember, these REM statements are there only as reminders to the programmer. They will never appear during program execution.

```
100  REM PROGRAM TO CALCULATE CAPACITIVE REACTANCE
110  REM C IS THE CAPACITANCE (IN MICROFARADS)
120  REM F IS THE FREQUENCY (IN HERTZ)
130  REM X IS THE CAPACITIVE REACTANCE (CALCULATED)
```

The INPUT statement(s) come next. Here we have two options. We can write a single INPUT statement that will accept both values:

```
140 INPUT "ENTER CAPACITANCE (UF) AND FREQUENCY (HZ): ",C,F
```

Or, we can write two input statements, one for the entry of each item needed:

```
140  INPUT "ENTER CAPACITANCE (IN MICROFARADS): ",C
150  INPUT "ENTER OPERATING FREQUENCY (IN HERTZ): ",F
```

This is usually the best approach, for reasons of clarity (the programmer can best see how the program operates and the program's user is best able to understand exactly what information is being requested). This is the method we will use in this program.

Notice we have used the form of the INPUT statement where the prompt string is followed by a comma. Remember that this supresses the printing of the question mark following the prompt string. We could also have structured the prompts so that the printing of the question mark would have been appropriate:

```
140  INPUT "WHAT IS THE CAPACITOR VALUE (MICROFARADS)";C
150  INPUT "WHAT IS THE OPERATING FREQUENCY (HERTZ)";F
```

Either set of INPUT statements could be used and the end result of using either is the same: two items will be solicited, one at a time, and assigned to their appropriate variables. The choice of which to use is the programmer's, and will depend on how the programmer prefers to write prompts.

Now we are ready to perform the calculation. Notice how the order of operations is controlled using parentheses.

```
160 LET X = 1000000 / (2 * 3.1416 * F * C)
```

Finally, we are ready to display our results. There are many ways in which the results could be displayed. However, good programming practice has certain requirements:

1. Values displayed should always be captioned. That is, there should be no question about what a numeric value represents. This can be done by printing a descriptive message along with the value (i.e., VALUE OF THE CAPACITOR IS XXXXXX, where XXXXXX is the numeric value), or, if there are a series of values to be printed, they may be in a columnar format, where there is an appropriate column heading, and all data appearing in that column is described by the heading.
2. Data should be presented in as uncluttered an environment as possible. There should be no extraneous information on the screen (or on the paper if we are dealing with printed output). Erase the screen (or advance to a new page of paper) and reprint (if necessary) any information that should appear.
3. Use blank lines, columns, and punctuation to make the reading of your data clear. Group related information together, separate entered data from calculated data (if appropriate), and use the same data presenta-

tion formats repeatedly when presenting similar data. In other words, if the users of your data are used to finding a name as the first item on a page, don't place that data in a different position on subsequent pages.

So, following these rules, first we clear the screen:

```
160 CLS
```

Now we begin the printing operations:

```
170  PRINT "THE CAPACITOR VALUE (MICROFARADS) WAS ";C
180  PRINT "THE OPERATING FREQUENCY (HERTZ) WAS ";F
190  PRINT
200  PRINT
210  PRINT "CAPACITIVE REACTANCE EQUALS ";X;" OHMS."
220  PRINT
230  PRINT
240  PRINT
```

Lines 170 and 180 print a caption (the alphanumeric string appearing between the double quotes) followed by the value the caption is describing. The PRINT statements with no parameters cause a line to be skipped (i.e., they print a blank line). This causes the information regarding the entered values to be grouped together. The final value printed, the capacitive reactance, is separated from the rest of the output by two blank lines to set it apart and give it more importance. Lines 220–240 print three blank lines, so that when the program ends, the system messages that the computer normally displays at this point will not appear to be part of the program's output.

Line 210 is somewhat different from the previous PRINT statements. It prints caption material on either side of the numeric value (X). When this statement is executed output will look like this:

```
CAPACITIVE REACTANCE EQUALS XX.XX OHMS.
```

(Where XX.XX represents the current numeric value of the variable X. The actual number of digits printed will depend on the variable's current value and the version of BASIC in use.)

This technique is often used to make the output more conversational. Most people find that small amounts of data presented in sentences are easier to read and understand. Let's rewrite the entire output section of this program as follows:

```
170  PRINT "CAPACITOR VALUE WAS ";C;" MICROFARADS."
180  PRINT "OPERATING FREQUENCY WAS ";F;" HERTZ."
190  PRINT
200  PRINT
210  PRINT "CAPACITIVE REACTANCE EQUALS ";X;" OHMS."
220  PRINT
230  PRINT
240  PRINT
```

Using these print statements, the output would look like this:

```
CAPACITOR VALUE WAS 0.22 MICROFARADS.
OPERATING FREQUENCY WAS 1500 HERTZ.


CAPACITIVE REACTANCE IS 482.286 OHMS
```

(Naturally, the numeric values shown would depend on the values entered in response to the input statements.)

Finally, we are ready to mark the end of the program:

```
250 END
```

Listing 13-1 shows this program in its entirety.

LISTING 13-1: COMPLETE LISTING OF THE CAPACITIVE REACTANCE PROGRAM

```
100  REM PROGRAM TO CALCULATE CAPACITIVE REACTANCE
110  REM C IS THE CAPACITANCE (IN MICROFARADS)
120  REM F IS THE FREQUENCY (IN HERTZ)
130  REM X IS THE CAPACITIVE REACTANCE (CALCULATED)
140  INPUT "WHAT IS THE CAPACITOR VALUE (MICROFARADS)";C
150  INPUT "WHAT IS THE OPERATING FREQUENCY (HERTZ)";F
160  LET X = 1000000 / (2 * 3.1416 * F * C)
170  PRINT "CAPACITOR VALUE WAS ";C;" MICROFARADS."
180  PRINT "OPERATING FREQUENCY WAS ";F;" HERTZ."
190  PRINT
200  PRINT
210  PRINT "CAPACITIVE REACTANCE EQUALS ";X;" OHMS."
220  PRINT
230  PRINT
240  PRINT
250  END
```

Example 13-3 How Data Input Relates to a Circuit Analysis Problem

Task: Write a program that will calculate the combined value of four dissimilar resistors in parallel. Output should consist of the values of the four resistors and their combined parallel resistance.

Algorithmic analysis: Since this program may be run repeatedly with different data, the values of the four resistors will be entered using INPUT statements. The formula for calculating parallel resistance is

$$R_t = \frac{1}{1/R_1 + 1/R_2 + 1/R_3 + 1/R_4}$$

We will format the output in the form of a sentence.

Figure 13-2 shows the flowchart for this algorithm.

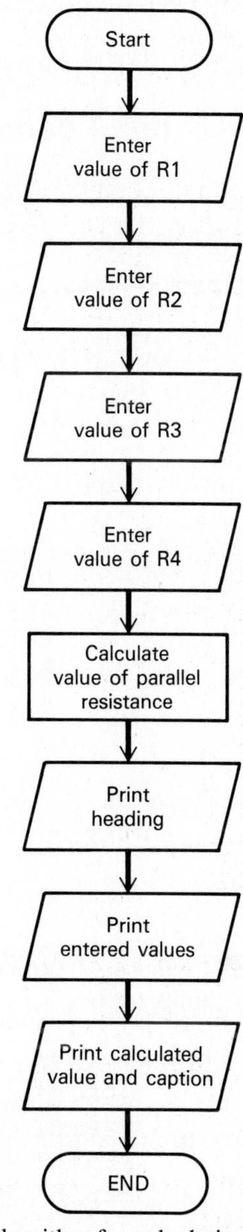

Fig. 13-2 Flowchart for the algorithm for calculating parallel resistances.

Program construction: Write the introductory REMs:

```
100  REM THIS PROGRAM CALCULATES THE COMBINED RESISTANCE
100  REM OF FOUR RESISTORS IN PARALLEL.
120  REM
130  REM VARIABLES USED:
140  REM R1 FIRST RESISTOR (OHMS ASSUMED)
150  REM R2 SECOND RESISTOR (OHMS ASSUMED)
160  REM R3 THIRD RESISTOR (OHMS ASSUMED)
170  REM R4 FOURTH RESISTOR (OHMS ASSUMED)
180  REM R COMBINED PARALLEL RESISTANCE, IN OHMS
```

Write the INPUT statements to accept the four resistor's values:

```
190  INPUT "ENTER THE FIRST RESISTOR'S OHMIC VALUE: ",R1
200  INPUT "ENTER THE SECOND RESISTOR'S OHMIC VALUE: ",R2
210  INPUT "ENTER THE THIRD RESISTOR'S OHMIC VALUE: ",R3
220  INPUT "ENTER THE FOURTH RESISTOR'S OHMIC VALUE: ";R4
```

Write the statement to calculate R:

```
230 LET R = 1/((1/R1) + (1/R2) + (1/R3) + (1/R4))
```

Write the output section:

```
240  CLS
250  PRINT "THE FOUR RESISTOR VALUES ENTERED WERE:"
260  PRINT "             RESISTOR 1: ";R1;" OHMS"
270  PRINT "             RESISTOR 2: ";R2;" OHMS"
280  PRINT "             RESISTOR 3: ";R3;" OHMS"
290  PRINT "             RESISTOR 4: ";R4;" OHMS"
300  PRINT
310  PRINT
320  PRINT "THE VALUE OF THESE RESISTANCES IN PARALLEL IS ";
330  PRINT R;" OHMS."
340  PRINT
350  PRINT
```

Out put will look like this [assume R_1 is 1000, R_2 is 200, R_3 is 100, and R_4 is 250 ohms (Ω)]:

```
THE FOUR RESISTOR VALUES ENTERED WERE:
             RESISTOR 1: 1000 OHMS
             RESISTOR 2: 200 OHMS
             RESISTOR 3: 100 OHMS
             RESISTOR 4: 250 OHMS
```

```
THE VALUE OF THESE RESISTANCES IN PARALLEL IS 50 OHMS.
```

Examine line 320 carefully. The last item in this line is a semicolon. Remember that this causes BASIC to leave the cursor on the same line, so that the next printing operation will take place in the next available space of *the same line*. That is why the value of *R* (50) and the word "OHM" printed on the same line as the text printed in line 320.

Finally, close the program.

```
360 END
```

Listing 13-2 shows the complete program.

LISTING 13-2: COMPLETE PROGRAM TO CALCULATE PARALLEL RESISTANCE

```
100  REM THIS PROGRAM CALCULATES THE COMBINED RESISTANCE
110  REM OF FOUR RESISTORS IN PARALLEL.
120  REM
130  REM VARIABLES USED:
140  REM R1  FIRST RESISTOR (OHMS ASSUMED)
150  REM R2  SECOND RESISTOR (OHMS ASSUMED)
160  REM R3  THIRD RESISTOR (OHMS ASSUMED)
170  REM R4  FOURTH RESISTOR (OHMS ASSUMED)
180  REM R COMBINED PARALLEL RESISTANCE IN OHMS
190  INPUT "ENTER THE FIRST RESISTOR'S OHMIC VALUE: ",R1
200  INPUT "ENTER THE SECOND RESISTOR'S OHMIC VALUE: ",R2
210  INPUT "ENTER THE THIRD RESISTOR'S OHMIC VALUE: ",R3
220  INPUT "ENTER THE FOURTH RESISTOR'S OHMIC VALUE: ";R4
230  LET R = 1/((1/R1) + (1/R2) + (1/R3) + (1/R4))
240  CLS
250  PRINT "THE FOUR RESISTOR VALUES ENTERED WERE:"
260  PRINT "          RESISTOR 1: ";R1;" OHMS"
270  PRINT "          RESISTOR 2: ";R2;" OHMS"
280  PRINT "          RESISTOR 3: ";R3;" OHMS"
290  PRINT "          RESISTOR 4: ";R4;" OHMS"
300  PRINT
310  PRINT
320  PRINT "THE VALUE OF THESE RESISTANCES IN PARALLEL IS ";
330  PRINT R;" OHMS."
340  PRINT
350  PRINT
360  END
```

13-4 THE READ AND DATA STATEMENTS

The programming examples so far assumed that the data would change with each iteration. Now we will examine *the technique of having a program contain data which does not change often.*

The READ and DATA statements are always used together. The READ statement contains the names of the variables to which values are to be assigned. The DATA statement contains the list of values to be assigned to the variables appearing in the DATA statement. There must be at least one DATA statement in a program containing a READ statement, but there may be multiple DATA statements associated with a given READ statement.

When a READ statement is executed, BASIC assigns a value to each variable named in the READ statement, taking these values, in the order in which they appear, starting with the first item in the DATA statement with the lowest line number. BASIC keeps track of which values in the DATA statements have been used, and if a READ statement is executed again, the next unused value or set of values appearing in a DATA statement is used for assignment.

Syntax:

READ {avar1 or nvar1} [{,} {avar2 or nvar2}] [· · ·]
DATA {alit1 or nlit1} [{,} {alit2 or nlit2}] [· · ·]

The READ statement must contain at least one variable name following the keyword READ. However, several variable names, of mixed types if appropriate, may appear, separated by commas. Execution of this statement will cause BASIC to search the program for the first unused value in a data statement. The first such value found will be assigned to the first variable named in the READ statement. Naturally, the value contained in the DATA statement must agree in type to the variable named in the READ statement (i.e., if the variable named is an alphanumeric variable, then the value appearing in the DATA statement must conform to the rules for alphanumeric literals). If additional variables appear in the READ statement, subsequent values appearing in DATA statements will be checked and assigned to the variables named.

The DATA statement or statements contain the values which are to be assigned to the variables appearing in the READ statements. DATA statements do not execute; they mark a given line of a program as being one which contains values for subsequent executions of READ statements. As a result, DATA statements may appear *anywhere* in a program. Beginning programmers usually put their DATA statements immediately following the READ statement that is expected to use the values contained. Experienced programmers usually place all the data in one place in the program, usually very near the end. As far as BASIC is concerned, it makes no difference. However, one of the reasons for using the DATA statement is to simplify the process of making modifications to the information carried by the program. Placing the data near the end of the program, all in one location, makes such modifications simpler and less likely to be performed inaccurately.

Table 13-5 shows some examples of how the READ and DATA statements work.

TABLE 13-5 EXAMPLES OF READ AND DATA STATEMENTS

Statement	Result
READ NAME$ . . . DATA "JOHN"	Upon execution, locates the first unused value in a DATA statement. If the type of value found in the DATA statement ("JOHN") agrees with the type of variable named in the READ statement (NAME$), then the value will be assigned to the named variable.
READ NAME$, HOURS . . . DATA "JUDY",40	Upon execution, locates the first unused value in a DATA statement ("JUDY"). If this value agrees with the variable type (NAME$), the value will be assigned. If there are additional variables named in the READ statement (HOURS), additional values will be taken from the DATA statement(s), and if these values match in type, they will be assigned to the remaining variables in the READ statement.
READ V1, V2, V3, V4 . . . DATA 17,29 DATA -5 DATA 53.7 DATA 28, −86,54,.7 DATA 3 DATA 99 DATA 23E-2 DATA .0876	Upon execution, assigns the first available DATA statement value (17) to V1, the second available value (29) to V2, the third available value (-5) to V3, and the fourth available value (53.7) to V4 (after type-checking). Notice that the first two values appear in the first DATA statement (separated by commas) but that the third and fourth values appear in DATA statements of their own. This does not make any difference to BASIC; DATA statement values are assigned in the sequence found, no matter how many DATA statements are involved. If the READ statement were executed again, the values of 28, −86, 54, and .7 would be assigned to V1, V2, V3, and V4, respectively. If the READ statement were executed one more time, the values 3, 99, 23E−2 (23×10^{-2}), and .0876 would be assigned to the variables V1, V2, V3, and V4.

13-5 USING THE READ AND DATA STATEMENTS

Examine the following example to see how READ and DATA statements can be used as alternatives to an INPUT statement.

Example 13-4 The Network Problem Revisited

Task: Modify the program that calculates the combined value of four resistors to use the READ and DATA statements instead of the INPUT statement.

Algorithmic analysis: Since there is no change in the algorithm of the program (we are changing only the method of obtaining data), the analysis of the algorithm remains the same as before. The flowchart developed in Fig. 13-2 still applies.

Program construction: Use the REM statements from the previous example:

```
100 REM THIS PROGRAM CALCULATES THE COMBINED RESISTANCE
110 REM OF FOUR RESISTORS IN PARALLEL.
120 REM
130 REM VARIABLES USED:
140 REM R1   FIRST RESISTOR (OHMS ASSUMED)
150 REM R2   SECOND RESISTOR (OHMS ASSUMED)
160 REM R3   THIRD RESISTOR (OHMS ASSUMED)
170 REM R4   FOURTH RESISTOR (OHMS ASSUMED)
180 REM R COMBINED PARALLEL RESISTANCE IN OHMS
```

Replace the input statements with a read statement:

```
190 READ R1, R2, R3, R4
```

At this point we will write the data on which the program is to act:

```
200 DATA 200,200,100,50
```

Notice the difference between using the READ and DATA statements for data entry and using the INPUT statement for data entry. We are including data within the program *at the time the program is being written*. Using the INPUT statement allows data to be entered *at the time the program is executed*.

Perform the calculations (no change):

```
230 LET R = 1/((1/R1) + (1/R2) + (1/R3) + (1/R4))
```

Print the results (no changes):

```
240 CLS
250 PRINT "THE FOUR RESISTOR VALUES ENTERED WERE:"
260 PRINT "              RESISTOR 1: ";R1;" OHMS"
270 PRINT "              RESISTOR 2: ";R2;" OHMS"
280 PRINT "              RESISTOR 3: ";R3;" OHMS"
290 PRINT "              RESISTOR 4: ";R4;" OHMS"
300 PRINT
310 PRINT
320 PRINT "THE VALUE OF THESE RESISTANCES IN PARALLEL IS ";
330 PRINT R;" OHMS."
340 PRINT
350 PRINT
```

Close the program:

```
360 END
```

The program is shown in its entirety in Listing 13-3.

LISTING 13-3: REVISED PROGRAM FOR CALCULATING PARALLEL RESISTANCES, USING THE READ AND DATA STATEMENTS

```
100  REM THIS PROGRAM CALCULATES THE COMBINED RESISTANCE
110  REM OF FOUR RESISTORS IN PARALLEL.
120  REM
130  REM VARIABLES USED:
140  REM R1  FIRST RESISTOR (OHMS ASSUMED)
150  REM R2  SECOND RESISTOR (OHMS ASSUMED)
160  REM R3  THIRD RESISTOR (OHMS ASSUMED)
170  REM R4  SECOND RESISTOR (OHMS ASSUMED)
180  REM R COMBINED PARALLEL RESISTANCE IN OHMS
190  READ R1, R2, R3, R4
200  DATA 200,200,100,50
230  LET R = 1/((1/R1) + (1/R2) + (1/R3) + (1/R4))
240  CLS
250  PRINT "THE FOUR RESISTOR VALUES ENTERED WERE:"
260  PRINT "            RESISTOR 1: ";R1;" OHMS"
270  PRINT "            RESISTOR 2: ";R2;" OHMS"
280  PRINT "            RESISTOR 3: ";R3;" OHMS"
290  PRINT "            RESISTOR 4: ";R4;' OHMS"
300  PRINT
310  PRINT
320  PRINT "THE VALUE OF THESE RESISTANCES IN PARALLEL IS ";
330  PRINT R;" OHMS."
340  PRINT
350  PRINT
360  END
```

Notice that lines 210 and 220 are no longer in this program. While we could renumber the remaining program lines if we wished to, there is no need to do so. BASIC will continue execution with the next higher line number that exists, unless we tell it to do otherwise.

We have not yet realized the full power of the READ and DATA statement combination. This is because we do not yet know how to write a program that repeats its operations on a series of data values without rerunning the program each time. The next chapter deals with controlling program execution and will demonstrate this power.

SUMMARY

Programs are made more versatile and powerful when the data to be used in the calculations can be supplied by the user. An important statement in BASIC which supports data entry during program execution is the INPUT statement. It can take a number of allowable forms. When the data to be used by the program does not change too often, the READ and DATA statements are a useful alternative to the INPUT statement.

REVIEW PROBLEMS

1. Give some examples of data that would change frequently in a system that keeps track of a PC board manufacturing company's parts inventory.

2. Give some examples of data that would be likely to change, but not frequently, for the same inventory system.

3. Give some examples of data that would most likely never change for the same inventory system.

4. Line 230 of both parallel resistance programs reads

```
230 LET R = 1/((1/R1) + (1/R2) + (1/R3) + (1/R4))
```

a. Are the inner parentheses (around the expressions 1/R*X*) needed to calculate the correct values? If not, why do you think they were included?

b. Rewrite line 230 to eliminate the inner parentheses.

5. Give two examples of suitable use of an INPUT statement and two examples of suitable use of the READ and DATA statements.

6. For the following examples, write syntactically correct INPUT, LET, or READ and DATA statements, whichever seem suitable, for the data being sought. INPUT statements should include suitable prompts; LET, READ, and DATA statements should include correctly written and logical data values. In either case, be sure to use appropriate variable names for the values to be stored.

a. Entry of today's date in the format MM/DD/YY (e.g., 7/2/87).

b. Entry of today's date in the format MONTH DAY, YEAR (e.g., MAY 23, 1984).

c. Entry of the operator's ID number (all digits).

d. Entry of the names of the days of the week into the variables DAY1$, DAY2$, DAY3$, etc.

e. Entry of the heading to be printed at the top of an engineering summary report in a program that serves no other function.

f. Entry of the number of stages in an amplifier for a program that calculates total gain.
g. Entry of the number of identical parallel resistors and their value, to be processed by a program that calculates averages for all members of a class.
h. Entry of the number of radios sold in the month of March.
i. Entry of the number of different suppliers of linear ICs normally carried by a small electronics distributor.
j. Entry of the value of PI for a program that calculates inductive reactance.

7. Given the following program segment:

```
250  READ A, B, C$
260  READ X, A, Y
270  DATA 6,2,"ABCDEFG",9,1,7
280  PRINT A
290  PRINT X
300  PRINT C$
```

a. What will be printed as a result of the execution of line 280?
b. What will be printed as a result of the execution of line 290?
c. What will be printed as a result of the execution of line 300?

8. Given the following program segment:

```
170  DATA 9, 12, 23,"ABC"
180  DATA 1,7,3
190  READ X, Y, Z
200  DATA 22,33,44
210  READ A$, A, B, X
220  READ X, Q, P
230  PRINT A
240  PRINT Z
250  PRINT X
260  PRINT Y/P
```

a. What is printed as a result of the execution of line 230?
b. What is printed as a result of the execution of line 240?
c. What is printed as a result of the execution of line 250?
d. What is printed as a result of the execution of line 260?

9. Consider the following program segment:

```
750  READ A1, A2, A3
760  DATA 1,2,3,4,5,6
770  READ B1, B2, B3, B4
775  DATA  7,8,9,10
780  PRINT A1, A2, B3
```

```
790  READ A1 , A2 , A3
800  DATA 11 ,12 ,13
810  PRINT B4 , B3 , A1
820  DATA 60 ,70 ,80
830  READ B4 , B3 , A1
```

a. What is printed as a result of the execution of line 780?
b. What is printed as a result of the execution of line 810?
c. What are the final values for the variables A1, A2, A3, B1, B2, B3, and B4?

REVIEW QUESTIONS

1. Why do we not want to have to change program lines whenever a program is to be rerun with different data?
2. Why do experienced programmers prefer to locate all the infrequently changing data in a common location within a program? What is that location?
3. What is meant by the term "iteration"?
4. What is the purpose of the INPUT statement?
5. What is the purpose of the prompt string?
6. What is meant by the term "delimiter"? What are the common delimiters used by BASIC?
7. What is the purpose of the READ and DATA statements? Why are they always discussed together?

14 PROGRAM FLOW

In previous chapters we mentioned the fact that BASIC statements are executed in ascending numerical order, that is, from the lowest line number to the highest line number, unless explicitly commanded to do otherwise. We also discussed that efficient use of the computer occurred when we were able to use the same program over and over again, substituting different data for each iteration (or building upon the data generated in the previous iteration). In this chapter we will explore the BASIC commands that make these techniques possible.

14-1 THE GOTO STATEMENT AND UNCONDITIONAL PROGRAM BRANCHING

In some programs, execution is never to cease. When one iteration of the program has been completed, the program is to recycle back to the beginning. This repetition is to continue until such time as the computer is turned off. While this is most often the case with computers that have been dedicated to a single function (usually control computers that oversee some technical function such as controlling traffic lights or checking the operation of a heating system), there are applications in which general purpose computers, capable of performing numerous functions in a time-sharing mode, have similar programming. An example would be the program that allows you to get information about your bank account from a small terminal at the bank. When you have finished asking questions about your account, the program starts at the beginning again, ready for the next customer's queries.

BASIC provides the programmer with the GOTO statement to perform such an unconditional branch. It allows the programmer to change the next statement to be executed from the normal, next higher numerical line number to the line number of the programmer's choice. Once execution has been redirected, the normal order of execution resumes; statements are executed starting with the destination line number, continuing in ascending numerical order.

Purpose: The purpose of the GOTO statement is to provide a means of interrupting the normal sequential execution of statements by redirecting execution to continue from an alternative line number.

Syntax:

GOTO {lnum}

Explanation:

When this statement is executed, BASIC changes the normal order of line execution and executes the line named in the GOTO statement next, regardless of its position in the program. Execution continues from the destination line in normal ascending order. An example of this is

```
GOTO 100
```

Example 14-1 Repeating network calculations

Listing 14-1 is the program we used earlier to calculate the combined resistance of four resistors in parallel, but with an addition at line 355 that sends the program back to the beginning after each set of resistances has been calculated and printed. (We have also removed some of the REM statements between lines 110 and 190 for brevity.) *Note:* This program will not end unless the computer is reset.

LISTING 14-1: REVISED PROGRAM FOR CALCULATING PARALLEL RESISTANCES

```
100 REM THIS PROGRAM CALCULATES THE COMBINED RESISTANCE
110 REM OF FOUR RESISTORS IN PARALLEL.
190 INPUT "ENTER THE FIRST RESISTOR'S OHMIC VALUE: ",R1
200 INPUT "ENTER THE SECOND RESISTOR'S OHMIC VALUE: ",R2
210 INPUT "ENTER THE THIRD RESISTOR'S OHMIC VALUE: ",R3
220 INPUT "ENTER THE FOURTH RESISTOR'S OHMIC VALUE: ",R4
230 LET R = 1/((1/R1) + (1/R2) + (1/R3) + (1/R4))
240 CLS
250 PRINT "THE FOUR RESISTOR VALUES ENTERED WERE:"
260 PRINT "          RESISTOR 1: ";R1;" OHMS"
270 PRINT "          RESISTOR 2: ";R2;" OHMS"
280 PRINT "          RESISTOR 3: ";R3;" OHMS"
290 PRINT "          RESISTOR 4: ";R4;" OHMS"
300 PRINT
310 PRINT
320 PRINT, "THE VALUE OF THESE RESISTANCES IN PARALLEL IS ";
330 PRINT R;" OHMS."
340 PRINT
350 PRINT
355 GOTO 190
360 END
```

Depending upon the nature of the programming task to be performed, we may or may not know the exact number of times a program or section of a program is to repeat. For instance, consider a program that is to calculate the average of six voltage readings taken. We may assume (for the purposes of this example) that there will always be exactly six voltage readings to be averaged, even though some of those readings might equal zero.

There are two possible approaches to obtaining the needed data: use six data entry statements (these might be INPUT statements or READ statements) or use one data entry statement in a control structure that causes it to be executed six times. Figure 14-1 illustrates the algorithm of using the six data entry statements. Figure 14-2 illustrates the use of a control structure causing the one data entry statement to be executed six times.

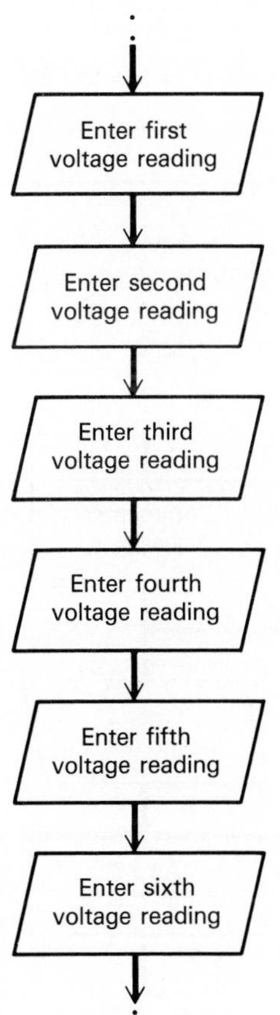

Fig. 14-1 Flowchart for entering six voltage readings, using six data entry operations.

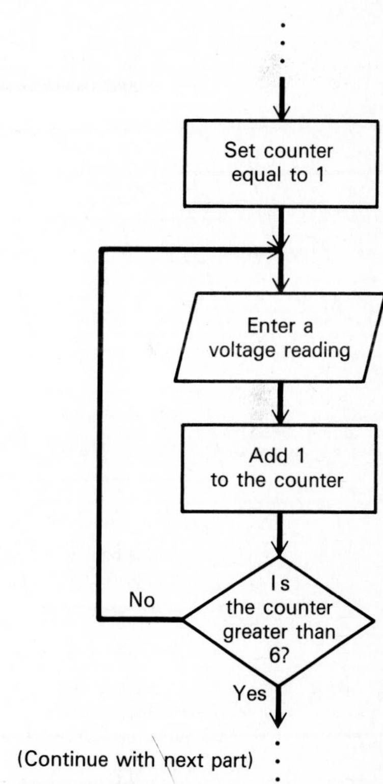

Fig. 14-2 Flowchart for entering six voltage readings using a control structure.

Compare the two algorithms. If the needs of the program were to change for some reason (i.e., the engineering department wanted an additional voltage reading to be taken and averaged), additional steps would have to be added to the method described by Fig. 14-1 (see Fig. 14-3). But notice that the Fig. 14-2 algorithm only needs to have the ending value changed from six to seven (see Fig. 14-4). Consider the changes that would have to be made to both of the algorithms if the engineering department wanted to average twelve voltage readings (instead of six or seven). The length of the program requiring individual data entry statements would nearly double! The length of the program using the control structure to execute the single data entry statement multiple times would remain the same; only the number of times that the data entry statement is executed would change.

BASIC provides a control structure such as the one described in Figs. 14-2 and 14-4. It is implemented as the FOR-NEXT loop.

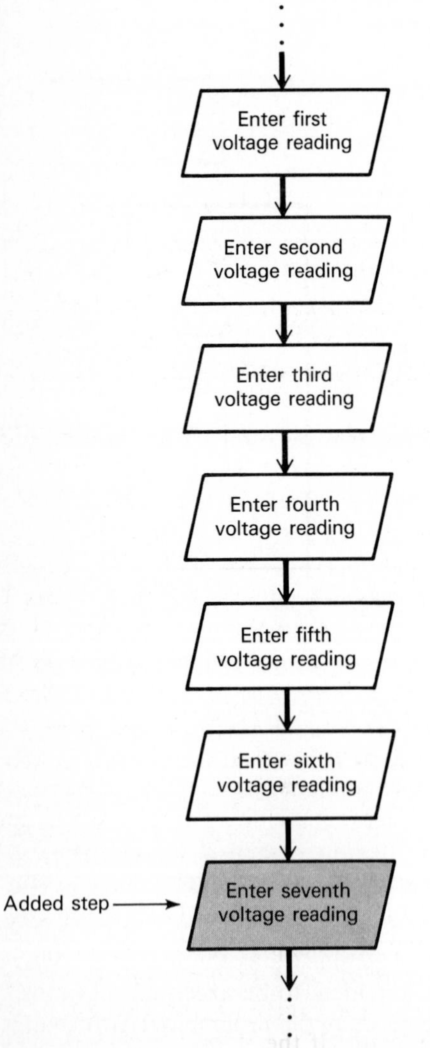

Fig. 14-3 Flowchart for entering seven voltage readings, using seven data entry operations.

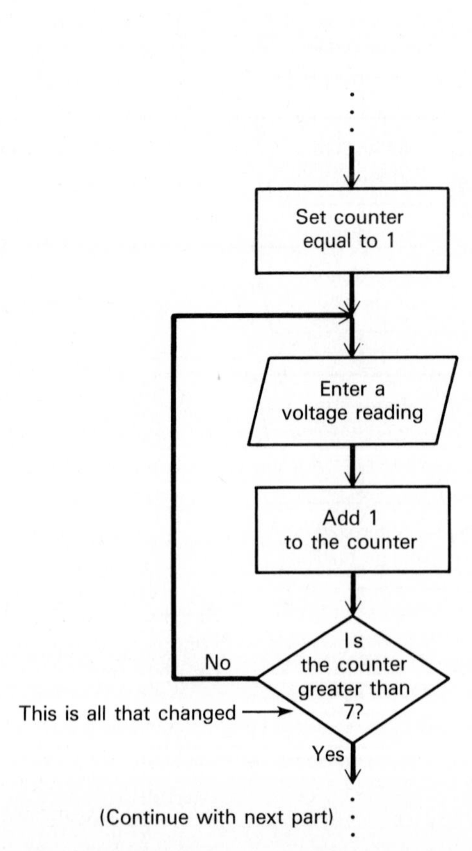

Fig. 14-4 Flowchart for entering seven voltage readings using a control structure.

Purpose: The purpose of the FOR and NEXT statements is to create an iterative (repetitive) loop which will repeat the BASIC statements physically located between the FOR statement and the corresponding NEXT statement until parameters (contained in the FOR statement) are satisfied.

Syntax:

```
FOR {nvar1} = {nexpr2} TO {nexpr3} [STEP {nexpr4}]
    (Statement)
    (Statement)
      .
      .
      .
  NEXT [{nvar1}]
    (Continue here when FOR statement is satisfied)
```

Explanation:

Nvar1 is a numeric variable name. Some forms of BASIC restrict the type of numeric variable to a single-precision floating-point variable, but this is not universal and most forms of BASIC permit any numeric variable to be used. This variable is known as the *index variable*. The value of the index variable will be varied by the action of the FOR-NEXT loop. This index variable performs the same function as the counter in Figs. 14-2 and 14-4.

Nexpr2 (which of course may be a nvar, nlit, or nexpr) is the value which will automatically be assigned to the index variable upon entering the loop. In Fig. 14-4 we used a starting value of 1. This starting value will be assigned to the index variable *only when the loop is entered.*

Once the loop has been entered, the BASIC statements between the FOR statement and its corresponding NEXT statement are executed as usual. References may be made, if desired, to the current value of the index variable; its value may be used just as the value of any other numeric variable may be used, but *no new value should be assigned to it*. Doing so will usually upset the operation of the loop. The index variable may be used in any statement which does not alter its value.

When BASIC encounters the NEXT statement, the value of nexpr4 is added to the current value of the index variable. Notice that nexpr4 (following the keyword clause STEP) is optional. If the STEP clause is omitted, a value of 1 will be used (1 is the *default* value).

After the STEP value has been added to the index variable, the index variable's value is compared to the value of nexpr3. If the index variable's value *exceeds* (is strictly greater than) the current value of nexpr3, the FOR statement is said to be "satisfied" and execution transfers to the first statement following the NEXT statement. If the FOR statement has *not* been satisfied, execution continues with the statement immediately following the FOR statement; that is, the statements between the FOR statement and the NEXT statement are executed again. When BASIC again reaches the NEXT statement, the STEP value is again added to the index variable and the index variable is again compared to the value of nexpr3.

This repetition will continue until the FOR statement has been satisfied.

Example 14-2 A Typical FOR-NEXT Loop

Consider the following program fragment:

```
 90  (Statement)
100  FOR I = 1 TO 6
110  INPUT "ENTER A TEST GRADE: ",G
120  (Statement)
130      .
140      .
150  NEXT I
160  (Continue here when FOR conditions have been satisfied)
```

Line 100 sets up the FOR-NEXT loop. I is the index variable. Upon entry to the loop (presumably from line 90), an initial value of 1 is assigned to I.

Lines 110 to 140 are executed in the normal manner. Line 110 solicits the entry of a test grade. Lines 120 to 140 would manipulate this value in some manner (it is not necessary to analyze these statements to understand the operation of the FOR-NEXT loop).

When line 150 is executed, the STEP value is added to I. Since we did not explicitly state a STEP value, the default value of 1 is used. Therefore, at this point, I has a value of 2 (the initial value of 1 plus the STEP value of 1).

This new value of I is compared to the value 6. Remember that the value following the keyword clause TO represents the ending value of the loop, i.e., the value against which the index variable is compared to determine whether the FOR conditions have been satisfied. Since the current value of I (2) does not exceed the ending value (6), execution continues with line 110.

When BASIC once again reaches line 150, the STEP value is again added to the index variable. I now has a value of 3 (previous value of 2 plus the STEP value of 1). This value is again compared to the ending value (6), and since it does not exceed the ending value, execution continues at line 110.

This process is repeated, with I attaining values of 4, 5, and 6. When line 150 is encountered during the iteration when I has reached a value of 6, the STEP value is again added to I. I has now reached a value of 7 This time, when the value of I (7) is compared to the ending value (6), the index variable *does* exceed the ending value. Instead of transferring execution to line 110, execution continues with line 160. The FOR condition has been satisfied.

Usually, the FOR-NEXT statement is written so that nexpr2 is less than nexpr3, and the value of the index variable increases. We may also write the FOR-NEXT statement so that nexpr2 is greater than nexpr3. In this case we must specify a *negative* step value. The negative value is added to the index variable on each pass through the loop, thus *diminishing* the index variable. When the index variable is *strictly less than* nexpr3, the loop is satisfied.

Example 14-3 Index Decrement

The following program shows the values which the index assumes during each iteration of a FOR-NEXT loop. The index is *decremented* by 1 each time.

```
100  FOR I = 10 TO -3 STEP -1
120  PRINT I
130  NEXT I
140  END
```

This program will print the values 10, 9, 8, 7, 6, 5, 4, 3, 2, 1, 0, −1, −2, and −3 on subsequent lines.

Example 14-4 Using a FOR-NEXT Loop for Calculating the Gain of a Noninverting Operational-Amplifier Circuit

Listing 14-2 (see Fig. 14-5) shows a short program that calculates the closed-loop voltage gain of a noninverting operational amplifier circuit as the value of R2 is varied while keeping the value of R1 constant.

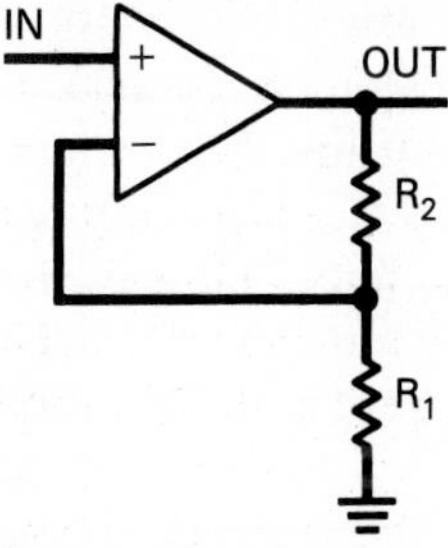

Fig. 14-5 Noninverting operational amplifier.

LISTING 14-2: CALCULATING THE CLOSED-LOOP VOLTAGE GAIN OF A NONINVERTING OPERATIONAL-AMPLIFIER CIRCUIT WHILE VARYING THE VALUE OF R2 WITH A CONSTANT VALUE OF R1

```
200  REM THIS PROGRAM CALCULATES THE CLOSED LOOP VOLTAGE GAIN OF A
210  REM NONINVERTING OP-AMP CIRCUIT. THE VALUE OF R1 WILL
220  REM BE KEPT CONSTANT AT 100K. THE VALUE OF R2 WILL BE
```

LISTING 14-2: *(continued)*

```
230  REM VARIED BETWEEN 0 OHMS AND 1 MEGOHM IN STEPS OF 50K.
240  PRINT "GAIN OF A NONINVERTING OPERATIONAL-AMPLIFIER CIRCUIT"
250  PRINT "R1 REMAINS CONSTANT AT 100K OHMS. R2 VARIES AS SHOWN."
260  PRINT
270  PRINT "R2 (OHMS)","GAIN"
280  LET R1 = 100000
290  FOR R2 = 0 TO 1000000 STEP 50000
300     LET GAIN = 1 + (R2/R1)
310     PRINT R2,GAIN
320  NEXT R2
330  PRINT
340  PRINT "END OF GAIN TABLE."
350  END
```

Lines 200 through 230 are remarks, describing the overall action of the program. Lines 240 through 260 print a report heading and a blank line. Line 270 prints headings for two columns of figures.

Line 280 initializes the value of the variable R1 to 100000. We must remember to do this or BASIC will use its default value when R1 is referenced in line 300. Since most BASICS default uninitialized numeric variables to a value of zero, line 300 would result in a DIVISION BY ZERO error message.

Line 290 is the beginning of the FOR-NEXT loop. The initial value of 0 is assigned to the variable R2. Line 300 computes a value for GAIN; this value and the current value of R2 is printed by the PRINT statement of line 310. When line 320 is encountered, the step value (50000) is added to the current value of the index variable, R2. At the first iteration, R2 has a value of 50000 (0 plus 50000). Since R2 does not exceed the ending value (1000000) execution resumes at line 300.

This process repeats until the iteration in which GAIN has been calculated on the basis of R2 = 1000000. At the conclusion of this iteration, R2 will attain a value of 1050000, which *exceeds* the ending value. Execution will continue at line 330 which will print a blank line, line 340 which will print a closing message, and line 340, the end of the program.

Notice how lines 300 and 310 were indented. This was done so that the statements that are part of the FOR/NEXT loop starting at line 290 could be clearly seen. The indentation is *not* required by BASIC, nor is it done automatically by BASIC. When you are writing your own programs, you will find that the program's operation is easier to follow if you use indentation to show when groups of lines are associated. We will use this notation in all the programming examples that follow.

Why do we initialize the value of R1 *before* the FOR-NEXT loop? We could have placed the LET statement of line 280, at line 295 instead. This would have satisfied the requirement for R1 having a value before the calculation at line 300. However, we would be causing BASIC to assign a new value to R1 for each iteration of the loop; in this case, 200 times.

Since we are assigning the same value each time, we have executed 199 unnecessary operations. By placing the initialization outside the loop, we perform the assignment of the initial value only once.

Example 14-5 Nested FOR-NEXT Loops

In this programming example, we have two FOR-NEXT loops. Notice that one loop (the one whose index variable is R2) is wholly contained within the loop whose index variable in R1. This is called *nesting* of loops and is permitted *as long as one loop is completely within the other.* Refer to Fig. 14-6. This shows the relationships permitted in nested loops. Loops A, B, and C are permissible, since there is no crossing of the loops—an inner loop is fully contained within an outer loop or loops. Figure 14-7 shows two loops, loops D and E, which are *not* permitted, since the control structures overlap.

Permitted FOR-NEXT loop structures

FOR
FOR
NEXT
NEXT
Loop A

FOR
FOR
NEXT
FOR
NEXT
NEXT
Loop B

FOR
FOR
FOR
NEXT
FOR
NEXT
NEXT
FOR
NEXT
NEXT
Loop C

Fig. 14-6 Legal nesting of loops.

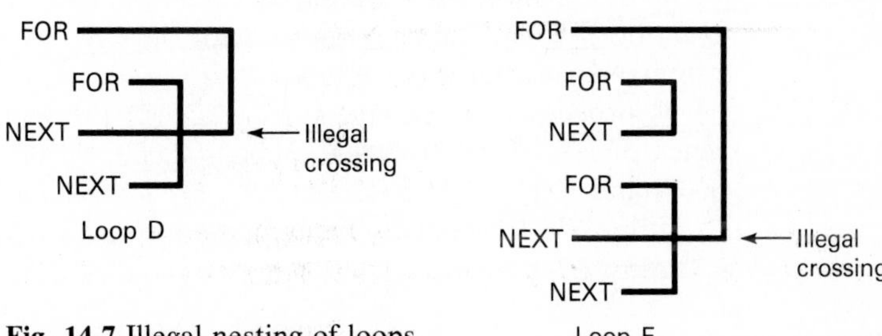

Fig. 14-7 Illegal nesting of loops.

The program which follows is a modification of the program we just analyzed. It will print closed loop gain calculations, while varying both R1 and R2.

LISTING 14-3: CALCULATING THE CLOSED-LOOP VOLTAGE GAIN OF A NONINVERTING OPERATIONAL-AMPLIFIER CIRCUIT WITH VARYING VALUES FOR BOTH R1 AND R2

```
200  REM  THIS PROGRAM CALCULATES THE CLOSED LOOP VOLTAGE GAIN OF A
210  REM   NONINVERTING OP-AMP CIRCUIT. THE VALUE OF R1 WILL BE
220  REM  VARIED BETWEEN 10K AND 100K IN STEPS OF 10K. THE VALUE OF
230  REM  R2 WILL BE VARIED BETWEEN 0 OHMS AND 100K IN STEPS OF 20K.
240  FOR R1 = 10000 TO 100000 STEP 10000
250    PRINT "GAIN OF A NONINVERTING OPERATIONAL-AMPLIFIER CIRCUIT"
260    PRINT "R1 EQUALS "; R1; "OHMS. R2 VARIES AS SHOWN."
270    PRINT
280    PRINT "R2 (OHMS)","GAIN"
290    FOR R2 = 0 to 100000 STEP 20000
300      LET GAIN = 1 + (R2/R1)
310      PRINT R2,GAIN
320    NEXT R2
330    PRINT
340  NEXT R1
350  PRINT
350  PRINT "END OF GAIN TABLE."
360  END
```

Notice that the inner loop (controlling the values for R2) is similar to the previous program. What has changed is that there is an outer loop controlling the value for R1.

In the first iteration, R1 receives a value of 10000 in line 240. Lines 250 through 270 print a heading for this particular table. Notice that line 260 prints the current value of R1 surrounded by a suitable caption.

The inner loop at line 290 is entered, and six gains are calculated and printed for R2 values of 0, 20000, 40000, 60000, 80000, and 100000 ohms. Throughout these six calculations, the value of R1 has remained at 10000.

When the inner loop is satisfied, execution continues at line 330, printing a blank line, line 340 closes the outer loop, adding the step value to R1. R1 now has a value of 20000. Execution continues at line 250, printing a new table heading with the current value of R1, and then reentering the inner loop, calculating six gains with varying values of R2 against the current value of R1.

This process continues until R1 exceeds the value of 100000 (i.e., for values of R1 = 10000, 20000, 30000, 40000, 50000, 60000, 70000, 80000, 90000, and 100000). Then the outer loop is satisfied and execution continues at line 350, printing a closing message and ending the program.

14-3 CONDITIONAL EXECUTION

At the beginning of this chapter we said that in many cases we know exactly how many times a given part of a program is to repeat and that, therefore, we could use a control structure that counts how many times the program segment has been executed and then goes on. There are times when the exact number of iterations is not known. For example, consider the voltage averaging problem again. We know that for each iteration of the routine, six voltage readings will be entered, but how many sets of voltages (that is, readings for how many circuits) are to be processed? The answer is a general one; additional sets of six voltage readings should be processed as long as unprocessed sets of readings remain. One of the ways we can determine when all the data has been processed is by entering a *key value* when all the legitimate sets of voltages have been entered. This key value, when detected, sets off a series of events inside the program that ultimately causes the program to end.

The key value is used as a *signal* to the program that you are all finished, so the value selected should be one that the data would not normally attain. This usually requires some analysis of the data that is being entered. For instance, if we were dealing with test grades instead of voltages, we could select any value less than zero or greater than one hundred as a key value. They represent values a test grade cannot normally attain. Therefore, we might select 999 or a negative value as a signal that we are done.

However, as we are dealing with a voltage reading, it is possible that the value can be either positive or negative. In order to use the key value technique we must determine what the possible voltage readings are and select a key value that is outside this range. If an analysis of the circuit determined that it is not possible to have a voltage reading greater than 10 volts, we may use any value greater than 10 as a key value. The value that is ultimately selected should be one that is easy to remember.

Thus, what we want the program to do is monitor the first voltage value (of a set of six voltage values) entered; if a value greater than 10 is detected, the program is to consider its task completed. Otherwise, the program is to use the value entered and the five values following as another set of input values to be averaged.

When comparing two quantities, keep in mind that there are really only three relational possibilities: the quantities can be equal, quantity 1 can be less than quantity 2, or quantity 1 can be greater than quantity 2. BASIC provides a mechanism for asking a question about the relationship between two quantities, and performing one action if the question is answered "true" and an alternate action if the question is answered "false."

The phrasing of the question to be asked makes use of *relational operators*. These are symbols that are probably quite familiar to you:

=	equal
>	greater than
<	less than

The stating of the condition is as follows:

{nexpr1} {relationsl operator} {nexpr2} or
{aexpr1} {relational operator} {aexpr2}

Some valid relations might be:

RTOTAL > 10000	Is the value of the variable RTOTAL greater than 10000?
NAME$ = "RACHEL"	Is the value of the variable NAME$ equal to the literal "RACHEL"?
SALES < QUOTA	Is the value of SALES less than the value of QUOTA?

Relational operators may be combined. The following are also validly written conditions:

VOLTAGE >= 90	Is the value of the variable Voltage greater than or equal to 90?
MONTH$ <> "DECEMBER"	Is the value of the variable MONTH$ *not equal* to the literal "DECEMBER"?
A * B <= D/X	Is the value of A times B less than or equal to the value of D divided by X?

Now that we can write conditions, let us introduce the statement that BASIC uses to evaluate these conditions and act accordingly.

14-3-1 The IF Statement

Purpose: The purpose of the IF statement is to provide a mechanism for the comparison of two numeric or two alphanumeric values and to perform one action if the condition evaluates as true and an alternate action if the condition evaluates as false.

Syntax:

Syntax *a*: IF {condition} THEN {any legal BASIC statement}
(Following statement)

Syntax *b*: IF {condition} THEN {lnum}
(Following statement)

Explanation:

Syntax a: The condition is evaluated. If the relationship is true, the statement following the THEN clause is executed. If the THEN clause is a branching instruction, execution continues from that point in the normal manner. If the THEN clause contains any other kind of statement, the statement is executed and execution then continues with the statement following the IF statement.

If the relationship is false, the THEN clause is bypassed (no matter what type of statement it is) and execution continues directly with the statement following the IF statement.

Syntax b: This form of the IF statement is similar to the general form of syntax *a,* and exists because most often the THEN action is a GOTO statement. If this is the case, the keyword GOTO may be omitted and the destination line number where execution is to continue if the condition evaluates as true, is simply stated.

Table 14-1 shows examples of the IF statement.

TABLE 14-1 (THE IF STATEMENT)

```
IF X > 7 THEN PRINT "FINISHED."
LET X = X + 1
```

Compares the current value of the variable X to 7. If the statement "X is greater than 7" is true, then the word "FINISHED" is printed. If the condition is not true, the PRINT operation is bypassed. In either case, the next operation to occur is the LET statement. Execution continues from there in the normal line-order sequence.

```
100  IF SALES < QUOTA THEN GOTO 500
110  PRINT "SALES QUOTA MET."
.
.
.
500  PRINT "SALES DID NOT MEET QUOTA."
```

Compares the current value of the variable SALES to the current value of the variable QUOTA. If SALES is less than QUOTA (condition is true), execution continues at line 500. If SALES is greater than or equal to quota (condition is false), execution continues at line 110 in the normal fashion.

```
600  IF NAME$ = "END" THEN 999
610  PRINT "NAME ENTERED WAS ";NAME$
.
.
.
999  END
```

Compares the current value of NAME$ to the literal "END". If the values match, the program takes this as a signal to end; execution branches to line 999, which is an END statement. If the condition is false (if NAME$ had any other value), execution continues with line 610, in the normal fashion.

```
250  IF QUANTINSTOCK <= REORDERPOINT THEN 1500
260  REM SUFFICIENT QUANTITY IN STOCK. DO NOT REORDER YET
.
.
.
1500  REM PROCESS THE REORDER.
```

Compares the current value of QUANTINSTOCK. If this value is less than or equal to the value in REORDERPOINT, the program branches to the area where reorders are handled. Otherwise, if no reorder is needed, execution continues at line 260.

14-3-2 Testing Multiple Conditions

Sometimes we wish to test if a combination of conditions is true; a computer-assisted printed circuit design program might need to test if ICNAME$ = "NE555" AND PACKAGE$ = "8 PIN DIP". An automatic circuit testing machine may need to test if VOLTAGE1 > NORMALV1 OR VOLTAGE 2 > NORMALV2. This kind of testing can be performed in a single *compound IF statement*. It is compound because more than one condition is tested.

Additional relational operators are used in a compound IF statement. They are:

AND Indicates that *both* conditions must be true for the entire condition to be considered true.

OR Indicates that *either* condition must be true for the entire condition to be considered true.

There is another relational operator that is available, but its use is not very common in simple data processing. The NOT operator is used frequently when comparing one binary value with another. Its operation, at our current level of programming, can be duplicated by rewriting the other relational operators involved.

NOT Indicates that the condition is to be negated after it has been evaluated; if the condition is true, treat it as though it were false. If the condition is false, treat it as though it were true.

Compound IF statements will become clearer when you have seen some examples. Refer to Table 14-2.

TABLE 14-2 EXAMPLES OF THE COMPOUND IF STATEMENT

```
800  IF YEARHIRED > 1983 AND RANKLEVEL > = 3 THEN 1000
810  PRINT "EMPLOYEE HAS INSUFFICIENT YEARS OF SERVICE AND RANK"
 .
 .
 .
1000 PRINT "EMPLOYEE MEETS PROMOTION STANDARDS."
```

If YEARHIRED is strictly greater than 1983 and if RANKLEVEL is greater than or equal to 3, then continue execution at line 1000. Otherwise, if either condition is not true (that is, unless both conditions are true), continue execution with line 810.

```
300  IF R1 = 0 OR R2 = 0 OR R3 = 0 THEN 400
310  REM DIMENSIONS OK-NONE ARE ZERO.
 .
 .
 .
400  PRINT "AN ILLEGAL DIMENSION (ZERO) HAS BEEN DETECTED. REENTER"
```

TABLE 14-2 (*continued*)

If the variable R1 equals 0, or the variable R2 equals 0, or the variable R3 equals 0, this IF statement evaluates as true, and execution continues with line 400. Otherwise, if all three tests are false, continue with line 310.

```
550  IF (SW1 = 0 AND V1 > 6) OR (SW1 = 1 AND V1 > 8) OR (SW2 = 0) THEN 700
560  PRINT "CIRCUIT PARAMETERS DO NOT MEET NORMAL STANDARDS."
.
.
.
700  PRINT "NORMAL PARAMETERS FOR CURRENT SWITCH POSITION DETECTED."
```

If SW1 (a number representing the position of switch 1) equals zero and V1 (the voltage measured at test point 1) is greater than 6, the IF is satisfied; execution continues at line 700. If this first clause evaluates false, test for SW1 equal to 1 and V1 greater than 8. If the second clause evaluates as true, the IF is still satisfied; continue execution at line 700. Finally, if neither clause 1 or clause 2 evaluates as true, test SW2 for a value equal to 0. If this clause is true, the IF statement is still satisfied. If NONE of the clauses are true, execute lines beginning with 560.

The individual clauses were parenthesized to make the order of evaluation clearer; the result, in this case, would have been the same since AND conditions are evaluated before OR conditions, just as multiplication is evaluated before addition.

Caution should be exercised in the use of compound IF statements. While combinations of conditions can be tested in this manner, sometimes program clarity suffers. If this is the case, additional explanatory REM statements are called for, or perhaps the compound IF statement should be broken down into several simpler IF statements. Often, breaking down the complex statement allows for more informative messages, since we know exactly which values are being tested and can therefore print messages about those that are outside what was expected.

SUMMARY

Normally, BASIC statements are executed starting from the lowest line number and proceeding to the highest line number in ascending numerical order. A capability which is very useful in BASIC is the ability to alter this sequence either with a direct command or as the result of a calculation. The unconditional branch is supported by the GOTO statement and allows the programmer to change the next statement to be executed. In this way the normal numerical sequence may be changed. Conditional branch control structures allow the computer to decide which statement is to be executed next. Such structures depend on the outcome of a calculation. There are two statements in BASIC which can be used for conditional control. The FOR-NEXT statement can be used to determine the number of times that a group of statements is executed. The resultant sequence of operations is referred to as a loop. Loops may be nested if there are no loop crossovers. The IF statement can be used to determine if a group of statements is to be executed at all. This is referred to as conditional execution. Relational operators are used within the expression portion of an IF statement to implement the control structure.

REVIEW PROBLEMS

1. Describe the result of executing each of the following FOR-NEXT loops:

a.
```
100  FOR I = 1 to 5
110    PRINT "THE VALUE OF I IS";I
120  NEXT I
```

b.
```
300  FOR COUNTER = 6 TO 9
310    PRINT COUNTER, COUNTER * COUNTER
320  NEXT COUNTER
```

c.
```
400  FOR POINT = 4 TO 13 STEP 5
410    PRINT "POINT HAS A VALUE OF ";POINT
420  NEXT POINT
430  PRINT "CLOSING VALUE OF POINT IS ";POINT
```

d.
```
200  Z = 0
210  FOR X = 50 TO 60 STEP 2
220  Z = Z + X
230  NEXT X
240  PRINT Z
```

e.
```
160  SUM = 0
170  FOR Q = 10 TO 1 STEP -1
180  SUM = SUM + Q
190  PRINT "AFTER ADDING ";Q;" THE SUM EQUALS
     ";SUM
200  NEXT Q
210  PRINT "THE VALUE THAT WOULD HAVE BEEN ADDED
     NEXT WAS ";Q
```

REVIEW QUESTIONS

1. In what order does BASIC normally execute statements?

2. What is meant by an unconditional program branch?

3. What BASIC statement causes an unconditional program branch?
4. What is meant by a conditional program branch?
5. What is meant by a program loop?
6. What is the purpose of the FOR-NEXT loop?
7. What is an index variable?
8. May the value of the index variable be used within the loop? Must the value of the index variable be used? May the value of the index variable be changed? Why or why not?
9. How can the FOR-NEXT loop be made to count down instead of up?
10. What is the meaning of the term "default"?
11. What is meant by a key value? How should a key value be selected? Give some examples of situations and suitable key values.
12. What is a relational operation? What are the common relational operators used by BASIC?
13. What are the two possible results of testing a relationship (i.e., performing a comparison)?
14. What is the purpose of the IF statement?
15. What are the four parts of the IF statement?
16. What is a compound IF statement?
17. What are the relational operators that permit compounding an IF statement?
18. What is the order of operations in the evaluation of a compound IF statement?
19. What limits the number of comparisons in a compound IF statement?
20. When might you use multiple IF statements instead of a single compound IF statement?

This chapter describes the BASIC equivalent of a group of instructions which (1) may be called from any point in the program, (2) will be executed, and (3) when completed, will return control to the instruction following the original point of invocation.

15-1 THE GOSUB AND RETURN STATEMENTS

GOSUB and RETURN provide the user with the statements needed to carry out the control sequence outlined above.

Purpose The purpose of the GOSUB and RETURN statements is to provide a branching function that will return to the origin of the branch, without having to specify the location of the origin, so that the same block of program code can be accessed (branched to) from a variety of different places in the same program. This structure is known as a *subroutine*.

Syntax

```
{lnum} GOSUB {lnum}
       (Next sequential statement)
       .
       .
       .
{lnum} REM Start of subroutine
       .
       .
       .
       RETURN
```

Explanation

The GOSUB statement performs two operations:

1. Saves the location (line number) of the BASIC statement that would normally be executed next.
2. Performs a branch to a specified line number.

The RETURN statement causes a branch back to the location that was saved by the GOSUB statement.

15-2 USING THE GOSUB AND RETURN STATEMENTS

Example 15-1 A Simple Subroutine

Examine the following program segment (this is not a complete program—only a fragment). The dots preceding line 300 indicate that there are other statements located here, but their content is not relevant at this time.

```
      .
      .
      .
 300  GOSUB 1500
 310  PRINT "POWER DISSIPATED EQUALS ";P
 320  GOTO 9999
1500  REM BEGINNING OF A SUBROUTINE TO CALCULATE POWER
1510  REM GIVEN VOLTAGE AND CURRENT. VOLTAGE VALUE IS
1520  REM ASSUMED TO BE IN VARIABLE V; CURRENT VALUE
1530  REM IS ASSUMED TO BE IN VARIABLE I. THIS SUBROUTINE
1540  REM RETURNS THE POWER IN VARIABLE P.
1550  P = V * I
1560  RETURN
9999  END
```

When line 300 is executed, BASIC stores (internally) the location of the line that would normally be executed next (line 310 in this example). BASIC then performs a branch to line 1500, in the same manner as if a GOTO has been executed. Statements are executed in the normal fashion until line 1560 is encountered. At this point, BASIC looks up the location of the line that it stored when the GOSUB was executed and performs a branch back to that stored line (line 310). Execution then continues from there.

Example 15-2 Using Subroutines to Advantage

Task: You are in charge of monitoring power consumption in various areas of a manufacturing plant. Recording devices have been installed that take periodic voltage and current readings for the two work areas of the PC Board Fabrication division and the three work areas of the Device

Assembly division. You must determine what percentage of the total power is consumed by each of the departments. Output should be as shown in Figure 15-1.

```
TOTAL POWER CONSUMPTION: XXXXXX WATTS.

PC DIVISION POWER CONSUMPTION: XXXXX WATTS.
   PERCENTAGE OF TOTAL: XXX.XX%.

PC BOARD AREA 1: XXXXX WATTS.
   PERCENT OF DIVISION: XXX.XX%.

PC BOARD AREA 2: XXXXX WATTS.
   PERCENT OF DIVISION: XXX.XX%.

DEVICE ASSEMBLY DIVISION POWER CONSUMPTION: XXXXX WATTS.
                                    (ETC)
```

Fig. 15-1 Sample output for the power consumption analysis program.

Algorithmic Analysis: This program breaks down into broad operations, as seen in Figure 15-2. Notice how in this flowchart, we display the operations in a more general manner. Instead of showing each individual operation (steps that are analogous to individual BASIC instructions) we show steps in a more general, logical format.

For each area we must calculate its power consumption and two percentages—the percentage of the division's power consumption and the percentage of the total power consumption. We must also calculate the percentage of the total power consumption for each division. We will use one subroutine to calculate all the power consumptions and another subroutine to calculate all the percentages.

Program Development: Construct the opening REM statements:

```
100  REM THIS PROGRAM COMPUTES TOTAL, DIVISIONAL,
110  REM AND AREA POWER CONSUMPTIONS AND EXPRESSES
120  REM AREA POWER CONSUMPTION IN WATTS AND AS A
130  REM PERCENTAGE OF TOTAL AND DIVISIONAL POWER CONSUMPTION
```

Construct the portion of the program to collect each department's voltage and current readings.

```
140  REM COLLECT DATA
150  CLS
160  PRINT "ENTERING VALUES FOR PC BOARD DIVISION"
170  INPUT "ENTER VOLTAGE READING FOR AREA 1: ",V
180  INPUT "ENTER CURRENT READING FOR AREA 1: ",I
190  REM CALCULATE AREA 1 POWER CONSUMPTION
```

We can use the subroutine we developed in the previous example to calculate the power:

```
200 GOSUB 1500
```

Remember, the subroutine starting at line 1500 returns a value in variable P. *We must store this value before calling the subroutine again, or the value just computed will be lost.*

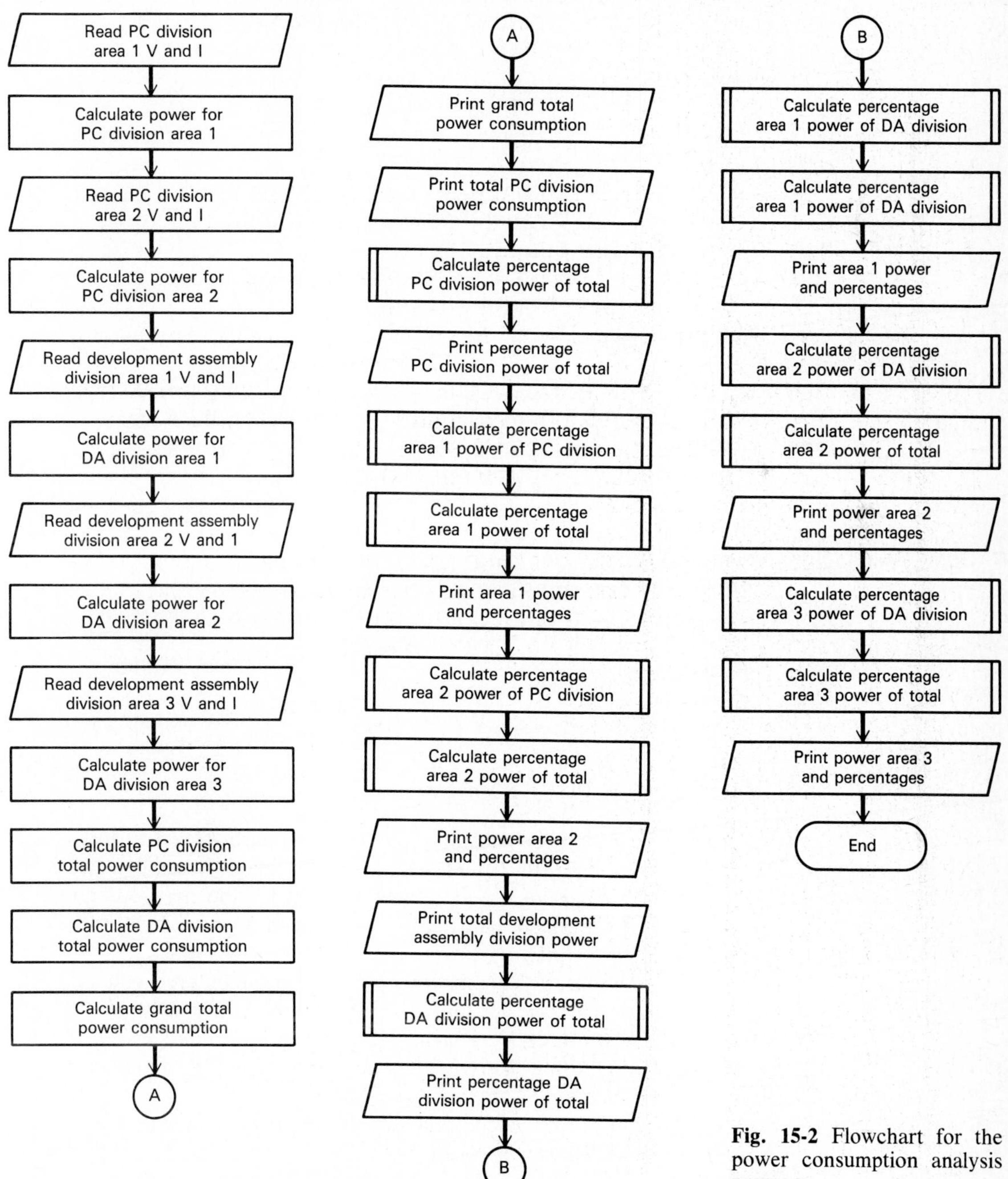

Fig. 15-2 Flowchart for the power consumption analysis program.

```
210  PPC1 = P
```

Now obtain and process the voltage and current readings for the other areas.

```
220  INPUT "ENTER VOLTAGE READING FOR AREA 2: ",V
230  INPUT "ENTER CURRENT READING FOR AREA 2: ",I
240  REM CALCULATE AREA 2 POWER CONSUMPTION
250  REM CALCULATE POWER FOR AREA 2
260  GOSUB 1500
270  PPC2 = P
280  PRINT
290  PRINT "ENTERING VALUES FOR DEVICE ASSEMBLY DIVISION"
300  INPUT "ENTER VOLTAGE READING FOR AREA 1: ",V
310  INPUT "ENTER CURRENT READING FOR AREA 1: ",I
320  REM CALCULATE AREA 1 POWER CONSUMPTION
330  REM CALCULATE POWER FOR AREA 1
340  GOSUB 1500
350  PDA1 = P
360  INPUT "ENTER VOLTAGE READING FOR AREA 2: ",V
370  INPUT "ENTER CURRENT READING FOR AREA 2: ",I
380  REM CALCULATE AREA 2 POWER CONSUMPTION
390  REM CALCULATE POWER FOR AREA 2
400  GOSUB 1500
410  PDA2 = P
420  INPUT "ENTER VOLTAGE READING FOR AREA 3: ",V
430  INPUT "ENTER CURRENT READING FOR AREA 3: ",I
440  REM CALCULATE AREA 3 POWER CONSUMPTION
450  REM CALCULATE POWER FOR AREA 3
460  GOSUB 1500
470  PDA3 = P
480  PPCDIV = PPC1 + PPC2
490  PDADIV = PDA1 + PDA2 + PDA3
500  PTOTAL = PPCDIV + PDADIV
```

We now have the power consumptions for PC Board Area 1 in PPC1, for PC Board Area 2 in PPC2, and for the three Device Assembly Areas in PDA1, PDA2, and PDA3, respectively. Totals for the divisions and the overall total have been calculated and placed in variables PPCDIV, PDADIV, and PTOTAL.

Notice how we used the same variables for all the entered voltages and currents. This was done so that the subroutine at line 1500 would find these values where it expects them. *We can use the same variables since we do not need to retain the individual area's voltage and current readings once we have calculated the power consumption.*

Why was the power calculating subroutine located at line 1500? This was an arbitrary choice; it could have been located almost anywhere in the program. However, all of a program's subroutines are often grouped near the physical end of the program, before the END statement. Another rule of thumb is to start numbering subroutines at whole-hundred line numbers. The percentage calculating subroutine will start at line 1400 in this example.

```
1400  REM SUBROUTINE TO CALCULATE A PERCENTAGE. INCOMING VALUES
1410  REM ARE EXPECTED IN THE VARIABLES NUMERATOR AND DENOMINATOR.
1420  REM THE RESULTING PERCENTAGE IS RETURNED IN THE VARIABLE
1430  REM PERCENT.
1440  PERCENT = 0
1450  REM CHECK DENOMINATOR FOR ZERO TO AVOID DIVISION BY ZERO
1460  IF DENOMINATOR = 0 THEN GOTO 1480
1470  PERCENT = (NUMERATOR/DENOMINATOR) * 100
1480  RETURN
```

This subroutine expects the values it will work on to be in the variables NUMERATOR and DENOMINATOR. This must be handled prior to entering the subroutine. It checks the value of DENOMINATOR for a value of zero. If this value is found, the division is bypassed because division by zero would raise an error condition and BASIC would stop executing the program. If DENOMINATOR is non – zero, then the percentage calculation is performed. Either the correct percentage will be returned in the variable PERCENT, or a value of zero will be returned, if DENOMINATOR was zero.

Now for the output section of the main program:

```
510  REM OUTPUT SECTION
520  CLS
530  PRINT "TOTAL POWER CONSUMPTION: "; PTOTAL; " WATTS."
540  PRINT
550  PRINT
560  PRINT "PC DIVISION POWER CONSUMPTION: "; PPCDIV; " WATTS."
570  REM CALCULATE PERCENTAGE OF TOTAL
580  NUMERATOR = PPCDIV
590  DENOMINATOR = PTOTAL
600  GOSUB 1400
610  PRINT "     PERCENTAGE OF TOTAL: "; PERCENT; " %."
```

This part of the program prints the total power consumption and the consumption for the PC Board division. Lines 580 and 590 place appropriate values into the variables NUMERATOR and DENOMINATOR. Line 600 transfers execution to the subroutine at line 1400. When the subroutine has finished its task, execution resumes at line 610 which prints the percentage calculated by the subroutine.

The next part of the program will cause the area power consumptions and their percentages to be printed:

```
620  PRINT
630  PRINT "PC BOARD AREA 1: ";PPC1; " WATTS."
640  NUMERATOR = PPC1
650  DENOMINATOR = PPCDIV
660  GOSUB 1400
670  PRINT "     PERCENT OF DIVISION: "; PERCENT; "%."
680  DENOMINATOR = PTOTAL
690  GOSUB 1400
700  PRINT "     PERCENT OF TOTAL: "; PERCENT; "%."
```

Notice that before calling the subroutine in line 690, the program only needed to assign a new value to DENOMINATOR. It was not necessary to assign a new value to NUMERATOR because the value previously assigned in line 640 was not changed by the subroutine. The program proceeds to calculate the percentage of this area's (PC board area 1) power consumption with respect to the total power consumption.

The remaining program lines follow the same pattern:

```
 710  PRINT
 720  PRINT "PC BOARD AREA 2: ";PPC2; " WATTS."
 730  NUMERATOR = PPC2
 740  DENOMINATOR = PPCDIV
 750  GOSUB 1400
 760  PRINT "     PERCENT OF DIVISION: "; PERCENT; "%."
 770  DENOMINATOR = PTOTAL
 780  GOSUB 1400
 790  PRINT "     PERCENT OF TOTAL: "; PERCENT; "%."
 800  PRINT
 810  PRINT
 820  PRINT
 830  PRINT "DEVICE ASSEMBLY DIVISION POWER CONSUMPTION: "; PDADIV;
 840  PRINT " WATTS."
 850  REM CALCULATE PERCENTAGE OF TOTAL
 860  NUMERATOR = PDADIV
 870  DENOMINATOR = PTOTAL
 880  GOSUB 1400
 890  PRINT "     PERCENTAGE OF TOTAL: "; PERCENT; "%."
 900  PRINT
 910  PRINT "DEVICE ASSY. AREA 1: ";PDA1; " WATTS."
 920  NUMERATOR = PDA1
 930  DENOMINATOR = PDADIV
 940  GOSUB 1400
 950  PRINT "     PERCENT OF DIVISION: "; PERCENT; "%."
 960  DENOMINATOR = PTOTAL
 970  GOSUB 1400
 980  PRINT "     PERCENT OF TOTAL: "; PERCENT; "%."
 990  PRINT
1000  PRINT
```

```
1010  PRINT "DEVICE ASSY. AREA 2: ";PDA2; " WATTS."
1020  NUMERATOR = PDA2
1030  DENOMINATOR = PDADIV
1040  GOSUB 1400
1050  PRINT "     PERCENT OF DIVISION: "; PERCENT; "%."
1060  DENOMINATOR = PTOTAL
1070  GOSUB 1400
1080  PRINT "     PERCENT OF TOTAL: "; PERCENT; "%."
1090  PRINT
1100  PRINT
1110  PRINT "DEVICE ASSY. AREA 3: ";PDA3; " WATTS."
1120  NUMERATOR = PDA3
1130  DENOMINATOR = PDADIV
1140  GOSUB 1400
1150  PRINT "     PERCENT OF DIVISION: "; PERCENT; "%."
1160  DENOMINATOR = PTOTAL
1170  GOSUB 1400
1180  PRINT "     PERCENT OF TOTAL: "; PERCENT; "%."
1190  PRINT
1200  PRINT
1210  PRINT
1220  REM OUTPUT COMPLETED.
```

One more statement is needed. If the program were left as is (with line 1400 after line 1220), the next statement to be executed would be line 1400, the beginning of the percentage subroutine. An error would be generated when line 1480 (the RETURN statement) is executed. BASIC would not know what line to RETURN to, as the subroutine was not entered via a GOSUB statement. The program would stop running with a "RETURN THOUT GOSUB IN LINE 1480" error message.

To avoid this, the program includes a branch around the subroutines, to the END statement:

```
1230  GOTO 9999
```

And finally,

```
9999  END
```

The complete program can be found in Listing 15-1.

LISTING 15-1: COMPLETE LISTING OF POWER CONSUMPTION PROGRAM, VERSION 1

```
100  REM THIS PROGRAM COMPUTES TOTAL, DIVISIONAL,
110  REM AND AREA POWER CONSUMPTIONS AND EXPRESSES
120  REM AREA POWER CONSUMPTION IN WATTS AND AS A
130  REM PERCENTAGE OF TOTAL AND DIVISIONAL POWER CONSUMPTION
```

LISTING 15-1: ***(continued)***

```
140  REM COLLECT DATA
150  CLS
160  PRINT "ENTERING VALUES FOR PC BOARD DIVISION"
170  INPUT "ENTER VOLTAGE READING FOR AREA 1: ",V
180  INPUT "ENTER CURRENT READING FOR AREA 1: ",I
190  REM CALCULATE AREA 1 POWER CONSUMPTION
200  GOSUB 1500
210  PPC1 = P
220  INPUT "ENTER VOLTAGE READING FOR AREA 2: ",V
230  INPUT "ENTER CURRENT READING FOR AREA 2: ",I
240  REM CALCULATE AREA 2 POWER CONSUMPTION
250  REM CALCULATE POWER FOR AREA 2
260  GOSUB 1500
270  PPC2 = P
280  PRINT
290  PRINT "ENTERING VALUES FOR DEVICE ASSEMBLY DIVISION"
300  INPUT "ENTER VOLTAGE READING FOR AREA 1: ",V
310  INPUT "ENTER CURRENT READING FOR AREA 1: ",I
320  REM CALCULATE AREA 1 POWER CONSUMPTION
330  REM CALCULATE POWER FOR AREA 1
340  GOSUB 1500
350  PDA1 = P
360  INPUT "ENTER VOLTAGE READING FOR AREA 2: ",V
370  INPUT "ENTER CURRENT READING FOR AREA 2: ",I
380  REM CALCULATE AREA 2 POWER CONSUMPTION
390  REM CALCULATE POWER FOR AREA 2
400  GUSUB 1500
410  PDA2 = P
420  INPUT "ENTER VOLTAGE READING FOR AREA 3: ",V
430  INPUT "ENTER CURRENT READING FOR AREA 3: ",I
440  REM CALCULATE AREA 3 POWER CONSUMPTION
450  REM CALCULATE POWER FOR AREA 3
460  GOSUB 1500
470  PDA3 = P
480  PPCDIV = PPC1 + PPC2
490  PDADIV = PDA1 + PDA2 + PDA3
500  PTOTAL = PPCDIV + PDADIV
510  REM OUTPUT SECTION
520  CLS
530  PRINT "TOTAL POWER CONSUMPTION: "; PTOTAL; " WATTS."
540  PRINT
550  PRINT
560  PRINT "PC DIVISION POWER CONSUMPTION: "; PPCDIV; " WATTS."
570  REM CALCULATE PERCENTAGE OF TOTAL
580  NUMERATOR = PPCDIV
590  DENOMINATOR = PTOTAL
```

```
600  GOSUB 1400
610  PRINT "     PERCENTAGE OF TOTAL: "; PERCENT; " %."
620  PRINT
630  PRINT "PC BOARD AREA 1: ";PPC1; " WATTS."
640  NUMERATOR = PPC1
650  DENOMINATOR = PPCDIV
660  GOSUB 1400
670  PRINT "     PERCENT OF DIVISION: "; PERCENT; "%."
680  DENOMINATOR = PTOTAL
690  GOSUB 1400
700  PRINT "     PERCENT OF TOTAL: "; PERCENT; "%."
710  PRINT
720  PRINT "PC BOARD AREA 2: ";PPC2; " WATTS."
730  NUMERATOR = PPC2
740  DENOMINATOR = PPCDIV
750  GOSUB 1400
760  PRINT "     PERCENT OF DIVISION: "; PERCENT; "%."
770  DENOMINATOR = PTOTAL
780  GOSUB 1400
790  PRINT "     PERCENT OF TOTAL: "; PERCENT; "%."
800  PRINT
810  PRINT
820  PRINT
830  PRINT "DEVICE ASSEMBLY DIVISION POWER CONSUMPTION: "; PDADIV;
840  PRINT " WATTS."
850  REM CALCULATE PERCENTAGE OF TOTAL
860  NUMERATOR = PDADIV
870  DENOMINATOR = PTOTAL
880  GOSUB 1400
890  PRINT "     PERCENTAGE OF TOTAL: "; PERCENT; "%."
900  PRINT
910  PRINT "DEVICE ASSY. AREA 1: ";PDA1; " WATTS."
920  NUMERATOR = PDA1
930  DENOMINATOR = PDADIV
940  GOSUB 1400
950  PRINT "     PERCENT OF DIVISION: "; PERCENT; "%."
960  DENOMINATOR = PTOTAL
970  GOSUB 1400
980  PRINT "     PERCENT OF TOTAL: "; PERCENT; "%."
990  PRINT
1000 PRINT
1010 PRINT "DEVICE ASSY. AREA 2: ";PDA2; " WATTS."
1020 NUMERATOR = PDA2
1030 DENOMINATOR = PDADIV
1040 GOSUB 1400
1050 PRINT "     PERCENT OF DIVISION: "; PERCENT; "%."
```

LISTING 15-1: *(continued)*

```
1060  DENOMINATOR = PTOTAL
1070  GOSUB 1400
1080  PRINT "    PERCENT OF TOTAL: "; PERCENT; "%."
1090  PRINT
1100  PRINT
1110  PRINT "DEVICE ASSY. AREA 3: ";PDA3; " WATTS."
1120  NUMERATOR = PDA3
1130  DENOMINATOR = PDADIV
1140  GOSUB 1400
1150  PRINT "    PERCENT OF DIVISION: "; PERCENT; "%."
1160  DENOMINATOR = PTOTAL
1170  GOSUB 1400
1180  PRINT "    PERCENT OF TOTAL: "; PERCENT; "%."
1190  PRINT
1200  PRINT
1210  PRINT
1220  REM OUTPUT COMPLETED.
1230  GOTO 9999
1400  REM SUBROUTINE TO CALCULATE A PERCENTAGE. INCOMING VALUES
1410  REM ARE EXPECTED IN THE VARIABLES NUMERATOR AND DENOMINATOR.
1420  REM THE RESULTING PERCENTAGE IS RETURNED IN THE VARIABLE
1430  REM PERCENT.
1440  PERCENT = 0
1450  REM CHECK DENOMINATOR FOR ZERO TO AVOID DIVISION BY ZERO
1460  IF DENOMINATOR = 0 THEN GOTO 1480
1470  PERCENT = (NUMERATOR/DENOMINATOR) * 100
1480  RETURN
1500  REM BEGINNING OF A SUBROUTINE TO CALCULATE POWER
1510  REM GIVEN VOLTAGE AND CURRENT. VOLTAGE VALUE IS
1520  REM ASSUMED TO BE IN VARIABLE V; CURRENT VALUE
1530  REM IS ASSUMED TO BE IN VARIABLE I. THIS SUBROUTINE
1540  REM RETURNS THE POWER IN VARIABLE P.
1550  P = V * I
1560  RETURN
9999  END
```

Program Efficiency: Examine the following portion of the program.

```
640  NUMERATOR = PPC1
650  DENOMINATOR = PPCDIV
660  GOSUB 1400
670  PRINT "    PERCENT OF DIVISION: "; PERCENT; "%."
680  DENOMINATOR = PTOTAL
690  GOSUB 1400
700  PRINT "    PERCENT OF TOTAL: "; PERCENT; "%."
```

This segment performs most of the processing for one area. The same operation, using different variables, can be found in lines 730 through 790, 920 through 980, 1020 through 1080, and 1120 through 1180. Whenever this kind of condition exists, that is, where the same operation is performed on different data, it can often be replaced with a subroutine structure.

Examine how the program could be made more efficient. The values that such a subroutine would need to work with would be:

Area's power consumption
Division's power consumption
Total power consumption

The program steps can be arranged to pass these values to the subroutine in variables called PAREA, PDIV, and PTOTAL. PTOTAL is the same variable as before; AREA and PDIV are new. The new subroutine will not use NUMERATOR or DENOMINATOR.

```
1600  REM NEW SUBROUTINE FOR PROCESSING PERCENTAGES. WE EXPECT
1610  REM APPROPRIATE VALUES IN THE VARIABLES PAREA, PDIV,
1620  REM AND PTOTAL.
1630  PERCENT = 0
1640  IF PDIV = 0 THEN GOTO 1660
1650  PERCENT = (PAREA / PDIV) * 100
1660  PRINT "     % OF DIVISION: ";PERCENT;"%";
1670  PERCENT = 0
1680  IF PTOTAL = 0 THEN GOTO 1700
1690  PERCENT = (PAREA / PTOTAL) * 100
1700  PRINT "     % OF TOTAL: ";PERCENT;"%"
1710  RETURN
```

Notice that now, in addition to calculating the percentage, the printing of the two parts of the percentage line is performed as part of the subroutine.

The old subroutine at line 1400 for calculating the divisional percentages is still needed but the new subroutine cannot be used because the new subroutine *also* prints values (lines 1660 and 1700).

The start of the program (where the values were entered) remains the same, but now examine the output portion of the program:

```
510  REM OUTPUT SECTION
520  CLS
530  PRINT "TOTAL POWER CONSUMPTION: "; PTOTAL; " WATTS."
540  PRINT
550  PRINT
560  PRINT "PC DIVISION POWER CONSUMPTION: "; PPCDIV; " WATTS."
570  REM CALCULATE PERCENTAGE OF TOTAL
580  NUMERATOR = PPCDIV
590  DENOMINATOR = PTOTAL
```

```
 600  GOSUB 1400
 610  PRINT "     PERCENTAGE OF TOTAL: "; PERCENT; " %."
 620  PRINT
 630  PRINT "PC BOARD AREA 1: ";PPC1; " WATTS."
 640  PAREA = PPC1
 650  PDIV = PPCDIV
 660  REM TOTAL POWER IS ALREADY IN VARIABLE PTOTAL
 670  GOSUB 1600
 710  PRINT
 720  PRINT "PC BOARD AREA 2: ";PPC2; " WATTS."
 730  PAREA = PPC2
 740  REM NO CHANGE NEEDED TO PDIV SINCE AREA PC2 IS IN SAME DIVISION
 750  GOSUB 1600
 800  PRINT
 810  PRINT
 820  PRINT
 830  PRINT "DEVICE ASSEMBLY DIVISION POWER CONSUMPTION: "; PDADIV;
 840  PRINT " WATTS."
 850  REM CALCULATE PERCENTAGE OF TOTAL
 860  NUMERATOR = PDADIV
 870  DENOMINATOR = PTOTAL
 880  GOSUB 1400
 890  PRINT "     PERCENTAGE OF TOTAL: "; PERCENT; " %."
 900  PRINT
 910  PRINT "DEVICE ASSY. AREA 1: ";PDA1; " WATTS."
 920  PAREA = PDA1
 930  PDIV = PDADIV
 940  GOSUB 1600
 990  PRINT
1000  PRINT
1010  PRINT "DEVICE ASSY. AREA 2: ";PDA2; " WATTS."
1020  PAREA = PDA2
1030  GOSUB 1600
1090  PRINT
1100  PRINT
1110  PRINT "DEVICE ASSY. AREA 3: ";PDA3; " WATTS."
1120  PAREA = PDA3
1130  GUSUB 1600
1190  PRINT
1200  PRINT
1210  PRINT
1220  REM OUTPUT COMPLETED.
1230  GOTO 9999
```

Screened elements indicate no change from the old subroutine.

The complete program can be seen in Listing 15-2. Lines from the original program that are no longer needed have been deleted; notice how much shorter the new version of the program is.

LISTING 15-2: COMPLETE LISTING OF POWER CONSUMPTION PROGRAM, VERSION 2

```
100  REM  THIS PROGRAM COMPUTES TOTAL, DIVISIONAL,
110  REM  AND AREA POWER CONSUMPTIONS AND EXPRESSES
120  REM  AREA POWER CONSUMPTION IN WATTS AND AS A
130  REM  PERCENTAGE OF TOTAL AND DIVISIONAL POWER CONSUMPTION
140  REM  COLLECT DATA
150  CLS
160  PRINT  "ENTERING VALUES FOR PC BOARD DIVISION"
170  INPUT  "ENTER VOLTAGE READING FOR AREA 1: ",V
180  INPUT  "ENTER CURRENT READING FOR AREA 1: ",I
190  REM  CALCULATE AREA 1 POWER CONSUMPTION
200  GOSUB  1500
210  PPC1 = P
220  INPUT  "ENTER VOLTAGE READING FOR AREA 2: ",V
230  INPUT  "ENTER CURRENT READING FOR AREA 2: ",I
240  REM  CALCULATE AREA 2 POWER CONSUMPTION
250  REM  CALCULATE POWER FOR AREA 2
260  GOSUB  1500
270  PPC2 = P
280  PRINT
290  PRINT  "ENTERING VALUES FOR DEVICE ASSEMBLY DIVISION"
300  INPUT  "ENTER VOLTAGE READING FOR AREA 1: ",V
310  INPUT  "ENTER CURRENT READING FOR AREA 1: ",I
320  REM  CALCULATE AREA 1 POWER CONSUMPTION
330  REM  CALCULATE POWER FOR AREA 1
340  GOSUB  1500
350  PDA1 = P
360  INPUT  "ENTER VOLTAGE READING FOR AREA 2: ",V
370  INPUT  "ENTER CURRENT READING FOR AREA 2: ",I
380  REM  CALCULATE AREA 2 POWER CONSUMPTION
390  REM  CALCULATE POWER FOR AREA 2
400  GOSUB  1500
410  PDA2 = P
420  INPUT "ENTER VOLTAGE READING FOR AREA 3: ",V
430  INPUT "ENTER CURRENT READING FOR AREA 3: ",I
440  REM  CALCULATE AREA 3 POWER CONSUMPTION
450  REM  CALCULATE POWER FOR AREA 3
460  GOSUB  1500
470  PDA3 = P
480  PPCDIV = PPC1 + PPC2
490  PDADIV = PDA1 + PDA2 + PDA3
500  PTOTAL = PPCDIV + PDADIV
510  REM  OUTPUT SECTION
520  CLS
530  PRINT "TOTAL POWER CONSUMPTION: "; PTOTAL; " WATTS."
540  PRINT
550  PRINT
```

```
560  PRINT "PC DIVISION POWER CONSUMPTION: "; PPCDIV; " WATTS."
570  REM CALCULATE PERCENTAGE OF TOTAL
580  NUMERATOR = PPCDIV
590  DENOMINATOR = PTOTAL
600  GOSUB 1400
610  PRINT "     PERCENTAGE OF TOTAL: "; PERCENT; " %."
620  PRINT
630  PRINT "PC BOARD AREA 1: ";PPC1; " WATTS."
640  PAREA = PPC1
650  PDIV = PPCDIV
660  REM TOTAL POWER IS ALREADY IN VARIABLE PTOTAL
670  GUSUB 1600
710  PRINT
720  PRINT "PC BOARD AREA 2: ";PPC2; " WATTS."
730  PAREA = PPC2
740  REM NO CHANGE NEEDED TO PDIV SINCE AREA PC2 IS IN SAME DIVISION
750  GOSUB 1600
800  PRINT
810  PRINT
820  PRINT
830  PRINT "DEVICE ASSEMBLY DIVISION POWER CONSUMPTION: "; PDADIV;
840  PRINT " WATTS."
850  REM CALCULATE PERCENTAGE OF TOTAL
860  NUMERATOR = PDADIV
870  DENOMINATOR = PTOTAL
880  GOSUB 1400
890  PRINT "     PERCENTAGE OF TOTAL: "; PERCENT; " %."
900  PRINT
910  PRINT "DEVICE ASSY. AREA 1: ";PDA1; " WATTS."
920  PAREA = PDA1
930  PDIV = PDADIV
940  GOSUB 1600
990  PRINT
1000 PRINT
1010 PRINT "DEVICE ASSY. AREA 2: ";PDA2; " WATTS."
1020 PAREA = PDA2
1030 GOSUB 1600
1090 PRINT
1100 PRINT
1110 PRINT "DEVICE ASSY. AREA 3: ";PDA3; " WATTS."
1120 PAREA = PDA3
1130 GOSUB 1600
1190 PRINT
```

LISTING 15-2: *(continued)*

```
1200  PRINT
1210  PRINT
1220  REM OUTPUT COMPLETED.
1230  GOTO 9999
1400  REM  SUBROUTINE TO CALCULATE A PERCENTAGE. INCOMING VALUES
1410  REM  ARE EXPECTED IN THE VARIABLES NUMERATOR AND DENOMINATOR.
1420  REM  THE RESULTING PERCENTAGE IS RETURNED IN THE VARIABLE
1430  REM  PERCENT
1440  PERCENT = 0
1450  REM  CHECK DENOMINATOR FOR ZERO TO AVOID DIVISION BY ZERO
1460  IF DENOMINATOR = 0 THEN GOTO 1480
1470  PERCENT = (NUMERATOR/DENOMINATOR) * 100
1480  RETURN
1500  REM  BEGINNING OF A SUBROUTINE TO CALCULATE POWER
1510  REM  GIVEN VOLTAGE AND CURRENT. VOLTAGE VALUE IS
1520  REM  ASSUMED TO BE IN VARIABLE V; CURRENT VALUE
1530  REM  IS ASSUMED TO BE IN VARIABLE I. THIS SUBROUTINE
1540  REM  RETURNS THE POWER IN VARIABLE P.
1550  P = V * I
1560  RETURN
1600  REM  NEW SUBROUTINE FOR PROCESSING PERCENTAGES. WE EXPECT
1610  REM  APPROPRIATE VALUES IN THE VARIABLES PAREA, PDIV,
1620  REM  AND PTOTAL.
1630  PERCENT = 0
1640  IF PDIV = 0 THEN GOTO 1660
1650  PERCENT = (PAREA / PDIV) * 100
1660  PRINT "     % OF DIVISION: ";PERCENT;"%";
1670  PERCENT = 0
1680  IF PTOTAL = 0 THEN GOTO 1700
1690  PERCENT = (PAREA / PTOTAL) * 100
1700  PRINT "     % OF TOTAL: ";PERCENT;"%"
1710  RETURN
9999  END
```

15-3 OTHER SUBROUTINE FEATURES

Compare the two subroutines in the new version; one starting at line 1400 calculates the percentages only for the division's power consumption and one at line 1600 calculates the remaining percentages. Both include an operation in which PERCENT is set equal to 0; a test is made to see whether the divisor is zero; and finally, a calculation for PERCENT (if the divisor is not zero).

Why can't these two subroutines be rewritten so that duplication is eliminated? Consider the following:

```
1400  REM SUBROUTINE TO CALCULATE A PERCENTAGE. INCOMING VALUES
1410  REM ARE EXPECTED IN THE VARIABLES NUMERATOR AND DENOMINATOR.
1420  REM THE RESULTING PERCENTAGE IS RETURNED IN THE VARIABLE
1430  REM PERCENT.
1440  PERCENT = 0
1450  REM CHECK DENOMINATOR FOR ZERO TO AVOID DIVISION BY ZERO
1460  IF DENOMINATOR = 0 THEN GOTO 1480
1470  PERCENT = (NUMERATOR/DENOMINATOR) * 100
1480  RETURN
1600  REM NEW SUBROUTINE FOR PROCESSING PERCENTAGES. WE EXPECT
1610  REM APPROPRIATE VALUES IN THE VARIABLES PAREA, PDIV,
1620  REM AND PTOTAL.
1630  NUMERATOR = PAREA
1640  DENOMINATOR = PDIV
1650  GOSUB 1400
1660  PRINT "    % OF DIVISION: ";PERCENT;"%";
1670  DENOMINATOR = PTOTAL
1680  GOSUB 1400
1700  PRINT "    % OF TOTAL: ";PERCENT; "%"
1710  RETURN
```

The subroutine at line 1600 executes as follows:

1. When called, the point of return (line number) is stored. Call this lnuml.
2. Execution continues at line 1600. Another GOSUB statement appears at line 1650. BASIC again saves the return point; in this case, line 1660. Call this lnum2.
3. Execution continues at line 1400 until the RETURN statement at line 1480 is executed. Execution continues from the line number most recently saved by a GOSUB; in this example it is lnum2 or line 1660.
4. Execution resumes at line 1660 until the GOSUB at line 1680 is executed. BASIC saves line 1700 as the line to return to. This replaces old lnum2 with 1700.
5. The subroutine at line 1400 is executed until the RETURN at line 1480 is executed. Execution is transferred to lnum2, (line 1700 in our example).
6. Finally when line 1710 is executed, execution continues at lnum1, the line number that was saved when the subroutine at line 1600 was first entered.

This demonstrates a very important property of subroutines: *a subroutine may call another subroutine* (which may call still another subroutine).

Each RETURN statement will cause a return to the location in the program saved by the most recently executed GOSUB statement.

15-3-1 Recursion

A subroutine may even call itself! There is, however, a very real danger in this. If the subroutine calls or returns aren't conditional, the subroutine will never complete its recursion. The BASIC program will stop running when it has used up all its memory in saving return destinations.

Examine the following subroutine:

```
1000  REM SUBROUTINE TO CALCULATE N FACTORIAL
1010  REM N% HAS VALUE-TOTAL WILL HAVE RESULT.
1020  IF N% <= 2 THEN GOTO 1060
1030  N% = N% - 1
1040  TOTAL = TOTAL * N%
1050  GOSUB 1000
1060  RETURN
```

Assume that there was a GOSUB 1000 statement in line 500 of the main program and that the line number that was saved as the return destination was 510; call this 1num1. In addition, it is assumed that variable N% will have a positive value when the subroutine is first invoked. N% will be a whole number because it is specified as an integer variable (suffix of "%"). In addition, TOTAL must be given the same value as the starting value of N%.

In line 1020 N% is tested to see if it is less than or equal to 2. Presumably the subroutine starts with a larger value of N, but a value of 2 is possible. If so the program branches to line 1050, which causes a return to lnum1 in the main routine.

However, assume that for this run, N% has a value of 4. If this is so, 1 will be subtracted from N% in line 1030, and the value in TOTAL will be multiplied by this result (line 1040). TOTAL now has a value of 12 (4 times 3), and N% has a value of 3.

When line 1050 is executed BASIC saves 1060 as the return line number. (Call this lnum2.) Execution continues at line 1000.

N% is still not equal to 1, so we again subtract 1 from N% (giving a value of 2) and multiply TOTAL by this value. TOTAL now has a value of 24 (12 times 2).

When line 1050 is executed, BASIC once again saves 1060 as the return line number. This is separate from the last time BASIC did this so we will call this lnum3. However, both lnum2 and lnum3 indicate 1060 as the return destination. Once again, execution continues at line 1000.

Now the value of N% is 2 and the IF statement evaluates as true. We branch to line 1060 which is a RETURN statement. Note that this is the first time we have executed the RETURN statement. The most recent destination line stored is lnum3 which is line 1060. BASIC branches to line 1060. It does not matter that we were already there; the RETURN causes a branch to the line most recently saved by a GOSUB. Line 1060 causes the next most recently stored line number to be retrieved. This is lnum2, which is also line 1060; execution continues. The next time line 1060 is executed, lnum1 is picked up; this restores program control to the main routine at line 510.

This process would have been repeated many more times if the initial value of N% had been larger.

SUMMARY

A very important control structure in BASIC is the subroutine. It can be used to

- Call or invoke a group of instructions from any point in a program
- Execute those instructions without losing track of its original place in the program
- Return to the main program when the group of instructions is completed

REVIEW PROBLEMS

In each of the following problems write subroutines that perform the indicated tasks. Specify, using remarks (REMs), which variables are expected to contain known values at the time of entry, and which variables contain the results.

1. A subroutine that calculates power, given the applied voltage and resistance of a circuit.

2. A subroutine that calculates the effective capacitance of two capacitors in connected in series. Neither capacitor may have a value of zero. The effective capacitance is equal to the sum of the capacitances divided by the product of the capacitances.

3. A subroutine that calculates the value of a resistor that must be placed in parallel with a given resistance to achieve a given total resistance.

4. A subroutine that prints the heading for the power consumption report program. The heading would be printed at the top of each page of the report and contain the name of the company (make one up), name of the report, and the date, suitably formatted. The subroutine should also reset the value of the variable LINECNTR to zero.

5. Given the following information, write a subroutine that receives as input the maximum voltage to be applied to a circuit and returns the minimum power rating of the resistor to use.

Resistor's Power Rating	Maximum Permitted RMS Voltage
¼ watt	250 V
½ watt	350 V
1 watt	500 V

6. A subroutine that converts frequency to wavelength (in meters) and prints the result of the conversion in a suitable sentence.
7. A subroutine that calculates percent regulation of a power supply.
8. A subroutine which simulates the action of an AND gate.
9. A subroutine which simulates the action of a NAND gate.
10. A subroutine which will simulate BOTH an AND gate and a NAND gate depending upon the value of variable FUNCTION: if FUNCTION = 0, simulate an AND gate; otherwise simulate a NAND gate. You may use more than one subroutine if you wish.

REVIEW QUESTIONS

1. What is a subroutine?
2. When is it efficient programming to use a subroutine?
3. What BASIC statement is used to enter a subroutine? To exit a subroutine?
4. What is the difference in effect between the GOSUB statement and the GOTO statement?
5. Can one subroutine call another subroutine? What is this called?
6. Can a subroutine call itself? What is the danger in doing this?
7. Can a subroutine contain more than one RETURN?
8. Can a program contain more than one subroutine?
9. Can a GOSUB be made conditional? Write an example of such a conditional GOSUB.
10. Can a RETURN be made conditional? Write an example of such a conditional RETURN.

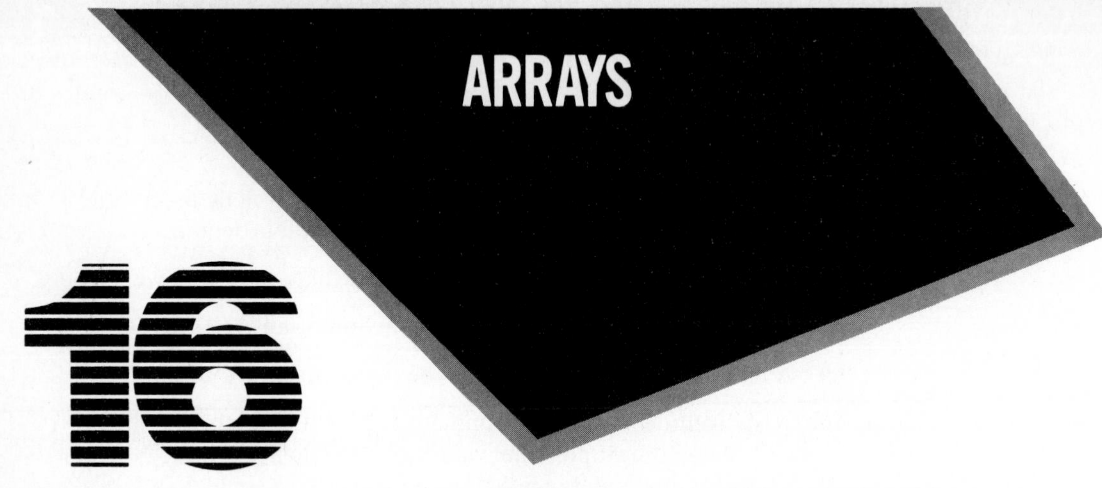

16 ARRAYS

Many data-processing applications use data in lists; a list of part numbers, a list of components needed to assemble a device, and a list of specifications are some examples. These lists are often filled with values taken from a data file. This data file is a collection of related records, recorded on a storage medium, usually disk (or diskette on smaller systems), or tape. This chapter explains how BASIC creates, maintains, and uses these lists, once they have been brought back into memory.

16-1 THE DATA ARRAY

Consider the problem of parts-shopping for a project. A list may help you remember all the required items. Table 16-1 contains such a list.

TABLE 16-1 SAMPLE PARTS SHOPPING LIST

SHOPPING LIST	
1. 2N3055 transistor	4. 14 pin DIP sockets
2. NE555 timer IC	5. 8 pin DIP sockets
3. SN7400 IC	6. wire-wrap terminals

The *name* of this list is *SHOPPING LIST.* There are six items, or members, in this list. They are numbered from one to six. The first member is "2N3055 transistor," the fourth member is "14 pin IC sockets," and the sixth member has the value "wire-wrap terminals." This list could be made longer by adding more lines and continuing the numbering sequence. The list could also be made shorter if fewer items are needed.

BASIC provides a similar structure in the form of *one-dimension arrays.* (It is possible to create multiple-dimension arrays; these are described later.) A one-dimension array is a list. Visualize such an array as being like the shopping list shown above. The *length* of the array defines the number of items it contains.

While the numbering of members in the SHOPPING LIST started with member number one, most forms of BASIC begin numbering members from *zero*. It is possible to ignore the additional member of the array, but this wastes storage space. (Learn to make use of the space in the manner in which it is allocated.)

BASIC requires that a name be assigned to the array. The rules for naming arrays are exactly the same as the rules for naming simple (non-array) variables, including the types of values (integer, single precision, double precision, or string) that will be contained. So, arrays that will contain string values must have names that end with the character "$"; arrays that will contain integers must end with a "%". All members of a given array must contain the *same type* of value; each member of the same array is a string, integer, single precision, or double precision value.

When BASIC performs an operation on a particular member of an array, the program must specify both the array's name and the member number. The member number is called the *subscript* and is stated in parentheses following the array name:

```
ARRAYNAME(SUBSCRIPT)
```

The subscript may be expressed using a numeric literal, a numeric variable, or a numeric expression. If a noninteger value is used as a subscript, the value will be truncated to an integer, since subscripts must be integers.

Before using an array, BASIC must be told how large the array will be. This allows BASIC to set aside enough memory to store the values that will be associated with the array.

16-2 THE DIM STATEMENT

Purpose: To direct BASIC as to how much memory must be allocated for an array or a series of arrays.

Remember—most BASICS give the first element of an array the subscript (member number) zero.

Syntax:

```
DIM {ARRAYNAME1(NUMBER OF ELEMENTS)} [,{ARRAYNAME2(NUMBER OF ELE-
MENTS},...]
```

Explanation: For each array to be used, specify the maximum number of elements (members) that the array will contain.

See Table 16-2 for examples of the writing of the DIM statement.

TABLE 16-2 USING THE DIM STATEMENT

DIM SHOPPINGLIST$(6)	Sets aside memory for an array called SHOPPINGLIST$, which will contain a maximum of 7 members (member 0 through member 6). Members may contain string values.
DIM VOLTAGE(4), CURRENT(8)	Sets aside memory for two arrays: VOLTAGE and CURRENT, both of which contain single precision numeric values (default). VOLTAGE has 5 members (subscripts of zero through 4). CURRENT has 9 members (subscripts zero through 8).
DIM A%(5),B#(2),C(27)	Allocates memory for three arrays, A%, containing integer values, has 6 members, B#, containing double precision values, has 3 members, and C, containing single precision values, has 28 members.

16-3 USING AN ARRAY IN A PROGRAM

Arrays provide efficient ways to organize the data which is to be used in a program. The example which follows describes one application.

Example 16-1 Translating the Color Code for Resistors

Task: Design a program that will convert a numeral (from 0 to 9) to the color which represents that numeral for the first two bands of the color code used for carbon resistors.

Algorithmic Analysis: Create an ordered list of the colors and place this list in an array called COLORCODE$. Read (accept) the numerals through an INPUT statement; then, if the number entered is valid, print the name of the color that corresponds to that number. Continue to solicit numbers until a value greater than 9 is entered.

See Figure 16-1 for the flowchart of this program.

Program Construction: Write the introductory REMs:

```
100  REM PROGRAM ACCEPTS A NUMERAL AND PRINTS THE COLOR CODE
110  REM FOR BANDS 1 OR 2 OF A CARBON RESISTOR.
```

Now, dimension and initialize (give starting values to) the COLORCODE$ array. Experienced programmers will often place all the initialization operations at the physical end of the program, and branch to this section at the beginning of the program. This is because the initialization

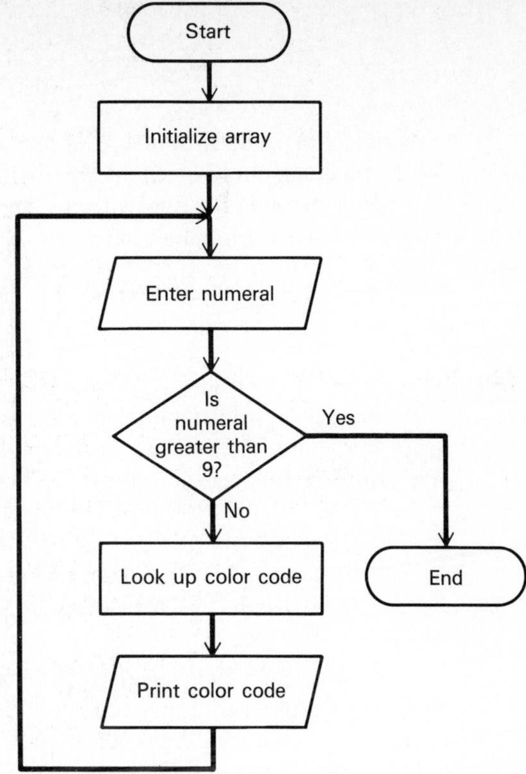

Fig. 16-1 Flowchart for decoding resistor color code bands 1 and 2.

will generally occur only once during the execution of the program; placing the section of the program that performs this operation at the end of the program puts it out of the way and allows the repetitive operations to be more prominently shown at the beginning. Therefore, the program is arranged as follows:

```
120  GOSUB 900
```

Label this section:

```
900  REM  INITIALIZATION SECTION
```

Dimension the COLORCODE$ array:

```
910  DIM  COLORCODE$(9)
```

Notice that while the highest permitted subscript will be 9, there are 10 members in this array: COLORCODE$(0) through COLORCODE$(9).

Next, create the program segment which reads values into the array. As the names of the colors are not likely to change, place the names of the colors in DATA statements, and assign them by using a READ statement.

```
920  FOR I = 0 TO 9
930  READ COLORCODE$(I)
940  NEXT I
```

Notice how a loop is used to read the 10 values for COLORCODE$. With each iteration of the loop formed by lines 920 through 940, I is increased by one, starting with a value of 0. Line 930 will be executed 10 times, first with I having a value of 0, then 1, then 2, and so on through 9.

Now, return to the main program.

```
950  RETURN
```

Before we continue constructing the main program, describe the program statements needed to build the DATA statements that will contain the values to be accessed by the READ in line 930.

```
960  DATA "BLACK","BROWN","RED","ORANGE"
970  DATA "YELLOW","GREEN","BLUE","PURPLE"
980  DATA "GRAY","WHITE"
```

This data could have been written in 10 DATA statements, or it could have been broken into any other number of DATA statements, as long as each value (appearing between double quotes) is separated from the next value on the same line by a comma. The last value on a line must *not* be followed by a comma.

Obtain a value to translate:

```
130  PRINT "ENTER THE NUMERAL WHO'S COLOR CODE YOU WANT"
140  INPUT "OR A NUMBER GREATER THAN 9 TO END: ",NUM
```

Test to see if a number greater than 9 was entered.

```
150  IF NUM > 9 THEN GOTO 999
```

Print the corresponding color's name. In this case, the color code for the numeral "3" is the third member of the COLORCODE$ array.

```
160  PRINT
170  PRINT "NUMBER ";NUM;" IS REPRESENTED BY THE COLOR ";COLORCODE$(NUM)
180  PRINT
```

Now, go back and repeat the operation:

```
190  GOTO 130
```

Finally, remember the END statement we need at line 999:

```
999  END
```

Listing 16-1 contains the program in its entirety.

LISTING 16-1: COMPLETE PROGRAM TO TRANSLATE A NUMERAL TO THE COLOR CODE FOR THE FIRST TWO BANDS OF A CARBON RESISTOR

```
100  REM  PROGRAM ACCEPTS A NUMERAL AND PRINTS THE COLOR CODE
110  REM  FOR BANDS 1 OR 2 OF A CARBON RESISTOR
120  GOSUB 900
130  PRINT "ENTER THE NUMERAL WHO'S COLOR CODE YOU WANT"
140  INPUT "OR A NUMBER GREATER THAN 9 TO END: ",NUM
150  IF NUM > 9 THEN GOTO 999
160  PRINT
170  PRINT "NUMBER ";NUM;" IS REPRESENTED BY THE COLOR ";COLORCODE$(NUM)
180  PRINT
190  GOTO 130
900  REM  INITIALIZATION SECTION
910  DIM  COLORCODE$(9)
920  FOR I = 0 TO 9
930  READ COLORCODE$(I)
940  NEXT I
950  RETURN
960  DATA "BLACK","BROWN","RED","ORANGE"
970  DATA "YELLOW","GREEN","BLUE","PURPLE"
980  DATA "GRAY","WHITE"
999  END
```

Example 16-2 Expanding the Program

Task: Expand the program just written to translate numeric entries for a resistor's resistance and tolerance into the colors for the four bands.

Algorithmic Analysis: The resistor's value will be entered in ohms, then its tolerance in percent. Values between .1 and 22,000,000 ohms, and tolerances of 5, 10, or 20 percent will be accepted as valid. An entry of 0 ohms will be used as a signal that data entry is complete.

The first task will be to determine the order of magnitude of the resistance value. This is accomplished by using a series of IF statements, test to see if the resistance is less than 10,000,000, 1,000,000, 100,000, and so on through 1. This will define the value for the third band, and a numeric value for the first two digits of the value. The first two bands can then be computed. The tolerance value will be tested to determine the color of the fourth band (if any).

Figure 16-2 shows the flowchart for these operations.

Program Construction: Begin with the introductory REMs:

```
100  REM PROGRAM TO CONVERT A NUMERIC ENTRY OF A RESISTOR'S
110  REM VALUE TO ITS COLOR CODE EQUIVALENT.
120  REM PERMITTED VALUES:
130  REM RESISTANCE: .1 THROUGH 22 MEGOHMS
140  REM TOLERANCE: 5, 10, OR 20 PERCENT
150  REM A RESISTANCE VALUE OF ZERO TERMINATES THE PROGRAM.
```

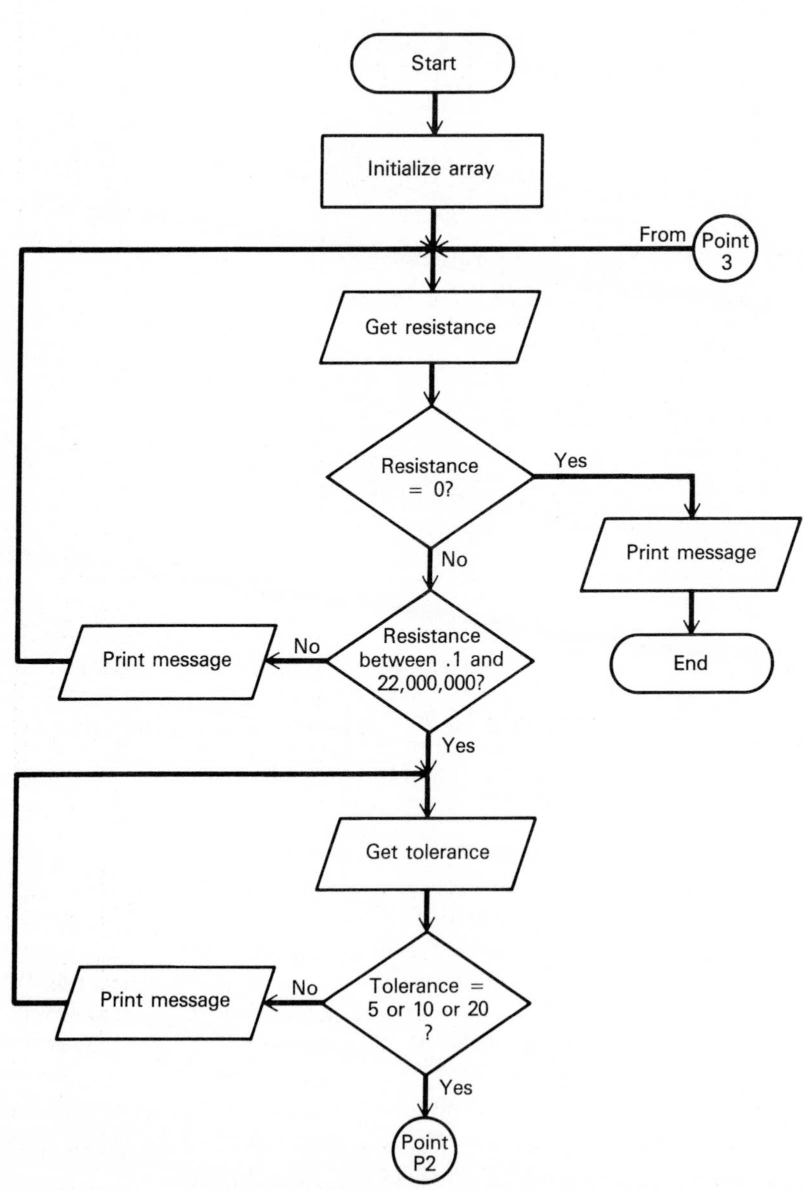

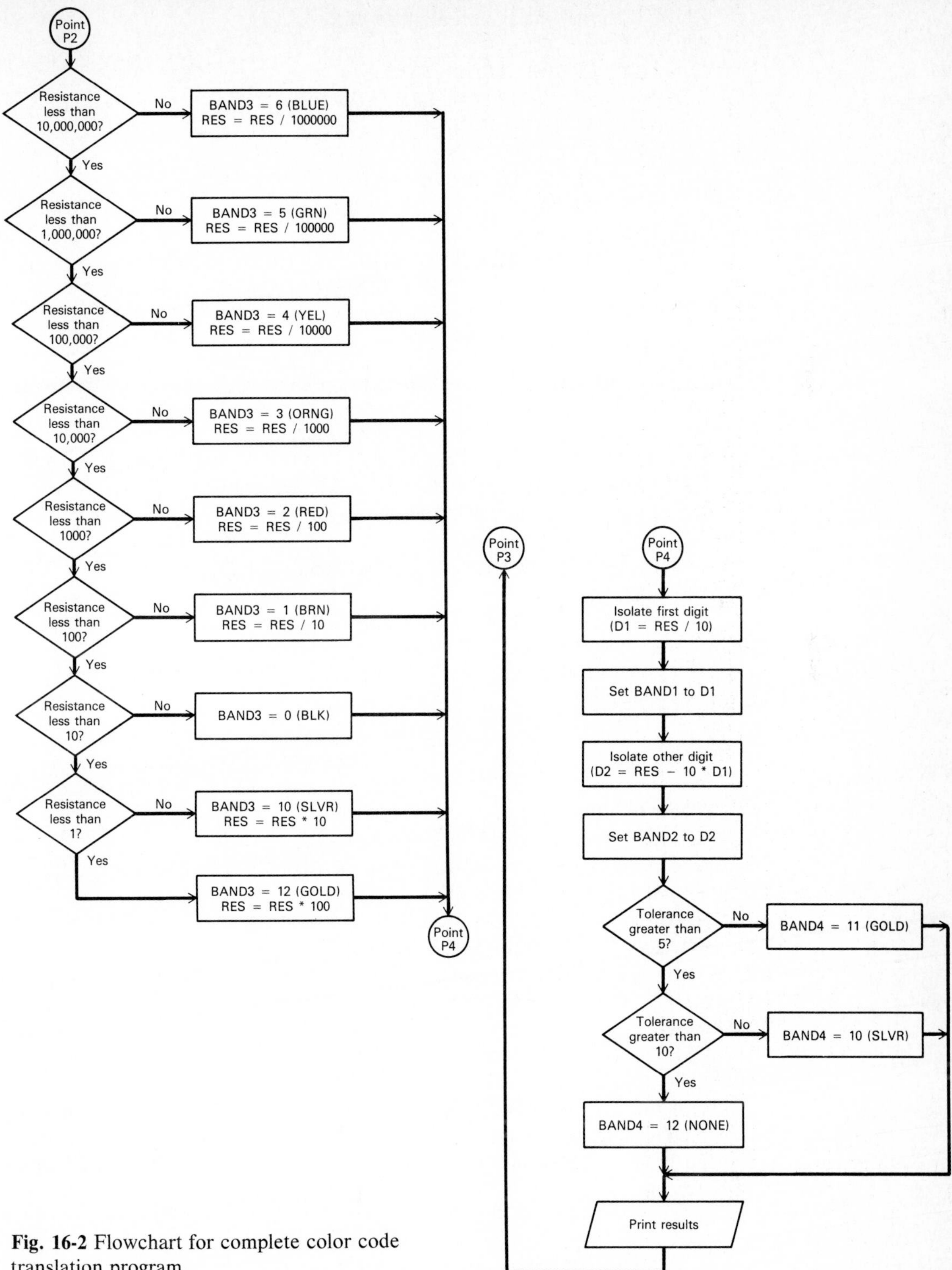

Fig. 16-2 Flowchart for complete color code translation program.

GOSUB to the initialization subroutine:

```
 160  GOSUB 1000
1000  REM  INITIALIZATION ROUTINE
1010  DIM COLORCODE$(12)
1020  FOR I = 0 TO 12
1030  READ COLORCODE$(I)
1040  NEXT I
1050  RETURN
1060  DATA "BLACK","BROWN","RED","ORANGE"
1070  DATA "YELLOW","GREEN","BLUE","PURPLE"
1080  DATA "GRAY","WHITE","SILVER","GOLD"
1090  DATA "NONE"
```

The size of COLORCODE$ has been increased to 13 members so that it may include the values "SILVER," "GOLD," and "NONE." These values will be used for the *multiplier* and *tolerance* bands.

Solicit the resistance value and check for validity or signal value:

```
170  INPUT "ENTER RESISTANCE VALUE (OHMS) OR ZERO TO QUIT: ",R
180  IF R = 0 THEN 9998
190  IF R >= .1 AND R <= 22000000 THEN GOTO 250
200  REM  INVALID VALUE DETECTED
210  PRINT "RESISTANCE VALUE MUST BE BETWEEN .1 OHMS AND"
220  PRINT "22 MEGOHMS. PLEASE REENTER."
230  PRINT
240  GOTO 170
```

Solicit the tolerance and screen for validity:

```
250  REM  GET THE TOLERANCE
260  INPUT "ENTER TOLERANCE; 5, 10, OR 20 PERCENT: ",TOL
270  REM  SCREEN TOLERANCE
280  IF TOL = 5 OR TOL = 10 OR TOL = 20 THEN GOTO 340
290  REM  INVALID TOLERANCE DETECTED
300  PRINT "TOLERANCE VALUE MUST BE 5, 10, OR 20 PERCENT."
310  PRINT "PLEASE REENTER."
320  PRINT
330  GOTO 260
```

With the resistor value defined, write the program segment which can be used to determine the order of magnitude of the resistance. Start testing at the largest values and work toward the smallest value. This simplifies the testing.

```
340  IF R < 10000000 THEN GOTO 400
350  REM  BAND 3 MUST BE BLUE
```

```
360  BAND3 = 6
370  R = R/1000000
380  GOTO 800
```

In line 340, the program tests the value of R against 10 million. If the value is less, it branches to line 400. Otherwise the program concludes that the value is between 10 million and 22 million (the highest value allowed by the limits in line 190). Set the variable BAND3 to 6 (color code for a multiplier of 1,000,000). Next, perform an integer division (i.e., throw away the remainder) of R by 1000000 to produce a two-digit value representing the first two bands. This is repeated for each of the subsequent tests in the program then proceeds to process the two-digit value at line 1000 in the program.

Now construct the rest of the tests:

```
400  IF R < 1000000 THEN GOTO 450
410  REM  BAND 3 MUST BE GREEN
420  BAND3 = 5
430  R = R/100000
440  GOTO 800
450  IF R < 100000 THEN GOTO 500
460  REM  BAND 3 MUST BE YELLOW
470  BAND3 = 4
480  R = R/10000
490  GOTO 800
500  IF R < 10000 THEN GOTO 550
510  REM  BAND 3 MUST BE ORANGE
520  BAND3 = 3
530  530  R = R/1000
540  GOTO 800
550  IF R < 10000 THEN GOTO 600
560  REM  BAND 3 MUST BE RED
570  BAND3 = 2
580  R = R/100
590  GOTO 800
600  IF R < 100 THEN GOTO 650
610  REM  BAND 3 MUST BE BROWN
620  BAND3 = 1
630  R = R/10
640  GOTO 800
650  IF R < 10 THEN GOTO 700
660  REM  BAND 3 MUST BE BLACK
670  BAND3 = 0
680  REM  NO ADJUSTMENT TO R NEEDED
690  GOTO 800
700  IF R < 1 THEN GOTO 750
710  REM  BAND 3 MUST BE SILVER
720  BAND3 = 10
```

```
730  R = R * 10
740  GOTO 800
750  REM  SINCE VALUE IS LESS THAN 1 OHM,
760  REM BAND 3 MUST BE GOLD
770  BAND3 = 11
780  R = R * 100
```

The values for the first two bands are computed. A two-digit number in variable R represents these two bands. If R is divided by 10 and the remainder discarded, the first digit (representing the first band) remains. Multiplying the numeric value of the first band by 10 and subtracting that value from R derives the value of the second band:

```
800  REM  CALCULATE VALUES FOR BAND1 AND BAND2
810  BAND1 = R / 10
820  BAND2 = R - (BAND1 * 10)
```

It remains to determine the color for the tolerance band. Since there are only three possible values (5 percent, 10 percent, or 20 percent) one can use IF statements to determine the correct value for BAND4:

```
830  REM  CALCULATE VALUE FOR BAND4
840  IF TOL > 5 GOTO 880
850  REM  TOLERANCE MUST BE 5% - GOLD BAND
860  BAND4 = 11
870  GOTO 950
880  IF TOL > 10 GOTO 920
890  REM  TOLERANCE MUST BE 10% - SILVER BAND
900  BAND4 = 10
910  GOTO 950
920  REM  TOLERANCE NOT 5% AND NOT 10% - MUST BE 20% -
     NO BAND
930  BAND4 = 12
```

Print it out:

```
950  REM  OUTPUT SECTION
960  PRINT "COLOR CODE WOULD BE: ";COLORCODE$(BAND1)
970  PRINT  COLORCODE$(BAND2),COLORCODE$(BAND3), COLORCODE$(BAND4)
980  PRINT
990  GOTO 170
```

Finally, make the arrangements for the termination of the program:

```
9998  PRINT "PROGRAM HAS BEEN TERMINATED BY OPERATOR."
9999  END
```

The complete program is shown in Listing 16-2.

LISTING 16-2: COMPLETE PROGRAM FOR THE DETERMINATION OF A RESISTORS FOUR BAND COLOR CODE, GIVEN ITS RESISTANCE AND TOLERANCE

```
100  REM  PROGRAM TO CONVERT A NUMERIC ENTRY OF A RESISTOR'S
110  REM  VALUE TO ITS COLOR CODE EQUIVALENT.
120  REM  PERMITTED VALUES:
130  REM  RESISTANCE:     .1 THROUGH 22 MEGOHMS
140  REM  TOLERANCE:     5, 10, OR 20 PERCENT
150  REM  A RESISTANCE VALUE OF ZERO TERMINATES THE PROGRAM.
160  GOSUB  1000
170  INPUT  "ENTER RESISTANCE VALUE (OHMS) OR ZERO TO QUIT: ",R
180  IF R = 0 THEN 9998
190  IF R >= .1 AND R <= 22000000 THEN GOTO 250
200  REM  INVALID VALUE DETECTED
210  PRINT  "RESISTANCE VALUE MUST BE BETWEEN .1 OHMS AND"
220  PRINT  "22 MEGOHMS. PLEASE REENTER."
230  PRINT
240  GOTO 170
250  REM  GET THE TOLERANCE
260  INPUT  "ENTER TOLERANCE; 5, 10, OR 20 PERCENT: ",TOL
270  REM  CHECK TOLERANCE
280  IF TOL = 5 OR TOL = 10 OR TOL = 20 THEN GOTO 340
290  REM  INVALID TOLERANCE DETECTED
300  PRINT  "TOLERANCE VALUE MUST BE 5, 10, OR 20 PERCENT."
310  PRINT  "PLEASE REENTER."
320  PRINT
330  GOTO 260
340  IF R < 10000000 THEN GOTO 400
350  REM  BAND 3 MUST BE BLUE
360  BAND3 > 6
370  R = R/1000000
380  GOTO 800
400  IF R < 1000000 THEN GOTO 450
410  REM BAND 3 MUST BE GREEN
420  BAND3 = 5
430  R = R/100000
440  GOTO 800
450  IF R < 100000 THEN GOTO 500
460  REM  BAND 3 MUST BE YELLOW
470  BAND3 = 4
480  R = R/10000
490  GOTO 800
500  IF R < 10000 THEN GOTO 550
510  REM  BAND 3 MUST BE ORANGE
520  BAND3 = 3
```

```
530  R = R/1000
540  GOTO 800
550  IF R < 1000 THEN GOTO 600
560  REM  BAND 3 MUST BE RED
570  BAND3 = 2
580  R = R/100
590  GOTO 800
600  IF R < 100 THEN GOTO 650
610  REM  BAND 3 MUST BE BROWN
620  BAND3 = 1
630  R = R/10
640  GOTO 800
650  IF R < 10 THEN GOTO 700
660  REM  BAND 3 MUST BE BLACK
670  BAND3 = 0
680  REM  NO ADJUSTMENT TO R NEEDED
690  GOTO 800
700  IF R < 1 THEN GOTO 750
710  REM  BAND 3 MUST BE SILVER
720  BAND3 = 10
730  R = R * 10
740  GOTO 800
750  REM  SINCE VALUE IS LESS THAN 1 OHM,
760  REM  BAND 3 MUST BE GOLD
770  BAND3 = 11
780  R = R * 100
800  REM  CALCULATE VALUES FOR BAND1 AND BAND2
810  BAND1 = R x 10
820  BAND2 = R - (BAND1 * 10)
830  REM  CALCULATE VALUE FOR BAND4
840  IF TOL > 5 GOTO 880
850  REM  TOLERANCE MUST BE 5% - GOLD BAND
860  BAND4 = 11
870  GOTO 950
880  IF TOL > 10 GOTO 920
890  REM  TOLERANCE MUST BE 10% - SILVER BAND
900  BAND4 = 10
910  GOTO 950
920  REM  TOLERANCE NOT 5% AND NOT 10% - MUST BE 20% - NO BAND
930  BAND4 = 12
950  REM  OUTPUT SECTION
960  PRINT  "COLOR CODE WOULD BE: ";COLORCODE$ (BAND1),
970  PRINT  COLORCODE$(BAND2),COLORCODE$(BAND3), COLORCODE$(BAND4)
980  PRINT
990  GOTO 170
```

LISTING 16-2: ***(continued)***

```
1000  REM INITIALIZATION ROUTINE
1010  DIM COLORCODE$(12)
1020  FOR I = 0 TO 12
1030  READ COLORCODE$(I)
1040  NEXT I
1050  RETURN
1060  DATA "BLACK","BROWN","RED","ORANGE"
1070  DATA "YELLOW","GREEN","BLUE","PURPLE"
1080  DATA "GRAY","WHITE","SILVER","GOLD"
1090  DATA  "NONE"
9998  PRINT  "PROGRAM HAS BEEN TERMINATED BY OPERATOR."
9999  END
```

Example 16-3 Another Approach to the Same Problem

Often, there is more than one way to approach a problem. Consider this approach as an alternate to the algorithm presented in Example 16-2. The flowchart is shown in Fig. 16-3; the complete listing is in Listing 16-3.

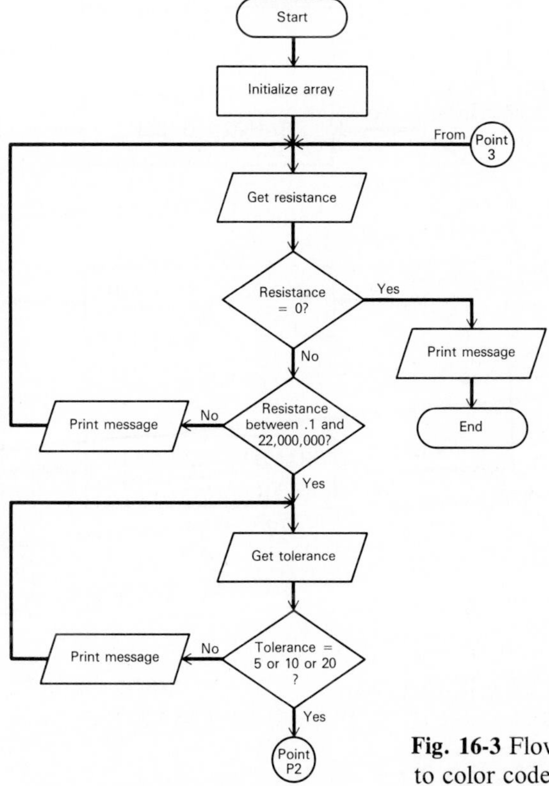

Fig. 16-3 Flowchart for alternate approach to color code program.

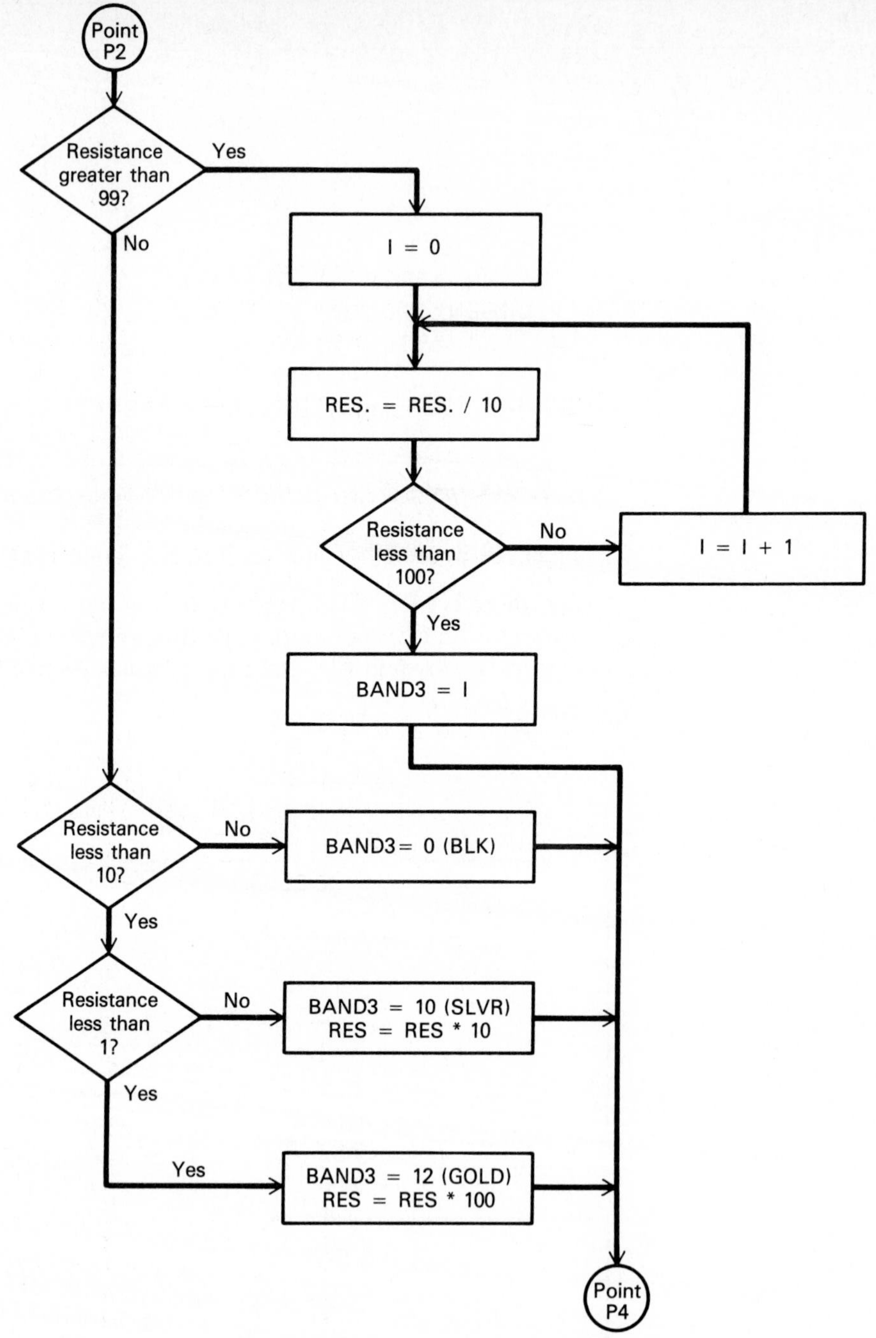

Fig. 16-3 *(continued)*

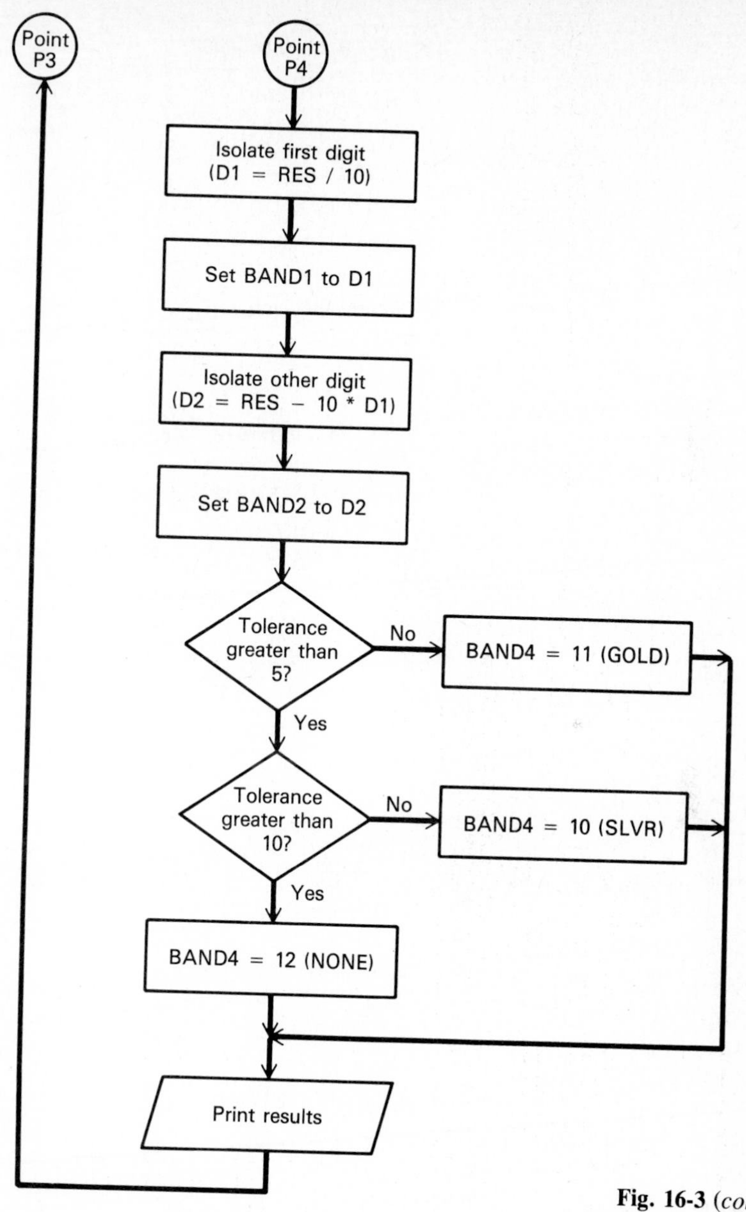

Fig. 16-3 *(continued)*

LISTING 16-3: ALTERNATE APPROACH TO THE COLOR CODE TRANSLATION PROGRAM*

```
100  REM PROGRAM TO CONVERT A NUMERIC ENTRY OF A RESISTOR'S
110  REM VALUE TO ITS COLOR CODE EQUIVALENT.
120  REM PERMITTED VALUES:
130  REM RESISTANCE:  .1 THROUGH 22 MEGOHMS
140  REM TOLERANCE:    5, 10, OR 20 PERCENT
150  REM A RESISTANCE VALUE OF ZERO TERMINATES THE PROGRAM.
```

```
160  GOSUB 1000
170  INPUT "ENTER RESISTANCE VALUE (OHMS) OR ZERO TO QUIT: ",R
180  IF R = 0 THEN 9998
190  IF R >= .1 AND R <= 22000000 THEN GOTO 250
200  REM INVALID VALUE DETECTED
210  PRINT "RESISTANCE VALUE MUST BE BETWEEN .1 OHMS AND"
220  PRINT "22 MEGOHMS. PLEASE REENTER."
230  PRINT
240  GOTO 170
250  REM GET THE TOLERANCE
260  INPUT "ENTER TOLERANCE; 5, 10, OR 20 PERCENT: ", TOL
270  REM CHECK TOLERANCE
280  IF TOL = 5 OR TOL = 10 OR TOL = 20 THEN GOTO 340
290  REM INVALID TOLERANCE DETECTED
300  PRINT "TOLERANCE VALUE MUST BE 5, 10, OR 20 PERCENT."
310  PRINT "PLEASE REENTER."
320  PRINT
330  GOTO 260
340  REM FIRST, TEST FOR VALUES LESS THAN 100 - PROCESS THEM
350  REM SEPARATELY
360  IF R > 99 THEN GOTO 600
370  IF R < 10 THEN GOTO 420
380  REM BAND 3 MUST BE BLACK
390  BAND3 = 0
400  REM NO ADJUSTMENT TO R NEEDED
410  GOTO 800
420  IF R < 1 THEN GOTO 470
430  REM BAND 3 MUST BE SILVER
440  BAND3 = 10
450  R = R * 10
460  GOTO 800
470  REM SINCE VALUE IS LESS THAN 1 OHM,
480  REM BAND 3 MUST BE GOLD
490  BAND3 = 11
500  R = R * 100
510  GOTO 800
600  REM NEW PART OF PROGRAM BEGINS HERE
610  REM I WILL BE USED AS A COUNTER TO KEEP TRACK OF HOW MANY
620  REM TIMES R CAN BE DIVIDED BY 10; THIS VALUE WILL BE THE
630  REM SAME AS THE BAND'S NUMBER CODE.
640  I = 0
650  R = R/10
660  I = I + I
670  IF R > 100 THEN GOTO 650
680  REM WE GET TO THIS POINT WHEN THE VALUE OF R IS LESS THAN
```

```
690  REM 99 - I.E.: TWO DIGITS. I CONTAINS PROPER COLOR CODE VALUE.
700  BAND3 = I
800  REM CALCULATE VALUES FOR BAND1 AND BAND2
810  BAND1 = R/10
820  BAND2 = R - (BAND1 * 10)
830  REM CALCULATE VALUE FOR BAND4
840  IF TOL > 5 GOTO 880
850  REM TOLERANCE MUST BE 5% - GOLD BAND
860  BAND4 = 11
870  GOTO 950
880  IF TOL > 10 GOTO 92
890  REM TOLERANCE MUST BE 10% - SILVER BAND
900  BAND4 = 11
910  GOTO 950
920  REM TOLERANCE NOT 5% AND NOT 10% - MUST BE 20% - NO BAND
930  BAND4 = 12
950  REM OUTPUT SECTION
960  PRINT "COLOR CODE WOULD BE: ";COLORCODE$(BAND1),
970  PRINT COLORCODE$(BAND2),COLORCODE$(BAND3), COLORCODE$(BAND4)
980  PRINT
990  GOTO 170
1000 REM INITIALIZATION ROUTINE
1010 DIM COLORCODE$(12)
1020 FOR I = 0 TO 12
1030 READ COLORCODE$(I)
1040 NEXT I
1050 RETURN
1060 DATA "BLACK","BROWN", "RED","ORANGE"
1070 DATA "YELLOW","GREEN","BLUE","PURPLE"
1080 DATA "GRAY","WHITE","SILVER","GOLD"
1090 DATA "NONE"
9998 PRINT "PROGRAM HAS BEEN TERMINATED BY OPERATOR."
9999 END
```

*Screened elements indicate no change from Listing 16-2.

16-4 MULTIPLE-DIMENSION ARRAYS

The arrays described to this point have all been *one-dimension arrays*—analogous to lists. *Two-dimension* arrays are also possible. Think of a two-dimension array as a *table* or *grid*. A two-dimension array is also sometimes called a *matrix*.

A two-dimension array is envisioned as having vertical *columns* and horizontal *rows*. Consider the following table (Table 16-3).

TABLE 16-3 MATRIX OF VALUES

	0	1	2	3	4
0	392	456	**142**	843	889
1	−24	539	23	−78	43
2	652	121	−3	6	**986**

This table contains three rows of five columns each. In order to access the member of this table that currently contains the value 142, its location, row 0, column 2 must be specified. Similarly, the value 986 is located in row 2, column 4.

In order to access other (individual) members of the array in a similar manner, a subscript containing two values separated by a comma is used. The location is specified by row first, then column.

```
ARRAYNAME(ROW,COLUMN)
```

The subscripts (for two dimensional arrays) can be specified using numeric literals, numeric variables, or numeric expressions, one for each of the two-dimensions, *separated by a comma.*

When dimensioning such arrays, the extents of both dimensions must be specified:

```
DIM VOLTAGE(11,4)
```

This statement sets aside storage for an array having 12 rows (row number 0 through row number 11) of 5 columns (column number 0 through column number 4) or a total of 60 members.

A program may contain both one- and two-dimension arrays, and both may be dimensioned in the same DIM statement.

```
DIM ICPARTNUMBER$(12),PCBOARD(12,4),STATION$(11)
```

16–5 USING A TWO-DIMENSION ARRAY

When the data that a program needs or generates is best represented in a matrix or table, it is a good candidate for the use of a two-dimension array.

Example 16-4 Table of Operational Amplifier Gain

Task: A table of the gain of a simple operational amplifier circuit (see Example 14-5) for all combinations of 4 different values of R1 and R2 is required. The values for R1 and R2 will be held in DATA statements. The output should resemble Fig. 16-4.

GAIN OF NONINVERTING OPERATIONAL AMPLIFIER				
VALUE OF R1 (OHMS)				
R2	1000	10000	100000	1000000
1000	XXXXXX	XXXXXX	XXXXXX	XXXXX
10000	XXXXXX	XXXXXX	XXXXXX	XXXXX
100000		(ETC.)		
1000000				

Fig. 16-4 Output data for Example 16-4.

Algorithmic Analysis: A two-dimension array called GAIN will be used to solve the problem. The 16 gain values we will calculate require an array with 4 rows and 4 columns (4 × 4). The task also requires a place to store the 4 values for R1 and the 4 values for R2. These will be placed in the GAIN(O,N) row and GAIN(N,O) column, respectively. Not only does this make good use of storage, it allows us to reference each resistance value by manipulating the subscripts of the GAIN array.

Two FOR-NEXT loops will be created to perform the subscript manipulation. By controlling the values of the index variables I and J, the program can successively calculate gains for each combination of R1 and R2, and store the resulting value in the GAIN array. The flowchart for this algorithm is shown in Fig. 16-5.

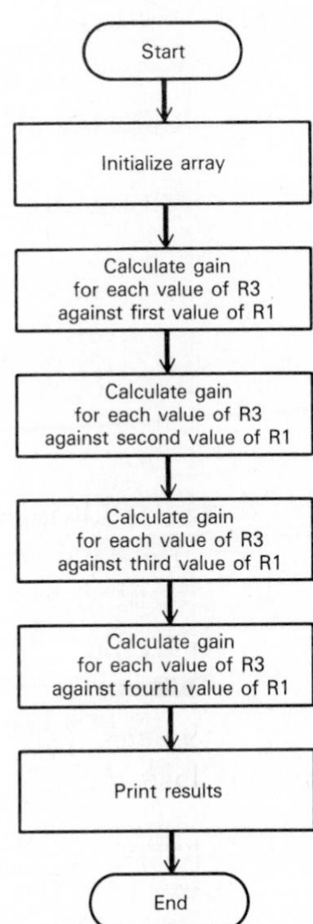

Fig. 16-5 Flowchart to calculate gain for the noninverting op-amp.

Program Construction: Introductory REMs and initialization:

```
100  REM PROGRAM TO PRINT A TABLE OF GAINS FOR A NON-INVERTING
110  REM OPERATIONAL AMPLIFIER FOR VARYING VALUES OF R1 AND R2.
120  REM THE VALUES OF R1 ARE IN THE DATA STATEMENT ON LINE 2140
130  REM THE VALUES OF R2 ARE IN THE DATA STATEMENT ON LINE 2160
140  REM BRANCH TO INITIALIZATION
150  GOSUB 2000

2000 REM INITIALIZATION
2010 DIM GAIN(4,4)
2020 I = 0
2030 REM READ VALUES FOR R1 INTO ROW 0, MEMBERS 1 THROUGH 4
2040 FOR J = 1 TO 4
2050 READ GAIN(I,J)
2060 NEXT J
2070 J = 0
2080 REM READ VALUES FOR R2 INTO COLUMN 0, MEMBERS 1 THROUGH 4
2090 FOR I = 1 TO 4
2100 READ GAIN(I,J)
2110 NEXT I
2120 RETURN
2130 REM NEXT LINE CONTAINS 4 VALUES FOR R1
2140 DATA  1000,10000,100000,1000000
2150 REM NEXT LINE CONTAINS 4 VALUES FOR R2
2160 DATA 1000,10000,100000,1000000
```

Calculate the gains for each of the combinations of R1 and R2:

```
160  REM CALCULATE GAINS
170  FOR I = 1 TO 4
180  FOR J = 1 TO 4
190  GAIN(I,J) = 1 + (GAIN(I,0)/GAIN(0,J))
200  NEXT J
210  NEXT I
```

The following remarks will help to explain the details of the program.

Entering the I loop at line 170, I is set to a value of 1. Immediately afterward, the J loop begins at line 180 which is initiated when J is set equal to 1. The J loop is the inner loop; it must be satisfied before the I loop is advanced.

The first calculation is performed at line 190. Substituting the numerical values for I and J, the calculation becomes:

```
GAIN(1,1) = 1 + (GAIN(1,0)/GAIN(0,1))
```

Substituting for the values entered in the GAIN array for R1 and R2:

```
GAIN(1,1) = 1 + (1000 / 1000)
```

Thus, Gain(1,1) is assigned a value of 2.

At line 200, the J loop is incremented. J now has a value of 2. Again, substituting values in the formula on line 190:

```
GAIN(1,2) = 1 + (GAIN(1,0) / GAIN(0,2))
GAIN(1,2) = 1 + (1000 / 10000)
GAIN(1,2) = 1.1
```

When the J loop has been satisfied (when GAIN(1,4) has been calculated), the I loop is incremented; I now has a value of 2. The J loop is reentered, reinitializing J to a value of 1, and the sequence repeats.

The next portion of the program causes the results to be printed:

```
220  REM OUTPUT SECTION
230  CLS
240  PRINT ,"GAIN OF NONINVERTING OPERATIONAL AMPLIFIER"
250  PRINT
260  PRINT ,"            VALUE OF R1 (OHMS)"
270  PRINT
280  PRINT ,"____________________________________________________________"
290  PRINT "   R2",GAIN(0,1),GAIN(0,2),GAIN(0,3),GAIN(0,4)
300  PRINT
310  REM NOW PRINT THE VALUES FOR R2 AND THE GAINS
320  FOR I = 1 TO 4
330  PRINT GAIN(I,0),GAIN(I,1),GAIN(I,2),GAIN(I,3),GAIN (I,4)
340  PRINT
350  NEXT I
```

The next statement (360) causes a branch to the close of the program:

```
 360  GOTO 9998
9998  PRINT "PROGRAM HAS COMPLETED ITS TASK."
9999  END
```

The complete listing can be found in Listing 16-4.

LISTING 16-4: COMPLETE LISTING OF TABLE OF GAINS PROGRAM

```
100  REM PROGRAM TO PRINT A TABLE OF GAINS FOR A NONINVERTING
110  REM OPERATIONAL AMPLIFIER FOR VARYING VALUES OF R1 AND R2.
120  REM THE VALUES OF R1 ARE IN THE DATA STATEMENT ON LINE 2140
130  REM THE VALUES OF R2 ARE IN THE DATA STATEMENT ON LINE 2160
140  REM BRANCH TO INITIALIZATION
150  GOSUB 2000
160  REM CALCULATE GAINS
```

LISTING 16-4: *(continued)*

```
170  FOR I = 1 TO 4
180  FOR J = 1 TO 4
190  GAIN(I,J) = 1 + (GAIN(I,0)/GAIN(0,J))
200  NEXT J
210  NEXT I
220  REM OUTPUT SECTION
230  CLS
240  PRINT ,"GAIN OF NONINVERTING OPERATIONAL AMPLIFIER"
250  PRINT
260  PRINT ,"          VALUE OF R1 (OHMS)"
270  PRINT
280  PRINT ,"____________________________________________________________"
290  PRINT "   R2",GAIN(0,1),GAIN(0,2),GAIN(0,3),GAIN(0,4)
300  PRINT
310  REM NOW PRINT THE VALUES FOR R2 AND THE GAINS
320  FOR I = 1 TO 4
330  PRINT GAIN(I,0),GAIN(I,1),GAIN(I,2),GAIN(I,3),GAIN(I,4)
340  PRINT
350  NEXT I
360  GOTO 9998
2000 REM INITIALIZATION
2010 DIM GAIN(4,4)
2020 I = 0
2030 REM READ VALUES FOR R1 INTO ROW 0, MEMBERS 1 THROUGH 4
2040 FOR J = 1 TO 4
2050 READ GAIN(I,J)
2060 NEXT J
2070 J = 0
2080 REM READ VALUES FOR R2 INTO COLUMN 0, MEMBERS 1 THROUGH 4
2090 FOR I = 1 TO 4
2100 READ GAIN(I,J)
2110 NEXT I
2120 RETURN
2130 REM NEXT LINE CONTAINS 4 VALUES FOR R1
2140 DATA 1000,10000,100000,1000000
2150 REM NEXT LINE CONTAINS 4 VALUES FOR R2
2160 DATA 1000,10000,100000,1000000
9998 PRINT "PROGRAM HAS COMPLETED ITS TASK."
9999 END
```

16-6 HIGHER-ORDER ARRAYS

A one-dimension array can be compared to a list and a two-dimension array to a table. Most versions of BASIC will permit arrays with even more dimensions; some as many as 31.

A three-dimension array is usually thought of as a book. A book has pages; each page contains a table. The third dimension then is equivalent to the page number, where the remaining two dimensions are the row and column of the table *on the given page*. A book of 30 pages, each page containing a table consisting of 20 rows of 15 columns, would be analogous to an array dimensioned as (29,19,14); remember the zero page, row, and column!

A four-dimension array can be compared to a bookcase full of books, each book having a unique number. Each book has pages; each page has a table. A data element is specified by stating the book number, page, row, and column.

For a five-dimension array, consider that there are a number of bookcases, each containing numbered books. To specify a given data element, the bookcase, book, page, row, and column are required.

For a six-dimension array, think of a library, with rows of bookcases. Referencing a given data element now requires knowing the bookcase row, bookcase number, book number, page number, row, and column.

These analogies may be carried on and on; seven dimensions adds additional floors of bookcase rows; eight dimensions has multiple buildings; and so on. These are only analogies, though, to help visualize the way in which the data is being stored. Often, data arrays requiring more than four dimensions are better broken down into multiple arrays.

SUMMARY

Programs execute more efficiently when items or data with common characteristics can be grouped together and assigned a common name. The array structure in BASIC can be used for this purpose. The subscript is used to indicate to BASIC which member of the array is to be accessed. The strength and flexibility of the array is a result of the ability to *compute* subscripts, manipulating them with any of the commands available in BASIC.

The DIM statement is used to tell the computer (BASIC) how much memory to set aside for the array.

A two-dimension array is used to represent data which has a tabular or grid arrangement. The array can be envisioned as having columns and rows of data in the form of a matrix.

The number of dimensions of an array depends on the dialect of BASIC, but may be extended beyond two when appropriate for the data structure.

REVIEW PROBLEMS

1. Determine how many members are in each of the following arrays and what their characteristics are.

a. DIM PARTS(30)

b. DIM DAYS(365)
c. DIM VOLTAGE(8)
d. DIM READINGS%(11,31)
e. DIM POWER#(3,15)
f. DIM PARTNAME$(23)
g. DIM MANUFACTURERS$(4,2,20)
h. DIM BOARDPOSITION%(28,45)
i. DIM TEST(9)
j. DIM BIGARRAY(2,3,4,5,6)

In the following problems write DIM statements for each of the indicated arrays. Be sure to choose suitable variable names and types, in addition to allocating sufficient members.

2. An array that will contain the number of 16 different transistors in stock.

3. An array that will contain the standard values for 10 percent tolerance resistors.

4. An array that will contain the standard values for 5 percent, 10 percent, and 20 percent tolerance resistors.

5. An array that will store the names of the 23 different parts contained on "PC board subassembly 123-76-99B".

6. An array that will contain the names and alphanumeric part number of the 23 different parts contained on "PC board subassembly 123-76-99B".

7. An array or arrays that will contain the names, alphanumeric part number, and quantity of the 23 different parts contained on "PC board subassembly 123-76-99B" (i.e., there may be 4, 1200-ohm ½-watt resistors, part number R1200.5, appearing on the board).

8. A single array that will contain the names and alphanumeric part number of the parts contained on each of the six different PC boards that are part of a given device. No board contains more than 40 components.

9. A single array that will contain the proper voltage and resistance readings for 37 test-points as shown on a schematic.

10. An array or arrays that will act as a parts list for a given device. The data to be contained includes a part name, alphanumeric part number, schematic designation (i.e., R27, Q118, etc.), and a numeric vendor code.

11. An array or arrays that could be used as part of a data base for cataloging computer programs on a collection of diskettes. Data includes program name, language it is written in, number of the diskette on which it appears, and date the program was written.

REVIEW QUESTIONS

1. What is an analogy for a one-dimension array? What does the dimension represent?
2. What is the subscript of the first member of a one-dimension array?
3. What do all members of an array have in common?
4. How may the subscript of an array be expressed? What type of value must a subscript be?
5. What is the purpose of the DIM statement?
6. What is an analogy for a two-dimension array? What do the two dimensions represent?
7. What is the subscript of the first member of a two-dimension array?
8. What is the strength in using arrays?
9. Can more than one array be used in a program? Can arrays of different dimensions be used in the same program? Can arrays of different numbers of dimensions be used in the same program?
10. Why is it good programming practice to use the ''zero'' members of an array?

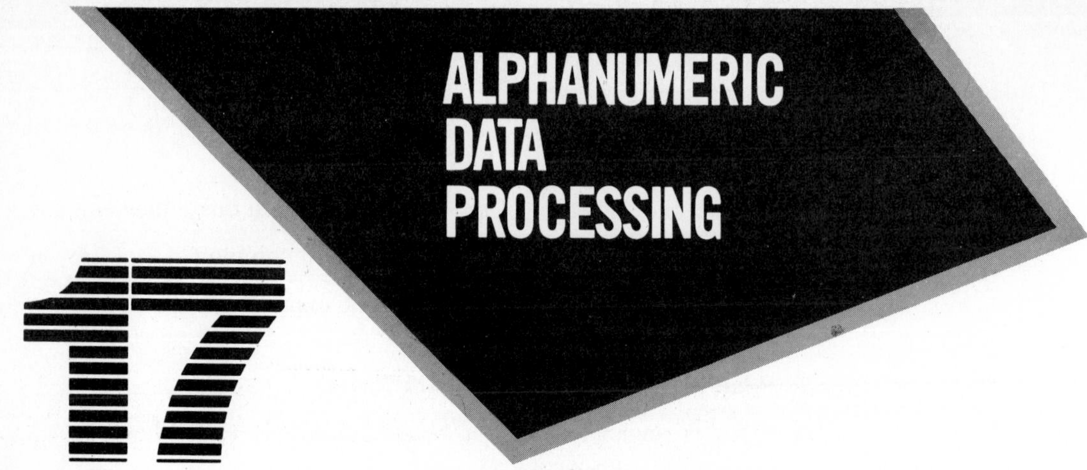

17 ALPHANUMERIC DATA PROCESSING

BASIC, being a general-purpose language, supports alphanumeric processing with a number of functions that permit the manipulation of data which is not numeric. While the degree of support varies from BASIC to BASIC, nearly all dialects support the functions described in this chapter.

17-1 STORAGE OF ALPHANUMERIC DATA

In Chapter 12 we discussed how numeric values were stored in memory; that integer values were generally stored in 2 bytes, 15 bits for the value, 1 bit for the sign; single and double precision floating-point values in exponential (base two) form. We did not at that time discuss how *strings* or groups of alphanumeric data were stored.

In the earlier sections of this text, ASCII codes were introduced (see Appendix). Each letter, symbol, numeral, punctuation mark, and special character was assigned a numeric code. The letter "A" has an ASCII code of 65 (decimal); the numeral "6" has an ASCII code of 54 (decimal). ASCII is a 7-bit code, so there are 128 different codes available with which to represent the characters we want to use. In addition, many computer manufacturers take advantage of the remaining 127 possible codes in an 8-bit byte and provide special graphics characters, foreign language characters (such as û or ñ), or special scientific characters (such as δ or ω). Remember, every character must be assigned a code—even the "space" which has an ASCII code of 32 (decimal).

An *alphanumeric string* (*string*) consists of a series of ASCII codes for the characters that are to be represented. Thus the characters in the string:

```
MARY HAD A LITTLE LAMB
```

would occupy 22 bytes of storage, and would look like this:

```
77 65 82 89 32 72 65 68 32 65 32 76 73 84 84 76 69 32 76 65 77 66
M  A  R  Y  sp H  A  D  sp A  sp L  I  T  T  L  E  sp L  A  M  B
```

with each ASCII code occupying one byte of storage.

In addition to storing the character codes, most BASICs store the length of the string, using a single byte of storage. Therefore, most forms of BASIC will permit a string to contain up to 255 characters.

Just as with numeric data, BASIC takes care of this conversion to ASCII and the storage details as well. Symbolic names are used to represent the data locations (just as they were used for numeric values).

Variables that are to contain alphanumeric data must carry the suffix character $ as the last character of the variable's name. This signals BASIC to store the value as alphanumeric characters (i.e., in ASCII) as opposed to using numeric storage conventions.

17-2 MANIPULATING ALPHANUMERIC DATA

Clearly, the operations that we would want to perform on alphanumeric data are different from those that are performed upon numeric data. It makes little sense to multiply one name by another, or to subtract the description of an item from it's location in a store. And yet, there are some operations that are similar to those performed on numeric data.

17-2-1 Concatenation

Concatenation means to connect together; the concatenation of two (or more) strings is to connect the end of the first string with the beginning of the second string. Most BASICS represent the operation of concatenation with the plus sign (+). This may be just a bit confusing, since the operation of adding one string to another (i.e., the plus representing addition) does not make sense. Just remember that *the plus symbol, when used between string values, represents concatenation and not addition.*

Concatenation is useful when alphanumeric data is stored in a number of different variables but is to be treated, at some point, as a single item. For instance, a component's type (Q, R, C, IC, etc.), and schematic designation (i.e., 127), would be stored in separate variables so that the data can be sorted or searched according to either of these pieces of data. However, they would be printed together as a single item of a parts list. Although the printing of this item could be done with the statement

```
PRINT PARTTYPE$(POINTER);SCHDESIG$(POINTER)
```

we might first combine the values into a single string and then print the value of the combined string:

```
PARTNO$ = PARTTYPE$(POINTER) + SCHDESIG$(POINTER)
    .
    .
    .
PRINT PARTNO$
```

The reason for doing this might not be clear. After all, it required an additional operation to create the concatenated string and print it, rather than printing the strings directly. The gain is that we are then able to more precisely format the output; we can determine, using functions that will be introduced shortly, the exact length of the string (i.e., "IC501" – 5 characters or "R1" – 2 characters) and concatenate exactly the right number of spaces to make all the part numbers print out in an even column.

17-2-2 String Comparisons

The IF statement has been used for comparing numeric values; we can test for greater than, less than, equal, and combinations such as greater than or equal, less than or equal, and less than or greater than (this is the same as not equal). We use the same IF statement and relational operators (<, >, and =) to compare strings. However, the results of such comparisons are somewhat different from the results of numerical comparisons.

First, BASIC compares the lengths of the two strings. A shorter string is *always* less than a longer string, *regardless* of the values contained in the strings. Therefore, the string "Z" is less than the string "AA", since "AA" has two characters and "Z" has only one. This upsets the way we would normally order these two strings, but we can correct this by equalizing the lengths of the strings first. If we concatenate enough spaces to the shorter string so that the length of the short string equals the length of the long string, the comparison will be made correctly.

If the lengths of the strings are equal, the comparison is made on a character by character basis, starting at the leftmost character of the strings. If the ASCII codes are the same, comparison continues with the next character. If the ASCII codes are not the same, the comparison ends, with the string containing the character with the higher-value ASCII code being considered greater than the other string.

See Figure 17-1 for some examples.

```
String 1: "XYZ"  (ASCII: 88 89 90)
String 2: "ABCD" (ASCII: 65 66 67 68)
```

1. Lengths of the two strings are compared: string 2 is longer than string 1.
2. Comparison ends; string 1 is less than string 2.

```
String 1: "XYZ " (ASCII: 88 89 90 32)
String 2: "ABCD" (ASCII: 65 66 67 68)
```

1. Compare lengths of strings; they are equal (string 1 has been padded with a blank on the right).
2. Compare ASCII codes of first character: 88 (string 1) vs. 65 (string 2).

3. 88 is greater than 65.
4. Comparison ends; string 1 is greater than string 2.

```
String 1: "SIX"   (ASCII: 83 73 88)
String 2: "SIX"   (ASCII: 83 73 88)
```

1. Both strings are of equal length.
2. Compare first character of each: ASCII 83 vs. ASCII 83
3. ASCII values equal. Compare next character.
4. ASCII 73 vs ASCII 73; values equal, compare next character.
5. ASCII 88 vs ASCII 88; values equal, no more characters to compare.
6. Strings compare as equal. (lengths the same, all characters compare as equal)

```
String 1: "DOG" (ASCII: 68 79 71)
String 2: "CAT" (ASCII: 67 65 54)
```

1. Both strings are of equal length—compare first character of each.
2. ASCII 68 is compared to ASCII 67; 68 is greater than 67.
3. Comparison is completed—string 1 is greater than string 2.

```
String 1: "ADAMS, A" (ASCII: 65 68 65 77 83 44 32 65)
String 2: "ADAMS, J" (ASCII: 65 68 65 77 83 44 32 74)
```

1. Both strings of equal length; compare first character.
2. ASCII 65 vs ASCII 65—equal. compare next character.
3. ASCII 68 vs ASCII 68—equal. compare next character.
4. ASCII 65 vs ASCII 65—equal. compare next character.
5. ASCII 77 vs ASCII 77—equal. compare next character.
6. ASCII 83 vs ASCII 83—equal. compare next character.
7. ASCII 44 vs ASCII 44—equal. compare next character.
8. ASCII 32 vs ASCII 32—equal. compare next character.
9. ASCII 65 vs ASCII 74—string 2 is greater than string 1.
10. Comparison ends; string 2 is greater than string 1.

Fig. 17-1 Examples of string comparisons.

17-2-3 The Length Function

It is often useful to be able to determine the length (number of characters) of a string. BASIC provides a function to do just that—the LEN function. BASIC computes the number of characters in a string and returns that value. The value can be assigned to another variable or can be used directly as a value to be included in further calculations.

X$ = "ABC DEF"   LEN(X$) would return a value of 7.
Z$ = "A B C D E F G"   LEN(Z$) would return a value of 13.

This is a clue as to how one can equalize the lengths of two strings before comparing them. Listing 17-1 shows one method of using a subroutine to equalize the length of two strings. The shorter string is expanded to the length of the longer string.

LISTING 17-1 A SUBROUTINE TO EQUALIZE THE LENGTHS OF TWO STRINGS

```
300  REM TWO STRINGS ARE IN VARIABLES S1$ AND S2$
310  REM IF STRINGS ARE SAME LENGTH, GOTO COMPARISON
320  IF LEN(S1$) = LEN(S2$) THEN GOTO 480
330  REM DETERMINE WHICH STRING IS LONGER - TRY STRING 1
340  IF LEN(S1$) > LEN(S2$) THEN 420
350  REM STRING 2 IS LONGER - PAD STRING 1 WITH BLANKS.
360  DIFFERENCE = LEN(S2$) - LEN(S1$)
370  FOR I = 1 TO DIFFERENCE
380  S1$ = S1$ + " "
390  REM ADD A SPACE TO THE END OF S1$
400  NEXT I
410  GOTO 480
420  REM STRING 1 IS LONGER; PAD STRING2 WITH BLANKS
430  DIFFERENCE = LEN(S1$) - LEN(S2$)
440  FOR I = 1 TO DIFFERENCE
450  REM ADD A SPACE TO THE END OF STRING 2
460  S2$ = S2$ + " "
470  NEXT I
480  REM BOTH STRINGS THE SAME LENGTH - NOW COMPARE THEM
490  RETURN
```

There are more efficient ways of doing this. We will discuss them shortly.

17-2-4 Extracting Parts of Strings — The LEFT$, RIGHT$, and MID$ Functions.

Sometimes, instead of wanting to put strings together (concatenate them) we wish to take them apart. For instance, we may know that the variable PARTNAME$ was constructed in such a way that the first 10 characters contain a part's standard number (e.g., "NE555"), padded with blanks if shorter, and truncated if longer than the 10 characters allowed, and the next 6 characters contain the part's schematic designation (e.g., "IC207"), also padded with blanks, or truncated, as necessary. There may be times when we want to consider only the part number or only the schematic designation and wish to extract that part of the string from PARTNAME$.

The LEFT$, RIGHT$, and MID$ functions allow the programmer to extract a given number of characters from the left end, right end, or middle of an existing string, respectively. Notice how the names of these strings end with a $. This is a reminder that these functions return a result which is itself a string. The LEN function returns a number which represents the length of a given string, but the value that is returned is a numeric value.

LEFT$, RIGHT$, and MID$ return the actual characters specified by the parameters of the function. The result may be used as a string or assigned to another string variable.

a. LEFT$ Function

Syntax: LEFT$(aexpr,nexpr) Where aexpr is the string from which you wish to extract characters, and nexpr is a numeric value representing the number of characters you wish to extract, starting with the *leftmost* character. The nexpr must be less than the length of aexpr or an error will result.

Figure 17-2 contains examples of how the LEFT$ function is used.

```
Z$ = LEFT$("MC68000MOTOROLA",10)
```

Z$ would then contain the value "MC68000MOT"

```
PARTNAME$ = LEFT$(DESCRIPT$(3,87),6)
```

PARTNAME$ would then contain the left 6 characters of DESCRIPT$(3,87), assuming that DESCRIPT$(3,87) was at least six characters long.

```
PADDED$ = LEFT(PARTNAME$ + "          ",10)
```

PADDED$ would then contain the leftmost 10 characters of the string starting with all the characters of PARTNAME$ concatenated with 10 blanks (spaces).

If PARTNAME$ was "SN74121", PADDED$ would contain "SN74121   " ("SN74121" followed by 3 spaces). If PARTNAME$ was "CD74HCT4031E" PADDED$ would contain "CD74HCT403" (the final 1E has been truncated).

Notice that even if PARTNAME$ were null (empty—no contents), PADDED$ would be given a value of 10 spaces, because the LEFT$ function would than be working on the concatenation of nothing (null string) with 10 spaces.

Fig. 17-2 Examples of the use of the LEFT$ function.

b. RIGHT$ Function

Syntax: RIGHT$(aexpr,nexpr) Where aexpr is the string from which to extract characters, and nexpr is a numeric value representing the number of characters to be extracted, starting from the *rightmost* character. The value of nexpr must be less than the length of aexpr or an error will result. Figure 17-3 contains examples of how the RIGHT$ function is used.

```
K$ = RIGHT$("PL-259 PLUG",6)
```

K$ would then contain "9 PLUG" (the rightmost 6 characters).

```
RIGHTJUSTIFY$ = RIGHT$("          "+PARTNAME$,20)
```

RIGHTJUSTIFY$ would contain the rightmost 20 characters of the string formed by the concatenation of 20 spaces to the contents of PARTNAME$.

This would be useful if we wanted to print a column of part names with the right edge of each name printing in the same position on subsequent lines. Just printing those names, even using commas for column alignment, would left-justify the names (print them flush on the left edge).

```
NEWWORD$ = RIGHT$( LEFT$(OLDWORD$,8), 5)
```

This uses two function calls—one to RIGHT$, one to LEFT$. Assume that OLDWORD$ contains the string "ONE MORE TIME." The LEFT$ function is evaluated first because it appears in the innermost set of parentheses. The leftmost 8 characters of OLDWORD$ are "ONE MORE." Then the RIGHT$ function is evaluated. It says, use the rightmost five characters of the leftmost 8 characters of OLDWORD$. The rightmost 5 characters of "ONE MORE" are " MORE" (don't forget, the space counts as a character).
This demonstrates that function may use expressions as parameters, and that these expressions may themselves contain calls to other functions.

Fig. 17-3 Examples of the use of the RIGHT$ function.

c. MID$ Function

Syntax a: MID$(aexpr,nexpr1,nexpr2) For the MID$ function aexpr is the string upon which MID$ is to work, nexpr1 is a numeric value which indicates the position of the first character to be extracted, and nexpr2 indicates the number of characters to be extracted. The value of nexpr1 must be less than or equal to the length of the string or an error will result. The value of nexpr2 must be less than or equal to the number of remaining characters, or an error will result.
Syntax b: MID$(aexpr1,nexpr1) Where aexpr is the string upon which MID$ is to work, and nexpr1 marks the first column to be extracted. This form of the MID$ function extracts the *remainder* of the string, starting from position nexpr1. The value of nexpr1 must be less than or equal to the length of the string or an error will result.

Figure 17-4 contains examples of how to use the MID$ function.

```
P$ = MID$("ABCDEFGHIJKLMNOPQRSTUVWXYZ",6,3)
```

P$ would be assigned a value of "FGH"; 3 characters, starting with character number 6 (F).

```
X$ = MID$(FULLSTRING$,4,12)
```

X$ would be assigned a value of the 12 characters beginning with character #4 of the string FULLSTRING$, assuming that FULLSTRING$ is at least 16 characters long (4 + 12) (otherwise an error condition is raised).

```
Q$ = MID$("ABCDEFGHIJKLMNOPQRSTUVWXYZ",20)
```

Q$ would be assigned a value of "TUVWXYZ"; the remainder of the string, beginning with the 20th character.

```
REMAINDER$ = MID$(ORIGINAL$,8)
```

REMAINDER$ would be assigned a value of the rest of the string ORIGINAL$, starting with the 8th character, assuming that ORIGINAL$ was at least 8 characters long (otherwise an error condition is raised).

Fig. 17-4 Examples of using the MID$ function.

17-3 PUTTING STRING FUNCTIONS TO USE

17-3-1 Centering Headings

Often we want to center a heading on the screen (or paper). We can count the number of characters in our heading, and pad the heading with blanks on the left until it is centered. Sometimes, we don't know the exact length of the heading; it may contain data that is calculated or entered during the execution of the program. In this case we must let the computer do the calculations.

Consider Listing 17-2:

LISTING 17-2 LISTING OF A SUBROUTINE TO CENTER A HEADING

```
100  REM ASSUME THE TEXT FOR THE HEADING IS IN THE VARIABLE HEADING$
110  REM AND THAT THE HEADING IS NO MORE THAN 80 CHARACTERS LONG.
120  REM ASSUME THAT A LINE MAY CONTAIN A MAXIMUM OF 80 CHARACTERS.
130  REM ASSUME THAT THE VARIABLE BL$ CONTAINS A STRING OF 40 SPACES.
140  HEADLENGTH = LEN(HEADING$)/2
150  REM PAD HEADING WITH 40 BLANKS ON LEFT(HALF THE LINE WIDTH)
160  TEMP$ = BL$ + HEADING$
170  HEADING$ = MID$(TEMP$,HEADLENGTH)
180  PRINT HEADING$
190  RETURN
```

Suppose HEADING$ had the value:

```
"CAPACITIVE REACTANCE OF A .01MFD CAPACITOR AT VARIOUS FREQUENCIES"
```

At line 140 HEADLENGTH is assigned a value of 32.5 (65/2).

After executing line 160, TEMP$ would be a string consisting of 40 spaces, followed by "CAPACITIVE REACTANCE OF A .01MFD CAPACITOR AT VARIOUS FREQUENCIES".

Line 170 says, take the string TEMP$, starting at character 32.5, for a remainder of the string, and assign this part of the string to the variable HEADING$.

One might ask, "What is character 32.5?" There is indeed, no such thing as character 32.5. However, when a noninteger is passed to a function that requires an integer, one of two things takes place: either the value is rounded to the nearest integer (0.5 or greater rounds to the next higher value), or, the value is truncated—the fractional part is discarded. If the version of BASIC being used rounds off, the MID$ function at line 170 would begin with column 33. If BASIC truncates, the MID$ function at line 170 would begin with column 32. This truncation can be handled by changing line 140 to:

```
140  HEADLENGTH = (LEN(HEADING$) / 2) + .5
```

Now, HEADLENGTH would arrive at line 170 with a value of 33 (32.5 + 0.5), and truncation would have no effect. If the length of HEADING$ had been even (for example 30), HEADLENGTH would arrive at line 170 with a value of 15.5 ((30 / 2) + 0.5), which would be truncated to 15.

Finally, at line 180 the heading is printed, padded with the correct number of blanks on the left to center the text on an 80-character line.

The entire operation could be condensed to a single statement:

```
PRINT MID$(BL$ + HEADING$, (LEN(HEADING$) / 2 + .5))
```

17-3-2 Locating a Character in a String—The INSTR Function

It is useful to know whether a character or group of characters is contained within a string, and if so, where in the string that character or group of characters is located. Some forms of BASIC provide the INSTR function which performs this task.

Syntax: INSTR(aexpr1,aexpr2) Where aexpr1 is the string to be searched, and aexpr2 is the character or group of characters being sought.

The INSTR function returns the number of the column of the *first* occurrence of aexpr2 in aexpr1. If aexpr2 is not found within aexpr1, INSTR returns a value of 0.

See Fig. 17-5 for examples of how to use the INSTR function.

```
K = INSTR("ABCDEFGHIJ","D")
```

K would be assigned the value 4; "D" is found in the fourth column of the string to be searched.

```
L = INSTR("ABCABCABC","ABC")
```

L would be assigned the value 1; the first occurrence of the string "ABC" is in column 1.

```
J = INSTR ("ABCABCABC","ABCD")
```

J would be assigned the value 0; the string "ABCD" does not occur anywhere within the string to be searched.

```
MANUFAC$=MID$(PARTNAME$, INSTR(PARTNAME$,",") + 1)
PARTNUM$=LEFT$(PARTNAME$, INSTR(PARTNAME$,",") - 1)
```

Assume that PARTNAME$ contains a part number and manufacturer, separated by a comma as in: "CA3040,RCA". MANUFAC$ would be assigned the portion of the string starting 1 column after the first comma (position 8) and ending with the end of the string: "RCA."

PARTNUM$ would be assigned the string beginning with the leftmost character of PARTNAME$ for 6 (position of the first comma, minus 1) characters: "CA3040."

Fig. 17-5 Examples of use of the INSTR function.

Example 17-1 Generating a Parts List

Task A program must be written to create a parts list which is to be included with the documentation accompanying an oscilloscope being sent to a customer. The report is to have the following format:

PARTS CONTAINED ON VERTICAL AMPLIFIER PC BOARD		
CAPACITORS:		
C1	.1 MFD 100V CERAMIC	C27.987SPR
C2	2000 MFD 50V TANTALUM	C43.913PAN
	(ETC)	
DIODES:		
D1	1N914 SWITCHING DIODE	S12.652IR
	(ETC)	

Data has been stored in arrays as follows:

PARTTYPE$ Contains name of part type—such as, TRANSISTOR or SWITCH. A member may be up to 35 characters long.

SCHDESIG$ Contains schematic designation—for example, Q204 or IC7. A member may be up to 7 characters long.

DESCRIPT$ Contains the complete parts description—.01 MFD 100 V CERAMIC. A member may be up to 25 characters long.

PARTNUM$ Contains the complete stocking part number—S12.652IR. A member may be up to 10 characters long.

So, if the data for C1 (above) is in member number 1, its data would be stored as follows:

```
PARTTYPE$(1) = "CAPACITOR"
SCHDESIG$(1) = "C1"
DESCRIPT$(1) = ".1 MFD 100V CERAMIC"
PARTNUM$(1) = "C27.987SPR"
```

The arrays are sorted so that the data appears in the order in which it is to be printed; all the capacitors, diodes, resistors, transistors, and so on are grouped together in schematic-designation order.

Finally, there are a total of 86 parts contained on this board.

Algorithmic Analysis Since the data is already contained in arrays as previously described, the primary task is formatting the output. The following observations can be made:

1. The heading is centered in an 80-column field; assume the uncentered heading to be in a variable HEADING$.
2. The part type is printed only once, as a heading, in column 1, each time the type of part changes. The heading is printed in its plural form, followed by a colon (:).

3. The schematic designation begins in column 1.
4. The part description begins in column 15.
5. The part number begins in column 50.

Because the schematic designation and part description may vary in length, one cannot simply append a fixed number of blanks to achieve the necessary spacing. Instead, the number of blanks to be appended to achieve the fixed length desired must be calculated. The schematic designation and its blanks will occupy columns 1 through 14; the parts description, columns 15 through 49; and the part number, columns 50 and beyond. Thus, if all the schematic designations are 14 characters long and all the parts descriptions 35 characters long by right-padding with blanks, we can then concatenate the padded designation, description, and part number and print the result.

Two possibilities exist:

1. Generate the padded versions of the data and store this version back in the same array for the SCHDESIG$ and DESCRIPT$ arrays; then generate and store complete output lines in still another array; then print the contents of the lines array.
2. Generate the output line at print-time; perform all the padding and concatenations just before printing. This leaves the original data unchanged and does not require storage for more than one output line at a time.

If there was further use for the data in its padded form, or if a copy of the documentation was to be saved on disk, we might choose the first method which ends with all of the output lines in an array that can easily be stored to disk.

However, if the only goal is to generate the print report, approach 2 is our better choice. It does not waste time storing the padded versions of the data, and it does not waste storage in keeping the output lines. The design shown here uses approach 2. Figure 17-6 shows the overall approach to this problem.

Program Construction Since the padding function is used several times on different pieces of data, a subroutine will be used to perform the operation. The string to be padded will be found in the variable UNPADDED$. Additionally, the desired length of the string will be located in the variable DESLEN. The result to be returned is stored under the variable name PADDED$.

Opening REMs:

```
2000  REM  SUBROUTINE TO PAD A STRING WITH BLANKS TO A DESIRED
2010  REM LENGTH. INPUT STRING IS IN UNPADDED$, DESIRED LENGTH
2020  REM  IS IN DESLEN. PADDED STRING IS RETURNED IN PADDED$.
2030  REM  VARIABLE BLKS$ IS ASSUMED TO CONTAIN 40 BLANKS.
2040  L = LEN(UNPADDED$) + 40
2050  REM  AS SAFETY, TEST FOR A ILLEGAL STRING LENGTH
2060  IF L <= 255 AND DESLEN <= 255 THEN GOTO 2100
```

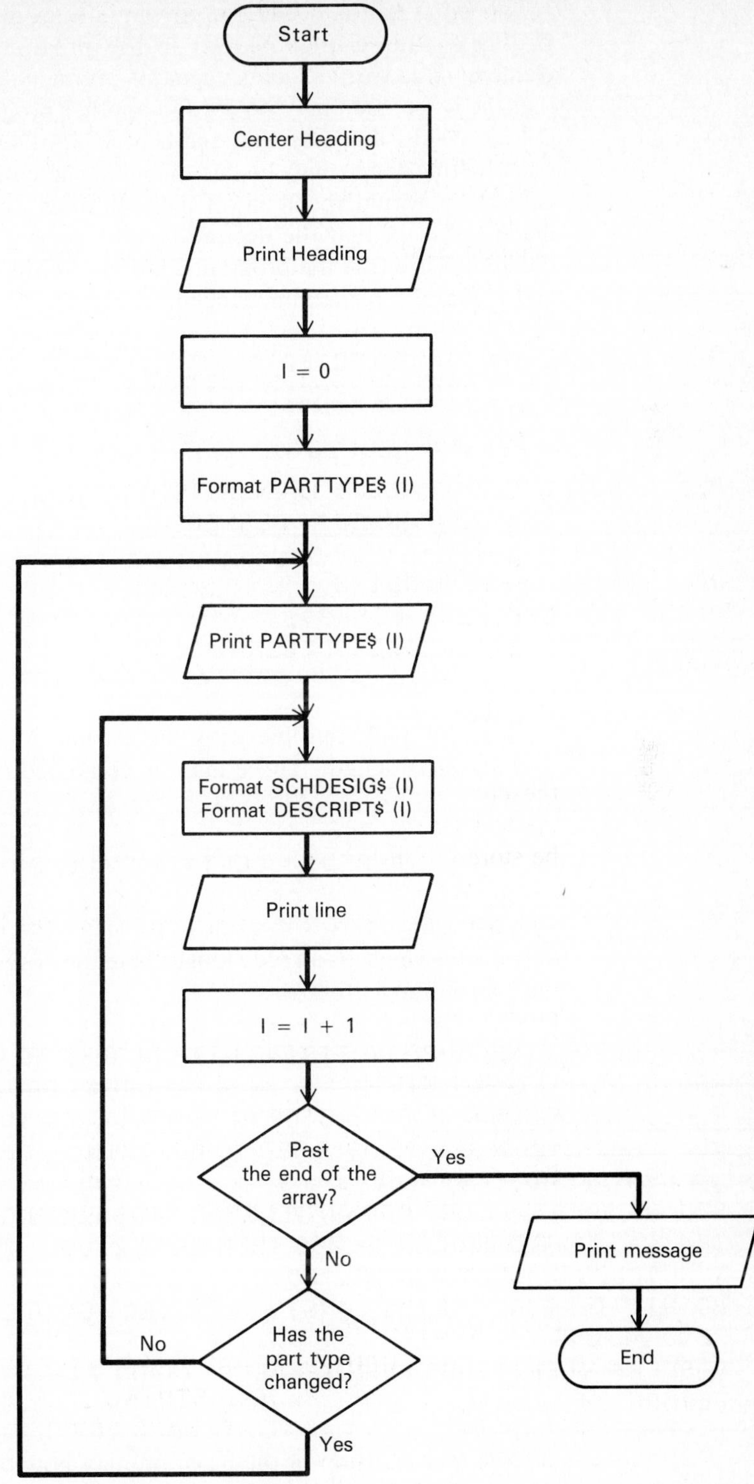

Fig. 17-6 Algorithm for Parts List Generator.

This latter test is needed to prevent strings in excess of 255 characters. Ordinarily this cannot happen in the program (the length of the data elements is known). Such safeguards are included in BASIC programs so that the same code may be used in another program without modification.

Line 2040 calculates the length of UNPADDED$ + BLKS$, without constructing the string. In this manner, one can determine if such a concatenation would result in an illegally long string. Similarly, a check is made to verify that the desired length was not greater than 255. If both conditions are true the program continues. Otherwise a message is printed and the data returned unchanged.

```
2070  REM ILLEGAL LENGTH DETECTED.
2080  PRINT "ILLEGAL STRING LENGTH DETECTED. DATA LEFT UNCHANGED."
2090  GOTO 2170
2100  IF LEN(UNPADDED$) < DESLEN THEN GOTO 2140
2110  REM LENGTH IS OK OR NEEDS TRUNCATION
2120  PADDED$ = LEFT$(UNPADDED$, DESLEN)
2130  GOTO 2170
2140  REM STRING NEEDS PADDING
2150  PADDED$ = UNPADDED$ + BLKS$
2160  PADDED$ = LEFT$(PADDED$,DESLEN)
2170  RETURN
```

Line 2150 pads the line with blanks; line 2160 trims the padded string to the desired length. These may be combined into a single BASIC statement:

```
2110  PADDED$ = LEFT$(UNPADDED$ + BLKS$,DESLEN)
```

In fact, since this will result in the desired string of length, even if the unpadded string was already longer than the desired length, one can rewrite the subroutine as follows:

```
2000  REM SUBROUTINE TO PAD A STRING WITH BLANKS TO A DESIRED
2010  REM LENGTH. INPUT STRING IS IN UNPADDED$, DESIRED LENGTH
2020  REM IS IN DESLEN. PADDED STRING IS RETURNED IN PADDED$.
2030  REM VARIABLE BLKS$ IS ASSUMED TO CONTAIN 40 BLANKS.
2040  L = LEN(UNPADDED$) + 40
2050  REM AS SAFETY, TEST FOR AN ILLEGAL STRING LENGTH
2060  IF L <= 255 AND DESLEN <= 255 THEN GOTO 2100
2070  REM ILLEGAL LENGTH DETECTED.
2080  PRINT "ILLEGAL STRING LENGTH DETECTED. DATA LEFT UNCHANGED."
2090  GOTO 2130
2100  PADDED$ = LEFT$(UNPADDED$ + BLKS$, DESLEN)
2130  RETURN
```

The main portion of the program may now be written.

```
 100  REM PROGRAM TO CONSTRUCT THE PARTS LIST
```

```
110  REM DATA IS ALREADY ASSUMED TO BE IN THE PARTTYPE$,
120  REM SCHDESIG$, DESCRIPT$, AND PARTNUM$ ARRAYS.
130  HEADING$ = "PARTS CONTAINED ON VERTICAL AMPLIFIER PC BOARD "
140  REM SET BLKS$ = 40 SPACES
150  BLKS$ = "
160  REM CENTER THE HEADING AND PUT IT BACK IN HEADING$
170  HEADING$ = MID$(HEADING$ + BLKS$, LEN(HEADING) /2)
180  REM PRINT IT ...
190  CLS
200  PRINT HEADING$
210  REM BUILD THE LOOP TO CONTROL OUTPUT OF THE 86 PARTS
220  I = 0
230  TYPE$ = PARTTYPE$(I)
240  PRINT
250  REM CONSTRUCT AND PRINT THE PLURAL FORM FOLLOWED BY A COLON
260  PRINT TYPE$;"S: "
270  PRINT
280  REM PAD THE DATA
290  DESLEN = 14
300  UNPADDED$ = SCHDESIG$(I)
310  GOSUB 2000
320  PART1$ = PADDED$
330  DESLEN = 35
340  UNPADDED$ = DESCRIPT$(I)
350  GOSUB 2000
360  PART2$ = PADDED$
370  REM PART1$ HAS PADDED SCHEMATIC DESIGNATION,
380  REM PART2$ HAS PADDED DESCRIPTION.
390  REM NOW PRINT IT
400  PRINT PART1$;PART2$;PARTNUM$(I)
410  REM ADVANCE THE INDEX VARIABLE (I) AND TEST FOR COMPLETION
420  I = I + 1
430  IF I > 86 THEN 9998
440  REM NOT YET DONE
```

At this point the program tests whether the part now pointed to by I is of the same type as the previous part, or whether a new heading should be printed. Recall that the previous part type was saved in the variable TYPE$. So, if TYPE$ still equals PARTTYPE$(I), a new heading is not required.

```
450  IF TYPE$ = PARTTYPE$(I), THEN GOTO 280
460  REM PRINT A NEW TYPE
470  GOTO 230
```

The program finishes with the closing message and end statement:

```
9998  PRINT "REPORT COMPLETED"
9999  END
```

The complete listing can be found in Listing 17–3.

LISTING 17-3 PROGRAM TO PRODUCE PARTS LIST REPORT

```
100  REM  PROGRAM TO CONSTRUCT THE PARTS LIST
110  REM  DATA IS ALREADY ASSUMED TO BE IN THE PARTTYPE$,
120  REM  SCHDESIG$, DESCRIPT$, AND PARTNUM$ ARRAYS.
130  HEADING$ = "PARTS CONTAINED ON VERTICAL AMPLIFIER PC BOARD "
140  REM  SET BLKS$ = 40 SPACES
150  BLKS$ = "
160  REM  CENTER THE HEADING AND PUT IT BACK IN HEADING$
170  HEADING$ =                                                "
180  REM  PRINT IT...
190  CLS
200  PRINT HEADING$
210  REM  BUILD THE LOOP TO CONTROL OUTPUT OF THE 86 PARTS
220  I = 0
230  TYPE$ = PARTTYPE$(I)
240  PRINT
250  REM  CONSTRUCT AND PRINT THE PLURAL FORM FOLLOWED BY A COLON
260  PRINT TYPE$;"S:"
270  PRINT
280  REM  PAD THE DATA
290  DESLEN = 14
300  UNPADDED$ = SCHDESIG$(I)
310  GOSUB 2000
320  PART1$ = PADDED$
330  DESLEN = 35
340  UNPADDED$ = DESCRIPT$(I)
350  GOSUB 2000
360  PART2$ = PADDED$
370  REM  PART1$ HAS PADDED SCHEMATIC DESIGNATION,
380  REM  PART2$ HAS PADDED DESCRIPTION.
390  REM  NOW PRINT IT
400  PRINT  PART1$;PART2$;PARTNUM$(I)
410  REM  ADVANCE THE INDEX VARIABLE(I) AND TEST FOR COMPLETION
420  I = I + 1
430  IF I > 86 THEN 9998
440  REM  NOT YET DONE
450  IF TYPE$ = PARTTYPE$(I) THEN GOTO 280
460  REM  PRINT A NEW TYPE
470  GOTO 230
2000 REM  SUBROUTINE TO PAD A STRING WITH BLANKS TO A DESIRED
2010 REM  LENGTH. INPUT STRING IS IN UNPADDED$, DESIRED LENGTH
2020 REM  IS IN DESLEN. PADDED STRING IS RETURNED IN PADDED$.
2030 REM  VARIABLE BLKS$ IS ASSUMED TO CONTAIN 40 BLANKS.
2040 L = LEN(UNPADDED$) + 40
```

LISTING 17-3 *(continued)*

```
2050  REM AS SAFETY, TEST FOR AN ILLEGAL STRING LENGTH
2060  IF L <= 255 AND DESLEN <= 255 THEN GOTO 2100
2070  REM ILLEGAL LENGTH DETECTED.
2080  PRINT "ILLEGAL STRING LENGTH DETECTED. DATA LEFT UNCHANGED."
2090  GOTO 2130
2100  PADDED$ = LEFT$(UNPADDED$ + BLKS$, DESLEN)
2130  RETURN
9998  PRINT "REPORT COMPLETED"
9999  END
```

17-3-4 Searching

In many data processing applications it becomes necessary to determine if a particular value is represented among a group of values, generally stored in an array. As an example, using the arrays described for programming Example 17-1, one may wish to locate the part number for the component whose schematic designation is D1. One way to do this is to start with the first member of the SCHDESIG$ array, compare the value found to "D1", then, if a match occurs, look in the corresponding member of PARTNUM$ for the part number. However, if a match is not found, the variable being used as the index is incremented. This checks to see if the upper bounds of the array have been exceeded. If not, the test (match) is repeated. This process is continued until either the desired member is located or every member of the array is checked. This method of searching is called *linear searching* because the array is examined one item at a time, in order.

In this example, there were 86 members in the array. On the average, half the members of an array must be tested before a particular item is located. With a relatively small array such as this, the inefficiency of such a searching technique is offset by its simplicity. A subroutine that implements a linear search is shown below.

```
3000  REM SUBROUTINE TO LOCATE A SPECIFIED VALUE IN THE
3010  REM SCHDESIG$ ARRAY. THE VALUE TO BE LOCATED IS IN
3020  REM FIND$. POINTER CONTAINS THE MEMBER OF THE ARRAY IF
3030  REM FIND$ IS FOUND. POINTER WILL CONTAIN 999 IF THE VALUE
3040  REM IS NOT FOUND.
3050  I = 0
3060  REM LOOK FOR FIND$ IN THE FIRST CHARACTERS OF SCHDESIG$(I)
3070  IF INSTR ((LEFT$(SCHDESIG$(I),LEN(FIND$))),FIND$) = 1 THEN 3200
```

Examine line 3070 in detail. The two parameters for the INSTR function are LEFT$(SCHDESIG$(I),LEN(FIND$)) for the string that is to be searched, and FIND$ for the string we are searching for. If the string

FIND$ is found starting in column one of SCHDESIG$, the IF statement succeeds and execution continues at line 3200.

But why not simply use: IF FIND$ = SCHDESIG$(I)? As noted earlier, string comparisons will not work correctly if the lengths of the strings are not the same. One way around this would require BASIC statements which equalize the lengths of the two strings before comparing; by using the INSTR function this is not needed.

Why test for a value of 1? Why not test for 0 indicating that the FIND$ was not located anywhere within SCHDESIG$(I)? Consider the following possibility:

```
SCHDESIG$(I) = "IC501"    FIND$ = "C50"
```

With these values, the INSTR function will return a value of 2; the string "C50" was found in SCHDESIG$(I) beginning in column 2, but clearly, this is not the correct match. This raises another question. Consider these values:

```
SCHDESIG$(I) = "C500"    FIND$ = "C50"
```

Now, the INSTR function returns the value of 1; the string "C50" was found beginning in column 1. How can this problem be corrected?

If a blank is appended to the end of both FIND$ and the end of SCHDESIG$(I) before comparing, the problem is solved. Consider:

Original data:	SCHDESIG$(I) = "C500"	FIND$ = "C50"
Data passed to INSTR:	SCHDESIG$(I) = "C500 "	FIND$ = "C50 "

Now the INSTR function fails and returns a value of 0; "C50 " is not found in SCHDESIGN$(I). For the data which truly matches:

Original data:	SCHDESIG$(I) = "C50"	FIND$ = "C50"
Data passed to INSTR:	SCHDESIG$(I) = "C50 "	FIND$ = "C50 "

The INSTR function will return the value of 1. Therefore, change line 3070:

```
3070  IF INSTR(SCHDESIG$(I)+" ",FIND$+" ") = 1 THEN GOTO 3200
```

Proceeding:

```
3100  REM NO MATCH
3110  I = I + 1
3120  REM TEST TO SEE IF WE POINT BEYOND MEMBER 85
3120  IF I <= 85 THEN GOTO 3060
3130  REM WE HAVE TESTED ALL MEMBERS WITH NO FIND
```

```
3130  PRINT "THE STRING";FIND$;" NOT FOUND IN THE ARRAY."
3140  POINTER = 999
3150  GOTO 3230
3200  REM A MATCH WAS FOUND
3210  PRINT " A MATCH FOR STRING ";FIND$;" WAS FOUND IN MEMBER ";I
3220  POINTER = I
3230  RETURN
```

The complete listing can be examined in Listing 17–4

LISTING 17-4 LINEAR SEARCH SUBROUTINE

```
3000  REM SUBROUTINE TO LOCATE A SPECIFIED VALUE IN THE
3010  REM SCHDESIG$ ARRAY. THE VALUE TO BE LOCATED IS IN
3020  REM FIND$. POINTER CONTAINS THE MEMBER OF THE ARRAY IF
3030  REM FIND$ IS FOUND. POINTER WILL CONTAIN 999 IF THE VALUE
3040  REM NOT FOUND.
3050  I = 0
3060  REM LOOK FOR FIND$ IN THE FIRST CHARACTERS OF SCHDESIG$(I)
3070  IF INSTR(SCHDESIG$(I)+ " ",FIND$+" ") = 1 THEN GOTO 3200
3100  REM NO MATCH
3110  I = I + 1
3120  REM TEST TO SEE IF WE POINT BEYOND MEMBER 86
3120  IF I <= 85 THEN GOTO 3060
3130  REM WE HAVE TESTED ALL MEMBERS WITH NO FIND
3130  PRINT "THE STRING ";FIND$;" NOT FOUND IN THE ARRAY."
3140  POINTER = 999
3150  GOTO 3230
3200  REM A MATCH WAS FOUND
3210  PRINT " A MATCH FOR STRING ";FIND$;" WAS FOUND IN MEMBER ";I
3220  POINTER = I
3230  RETURN
```

17-3-5 Binary Search

Consider what happens when there are many array members to be searched. If the data is stored in no particular order, the program being executed would have to search through the entire list to determine if a given string was not present; this would average N/2 tries to locate any data item that *was* on the list. If N is a large number, say 16,000, an average of 8000 comparisons would be needed to locate an item. In the worst case all 16,000 items would have to be tested before it could be known for certain that a string was not in the list.

If, however, the data in the array is organized in alphabetical order (or if the data is numeric, in numerical order), a much more efficient searching method, called a *binary search,* is possible. This searching technique is not called "binary" because it works in the binary number system; it is called "binary" because with each try it eliminates ½ of the remaining elements from being considered as possible locations for the item that is being sought.

A game called "higher-lower" illustrates the method. You think of a number; a friend then tries different numbers, trying to guess the number you selected. With each guess you must truthfully answer whether the actual value is higher than or less than what your friend guessed. If your friend is clever, he can use this same technique to minimize the number of guesses needed to determine the number you had in mind.

Consider the following ordered list of 16 values:

Value Number	Value	Value Number	Value
1	2	9	17
2	4	10	20
3	6	11	25
4	7	12	29
5	8	13	36
6	9	14	37
7	11	15	39
8	14	16	41

Suppose the value being sought is 36. First, look at the value in the center of the list; in this case the value of the eighth item is 14. As the number being sought is greater than this value, items 1 through 7 need not be checked, because they all contain values less than 36. Next (second try), examine the item halfway between member 8 and member 16; member 12. Member 12 contains 29, which is still less than 36. The next try (third) is midway between member 12 and member 16; member 14 contains a 37. This is the required value—it is greater than 36. If the value is in the list it must lie between members 12 and 14. On the fourth try the exact value is found in location 13.

What happens when the value is *not* in the table, such as value 10? Again, the first try is item 8, with a value of 14, which is greater than the value being sought (10). The next try is halfway between member 1 and 8—member 4 (second try). Member 4 contains a 7; less than the value being sought. The third try is midway between member 4 and member 8; member 6 contains a 9; still less than 10. The fourth try is with member 7; since there is still no match, one may conclude that the value 10 is not on the list.

If the list were expanded up to 32 members, only one more try is needed to locate a value or determine that a value is not in the list. Six tries would suffice for a list of up to 64 values; seven would be needed for 128 values, and only 8 tries for a list of as many as 256 items.

The number of tries needed to locate a value that is present in the list of selected values is never more than: integer portion of ($\log_2$ (number of values -1) $+ 1$). If the value has not been found in the indicated number of tries, one can safely conclude that the test value is not on the list. If the SCHDESIG$ array is ordered alphabetically, a binary search technique can be used to locate desired strings. The binary search subroutine shown below could be used in place of the linear search routine.

```
3000  REM SUBROUTINE TO LOCATE A SPECIFIED VALUE IN THE
3010  REM SCHDESIG$ ARRAY. THE VALUE TO BE LOCATED IS IN
3020  REM FIND$. POINTER CONTAINS THE MEMBER OF THE ARRAY IF
3030  REM FIND$ IS FOUND. POINTER WILL CONTAIN 999 IF THE VALUE
3040  REM NOT FOUND.
3050  REM SCHDESIG$ MUST BE IN ALPHABETICAL ORDER FOR THIS TO WORK!
```

Several variables are needed to hold values which are produced as calculations and examinations of the array. HITRY% and LOWTRY% will be used to keep track of the highest- and lowest-numbered members tried. TRIESCOUNTER% will be used to keep track of how many attempts we have made at locating the value. This will determine when we may stop searching.

How many tries must we perform before we have determined that a value is not represented in the array? Using the formula shown previously:

integer portion of($\log_2$ (number of values − 1) + 1)
integer portion of($\log_2$ (86 − 1) + 1)
= 7 tries

Initializing our variables:

```
3060  TRIESCOUNTER% = 0
3070  HITRY% = 85
3080  LOWTRY% = 0
3090  THISTRY% = (HITRY%+LOWTRY%)/2
```

Test the value at SCHDESIG$(THISRY%):

```
3100  IF INSTR(SCHDESIG$(I)+ " ",FIND$+" ") = 1 THEN GOTO 3400
3110  REM NO MATCH
3120  TRIESCOUNTER% = TRIESCOUNTER% + 1
3130  REM TEST FOR TRIES > 7; IF SO, BRANCH OUT.
3140  IF TRIESCOUNTER% > 7 THEN 3300
```

The program determines which half of the array to search. If the value of SCHDESIG$(THISTRY%) is *less* than FIND$, the next try should be into the lower half of the array. Conversely, if the value of SCHDESIG$(THISTRY%) is *greater* than FIND$ the upper half of the array is searched next.

In order to perform string comparisons, the lengths of the test strings must be checked for equality. This would best be done before entering the search subroutine. Knowing that the maximum length of the members of

SCHDESIG$ is seven characters, it is a simple matter to pad all the entries to seven characters using the padding subroutine developed earlier in Example 17-1 (lines 2000 through 2130). FIND$ should also be tested to be sure it is not more than seven characters long; if it is, then there is no match for it in SCHDESIG$. If FIND$ is less than seven, pad it to seven characters too. The following accomplishes all of this (before starting the search itself):

```
1000 REM EQUALIZE LENGTHS OF STRINGS - DO THIS SECTION ONCE
1010 DESLIN = 7
1020 FOR I = 0 TO 85
1030 UNPADDED$ = SCHDESIG$(I)
1040 GOSUB 2000
1050 SCHDESIG$(I) = PADDED$
1060 NEXT I
1070 RETURN

1100 REM TEST AND PAD FIND$ IF APPROPRIATE.
1110 REM PERFORM THIS SUBROUTINE EACH TIME FIND$ CHANGES.
1120 IF LEN(FIND$) <= 7 THEN 1160
1130 REM FIND$ TOO LONG
1140 PRINT "THE SEARCH STRING IS TOO LONG."
1150 GOTO 1180
1160 REM TRIM FIND$ TO SEVEN CHARACTERS
1170 FIND$ = LEFT$(FIND$ + "       ",7)
1180 RETURN
```

Now that the strings are the same length, a simpler string comparison may be used in place of the one shown in line 3100.

```
3100 IF SCHDESIG$(THISTRY%) = FIND$ THEN GOTO 3400
```

Returning to the search:

```
3150 IF SCHDESIG$(THISTRY%) < FIND$ THEN GOTO 3190
3160 REM  TRY UPPER HALF
3170 LOWTRY% = THISTRY%
3180 GOTO 3090
3190 REM  TRY LOWER HALF
3200 HITRY% = THISTRY%
3210 GOTO  3090
```

Thus, the program will continue to narrow the range between HITRY% and LOWTRY%, until the value is found, or the number of tries is exhausted. Taking care of these eventualities:

```
3300 REM  TRIES EXHAUSTED; VALUE NOT FOUND
3310 PRINT "VALUE"FIND$;" NOT FOUND IN ARRAY."
```

```
3320  POINTER = 999
3330  GOTO 3500

3400  REM MATCH FOUND
3410  PRINT "MATCH FOUND IN MEMBER ";THISTRY%
3420  POINTER = THISTRY%

3500  RETURN
```

Listing 17–5 shows this subroutine in its entirety, but without the lines of code needed to equalize the length of the strings. Compare it with the linear search. As you see, the binary search is more complex, but provides a much greater efficiency for searching sorted datasets.

LISTING 17-5 BINARY SEARCH

```
3000  REM SUBROUTINE TO LOCATE A SPECIFIED VALUE IN THE
3010  REM SCHDESIG$ ARRAY. THE VALUE TO BE LOCATED IS IN
3020  REM FIND$. POINTER CONTAINS THE MEMBER OF THE ARRAY IF
3030  REM FIND$ IS FOUND. POINTER WILL CONTAIN 999 IF THE VALUE
3040  REM NOT FOUND.
3050  REM SCHDESIG$ MUST BE IN ALPHABETICAL ORDER FOR THIS TO WORK!
3060  TRIESCOUNTER% = 0
3070  HITRY% = 85
3080  LOWTRY% = 0
3090  THISTRY% = (HITRY%+LOTRY%)/2
3100  IF SCHDESIG$(THISTRY%) = FIND$ THEN GOTO 3400
3110  REM NO MATCH
3120  TRIESCOUNTER% = TRIESCOUNTER% + 1
3130  REM TEST FOR TRIES > 7; IF SO, BRANCH OUT.
3140  IF TRIESCOUNTER% > 7 THEN 3300
3150  IF SCHDESIG$(THISTRY%) < FIND$ THEN GOTO 3190
3160  REM TRY UPPER HALF
3170  LOWTRY% = THISTRY%
3180  GOTO 3090
3190  REM TRY LOWER HALF
3200  HITRY% = THISTRY%
3210  GOTO 3090
3300  REM TRIES EXHAUSTED; VALUE NOT FOUND
3310  PRINT "VALUE ";FIND$;" NOT FOUND IN ARRAY."
3320  POINTER = 999
3330  GOTO 3500
3400  REM MATCH FOUND
3410  PRINT "MATCH FOUND IN MEMBER ";THISTRY%
3420  POINTER = THISTRY%
3500  RETURN
```

SUMMARY

An important element of BASIC is its ability to perform operations and calculations on alphanumeric or character-type data. One operation is that of concatenation, or the joining together of alphanumeric strings. In addition, strings may be compared. If they are of the same length, then they are compared character by character according to their ASCII code value. Results of such comparisons can be used to determine if a given string is less than, equal to, or greater than a test string. The length (LEN) function determines the number of characters in a string. To extract parts of a string, the programmer may use the LEFT$, RIGHT$, or MID$ function. These extract a given number of characters from the left end, right end, or middle of a string, respectively.

REVIEW PROBLEM

1. For each of the following string operations, determine the value that would be returned (i.e., the value that would be assigned to a variable named to the left of the equals sign).

```
Given: TEMP$ = "ABCDEFGHIJKLMNOPQRSTUVWXYZ"
          X$ = "12345678901234567890"
          Y$ = "ABC123DEF456ABC123"
         N1$ = "123.4"
         N2$ = "987.6"
```

```
a.  = X$ + Y$
b.  = TEMP$ + "END OF STRING"
c.  = LEN(N1$)
d.  = LEFT$(X$, 6)
e.  = RIGHT$(TEMP$, 21)
f.  = N1$ + N2$
g.  = MID$(TEMP$, LEN(Y$) - 8, 4)
h.  = INSTR(X$, N1$)
i.  = MID$(Y$, 4, 3) + MID$(Y$, 10, 3)
j.  = INSTR(Y$, MID$(N1$, 1, 3))
```

REVIEW QUESTIONS

1. What distinguishes alphanumeric values from numeric values?
2. What is ASCII? How many different codes are available in standard ASCII? In extended ASCII?

3. What is concatenation? How is the operation of concatenation indicated?
4. Where might the operation of concatenation be useful?
5. What is the first aspect of two strings that is taken into consideration when the two strings are compared?
6. At which end of a string does the character-by-character comparison of ASCII codes begin? Why?
7. What operation does the LEN function perform? Are spaces within the string counted?
8. What is meant by "padding" a string?
9. What operation does the LEFT$ function perform?
10. What operation does the RIGHT$ function perform?
11. What operation does the MID$ function perform?
12. Why do the LEFT$, RIGHT$, and MID$ functions have names that end with the character $, but the LEN function does not?
13. What is truncation? How does truncation differ from rounding?
14. In general, how can a BASIC dialect that normally truncates be made to round off instead?
15. What operation does the INSTR function perform?
16. What are the two parameters of the INSTR function?
17. What are the characteristics of a linear search? When might a linear search be used?
18. What are the characteristics of a binary search? When might a binary search be used?
19. Why is a binary search so named?
20. Why might we be willing to trade off program inefficiency for ease of programming? When might we be willing to do this?

18 SEQUENTIAL FILES

By now it should be clear that the methods of data entry thus far discussed are not particularly well-suited to working with very large amounts of data. The INPUT statement is practical for data that must be entered at run time, and the READ/DATA statements are fine for relatively small amounts of unchanging data, but many programs operate on very large amounts of raw information. In such cases, the data is frequently stored separately from the program. This allows the stored data to be changed without modifying the program at all. It also allows the data to be collected and stored using a program separate from the program processing the data; thus several people can be involved with entering data from separate systems. This data can then be combined and processed together. This stored data is kept in a *file*.

18-1 THE NATURE AND NEED FOR FILES

Reconsider the parts list program introduced in the previous chapter. The example dealt with the parts for only a single printed-circuit board. In a device such as an oscilloscope six or seven boards might be included with three or four hundred components in all. However, even once the design has been established, changes to the components' data are necessary. Manufacturers or suppliers may change, circuits may undergo revisions, and parts may be discontinued and need to be replaced with substitutions. Clearly, including the data in the program, even with READ/DATA statements, opens the door for errors to be introduced into the program each time such a change is made.

However, we would not want to have to reenter all the parts data via INPUT statements each time the program is to be run. While this would allow for the changes to be made, it would take far too much time and also be error-prone.

Ideally, some method would exist for storing the data separately from the program, but in such a manner that the data can be accessed by the program and readily edited when the need arises.

A *file* is a collection of related data, independent of the program or programs that will access it, stored in a machine-readable form (see Chapter 8). Files are most frequently maintained on disk or magnetic tape, but other storage media may also be used, such as punched card, paper tape, optical disk, and computer-readable microform.

In a sense, a file might seem similar to a storage form of an array. In some cases, this comparison would be accurate. However, a file is much more flexible; unlike an array, a file may contain different *types* of data, and there may be both numeric and alphanumeric data contained in a single file. For example, the contents of the PARTTYPE$, SCHDESIG$, DESCRIPT$, and PARTNUM$ arrays may be included in a file. In addition, the file may contain information about the source of a particular part (i.e., manufacturer or distributor information), number of such parts to be kept in stock, purchase and reselling prices, and even information such as failure rate figures obtained from warranty service reports.

Notice that the file now contains information that might not seem to be directly related to the original function. There is no reason, though, that all the information contained in a file must be used by a single application. The same file can be used by a number of different departments; in the example, not only the department responsible for creating the equipment documentation (i.e., the parts list) but also the departments responsible for purchasing parts, maintaining proper amounts of inventory, selecting vendors based on parts reliability, and so on, may use the file. This makes for efficient use of storage space, as it is not necessary for all departments to separately store data they use. Such items as the part's type, description, and part number are stored once, but are accessed by several programs.

18-2 THE OPEN STATEMENT

Purpose In order to make use of a file in BASIC, the computer must be instructed to make the necessary arrangements to be able to read from, or write to the selected storage device. The OPEN statement carries information the computer needs to make the data transfer possible. An OPEN statement must be executed before any I/O from the associated file is attempted. More than one file may be open at a given time, with the number of files allowed to be open determined by the computer in use.

The OPEN statement itself causes no file data to be transferred; it only causes the computer to set up the necessary conditions for such transfers to take place. It can be thought of as establishing a connection or link between the computer and the file.

18-2-1 Syntax of the OPEN Statement

```
OPEN {"mode"}, {# filenumber}, {"filename"}
```

where *mode* is the first letter of *O*utput, *I*nput, or *A*ppend, depending upon the operation you wish to perform (reading from the file, writing to a file, or adding to the end of an existing file, respectively), and must appear in quotes as shown.

 # filenumber is a number (must be an integer) which will be used by the Input and Output statements to reference the file (instead of the file's name).

filename is the name under which the file exists (or should be created), and, as shown, must appear in quotes, or be contained in an alphanumeric variable.

Figure 18-1 contains examples of the OPEN statement.

```
OPEN "I", #1,"VOLTAGES"
```

Open the file named VOLTAGES, and prepare to enter data from the file. The file will be referred to as #1 in the program's data entry statements. If the file VOLTAGES does not exist, an error condition is raised.

```
OPEN "O", #4, "PARTSPEC"
```

Search for the file named PARTSPEC. If it already exists, prepare to replace the data in the file already with data coming from output statements in the program. If the file does not already exist, create a file with the name PARTSPEC, then proceed as above. The file will be referred to as #4 in the program's output statements.

```
OPEN "A", #2, "EQUIPMNT"
```

Search for the file named EQUIPMNT. If the file exists, prepare to add data to the end of the data already in the file. If the file EQUIPMNT does not exist, create such a file, then prepare to place data in it. This file will be referred to as #2 in the program's output statements.

Fig. 18-1 Examples of the OPEN statement.

18-3 FILE TRANSFERS OR I/O

Once the OPEN statement has been executed, the actual business of data transfer can take place.

File I/O is nearly identical with keyboard/screen I/O. A special form of the INPUT statement is used to obtain data from an existing file; a different statement, the WRITE statement, is used to write data to a file.

18-3-1 The INPUT # Statement for Input from a File

```
INPUT {# filenumber}, {varname1} [,varname2...]
```

where: # filenumber is the number assigned to the file in the OPEN statement.
varnames are the variable into which data from the file is to be placed.

Figure 18-2 demonstrates the use of the INPUT # statement.

```
INPUT #3,A$,B
```

Access the file opened as file #3 and read two data items from it. Expect the first to be alphanumeric, and the second to be numeric.

```
INPUT #1,VOLTAGE, CURRENT, PART$
```

Access the file opened as file number 1 and read three data items from it. Expect the first two to be numeric and the third item to be alphanumeric.

Fig. 18-2 Demonstrating the use of the INPUT # statement.

18-3-2 The WRITE Statement

```
WRITE {# filenumber}, {varname1} [,varname2,..]
```

where: # filenumber is the number assigned to the file in the OPEN statement.
varnames are the program variables from which data for the file is to be taken.

The WRITE statement works very much like the PRINT statement with the following exception:

The WRITE statement causes the *values* of string variables to be written, surrounded by quotes and separated by commas, just as one would write them if included in a DATA statement. Numeric values are separated by commas only. Consider the following variables and their values:

NAME$ = "2N3055"
QUANTITY = 17
FUNCTION$ = "POWER REGULATOR"

If the following statements were executed,

```
OPEN "O",#1,"SPECFILE"
WRITE #1,NAME$,QUANTITY,FUNCTION$
```

The file SPECFILE would contain the following:

```
"2N3055",17,"POWER REGULATOR"{carriage return, line feed}
```

The carriage return and line feed tell BASIC that this was where the WRITE statement left off. The INPUT # statement treats the end of line in the same way as does the READ statement; data continues to be read from the file until the input list is satisfied.

Figure 18-3 demonstrates the use of the WRITE statement.

```
WRITE #1,VOLTAGE, CURRENT, PART$
```

(where VOLTAGE = 98.23, CURRENT = .233, and PART$ = "R21") Writes three values to the file opened as file number 1: two numeric values, separated by commas, and one alphanumeric value, surrounded by quotes, followed by a carriage return and a line feed:

```
98.23,.233,"R21"{CR LF}
```

```
WRITE #5,R1,R2,R3,R3,R5
```

(where R1=120, R2=120, R3=4700, R4=820, and R5=1200) Writes five numeric values to the file opened as number 4, separated by commas, and followed by a carriage return and a line feed:

```
120,120,4700,820,1200{CR LF}
```

Fig. 18-3 Demonstrating the use of the WRITE statement.

Example 18-1 Getting Data from a File

Task: Write the portion of the program, to work with the program designed in Example 17-1, that will read the data from a diskette file and place the data into arrays.

Algorithmic Analysis: Assume that a file exists, named PARTDATA, which contains the contents of the four arrays PARTTYPE$, SCHDESIG$, DESCRIPT$, and PARTNUM$ as they were originally described in Example 17-1.

In order to make use of the data in the file its organization must be known. For example, in what order was the data recorded? In this case there are two distinct possibilities:

1. All the members of PARTTYPE$ followed by all the members of SCHDESIG$, followed by all the members of DESCRIPT$, followed by all the members of PARTNUM$.
2. Using I as a pointer, PARTTYPE$(I), SCHDESIG$(I), DESCRIPT$(I), and PARTNUM$(I), followed by PARTTYPE$(I+1), SCHDESIG$(I+1), etc., until all the members have been recorded.

Which strategy to use will depend on how the data is to be manipulated. If the data will always be read in its entirety, it makes little difference which method to use. Sometimes it is better to read in one set of values at a time, manipulate those values, then perhaps write the new values into a new file. In this case it makes sense to have all the I'th members of the array together. We will assume that the data has been organized as in method number two.

In addition, it is helpful to know how many members have been stored; it allows one to use a FOR/NEXT loop in retrieving the data, rather than having to check for a signal value. So, in addition, the very first data item in the file includes the number of members in the arrays. If the arrays were of different lengths or number of dimensions, this data would also be recorded so that the reading program could set up the same storage environment.

Program Development: The data read-in routine is contained in a subroutine which starts at line 5000.

```
5000  REM SUBROUTINE TO BRING THE DATAFILE PARTDATA INTO THE
5010  REM ARRAYS. THE FIRST ITEM IN THE DATAFILE WILL CONTAIN
5020  REM NUMBER OF MEMBERS IN THE ARRAYS. THE ARRAYS MUST NOT
5030  REM HAVE BEEN DIMENSIONED PRIOR TO THIS SUBROUTINE.
5040  OPEN "I",#1,"PARTDATA"
```

The OPEN statement in line 5040 prepares the computer to read data ("I" for input) from the file named PARTDATA. The computer is instructed that this file will be referenced by the number "1" in future input statements.

```
5050  INPUT #1,N
```

Line 5050 causes the first item in the file to be read and placed into the variable "N." N is a numeric variable; the same kind of data type checking that occurs with data entry from the keyboard occurs with data being read from the diskette. If the first data item in the file PARTDATA is numeric, its value will be assigned to the variable N, where it can be used in subsequent statements.

If N represents the number of members in the arrays, then the highest member number must be $N - 1$ since the first member is stored in member number (0). After adjusting the value of N the dimension of the arrays can be declared:

```
5060  N = N - 1
5070  DIM PARTTYPE$(N),SCHDESIG$(N),DESCRIPT$(N),PARTNUM$(N)
```

Next is the portion of the program that actually reads the data:

```
5080  FOR I = 0 TO N
5090  INPUT #1, PARTTYPE$(I),SCHDESIG$(I),DESCRIPT$(I),PARTNUM$(I)
5100  NEXT I
```

It is now possible to return to the main program:

```
5110  RETURN
```

Examine this subroutine in its entirety in Listing 18-1.

LISTING 18-1 SUBROUTINE TO READ THE PARTDATA FILE INTO ARRAYS

```
5000  REM SUBROUTINE TO BRING THE DATAFILE PARTDATA INTO THE
5010  REM ARRAYS. THE FIRST ITEM IN THE DATAFILE WILL CONTAIN
5020  REM NUMBER OF MEMBERS IN THE ARRAYS. THE ARRAYS MUST NOT
5030  REM HAVE BEEN DIMENSIONED PRIOR TO THIS SUBROUTINE.
5040  OPEN "I",1,"PARTDATA"
5050  INPUT #1,N
5060  N = N - 1
5070  DIM PARTTYPE$(N),SCHDESIG$(N),DESCRIPT$(N),PARTNUM$(N)
5080  FOR I = 0 TO N
5090  INPUT #1, PARTTYPE$(I),SCHDESIG$(I),DESCRIPT$(I),PARTNUM$(I)
5100  NEXT I
5110  RETURN
```

18-4 FILE MAINTENANCE COMMANDS

The commands already introduced are file access commands; they allow a programmer to prepare, read from, or write to a file. The next three commands are maintenance commands; they perform the functions of closing a file, deleting an entire file, and renaming a file.

18-4-1 The CLOSE Command

Purpose Disk I/O is buffered; although the program may contain a statement which instructs the computer to write to a file, the computer's operating systems will accumulate your writes in memory (in a buffer) until there is a complete sector to be written. A similar procedure is followed for reads: when a read command is issued, an entire disk sector is read and brought into a buffer; then the desired portion is assigned to the named variables. The next time a read is performed it is possible that the data you are trying to read is already in memory (in the buffer); the disk does not have to be accessed.

The file is *closed* in order to assure that all the data in the write buffer has been actually written to the disk. Closing the file also releases the memory used as the disk buffer, and updates the disk directory.

Syntax

```
CLOSE {# FILENUM} [,# FILENUM...]
```

Where # FILENUM is the file to be closed. More than one file can be closed with a single CLOSE statement.

```
CLOSE
```

Closes ALL open files.

Figure 18-4 demonstrates the use of the CLOSE statement.

```
CLOSE #1,#2
```

Closes the files that were opened as number 1 and number 2; does not affect any other open files.

```
CLOSE
```

Closes any files that are open.

Fig. 18-4 Demonstration of the use of the CLOSE statement.

18-4-2 The KILL Command

Purpose The KILL command causes the named file to be deleted. The KILL command will let one erase only files that have been previously closed; trying to KILL an OPEN file will generate an error message.

Syntax

```
KILL {"FILENAME"}
```

Where "FILENAME" is the complete name of the file you wish to erase.

Figure 18-5 demonstrates the use of the KILL statement.

```
KILL "TEMPFILE"
```

Erases the file named TEMPFILE, assuming that TEMPFILE is not currently open.

```
KILL "PROGRAM.BAS"
```

Erases the file "PROGRAM.BAS." Many BASICS save program files with the extension ".BAS" as part of the file name. In order to use the KILL command to erase such a program, the complete name, including extension must be specified.

Fig. 18-5 Demonstration of the KILL statement.

18-4-3 The NAME Command

Purpose The NAME command can be used to change the name of a file.
Syntax

```
NAME {filename1} AS {filename2}
```

where: filename1 is the current name of the file.
filename2 is the desired name of the file.

The NAME command works only on files that are not currently open; a file in use must be closed before it can be renamed.

Figure 18-6 demonstrates the use of the NAME command.

```
NAME "TEMPFILE" AS "NEWDATA"
```

Changes the name of the file currently known as TEMPFILE to NEWDATA. TEMPFILE must not be open when the NAME command is issued.

```
NAME "PROG1.BAS" AS "PROG2.BAS"
```

Changes the name of the BASIC program currently known as PROG1 to PROG2. PROG1 may not be in use while it is being renamed.

Fig. 18-6 Demonstration of the NAME command.

Example 18-2 Output to a File

The program shown in Example 18-1 processes data that is already contained in a file. How did the data get *into* the file?

Task: To write a program that will issue prompts, and accept data to build the PARTDATA file as described above.

Algorithmic Analysis: It has been decided to store the data regarding the same member of each of the four arrays together; that is, PARTTYPE$(I), SCHDESIG$(I), DESCRIPT$(I), and PARTNUM$(I) will be accepted (via INPUT statements) and then written to the file using a WRITE statement. Since the program will be accepting only one set of values at a time, arrays are not required; the current values can be accepted into simple variables, the values written to the file, and then the next set of values can be obtained.

Ultimately the computer needs to know how many sets of data have been entered. If the number of all the sets which have been entered are counted, that value will be available when the process is complete. However, we can no longer write this information at the beginning of the file where it is expected to be located. There are three choices:

1. Force the operator to specify how many sets of data are coming; this value can be written at the beginning of the file, before any other data has been written.
2. Write data to disk in a temporary file, keeping a count of all data. When finished, proceed as follows: open a new file, write the number of items that are present to the new file, then transfer the entire contents of the temporary file to the new file.
3. Accumulate the data, as it is entered, into arrays, keeping count of the number of items; when entry is completed, write the number of entries and the actual data from the arrays.

All three methods have merits and disadvantages, and all three methods are routinely used, depending upon the circumstances. Method one is the least complex; however, it requires the operator to know how many data items are coming. It does not permit the operator to terminate entry until the number of items specified has actually been entered; otherwise, the count would be wrong.

Method two allows any number of entries to be made before terminating because a count of data which is actually entered is maintained. It has the advantage of writing data to disk (into the temporary file) as data is entered; therefore, there is less risk of data being lost should there be a power failure (data in RAM would be lost but data which has been written to disk can usually be recovered). It also allows large amounts of data to be entered; the program is not required to maintain all the data in RAM, only the items that have not yet been written to disk. The problem with this technique is that there must be enough space on the disk for twice the amount of data to be entered. The temporary file occupies nearly the same amount of space as the final file (the same amount less the space needed to record the number of data items present); both are present until the temporary file's contents have been completely transferred to the permanent file and the temporary file deleted.

The third method accumulates the data entered in RAM instead of writing it to disk. Disk capacity need only be sufficient to store the data and the count. However, RAM must be large enough to contain all the data (and of course, the program and operating system) at the same time. In addition, should there be a power failure during data entry, the data in RAM would most likely be lost.

Method two affords the most data security and is the technique to be used in this example.

Program Construction:

Introductory REMs:

```
100  REM PROGRAM TO WRITE A DATA FILE IN THE FOLLOWING FORMAT:
110  REM NUMBER OF SETS OF DATA; NUMERIC VALUE
120  REM EACH SET OF DATA CONSISTS OF FOUR STRING VALUES:
130  REM   1.   PART TYPE
140  REM   2.   SCHEMATIC DESIGNATION
150  REM   3.   DESCRIPTION
160  REM   4.   PART NUMBER
170  REM DATA WILL BE ACCEPTED VIA INPUT STATEMENTS, THEN WRITTEN
180  REM TO THE FILE. ENTRY OF PART TYPE = "END" WILL TERMINATE
190  REM THE ENTRY PHASE AND CAUSE THE DATA TO BE WRITTEN FROM ITS
200  REM TEMPORARY FILE TO ITS PERMANENT FILE.
```

Write the OPEN statement for the temporary data file and initialize the record counter:

```
210  OPEN "O",#1,"TEMPDATA"
220  RECCNTR = 0
```

Begin accepting data, until the signal value is found:

```
230  CLS
240  PRINT  "DATA SET NUMBER "; RECCNTR + 1
250  PRINT
260  INPUT "ENTER PART TYPE: "; PARTTYPE$
270  IF PARTTYPE$ = "END" THEN GOTO 1000
```

Reviewing the specifications given for the data in Example 17–2 will reveal that certain maximum lengths were stated for the data. The data should be checked to see that it does not exceed these parameters:

```
280  IF LEN(PARTTYPE$) <= 35 THEN 320
290  PRINT "LENGTH OF PART TYPE MUST BE 35 CHARACTERS OR LESS."
300  PRINT  "PLEASE REENTER."
310  GOTO  250
```

Do the same for the other three data items:

```
320  PRINT
330  INPUT "ENTER THE SCHEMATIC DESIGNATION: "; SCHDESIG$
340  IF LEN(SCHDESIG$) <= 7 THEN GOTO 380
350  PRINT  "LENGTH OF SCHEMATIC DESIGNATION MUST BE 7 CHARACTERS"
360  PRINT "OR LESS. PLEASE REENTER."
370  GOTO 320

380  PRINT
390  INPUT "ENTER THE PART DESCRIPTION: ";DESCRIPT$
400  IF LEN(DESCRIPT$) <= 25 THEN GOTO 440
410  PRINT  "LENGTH OF PART DESCRIPTION MUST BE 25 CHARACTERS OR"
420  PRINT  "LESS. PLEASE REENTER."
430  GOTO  380

440  PRINT
450  INPUT  "ENTER THE PART NUMBER: "; PARTNUM$
460  IF LEN(PARTNUM$) <= 10 THEN GOTO 500
470  PRINT  "LENGTH OF PART NUMBER MUST BE 10 CHARACTERS OR LESS."
480  PRINT "PLEASE REENTER."
490  GOTO 440

500  REM  DATA IN PARTTYPE$, SCHDESIG$, DESCRIPT$, AND PARTNUM$
```

At this point valid-length data exists in each of the variables. It would be a good idea to present the data entered back to the operator and request validation. If the operator then detects an error, the value may be reentered before it is written to the file:

```
510  CLS
520  PRINT "THIS IS THE DATA RECEIVED FOR DATA ITEM ";RECCNTR+1
530  PRINT
540  PRINT "PART TYPE:  "; PARTTYPE$
550  PRINT "SCHEMATIC DESIGNATION: "; SCHDESIG$
560  PRINT "PART DESCRIPTION: "; DESCRIPT$
570  PRINT  "PART NUMBER:  "; PARTNUM$
580  PRINT
590  PRINT
600  INPUT  "ARE THERE ANY ERRORS YOU WISH TO CORRECT (Y/N)", X$
610  IF X$ = "N" THEN GOTO 700
620  REM  AN ERROR WAS DETECTED. OPERATOR WANTS TO REENTER
630  PRINT  "DELETING THIS DATA...RETURNING FOR REENTRY"
640  INPUT  "PRESS THE RETURN KEY TO CONTINUE...";X$
650  GOTO  230

700  REM  VALID DATA IN PARTTYPE$, SCHDESIG$, DESCRIPT$, AND PARTNUM$
```

This information can now be written into the temporary file:

```
710  WRITE #1,PARTTYPE$,SCHDESIG$,DESCRIPT$, PARTNUM$
```

Increment the record counter to reflect the number of records written to the file, and go back to the top to get the next set of data:

```
720  RECCNTR = RECCNTR + 1
730  GOTO  230
```

The next sequence deals with the part of the program that closes the temporary file and transfers the data to the permanent file:

```
1000  REM  TRANSFER DATA
1010  CLOSE #1
1020  OPEN "I",#1,"TEMPDATA"
1030  OPEN "O",#2,"PARTDATA"
```

Two files have been opened: TEMPDATA was opened for input and PARTDATA was opened for output.

```
1040  REM  WRITE THE NUMBER OF RECORDS
1050  WRITE #2, RECCNTR
1060  REM  SET UP A LOOP TO READ FROM TEMPDATA AND WRITE TO PARTDATA
1070  FOR I = 1 TO RECCNTR
1080  PRINT "NOW PROCESSING RECORD NUMBER ";I
1090  INPUT #1,PARTTYPE$,SCHDESIG$,DESCRIPT$,PARTNUM$
1100  WRITE #2,PARTTYPE$,SCHDESIG$,DESCRIPT$,PARTNUM$
1110  NEXT I
```

```
1120  REM ALL DATA TRANSFERRED - CLOSE FILES
1130  CLOSE #1,#2
```

Delete the temporary file and end the program:

```
1140  KILL "TEMPDATA"
1150  PRINT "ALL DATA TRANSFERRED - DELETE THE TEMPORARY DATA FILE"
1160  PRINT "WHEN DATA IN MAIN FILE HAS BEEN VERIFIED."
1170  END
```

The complete listing of this program is in Listing 18-2.

LISTING 18-2 WRITING THE PARTDATA FILE

```
100  REM PROGRAM TO WRITE A DATA FILE IN THE FOLLOWING FORMAT:
110  REM NUMBER OF SETS OF DATA; NUMERIC VALUE
120  REM EACH SET OF DATA CONSISTS OF FOUR STRING VALUES:
130  REM     1.  PART TYPE
140  REM     2.  SCHEMATIC DESIGNATION
150  REM     3.  DESCRIPTION
160  REM     4.  PART NUMBER
170  REM DATA WILL BE ACCEPTED VIA INPUT STATEMENTS, THEN WRITTEN
180  REM TO THE FILE. ENTRY OF PART TYPE = "END" WILL TERMINATE
190  REM THE ENTRY PHASE AND CAUSE THE DATA TO BE WRITTEN FROM ITS
200  REM TEMPORARY FILE TO ITS PERMANENT FILE.
210  OPEN "O",#1,"TEMPDATA"
220  RECCNTR = 0
230  CLS
240  PRINT "DATA SET NUMBER "; RECCNTR + 1
250  PRINT
260  INPUT "ENTER PART TYPE: "; PARTTYPE$
270  IF PARTTYPE$ = "END" THEN GOTO 1000
280  IF LEN(PARTTYPE$) <= 35 THEN 320
290  PRINT "LENGTH OF PART TYPE MUST BE 35 CHARACTERS OR LESS."
300  PRINT "PLEASE REENTER."
310  GOTO 250
320  PRINT
330  INPUT "ENTER THE SCHEMATIC DESIGNATION: "; SCHDESIG$
340  IF LEN(SCHDESIG$) <= 7 THEN GOTO 380
350  PRINT "LENGTH OF SCHEMATIC DESIGNATION MUST BE 7 CHARACTERS"
360  PRINT "OR LESS. PLEASE REENTER."
370  GOTO 320
380  PRINT
390  INPUT "ENTER THE PART DESCRIPTION: ";DESCRIPT$
400  IF LEN(DESCRIPT$) <= 25 THEN GOTO 440
```

```
410  PRINT "LENGTH OF PART DESCRIPTION MUST BE 25 CHARACTERS OR"
420  PRINT "LESS. PLEASE REENTER."
430  GOTO 380
440  PRINT
450  INPUT "ENTER THE PART NUMBER: "; PARTNUM$
460  IF LEN(PARTNUM$) <= 10 THEN GOTO 500
470  PRINT "LENGTH OF PART NUMBER MUST BE 10 CHARACTERS OR LESS."
480  PRINT "PLEASE REENTER."
490  GOTO 440
500  REM  DATA IN PARTTYPE$, SCHDESIG$, DESCRIPT$, AND PARTNUM$
510  CLS
520  PRINT "THIS IS THE DATA RECEIVED FOR DATA ITEM ";RECCNTR+1
530  PRINT
540  PRINT "PART TYPE: "; PARTTYPE$
550  PRINT "SCHEMATIC DESIGNATION: "; SCHDESIG$
560  PRINT "PART DESCRIPTION: "; DESCRIPT$
570  PRINT "PART NUMBER: "; PARTNUM$
580  PRINT
590  PRINT
600  INPUT "ARE THERE ANY ERRORS YOU WISH TO CORRECT (Y/N)", X$
610  IF X$ = "N" THEN GOTO 700
620  REM  AN ERROR WAS DETECTED. OPERATOR WANTS TO REENTER
630  PRINT "DELETING THIS DATA... RETURNING FOR REENTRY"
640  INPUT  "PRESS THE RETURN KEY TO CONTINUE...";X$
650  GOTO  230
700  REM VALID DATA IN PARTTYPES$,SCHDESIG$,DESCRIPT$,AND PARTNUM$
710  WRITE #1,PARTTYPE$,SCHDESIG$,DESCRIPT$,PARTNUM$
720  RECCNTR = RECCNTR + 1
730  GOTO  230
1000 REM  TRANSFER DATA
1010 CLOSE #1
1020 OPEN "I",#1,"TEMPDATA"
1030 OPEN "O",#2,"PARTDATA"
1040 REM  WRITE THE NUMBER OF RECORDS
1050 WRITE #2, RECCNTR
1060 REM  SET UP A LOOP TO READ FROM TEMPDATA AND WRITE TO PARTDATA
1070 FOR I = 1 TO RECCNTR
1080 PRINT "NOW PROCESSING RECORD NUMBER ";I
1090 INPUT #1,PARTTYPE$,SCHDESIG$,DESCRIPT$,PARTNUM$
1100 WRITE #2,PARTTYPE$,SCHDESIG$,DESCRIPT$,PARTNUM$
1110 NEXT I
1120 REM  ALL DATA TRANSFERRED - CLOSE FILES
1130 CLOSE #1,#2
1140 KILL "TEMPDATA"
1150 PRINT "ALL DATA TRANSFERRED - DELETE THE TEMPORARY DATA FILE"
```

LISTING 18-2 (*continued*)

```
1160 PRINT "WHEN DATA IN MAIN FILE HAS BEEN VERIFIED."
1170 END
```

18-5 UPDATING AN EXISTING SEQUENTIAL FILE

The previous program wrote a file all at once; that is, all the data for the file was entered at one time. Often, a file is created cumulatively; as data becomes available, it is added to the file. The file is said to be *updated*. Such updates may take one of several forms:

1. Records may be added to the end of the file. In Example 18-2 this would mean that additional parts have been added to the device's circuits.
2. Records already in the file may be deleted. This would occur if the circuits were modified.
3. Data already in the file may need to be altered. A value may be changed as the result of a circuit modification or an erroneous entry may have slipped through.

There are two general strategies that can be used to update an existing sequential file:

1. The entire file can be read into an array or arrays in memory. Each desired data item may then be appropriately altered. Finally, when all the changes and additions have been made, the entire data set is written back to the file, replacing the old data. This works well when the data file is not very large or when the records are in a particular order (e.g., ascending schematic designation order) which must be preserved, even if additional items are added. Because the data is in memory, it can easily be sorted or reordered as needed. One problem with this method is that the entire file must be completely read and completely written back, even if only a single data modification is needed. Another shortcoming is that there must be sufficient system memory to store all data in the file, the program that performs the updates, and BASIC and its operating system.
2. The data file can be read one record at a time, modified, and then written to a new data file. New records are added, in their correct position, by signaling that a new record should be added instead of updating the next old record. When the last old record has been read, the old data file is deleted, and the new data file is renamed with the old file's name, thus becoming the current file. At any time during the updating process, the program can stop presenting old records for modification and simply rewrite the remaining records directly to the new file. Therefore, making a few modifications, particularly to records located near the beginning of the file, can be done reasonably efficiently.

Further, the system need not provide more memory than required to store a single record, because only a single record is read in at any given time, no matter how large the file actually is. The disadvantages include the need for enough space on the file storage device for two copies of the entire file (the old copy remains intact until the new copy is completely written), and the need to both read and write every record, whether modifications are needed or not.

There is an additional complication to be examined. Because the program will allow the number of parts records to vary (i.e., new records may be added or existing records may be deleted), the program will not know until the very end how many records are to be processed. The problem is that the first data item in the file indicates the number of records the file contains. This requires knowing how many records there will be (taking into account current records) and the number of deletions and additions. There are three choices:

1. Rewrite the entire file once more, just to change the first item to its correct value.
2. Place the number of file records in another file which contains *only* this single value. The program would then read this new file first, use the resultant value while processing the file being modified, and then revise the value as records are added or deleted. Finally, this single value would be rewritten to its file at the end of the processing.
3. Eliminate the need for a separate count of the number of records by using a key or flag value in the file to indicate that the last real record has been processed. This has the added advantage of its no longer being necessary to keep track of how many deletions or insertions have been made. When processing is complete, the end of file marker is simply written to the file.

Because a file format that requires the number of records as the first item in the file is already in place, the first method will be described. However, remember the other two methods for future designs. In general, method two is a good choice; it would also simplify the file creation program because it does not require rewriting the temporary file.

Example 18-3 Complete File Manipulation

Task: Write a program that allows the addition, deletion, and editing of the PARTDATA file (of Example 18-2).

Algorithmic Analysis: In order to maintain the order of the data file as it has been organized, one set of data at a time is read and the operator is offered the following five options.

1. Leave the data as it is; proceed to the next item.
2. Edit data except for the schematic designation or part type.

3. Delete the record from the new file.
4. Insert a new record *prior* to the current record.
5. Cease all editing; write the current record and all subsequent records to the new file and finish operations.

The schematic designation or part type will *not* be altered, as this might change the position the data should occupy in the file. If this data must be changed, the record must be deleted and then reinserted at its correct position.

The flowchart for this algorithm is in Figure 18-7.

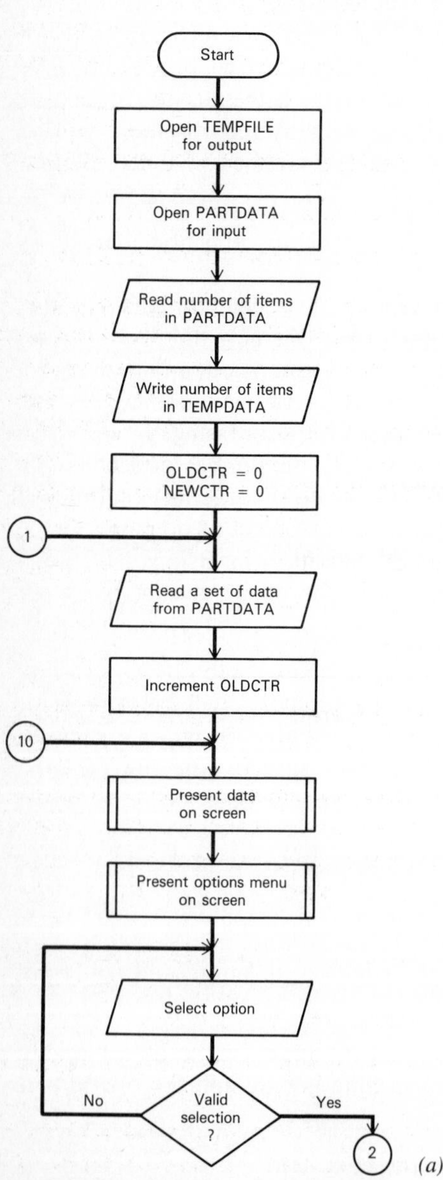

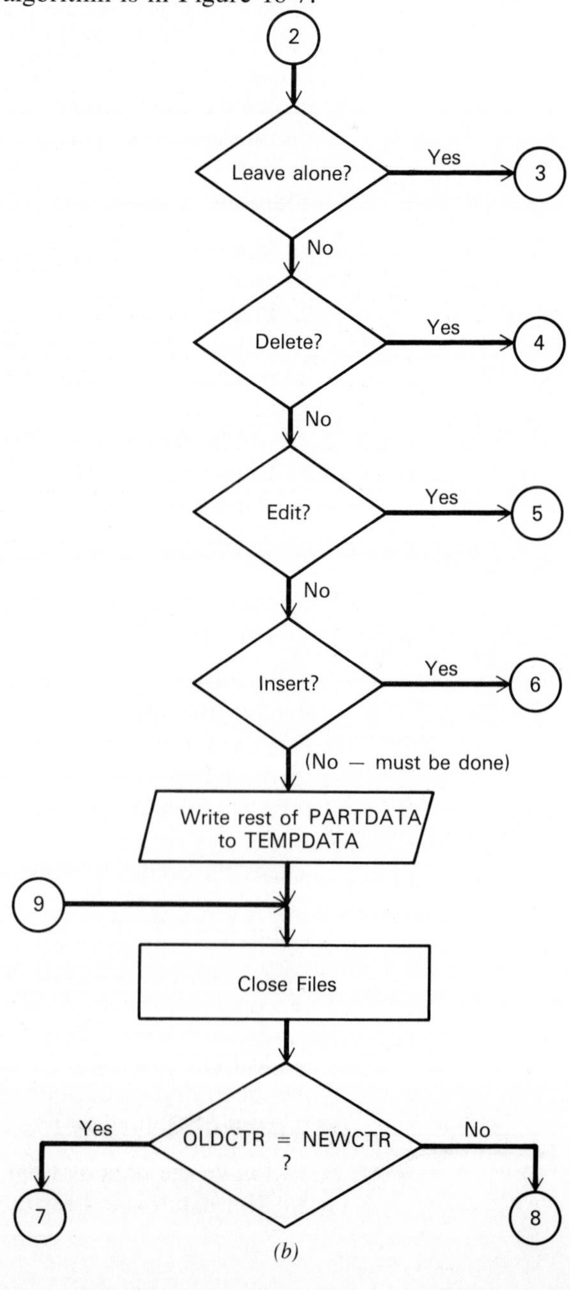

Fig. 18-7 Algorithm for the PARTDATA file update program.

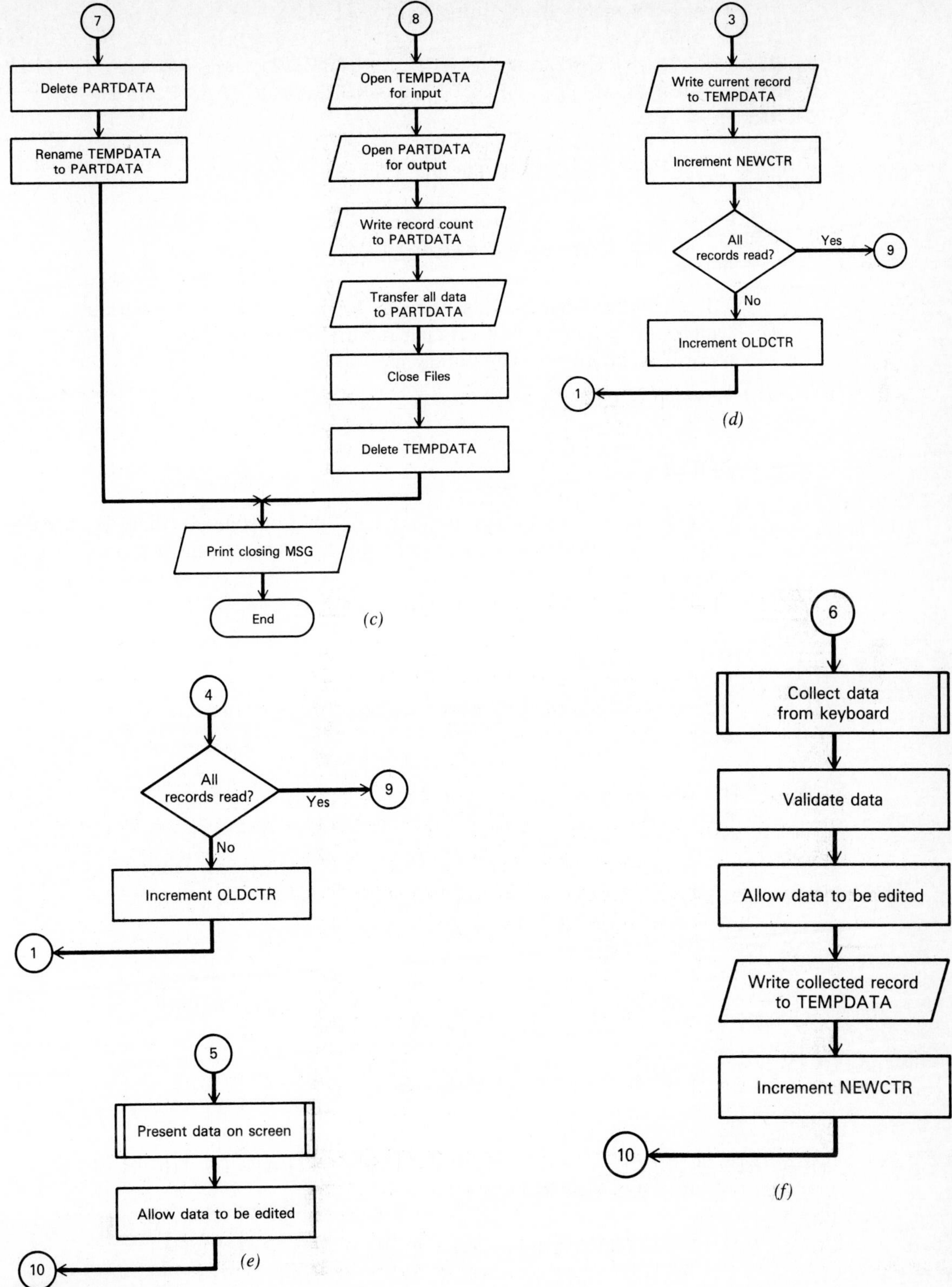

Fig. 18-7 *(continued)*

Program Construction: Introductory REMs:

```
100  REM PROGRAM TO ALLOW DYNAMIC UPDATES OF THE PARTDATA FILE
110  REM PROGRAM ALLOWS DELETION, INSERTION, AND EDITING OF
120  REM RECORDS.
```

Open the existing data file and a temporary file:

```
130  OPEN "I",#1,"PARTDATA"
140  OPEN "O" ,#2,"TEMPDATA"
```

Read the number of data items to follow. Initialize two variables that will count the number of original records processed, and the number of records written to the temporary file:

```
150  INPUT #1,N
160  OLDCTR = 0
170  NEWCTR = 0
```

Although records in this file may be added or deleted, there is at least a chance that the record count will stay the same. If this is true, it is not necessary to update the count. Therefore, the computer will write this value to the temporary file; it will be changed as needed.

```
180  WRITE #2,N
```

Now we begin the process of reading a record, presenting the options, and processing accordingly:

```
190  REM USE SUBROUTINE TO READ DATA FROM FILE #1
200  GOSUB 2600

2600  REM SUBROUTINE TO READ FROM FILE #1 AND ADVANCE COUNTER
2610  INPUT #1,PARTTYPE$,SCHDESIG$,DESCRIPT$,PARTNUM$
2620  OLDCTR = OLDCTR + 1
2630  RETURN
```

Display the contents of the current record via a subroutine call:

```
210  CLS
220  REM PRESENT CURRENT VALUES
230  GOSUB 2000

2000  REM SUBROUTINE TO DISPLAY THE CONTENTS OF THE CURRENT
2010  REM RECORD ON THE SCREEN
2020  PRINT
2030  PRINT "ORIGINAL FILE RECORD NUMBER "; OLDCTR
```

```
2040 PRINT
2050 PRINT "CURRENT PART TYPE: "; PARTTYPE$
2060 PRINT
2070 PRINT "CURRENT SCHEMATIC DESIGNATION: "; SCHDESIG$
2080 PRINT
2090 PRINT "CURRENT DESCRIPTION: "; DESCRIPT$
2100 PRINT
2110 PRINT "CURRENT PART NUMBER: "; PARTNUM$
2120 PRINT
2130 PRINT
2140 RETURN
```

Print the options menu via a subroutine call. Be sure to test for validity of the choice entered:

```
230 REM PRESENT OPTIONS
240 GOSUB 2200
```

```
2200 REM SUBROUTINE TO PRESENT OPTIONS MENU
2210 PRINT
2220 PRINT "YOU HAVE THE FOLLOWING OPTIONS:"
2230 PRINT
2240 PRINT "1.   LEAVE CURRENT RECORD AS IS; GO ON.
2250 PRINT "2.   DELETE THE CURRENT RECORD."
2260 PRINT "3.   EDIT THE CURRENT RECORD."
2270 PRINT "4.   INSERT A RECORD BEFORE THE CURRENT RECORD."
2280 PRINT "5.   CEASE OPERATIONS - KEEP ALL REMAINING RECORDS."
2290 PRINT
2300 INPUT "ENTER YOUR CHOICE OF OPERATION (1-5): ";OPERATION
2310 IF OPERATION >= 1 AND OPERATION <= 5 THEN 2350
2320 PRINT "OPERATION CODE MUST BE BETWEEN 1 AND 5."
2330 GOTO 2290
2350 RETURN
```

This subroutine returns with a value between 1 and 5 in the variable OPERATION. Process accordingly:

```
 250 REM PROCESS OPERATION
 260 IF OPERATION <> 1 THEN GOTO 310
 265 REM WRITE CURRENT RECORD, THEN SKIP TO NEXT.
 270 GOSUB 2500
```

```
2500 REM WRITE VARIABLES TO FILE #2 AND ADVANCE COUNTER
2510 WRITE #2,PARTTYPE$,SCHDESIG$,DESCRIPT$, PARTNUM$
2520 NEWCTR = NEWCTR + 1
2530 RETURN
```

```
280  REM  TEST FOR ALL RECORDS READ FROM ORIGINAL FILE
290  IF OLDCTR = N THEN GOTO 900
395  GOSUB 2600
300  GOTO 210
```

Test operation for "delete" code. Confirm before actually performing a deletion. Remember, to delete means simply not to write the current record to the temporary file before reading the next record from the original file:

```
310  IF OPERATION <> 2 THEN GOTO 400
320  REM  DELETE CURRENT RECORD - CONFIRM FIRST!
330  INPUT  "PLEASE CONFIRM: DELETE CURRENT RECORD? (Y/N):"; X$
340  IF X$ <> "Y" THEN GOTO 210
350  REM  DELETION CONFIRMED
360  REM TEST FOR ALL RECORDS READ FROM ORIGINAL FILE
370  IF OLDCTR = N THEN GOTO 900
380  GOSUB 2600
390  GOTO 210
```

Test for operation "edit":

```
400  IF OPERATION <> 3 THEN GOTO 690
410  REM  EDIT
420  REM  CLEAR THE SCREEN AND RE-PRESENT:
430  CLS
440  PRINT "     ---- EDIT SCREEN ----     "
450  PRINT
460  PRINT "YOU MAY CHANGE THE DESCRIPTION AND THE PART NUMBER"
470  PRINT "ONLY. PART TYPE AND SCHEMATIC DESIGNATION MAY ONLY "
480  PRINT  "BE CHANGED BY DELETING THE CURRENT RECORD AND "
490  PRINT  "INSERTING IT WHERE IT BELONGS."
500  PRINT
510  GOSUB 2000
```

Give the operator a chance to change the data:

```
520  PRINT
530  INPUT  "ENTER NEW DESCRIPTION OR [RETURN] TO LEAVE UNCHANGED";X$
540  IF X$ = "  " THEN 600
550  IF LEN(X$) <= 25 THEN GOTO 590
560  PRINT  "DESCRIPTION LENGTH MAY NOT EXCEED 25 CHARACTERS."
570  PRINT "PLEASE REENTER."
580  GOTO 520
590  DESCRIPT$ = X$
600  PRINT
610  INPUT "ENTER NEW PART NUMBER OR [RETURN] TO LEAVE UNCHANGED";X$
620  IF X$ = "  " THEN 700
```

```
630  IF LEN(X$) <= 10 THEN GOTO 680
640  PRINT "PART NUMBER LENGTH MAY NOT EXCEED 10 CHARACTERS."
650  PRINT "PLEASE REENTER."
660  GOTO 600
670  PARTNUM$ = X$
```

After allowing the data to be changed, it is presented again with the five options; if a mistake was made requiring further modifications the edit process can be performed again. Notice that the program included means to screen for legal lengths of data according to the original specifications.

```
680  GOTO 210
```

Process for operation "insert." An insertion consists of obtaining new data and writing it to the temporary file without changing the current record:

```
 690  IF OPERATION <> 4 THEN GOTO 790
 700  REM  INSERT RECORD - GET NEW DATA
 710  CLS
 720  PRINT "---- INSERT A RECORD ----"
 730  REM  PERFORM DATA ENTRY AS SUBROUTINE
 740  GOSUB 3000

3000  REM  SUBROUTINE TO ADD DATA FOR INSERTION
3010  REM  CODE TAKEN FROM EXAMPLE 18.2!
3020  PRINT
3030  INPUT  "ENTER PART TYPE: "; PT$
3040  IF LEN(PT$) <= 35 THEN 3090
3050  PRINT  "LENGTH OF PART TYPE MUST BE 35 CHARACTERS OR LESS."
3060  PRINT  "PLEASE REENTER."
3070  GOTO  3020
3090  PRINT
3100  INPUT  "ENTER THE SCHEMATIC DESIGNATION: "; SC$
3110  IF LEN(SC$) <= 7 THEN GOTO 3150
3120  PRINT  "LENGTH OF SCHEMATIC DESIGNATION MUST BE 7 CHARACTERS"
3130  PRINT  "OR LESS. PLEASE REENTER."
3140  GOTO  3090
3150  PRINT
3160  INPUT "ENTER THE PART DESCRIPTION: ";DE$
3170  IF LEN(DE$) <= 25 THEN GOTO 3190
3180  PRINT (LENGTH OF PART DESCRIPTION MUST BE 25 CHARACTERS OR"
3190  PRINT "LESS. PLEASE REENTER."
3195  GOTO  3150
3196  PRINT
3200  INPUT  "ENTER THE PART NUMBER: "; PN$
3210  IF LEN(PN$) <= 10 THEN GOTO 3250
```

```
3220 PRINT "LENGTH OF PART NUMBER MUST BE 10 CHARACTERS OR LESS."
3230 PRINT "PLEASE REENTER."
3240 GOTO 3200
3250 REM DATA IN PT$, SC$, DE$, AND PN$
3260 CLS
3270 PRINT "THIS IS THE DATA RECEIVED FOR INSERTION:"
3280 PRINT
3290 PRINT "PART TYPE: "; PT$
3300 PRINT "SCHEMATIC DESIGNATION: "; SC$
3310 PRINT "PART DESCRIPTION: "; DE$
3320 PRINT "PART NUMBER: "; PN$
3330 PRINT
3340 PRINT
3350 INPUT "ARE THERE ANY ERRORS YOU WISH TO CORRECT (Y/N)", X$
3360 IF X$ = "N" THEN GOTO 3410
3370 REM AN ERROR WAS DETECTED. OPERATOR WANTS TO REENTER
3380 PRINT "DELETING THIS DATA...RETURNING FOR REENTRY"
3390 INPUT "PRESS THE RETURN KEY TO CONTINUE...";X$
3400 GOTO 3000
3410 REM CHANGES ACCEPTED - RETURN
3420 RETURN
```

This code is almost identical to the code developed for the data entry program developed in Example 18-2 because the same functions need to be performed.

After the new data has been accepted, it must be written. Because it is in variables other than those which have been used, a new WRITE statement is required,

```
750 REM WRITE NEW DATA TO TEMPORARY FILE
760 WRITE #2, PT$,SC$,DE$,PN$
770 NEWCTR = NEWCTR + 1
```

Re-present the screen with the same current record, in case more records need to be inserted:

```
780 GOTO 210
```

If the operation was = 5, we arrive at line 790; write all the remaining records to the temporary file:

```
790 REM OPERATION 5 - WRITE ALL REMAINING RECORDS
800 REM WRITE THE CURRENT RECORD
810 GOSUB 2500
820 REM READ AND WRITE REMAINDER:
830 IF OLDCTR = N  THEN GOTO 900
840 GOSUB 2600
```

```
850  GOSUB 2500
860  GOTO 830

900  REM ALL RECORDS WRITTEN TO TEMPORARY FILE
```

All the records in the original file have been transferred to the temporary file. It is also possible to arrive at line 900 if the procedure reaches the end of the file before a read operation has been tried (from lines 290 or 370). In either case, if OLDCTR = NEWCTR, the value originally placed at the beginning of the temporary file is correct and need not be rewritten. Otherwise, all the records must be transferred to a new file with the correct number of records at its head:

```
910  REM DETERMINE IF FILE NEEDS TO BE REWRITTEN
920  IF OLDCTR = NEWCTR THEN GOTO 9900
930  REM FILE NEEDS TO BE RE-WRITTEN
940  CLOSE #1,#2
950  OPEN "I",#1,"TEMPDATA"
960  OPEN "O",#2,"PARTDATA"
970  WRITE #2,NEWCTR
```

The program must contain instructions to read the (incorrect) number of records stored in TEMPDATA or the remaining data will not be read correctly. We have no use for this data, but it must be read so that we are correctly positioned to read the next data item in the file.

```
 980  INPUT #1,N
 990  FOR I = 1 TO NEWCTR
1000  INPUT #1,PARTTYPE$,SCHDESIG$,DESCRIPT$,PARTNUM$
1010  PRINT "COPYING RECORD NUMBER ":I
1020  WRITE #2,PARTTYPE$,SCHDESIG$,DESCRIPT$,PARTNUM$
1030  NEXT I
1040  CLOSE #1,#2
1050  PRINT "ALL RECORDS NOW IN FILE PARTDATA."
1060  PRINT "DELETING THE TEMPORARY FILE..."
1070  KILL "TEMPDATA"
1080  GOTO 9950
```

A few more lines are added in case the temporary file did not have to be rewritten:

```
9900  PRINT "TEMPORARY FILE DOES NOT HAVE TO BE RE-WRITTEN."
9910  PRINT "RENAMING TEMPDATA TO PARTDATA AFTER DELETING THE"
9920  PRINT "OLD PARTDATA FILE."
9930  KILL "PARTDATA"
9940  NAME "TEMPDATA" AS "PARTDATA"
9950  PRINT "OPERATIONS COMPLETED"
```

```
9960  PRINT
9998  PRINT "PROGRAM TERMINATING NORMALLY."
9999  END
```

The complete listing for this program is shown in Listing 18-3.

LISTING 18-3 SEQUENTIAL FILE UPDATE PROGRAM

```
100  REM PROGRAM TO ALLOW DYNAMIC UPDATES OF THE PARTDATA FILE
110  REM PROGRAM ALLOWS DELETION, INSERTION, AND EDITING OF
120  REM RECORDS.
130  OPEN "I",#1,"PARTDATA"
140  OPEN "O",#2,"TEMPDATA"
150  INPUT #1,N
160  OLDCTR = 0
170  NEWCTR = 0
180  WRITE #2,N
190  REM USE SUBROUTINE TO READ DATA FROM FILE #1
200  GOSUB 2600
210  CLS
220  REM PRESENT CURRENT VALUES
230  GOSUB 2000
230  REM PRESENT OPTIONS
240  GOSUB 2200
250  REM PROCESS OPERATION
260  IF OPERATION <> 1 THEN GOTO 310
265  REM WRITE CURRENT RECORD, THEN SKIP TO NEXT.
270  GOSUB 2500
280  REM TEST FOR ALL RECORDS READ FROM ORIGINAL FILE
290  IF OLDCTR = N THEN GOTO 900
295  GOSUB 2600
300  GOTO 210
310  IF OPERATION <> 2 THEN GOTO 400
320  REM DELETE CURRENT RECORD - CONFIRM FIRST!
330  INPUT "PLEASE CONFIRM: DELETE CURRENT RECORD? (Y/N):"; X$
340  IF X$ <> "Y" THEN GOTO 210
350  REM DELETION CONFIRMED
360  REM TEST FOR ALL RECORDS READ FROM ORIGINAL FILE
370  IF OLDCTR = N THEN GOTO 900
380  GOSUB 2600
390  GOTO 210
400  IF OPERATION <> 3 THEN GOTO 690
410  REM EDIT
420  REM CLEAR THE SCREEN AND RE-PRESENT:
430  CLS
440  PRINT "    ---- EDIT SCREEN ----"
```

LISTING 18-3 ***(continued)***

```
450  PRINT
460  PRINT  "YOU MAY CHANGE THE DESCRIPTION AND THE PART NUMBER"
470  PRINT  "ONLY. PART TYPE AND SCHEMATIC DESIGNATION MAY ONLY "
480  PRINT  "BE CHANGED BY DELETING THE CURRENT RECORD AND "
490  PRINT "INSERTING IT WHERE IT BELONGS."
500  PRINT
510  GOSUB 2000
520  PRINT
530  INPUT  "ENTER NEW DESCRIPTION OR [RETURN] TO LEAVE UNCHANGED";X$
540  IF X$ =    THEN 600
550  IF LEN(X$) <= 25 THEN GOTO 590
560  PRINT "DESCRIPTION LENGTH MAY NOT EXCEED 25 CHARACTERS."
570  PRINT  "PLEASE REENTER."
580  GOTO 520
590  DESCRIPT$ = X$
600  PRINT
610  INPUT "ENTER NEW PART NUMBER OR [RETURN] TO LEAVE UNCHANGED";X$
620  IF X$ =    THEN 700
630  IF LEN(X$) <= 10 THEN GOTO 680
640  PRINT  "PART NUMBER LENGTH MAY NOT EXCEED 10 CHARACTERS."
650  PRINT "PLEASE REENTER."
660  GOTO 600
670  PARTNUM$ = X$
680  GOTO 210
690  IF OPERATION <> 4 THEN GOTO 790
700  REM  INSERT RECORD - GET NEW DATA
710  CLS
720  PRINT "     ---- INSERT A RECORD ----"
730  REM PERFORM DATA ENTRY AS SUBROUTINE
740  GOSUB 3000
750  REM  WRITE NEW DATA TO TEMPORARY FILE
760  WRITE #2, PT4,SC$,DE$,PN$
770  NEWCTR = NEWCTR + 1
780  GOTO 210
790  REM  OPERATION 5 - WRITE ALL REMAINING RECORDS
800  REM  WRITE THE CURRENT RECORD
810  GOSUB 2500
820  REM  READ AND WRITE REMAINDER:
830  IF OLDCTR = N THEN GOTO 900
840  GOSUB 2600
850  GOSUB 2500
860  GOTO 830
900  REM  ALL RECORDS WRITTEN TO TEMPORARY FILE
910  REM  DETERMINE IF FILE NEEDS TO BE REWRITTEN
920  IF OLDCTR = NEWCTR THEN GOTO 9900
```

```
930  REM FILE NEEDS TO BE RE-WRITTEN
940  CLOSE #1,#2
950  OPEN "I",#1,"TEMPDATA"
960  OPEN "O",#2,"PARTDATA"
970  WRITE #2,NEWCTR
980  INPUT #1,N
990  FOR I = 1 TO NEWCTR
1000 INPUT #1,PARTTYPE$,SCHDESIG$,DESCRIPT$,PARTNUM$
1010 PRINT  "COPYING RECORD NUMBER ";I
1020 WRITE #2,PARTTYPE$,MSCHDESIG$,DESCRIPT$,PARTNUM$
1030 NEXT I
1040 CLOSE #1,#2
1050 PRINT "ALL RECORDS NOW IN FILE PARTDATA."
1060 PRINT "DELETING THE TEMPORARY FILE..."
1070 KILL "TEMPDATA"
1080 GOTO 9950

2000 REM  SUBROUTINE TO DISPLAY THE CONTENTS OF THE CURRENT
2010 REM  RECORD ON THE SCREEN
2020 PRINT
2030 PRINT "ORIGINAL FILE RECORD NUMBER "; OLDCTR
2040 PRINT
2050 PRINT "CURRENT PART TYPE: "; PARTTYPE$
2060 PRINT
2070 PRINT  "CURRENT SCHEMATIC DESIGNATION: "; SCHDESIG$
2080 PRINT
2090 PRINT  "CURRENT DESCRIPTION: "; DESCRIPT$
2100 PRINT
2110 PRINT  "CURRENT PART NUMBER: "; PARTNUM$
2120 PRINT
2130 PRINT
2140 RETURN

2200 REM  SUBROUTINE TO PRESENT OPTIONS MENU
2210 PRINT
2220 PRINT "YOU HAVE THE FOLLOWING OPTIONS:"
2230 PRINT
2240 PRINT  "1.  LEAVE CURRENT RECORD AS IS; GO ON."
2250 PRINT  "2.  DELETE THE CURRENT RECORD."
2260 PRINT  "3.  EDIT THE CURRENT RECORD."
2270 PRINT  "4.  INSERT A RECORD BEFORE THE CURRENT RECORD."
2280 PRINT  "5.  CEASE OPERATIONS - KEEP ALL REMAINING RECORDS."
2290 PRINT
2300 INPUT "ENTER YOUR CHOICE OF OPERATION (1-5): ";OPERATION
```

```
2310 IF OPERATION >= 1 AND OPERATION <= 5 THEN 2350
2320 PRINT "OPERATION CODE MUST BE BETWEEN 1 AND 5."
2330 GOTO 2290
2350 RETURN

2500 REM WRITE VARIABLES TO FILE #2 AND ADVANCE COUNTER
2510 WRITE #2,PARTTYPE$,SCHDESIG$,DESCRIPT$, PARTNUM$
2520 NEWCTR = NEWCTR + 1
2530 RETURN

2600 REM SUBROUTINE TO READ FROM FILE #1 AND ADVANCE COUNTER
2610 INPUT #1,PARTTYPE$,SCHDESIG$,DESCRIPT$,PARTNUM$
2620 OLDCTR = OLDCTR + 1
2630 RETURN

3000 REM SUBROUTINE TO ADD DATA FOR INSERTION
3010 REM CODE TAKEN FROM EXAMPLE 18.2!
3020 PRINT
3030 INPUT "ENTER PART TYPE: "; PT$
3040 IF LEN(PT$) <= 35 THEN 3090
3050 PRINT "LENGTH OF PART TYPE MUST BE 35 CHARACTERS OR LESS."
3060 PRINT "PLEASE REENTER."
3070 GOTO 3020
3090 PRINT
3100 INPUT "ENTER THE SCHEMATIC DESIGNATION: "; SC$
3110 IF LEN(SC$) <= 7 THEN GOTO 3150
3120 PRINT "LENGTH OF SCHEMATIC DESIGNATION MUST BE 7 CHARACTERS"
3130 PRINT "OR LESS. PLEASE REENTER."
3140 GOTO 3090
3150 PRINT
3160 INPUT "ENTER THE PART DESCRIPTION: ";DE$
3170 IF LEN(DE$) <= 25 THEN GOTO 3190
3180 PRINT "LENGTH OF PART DESCRIPTION MUST BE 25 CHARACTERS OR"
3190 PRINT "LESS. PLEASE REENTER."
3195 GOTO 3150
3196 PRINT
3200 INPUT "ENTER THE PART NUMBER: "; PN$
3210 IF LEN(PN$) <= 10 THEN GOTO 3250
3220 PRINT "LENGTH OF PART NUMBER MUST BE 10 CHARACTERS OR LESS."
3230 PRINT "PLEASE REENTER."
3240 GOTO 3200
3250 REM DATA IN PT$, SC$, DE$, AND PN$
3260 CLS
3270 PRINT "THIS IS THE DATA RECEIVED FOR INSERTION:"
```

```
3280  PRINT
3290  PRINT "PART TYPE: "; PT$
3300  PRINT "SCHEMATIC DESIGNATION: "; SC$
3310  PRINT "PART DESCRIPTION: "; DE$
3320  PRINT "PART NUMBER: "; PN$
3330  PRINT
3340  PRINT
3350  INPUT "ARE THERE ANY ERRORS YOU WISH TO CORRECT (Y/N)", X$
3360  IF X$ = "N" THEN GOTO 3410
3370  REM AN ERROR WAS DETECTED. OPERATOR WANTS TO REENTER
3380  PRINT "DELETING THIS DATA... RETURNING FOR REENTRY"
3390  INPUT "PRESS THE RETURN KEY TO CONTINUE...";X$
3400  GOTO 3000
3410  REM CHANGES ACCEPTED - RETURN
3420  RETURN

9900  PRINT "TEMPORARY FILE DOES NOT HAVE TO BE RE-WRITTEN."
9910  PRINT "RENAMING TEMPDATA TO PARTDATA AFTER DELETING THE"
9920  PRINT "OLD PARTDATA FILE."
9930  KILL "PARTDATA"
9940  NAME "TEMPDATA" AS "PARTDATA"
9950  PRINT "OPERATIONS COMPLETED"
9960  PRINT
9998  PRINT "PROGRAM TERMINATING NORMALLY."
9999  END
```

SUMMARY

When programs operate on or generate large amounts of data, such data are more conveniently stored in a file. To deal with such files, a program must do the following:

1. Establish communication with the file, using an OPEN statement.
2. Transfer data to or from the file, using WRITE or INPUT statements.
3. Close the transaction, using the CLOSE statement.

To update (sequential) files, two strategies are possible:

1. Read the entire file into memory, modify the memory as needed, and transfer (write) the new contents to the secondary storage system.
2. Read the file one record at a time, modify the record as needed, and write the modified record to another file.

REVIEW PROBLEMS

1. Write syntactically correct OPEN statements for the following:
   a. A file which contains a collection of the titles of computer software owned by the school, to be opened for reading.
   b. A file which contains the specifications of parts contained in a typical personal computer to be opened for reading.
2. Suggest what the typical contents of the following files might be:
   a. A file that contains data regarding the parts in stock at your local electronics component distributor.
   b. A file that contains data needed by a CAD program to draw printed-circuit boards. Do not include data that is specific to a particular design; just the data that the program might need when it is started is included.
   c. A file that is used to record power consumption for later analysis.

REVIEW QUESTIONS

1. Why is keyboard input not always a practical method of entering data to a computer?
2. What is a file?
3. Name some common files and typical contents.
4. What are the differences between a file and an array?
5. What is the purpose of the OPEN statement?
6. What is the significance of the file number?
7. What statement is used to write data to a file?
8. What statement is used to obtain data from a file?
9. What are the difficulties involved in creating a sequential file?
10. Describe the significance of delimiters contained in file data and how their presence or absence must be accommodated.
11. What are the difficulties involved with the updating of a sequential file? What are the three general forms such updates take?
12. Describe the method of updating a sequential file which requires reading the entire file at once. What are the advantages and disadvantages of this method?

13. Describe the method of updating a sequential file which requires reading the file one record at a time. What are the advantages and disadvantages of this method?

14. What is the purpose of the end-of-file marker? What rules would you suggest for the selection of values for the end-of-file marker?

Refer to the description of the program that allows dynamic updating of a sequential file:

15. What is meant by "dynamic" updating?

16. What is meant by the "current" record?

17. Why did we insist that a record deletion be verified? What other types of actions would be good candidates for such verification?

18. Why were so many of the functions performed by this program placed in subroutines? Could the program have been written without using subroutines?

19. Describe a method of program development that would eliminate the problem of having written a program with a function that was not originally placed in a subroutine, causing the program to be rewritten so that the function *is* contained in a subroutine.

19 GETTING STARTED IN PASCAL

Pascal promotes orderly thinking, which is a great advantage in the solving of programming problems. This language was first developed by Niklaus Wirth in 1971. Professor Wirth wanted to teach students how to write programs in an orderly and efficient manner, and in his view other languages suffered from certain limitations. Thus he created a language that did not require students to worry about certain details in their programs, permitting them to concentrate on the solutions to problems (algorithms).

This chapter will introduce you to the language. You will find that it is not difficult to read and understand a program written in Pascal. However, you may want to read this chapter twice, the second time after you have learned the language's syntactical details. You may also want to refer back to this chapter when studying the material that follows it. In particular, you may want to check the overall organization of a program written in Pascal. As you do this, you will begin to understand and appreciate how a program is designed.

19-1 A FIRST PROGRAM

Imagine that you are seated in front of a computer terminal. Such terminals include two components. One is a keyboard much like a typewriter keyboard. This is called the *standard computer input device*. The second component looks like a television screen and is called the *monitor,* which is the *standard computer output device*. The keyboard allows you to enter data into the computer, and the monitor allows you to see the results produced by the computer. (When the word "terminal" is used here, it will be clear from the context as to whether the reference is to the keyboard or to the monitor.) With this brief description in mind, consider a Pascal program such as the one shown in the following example.

Example 19-1 The First Step

A PASCAL program includes the following statements:

```
PROGRAM Startoff (OUTPUT);

(* This is a sample program and what you are now reading
   is a comment. Comments are ignored by the computer.
   They are very useful when you want to include expla-
   nations of the solution method. Comments begin with
   special characters and are terminated with special
   characters.*)

BEGIN
   WRITELN ('This is my first successful program.')
END.
```

This program includes three components: the *program header,* a sample *comment,* and the *main body.* Generally, a Pascal program will contain other parts. This simple example, however, contains a minimum of two elements which every Pascal program must have: the program header and the main body.

The program header starts with the keyword PROGRAM (*keywords* are certain special names the Pascal compiler uses to translate the source program into a form the computer can use). Next, the *name* you have assigned to the program must appear. In this case the name is "startoff." Names, also called *identifiers,* are assigned to programs and to computer memory locations. Next, you notice a second keyword, OUTPUT, located within a pair of parentheses. This keyword indicates to the compiler that this program is going to send data to the standard output device. If the program were going to receive data from the standard input device, then you would also find the keyword INPUT within these parentheses:

```
PROGRAM startoff (INPUT, OUTPUT);
```

The second program component found in this example is called a *comment.* A comment is not an instruction to the machine. It is used to help someone reading the program understand what the program will accomplish. Comments may be used anywhere in the program, but ordinarily not before every instruction, since overuse of comments tends to obscure the instructions themselves. A comment begins with the characters "(*". Everything which follows these symbols, up to and including the symbols "*)," is considered to be part of the comment and is ignored by the computer. The symbol "{" can also be used to start a comment in some computer installations. The symbol "}" would then be used to terminate the comment. This text will use only "(*" and "*)" to enclose comments.

The third element of the program in this example is the main body of the program. In other books, and later on in this text, you will find the term "main program," which is shorthand for "main body of the program." This part of the overall program starts at the keyword BEGIN and terminates at the keyword END. Between these two keywords you will find all the statements that comprise the program.

Each statement in a program must end with the symbol ";". If you look back at this program, you may say, "Aha, I have detected an error in this example." You may have already noticed that the statement "WRITELN (' This . . . program')" does not end with a semicolon. The reason for this is that the last statement before the END of the program need not terminate in a semicolon. The keyword END *must* be followed by a period (.) to signify to the compiler that this is the physical end of the program and that it should not expect any additional statements.

In this example, what the program is intended to do is pretty obvious. The most important statement (as far as the program is concerned) is:

```
WRITELN(' This is my first successful program.')
```

This English-like statement is almost self-explanatory and is interpreted as follows: Write (or display) a line of data. The data of interest is included within the parentheses. In this instance, the computer echoes the characters which are contained within the single quotation marks ('). Therefore, you will see a single line of characters which reads "This is my first successful program."

PROBLEMS FOR SECTION 19-1

1. Using the program described in Example 19-1 as a guide, write a complete Pascal program which will print the following data on the terminal:

   Your name
   Your address
   Your student identification number

   Each item is to appear on a separate line. Assume that there are 80 possible positions on your monitor where characters can appear. For each line of information, center the characters.

2. Using the program described in Example 19-1 as a guide, write a program which will create an image (graphic picture) on the terminal of your computer. To do this, use the letter "x" (or some other symbol) to create the picture. For example, program the computer to draw the symbol for a resistor, and the text below it, as follows:

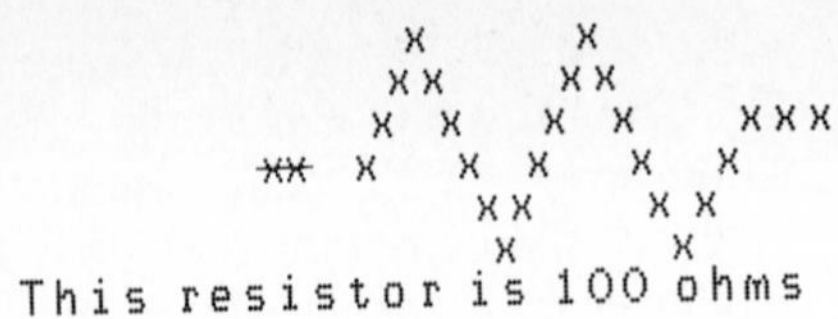
This resistor is 100 ohms

19-2 The Format or Organization of a Pascal Program

The simple program shown in Example 19-1 included two elements basic to all Pascal programs: a program header, and the main body. Pascal programs also contain other types of elements, as the following example demonstrates.

Example 19-2 A Simple but Useful Program

You are the manager of quality control for a company that produces electromagnetic clutches. These clutches are engaged at varying levels of current which are passed through the clutch coil. One of your assistants tests the clutches by gradually increasing the driving current until the clutch operates. The value of the current at which this takes place is recorded using pencil and paper. The program shown in Fig. 19-1 allows you to enter the test results into a computer and calculates the average of the numbers (current values) that are entered.

```
program clutchresults(Input,Output);
(* This program accepts test values from a user and returns the
average value.*)

(* The variables of the program follow. *)
VAR
   numberoftests, index: integer;
   clutchcurrents: ARRAY[1..100] OF real;
   average: real;

(* The following procedure accepts test values entered into the
computer by the user. *)

procedure acceptdata(VAR testvalue:real);
   BEGIN
      WRITE(' What is the next test result? ');
      READLN(testvalue)
   END; (*End of operation which accepts data from a user.*)

(* The following procedure computes an average by dividing the value
of the variable named 'sum' by the number of points which are included
in the sum. *)
```

Fig. 19-1 A Pascal program which accepts test data from a user, calculates the average of the data, and displays the results at the user's terminal.

```
procedure averager(VAR datain:array[1..100] of real;
VAR  result:real; noofpoints:integer);

VAR
  sum:real;
  index:integer;
BEGIN
  sum := 0.0;
  for index := 1 to noofpoints do
      sum := sum + datain[index];
  result := sum/noofpoints
END; (* end of averaging procedure *)

(* start of the main program *)
BEGIN
(* Set the variables to their starting values ("initialize') *)
   numberoftests := 0;
   index := 1;
(* Get results from the user as long as:
   (1) the numbers are positive, or
   (2) there are no more than 100 test results. *)

   acceptdata(testvalue);
   while ((testvalue >= 0.0) and (index <= 100)) do
   begin
     clutchcurrents[index] := testvalue;
     index := index + 1;
     numberoftests := numberoftests + 1;
     acceptdata(testvalue)
   end; (* end of while operation *)

(* The last logical operation is to instruct the computer to calculate
the average, and then to display the results on the terminal. *)

averager(clutchcurrents,average,numberoftests);
writeln(' The computer averaged ',numberoftests,'points');
writeln(' The average is ',average,' amps.')
END. (* of main body of the program. *)
```

Fig. 19-1 *(continued)*

This program contains a number of new elements. The rules for these statements will be introduced in the chapters that follow. However, below you will find a summary of some of the important components:

1. The program heading.
2. A new program section is introduced next. It is called a *declaration*

section and is headed by the keyword VAR.

3. After the section headed by VAR, you will notice two sections both headed by the keyword PROCEDURE. A PROCEDURE defines a set of operations which are to be performed. Procedures are like miniprograms. They can be *called into action,* or *invoked,* from statements in the main body (or from other procedures). Procedures are terminated by END statements, as indicated in the figure. With the exception of a few special cases the PROCEDURE subprogram must physically appear in the Pascal program before it can be used (invoked).
4. The procedures are followed by the main body of the program. This is signaled by the comment "(*start of the main program*)". This comment is useful to someone trying to read your program. In programs containing many procedures, the start of the main body can sometimes be a little hard to find. The comment directs the reader to the best place in the program to begin reading. This comment is not necessary in short programs.

To follow this program, direct your attention to the main body—"(*start of the main program*)". The main body is delimited by the keywords BEGIN and END. Here are some hints which will help you understand the statements which are unfamiliar:

1. The test values are going to be stored in a list. Such a list is called an ARRAY in Pascal. The ARRAY is given a name (or identifier) which, in this case, is "clutchcurrents." The computer will set aside space for a maximum of 100 test currents to be entered as real numbers (i.e., with decimal points in the number)—see the statement at the beginning of the program which says "clutchcurrents:ARRAY [1..100] OF REAL;".
2. In order to keep track of the positions in the list, a memory location named "index" is used. You must instruct the computer to start the list at the first position, hence the statement "index := 1;". This is called an *assignment statement.* In such statements the memory location named on the left of ":=" is assigned whatever value appears (or is calculated) after ":=".
3. To calculate the average, the computer must keep track of the number of tests which have been entered. Before the program starts, no test currents have been entered, which is why you see "number_of_tests := 0;". The value assigned to this quantity (variable) is initialized at 0. (A great many details must be specified for the computer. Subtle programming errors stem from the failure to set starting or initial values for the variables in a program.)
4. Next, the computer requests a test value from the user. This happens when the computer executes the instructions which result from the statement "acceptdata (testvalue);". This latter term calls into operation (invokes) the procedure "acceptdata(VAR testvalue:REAL);". Examine this procedure. It contains at least one familiar instruction—"WRITE ('. . . result?');". The question "What is the next test result?"

appears on the terminal. The next instruction, "READLN · · · test-value)", accepts a keyboard entry from the user. The data is moved from the terminal to the computer when the user strikes the carriage return key. The real (fixed-point decimal) number is assigned to the memory locations within the computer which contain values for the data identified as "testvalue."

5. The next portion of the main program carries out a repeated sequence of operations. This sequence starts at the keyword WHILE and continues to the keyword END. (The comment "(*end of WHILE operations*)" notes the end of the sequence of operations.) The sequence of operations includes the following instructions and their associated purposes:

clutchcurrents[index] := testvalue;	Add a new test value to the list
index := index + 1;	Get ready to put a test value in the next unoccupied position in the list
numberoftests := numberoftests + 1;	Add 1 to the number of tests which have been carried out
acceptdata(testvalue)	Get a new test result from the user

This sequence continues until one of two things happens: The user enters a negative value for a test result, or 100 tests have been entered. The use of a negative number to signal, or *flag,* the end of a list is a standard trick which can be used to indicate the end of a list of numbers when you do not know how many items to expect. The value of the flag can be any value that cannot result from the test data. It is assumed that no more than 100 results will ever be entered at one time. This is a number which provides an aboslute upper limit on the number of tests which can be accepted.

6. When all data has been entered, the computer carries out three final operations, which are (together with explanations) as follows:

```
averager(clutchcurrents, average, numberoftests);
```

This invokes the procedure "averager" which calculates the average value of all items on the list. It does so by summing all items and dividing the sum by the number of tests which have been entered.

```
WRITELN('The computer averaged', numberoftests,
'points');
```

This prints "The computer averaged" on the terminal, followed by the value of the quantity identified by "numberoftests," followed by the word "points." Thus, you should see

```
"The computer averaged ___ points"
```

where "___" will show the number of points which were averaged.

```
WRITELN('The average is', average, 'amps')
```

This is very similar to the instruction just cited, where

```
"The average is ___ amps"
```

appears on the terminal with the blanks replaced with the average value of testresults.

The program included in Example 19-2 and shown in Fig. 19-1 contains simple instances of the elements you can expect to find in a Pascal program. In addition, it shows the order in which you should encounter these elements. This is summarized in Fig. 19-2. The format for a program is broken down into a sequence of detailed components.

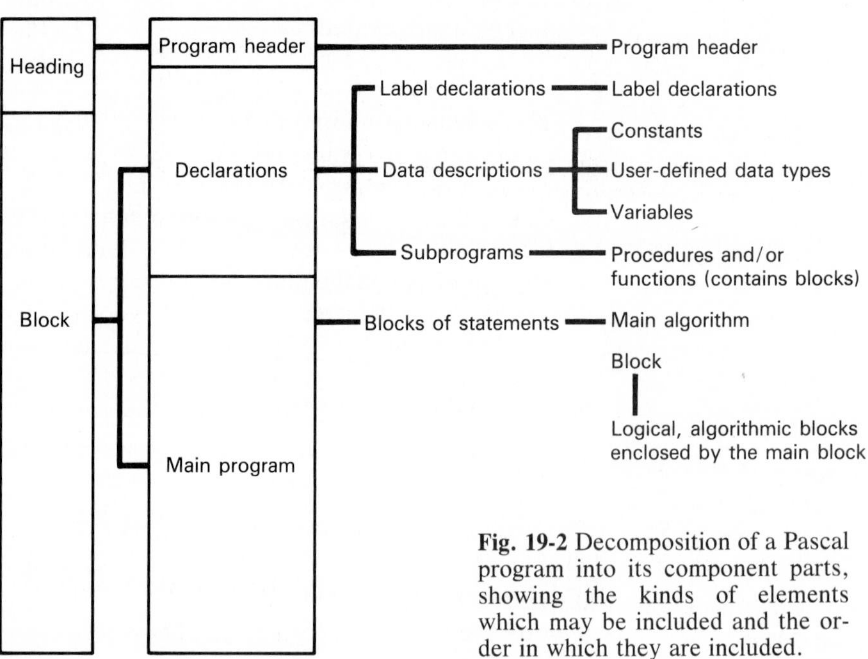

Fig. 19-2 Decomposition of a Pascal program into its component parts, showing the kinds of elements which may be included and the order in which they are included.

19-2-1 The Program Header

The rules governing the program header are contained within the syntax diagram shown in Fig. 19-3. In this diagram, *identifier* includes *symbols* belonging to the language, *reserved words, standard identifiers,* or *user-defined identifiers*.

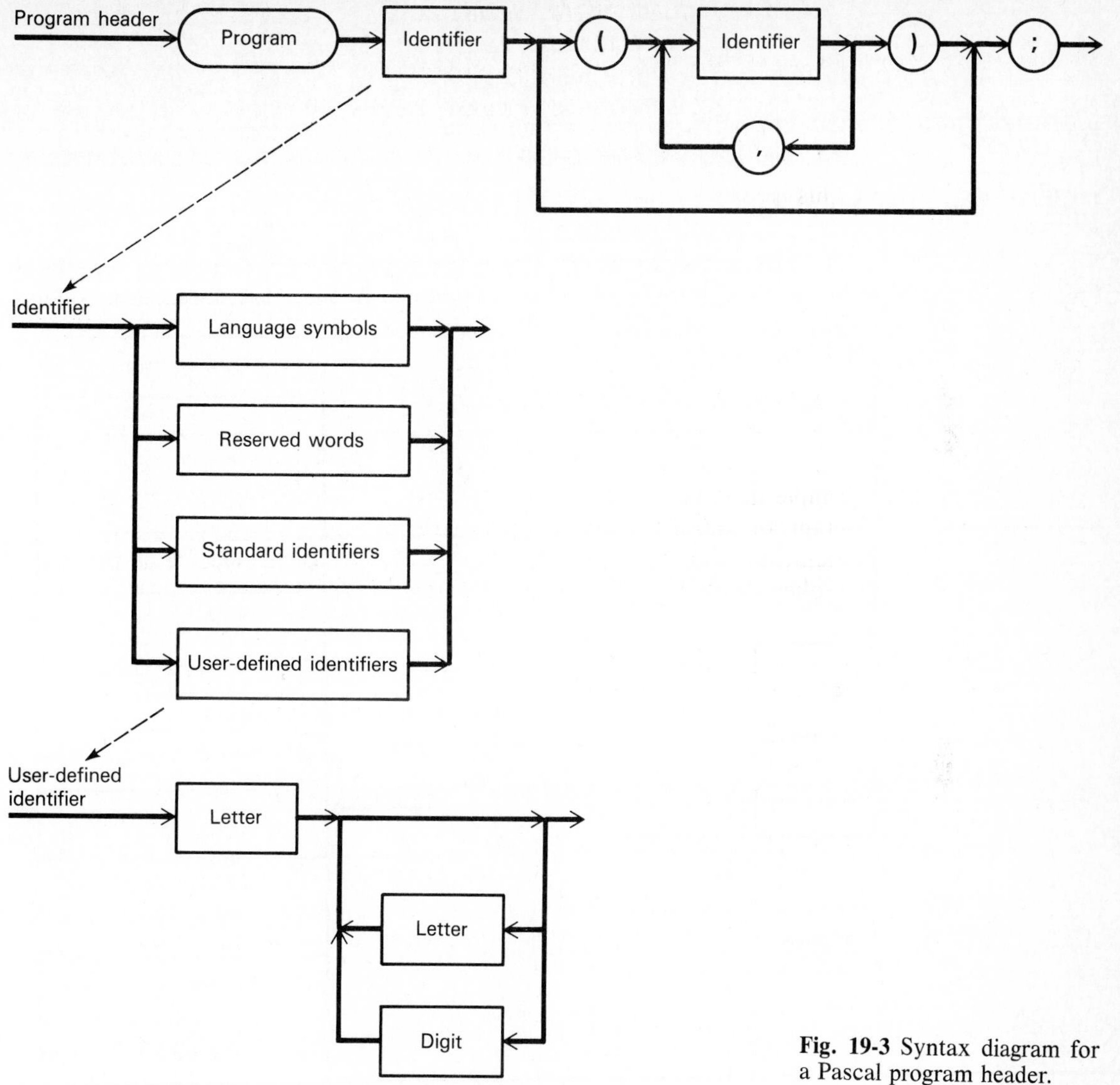

Fig. 19-3 Syntax diagram for a Pascal program header.

Example 19-3 Good and Bad Program Headings

Here are some correct program headers:

```
PROGRAM myprogram;
PROGRAM yourprogram(INPUT);
PROGRAM HISPROGRAM(INPUT, OUTPUT);
PROGRAM HERPROGRAM(OUTPUT, INPUT, herdatafile);
```

Can you tell which of the following headers are incorrect? (*Hint:* Review the syntax diagrams of Fig. 19-3.)

```
PROGRAM case1.1;
PROGRAM case2
PROGRAM case3;
PROGRAM case4(INPUT OUTPUT);
```

19-2-2 The Program Block

The second major part of a Pascal program is the *program block* (or simply block). The format of a block is detailed in Fig. 19-4; block components

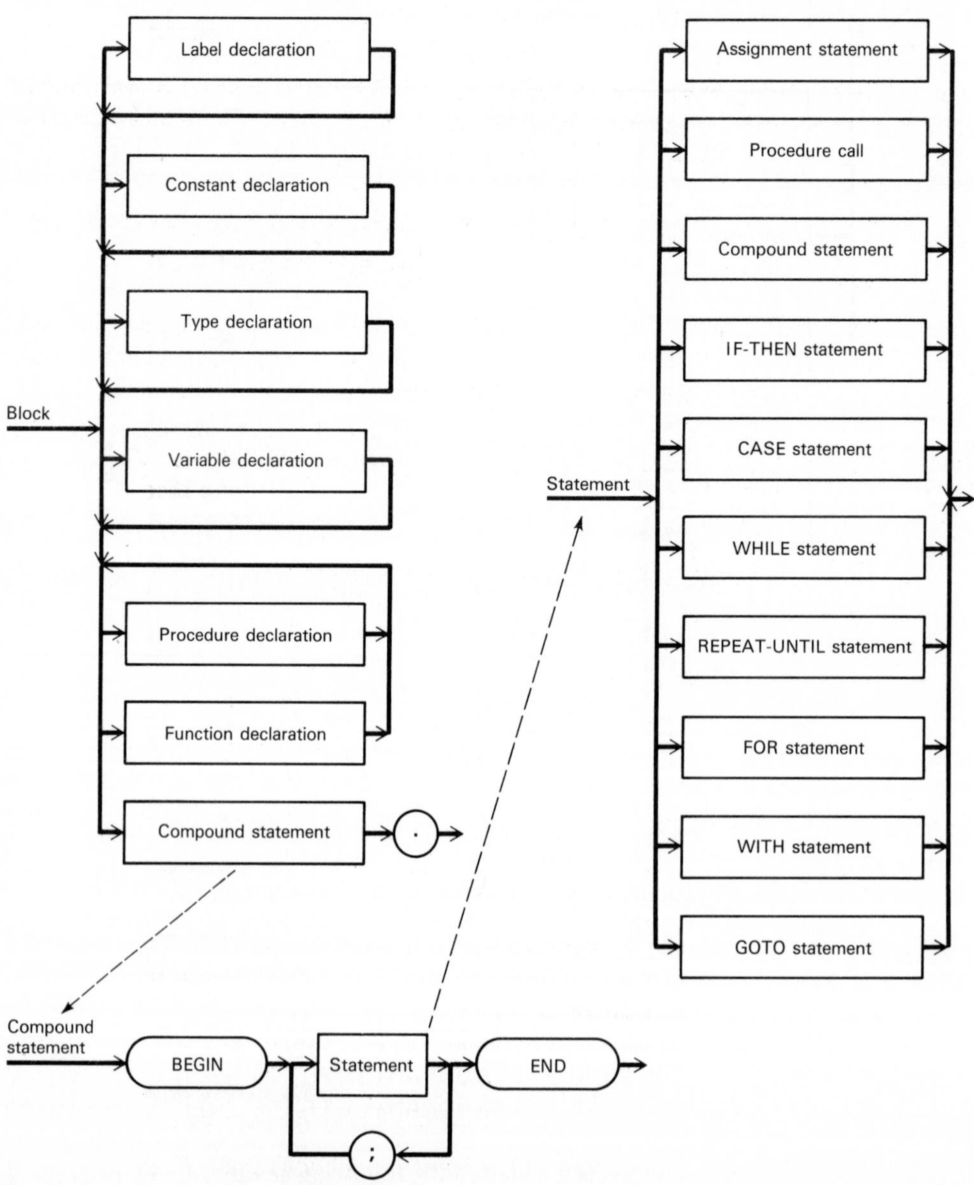

Fig. 19-4 Syntax diagram for the body of a Pascal program.

will be described in subsequent chapters. Notice in Fig. 19-4 that a block may include such Pascal elements as *label, constant, type, variable, procedure,* or *function declarations,* and a *compound statement.* The block is terminated by a period. If an element does appear, such as a type declaration, then it *must appear in the order it is in Fig. 19-4.*

SUMMARY

This chapter introduces the basic elements of a Pascal program. In particular, the format or organization of a Pascal program includes the program header, a declaration section, and a main program. The declaration section contains label declarations, constants, user-defined data types, variables, and procedures and/or functions which may be required by the program.

REVIEW PROBLEMS

1. Write the program header for a program named "wirelist" which will need to use the standard input/output in addition to data which is expected from a file (review Chapter 9) named "wraplist."
2. Modify the procedure "acceptdata" (Fig. 19-1) so that the computer echoes the value of the variable named "testvalue" on the terminal minitor.

REVIEW QUESTIONS

1. What is an algorithm?
2. What two elements must appear in all Pascal programs?
3. What parts of a Pascal program are optional?
4. Name three types of identifiers which are recognized in Pascal.
5. Is the following program order correct?

   Header
   Label declaration
   Constant declaration
   Procedure declaration
   Function declaration
   Main body
6. Make a list of the types of Pascal statements.
7. What two keywords must appear in every block?
8. What symbol separates statements in a Pascal program?

20 DATA: SIMPLE AND STRUCTURED

Pascal, like other HLLs, makes it possible for a user to control a digital computer without an understanding of the detailed operation of the machine itself. The commands written in this language bear some similarity to English and are translated into binary numbers that control the operation of the machine. Users can thus concentrate on solving a problem or designing an algorithm. Learning how to get things done on a computer is in great part dependent on learning the HLL which controls the machine. In order to learn Pascal, you must know:

- The symbols used in the language
- The types of data it will accept
- How to specify what is to be done
- How to determine the order in which the machine should execute instructions

This chapter will describe the Pascal character set as well as the data types you can expect to excounter.

20-1 DATA NAMES

20-1-1 Letters, Symbols, and Words

In order to learn a language, start with the letters and symbols of which it is composed. In addition to letters and digits, the set of allowed characters usually includes all those found on the computer keyboard. These symbols may be those found in the ASCII character set made up of 128 ASCII symbols. The letters, digits, and symbols of Pascal are combined to form the *words* and *statements* belonging to this HLL. Words are formed by combining letters and digits.

20-1-2 Identifiers

Identifiers are the names of words found in Pascal. Figure 20-1 contains a breakdown of the kinds of identifiers you might find. Each of these will be briefly described.

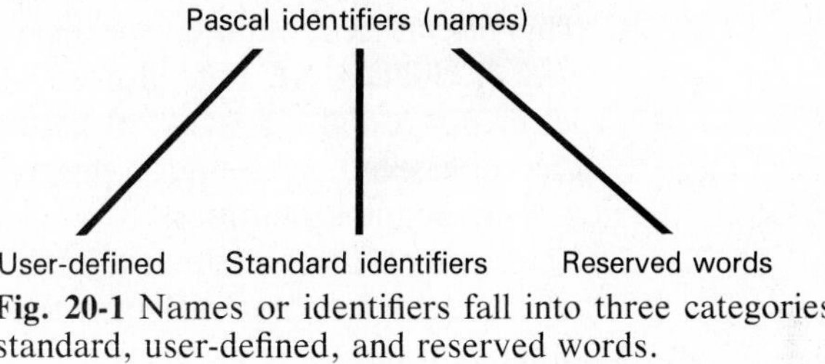

Fig. 20-1 Names or identifiers fall into three categories: standard, user-defined, and reserved words.

a. Identifiers Defined by a User

Users can create their own names or identifiers. This can be done by following certain rules:

1. A user-defined identifier must start with a letter.
2. A name may contain both letters and digits.
3. A user-defined identifier can have any number of letters and digits. A word of caution: compilers may use only the first eight letters and numbers to distinguish identifiers. Therefore, when creating names, be sure your identifiers differ by at least one letter or digit in the first eight places.

Example 20-1 Naming Names

The following are Pascal identifiers:

```
EXAMPLE1
EXAMPLE2
voltage
current
thevoltageatstation1
wastevalvestatus
```

It is evident from the above rules and examples that highly descriptive user-defined identifiers can be devised which can be very helpful to anyone reading the program. The program can take on aspects of a story, and the algorithm becomes self-explanatory.

Of course, it is also possible to create incorrect identifiers. A short list of such potentially unacceptable identifiers is shown below. Can you tell what is wrong in each case? Do not look at the answers (which follow) until you think you have the answer or you give up.

1. the first station
2. next*answer

3. outofdata
4. 1January1986
5. while

Here are the reasons the above identifiers are wrong:

1. This identifier contains spaces (or blanks), sometimes called *white space*. Spaces are not allowed in an identifier. A blank is neither a letter nor a digit. Spaces, of course, are one of the permissible Pascal characters and are found in programs, but they must never be included in user-defined identifiers.
2. The symbol "*" is neither a letter nor a digit and thus must not appear in an identifier. You will see this symbol used in programs, but for other purposes.
3. Nothing wrong with this one.
4. An identifier must never start with a digit, but only with a letter.
5. This is a special name in Pascal and is called a *reserved word*. It cannot be used for user-defined names. Reserved words will be described later.

b. Standard Identifiers

Identifiers that are automatically recognized are called *standard identifiers*. Fig. 20-2 shows five categories with the standard identifiers belonging to

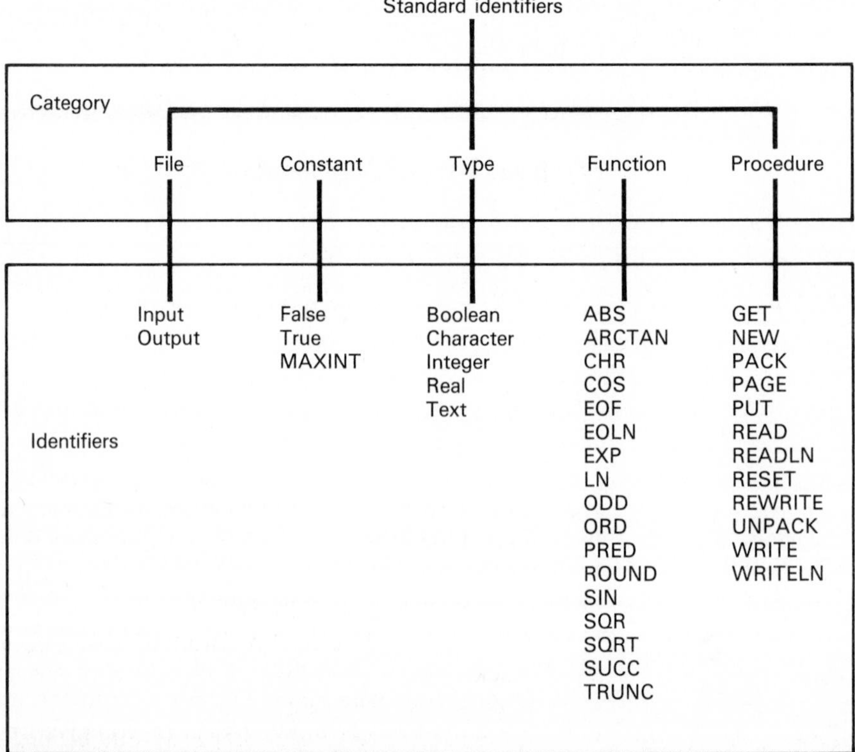

Fig. 20-2 Breakdown of standard identifiers.

each one. It is possible to create a *user-defined* identifier using the same name as one of these standard identifiers. However, the computer will no longer recognize the name as a standard identifier. Using that name as a standard identifier in the program may result in a serious error because the computer uses the programmer's definition instead of the standard meaning. *For safety, avoid creating an identifier having the same name as a standard identifier.*

c. Reserved Words and Symbols

The last type of identifier (name) shown in Fig. 20-1 is the reserved word or symbol. These symbols and words have special meanings and cannot be changed by you. Reserved words include AND, ARRAY, BEGIN, CASE, CONST, DIV, DO, DOWNTO, ELSE, END, FILE, FOR, FUNCTION, GOTO, IF, IN, LABEL, MOD, NIL, NOT, OF, OR, PACKED, PROCEDURE, PROGRAM, RECORD, REPEAT, SET, THEN, TO, TYPE, UNTIL, VAR, WHILE, WITH (*lowercase letters are permitted*). There is also a group of reserved symbols in Pascal which are shown in Table 20-1.

TABLE 20-1 RESERVED SYMBOLS IN PASCAL

+	−	*	/	:=
.	,	;	:	=
<>	<	<=	>=	>
↑	(	)	[	]
(*	{	*)	}	..

These symbols will be used to describe operations to be performed within the program.

PROBLEMS FOR SECTION 20-1

1. Are these user-defined identifiers correct?

message	1st
MESSAGE	month/day/year
RECORD	notbusy
ItseasytolearnPascal	waiting?

2. Create identifiers for the following:

a. The Greek letter π.
b. A signal to be received from a temperature-measuring instrument at the top of Mount McKinley.
c. The number of 10-K Ω resistors that your company presently has in stock.
d. A person's heart rate.
e. An alarm whose value depends on the pressure of a boiler in a building.

3. Which of the following are reserved words?

   RECORD1 OUT
   IF ANDNOT
   IN

4. Write as many reserved symbols as you can. Check your answer against Table 20-1.

   If you wrote 25 correctly, you are a champion.
   If you wrote 20 to 25 correctly, you are an expert.
   If you wrote 15 to 19 correctly, you are on the way.
   If you wrote 10 to 14 correctly, you need more review.
   If you wrote 5 to 9 correctly, "get with it." It is not that hard.
   If you wrote less than 5 correctly, that is bad news.

5. Which reserved words begin with the letter "P"?

6. Which reserved word, other than WHILE, also begins with the letter "W"?

7. What kind of names are the following:

   WRITELN BEGAN
   OUTPUT ARRAY
   LABEL EOF
   STATUS TRUE

8. A short Pascal program follows. Name the reserved words, reserved symbols, standard identifiers, and user-defined identifiers.

```
PROGRAM ADDER(INPUT,OUTPUT);
VAR X, Y, SUM: REAL;
BEGIN
WRITELN('PLEASE TELL ME THE NOS. TO ADD...');
READ(X, Y);
SUM := X + Y;
WRITELN('I GET', SUM)
END.
```

20-2 DATA TYPES

There are two things to know about numbers used in Pascal programs. One concerns the way in which they are stored in memory; the second concerns the kinds of operations which can be performed on these numbers. With regard to the latter, for example, two characters such as "A" and "S" may be joined together (*concatenated* to form "AS"), but it makes no sense to perform arithmetic addition on this data. In HLLs, *data types are defined for each combination of memory storage allocations and sets of allowed operations on such data*. Pascal includes many data types; it also allows the user to create new data types. It is known as a *strongly typed* language, which means that operations can only be performed on similar data types. This helps reduce errors.

This chapter will introduce simple data types as well as structured data types which are combinations of the simple types.

20-2-1 The INTEGER Type

In very simple terms, integers are numbers without decimal points. All of the following are integers in Pascal: −25, 100, +15000. The number −2.1 is not an integer because it has a decimal point. The number 20,150 is not an integer because commas are not permitted in integers. However, integers may include minus signs (−). What is the range of integers in Pascal? The answer to this question depends on which computer is being used. To get around this variability, Pascal uses MAXINT to stand for the largest integer provided by your installation. The range of the INTEGER data type extends from −MAXINT to +MAXINT. If you do not know the value of MAXINT for your computer, it is possible to find out. When you are familiar with the process for creating an executable program for your computer, try the following program:

```
PROGRAM TEST(OUTPUT);
(*This simple Pascal program will tell you
the value of maxint for your installation*)
BEGIN
   WRITELN(MAXINT)
END.
```

How are integer data types specified? Each identifier that is to be an INTEGER data type is written, separated by commas. Following the last identifier, the symbol ":" appears, followed in turn by the standard identifier INTEGER (lowercase may be used). The symbol ";" terminates the line. The following is a list of examples:

```
index, counter, sum, total: INTEGER;
partscount, numberofresistors: INTEGER;
wiresource, wiredestination: INTEGER;
```

Include as many lines as are necessary. A diagram for specifying INTEGER data types is shown in Fig. 20-3. (In particular, follow the solid lines in this diagram.)

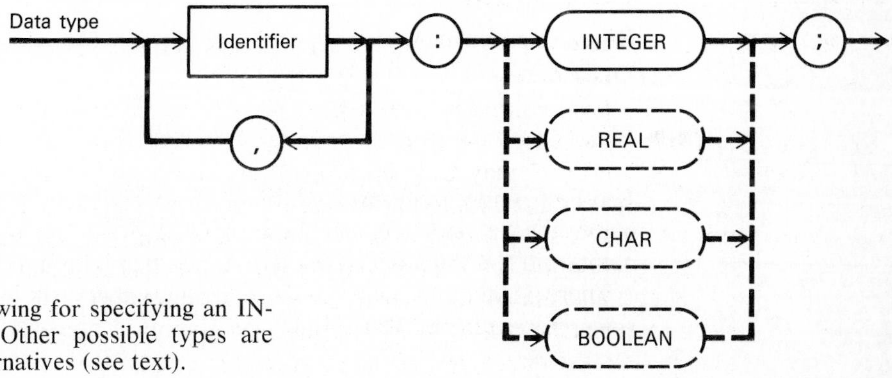

Fig. 20-3 Syntax drawing for specifying an INTEGER data type. Other possible types are shown as dotted alternatives (see text).

PROBLEMS FOR SECTION 20-2-1

1. Which of the following are integers?

25,325
−2
+50
−1.256
3.0E−01
MAXINT
250

2. Write the term which expresses the fact that "dollars," "cents," "route," "termination," and "estimatedtime" are INTEGER identifiers.

3. For each of the following INTEGER declaration, determine if there is anything wrong and, if so, what?

```
mostly, one, two: INTEGER;
record, fielder, dialsetting: INTEGER;
once, twice, threetimes: INTEGER
```

20-2-2 The REAL Data Type

A real number is recognized by the presence of a decimal point. This is the normal form of a *floating-point* number. The smallest and largest real number varies from one computer to another. There is no standard identifier similar to MAXINT for real numbers. Some rules to remember concerning real numbers are as follows:

1. A real number must have a decimal point.
2. There must be at least one digit to the left of the decimal point.
3. There must be at least one digit to the right of the decimal point.

Here are some examples of real numbers in Pascal:

+100.6
−1.2
1052.8315

Here are some examples which are incorrect. Can you tell why?

+.25
−2.
+15

The first is incorrect because there is no digit to the left of the decimal point, the second because there is no digit to the right of the decimal point, and the third because there is no decimal point.

There is another way to write real numbers. It involves the use of *scientific notation.* The number in this case consists of a *mantissa,* or *characteristic,* and an *exponent.* An example of a real number written in scientific notation is

$$-2.581E-02$$

where -2.581 is the mantissa and -02 is the exponent. The exponent follows the letter "E." A number of installations limit the mantissa to six digits and the exponent to two digits.

REAL data types are specified in exactly the same way as INTEGER data types. Therefore, Fig. 20-3 is also valid for REAL data types. There is only one difference, but it is crucial. The standard identifier REAL is used in place of INTEGER. Some examples will make this clear:

```
tolerance, threshold, range, domain: REAL;
controlvoltage, frequency, amplitude, phase: REAL;
```

PROBLEMS FOR SECTION 20-2-2

1. Write each of these floating-point numbers in scientific notation:

   0.157
   −200.1
   153.2
   −41062.3

2. Write each of the following numbers in floating-point form:

   −2.5E+05
   16.5E−01
   2.14E0

3. Write a declaration which specifies the user-defined identifiers "small," "large," "medium," and "gross" as REAL data types.

4. Is there anything wrong with the following declarations?

```
station1temp, station2temp, station3temp,: REAL
round, new, reference, error: REAL
```

20-2-3 BOOLEAN Data Types

Some data requires only two values, which are often called *false* and *true*. A switch, for example, can be either on or off. If it is on, you can say that the switch has the value "true." If it is off, you can say that the switch has the value "false." Many kinds of data can be described in this way. Data which require only the values true and false are called BOOLEAN quantities. You specify such data in a manner similar to that for data types just described. Once again Fig. 20-3 can be used to declare such data. In this case the word INTEGER is replaced by BOOLEAN. Some examples of terms which result are:

```
test, flag, semaphore, overflow: BOOLEAN;
trafficlight, carsignal: BOOLEAN;
```

You may use as many of these declarations as needed. It is not necessary to put all identifiers on one line.

PROBLEMS FOR SECTION 20-2-3

1. Write a declaration which specifies the following identifiers as BOOLEAN. Write the declaration so that each identifier appears on a separate line. The identifiers are "wastevalve," "mixingmotor," "overflowsensor," "powerfailsignal," and "interlock."

2. Find all the errors in the following declarations:

```
switch off, clutchengaged, no*current: BOOLEAN;
buffer full, tapeready, page: BOOLEAN;
packed, ready, ontime: BOOLEAN
```

20-2-4 CHAR Data Types

A character is generally any symbol available to the programmer on the computer. When data consists of characters, these will appear within a single quotation mark, or apostrophe. Some examples of character type data are:

'a'
'B'
' ' (the "blank" character)

The quotation mark character itself is represented as double quotation marks (' ' ' '). Figure 20-3 can once again be used as the model for declaring a character data type, where CHAR is used in place of INTEGER. Some CHAR declaration examples follow:

```
firstletter, lastletter, sampleletter: CHAR;
thissymbol, thatsymbol: CHAR;
```

Characters, like real numbers or integers, have an order that is imposed by the code used. You must check your installation to determine this order. Although not universally adopted, it is often the following:

$$'A' < 'B' < 'C' < \cdots < 'Z'$$

and

$$'0' < '1' < '2' < \cdots < '9'$$

In the latter example, '1' (etc.) is the symbol for the number 1 but is not equal to (does not have the value of) the number 1.

It is also important to note that CAT is *not* a character; it is a *string* of characters. Dealing with linked characters (the string) is discussed later.

PROBLEM FOR SECTION 20-2-4

1. What, if anything, is wrong with each of the following?

```
'a', firstchar: CHAR;
ch, falsech, truech: CHAR
c1, c2, c3: CHAR;
```

20-3 COMPLETE TYPE DECLARATIONS

Four simple Pascal data types have been described to this point. Other types will be added later in the chapter. It is now possible to incorporate such data types into a complete declaration. There are three ways to do this: you can use the CONST declaration, the VAR declaration, or the TYPE declaration. The TYPE declaration allows you to define *new* data types.

Data in a computer takes one of two forms. Its value can vary during the execution of a program, in which case the data items are considered *variables,* or its value remains fixed during the program, in which case the data items are called *constants.* If these data types do not meet programming needs, it is possible to define a completely new data type. This can be done by listing *all* the values such data can take. You must also specify the order (from smallest to largest value) of the new data type. Three different declaration statements are used respectively for these three circumstances.

20-3-1 Implicit Type Declaration (CONST)

It is often advantageous to use an identifier in place of a constant data value. For example, the mathematical constant π has the approximate value 3.14159. PI used in place of 3.14159 would obviously make the program easier to read. The CONST mechanism in Pascal provides for such a substitution. Refer to the syntax diagram of Fig. 20-4 for guidance in the use of a CONST declaration. Notice that for each object in the diagram that is unfamiliar (i.e., "literal"), a drawing is included. The following examples should be studied by checking them against the CONST syntax diagram.

Example 20-2 A CONST Declaration

```
CONST
    largest = 10;
    smallest = -largest;
```

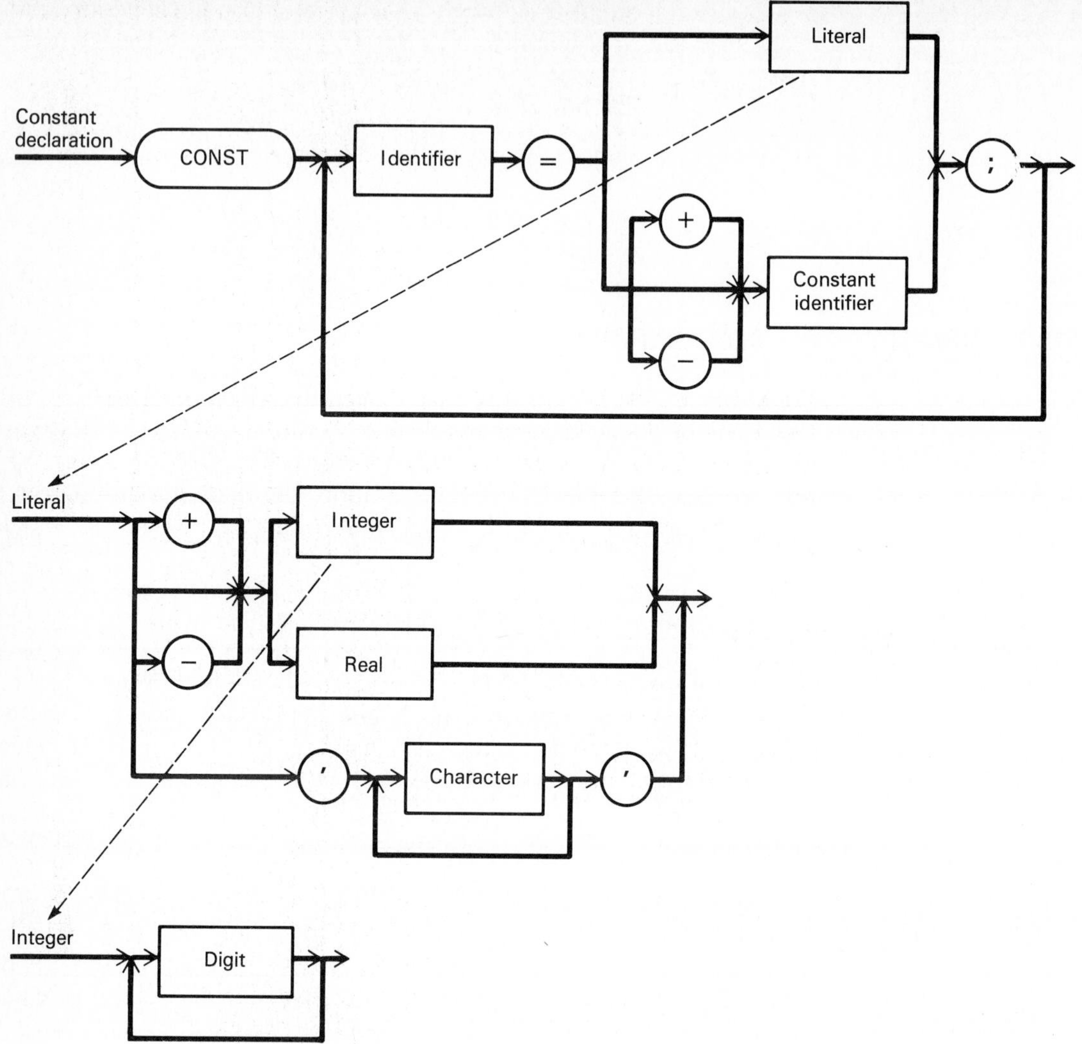

Fig. 20-4 Syntax diagrams for declaring data types using a CONST construction.

Notice from Fig. 20-4 that the CONST declaration consists of two major elements. Identifiers appear on the left of the "=" sign. To the right of the = sign, one of four kinds of data can appear: integer data (no decimal point present), real data (contains decimal point), character data (a string of characters enclosed within single quotation marks), or the name of another constant identifier. (In the last case, the constant identifier should have appeared on the left-hand side of a prior line.) Each line is terminated by a semicolon (;). In the example shown above, the identifier "largest" is equivalent to the integer 10. The identifier "smallest" is associated with the negative value of the identifier largest. It is therefore equivalent to −10.

Example 20-3 Another CONST Declaration

Consider the following program fragment:

```
CONST
    one = 1;
    two = 2;
    three = 3;
    pi = 3.14159;
```

The programs can use the identifiers "one," "two," etc., to represent the integers 1, 2, etc. This, obviously, makes the program easier to read. In like manner, "pi" is easier to deal with than the numerical value it represents.

PROBLEMS FOR SECTION 20-3-1

1. Write a simple CONST declaration statement which defines the following data types:

```
eachstep = 1
pi = 3.14159
poslimit = +10
neglimit = -10
threshold = 0.0
```

2. Correct all the errors you can find in the following CONST declaration:

```
CONST
    fourteen = 14.;
    oK = 1
    error = -1;
    epsilon = small;
    small = 0.01;
    exp = 25.1;
    round off = 0.5;
```

3. Define an entity which has the name "noofcharsonaline" and has a value of 80.

20-3-2 The VAR Declaration

Data which changes or varies during the course of a program is defined by using a VAR declaration. The syntax for this declaration is shown in Fig. 20-5. The following examples conform to the syntax diagram of the VAR declaration.

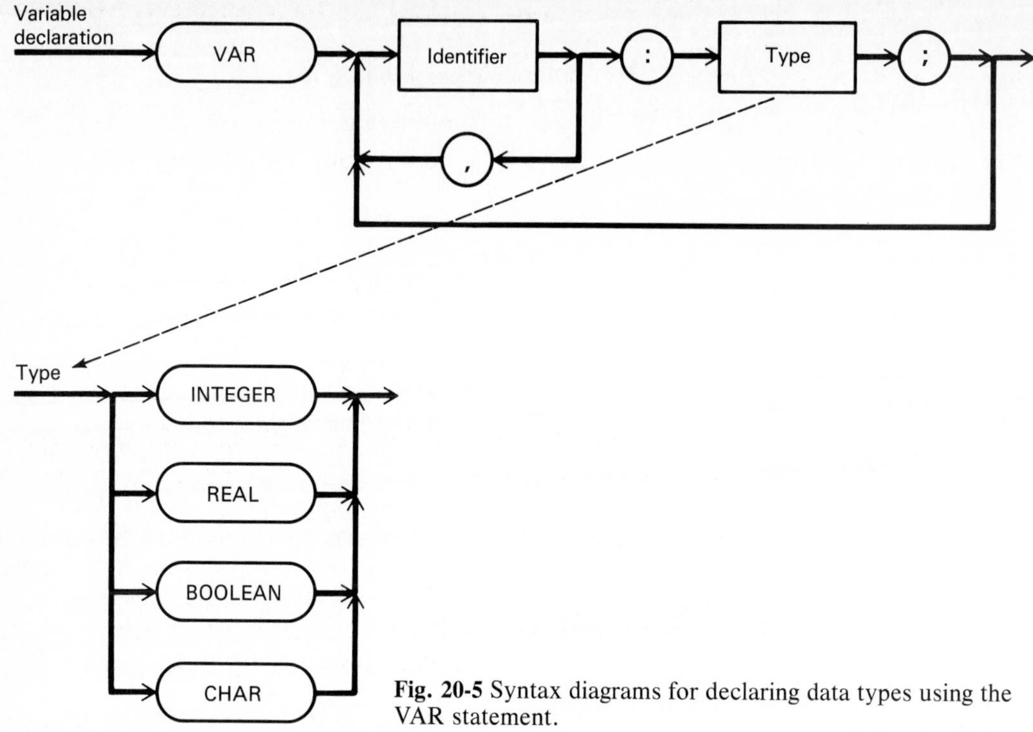

Fig. 20-5 Syntax diagrams for declaring data types using the VAR statement.

Example 20-4 The VAR Declaration

Consider the following program fragment.

```
VAR
  xposition, yposition, timedelay, drilldepth: REAL;
  xmotoron, ymotoron, zmotoron: BOOLEAN;
  boardno, noofholes: INTEGER;
  stopch, startch: CHAR;
```

Note that the fragment starts with the word VAR. This is followed by a number of lines, each consisting of identifiers separated by commas, a colon (:) after the last identifier, a data type (REAL, BOOLEAN, INTEGER, CHAR), and a semicolon (;) which terminates the line. Study this example, using Fig. 20-5 as a guide.

PROBLEMS FOR SECTION 20-3-2

1. Use a VAR declaration to define the following variables:

   "frequency," "hipass," "lowpass," and "bandpass" are REAL variables

"omega," "f," "leftbracket," and "rightbracket" are CHAR variables
"error," "endofdata," "hipassswitch," "lowpassswitch," and "bankpassswitch" are BOOLEAN variables
"noofstages," "n," "index," and "power" are INTEGER variables

2. Correct all the errors in the following VAR declaration:

```
VAR
    start, finish, and middle: BOOLEAN
    one, two, three: INTEGER
    function, abscissa, ordinate: REAL
```

20-3-3 The TYPE Definition

There are times when it is convenient to define a new data type. There are three ways this can be done. All methods employ the user-defined *TYPE declaration.* In one method, the identifier is named, and all the values it can take are enumerated. The second method also includes the identifier. In this case the identifier is made into one of the data types already described. The third method also specifies values. In this case the values are described by a subrange. Each of the three methods mentioned will be described in detail, with examples.

a. Defining a New Data Type by Enumeration

Figure 20-6 is the syntax diagram describing the TYPE declaration that specifies all values that the new data type can take.

In Pascal the term "scalar" applies to data types which have a specified order. The types INTEGER, REAL, BOOLEAN, and CHAR are considered scalar types. Why? INTEGER data types include all the integers from

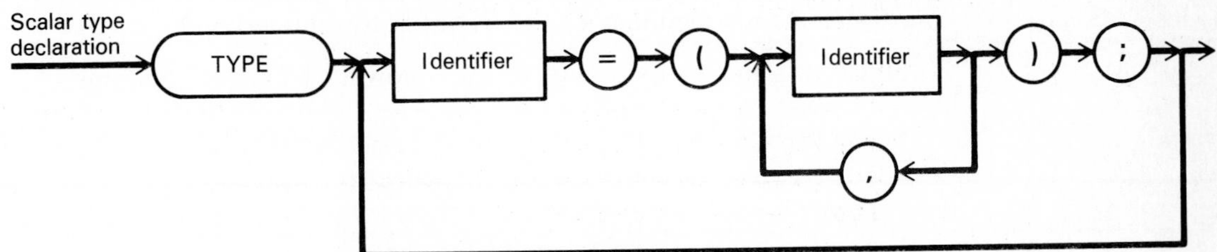

Fig. 20-6 Syntax diagram for a user-defined scalar type.

−MAXINT to +MAXINT. Since these integers have an order (i.e., −10, −9, . . ., 0, 1, . . ., 10), they come within the definition of a scalar. The same is true for the REAL data type. The BOOLEAN data type takes two values, false and true. False is considered to be first in order (smaller), and true is second in order for this type of data. The characters of the computer (CHAR data types) are also ordered, often with the sequence

$$a < b < c < \dots$$

Example 20-5 A User-Defined Scalar Type Using Enumeration

A given program is intended to analyze an electrical network. It may be convenient to define a new type of data called a "component" type. Its values might be "resistor," "capacitor," and "inductor," in that order. Following the diagram of Fig. 20-6 this data would be declared as follows:

```
TYPE
    component = (resistor, capacitor, inductor);
```

The values resistor, capacitor, and inductor are ordered, and within the program each data element of the newly created type is given an ordinal value. The first has ordinal value 0, the second has a value of 1, and this continues until all values have been assigned an ordinal value. In this way it is possible to perform certain operations, comparison operations in particular, on such user-defined data.

PROBLEMS FOR SECTION 20-3-3*a*

1. Write a TYPE declaration which defines a data type called "day." This new data type should take values which are equivalent to the days of the week.
2. A program has been written which automatically sorts resistors into boxes which correspond to their values; each box holds a resistor of a different value. To do this requires a resistor color code which is defined as a new data type. Using the identifier "colorcode," write a TYPE statement which defines the identifier by enumeration.
3. Correct the errors (if any) in the following TYPE declarations:

```
TYPE
    wiresize = (AWG#18, AWG#20, AWG#22);
    month = (1, 2, 3, 4, 5, 6, 7, 8, 9, 10, 11, 12);
```

b. Other Names for Standard Data Type Identifiers

A second method for defining user-defined data is diagrammed in Fig.

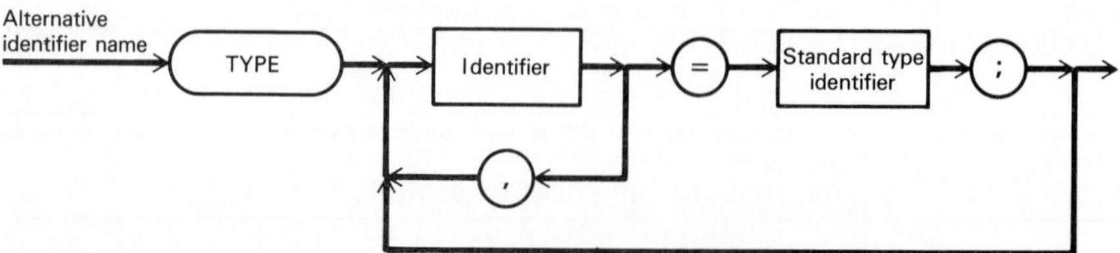

Fig. 20-7 Diagram for an alternative method for defining *new* data types by replacement of names with a standard identifier.

20-7. The syntax described in this figure is used in conjunction with a VAR declaration to define a new data type.

Example 20-6 Alternative Data Typing

A program automatically decodes messages which have been previously coded by simply substituting other letters of the alphabet for each letter of the message. For example, the word "as" becomes "zh" if the coding algorithm consists of reversing the letters of the alphabet (that is, "a," the first letter, becomes a "z," the last letter). In this program a new data type called "coded" is defined using the TYPE declaration diagramed in Fig. 20-7. The variable "codeletter" is defined in a VAR declaration. The important parts of the program are:

```
TYPE
    coded = char;
VAR
    codeletter: coded;
```

In this way "coded" is really a CHAR data type. Therefore, codeletter (in VAR) is of type coded, and it is also a CHAR data type.

Defining data types as described in Example 20-6 can increase the flexibility and readability of programs. Extensions of this method to more complex situations will be described later in the chapter.

PROBLEMS FOR SECTION 20-3-3*b*

1. The days of the week and the months of the year may be treated in numerical form (as integers) in certain Pascal programs. The variables "birthday" and "birthmonth" will be defined using a VAR declaration. Write a TYPE declaration and a VAR declaration which will work for these definitions. Use "weekday" and "month" for the identifiers in the TYPE declaration.

c. User-Defined Scalar Subrange Types

In Pascal, it is possible to create a new data type as a subsequence of any scalar type (except REAL) which has already been defined. This is called a *scalar subrange* data type and is a third method for creating new types of data.

Example 20-7 A Scalar Subrange Type

A program keeps track of the line voltages at various points of a factory. These voltages must remain between 100 and 120 volts. To simplify the program, a new type of data can be created which is a subset of the INTEGER type, and includes all integers (voltages) between 100 and 120 volts. To do so, use the following declaration:

```
TYPE
voltageinrange = 100..120;
```

The declaration is interpreted or read as follows:

> voltageinrange is a user-defined data type which can take integer values between 100 and 120.

Notice the use of the reserved symbol ". ." in this example.

The general method for creating scalar subrange data types is shown in Fig. 20-8.

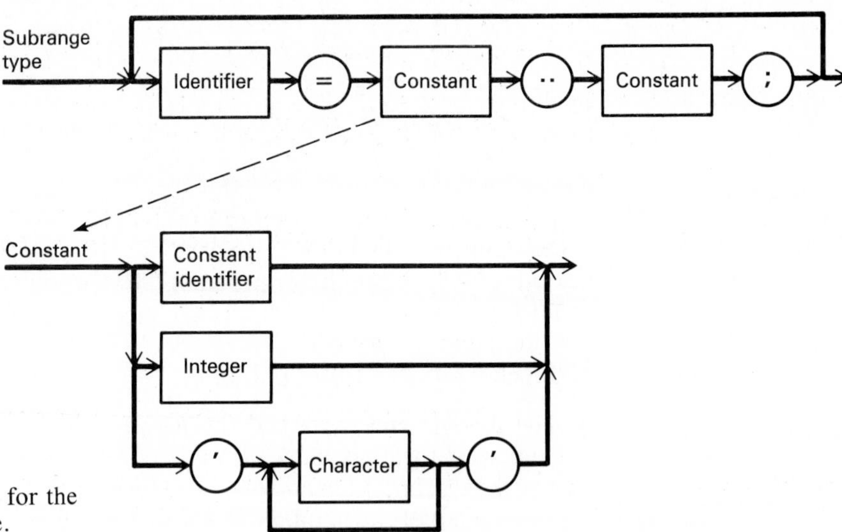

Fig. 20-8 Syntax diagram for the scalar subrange data type.

Example 20-8 More Scalar Subrange Examples

Here are additional scalar subrange definitions:

```
TYPE
lorange = 1..5;
hirange = 5..10;
letter = 'A'..'Z';
digit = '0'..'9';
```

PROBLEMS FOR SECTION 20-3-3*c*

1. Give five examples of a subrange type.
2. Find the errors in the following subrange declarations.

```
TYPE
scale = 10..1;
empty = 1..;
```

d. User-Defined Data Types Using a VAR Declaration

New data types may also be created using a VAR declaration. Figure 20-9 contains the syntax diagrams for defining enumerated or subrange scalar data types. This is a shorthand form which can be used in place of the TYPE-VAR method.

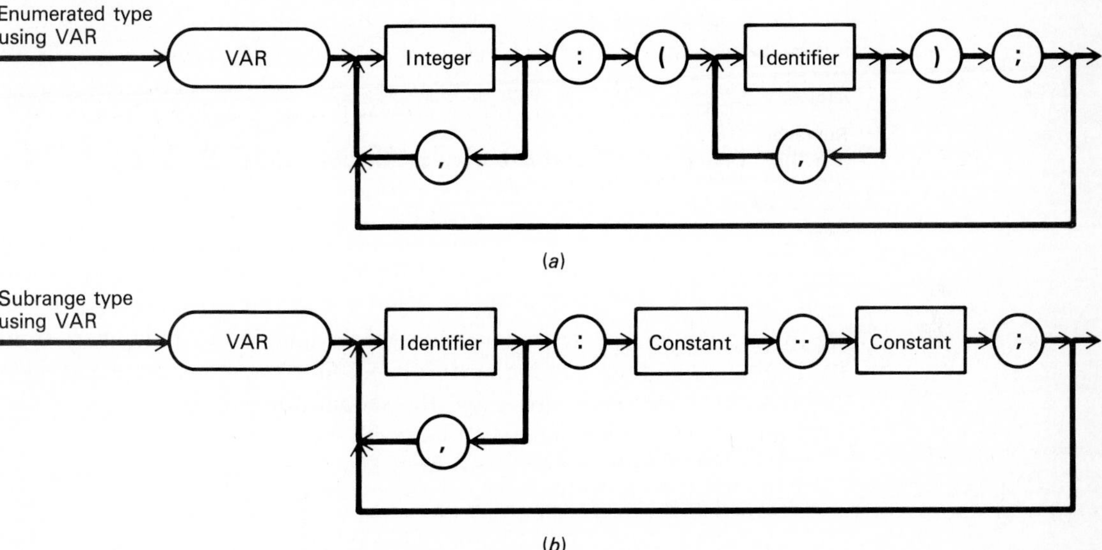

Fig. 20-9 Syntax diagrams showing how to create new data types using a VAR declaration. (*a*) Enumerated types. (*b*) Subrange types.

Example 20-9 Using the VAR Declaration to Create New Data Types

A computer is used to sort resistors using a color code. The colors of the code are going to be defined as a new type of data, and a VAR declaration will be used for this purpose.

```
VAR
colorcode: (black, brown, red, orange, yellow, green,
            blue, violet, gray, white);
```

This could also have been defined in an alternate manner using:

```
TYPE
colorcode= (black, brown, red, orange, yellow, green,
            blue, violet, gray, white);
```

and followed with a VAR declaration:

```
VAR
   bodycolor: colorcode;
   firstband: colorcode;
   secondband: colorcode;
   .
   .
   .
   tolerancecolor: colorcode;
```

(To define "bodycolor," "firstband," "secondband," etc. in a VAR declaration would require repetition of the enumerated list for each variable in the list.)

Example 20-10 Another Case of the VAR Declaration to Create a New Data Type

Subrange types can also be created using a VAR declaration. An electronic instrument contains two circuit boards. The first board, as well as the second board, has 100 wires. Wires identified with numbers from 1 to 100 are to be found on the first board, and wires identified with numbers from 101 to 200 are on the second board. It is possible to create two data types, one type for wires on board 1 and the second for wires on board 2. The VAR declaration which achieves this result is:

```
VAR
board1wire: 1..100;
board2wire: 101..200;
```

PROBLEMS FOR SECTION 20-3-3*d*

1. Use a VAR declaration to define the data types created in Example 20-8.

2. Is there anything wrong with the following?

```
TYPE
   week = (mon, tu, wed, th, fri, sat, sun);
VAR
   weekend: sat..sun;
```

3. Write a VAR declaration which defines a new data type. The identifier to be used is called "bignumber," and the corresponding data type can

take values from 1000 up to the largest integer which the computer can store.

4. (a) What is wrong with the following?

```
VAR
    COUNTS: 1..10;
    index: counts;
```

   (b) Use a TYPE declaration in conjunction with a VAR declaration to correct the error.

20-4 STRUCTURED DATA

The simple data types described in the preceding sections can be combined into larger units. These larger units are called *structured* types. They include *arrays, sets, records,* and *files*. Each of these will be discussed in the sections which follow.

20-4-1 Arrays

An *array* is a collection of data in which each element is the same type. It can be a collection of integer data, real data, boolean data, character data, or user-defined data elements. An *index* is used to access (read or write) the data within the array. All elements of the array are identified by a single name or identifier. To examine a given array element, use the name and the corresponding index number of the particular data item. To address the second data element of the array use the expression

```
arrayname[2]
```

in which "arrayname" is the name of the entire array.

The computer must be told how many data items the array will contain prior to the first instructions, i.e., at the beginning of the program block. In addition, the computer must know the type of data to expect within the array. This information appears in one of the data declarations of the program, and Fig. 20-10 includes the syntax for the ARRAY data type. The type of array described in this figure is called a *one-dimensional array*. One-dimensional arrays include a *single list,* or column, of data elements. Example 20-11 provides an instance in which the array declaration syntax is used.

Example 20-11 Declaring a One-Dimensional Array: Method 1

A list, or array, of characters is used to keep track of an error message. Such a message might be sent to a user when the computer detects the occurrence of an error. (The same idea can be used to store other types

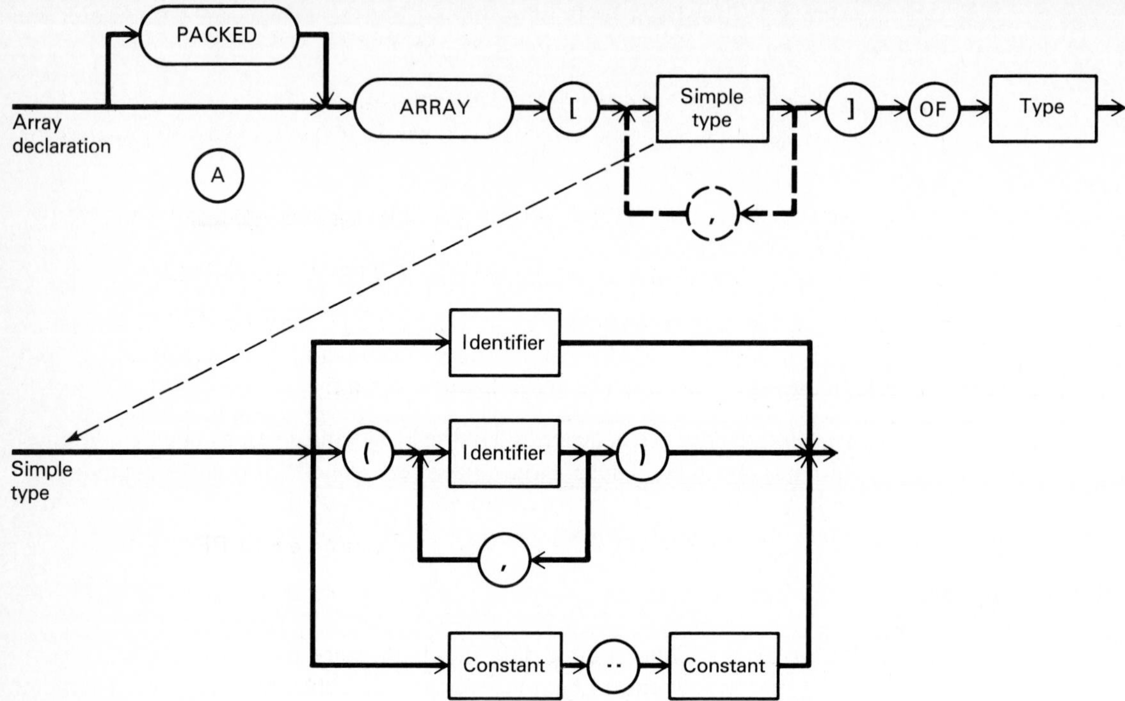

Fig. 20-10 Array syntax, one dimension.

of messages.) This array can be declared using a VAR declaration. One such declaration might have the following form:

```
VAR
    msgbuffer: ARRAY[1..32] OF CHAR;
```

The above statement means that a variable array named "msgbuffer" will contain 32 data items. Each of these will be a character data type. The syntax for the array follows the outline of Fig. 20-10. In particular, it follows the path identified by "A." An alternative way to declare such an array is:

```
CONST
    noofcharacters = 32;
VAR
    msgbuffer: ARRAY[1..noofcharacters] OF CHAR;
```

Using the identifier "noofcharacters" throughout a program makes it easier to read. If it is necessary to change the value associated with this parameter from 32 to, say, 64, using the method shown above reduces the required number of physical changes to the program source. Only one line needs to be changed, as indicated by:

```
CONST
    noofcharacters = 64;
```

Had the number 32 been used throughout the program, each of these locations would have had to be changed. In such cases errors may be accidentally introduced.

Example 20-12 Declaring a One-Dimensional Array: Method 2

The one-dimensional array of Example 20-11 may be declared using a combination of a TYPE and a VAR statement. It is equivalent to the previous method and has the following syntax:

```
CONST
    noofcharacters = 32;
TYPE
    msg = ARRAY[1..noofcharacters] OF CHAR;
VAR
    msgbuffer: msg;
```

Advantages of this method include the following:

- The new user-defined data type called "msg" may be used for any other variable which is an array consisting of 32 characters. For example, this simplifies the case where there are several different messages to be manipulated by the program:

```
VAR
    msg1: msg;
    msg2: msg;
    msg3: msg;
```

or the more concise version of this:

```
VAR
    msg1, msg2, msg3: msg;
```

- By using

```
CONST
    noofcharacters = 32;
```

all instances of the identifier "noofcharacters" can be easily changed if the program needs to be modified in this regard. Only one line of the program must be changed to affect all instances of this identifier.

Notice the word PACKED in Fig. 20-10. Up to now it has not been used in any of the Pascal statements which have been used as examples. This keyword can be used to advantage in those instances where the computer is able to store more than one item of data per storage location in the memory. For example, it may be possible to store two character data items for each location in a computer's memory. If the word PACKED is used in the array declaration, the machine will automatically store as much data as it can in each memory location—it *packs* the memory. Each data element therefore occupies a minimum of storage space, but this is accomplished at the expense of speed of operation of the program. Whenever an array element is accessed, it requires more time to do so when the data is packed than would otherwise be the case. In Examples 20-11 and 20-12 the syntax for the array could have been

```
PACKED ARRAY[1..noofcharacters] OF CHAR;
```

PROBLEMS FOR SECTION 20-4-1

1. Consider Examples 20-11 and 20-12 and assume that the array msgbuffer contains the data

   ```
   "This is a sample message. ________"
   ```

   where "_" = a space or blank. What is the data in each of the following locations: msgbuffer[1], msgbuffer[5], msgbuffer [10], msgbuffer[15], msgbuffer[20], msgbuffer[25], msgbuffer[30], and msgbuffer[35]?

2. What two pieces of information are required for each array in a program?

3. Using two different methods, write declarations needed to specify a one-dimensional array of integers. Provide space for 100 integers and use any convenient identifier.

4. Use a TYPE and a VAR declaration to specify an array which can store test results coming from digital voltmeter readings of a series of power supplies manufactured by the XYZ Company. Arrange the answer so that it is easy to change the number of test measurements in the program.

5. Specify an array of switch settings for a series of valves in a chemical processing plant. The switches can be either on or off. There may be as many as 37 such switches.

20-4-2 Multidimensional Arrays

There are occasions when a simple list is inconvenient for the needs of the problem being solved. Suppose, for example, that the computer is being programed to keep track of the voltages in a power transmission system (grid). This record might be required to include the readings from a reporting station (a point in the grid) and the time at which the measurement was taken. Using arrays of the kind considered up to now would require a multiplicity of such arrays. The first array might contain the voltages for all stations at the first measurement time, the second array might contain the voltages for all stations at the second measurement time, etc. Such a structure would reduce the computer's efficiency, as it would require considerable memory space and would slow operation during execution. A more efficient arrangement would use a single array with a *matrix,* or grid, configuration. An array organized in this way would require less memory and would operate faster than a system containing multiple one-dimensional arrays.

Example 20-13 Specifying a Two-Dimensional Array in Pascal

The measurement record of the voltages of an electric transmission system can be included in a *two-dimensional array.* The declaration statement for such an array is very similar to the declaration used for one-dimensional arrays. There is, however, a slight change in the syntax. The dotted path in Fig. 20-10 describes this difference. Call the name of the array "voltages." Declaring this array can be accomplished using either of the methods outlined in Sec. 20-4-1. Both methods (for the two-dimensional array) are shown below:

Method 1

```
CONST
   noofstations = 50;
   noofmeasurements = 24;
VAR
   voltages: ARRAY[1..noofstations, 1..noofmeasurements] OF REAL;
```

Method 2

```
CONST
   noofstations = 50;
   noofmeasurements = 24;
TYPE
   grid = ARRAY[1..noofstations, 1..noofmeasurements] OF REAL;
VAR
   voltages: grid;
```

The difference between specification of a two-dimensional array and a one-dimensional array shows up in the information included between the brackets—"[" and "]"—of the declaration statement. Notice, for the two-dimensional array, that the size of each dimension appears within the brackets, separated by a comma. The subrange "1 . . noofstations" specifies the number of rows of the array, and the subrange "1 . . noofmeasurements" specifies the number of columns of the array.

An index is used to access any data element in a two-dimensional array. Accessing the data in the cell which represents the voltage at station 1 at 1 P.M. is achieved using the expression

```
voltages[1, 2]
```

To access a given cell requires two pieces of information: the array identifier (name) and the index, which consists of two numbers. The two numbers of the index specify the row and column of the cell of interest. The number of distinct integers in the index indicates the number of dimensions of the array.

There are a number of instances in which three-dimensional structures are convenient representations of the data. In Example 20-13, 24 hours worth of data is indicated. This could represent one day's information regarding the system. Adding another dimension to the array permits further grouping of the data into multiple days.

Multidimensional arrays can also be packed in a way which is similar to the way one-dimensional arrays are packed. A typical example for such a case is:

```
voltages: PACKED ARRAY[1..50,1..24] OF INTEGER;
```

PROBLEMS FOR SECTION 20-4-2

1. Name five examples in which it is convenient to have a two-dimensional array. Write declarations for each case.
2. Name one example in which a three-dimensional array is useful. Write data declarations for this array, using two different methods.
3. Modify the data declarations of Example 20-13 so that it includes the additional dimension required by daily measurement.
4. Is the following allowed in Pascal?

```
CONST
   n = 10;
TYPE
   index = 1..n;
   matrix = ARRAY[index] OF ARRAY[index] OF REAL;
```

If it is correct, what is the format of the data? Can the matrix be defined in another way?

20-3 Sets

Sets are collections of objects of the same type. In this sense they are similar to arrays. The number of such objects varies from one machine to another, but usually the number is small, perhaps 256. The syntax of the SET type is shown in Fig. 20-11. The object type is referred to as the *base*

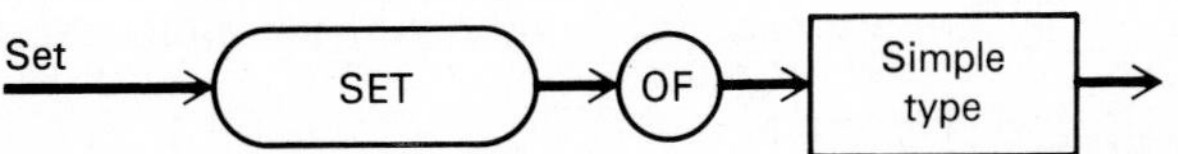

Fig. 20-11 Syntax diagram for the SET type of data structure.

type. The most important features of the set are the operations which can be performed on such data. These operations will be described in the next chapter, but it can be noted here that one of the more useful operations possible is the testing of data for its membership in the set. This is useful for those programs in which an operator may enter a special character that might represent potential commands to the program. All the special characters may be contained in a single set, and as each character is taken into the program, it can be tested for membership in the special set. If it is a member of the special character set, the program can be arranged to perform special operations or carry out appropriate commands.

Example 20-14 Specifying the SET Type

Special characters that can be entered into the computer from its keyboard are to be used to control or command the operation of a program. The special characters are

#, $, %, &, =, +, >, <, /, ↑, @

Control character sequences may be specified as variables, and the following declarations can be used to support this:

```
TYPE
    symbols = ('#', '$', '%', '=', '+', '>', '<', '/', '↑', '@');
    control = SET OF symbols;
VAR
    command1sequence, command2sequence, command3sequence: control;
```

In the program that uses this data structure, command squences will be encountered. These will be sets of symbols that can include any of those enumerated in the symbol list. The variables "command1sequence ···

command3sequence'' are sets and may include any number of symbols from none (0) up to 11. (When a set contains no elements, it is called a *null set.*)

PROBLEMS FOR SECTION 20-4-3

1. A certain set base type can have three values. How many combinations are possible for the corresponding SET type?

20-4-4 Records

Arrays (including multidimensional ones), and sets include data items of the same type. This section introduces a data arrangement which includes a *mixture* of data types. This type of structure is called a *record*. The individual parts of the record are called *fields*.

Record structures are often encountered in the course of developing applications programs. In industry, records are convenient for keeping information about parts which are used in various manufacturing or maintenance tasks. The format for a parts record might look as follows:

Part number
Part description
Serial number
Test data
Date

Such a record may contain different types of data for each subpart, or field. The part number might be a character string (array of characters), the part description might be a string of characters, the serial number might be an integer, and the test data might include real data while the date might contain alphanumeric data.

Pascal allows combinations of different types of data into a single structure called a record. Figure 20-12 presents the syntax for defining a record. In Fig. 26-12*a* the syntax is pictured. An example shows how this diagram is translated into a practical result.

Example 20-15 Declaring a RECORD Type

A program which is used by a company's test department keeps track of all production testing that is performed. Within the program it is convenient to include test data as a record structure. A typical record for such an application could be declared within the program as follows:

```
type testrecord =
RECORD
partname: PACKED ARRAY[1..10] OF CHAR;
```

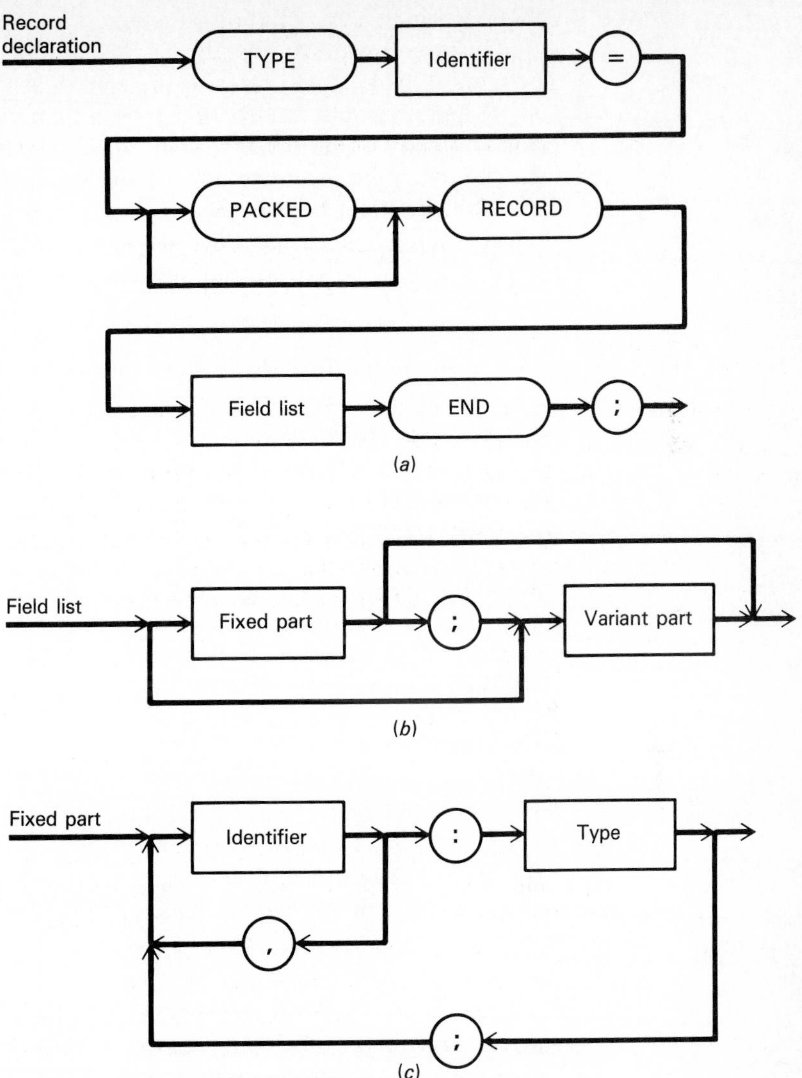

Fig. 20-12 Syntax diagram for defining a record. (*a*) General form. (*b*) Syntax for the field list. (*c*) Syntax for the fixed part of a record.

```
serialno: PACKED ARRAY[1..10] OF CHAR;
outtest: REAL;
load: INTEGER;
ripple: REAL;
date: INTEGER
END;
```

In this example, "partname" might refer to one of the many models of voltage or constant-current power supplies manufactured by the company. The field "serialno" would be its serial number; "outtest" is a test measurement which is the reading on either a voltmeter or an ammeter. These latter tests are made to ensure that the product meets its specifications. The name "load" could refer to the electrical load on the product under test, "ripple" would correspond to a measurement which indicates the error or quality of the product, and "date" would have its obvious meaning. The date field is shown as an INTEGER data type; a sample format for such data might be 090188, which stands for September 1, 1988.

Once such a record has been defined, variables with a corresponding format may now be introduced into the program. For example,

```
VAR
    voltsupply, currentsupply: testrecord;
```

defines two variables, namely, "voltsupply" and "currentsupply," both of which are RECORD variables. That is, the structure of these variables is determined by the "testrecord" declaration.

Both the diagram in Fig. 20-12*a* and Example 26-15 emphasize the general nature of a record. The definition of a RECORD type includes an identifier, followed by an equals sign (=). This in turn is followed by a list of all the different types of data included in the record. The list is terminated with the keyword END. A summary definition of a RECORD type is

```
identifier = RECORD field list END
```

To make a record useful, it will be necessary to be able to refer to any one of the items in the record. This is accomplished by accessing the item as follows:

```
record name.field identifier
```

Example 20-16 Referencing Parts of a Record

In Example 20-15 the record variables voltsupply and currentsupply were introduced; these are the names of the records whose format is given by testrecord. To refer to any part of these records the syntax shown above is used. The following list describes the phrases that could be used to access any field of the records voltsupply or currentsupply:

voltsupply.partname	currentsupply.partname
voltsupply.serialno	currentsupply.serialno
voltsupply.outtest	currentsupply.outtest
voltsupply.load	currentsupply.load
voltsupply.ripple	currentsupply.ripple
voltsupply.date	currentsupply.date

It is sometimes tedious to have to constantly write the record name when referring to the field elements. Pascal has a shorthand utility which can be used to avoid this. Pascal programs may include the keyword WITH, and when this is encountered, the record name is automatically appended to the field identifiers.

Example 20-17 An Introduction to WITH

In the Pascal program briefly described in Examples 20-15 and 20-16, the following fragment appears:

```
WITH voltsupply DO
BEGIN
partname...<the remainder of the Pascal statement>
serialno...
outtest...
load...
ripple...
date...
END;
```

An important element of the fragment is the presence of the phrase "WITH voltsupply." This causes the identifier voltsupply to be associated with each of the field identifiers between the keywords BEGIN and END; voltsupply is automatically added to such identifiers, and thus partname is translated as "voltsupply.partname." The same is true for all other field identifier references in the fragment.

Notice the syntax for the record field list in Fig. 20-12*b*. It includes two parts, with the first part called the *fixed part* and the second part called the *variant part*. The syntax for the fixed part is detailed in Fig. 20-12*c*; however, there is no syntax diagram for the variant part. The introduction of a variant portion of the field list creates the possibility for greater flexibility in the definition of a record. There are cases in which it is convenient to be able to define a record with a fixed portion and several variable parts. The idea behind this is sketched in Fig. 20-13. The total

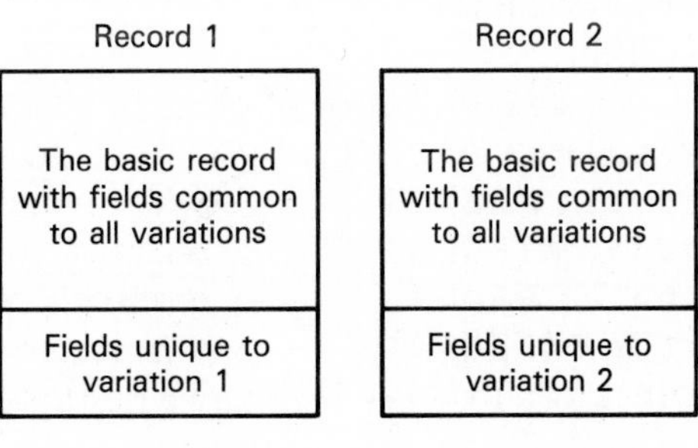

Fig. 20-13 Records can be made up of a set of fixed, or common, fields and additional fields which are unique to a given record.

record in this instance is called a *variant record*. The syntax for the field list of the variant portion of such records is diagramed in Fig. 20-14. The next example provides a practical application for a variant record.

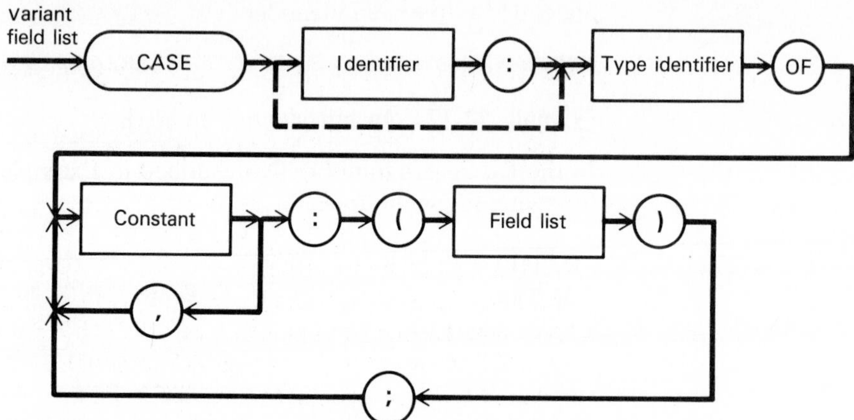

Fig. 20-14 Syntax diagram for the variant portion of a variant record.

Example 20-18 A Case of Variable Records

The product test measurements outlined in Example 20-15 must be subdivided into categories because the company manufactures two kinds of power supplies, low-voltage and high-voltage variants. For the high-voltage units an additional test (above those for the low-voltage group) is required. This is the high-voltage breakdown test. The unit either passes or fails this test, producing boolean results. In addition, the company manufactures two kinds of current supplies. One is a low-current model and the second is a high-current model. For the high-current supply a test must be performed to assure customers that a minimum electrical load can be supplied. The definition of the record to accommodate these variations is shown below:

```
TYPE
categories = (lowv, hiv, lowi, hii);

testrecord =
RECORD
partname: PACKED ARRAY[1..10] OF CHAR;
serialno: PACKED ARRAY[1..10] OF CHAR;
outtest: REAL;
load: INTEGER;
ripple: REAL;
date: INTEGER;
CASE supplytype: categories OF
```

```
lowv: ();
hiv: (breakdown: BOOLEAN;)
lowi: ();
hii: (compliance: REAL;)
END;
```

Several facts are important with regard to this variant definition:

- A user-defined data type called "categories" has been defined. It is an enumerated type (see Sec. 20-3-3*a*) which defines four elements: "lowv," "hiv," "lowi," and "hii." These correspond to the four kinds of power supplies, namely, low voltage, high voltage, low current, and high current. The variable supplytype can have one of the values of the data type categories. The keyword CASE signifies this fact.
- The RECORD is a variant form. The fixed portion of the field list includes "partname," "serialno," "outtest," "load," "ripple," and "date." In addition, there are four variants of this record, which are described by the four identifiers following the phrase "CASE ⋯." The first (lowv) is followed by the symbol "( )," which signifies that nothing is added to the record for the low-voltage case. For hiv (the high-voltage case) the record has one more field in addition to those of the fixed portion. This is specified by the identifier "breakdown," a boolean variable which takes true or false values that depend on passing or failing the voltage breakdown test. Lowi does not require additional fields, while hii adds compliance to the fixed field types. This latter field is to contain real data.
- The special field following the word CASE ("supplytype") is called the *tag field*. The value of the tag field (i.e., either lowv, hiv, lowi, or hii) determines which fields of the record are valid.

Additional variables with structures like those of the variant record type (testrecord) may be declared. One such example is:

```
VAR
    voltsupply, currentsupply: testrecord;
```

It is now possible to refer to the voltage breakdown test field as

```
voltsupply.breakdown
```

However, a note of caution is in order. In order to access this field (voltsupply.breakdown), the variable supplytype must have as its value hiv at the time that the above reference is used. It cannot be equal to lowv at the time and place in the program where voltsupply.breakdown appears. Whenever the data type categories assumes the value lowv, the breakdown field does not exist.

PROBLEMS FOR SECTION 20-4-4

1. Refer to Example 20-15. One of the fields in the record is identified by "outtest." Why is "output" *not* a good choice for this identifier?

2. What is a record?

3. One company uses a wire list program to keep track of the wiring connections in its various products. Each wire is to contain the following information:

   Name of the wire—a string of 16 alphanumeric characters
   Source—a string of 10 alphanumeric characters
   Destination—a string of 10 alphanumeric characters
   Wire size—an integer
   Length—a real number

   Define a RECORD that can be used to declare a data structure incorporating the wiring information.

4. Standard versions of Pascal have no provisions for a complex number data type. Complex numbers have a real part and an imaginary part. An example of such a number is $1.0 + j2.5$, in which the letter j identifies the imaginary portion of the number.

   To circumvent this limitation, declare a RECORD called "complex" which includes two fields, one corresponding to the real part of the complex number and the second corresponding to the imaginary portion of the complex number. Next, declare two variables, "complex1" and "complex2," which are both complex number types.

5. Create a variant RECORD type whose identifier is "partslist." The common fields are as follows:

   Resistors—an array of 200 integers
   Capacitors—an array of 200 integers
   Transistors—an array of 60 characters

   There are to be two options related to the parts list. The first contains no additional fields, and the second option is to include a parts list with the added "diodes" field as follows:

   Diodes—an array of 60 characters

20-4-5 Files

A *file* is a collection of data. The data is given a name which refers to the entire collection. Recall (see Chap. 8) that there are two kinds of files, sequential-access (SA) files and direct-access (DA) files. In standard versions of Pascal, all files are considered SA. That is, data to the file is accessed (read or written) one element at a time, in order. Some versions of Pascal, such as UCSD Pascal, include a provision for DA files. Because DA files are not available on all machines, they will not be described here. Files will be discussed in greater detail in Chap. 23. In this chapter, files will be described as just another data type.

Associated with a FILE data type are certain operations which can be performed. At this point the reading and writing operations will be described. Later, more file operations will be added.

Files may consist of *characters, arrays,* or *records*. They are *delimited,* or terminated, by a special mark called an *end-of-file (EOF) marker.* One syntax which is used to declare a file is shown in Fig. 20-15. It is important to note that files may be declared as variables in order to use them in a program.

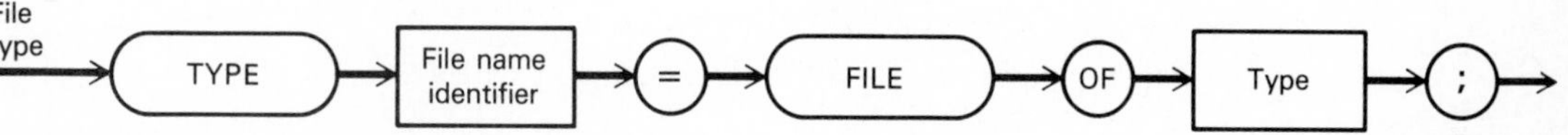

Fig. 20-15 Syntax diagram for declaring a file.

Example 20-19 Declaring a File, Method 1

A FILE type can be declared by following the syntax diagram of Fig. 20-15. In order to keep records in a power generating station, the readings of all meters are kept in a file. These meter readings are taken periodically, and a file of such readings can be declared as follows:

```
TYPE
    datfile = FILE OF REAL;
VAR
    meterreadings: datfile;
```

The type of elements within the file can include any legal type. A FILE OF INTEGER and a FILE OF CHAR are permitted. While a FILE OF FILE is perfectly legal, it is often not permitted in many compilers. It will therefore be avoided in this text.

Example 20-20 Defining a File, Method 2

As with other data types, files may be defined within a VAR declaration. For the meter readings file of Example 20-19, the following will also declare the appropriate file:

```
VAR
    meterreadings: FILE OF REAL;
```

A special instance of the file structure occurs when the file contains characters. This occurs frequently in the writing of computer programs.

Example 20-21 A Special Case of Files

A Pascal program helps to create the source code for other HLL programs—it is in the form of an *editing* program. The results (the source code statements) are to be kept in a file. This file can be declared as follows:

```
TYPE
    datfile = FILE OF CHAR;
VAR
    progtext: datfile;
```

In Pascal, a standard type called *TEXT* is provided for FILE OF CHAR. Therefore, it is possible to declare the source code results as

```
VAR
    progtext: TEXT;
```

This could also be defined as follows:

```
TYPE
    info = TEXT;
VAR
    progtext: info;
```

PROBLEMS FOR SECTION 20-4-5

1. Define the term "file."
2. List as many types of data as possible that can appear in a file.
3. What is the last element of a file?
4. Write all the declarations needed to define a file which contains records of the type found in Example 20-15.
5. Define a file of text which is to contain alphanumeric characters. This file will store part numbers and descriptions for one of the products manufactured by the XYZ Company.
6. What is lacking in the following definition?

```
TYPE
    switches = FILE OF BOOLEAN;
```

   Add a VAR declaration in order to be able to use the file (switches) in a program.

7. Describe the files defined by the following declarations:

```
CONST
   count = 100;
TYPE
   messages = PACKED ARRAY[1..count] OF CHAR;
VAR
   mail, greeting: FILE OF messages;
```

20-5 POINTERS

A file is a type of data structure that varies during execution of a program. It can get longer, for example, while other data structures have fixed lengths (i.e., INTEGER, REAL, ARRAY, RECORD). It is sometimes useful to have a data structure which is variable to make it possible for the number of data elements to change during the course of execution of the program. For example, wires may have to be added or deleted from a wiring list. It is convenient to be able to add or remove data from anywhere in the list. Figure 20-16 shows a picture of various kinds of lists. Each box

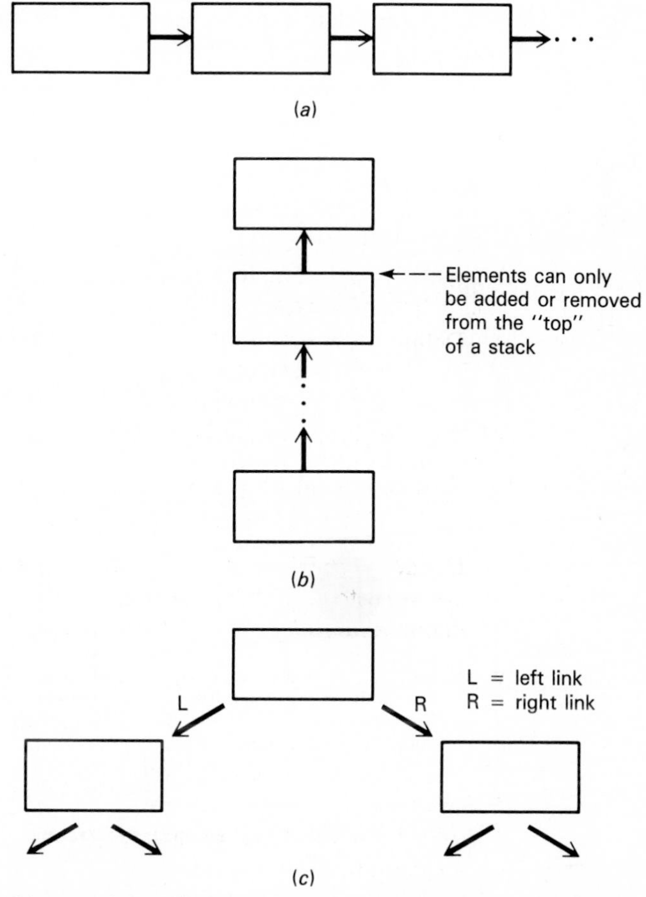

Fig. 20-16 Picture of data lists. (*a*) A singly linked list. (*b*) A stack. (*c*) A tree.

is a data element in the list, and all data elements are alike (i.e., REAL, INTEGER, ARRAY, RECORD). Such lists are actually groups of locations in the computer memory, and the arrows in the figure show how one group is logically connected to the next.

In order to build such lists, a new type of data element is required. This type is called a *pointer,* and it is a simple type (such as an integer). The syntax for a pointer definition is shown in Fig. 20-17.

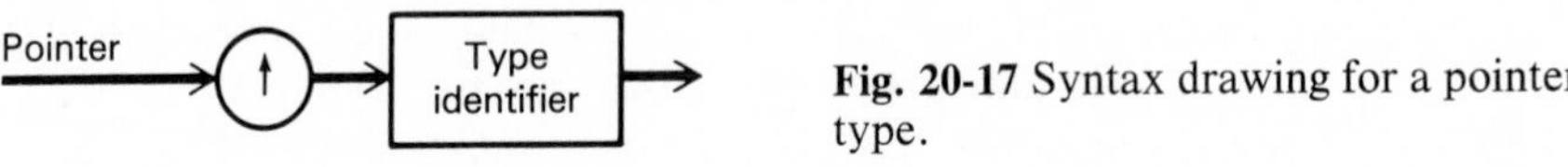

Fig. 20-17 Syntax drawing for a pointer type.

Example 20-22 Declaring Pointer Types

The name "pointer" is not a standard identifier. Notice that it is not found on the list of standard identifiers discussed in Sec. 20-1-2*b* (see also Fig. 20-2). To declare a pointer, use the following example as a guide:

```
TYPE
   listpointer = ↑listdata;
```

The symbol "↑" is a reminder that "listpointer" is a pointer data type. A pointer is really an *address* which is associated with one of the elements or data of the type defined by "listdata."

Pointers are used to build lists of the kind shown in Fig. 20-16. Lists will not be discussed in detail, as their application is beyond the scope of this text. However, they have been introduced because they are likely to be seen in a variety of Pascal programs. To further explain the idea of a pointer, note the following distinction. If "p" is a pointer, then p is the number (address) which is the value of the pointer, and p↑ is the value of the data found at the address specified by p. This is an important difference, and Fig. 20-18 is a sketch of the meaning of p and p↑ .

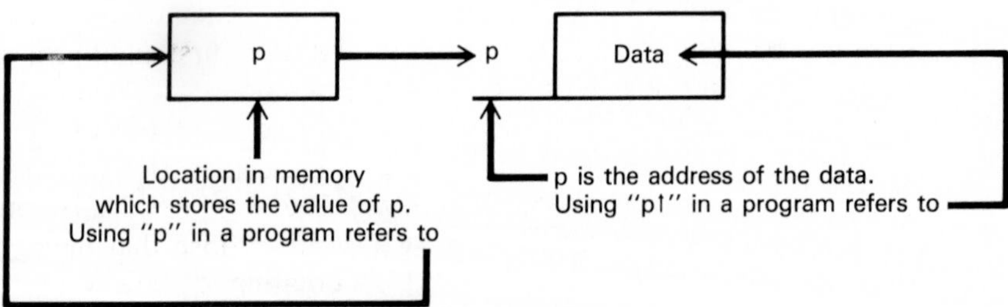

Fig. 20-18 A guide to the meaning of "p" and "p↑ ."

PROBLEMS FOR SECTION 20-5

1. Is there anything wrong with the following?

```
TYPE
pointer = ↑listelement;
listelement =
RECORD
nextelement: pointer;
elementdata: INTEGER;
END;
```

(The answer to this question contains important information about the way in which a Pascal program is to be written.)

2. Given the information in Fig. 20-19 what is the value of p and P↑ ?

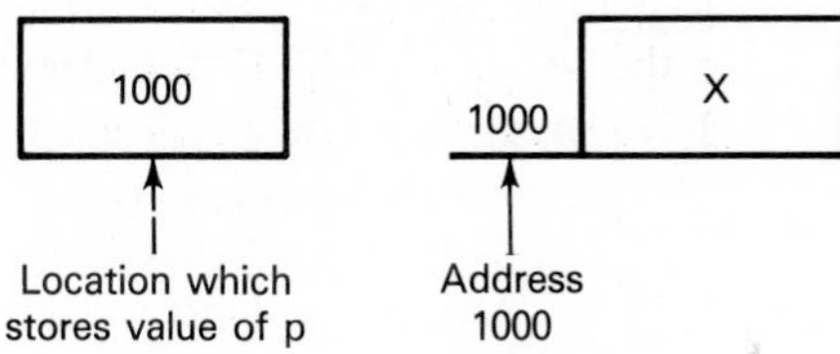

Fig. 20-19 Diagram for Prob. 2.

SUMMARY

Pascal is rich in the variety of types of data that it can use. The data can be considered to be objects. Each data element has two parts: the first is an identifier or name and the second is the type of data.

Letters and numbers may be used to create a name for the identifier, but the name must start with a letter. Otherwise, there are few restrictions on naming identifiers. It is a good idea to make sure that identifiers differ by at least one character within the first eight positions. Some installations recognize only the first eight characters when translating source code.

Some identifiers are considered to be standard and have special purposes or functions. Here again, it is a good idea not to use such standard identifiers for user-defined names because this can lead to subtle errors. Reserve words and symbols, or those that have special meanings, must not be used when you are creating identifiers.

Some types of data are considered simple and are sometimes called scaler data types. Scalar types consist of distinct, ordered values; that is, if P and Q are values of the scalar type, then $P > Q$, $P = Q$, or $P < Q$. Scalar types include the following:

INTEGER: Numbers (negative and positive) without decimal points
REAL: Numbers (negative and positive) which have a decimal point; they may be written in scientific notation (i.e., −2.OE-04 for the number −0.0002)
BOOLEAN: Data with one of two values, true or false (false < true)
CHAR: Includes alphanumeric characters, often those found in the ASCII set of symbols

In order to inform the computer of the data being used, data must be declared in the program. This is done using one or more declarations: CONST, VAR, or TYPE. The CONST construction provides a type to the data in an implicit way. Data defined using a CONST declaration does not change during the course of the program. VAR declarations are used to define data that changes or varies as the program is executed. The TYPE declaration can be used for two purposes: to use a new name for an existing data type, or to define a completely new type of data. This last capability is particularly powerful and important. It is usually carried out by enumeration, in which all possible values of the new data type are listed in order, starting with the smallest identified value and proceeding to the largest identified value. The data list can also be compiled using a shorthand notation called a subrange.

The simple data types can be combined into more complex arrangements called structured types. The ARRAY is a group of data of the same type where a single identifier refers to the entire structure. An index associated with the identifier is used to access one of the data elements. More than one index may be needed to exactly access the data in the array. If two indices are used, the array is said to be two-dimensional. The number of indices specifies the number of dimensions.

Sets are collections of objects of the same type. The type is called the base type. The number of objects in the set varies from one installation to another. The base type is limited to scalar types (not structured types). Sets are useful for certain kinds of operations (these will be discussed in the next chapter).

The RECORD type is available in order to combine objects of different types into a single data structure. The record is composed of fields. To access a component of a record, use a general phrase such as

```
record identifier.field identifier
```

In some circumstances the presence of the keyword WITH will cause the record identifier to be attached to the field identifier. Variations (or variants) of a record are possible. A series of tag fields associated with the keyword CASE allows records to consist of a set of common fields and a set of unique variations.

Files are also collections of data of the same type. These can only be accessed in strict sequence. These files are referred to as sequential-access, or SA, files. They are often associated with secondary storage systems such as disks or cassettes. File types should be declared in a VAR statement. When the file consists of the CHAR data type, it is called a text file. Because this type of file is used frequently, it has a special designation (or standard type), namely, a TEXT type. The TEXT designation is shorthand for FILE OF CHAR.

Finally, the pointer data type is a variable which is the address of another variable. Since the address of a variable is usually its name, a pointer value can be considered the name of a variable. It is often used to build even more complex data structures called lists. (Pointers will be used to describe various operations which are possible on files.)

REVIEW PROBLEMS

1. Make up names for five different identifiers. Include some with letters and some with numbers.

2. What is wrong, if anything, with the following user-defined Pascal identifiers?

   doit
   1chance
   first-pass
   eoln

3. Using the categories of user-defined, standard identifiers, and reserved objects, classify each of the following:

   DOWNTO
   DOWNTOEARTH
   ABS
   BOOLEAN
   [
   :=
   &
   COS
   LABEL

4. Give five examples of INTEGER data.

5. Give five examples of REAL data. Use decimal and scientific forms for each. Include negative and positive numbers.

6. Is there anything wrong with the following real numbers?

   −.321
   1.OE1
   12.3

7. Is there anything wrong with the following integers?

   12152
   −2.1
   3,122

8. Give three examples of CHAR data.

9. Is there anything wrong with the following?

```
CONST
    endpoint = lastvalue;
    lastvalue = 100;
```

10. Given the fragment show below, specify the names and types of all the data one can expect to find in the program.

```
VAR
    one, two, three, four, five: INTEGER;
    servo, error: REAL;
    msg1, msg2: CHAR;
```

11. Define a new data type. The data values are to be "red," "green," and "blue." These are the colors associated with a television receiver. Call the data type "guncolor." The ordering is not important.

12. Using a TYPE declaration, define a new data type which can take integer values from 1 to 100. Call this data "testresults."

13. (a) Using a VAR declaration, define a two-dimensional array of integers. The array is to be a 3 by 5 structure. Call the array "matrix." (b) Write the term needed to access the element in row 2, column 4.

14. What is the base type of the set defined by:

```
TYPE
    scalefactors = (1, 2, 4, 8, 16, 32);
    gain = SET OF scalefactors;
```

15. Write all the declarations needed to define a record. The record should consist of the following fields:

   datefield—an alphanumeric string of six characters
   stationno—an integer field
   temperature—a real number field
   pressure—a real number field

   Give the record any convenient name.

16. Declare a file which is to consist of the records defined in Prob. 15.

REVIEW QUESTIONS

1. What are identifiers?
2. Define the term ''scalar data.''
3. Name all the types of scalar data found in Pascal.
4. What does the standard identifier MAXINT mean?
5. What two values can BOOLEAN data have?
6. State the difference between the integer 1 and the character ''1.''
7. What is a common ordering for alphabetic and numeric characters?
8. What does the term ''structured data'' mean?
9. What does the term PACKED ARRAY mean?

21 OPERATIONS AND CONTROL

The preceding chapter included the important types of data used in Pascal. Certain operations can be performed on each of the data types which have been discussed. In this chapter the types of operations allowed for each data type will be described.

In addition to common operations (addition, subtraction, etc.), Pascal includes some operations which are more complex. One example of such an operation is computing the square root of a real (or integer) quantity. Such operations are called *functions,* and Pascal supports a number of such functions. These functions will also be discussed.

One of the most important operations is called *assignment*. After making a calculation, the computer can be instructed to *assign* the result to another object or variable. Such a variable is usually one which has been declared previously, as described in the preceding chapter.

Two important elements are associated with an HLL: the particular instructions that are to be performed and the sequence or order in which such commands are to be carried out. The assignment statement is the chief mechanism for indicating *which* instruction is to be executed. A number of control statements are used to determine which of the calculations in a given program are to be performed and the *order* in which they are to be executed. Control of the sequence of operations will also be described in this chapter.

21-1 OPERATIONS AND CALCULATIONS

A calculation can be decomposed into its component parts. An *expression* is a combination of *simple expressions*. Terms are themselves combinations of *factors,* and the latter are either *constants, variables* that have been declared, or *expressions within a set of parentheses*. This implies that the definition of an expression can be *recursive;* that is, the definition of an expression can include itself.

Example 21-1 Analyzing an Expression

The algebraic expression

$$xy + \frac{p}{q}$$

may be broken down into terms, factors, and variables; the result is shown in Fig. 21-1.

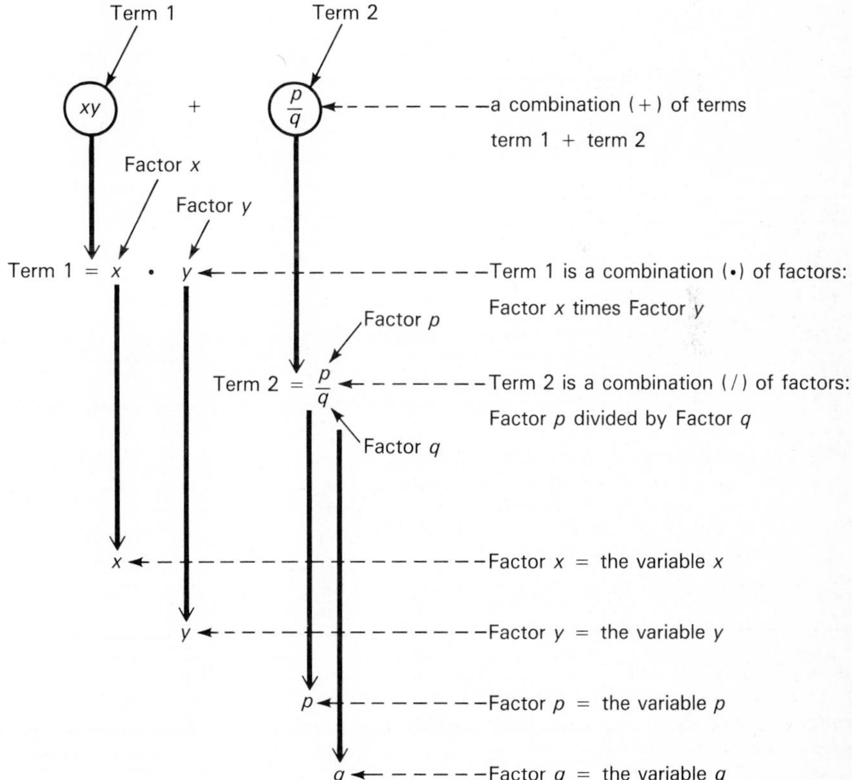

Fig. 21-1 Analysis of an expression.

21-1-1 Integer Operations

Table 21-1 shows the operators that can be used for integer data. Notice that there are two kinds of operations. One group is the *arithmetic* operations and includes the common operations addition, subtraction, multiplication, and division. The second group includes *relational* operations. Such operations may be used to *compare* two integers, including the values taken by integer variables. A good way to interpret such operations is in the form of a question which depends on the comparison being made (e.g., Is the first integer greater than the second integer?).

TABLE 21-1 INTEGER OPERATIONS

Operator or Operation	Symbol	Examples	Notes
Unary plus	+	+5 +intdata	
Unary minus	−	−3 −jones	
Addition	+	5 + 1 index + offset	
Subtraction	−	4 − 7 cost − 60	
Multiplication	*	5 * 8 nooftens * 10	
Division	DIV	5 DIV 2 counts DIV scale	Any remainder is discarded; the answer is truncated
Division	/	5/2 sum/numbertrials	The remainder is retained; the answer is a REAL data type
Modulus	MOD	7 MOD 2	What occurs: 7 is divided by 2. The answer is 3 with a remainder of 1. The result of the operation is the remainder (1) and is retained as an INTEGER data type. An equivalent value of (x MOD y) is x − (x DIV y) * y
Compare two integers for equality	=	first = second	Result is a BOOLEAN data type. If the integer variable "first" is equal to the integer variable "second," the result is true; else the result is false
Compare two integers for inequality	<>	first <> second	Result is BOOLEAN data. If the integer variable first is not equal to the integer variable second, result is true; otherwise result is false
Determine if one integer is less than another integer	<	first < second	Result is BOOLEAN data. If integer variable first is less than integer variable second, result is true; otherwise result is false

TABLE 21-1 *(continued)*

Operator or Operation	Symbol	Examples	Notes
Determine if one integer is less than or equal to another integer	<=	first <= second	Result is BOOLEAN data. If integer variable first is less than or equal to integer variable second, result is true; else result is false
Determine if one integer is greater than another integer	>	first > second	Result is BOOLEAN data. If integer variable first is greater than integer variable second, result is true; else result is false
Determine if one integer is greater than or equal to another integer	>=	first >= second	Result is BOOLEAN data. If integer variable first is greater than or equal to integer variable second, result is true; otherwise result is false
Determine if an integer is a member of a set	IN	intvar IN testset	Result is BOOLEAN data. If ''intvar'' is a member of the set ''testset,'' the result is true; else the result is false

Example 21-2 Some Integer Operations

Shown in the accompanying table are examples of integer operations, the values of the integer variables at the time these calculations are performed, and the results. Study the examples and do not look at the answers. Try to obtain the same results independently.

Integer Operation	Values at Time of Execution	Result
+intvar1	intvar1 = −25	−25
−intvar1	intvar1 = −25	+25
intvar1 + intvar 2	intvar1 = 50 intvar2 = −25	25
intvar1 − intvar2	intvar1 = −100 intvar2 = −50	−50
intvar1 * intvar2	intvar1 = 5 intvar2 = 18	90
intvar1 DIV intvar2	intvar1 = 25 intvar2 = 12	2
intvar1/invar2	intvar1 = 25 intvar2 = −4	−6.25
intvar 1 MOD intvar2	intvar1 = 8 intvar2 = −3	2
intvar1 = intvar2	intvar1 = −10 intvar2 = 10	False

Integer Operation	Values at Time of Execution	Result
intvar1 <> intvar2	intvar1 = −18 intvar2 = 50	True
intvar1 < intvar2	intvar1 = −25 intvar2 = −18	True
intvar1 <= intvar2	intvar1 = 180 intvar2 = 256	True
intvar1 > intvar2	intvar1 = −50 intvar2 = −75	True
intvar1 >= intvar2	intvar1 = −164 intvar2 = 10	False
testint IN testset	testint = 5 testset = (1, 3, 5, 7)	True

a. Advanced Topics in Integer Operations

The operations described above included two integers separated by a single operator. It is possible to write more complex expressions that involve more than one operation. A simple example is

```
intvar1 + intvar2 + intvar3
```

Example 21-3 More Integer Examples

Shown in the accompanying table are integer expressions involving more than one integer operation. Included are the operations to be performed, the value of the integer variables at the time of the execution, and the results. Cover the answer and try to arrive at the same result.

Integer Operation	Values at the Time of Execution	Result
5 + intvar1 − intvar2	intvar1 = −5 intvar2 = −7	7
3 * intvar1 * intvar2	intvar1 = 2 intvar2 = −2	−12
intvar1 DIV intvar2 / 3	intvar1 = 50 intvar2 = 8	2.0 (a REAL data type)

b. Operational Hierarchy

In Example 21-3 operations were performed in the order in which they were encountered.

Example 21-4 A Confusing Case

It is necessary to write a fragment of a Pascal program which carries out the following calculation:

$$\frac{\text{intvar1} + \text{intvar2}}{2} \tag{1}$$

In this example, intvar1 and intvar2 are integer variables. Assuming that the "/" operation is used for division, the following Pascal statement is used to represent the calculation to be performed:

$$\text{intvar1} + \text{intvar2} / 2 \tag{2}$$

Is this correct? If, for example, it was required to calculate

$$\text{intvar1} + \frac{\text{intvar2}}{2} \tag{3}$$

would the Pascal expression cited in Eq. (2) perform the necessary computation? If so, then the same Pascal expression has been used to represent two very different algebraic expressions [Eqs. (2) and (3)]. In order to properly represent (1), parentheses are added to Eq. (2) (intvar1 + intvar2) / 2.

Confusion has been generated as a result of the problem raised in Example 21-4, and in order to avoid such errors, a set of computational rules is needed. These rules are called the *hierarchy of operations*. Table 21-2 lists the hierarchy of operations for INTEGER data types.

TABLE 21-2 HIERARCHY OF INTEGER OPERATIONS

Priority	Operations
1 (highest)	Expressions within parentheses
2	*, /, DIV, MOD
3	+, −
4	=, <, >, <=, >=, <>, IN

Calculations within an expression are carried out from left to right. If expressions are included within parentheses, then these are evaluated ahead of all others (with a left-to-right sequence for all parenthetical expressions). If there are parenthetical expressions enclosed within a set of parentheses, then the innermost parenthetical expression is evaluated first.

Next, perform any of the operations *, /, MOD, or DIV. Again work from left to right. After these, evaluate operations involving + or −. Finally, perform all relational operations (=, <, >, <=, >=, <>, IN).

PROBLEMS FOR SECTION 21-1-1

1. Write Pascal integer expressions for the following algebraic expressions:

   (a) Integer1 + integer2

(b) $1 - x + \frac{x^2}{2} - \frac{x^3}{6}$

(c) $\frac{ab}{3}$

(d) $a + bc$

(e) $\frac{-a + b}{c + d}$

2. Write algebraic expressions for the following Pascal expressions:

   a. g * mass1 * mass2 DIV (radius * radius)
   b. (x − 1) DIV (x + 1)
   c. x − 1 DIV x + 1
   d. a * x + b * y + c + 1
   e. n * (n + 1)/2
   f. (a DIV b − c) * d

3. Given the following facts:

   $$A = 6 \qquad B = -1 \qquad C = 10 \qquad D = 25$$

   Calculate the results of the following Pascal expressions:

   a. 2 + A = 4 * 2
   b. B + C DIV D
   c. D DIV C
   d. D/(A + B)
   e. D * B < B * C
   f. D MOD C
   g. B/C
   h. A * C >= B * D
   i. A * C − C <> C + D

4. Find the errors in the following integer expressions:

   a. −6.2 DIV 6
   b. a * −3
   c. −3(c)
   d. (a < b) + c

5. An array of integers contains 10 elements. Write a Pascal expression which multiplies the first element by the tenth element.

6. Given the following:

```
TYPE testdata
   RECORD =
               date: ARRAY[1..6] OF CHAR;
               number: INTEGER;
               value: REAL;
   END
```

   Write a Pascal expression which adds 1 to the number field.

21-1-2 Real Operations

With two exceptions, the operations shown in Table 21-1 are valid for REAL data types.

- The MOD operation does not apply to REAL data.
- The DIV operation does not apply to REAL data.

The Pascal
expression
3.2 MOD 5.8
is invalid, as is
realvar1 DIV realvar2

where "realvar1" and "realvar2" are REAL data types. In all other respects the operations shown in Table 21-1 apply to real data.

The hierarchy of real operations is the same as the hierarchy of integer operations. Notice, however, that the MOD and DIV operations should not be included.

An important rule to note when using +, −, or * operators is the following: If one of the operands (arguments) is an integer, then the integer is converted to a real number and the calculation is performed, producing a real result.

Example 21-5 Some Real Expressions in Pascal

Shown in the accompanying table are some algebraic expressions and their equivalent real Pascal equivalent forms.

Algebraic Expression	Pascal Form
$b^2 - 4ac$	b * b − 4.0 * a * c
$(a + b)^2$	(a + b) * (a + b)
$x + \frac{1}{4}$	x + 1.0/4.0 or x + 0.25

Example 21-6 A Real Expression Involving Structured Data Elements

A record of acceptance tests for an audio amplifier is included in a Pascal program. Part of this program contains the following:

```
TYPE testresults =
   RECORD
      date: ARRAY[1..6] OF CHAR;
      model: ARRAY[1..10] OF CHAR;
```

```
          out: REAL;
          scalefactor: REAL;
         END;
     VAR
         testrecord: testresults;
```

In order to be able to compare different units, the output (''out'') must be divided by the scale factor which was used at the time of the tests. A Pascal expression which will compute this is

```
testrecord.out/testrecord.scalefactor
```

Example 21-7 An Average Calculation

An array of five real numbers appears in a Pascal program. These may, for example, be temperature readings at five locations on an electronic product. Part of the program includes the following:

```
CONST
    last = 5;
VAR
    temps: ARRAY[1..last] OF REAL;
```

A Pascal expression which computes the average temperature is given by:

```
(temps[1] + temps[2] + temps[3] + temps[4] + temps[5])/5.0
```

PROBLEMS FOR SECTION 21-1-2

1. Write real Pascal expressions for the following algebraic expressions:

a. $x^2 - a^2$

b. $\frac{a^2}{4x^2}$

c. $4k - 6k_1k_2$

d. $\frac{1}{a_2}\left(\frac{r^2}{10}\right)$

e. $x + \frac{y}{z + w}$

2. Write algebraic expressions for the following real Pascal expressions:

a. 4.0 * k − 6.0 * K1 * K2
b. 1.15 * D * R1 * R2/(R1 − R2)
c. x * (x * x − y * y)/(x * x + y * y)
d. (−B + radical)/(2.0 * A)
e. (X + Y + Z)/2.0

3. What is wrong, if anything, with the following real Pascal expressions?

   a. 2.OZ + A
   b. (A + B)C * C
   c. 1.0/−2.0 * A * B
   d. −23.1R + RY
   e. 2.0 * PI * R * R

21-1-3 Boolean Operations

There are a number of operations on other data types which produce boolean results in addition to the comparison operations on integer and real data. Table 21-3 lists the operations which are possible when the data is boolean.

TABLE 21-3 BOOLEAN OPERATIONS IN PASCAL

Operator or Operation	Symbol	Example	Notes (Results Are Always Boolean)
Logical inversion	NOT	NOT first	If "first" is true, result is false. If first is false, result is true
Logical intersection	AND	first AND second	Result is true if "first" and "second" are both true; else result is false
Logical union	OR	first OR second	Result is true if either (or both) first and second is (are) true; else result is false
Compare for equality	=	first = second	Result is true if first and second have same boolean value; else result is false
Compare for inequality	<>	first <> second	Result is true if first and second have different boolean values; else result is false
Comparison (less than)	<	first < second	Result is true if first is false and second is true; otherwise result is false
Comparison (less than or equal)	<=	first <= second	Result is false if first is true and second is false; otherwise result is true
Comparison (greater than)	>	first > second	Result is true if first is true and second is false; otherwise result is false
Comparison (greater than or equal)	>=	first >= second	Result is false if first is false and second is true; otherwise result is true

Boolean data consists of ordered data which can have one of two values: One value is *false,* and this is considered to be smaller than the second value, which is *true*. This accounts for the results which are shown for the relational operators (=, <>, <, <=, >, >=).

It is possible to use the relational operator IN for boolean data. However, the results obtained by the IN operator can always be obtained by one of the others, and since this operator is not widely used, it has been omitted from Table 21-3.

Example 21-8 A Simple Boolean Expression

Boolean expressions are most important when used to perform *logical tests*. Such expressions often form part of a control statement. (Control statements are discussed later in the chapter.) In this example, part of a Pascal program is shown in order to indicate how a boolean expression might arise.

A certain company produces chemicals. Under certain circumstances emergencies arise and must be corrected before serious damage occurs. A computer used to operate such a plant would include in its software a number of checks to detect emergency conditions. Provisions would be needed to respond to such error conditions. The program elements which respond to these events are often referred to as *error escapes*.

In the following program segment two variables are declared:

wastevalve: This is the state of a valve which allows excess chemicals to be safely drained off.

overflosensor: This is an optical indicator which reports the level of certain chemicals in the production vat.

One type of emergency exists when the waste valve is shut (wastevalve = true) and the optical sensor shows a high level of chemical present in the vat (overflosensor = true). Part of the program includes the following:

```
VAR
    wastevalve,overflosensor: BOOLEAN;
```

The boolean expression which tests for the emergency is

```
wastevalve AND overflosensor
```

Evaluation of this expression (the result) depends on conditions at the time it is executed. The possible outcomes are summarized in the accompanying table.

Wastevalve	Overflosensor	Result of AND Operation	Note
True	True	True	Emergency exists.
True	False	False	No emergency.
False	False	False	No emergency, but possible equipment malfunction.
False	True	False	Vat is emptying as fast as possible (this should be signaled as a caution).

Just as with integer and real data, boolean elements can be combined into sequences of simple operations. An example illustrates one possibility for advanced boolean expressions and hierarchy.

Example 21-9 Sequences of Boolean Operations

A computer and its associated software keeps track of a company's resources. In particular, consider a case involving two stamping machines. These machines may be in one of the following categories:

- Out of service (in repair)
- In service and busy
- In service and idle

A boolean expression is needed whose results will alert the user to the availability of a stamping machine. The variables for such an expression could be the following:

mach1busy: machine 1 is in service and busy
mach2busy: machine 2 is in service and busy
mach1out: machine 1 is out of service
mach2out: machine 2 is out of service

One of the two machines is available for service if the following expression is true. To verify this result, be sure to carry out the indicated operations in the correct order (the order is NOT first, AND second, OR last):

```
NOT mach1out AND NOT mach1busy OR NOT mach2out AND NOT mach2busy
```

Example 21-9 clearly shows the need for a specified order, or hierarchy of operations, in which to carry out boolean operations. The hierarchy of operations for boolean expressions is similar to that for integer and real operations. Table 21-4 shows the hierarchy of boolean operations.

TABLE 21-4 HIERARCHY OF BOOLEAN OPERATIONS

Priority	Operations
1 (highest)	Expressions within parentheses
2	NOT
3	AND
4	OR
5	Relational (=, <, >, <=, >=, <>)

PROBLEMS FOR SECTION 21-1-3

1. Write a boolean expression, using Pascal, which satisfies the following table of values:

If First Is	If Second Is	Result Is
(a) False	False	False
(b) False	True	True
(c) True	False	True
(d) True	True	False

   Hint: The expression must be true if either the first or the second is true but not both the first and the second

2. Given the following facts (at the time of execution):

```
A = true    B = false    C = true
```

   Evaluate the result for each expression shown below:

   (a) (A AND (B AND NOT C))
   (b) NOT (A OR (B OR NOT C))
   (c) NOT (A OR B) = NOT A AND NOT B

21-1-4 Character Operations

Characters are scalar in nature. That is, they include an ordered set of elements. Many installations use the following order:

'A' < 'B' < 'C' < 'Z' ··· < 'a' < 'b' < ··· < 'Z',
and '0' < '1' < '2' < ··· < '9'

Given the ordering of the characters, it is possible to define certain operations on character data. These operations are listed in Table 21-5.

Characters are enclosed by single quotation marks (apostrophes) as follows:

'?'   '+'   '–'   'a'   ···

TABLE 21-5 CHARACTER OPERATIONS

Operator or Operation	Symbol	Example: "First," "Second" Are Character Data	Notes
Character or string equality	=	first = second	If first equals second, result is true; otherwise result is false
Character or string inequality	<>	first <> second	If first does not equal second, result is true; otherwise result is false
Character or string comparison (less than)	<	first < second	If first has smaller internal (computer) value than second, result is true; otherwise result is false
Character or string comparison (less than or equal)	<=	first <= second	If first is less than or equal to second, result is true; else result is false
Character or string comparison (greater than)	>	first > second	If first is greater than second, result is true; else result is false
Character or string comparison (greater than or equal)	>=	first>= second	If first is greater than or equal to second, result is true; else result is false

A sequence of characters such as 'ABC' is called a *character string* or simply a *string*. Some data, such as a carriage return or a line feed, is considered to be a *control character*.

Example 21-10 Comparing Characters

Shown in the accompanying table are some character expressions and the results of the operations.

If First Is	And Second Is	And Operation Is	Result Is
'a'	'Z'	<=	False
'A'	'C'	<	True

If First Is	And Second Is	And Operation Is	Result Is
'6'	'1'	<>	True
'2'	'2'	>=	True
'c'	'x'	>	False
'C'	'A'	=	False

Strings are compared character by character until the result of the operation is determined. Since a space (blank) is lower in the ASCII collation sequence than other letters and numbers, strings with fewer characters are considered smaller than their longer counterparts. (This assumes all characters up to the blank are the same.)

PROBLEMS FOR SECTION 21-1-4

1. Compute the results for the following character operations. Assume the computer uses an ASCII code ordering as described in the text.

   a. '=' <= '?'
   b. '%' >= '*'
   c. 'o' > '0'
   d. 'O' < '@'
   e. 'U' = 'U'
   f. 'w' <> 'V'

21-1-5 Operations on User-Defined Data

Recall that an important Pascal feature is the ability of a user to define new data types. To do so, the user has to specify the *values* that the data can take, and the *relative order* of these values. A brief example reviews the way this is done.

Example 21-11 A Review of User-Defined Data

```
TYPE
    sample = (first, second, third);
VAR
    results1, results2: sample;
```

With these declarations, each of the variables ("results1" and "results2") can take one of three values at any one time, namely, "first," "second," or "third." The order of the values is

first < second < third

because that is the order in which they are listed in the TYPE declaration.

For user-defined data the relational operators may be used to make comparisons (=, <>, <, <=, >, >=). The results of such comparisons are always boolean (true or false). Since these operators have equal precedence, the evaluation takes place from left to right as they are encountered within the expression.

Example 21-12 Operating on User-Defined Data

Given the following:

```
TYPE
    color = (red, orange, yellow);
VAR
    firstcolor, secondcolor: color;
```

The expression, involving the user-defined data,

```
(firstcolor = red) AND (secondcolor = yellow)
```

appears in a Pascal program. This will produce a true result if the variable "firstcolor" has the value "red" and the variable "secondcolor" has the value "yellow" at the time this expression is evaluated. In this expression, parentheses are used to set the priorities. That is, "(firstcolor = red)" is evaluated first, and "(secondcolor = yellow)" is calculated next, then the AND operation is performed.

PROBLEMS FOR SECTION 21-1-5

1. Write the declarations which are needed to define three kinds of data. The first kind consists of passive electronic parts and includes resistors, capacitors, and inductors. The second class contains active components and includes transistors, ICs, and diodes. The last type contain special parts including fuses, switches, and relays. Write an expression which tests whether or not a variable called "part" belongs to either the active parts list or the special parts list.

21-1-6 Operations on Sets

There are three operations that can be used with sets: union, intersection, and complement.

The *union* of two sets is a set which contains the members of *both* sets. the *intersection* of two sets is a set which contains only the members that are *common* to both the original sets. The *complement*, sometimes called the *difference*, of two sets is a set which includes all the elements of the first but modified so that all members of the second have been removed. The symbols for set operations are included in Table 21-6.

TABLE 21-6 PASCAL SET OPERATIONS

Operator or Operation	Symbol	Examples: "First," "Second" Are Set Type Data	Notes
Union	+	first + second	"+" does not mean "add"
Intersection	*	first * second	"*" does not mean "multiply"
Difference	−	first − second	"−" does not mean "subtract"
Equality	=	first = second	Boolean result: true if two sets have same members; false otherwise
Inequality	<>	first <> second	boolean result: false if two sets have same members; true otherwise
Included	<=	first <= second	Boolean result: true if all members of first are found in second; otherwise false
Containment	>=	first >= second	Boolean result: true if all members of second are found in first; otherwise false
Membership	IN	expr IN first	Boolean result: Expr (expression) is calculated. If result is found in the set first, the answer is true; otherwise it is false

Example 21-13 Examples of Set Operations

Set A includes

['A' . . 'Z', '0' . . '9']

and set B is the set shown in the accompanying table. In each case shown in the table various set operations are indicated, along with the results of such operations. In order to construct a set, the brackets "[" and "]" are used as shown above.

Set B	Operation	Result
[' " ', '#']	B + A	[' " ', '#', 'A' . . 'Z', '0' . . '9']
['P', 'Q', '5']	B * A	['P', 'Q', '5']
['&', 'A' . . 'Y']	B − A	['&']
['A' . . 'Z', '0']	B = A	False
['A' . . 'Z', '0']	B <> A	True
['A' . . 'Z', '0']	B <= A	True
['A' . . 'Z', '0' . . '9', '*']	B >= A	True
['(', 'A' . . 'Z']	B IN A	False

The hierarchy or order of set operations is shown in Table 21-7. All operations which have the same priority are carried out as they are encountered within the expression from left to right.

TABLE 21-7 HIERARCHY OF SET OPERATIONS

Priority	Operations
1 (highest)	All operations within parentheses
2	* (intersection)
3	+, − (union, complement)
4	=, <>, <=, >=, IN (relational and set membership)

PROBLEMS FOR SECTION 21-1-6

1. Given the following declarations:

```
CONST
    letters = ('a', 'e', 'i', 'o', 'u');
    null = ( );
TYPE
    vowels = SET OF letters;
    empty = SET OF null;
```

calculate

```
[vowels + empty]
```

2. Complete the following set calculations: A is [tin, lead, iron, steel], and B is [metals].

a. A + B
b. A * B
c. A − B
d. B − A
e. NOT (A IN B)

3. Given
set A is [1. .20],
set B is [15. .25],
and set C is [1, 3, 5, 7, 9, 11, 13, 15],
perform the following calculations:

a. (A <= B) OR (B <= C)
b. NOT (C IN A) AND (B <> A)

21-1-7 The Assignment Operation

Normally, when the computer completes the evaluation of an expression, it *assigns* the resultant value to one of the variables of the program. While the assignment operation has the lowest priority in the hierarchy of operations—it is performed last, after all other operations—it is a very important operation. Its syntax is shown in Fig. 21-2.

The symbol ":=" is called the *assignment operator.* The value of the expression to the right of the assignment operator is assigned to the variable on the left-hand side of the assignment operator. The := symbol is used to make sure that this operation is not confused with the mathematical equals sign (=). *Mathematical equality and assignment are very different.*

When you are using the assignment operation, it is very important to make sure that the data produced when the expression is evaluated is consistent with the data type that has been declared for the variable. If the expression produces real data, then the variable to which this result is assigned must be a real variable.

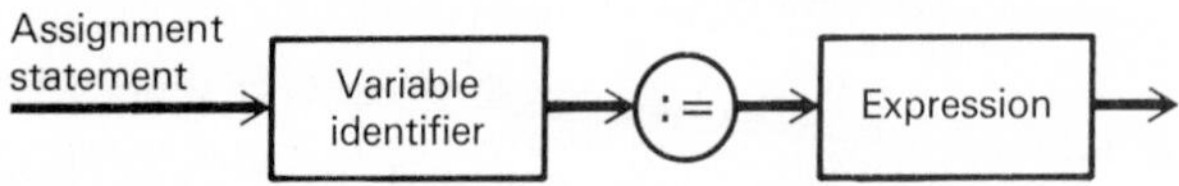

Fig. 21-2 Syntax of the assignment operation.

Example 21-14 Using the Assignment Operator

An array named "testresults" contains the output voltages of a regulated power supply which has been subjected to a number of tests. These readings may have been taken with the power supply in an oven, and the oven adjusted to five different temperature settings at which the power supply voltage is measured. The following program fragment shows how the assignment statement is used to compute the average of the values in the array.

```
VAR
testresults: ARRAY [1..5] OF REAL;
sum, average: REAL;
BEGIN (* Averaging calculation. *)
(* Make sure the variable sum starts at 0. *)
   sum := 0.0;
(* Sum the elements of the array. *)
sum := sum + testresults[1]; (* statement A *)
sum := sum + testresults[2]; (* statement B *)
sum := sum + testresults[3];
sum := sum + testresults[4];
sum := sum + testresults[5]; (* statement C *)
(* Compute the average by dividing the sum by the number
of readings (5). *)
   average := sum/5.0
END. (* averaging calculation. *)
```

Recall that the symbols "(*" and "*)" are used to enclose a comment. Anything between these symbols is ignored by the computer. In this example the sum is initially assigned a value of 0.0. This is not the only way to initialize the value of the sum. Consider a second method in which the statement

```
sum := testresults[1];
```

is used. Explain why this is valid.

Using the method outlined in the fragment, the value of "sum" is replaced by its initial value plus the value found in the first location of the array testresults. This is accomplished by "(* statement A *)" in the listing. Since sum was originally set to 0, the results produced by the execution of (* statement A *) should be 0 + testresults[1], or simply the real number found in testresults[1].

When the next statement, (* statement B *), is executed, the value of testresults[2] is added to the present value of the sum. Since the present value of the sum prior to the operation was the value of testresults[1], the new result (value of sum) will be testresults[1] + testresults[2]. The sequence of additions continues with the remaining statements. Once (* statement C *) has been completed, the value of the variable sum will be the sum of all elements in the array. The value of this sum is then divided by 5.0. This completes the calculation of the average of the array elements, and it is assigned to the variable "average."

Instead of the seven assignment statements used above, the entire calculation could be specified with a single assignment statement. The following shows how this is accomplished:

```
VAR
testresults: ARRAY [1..5] OF REAL;
average: REAL;
BEGIN (* COMPUTE AVERAGE *)
    average := (testresults[1]
              + (testresults[2]
              + (testresults[3]
              + (testresults[4]
              + (testresults[5])/5.0
END. (* average completed *)
```

The keywords BEGIN and END in the example define the boundaries of the program block.

PROBLEM FOR SECTION 21-1-7

1. Write Pascal program fragments similar to those in Example 21-14 to evaluate each of the following:

a. Area of a circle of radius *r*.
b. A boolean variable is to be assigned the value which results from the following combination: the result should be true if either A or B is true, but false if both A and B are true. The variables A and B are boolean data elements.
c. The remainder which results when two integers are divided.
d. The sine of an angle *x* using the formula

$$\sin x = x - \frac{x^3}{6} + \frac{x^5}{120}$$

e. Replace the elements of a two-dimensional array (two rows, three columns) by the square of the integers found in the array.

21-2 FUNCTIONS

When the square of a variable *x* is needed, the expression "x * x" may be used. Instead of having to write such expressions each time a square is needed, it is more convenient to let the computer perform the squaring operation. In order to instruct the computer to do so, a shorthand notation is used. The phrase SQR(x) is used to signify the squaring operation. When this is encountered in a program, it is interpreted as follows: "Square the value of the quantity found in the parentheses, and replace the phrase SQR(x) with the results." The SQR *function* is one example of certain useful functions included in Pascal. Each data type has certain functions which can be used, and each will be briefly described. *Such functions have the same priority as a parenthetical phrase; they have the highest priority in the evaluation of the expression.*

21-2-1 Functions of Integer Data

Table 21-8 lists the functions which can be performed on integer data. The table includes the kind of calculation being made, the keyword used, and the nature of the results. Notice that even though the operands (the data being operated upon) are integers, the results are often transformed into a new data type.

TABLE 21-8 FUNCTIONS ON INTEGER DATA

Type of Calculation	Symbol	Results	Example
Absolute value	ABS	Integer	ABS(3 − 15)
Arctangent (given the tangent of an angle, find the angle)	ARCTAN	Real	ARCTAN(X)
Convert an integer to its equivalent character form	CHR	Character	CHR (43) (answer is "+")
Find cosine of an angle	COS	Real	COS(10)

TABLE 21-8 (Continued)			
Find exponential value	EXP	Real	EXP(−1) that is, (e^{-1})
Find natural logarithm	LN	Real	LN(testno)
Test for odd integer	ODD	Boolean	ODD(3) yields a true result
Sine of an angle	SIN	Real	SIN(25)
Square of an integer	SQR	Integer	SQR(b) − 4 * A * C (b, A and C are integers)
Square root of an integer	SQRT	Real	SQRT(25) (answer is 5.0)

Example 21-15 Using an Integer Function

An assignment which represents the algebraic equation

$$F = aX^2 + bY + C$$

is given by

```
VAR
F, a, X, b, Y, c: INTEGER;
BEGIN
F := a * SQR (X) + b * Y + c
END.
```

PROBLEMS FOR SECTION 21-2-1

1. There is no direct way to compute the tangent of an angle in standard Pascal. Assuming that the variable "angle" is an INTEGER data type, write an assignment statement that will assign the tangent of angle to the variable "tanangle." (Use the functions in Table 21-8.)
2. Write a fragment of a program which converts all the integers of a one-dimensional array into characters. The array contains five data items.
3. Given an array with five items, compare the sum of the absolute error of these numbers within one assignment statement. Write a fragment that examines each member of the array. Compare the sum with the ideal value of 3, and convert the difference to a positive number.

21-2-2 Functions of Real Data

The functions ABS, ARCTAN, COS, EXP, LN, SIN, SQR, and SQRT included in Table 21-8 can accept real arguments (operands) as well as integer data. Thus, any one of these functions can be applied to real or integer data. Table 21-9 lists certain functions which can be used with real data in addition to those functions just mentioned.

TABLE 21-9 ADDITIONAL FUNCTIONS ON REAL OPERANDS

Type of Calculation	Symbol	Results	Example
Round off a real number	ROUND	Integer	ROUND(3.1) (answer = 3)
Find the integer portion of a real number	TRUNC	Integer	TRUNC(ABS(−2.9) (answer = 2)

Example 21-16 Calculating the Roots of a Quadratic Equation

Given the quadratic equation;

$$y = ax^2 + bx + c$$

find the two roots of this equation, assuming they both have real values. The following fragment solves this problem and makes use of the functions (of a real variable) just described.

```
VAR
    root1, root 2, a, X, b, c: REAL;
BEGIN (* start calculation of the roots of the
equation *)
    root1 := (-b + SQRT(SQR(b) - 4.0 * a * c))/(2.0 * a);
    root2 := (-b - SQRT(SQR(b) - 4.0 * a * c))/(2.0 * a)
END. (* calculation of the roots *)
```

PROBLEMS FOR SECTION 21-2-2

1. Solve Example 21-16 in a different way by calculating an intermediate variable that consists of the portion of the expression common to both roots. Explain an advantage of this solution over the one shown in the example.

2. Refer to the requirements of Example 21-16. Why is the following assignment statement incorrect?

```
root1 := (-b + SQRT(SQR(b) - 4.0 * a * c))/2.0 * a;
```

21-2-3 Functions of Boolean Data

There are some functions which produce boolean results; these have been discussed with regard to relational operations on INTEGER and REAL data types. Other functions with boolean results will be described in Chap. 23, which deals with the subject of input/output operations. There are some functions which accept boolean data, but these will not be discussed, as they go beyond the scope of pertinent material.

21-2-4 Functions of Character Data

There are three functions that can be applied to character data. These are listed in Table 21-10.

TABLE 21-10 FUNCTIONS WITH CHARACTER OPERANDS

Type of Calculation	Symbol	Results	Example
Find the number code for a character	ORD	Integer	ORD('a') (answer = 97 for ASCII code)
Find the character which precedes the data	PRED	Character if argument is character	PRED('Z') (answer = 'Y')
Find the character which follows the data	SUCC	Character if argument is character	SUCC('Y') (fill in the answer)

Example 21-17 Encrypting a Message

In the use of computers it is important to maintain the privacy of all users with regard to messages and data. For example, no one wants unauthorized people to have access to bank records. One way to maintain some security is to *code,* or *encrypt,* all communications with the computer. *Encryption* is a complicated topic, but this example provides one way in which to code messages. Assume that an array contains a 10-character string. In order to keep this message private, it is possible to replace each character with one which is coded. In this case the coded character will be the one which follows it in the ordered set of characters for the computer being used. (It is also possible to replace the character with the one which precedes it in the order.) The following program fragment shows how this is accomplished:

```
VAR
   message: ARRAY[1..10] OF CHAR;
BEGIN (* fragment which encodes a message *)
   message[1] := SUCC(message[1]);
   message[2] := SUCC(message[2]);
   message[3] := SUCC(message[3]);
   .
   .
```

```
      message[10] := SUCC(message[10])
   END. (* message encoding *)
```

If the coding algorithm is known, then it is a simple matter to decode any message. (It is possible to decode messages without knowledge of the algorithm, but this can take a very long time and includes material beyond the scope of this text.) If the characters in the array were

```
HLLs r fun
```

then the coding process would produce

```
IMMt!s!gvo
```

PROBLEMS FOR SECTION 21-2-4

1. Write a program fragment which decodes the message coded by the algorithm described in Example 21-17.
2. Using the ASCII code, what is ORD ('J') + 1?
3. Are the following equalities true?

```
PRED('C') = CHR(ORD('C') - 1)
ORD(CHR(I)) = I
```

21-2-5 Functions of User-Defined Data

Recall that a user may define a new data type. This can be done by using the TYPE or VAR declarations. To define a new (scalar) data type, the user must specify the values which the data can assume, and, in addition, the order of these values must be defined from the lowest to the highest values. Various operations on such data were described in Sec. 21-1-5. In summary, these included the relational operations >, >=,<, <=, =, and <>. In addition to the relational operations, three functions will accept user-defined data and produce results which are related to such data. The functions are as follows:

SUCC(V) This computes the successor, or next value, of V.

PRED(V) This function computes the predecessor of, or value which comes before, V.

ORD(V) This function computes a number which is V's position in the list that defines the data. It is called the *ordinal value*. The first data item in the user-defined data list has an ordinal value of 0.

Functions of the type listed above have the same priority as expressions within parentheses. Notice that the expression which appears within the parentheses of these functions would be computed before the function itself is evaluated.

PROBLEMS FOR SECTION 21-2-5

1. With a data type composed of:

```
(first, second, third, fourth, fifth)
```

find the following:

```
SUCC(first), SUCC(second),
PRED(fifth), PRED(first),
ORD(first), ORD(third - 1)
```

21-3 Program Flow and Control

The assignment operation (statement) is an important way to define the kinds of calculations to be performed. The computer evaluates each assignment statement in the order in which it is encountered in the program. A simple example illustrates the importance of having control over the sequence of statements to be executed.

Example 21-18 An Inefficient Program Fragment

Part of a program requires the computer to multiply each element of an array by 2. The array is one-dimensional and includes 100 real data items. Using only the statements discussed so far, a program fragment to do this might look as follows:

```
VAR
   values: ARRAY[1..100] OF REAL;
BEGIN (* Start of multiplication of array items by 2.
*)
   values[1] := 2.0 * values[1];
   values[2] := 2.0 * values[2];
   values[3] := 2.0 * values[3];
(* Included here would be a list of 97 other
assignment statements. *)
END. (* End of multiplication segment. *)
```

In addition to the time that it would take to write all the necessary assignment statements, it is very possible that silly, but significant, errors could be introduced. A much improved syntax would support some way to indicate such calculations in a shorthand manner. Such control mechanisms exist in Pascal and will be discussed in the following sections.

21-3-1 Control Statements

There are two basic types of program control: *conditional execution* of statements and *repetitive control* of statements. These two types of control are pictured in Fig. 21-3.

In Fig. 21-3*a*, conditional statement control is diagrammed. Within the program a test is included. It appears ahead of two potential sets of operations (or calculations) which are to be performed. The test has two possible boolean outcomes, true or false. The results of the test determine which set of operations will actually be performed. (The paths are labeled

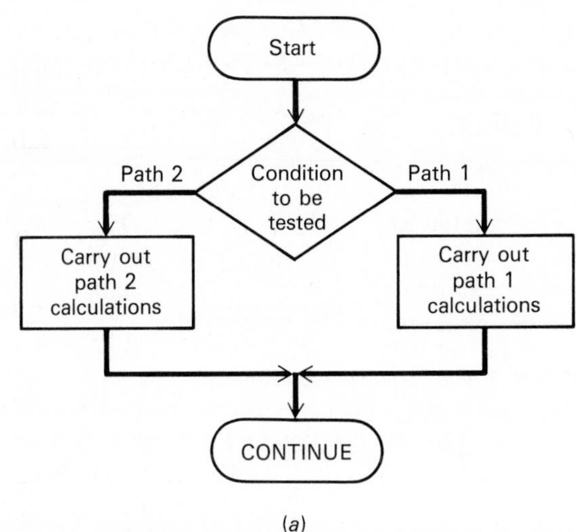

(*a*)

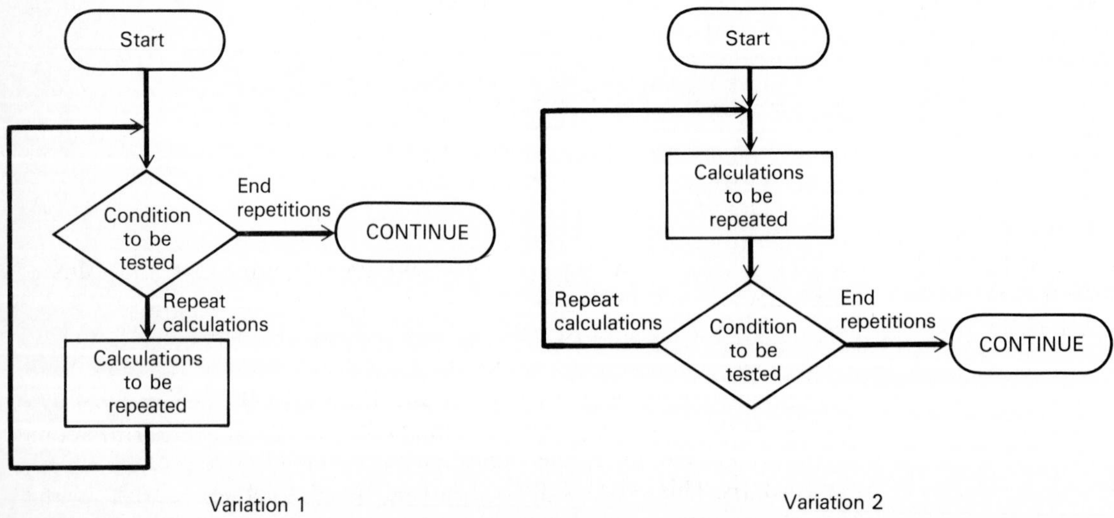

(*b*)

Fig. 21-3 Summary of program control. (*a*) Conditional execution. (*b*) Repetition control (two variations).

"path 1" and "path 2.") In some instances one of the paths will contain no operations; this can be described as a "do-nothing" path. The diagram may be viewed as a *switch*. If the switch (test) points one way, carry out the indicated calculations. If it points in the other direction, follow the instructions defined by that path.

One variation of conditional control found in Pascal is the *n-way switch*. Instead of the two possibilities shown in Fig. 21-3*a*, a number of paths (*n*) can be followed, with a like number of sets of calculations. The idea, however, is the same as that for the two-path system. The test will have *n* possible outcomes, and the path to be followed corresponds to the outcome of the test results.

Figure 21-3*b* is a pictorial representation of the statement repetition control structure or sequence. There are two slightly different variants. In general, a set of operations or calculations is to be performed in a repeated manner. A test is included as part of the structure, and the results of the test will ultimately determine how many times the calculations are to be carried out. The test results indicate if the operations are to be repeated, of if the program is to continue (transfer control) with the portion of the program following the set of operations.

In one variant, the test is performed before the statements are executed. This provides for the possibility that the number of repetitions is zero; do not carry out the calculations at all.

In the second variant, the calculations are performed at least once. In this case the test is performed at the end of the calculations.

The sequence of operations, either test-repeat, or repeat-test, appears to form a loop. This type of control is therefore referred to as a *loop*. One difficulty which can sometimes occur is getting trapped in a loop. If the condition which signals the end of the repetitions never occurs, the computer continues to carry out the calculations in an endless manner. This is a common error in HLL programs. Usually the calculations contain a statement that changes the data on which the exit test is performed. In this way the loop can be executed a specified number of times.

The statements which describe these operations are called *control statements*. Specific Pascal control statements will be described in the succeeding sections.

a. Conditional Control (IF-THEN-ELSE)

Figure 21-3*a* is a flow diagram for conditional control of two groups of instructions. The Pascal statement which implements such control is called the *IF-THEN-ELSE* statement.

There are three important elements in the diagram. The first is the *condition* to be tested. The second and third elements include the two groups of statements which are conditionally executed.

Within the statement the condition to be tested is identified by the keyword IF. This word will be followed by an expression which has a boolean, or true or false, result. Path 1 in Fig. 21-3*a* will be followed if the result is true.

Path 1 instructions follow the keyword THEN in the statement. If there is more than one instruction in this group (compound statement), the entire group will be bracketed by BEGIN and END (lowercase letters can also be used).

Path 2 instructions follow the keyword ELSE. Once again, if there is more than one instruction in the group, the entire structure will be bracketed by BEGIN and END.

It is possible that only one group of instructions will be present. That is, a group of instructions is to be either executed or omitted depending on the outcome of the IF expression. When that is the case, the ELSE portion of the statement will be left out. The Pascal statement becomes an IF-THEN statement. The test expression is written in such a way that a true result causes the statements after THEN to be executed.

The syntax for the IF-THEN-ELSE statement is shown in Fig. 21-4.

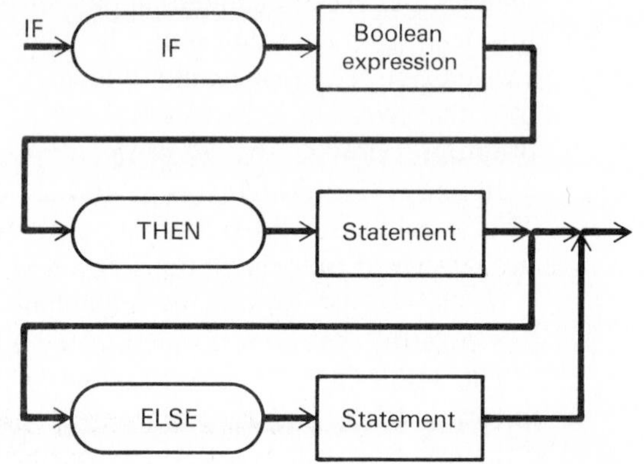

Fig. 21-4 Syntax of the IF-THEN-ELSE control structure.

Example 21-19 A Counting of Sorts

Assume that a company manufactures resistors, and as part of a large program to run the manufacturing in an efficient way, the number of resistors of a given type must be sorted according to their tolerance. (This problem could apply to any manufactured item in which part tolerance is an important consideration.) In this case, 10,000-ohm resistors are sorted according to the following tolerances: less than 5 percent, between 5 and 10 percent, and between 10 and 20 percent. (Resistors above 20 percent tolerance are discarded.) The following program fragment counts the number of resistors in each tolerance category.

```
CONST
resistorvalue = 10000.0;
VAR
nooffiveprcnt, nooftenprcnt, nooftwntyprcnt: INTEGER;
```

```
resistx: real;
BEGIN (* Program to count resistors in each tolerance
group. Initialize the number of elements in each
category to 0. *)
nooffiveprcnt := 0;
nooftenprcnt := 0;
nooftwntyprcnt := 0;

(* At this point in the program, the value of resistor
being sorted would be determined. These statements
are left out for simplicity. Its value is given by
resistx. Assume that no resistor has a tolerance of
greater than 20 percent. *)

IF ((resistx <= 1.05 * resistorvalue) AND
    (resistx >= 0.95 * resistorvalue)) (* statement A *)
THEN
nooffiveprcnt := nooffiveprcnt + 1(* statement B *)
ELSE
                                  (* statement C *)
IF ((resistx <= 1.10 * resistorvalue) AND
    (resistx >= 0.90 * resistorvalue))
THEN nooftenprcnt := nooftenprcnt + 1
ELSE nooftwntyprcnt := nooftwntyprcnt + 1(* statement D *)
END.
(* Remainder of program here. *)
```

Examine the program fragment and notice that "(* statement A *)" tests for a resistor value between 9500 and 10,500 ohms. This boolean expression will be true if the unknown resistor being tested lies within the 5 percent tolerance limit. A true result causes "(* statement B *)" to be executed, and this in turn increments the number of 5 percent resistors which have been counted. Control (the next statement executed) then passes to the remainder of the program, and the conditional control sequence is satisfied. The ELSE portion of the control statement would not be executed.

If the unknown resistor value lies outside the 5 percent tolerance limit, the ELSE portion of the statement is executed. This is identified by "(* statement C *)." Notice, the ELSE portion of the statement contains another IF statement! When the THEN or ELSE portions of the structure contain additional IF statements, the total (statement) structure is called a *compound* IF statement. This second IF portion tests to see if the resistor is within the 10 percent tolerance limit. If it is, the 10 percent counter ("nooftenprcnt") is incremented. If not, it automatically means that the resistor is in the 20 percent category. Hence, the ELSE statement "(* statement D *)" simply adds 1 to the counter represented by "nooftwntyprcnt." (Remember, no further tests are needed because it is assumed that all resistors are within 20 percent of the nominal resistor value.)

IF-THEN-ELSE statements do not include semicolons unless the statements to be executed are compound statements. It is incorrect to put a semicolon before THEN or after ELSE. Figure 21-5 shows a number of IF-THEN-ELSE possibilities and their corresponding logical flow diagrams. The formats for the compound IF-THEN-ELSE statements were chosen because they are easy to read and understand. Other forms are acceptable and may also be used.

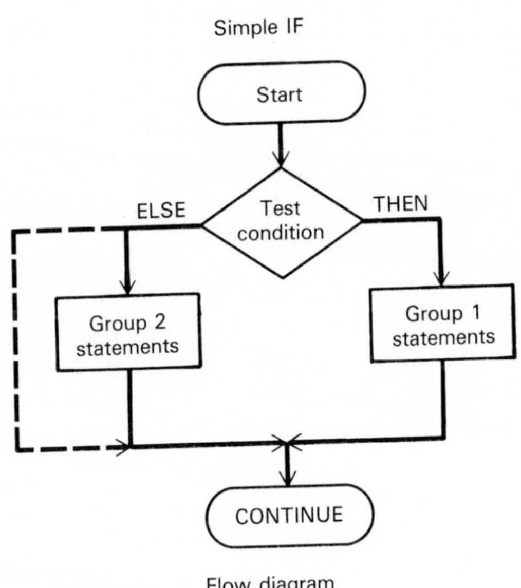

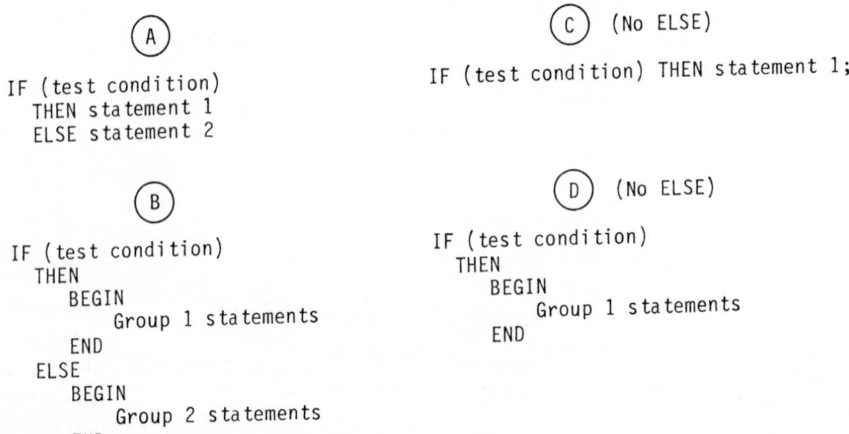

Fig. 21-5 Variations of the IF-THEN-ELSE statement.

Compound IF

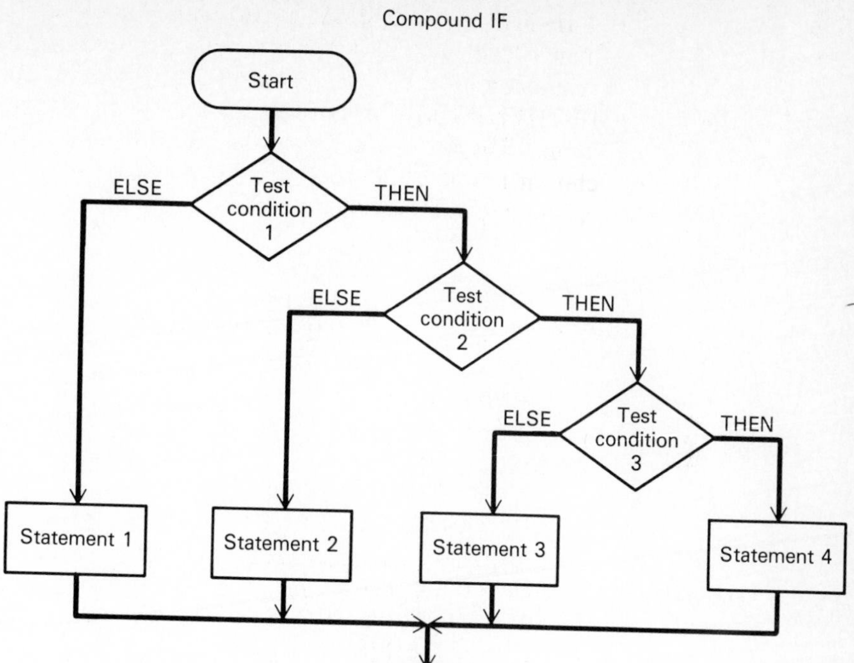

Syntax

```
IF (test condition 1)
  THEN
     IF (test condition 2)
       THEN
          IF (test condition 3)
            THEN
               Statement 4
            ELSE
               Statement 3
       ELSE
          Statement 2
     ELSE
        Statement 1
```

Fig. 21-5 *(continued)*

PROBLEMS FOR SECTION 21-3-1*a*

1. Given the IF-THEN-ELSE flow diagram of Fig. 21-6, write a Pascal statement which properly reflects the intended operations.
2. Is there any difference between the following IF-THEN-ELSE structures? If so, state the different results.

a. first form;

```
VAR
    A, B, C: REAL;
BEGIN
    C := 0.0;
    IF A < 5.0
        THEN
            BEGIN
                B := 0.5
                C := 600.0
            END
END.
```

b. second form;

```
VAR
    A, B, C: REAL;
BEGIN
    C := 0.0;
    IF A < 5.0
        THEN
                B := 0.5;
                C := 600.0

END.
```

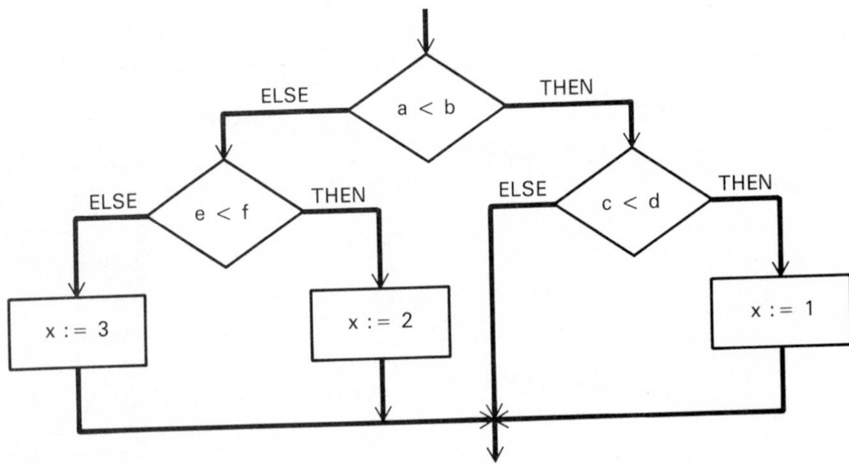

Fig. 21-6 Diagram for Prob. 1.

3. To draw flow diagrams for IF-THEN-ELSE statements and to understand what is being calculated, use the following rule:

> *The ELSE clause belongs to the nearest IF for which there is no ELSE clause.*

Using this rule, draw the flow diagram which corresponds to the following IF-THEN-ELSE fragment:

```
IF condition1
THEN
   IF condition2
     THEN x := 1.0
     ELSE x := 2.0
```

b. *n*-Way Switches—The CASE Statement

The IF-THEN-ELSE statement allows two choices or execution paths for each IF condition. Using this statement for cases involving more than two choices requires a complex IF structure. (A typical flow diagram for this case is shown in Fig. 21-5.) A more convenient method for cases involving multiple choices exists in Pascal and is called the *n-way switch*. The statement used for such instances is the *CASE* statement; its syntax is shown in Fig. 21-7.

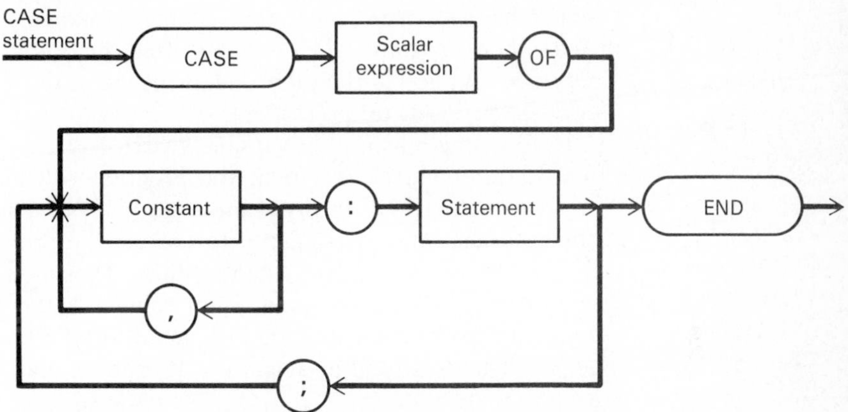

Fig. 21-7 Syntax of the CASE statement.

Example 21-20 Using the *n*-Way Switch (CASE Statement)

A program is designed to control a communication system with the computer. A switch on the front panel of the communications system selects the transmission frequency. There are five switch positions. The following list indicates the frequency to be selected for each switch position.

Setting	Frequency, Megahertz
1	1.0
2	1.35
3	2.0
4	2.55
5	3.1

The following example of the CASE statement shows how the frequency can be assigned as a function of the switch position.

```
CASE switch OF
            1: frequency := 1.0;
            2: frequency := 1.35;
            3: frequency := 2.0;
            4: frequency := 2.55;
            5: frequency := 3.1;
END
```

When the CASE statement is executed, the variable "switch" will have one of the values 1, 2, 3, 4, or 5. The variable switch has been assigned this value by some other statement (not shown) which instructs the computer to read or sense the actual position of the switch. If it has a value of 1, then the statement following number 1 is executed. The program then continues at the first statement following the keyword END. If the variable switch has the value 2, then the statement following number 2 is executed. Again, the program will continue after the END statement. The same argument applies to the other values of the variable switch; the complete description is left to the student.

If, for some reason, the variable switch has a value of 7 at the time the CASE statement is executed, the program will fail. The computer will come to a halt and an error message will be generated, in which case human intervention is required to correct the problem. It may be useful to precede the CASE statement with an IF statement which checks for improper values of the expression following the keyword CASE. The computer itself could then be instructed to take the necessary corrective action. This is a built-in diagnostic procedure and the computer supplies its own debugging.

Remember that each statement within the CASE statement can itself be a compound statement. That is, there may be many statements executed for each of the cited cases. These must be bracketed by the keywords BEGIN and END. In some instances, the CASE statement contains an elaborate sequence of operations in each branch. However, it is to be noted that this can lead to difficulties in reading and understanding the programmer's intentions.

One final rule concerning the CASE statement: *the scalar expression shown in Fig. 21-7 cannot produce a REAL data type as a result*. It cannot have a value of 1.5, for example, as each case to be executed must be associated with an integer.

PROBLEMS FOR SECTION 21-3-1*b*

1. Suggest some potential difficulties with the following program fragment.

```
TYPE
   coin = (penny, nickel, dime, quarter, halfdollar);
```

```
VAR
   value: INTEGER;
.
.
.
CASE coin OF
     penny: value := 1;
     nickel: value := 5;
     dime: value := 10;
     quarter: value := 25;
END;
```

2. Given the following parts of a Pascal program:

```
TYPE
   operation = (add, sub, mult, dvide);
VAR
   x, y: REAL;
```

Write a CASE statement which will support the following operations:

If the Operation Is	Then Calculate
add	x + y
sub	x − y
mult	x * y
divide	x / y

c. The GOTO Statement: Legal and Illegal

In general, it is best to use the structured statements, including loops and the CASE statement, to translate an algorithm into its Pascal form. There are, however, occasions when it is useful to be able to branch to a remote part of the program. The best examples of this are the responses which the program should make to *exceptions* or errors which it is designed to detect. *Exceptions* are unusual occurrences or unexpected outcomes within the program—usually some error condition—perhaps dependent on the failure of hardware such as the secondary storage system. (Chapter 23 contains information about input/output (I/O) and files. An error which may arise in regard to a file is an attempt to read from a file which does not exist.) A GOTO statement can be used to transfer computer control to that portion of the program which is dedicated to the treatment of errors that may occur.

Many programmers do *not* use GOTO statements because they tend to change the orderly sequence of operations. In addition, a programmer's intentions become difficult to follow. GOTO statements are included as part of our description of Pascal because they are likely to be encountered in a Pascal program.

The syntax of the GOTO statement is very easy to understand and use. A diagram of this syntax is shown in Fig. 21-8.

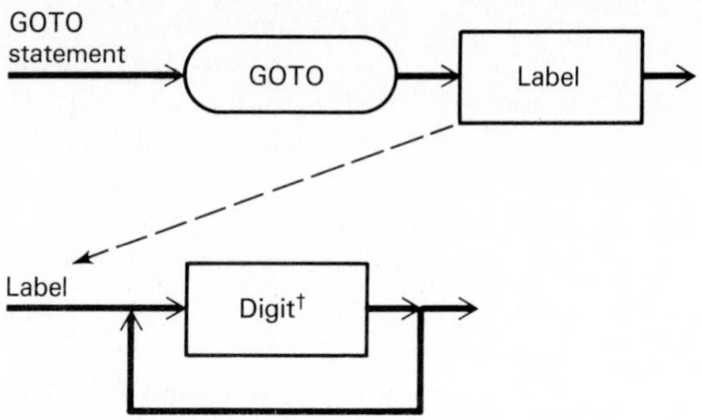

†Maximum of four digits

Fig. 21-8 Syntax of the GOTO statement.

The GOTO statement is not recognized in all versions of Pascal. In those versions where the compiler *does* support its use, an important application relates to *error recovery.* The following fragment shows how this is accomplished:

```
PROGRAM demo (INPUT, OUTPUT);
LABEL 100;
CONST
limit = 10.0;
VAR
result: REAL;
.
.
.
BEGIN
.
.
.
IF (result > limit)
    THEN GOTO 100;
.
.
.
100: (* start of error recovery *)
.
.
.
END.
```

In this program fragment a comparison is made (the IF statement) to determine if the variable "result" is greater than some predefined value of the constant "limit." In the program this could signal an error condition. When this occurs, control is transferred to the statement identified by the label 100. A group of instructions at that point in the program would specify what is to be done when the error is detected (such as print the message "Execution terminated because of error in result").

A word of caution is necessary. There are situations in which the jump specified by the GOTO is illegal. (This is another reason why their use should be avoided, if possible.) One such illegal case will be described. Recall from Chap. 19 that a Pascal program is composed of blocks. *It is illegal for a GOTO statement to transfer control from one separate block to another.* The control sequences shown is Fig. 21-9 indicate legal and illegal sequences.

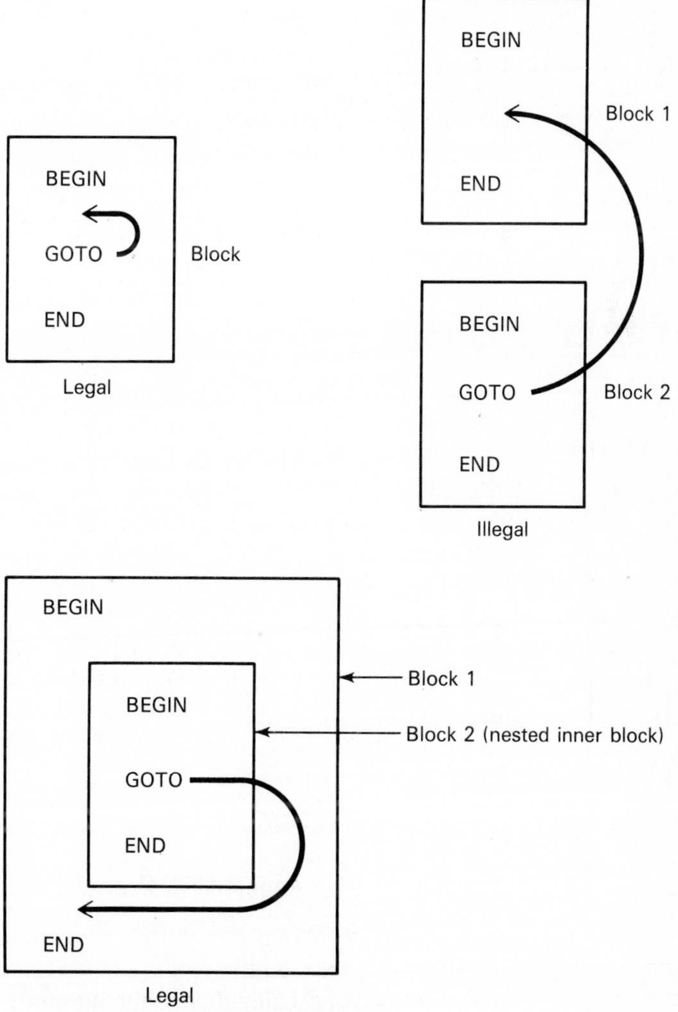

Fig. 21-9 Legal and illegal GOTO sequences.

PROBLEMS FOR SECTION 21-3-1*c*

1. Is the GOTO sequence of Fig. 21-10 legal or illegal?
2. Write all the necessary statements and declarations of a program fragment which will cause a jump to a label at which error recovery begins. The jump is to occur if the integer test is less than 40 or greater than 60. Use whatever variable names are convenient.

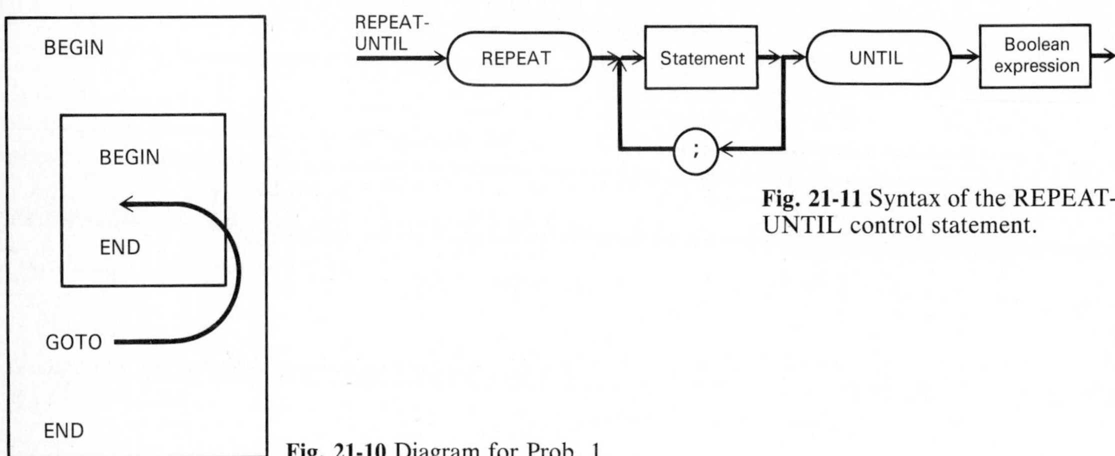

Fig. 21-11 Syntax of the REPEAT-UNTIL control statement.

Fig. 21-10 Diagram for Prob. 1.

21-3-2 REPEAT-UNTIL Loops

The IF-THEN-ELSE, CASE, and GOTO statements deal with selective execution of program statements. The next group of statements is concerned with repeated executions of instructions (recall Fig. 21-3*b*). The first of these is called the *REPEAT-UNTIL,* or simply *REPEAT* in some Pascal language manuals and books. The syntax for this statement is shown in Fig. 21-11. The sequence of operations (control) follows the flow diagram shown in Fig. 21-3*b* in which the Pascal statements that form the loop are executed before a test is performed to determine if they should be repeated. The statement to be executed may be compound; hence the symbol ";" appears in the syntax drawing. Statements to be executed may be bracketed by the keywords BEGIN and END. Although this is not a requirement, it often makes the program clearer and easier to read.

Example 21-21 Repeating a Previous Example

In Example 21-14, a program fragment indicated how to use the assignment statement to average the real values in an array. In that program the same operation was repeated on each member of the array. (Its value was added to a running sum.) Repeated operations on a group of data makes it a good candidate for using the REPEAT-UNTIL statement. Consider the fragment below, which averages the real values of 100 test results. (An array of 100 values is chosen because the direct method used in Example 21-14, although adequate for the five values used there, would be very cumbersome and prone to error when used with 100 elements.)

```
VAR
testresults: ARRAY[1..100] OF REAL;
sum, average: REAL;
index: INTEGER;
BEGIN
sum := 0.0;
index := 1;
REPEAT
sum := sum + testresults[index];
index := index + 1
UNTIL index > 100;
average := sum/100.0
END.
```

PROBLEMS FOR SECTION 21-3-2

1. Write a fragment which adds all numbers from 1 to 500, including all necessary declarations.
2. Describe the logical error in the following fragment:

```
VAR
number: REAL;
N: INTEGER;
BEGIN
number := 1.0;
N := 1;
REPEAT
(* Various operations on the variable number. *)
N := N - 1
UNTIL N > 500;
```

21-3-3 REPEAT-WHILE Loops

The second statement which can be used to control the number of repetitions of a group of instructions is called the *REPEAT-WHILE* statement. It can also be referred to as the *WHILE* statement. It is similar to the REPEAT statement with one important exception. For the WHILE control statement, the condition which terminates repetition is checked before any instructions are executed (see Fig. 21-3*b*, variation 1). Such is *not* the case for the REPEAT statement.

This kind of control structure is useful when calculations on the data may not have to be done at all. Suppose, for example, that some calculations are to be performed on all items of a data list. However, it is not known how many items are contained in the list. If there are no items on the list, then no calculations are performed. Checking the list for the presence of an item before any calculations are performed is a necessary first step. The WHILE statement is compatible with such a sequence of steps.

The syntax diagram for a WHILE statement is shown in Fig. 21-12. The keyword WHILE is a reminder that the terminating condition is checked before any statements are executed.

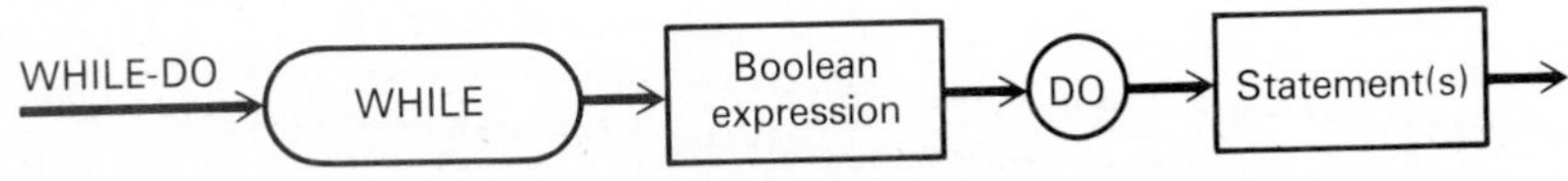

Fig. 21-12 Syntax diagram for the WHILE statement.

Example 21-22 Exercising a WHILE Statement

A message is to be coded (encrypted) prior to transmission over a telecommunications network in order to secure the information. The message is stored in an array in the form of a string of characters. The array contains a sufficient number of locations for the largest possible message. However, each message may have fewer than the maximum number of characters. The last character in a message is a carriage return. The ASCII code for this character is 13 (decimal).

There are 127 possible characters other than the carriage return in this form of the ASCII code. In order to encode the message the character is replaced by its complement. For example, the code for the letter "Z" is 90. This is replaced by "%." The code for "%" is 37, and the number 37 is obtained by subtracting 90 from 127. Thus, the number 37 is considered to be the complement of 90. All characters in the array are to be coded in this way, up to but not including the carriage return character. The coded characters are to replace the original characters in the array. The following fragment performs the required coding:

```
LABEL 100;
CONST
limit = 80;
cr = 13;
VAR
message: ARRAY[1..limit] OF CHAR;
codenumber, index: INTEGER;
BEGIN
index := 1;
WHILE message[index] <> CHR(cr) DO
```

```
  BEGIN
    codenumber := 127 - ORD(message[index]);
    message[index] := CHR(codenumber);
    index := index + 1;
    IF index > 80 THEN GOTO 100
  END;
(* Remainder of program appears here, including the
statements associated with the label 100. *)
END. (* of the entire program *)
```

Notice several features of this fragment:

- The program includes the ORD and CHR operations.
- The WHILE loop includes an IF-THEN operation which provides for a possible error that may arise. If, for some unknown reason, the message does not contain a carriage return character, the value of index will continue to increase without bound. In this case the computer will eventually attempt to access a memory location beyond the end of the array, causing unspecified side effects (unanticipated changes in the program results). The presence of the IF-THEN control path prevents such difficulties. The label 100 is not shown in the fragment, but instructions at that point would institute appropriate action.
- The program does not indicate how the message was initially read into the array. One way to accomplish this is to enter the message using the computer keyboard. Such operations will be described in a subsequent chapter.

PROBLEMS FOR SECTION 21-3-3

1. Replace the assignment statements (Example 21-22)

```
codenumber := 127 - ORD(message[index]);
message[index] := CHR(codenumber);
```

   with one assignment statement which achieves the same result.

2. Write a program fragment using the WHILE format which decodes the coded message that appears in the array "message" in Example 21-22.

3. It is possible to make a serious error using the coding method shown in Example 21-22. Try to find the error. To avoid this error, suggest another way to signal the end of a message (this problem is somewhat difficult). (*Hint:* What coded character is obtained when the message contains an "r"?)

4. Using a WHILE statement, write part of a program which will add all the numbers from 1 to 100.

21-3-4 FOR-TO and FOR-DOWNTO Loops

The flow diagrams of both the WHILE and REPEAT statements appear to take the form of a loop. This is visible in Fig. 21-3. There are a number of calculations to be performed in such sequences which are to be repeated a number of times. The number of repetitions is determined by the value or condition of some variable or variables in the program. Often, the data for these variables is changed within the loop itself. In such cases the program must include a decision block which determines if the loop is to be repeated. The WHILE and REPEAT statements have such decision blocks built into the syntax of the statement itself.

There are many instances in which it is possible to know, or calculate beforehand, the number of times that the loop is to be repeated. In such cases it is advantageous to let the computer keep track of the number of times that the loop has been executed. A special control statement in Pascal lets the computer track the loop count. This statement has one of two forms: (1) the *FOR-TO* form, or (2) the *FOR-DOWNTO* form. Both forms have a similar syntax, and the only difference is the counting direction. The direction is evident from the form of the statement. In the FOR-TO form the count proceeds from a low starting number to a higher terminating number. In the FOR-DOWNTO form the counting sequence is reversed (high initial value to low terminating value). The syntax for both forms of such a loop is shown in Fig. 21-13. Such statements operate according to the steps outlined in the flow diagram of Fig. 21-14.

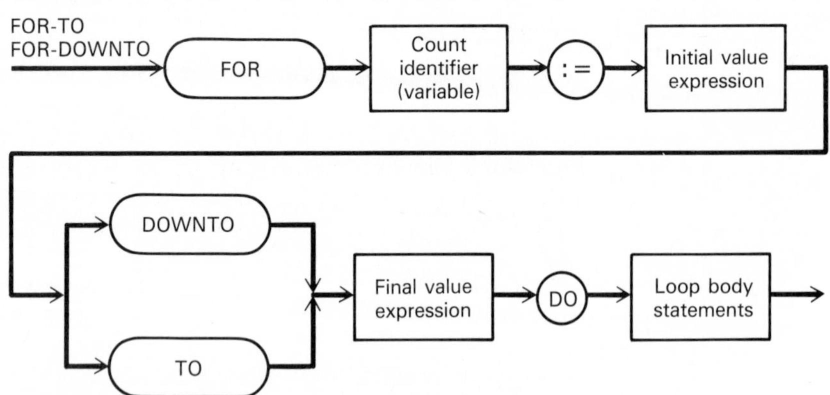

Fig. 21-13 Syntax of the FOR-TO and FOR-DOWNTO statements.

Example 21-23 Simplifying with FOR-TO

Example 21-14 described a method for computing the average of the elements of an array. The array contained five items and the program required seven assignment statements. These statements were used to initialize the sum of the elements to 0, and all five array items, and, finally,

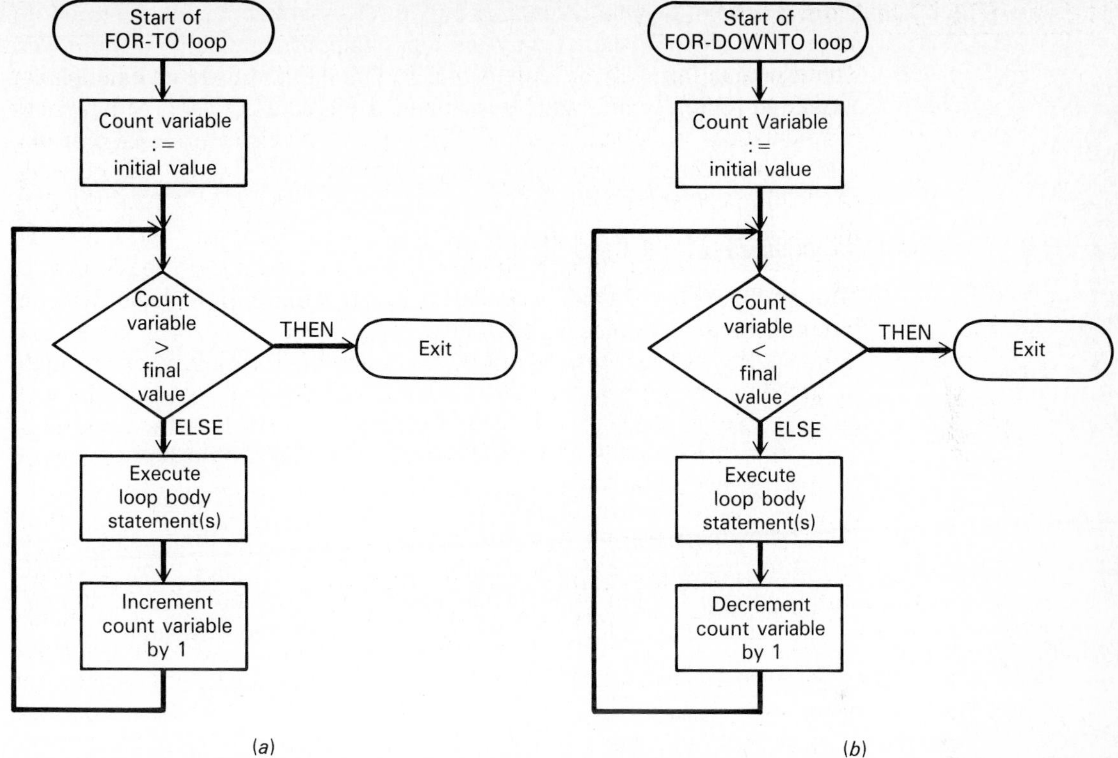

Fig. 21-14 Flow diagrams showing (*a*) how the FOR-TO statement operates and (*b*) how the FOR-DOWNTO statement functions.

compute the average. A FOR-TO loop can greatly simplify such cases involving a simple repetition of the same operations on a group of data. The main operation is repeated addition of all items in the array. The following program fragment computes the average of all members of an array.

```
CONST
lowest = 1;
highest = 5;
VAR
testresults: ARRAY[lowest..highest] OF REAL;
sum, average: REAL;
index: INTEGER;
BEGIN
sum := 0.0;
FOR index := lowest TO highest DO
sum := sum + testresults[index];
average := sum/5.0
END.
```

This version of the algorithm uses only three assignment statements. Moreover, it would *still* require only three assignment statements if there were 100 elements in the array rather than 5. The method used in Example 21-14 would require many more assignment statements.

Example 21-24 A Case of FOR-DOWNTO

Timing delays produced by an electronic timing circuit depend on the product of a resistance value and a capacitance value. The time delay produced by the circuit is given by the following formula:

$$\text{Delay time} = 0.693(\text{resistor value})(\text{capacitor value})$$

The following program fragment computes the delay time using a fixed value for capacitance and a variable value for resistance. The resistance varies from 1 million ohms (1 megohm) down to 1000 ohms in 500-ohm steps. Time delay values are stored in an array named "results."

```
CONST
largest = 2000;
smallest = 2;
capacitance = 0.001E-06;
VAR
index, i: INTEGER
results: ARRAY [1..largest] OF REAL;
resistance: REAL;
BEGIN
i := largest;
FOR index := largest DOWNTO smallest DO
BEGIN
     resistance := index * 500.0; (* statement A *)
     results[i] := 0.693 * resistance * capacitance;
     i := i - 1
END;
END.
```

Notice "(* statement A *)"; "index" is an INTEGER data type. The number 500.0 is a real quantity. Recall that when the multiplication operation (*) is used with one real and one integer quantity, the calculation is carried out as if both were real numbers. The result of this calculation is a real number, and it is assigned to the variable "resistance." This is one instance in which real and integer data may be mixed within an expression.

PROBLEMS FOR SECTION 21-3-4

1. Make all necessary changes to the program fragment in Example 21-23 so that is calculates the average of the items in an array which contains 100 data elements.

2. An array has data items which are sorted from the smallest value to the largest value. That is, the array named "results" has the smallest real data value in results[1], and the largest real data value in results[100].

   a. Write a program fragment using the FOR-TO structure which reverses the ordering of the data. The program should put the largest data value in results[1] and the smallest data value in results[100].
   b. Repeat part (a) using the FOR-DOWNTO loop.

3. Write a program fragment which calculates the sum of the squares of all even numbers from 1 to 100. Use a FOR-TO structure as the basis of the program.

21-3-5 Nesting

The statements within the body of a FOR-TO or FOR-DOWNTO structure can contain another FOR-TO or FOR-DOWNTO loop. Such a program construction is called a *nested* FOR-TO (or nested FOR-DOWNTO) arrangement. This is shown schematically in Fig. 21-15. Two loops are

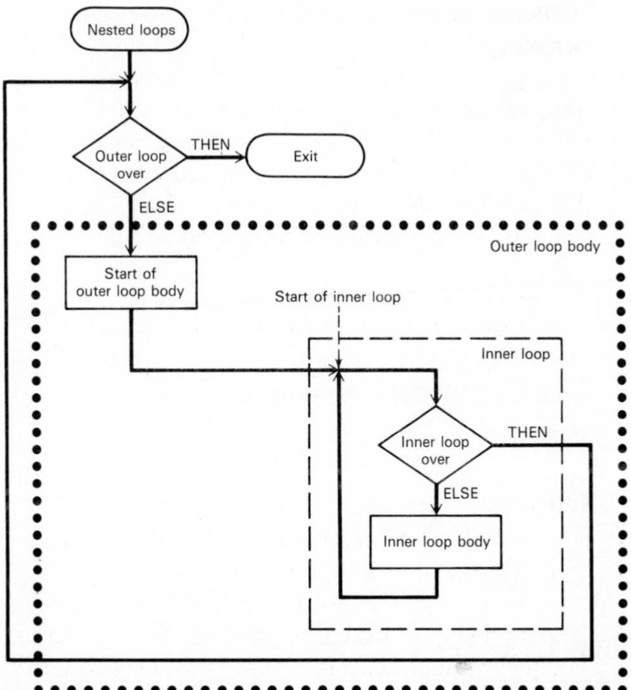

Fig. 21-15 Diagram of nested FOR-TO (FOR-DOWNTO) loops.

pictured. The enclosed loop is called the *inner loop* and the enclosing loop is called the *outer loop*. The inner loop completes all its repetitions for each repetition of the outer loop. Thus, if there are five repetitions of the inner loop and six repetitions of the outer loop, the inner loop will actually be executed 30 times. For each of the six repetitions of the outer loop, the inner loop complete five repetitions.

It is possible that the inner loop also contains a FOR-TO loop. This adds yet another level of nesting. In practice, programs rarely exceed three levels of nesting, although the actual number which is permitted varies from one computer installation to another.

Example 21-25 Nested Loops

A company manufactures flexible (floppy) disk storage systems. These systems are tested for many hours before being delivered to the customers. (This is referred to as *burn-in*.) A computer controls the testing process. Test data is recorded on the storage medium, the diskette, and is examined (read) for errors. The number of errors for each system is recorded, and if the average number of errors exceeds the company's specifications, the unit is considered unacceptable and will not be delivered. Part of the program which controls the test calculates the average number of errors for each system. The test data consists of a two-dimensional array where each row includes the data for one of the systems and each column contains the test data at a different point in time (each hour).

The program fragment shown below uses nested FOR-TO loops to compute the average number of errors for each floppy disk storage system undergoing testing. There are 20 systems being tested. The outer loop produces 20 repetitions of the calculation of the average, one for each floppy disk system. For each floppy disk system, the errors ("testresults[sysnumber, hour]") are added for all testing times. There are 100 test periods; the variable "hour" starts at 1 ("start") and ends at 100 ("finish"). An average is computed as follows:

```
average[sysnumber] := summation/((last - first) + 1.0);
```

This is stored in the array named "average" and is repeated for each system under test. The program fragment is as follows:

```
CONST
last = 20;
first = 1;
start = 1;
finish = 100;
VAR
sysnumber, hour: INTEGER;
testresults: ARRAY[first..last, start..finish] OF INTEGER;
average: ARRAY[(last + 1 - finish)] OF REAL;
```

```
summation: REAL;
BEGIN
FOR sysnumber := first TO last DO
   BEGIN
      summation := 0.0;
      FOR hour := start TO finish DO
         BEGIN
            summation := testresults [sysnumber, hour] + summation
         END;
      average[sysnumber] := summation/((last - first) + 1.0);
   END
END.
```

PROBLEM FOR SECTION 21-3-5

1. Sometimes data needs to be *smoothed*. To do so the operations described in Fig. 21-16 are performed. Suppose you are given an array of 100 data points which are to be smoothed. Write a Pascal fragment which carries out the smoothing algorithm. Begin with the second point on the list and end with the ninety-ninth point on the list.

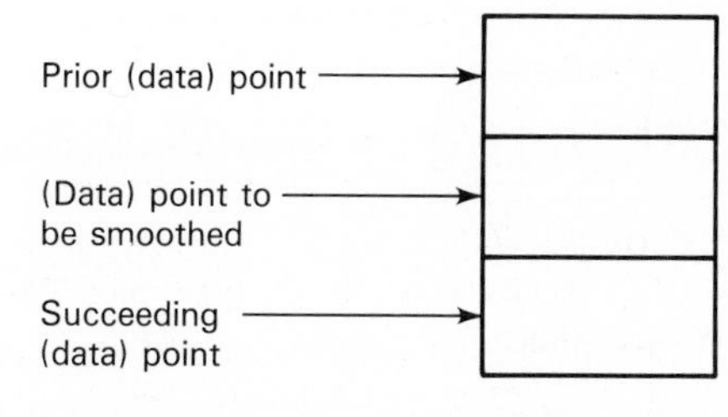

$$\text{Point to be smoothed} = \frac{\text{Prior point} + \text{point to be smoothed} + \text{succeeding point}}{3}$$

Fig. 21-16 Diagram for Prob. 1.

SUMMARY

This chapter describes various operations which can be performed on the data types previously discussed. The operational rules are discussed in addition to the order or hierarchy of operations. Even though it has a low priority, the assignment operation (or statement) is one of the most important in Pascal.

Because certain calculations are used frequently in solving problems, Pascal makes these available in a convenient form—that of functions. The rules and hierarchy of operations lead to the ability to write simple program fragments. However, it is also important to be able to control the sequence or order in which statements are executed. Two important control structures are described:

- Conditional execution, or the selective control of the statements to be carried out
- Repetition, or the number of times that a specific group of calculations is to be repeated

Statements which relate to such operations are called control statements. Within Pascal control statements include WHILE, UNTIL, CASE, GOTO, FOR-TO, and FOR-DOWNTO, and the syntax and rules governing such statements are described in this chapter.

REVIEW PROBLEMS

1. Analyze the following expressions in accordance with Fig. 21-1:

a. (a + b) (c + d)
b. a AND b OR c AND d

2. Write Pascal expresions for the following algebraic expressions:

a. $x(x - a)(x - b)(x - c)$
b. $e^x - e^{-x}$
c. $6x^5 - 5x^4 + 3x^3 - 2x + 5$
d. $\dfrac{\sin x}{\cos x}$
e. $\log(5x - 3)$, where log is the logarithm to the base 10.
f. πr^2

3. Write a boolean expression which satisfies the following table of values:

A	B	Result
False	False	False
False	True	True
True	False	True
True	True	False

4. Find the result of

$$6 + 8 * 2 + 8 \text{ DIV } 3$$

5. Given the following program fragment:

```
TYPE
    joblist = (joba, jobb, jobc, jobd, jobe);
```

Find:

SUCC(joba)
PRED(jobd)
ORD(jobe)

6. Given the following program fragment:

```
producta = [subassa, subassb, subassc, subassd];
productb = [subassa, subassc, subasse, subassf];
```

Compute:

producta + productb
producta * productb
producta – productb
productb – producta

7. Write a Pascal expression to calculate each of the following:

a. The absolute value of the real variable x.
b. The angle whose tangent is 0.5.
c. The character which is the equivalent of 50 (decimal).
d. The cosine of the angle represented by the real variable y.
e. e^{-x}
f. The natural log of 100.
g. Test the integer variable "number" to see if it has an odd value.
h. The sine of the angle represented by variable z.
i. The square of the sum of variables a and b.
j. The square root of 250.

8. The current i through a semiconductor diode is given (approximately) by one of two formulas:

$$i = I_0 \quad \text{if } V \leq 0.5$$

$$i = \frac{V - 0.5}{R} \quad \textit{if } V > 0.5$$

where I_0 = leakage current,
V = voltage across the diode
R = forward resistance

Write a Pascal statement or statements that will calculate the correct value of i. Assume that the computer has values for V, I_0, and R.

9. a. Draw flow diagrams describing the control sequences for the WHILE and REPEAT-UNTIL statements.
b. What is the most important difference between these two methods of control statement execution?

10. One way to find the square root of a positive number n (> 0) is to approximate the answer by repeated calculation of the formula

$$\text{New answer} = \frac{1}{2}\left(\frac{n}{\text{old answer}} + \text{old answer}\right)$$

Continue to evaluate the new answer until:

$$|n - (\text{new answer})^2| < 10^{-6}$$

("||" means "take the absolute value of"). Start with the answer = 1.0. Write all the Pascal statements needed to find the square root of a positive number *n*. Use a REPEAT-UNTIL statement to achieve this result.

11. A user has entered real numbers into the computer. These numbers are stored in an array called "voltagereadings." To signal the last entry, the user enters 0.0. There will never be more than 25 entries. (There may be fewer, even none, if the first entry is 0.0.) Write a program which calculates the largest entry.

12. Repeat Prob. 11. In this case find the smallest entry.

13. Given the following Pascal fragment:

```
PROGRAM mult
CONST
lastrow = 5;
lastcol = 5;
VAR
multarray: ARRAY[1..lastrow, 1..lastcol] OF INTEGER;
rowindex, colindex: INTEGER;
BEGIN
FOR rowindex := 1 TO lastrow DO
BEGIN
FOR colindex := 1 TO lastcol DO
multarray[rowindex, colindex] := rowindex * colindex
END;
END.
```

What is stored in the array when the program is finished?

14. a. Using a CASE statement, write a program fragment which performs the following assignments:

Region	Calculate
1	$y = 3x$
2	$y = 5x+1$
3	$y = 7x+2$

b. Repeat part (a) using an IF-THEN-ELSE construction.

15. Given the following facts:

```
TYPE testdata =
RECORD
  location: PACKED ARRAY[1..10] OF CHAR;
  Temperature: REAL
END;
VAR
  testarray: ARRAY[1..100] OF testdata;
```

Write a Pascal fragment which calculates the average temperature at 100 locations.

REVIEW QUESTIONS

1. Name all operations which can be performed on INTEGER data types.
2. Write down the hierarchy of integer operations.
3. Repeat questions 1 and 2 for REAL data types.
4. Name an important operation which cannot be performed directly on either integer or real data.
5. Name as many operations as possible which can be performed on boolean data.

22 PROCEDURES AND FUNCTIONS

An efficient way to construct electronic circuits is to use standard, prefabricated, integrated components. This technique can also be used to construct buildings, railroads, bridges, and other products. The same methods can be used to write computer programs. Companies that manufacture software products can achieve a high degree of efficiency if they design and produce such programs using standard off-the-shelf program modules. In Pascal this is made possible by means of elements called *procedures* and *functions*.

22-1 AN INTRODUCTION TO PROCEDURES AND FUNCTIONS

Figure 22-1 shows the general idea behind the modular concept. New programs are designed and developed by integrating existing modules

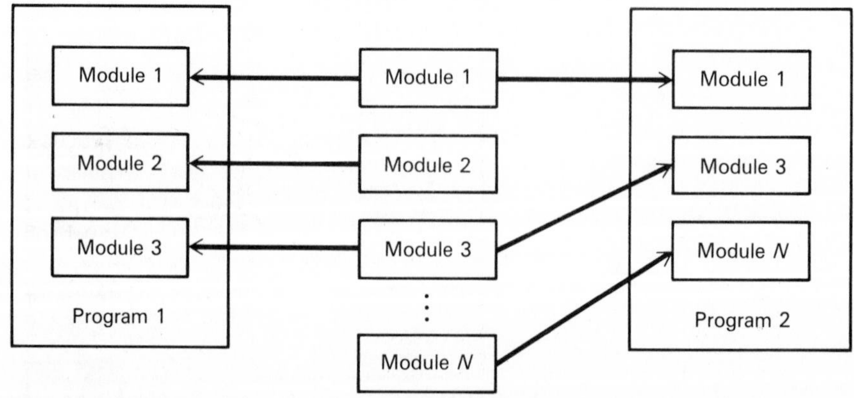

Fig. 22-1 New programs may be developed by integrating existing modules in different combinations.

(procedures and functions) into new arrangements and patterns. A procedure identifies a block of statements within a program. It is often referred to as a *subprogram*. Each time the name of the subprogram appears in a program, the entire block of statements is executed. The subprogram is said to be *invoked* when its name is used. New programs become easy to design if the relevant procedures already exist. For example, to put together a new program one might assemble several existing procedures as follows:

```
BEGIN
proc1;
proc2;
proc3;
proc4
END.
```

In this program, the four procedures (proc1, . . . , proc4) have been declared prior to their inclusion. In fact, they must appear at the beginning of the program—ahead of the statements shown in the example. If these programs have already been written and debugged (tested and verified), then the new program should not require any additional debugging effort. The statements shown above form the *main* program. Appearance of the name of the procedure (i.e., proc1) causes the statements of the subprogram (proc1) to be executed. When subprogram execution is complete, control of the program is transferred to the next statement in the main program. In the case shown above, the next statement invokes a new procedure (i.e., proc2).

Procedures also help to shorten programs. If a group of statements is to be used repeatedly in a program, the statements may be combined to form a procedure. The execution of such instructions requires only that the name of the procedure be invoked. A typical control sequence for this situation is shown in Fig. 22-2.

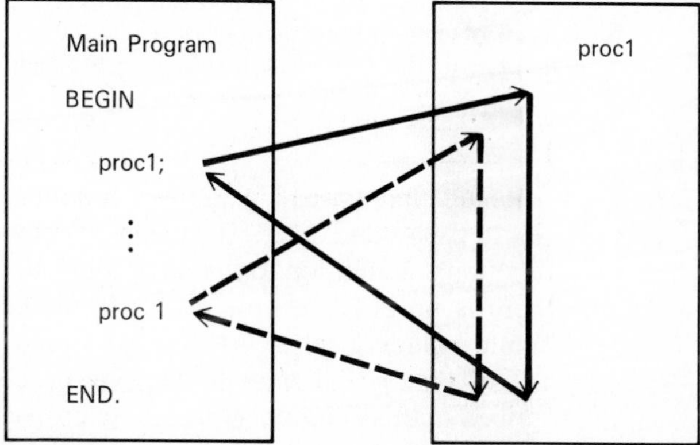

Fig. 22-2 A procedure can be called, or invoked, from many places in a program. When the subprogram is complete, the program continues at the point where the procedure was invoked.

To summarize, procedures are useful for a number of reasons;

- They can be used to build new programs in an efficient manner.
- A group of instructions can be collected within a procedure, and this group used repeatedly in a program. The resultant program will thus be shorter because the entire list of instructions need not be repeated each time it is used.
- Programs which use procedures are easier to read. This is important when the program size is large.

Functions are generally similar to procedures. They also include a group of instructions which are executed each time the name of the function is invoked. In addition, program control returns to the place where the function was used. However, there are some important differences between functions and procedures. These will be described later in the chapter. Figure 22-3 summarizes the operation of a call, or reference, to a function in a Pascal program.

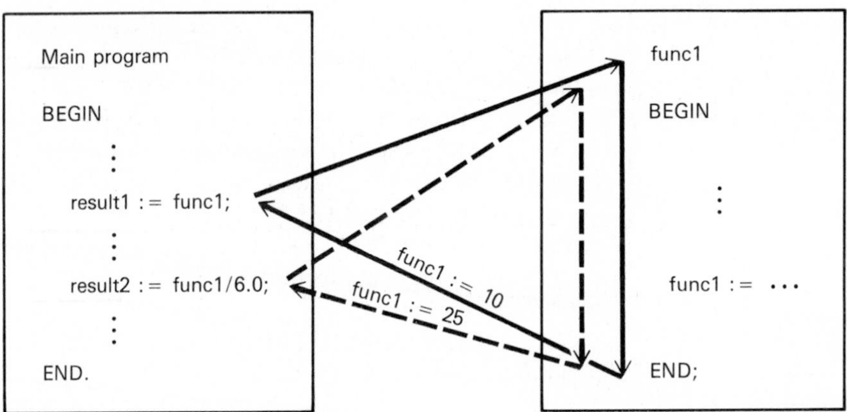

Fig. 22-3 Each time the name of a function is used within a program, the instructions associated with the function are executed. A value for the function is calculated and is substituted for the identifier in the calling program.

Recall that Pascal includes a number of *predefined* functions such as ABS, COS, and EXP. By using a function it is possible to create new functions in addition to the ones supplied in standard Pascal. For example, there is no provision for raising a number to a power. A useful function might include a set of instructions which performs this operation.

The syntax and rules for writing procedures and functions will be described in this chapter. A programmer may often have a library of functions and procedures which are written in flexible ways so that they are useful in a variety of circumstances. They are usually easy to integrate into new programs.

22-2 PROCEDURES

The syntax for procedures is shown in Fig. 22-4. It includes the following elements:

- *A name*. This is the identifier for the procedure.
- *A list of parameters*. These parameters are the variables which will be

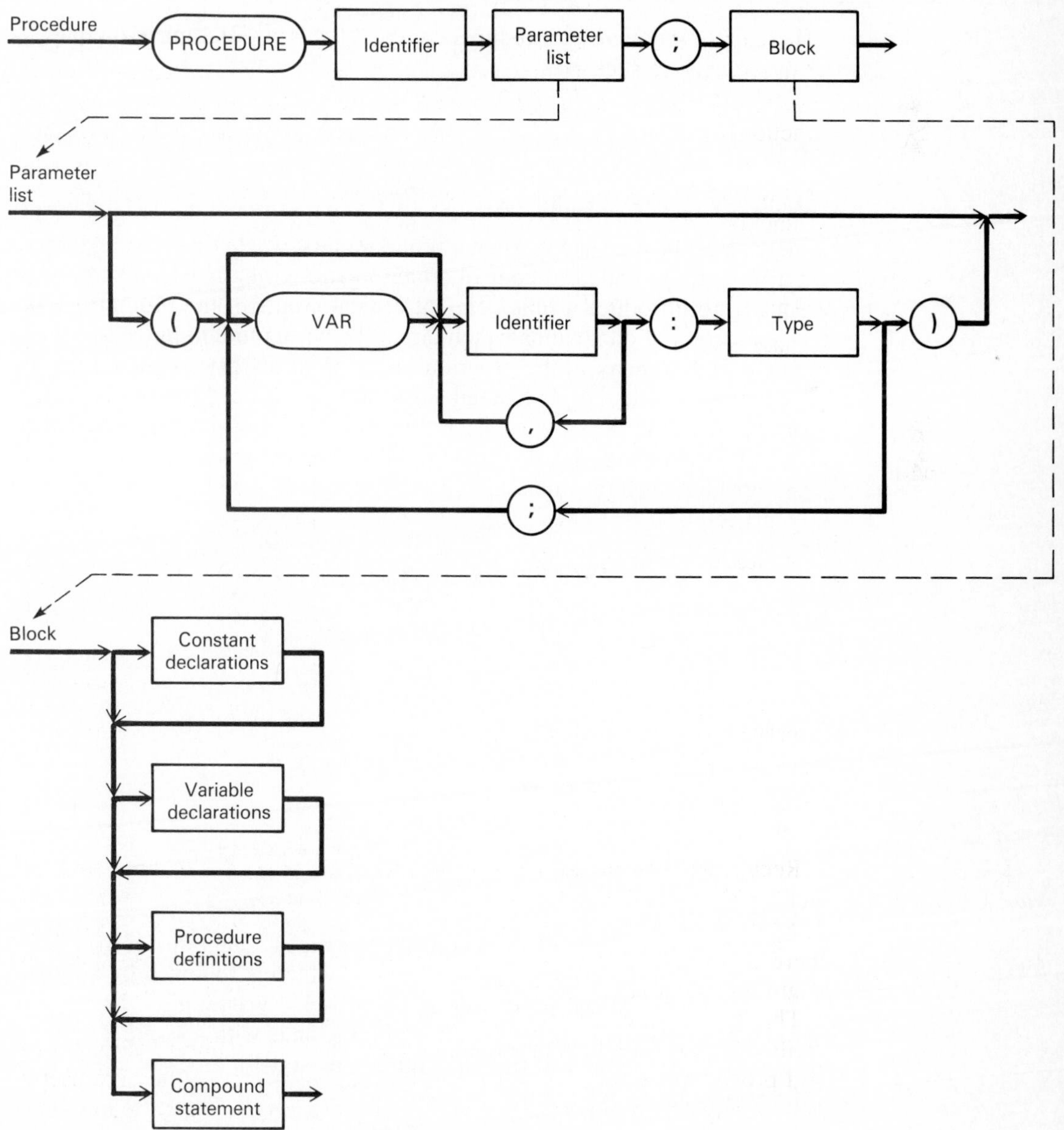

Fig. 22-4 Syntax diagram for a Pascal procedure.

used within the subprogram. When the procedure is invoked, values for these parameters will be included in the statement which calls the procedure.

- *A block* which includes various data declarations and the compound statement describing the calculations to be performed. The block may also include the definition of another procedure. This construction supports nested procedures.

22-2-1 Using a Procedure in a Program

There are many ways procedures can be used in a program. Example 22-1 describes one such way.

Example 22-1 A (Useful) Waste of Time

There are many occasions when a program must waste time. For example, in a program intended to control an automatic wiring machine, it may be required to introduce a time delay at critical points of the program. After the execution of commands which direct the wiring tool to move to a point to be wired, a delay in the program might be necessary to allow time for the tool to reach the designated position. The procedure shown below generates a time delay. That is, it appears to do nothing for a period of time. This time can be determined experimentally, and by varying the value of the constant ''delaytime,'' different delays will be introduced by the procedure.

```
PROCEDURE wastetime;
CONST
   delaytime = 100;
VAR
   index: INTEGER;
BEGIN
   index := 1;
REPEAT
      index := index + 1
   UNTIL index > delaytime
END. (* wastetime *)
```

Notice that this procedure is consistent with the diagrams of Fig. 22-4. It begins with the keyword PROCEDURE, which is followed by an identifier—the name of the procedure in this case—''wastetime.'' In this example there is no parameter list. The heading ends with a semicolon ('';'') symbol. The remainder of the procedure consists of a block of statements which include the following:

Constant declarations:

```
CONST
    delaytime = 100;
```

Variable declarations:

```
VAR
    index: INTEGER;
```

A compound statement which is bracketed by the keywords BEGIN and END

PROBLEM FOR SECTION 22-2-1

1. Write the procedure wastetime (Example 22-1), using two other methods. (*Hint:* Use a WHILE statement and a FOR loop.)

22-2-2 Calling a Procedure

To invoke a procedure simply insert the name of the procedure at those points in the program where the task is to be executed. Use the name of the procedure instead of repeating (copying) the statements to be executed. The procedure identifier acts as a shorthand for the statements.

Example 22-2 How to Actually Waste Time

Example 22-1 included a procedure which was capable of producing a time delay. Assume that the delay which results from this procedure is 0.010 s (10 ms). A delay of 100 ms is needed to allow an automatic wrapping tool to complete one wiring connection (wrap). How can this be accomplished using the procedure wastetime?

A simple way to do this is to invoke the procedure wastetime 10 times. Each execution introduces a 10-ms delay. Ten such executions produce the required 100-ms delay. Within the main program the following fragment will produce the delay:

```
VAR
    index: INTEGER;
BEGIN
    FOR index := 1 TO 10 DO
        wastetime
END.
```

The presence of the identifier wastetime in this fragment causes the procedure (wastetime) to be executed.

PROBLEM FOR SECTION 22-2-2

1. Modify the fragment in Example 22-2 so that the number of times that wastetime is called is specified by a constant identified as N. Set this constant equal to 10.

22-2-3 Transmitting Information to a Procedure

The procedure wastetime shown above can be improved and made more useful. The procedure includes a loop (REPEAT-UNTIL) construction which repeats the assignment statement "index := index + 1" a fixed number of times. In this case there are 100 repetitions. This procedure can be made more flexible (useful) if the number of repetitions is made a variable quantity and the variable is specified at the time at which the procedure is invoked.

Information which is transmitted to a procedure is called a *parameter.* All parameters are included in a list associated with the procedure, referred to as the *parameter list*. The syntax for a parameter list is shown in Fig. 22-4.

At the time that the procedure is invoked, a value (number) is computed for the parameter which is to be transmitted. This number is then substituted at each point in the procedure where the name of the parameter appears.

There are two names associated with a parameter. Within the procedure, the parameter identifier (name) is called the *formal* parameter. Within the program which calls the procedure, the parameter is called the *actual* parameter.

The procedure heading contains the list of parameters which it expects to receive at the time that it is invoked. A parameter list which contains a single formal parameter has the following form:

```
PROCEDURE identifier(parm:<parm data type>);
```

Notice how this conforms to the syntax of Fig. 22-4. The keyword PROCEDURE is followed by the procedure name. The parameter appears within the parentheses. Included within the parentheses is the formal name of the parameter ("parm" in the sample shown above) followed by a colon (:), followed in turn by the data type to be associated with the formal parameter. A semicolon completes the heading. If two parameters were needed in the procedure, the procedure heading might look as follows:

```
PROCEDURE identifier(parm1:<parm1type>; parm2:<parm2type>);
```

In this sample, parm1 and parm2 are the parameter names or identifiers.

Example 22-3 Making Better Use of Wasted Time

The procedure wastetime is to be modified. In the first version a control loop was executed a fixed number of times (100). In this version the number of loop repetitions will be supplied at the time the procedure is invoked. The modified procedure appears below:

```
PROCEDURE wastetime(delaytime: INTEGER);
VAR
INDEX: integer;
BEGIN
INDEX := 1;
REPEAT
   index := index + 1
UNTIL index > delaytime
END; (* wastetime *)
```

Assume that the procedure takes 10 ms to execute when the parameter "delaytime" is 100. In order to produce a delay of 100 ms, the procedure would be invoked as follows:

```
wastetime(1000);
```

The following sequence of events occurs when the procedure is invoked. When wastetime(1000) is executed, the value of the parameter delaytime is replaced by the number which appears within the parentheses, namely, 1000. The procedure wastetime is then executed with the formal parameter, delaytime, replaced by 1000 wherever this identifier appears within the subprogram.

Notice how a simple change in the procedure—making delaytime into a parameter—has greatly streamlined the way in which the procedure is invoked. Recall from Example 22-2 that a loop in the main program was required in order to generate the required delay. Other possibilities exist for invoking the delay in the present instance. For example, the following sequence will work just as well as the one described above:

```
(* a fragment of the main program *)
VAR
    latency: INTEGER;
.
.
.
BEGIN
LATENCY := 1000;
wastetime(latency);
END.
```

In this case the value of "latency" is 1000 at the time that wastetime is invoked. The integer data, latency, is replaced by a number, namely 1000, and this number is then transmitted to the procedure wastetime. The important fact is that a number is computed when the procedure is invoked, and this number is then used in place of the formal parameter. This method is termed *calling by value,* and the number (1000) is called the *actual value* of the parameter.

PROBLEM FOR SECTION 22-2-3

1. Write a procedure which will turn on a motor for a period of time given by a parameter named "turnon" and will then prevent the motor from being turned on again for a period of time identified by "turnoff." Both turnon and turnoff are to be parameters. Since actually turning on the motor requires special instructions, simply insert the comment "(* turn on motor *)" where the motor should logically be energized.

22-2-4 Getting Answers from a Procedure

Procedures would be of limited value if the results of calculations performed within the subprogram could not be *returned* to the calling program. In order to get results returned from a procedure, a different form of the parameter list must be used. A typical form for the procedure heading that may be used when results are to be returned appears as follows (for a single result):

```
PROCEDURE identifier(VAR parm:<parmtype>);
```

The most significant difference between this form and the previous form is the presence of the keyword VAR. In other words, to transmit results to the calling program, the parameter to be returned is declared to be a variable.

When the procedure is invoked, the *address* (and *not* its value) of the variable "parm" is transmitted to the procedure. This mechanism is referred to as *call by reference*. No value or number is calculated for the parameter. Instead, the address is transmitted. In this case the procedure can find (read) the data found at this address and replace that data with a new result (if necessary).

Since calling by reference transmits the address of data, *it can be used to transmit data to the procedure as well as receive results from the procedure*. Call by reference is thus useful when data is to be transmitted to a procedure, altered or changed by the actions of the procedure, and the new values returned to the calling program.

A word of caution is in order. If call by reference were the only method of communication, certain risks would exist. There would exist the possibility of changing the value of a variable which was not intended to be changed. This could result from some logical error in the procedure that might not be evident. The resultant changes (to the variable) are called *side effects* and are very difficult to discover, especially in large programs. The method of call by value provides some protection against possible side effects.

In summary, use call by value when data transmitted to a procedure should not be altered, and use call by reference when results must be returned to the calling program or where variables are to be altered by the actions of the procedure.

In general, it is possible to transmit parameters using both mechanisms within the same procedure heading. The following sample shows how this might appear:

```
PROCEDURE ident(VAR X,Y:REAL; VAR result:INTEGER; number:INTEGER);
```

In this case;

ident =	the name or identifier of the procedure
X and Y =	REAL data types which are called by reference
result =	an INTEGER data type which is called by reference
number =	an INTEGER data type transmitted to the procedure using call by value

Example 22-4 An Average Procedure

The preceding chapter described an algorithm for computing the average value of a group of numbers. A subprogram which calculates the average value of a group of real numbers stored in an array could be a useful addition to a library of utility programs. The following sample explains one possible method. The averaging procedure is shown below.

```
PROCEDURE average(VAR result: REAL;VAR indata:
                         datarray; noitems: INTEGER);
VAR
index: INTEGER;
sum: REAL;
BEGIN
sum := 0.0;
FOR index := 1 TO noitems DO
   sum := sum + indata[index];
result := sum/noitems
END; (* end of average procedure *)
```

The program (perhaps part of the main program) might contain the following fragment.

```
CONST
first = 1;
last = 100;
TYPE
datarray = ARRAY[first..last] OF REAL;
VAR
testdata: datarray;
answer: REAL;
howmany: INTEGER;
```

```
      .
      .
      .
BEGIN
howmany := 50;
average(answer, testdata, howmany);
END.
```

Notice the following with regard to the averaging procedure and the way in which it is invoked:

- The formal parameters are:

  "result," which is called by reference
  "indata," whose type is specified by "datarray"; this latter array is a simple structure which may include up to 100 real values
  "noitems," representing the number of items to be averaged, and which is called by value

- The actual parameters are:

  "answer," which is the variable where the averaged result from the procedure will be returned
  "testdata," whose type is the user-defined array type
  "howmany": this parameter is called by value, and the number 50 will be substituted when the procedure is invoked—notice that howmany is assigned the value 50 just before the procedure is called

- The procedure "average" accepts three parameters. These include the variable which will receive the results, the address of the array whose entries are to be averaged, and the number of items to be averaged. This last piece of information is really the number of items in the array which are to be included in the calculation of the average value.

- Within the procedure, a variable ("sum") keeps track of the sum of all valid data items. This variable is initially set to 0. A FOR loop control structure is used to add all the valid items. The average (called "result") is computed by dividing the sum of all valid data items by the number of items which were added to form the sum.

PROBLEMS FOR SECTION 22-2-4

1. a. In the program fragment shown below, identify the formal parameters and the actual parameters.
   b. Which parameters are called by reference and which ones are called by value?

```
(* In the program which invokes the procedure *)
TYPE
```

```
list = ARRAY[1..100] OF INTEGER;
VAR
a, b: list;
x, y: INTEGER;
P, Q: REAL;
BEGIN
join(a, b, x, y, p, q);
(* In the procedure join, the heading is *)
PROCEDURE join(VAR h, k: list; VAR l, m: INTEGER; w, v: REAL);
```

2. A company's products are inspected for quality in its test department. The machines being tested produce a table of results. Consider the table to be a one-dimensional array of data. Part of the information needed for the quality control report that must be developed includes the range of test values. Write a procedure which will examine a list of real values stored within an array, find the largest and smallest values in the list, and return these values to the program which invokes the procedure. For the formal identifiers use the following:

alist =	the array to be examined
largest =	the largest real number in the list
smallest =	the smallest real number in the list
noofitems =	the number of items in the list that must be examined

22-3 Functions

One useful function supplied as part of the standard version of Pascal is SQRT, which returns the square root of the argument that accompanies it. The syntax for invoking this function is

SQRT(x)

where "x" is the argument supplied by the user. The square root of x is computed and the resultant value is substituted for the entire expression SQRT(x). Functions such as SQRT are called *standard functions*. However, there are many potentially useful functions which are not supported by the standard version of Pascal. These must be developed by the users. Such functions are very similar to procedures, but there are a few differences in syntax. A list of such differences includes:

- The *name* (identifier) of the function *is assigned a value* somewhere within the subprogram. (Procedure names have no associated values.) Within the function subprogram, the function name will appear on the left-hand side of an assignment statement.
- Because a function has an associated value, *the data type for that value must be specified in the function heading statement*. Procedures have no such type associated with the procedure name.
- The keyword FUNCTION (as opposed to PROCEDURE) appears in the heading statement.

- A call (reference) to a function *always appears in an expression*. The function name never appears by itself, as is the case for procedures.

Aside from these important differences, functions and procedures are very similar, particularly with regard to the transmission of parameters.

Example 22-5 Writing a Function

Standard Pascal does not include a way to perform the algebraic operation

$$x^y$$

(Some nonstandard versions of Pascal have functions which can be used to help solve this problem; however, they may not be available for all computers.) The following procedure can be added to a library of special and useful functions which will perform the calculation cited above.

```
FUNCTION xpowery(x, y: INTEGER): INTEGER;
(* This function raises x to the y power. It expects
integer values for x and y. In addition, Y must be >=
0, and x<>0. *)

BEGIN
   IF (y = 0) THEN xpowery := 1
      ELSE
         BEGIN
            xpowery := x;
            WHILE Y > 1 DO
              BEGIN
                xpowery := x * xpowery
                y := y - 1
              END;
         END;
END; (* function xpowery *)
```

In the writing of the function to calculate x^y several questions need to be considered:

- What happens to the calculation when x or y or both are real numbers?
- What happens to the calculations when x and y are integers, but either or both are negative?

These are left for the student to consider (see the problems at the end of this section).

A sample of a program fragment which might invoke ''xpowery'' follows:

```
PROGRAM demo
VAR
    p, q, r: INTEGER;
BEGIN
    p := 2;
    q := 3;
    r := xpowery(p, q);
END.
```

(What is the value of the variable r in this fragment after the indicated operations have been completed?)

PROBLEMS FOR SECTION 22-3

1. Refer to Example 22-5. What is the value of r in the following?

```
r := xpowery(-3, 2);
```

What is the algebraic value of $(-3)^2$? Does the function "xpowery" correctly calculate $(-3)^2$? That is, does the result (r) returned by the function have the same value as the algebraic calculation?

2. Refer again to Example 22-5. What is the value of r in the following?

```
r := xpowery(3, -2);
```

Does this result equal the equivalent algebraic (hand) calculation 3^{-2}?

3. Modify the function "xpowery" so that it correctly calculates x^y when $y < 0$. To do so, make the following assumptions:
(a) x and y are integer quantities.
(b) The answer—the value assigned to xpowery—should be a real quantity. (Why?)

22-4 FUNCTIONS AND PROCEDURES AS PARAMETERS

In previous discussions, the parameters associated with functions and procedures have either been call by value or call by reference (variables). In addition to such parameters it is also possible to use an entire function or procedure as a parameter. The syntax for the function or procedure will be different. In the use of such parameters, the headings for procedures or functions will appear in one of the following forms:

PROCEDURE identifier (FUNCTION <identifier: type; other parameters>);
PROCEDURE identifier (PROCEDURE <identifier: other parameters>);
FUNCTION identifier (FUNCTION <identifier: type; other parameters>):<type>;
FUNCTION identifier (PROCEDURE <identifier: other parameters>):<type>;

Notice, when a function or procedure is included as a parameter, then the corresponding keyword must appear in front of the name (identifier) of the parameter.

Example 22-6 Explaining the Control Sequence When Using Functions as Parameters

The following procedure will add, subtract, multiply, or divide two real data elements. The operation which is actually performed depends on the function which is specified at the time that the procedure is invoked. Part of a Pascal program includes the following:

```
    FUNCTION sum(a, b: REAL): REAL;
       sum := a + b
    END; (* end of sum function *)

    FUNCTION diff(a, b: REAL): REAL;
       diff := a - b
    END; (* end of subtraction function *)

    FUNCTION product(a, b: REAL): REAL;
       product := a * b
    END; (* end of multiplication function *)

    FUNCTION ratio(a, b: REAL): REAL;
       ratio := a/b
    END; (* end of division function *)

PROCEDURE calculate(FUNCTION f: REAL; x, y: REAL; VAR result: REAL);
    result := f(x, y)
END; (* end of calculator procedure *)
```

Another part of the program, perhaps the main section, contains the following information:

```
PROGRAM calculatorsimulation;

VAR
   operand1, operand2: REAL;
   answer: real;

operand1 := 250.0;
operand2 := -125.3;
calculate(sum, operand1, operand2, answer);
calculate(diff, operand1, operand2, answer);
calculate(product, operand1, operand2, answer);
```

```
calculate(ratio, operand1, operand2, answer);

END. (* end of four-function calculator simulation *)
```

In the program fragment, the procedure named "calculate" is called four times. The first parameter of the procedure determines the function to be performed [i.e., sum (+), diff (−), product (*), ratio (/)]. The next two parameters indicate the numbers to be used in the calculations. The last parameter determines which variable is to be assigned the value returned by the calculations.

When "calculate (sum, . . .);" is executed, the function named "sum" is substituted for the formal parameter "f" in the procedure calculate. When this occurs, the statement "result := f(x, y);" (in procedure calculate) is interpreted as

```
result := sum(x, y);
```

This means that the function sum is invoked when the procedure calculate is executed.

The program segments shown above can be used to imitate the operations of an ordinary (four-function) hand-held calculator.

PROBLEMS FOR SECTION 22-4

1. Refer to Example 22-6. Within the program named "calculatorsimulation," compute the number which will be stored in the memory locations set aside for the variable "answer" for each invocation of the procedure calculate.

2. Use the functions and procedures defined in Example 22-6 to write a program fragment which calculates

$$\frac{x + y}{x - y}$$

22-5 THE SCOPE OF VARIABLES

Functions and procedures can be considered to be *tools* to a programmer. When a new program is needed, the procedures and functions of a software library may be combined to accomplish the programming task in an efficient manner.

Example 22-7 A Problem?

Shown below are the headings for two functions stored in the computer's library of Pascal subprograms:

```
FUNCTION func1(parm1: INTEGER; parm2: REAL): REAL;
FUNCTION func2(parm1: INTEGER; parm2: REAL): INTEGER;
```

Notice that the first function ("func1") and the second function ("func2") have certain similarities. In particular, they each contain two parameters with the same identifier ("parm1" and "parm2"). An immediate question and potential problem exists. Will the Pascal compiler set aside the same physical memory locations for parm1 when it translates func1 and func2? If so, such an arrangement would produce unanticipated results (side effects). It is evident that parm1 in func1 would interfere with parm1 of func2. Fortunately, such problems do not exist in standard versions of Pascal.

The reason for the absence of side effects posed in Example 22-7 lies in the *rules of scope*. In Pascal, groups of instructions are combined to form blocks. The main scope rule can be stated as follows:

> *A variable is known (accessible) to the Pascal compiler only within the block in which it is found.*

A variable which is defined within a procedure or a function can be accessed only when the program executes instructions within the subprogram. The variable is said to be a *local variable*. Another way of stating this is as follows:

> *The variable is local to the subprogram (procedure or function).*

Local variables have no effect outside the subprogram. The variables will *disappear* (its memory locations will be inaccessible) when the subprogram has been executed.

Blocks may be nested; that is, one block may be logically enclosed within another. A variable declared in the outer block is accessible to

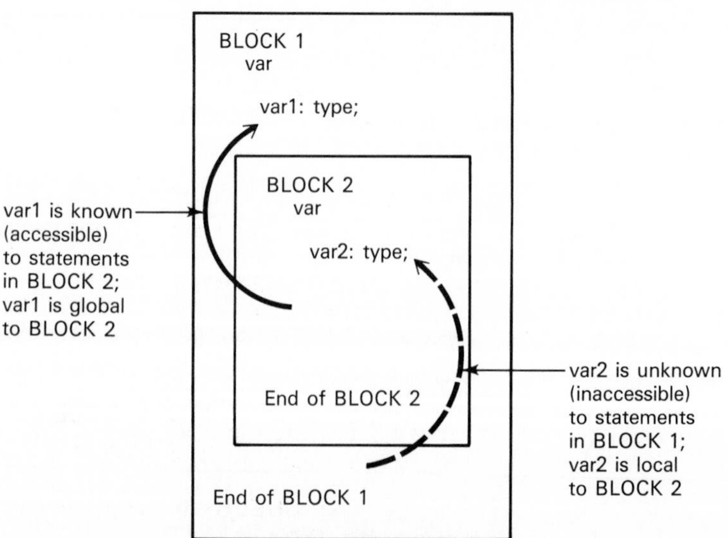

Fig. 22-5 Scope of Pascal variables.

statements in the inner block. Such a variable is said to be *global* to the inner block. Figure 22-5 depicts the nature of local and global variables.

Within a procedure or function, identifiers (parameter names) are local. They cannot have any effect on global variables even if they have the same names. If block 2 (Fig. 22-5) is a procedure, var2 cannot be accessed from block 1. However, once a variable is passed to the subprogram, it becomes accessible for the life of the function or procedure. If a function or procedure is passed (transmitted) to a subprogram, all variables accessible to the function or procedure are then known to the subprogram to which it has been passed.

Recall from Chap. 19 that a block may consist of:

Label declarations
Constant declarations
Type definitions
Variable declarations
Procedure declarations
Function declarations
One or more statements (at least one statement is necessary or the block does not exist)

PROBLEMS FOR SECTION 22-5

1. Examine the program fragment shown below. Copy and complete the following table after reviewing the fragment.

	Test	Inspect
A	local	global
B		
C		
D		
E		
F		
G		
H		
I		
J		
FIRST		

```
PROGRAM test;
CONST
   first = 1;
VAR
   A, B, C: INTEGER;
   D, E, F: REAL;

PROCEDURE inspect (VAR p: REAL);
VAR
```

```
      G, H: INTEGER;
      I, J: REAL;
    BEGIN
    .
    .
    .
    END; (* End of procedure inspect. *)

    BEGIN
      A := B + G;
    END. (* End of test. *)
```

2. In the program fragment in Prob. 1, what is wrong with the statement

```
A := B + G;
```

3. Given the following program fragment:

```
PROGRAM test2;
VAR
   A, B: INTEGER;
FUNCTION calculate(x, y: INTEGER): INTEGER;
VAR
   A, B: INTEGER;
BEGIN
   A := 25;
   B := 35;
END; (* calculate *)

BEGIN
   A := 10;
   B := 100;
END. (* test2 *)
```

What are the values of A and B when the program is complete?

22-6 FORWARD REFERENCES AND EXTERNAL PROCEDURES

In Pascal programs, functions and procedures must be defined (included) before they are actually invoked. This is shown in Fig. 22-6. There are occasions when there are so many functions or procedures that it becomes impossible to define a given subprogram before it is to be used. In order to overcome the problem, Pascal includes the *forward reference* provision. Simply stated, the keyword FORWARD is appended to the function or procedure heading. However, the heading is now moved to the beginning of the program.

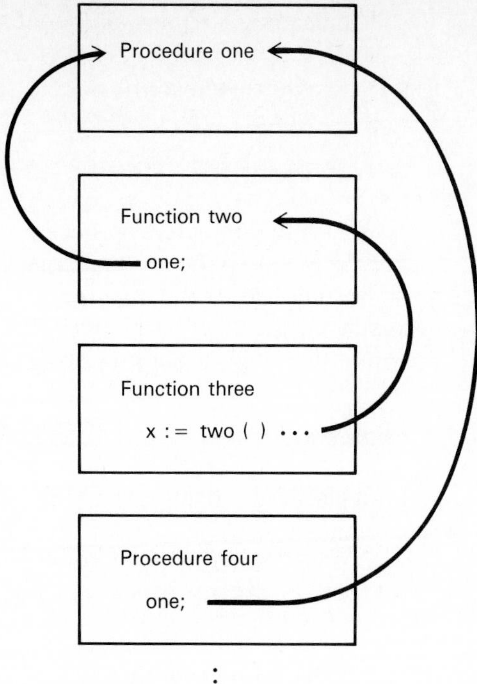

Fig. 22-6 Subprograms are normally defined before they are used or invoked.

Example 22-8 Using the FORWARD Reference

```
PROGRAM demo;
PROCEDURE one(x, y: INTEGER); FORWARD;
FUNCTION two(x, y: REAL): REAL; FORWARD;
   .
   .
   .
PROCEDURE one;
   .
   .
   .
FUNCTION two;
   .
   .
   .
END. (* demo *)
```

In the program fragment above, observe two facts:

- To declare a procedure or function which is to have a forward reference, *the subprogram heading is placed at the very beginning of the program.*

The heading contains all the information normally expected. The heading is followed by the keyword FORWARD.

- *When the complete subprogram appears within the body of the program, the heading is reduced to the name only.*

For some computers, procedures or functions in the library may have been previously written and compiled. Such subprograms do not have to be recompiled. To recognize such routines, the keyword EXTERN is appended to the subprogram. The procedure or function will not appear within the body of the program presently under development.

Example 22-9 Using the EXTERN Facility

```
PROGRAM demo;
PROCEDURE one(i: INTEGER): EXTERN;
   .
   .
   .
one(10);
   .
   .
   .
END. (* demo *)
```

Notice that the name is included at the beginning of the program. The keyword EXTERN is appended. The subprogram ("one") is not defined anywhere in the program. It is used (invoked) just as if it had been defined (i.e., "one(10);").

SUMMARY

Subprograms consist of procedures or functions. They identify a block of statements within a program. Each time the name of the subprogram appears in the program, the entire block of statements is executed. New programs may be designed very efficiently by combining such subprograms in new sequences.

The procedure includes the keyword PROCEDURE, the name or identifier, a list of parameters, and a block which contains data declarations and one or more statements. The parameters are called formal parameters. They mark positions within the subprogram where substitutions will be made when the procedure is used (executed). To invoke or call a procedure, simply insert the name of the procedure to be executed at the proper position in the program. In addition, include the actual parameters which are to be used in place of the formal ones.

Parameters exist in two varieties. If information (an actual parameter) is first evaluated and then transmitted to the subprogram, the parameter is said to be called by value or simply a value parameter. If the memory location (address) of the parameter is transmitted to the procedure, it is said to be called by reference. This second form of parameter allows the value of the parameter to be altered within the procedure body and returned to the calling program. This type of parameter must appear in the heading preceded by the keyword VAR.

A function subprogram is similar to a procedure. However, there is a value associated with the name of the function itself. Thus, the function identifier must appear on the left-hand side of an assignment statement within the body of the function subprogram. The value associated with the name of the function is returned to the calling program and replaces the same identifier found there.

Functions and procedures may also be transmitted as parameters to other functions or procedures.

An important idea presented in this chapter is the scope of a variable. Variables only "live" within the block in which they are defined. There are two characteristics which can be assigned to a variable in this regard. A variable may be either local or global. Local variables do not exist outside the block in which they are defined. However, if such a variable has the same name as a variable that is defined in a second block, the variable in the second block will not be affected by changes to the value of the variable in the first block. Global variables are known to all blocks which are nested within the defining block.

The FORWARD reference is used to avoid conditions in which subprograms are invoked before they are defined. The EXTERN option allows compiled subprograms within libraries to be used in Pascal programs.

REVIEW PROBLEMS

1. Write a procedure which calculates the equivalent resistive value for two resistors connected in parallel. Call the resistors R1 and R2. In the calling program, a variable named RT should be assigned the answer. The formula for calculating equivalent resistance is

$$R_T = \frac{R_1 R_2}{R_1 + R_2}$$

2. Using the procedure of Prob. 1, write a statement which could be used to calculate the equivalent resistance of a 1000-ohm resistor in parallel combination with a 200-ohm resistor.

3. Production expediters deal in part with scheduling of part assembly. If X, Y, and Z are the delivery times of three subassemblies (in weeks), write a function which will determine the subassembly with the longest lead time.

4. Given the following:

```
PROGRAM demo;
FUNCTION one(a: INTEGER): REAL;
BEGIN
.
.
.
END; (* one *)
procedure two(FUNCTION f: REAL; b, c: INTEGER);
VAR
   x, y, z: REAL;
BEGIN
.
.
.
END; (* two *)

BEGIN
.
.
.
End. (* demo *)
```

Describe the relationship of the variables x, y, and z to the function f in procedure "two."

REVIEW QUESTIONS

1. What is an efficient way to write new programs?
2. What is a procedure?
3. How many times can a procedure be called from a program?
4. The syntax for a procedure includes three important elements. Name and explain each one.

23 THE INS AND OUTS OF PASCAL

A computer would not be very useful if computational results could not be extracted from the machine; in addition, it would be severely limited if a user could not supply the data to be used in the program calculations. This chapter explains the Pascal statements that can be used to control movement of data between the computer and the users. Such control statements are referred to a *input/output,* or *I/O*.

This chapter includes a description of the communication between the standard input/output devices and the computer. In addition, it describes the rules which govern control of the other files, particularly those which can be found in the secondary storage system.

23-1 DATA AS FILES

Data is moved into or out of the computer in groups. The data being moved is identified by a single name and is referred to as a *file*. The name of the group is called the *file name*. Figure 23-1 translates these concepts into pictorial form. The figure shows a number of connections, or links, between the machine and the external world. Data moves to and from the computer via these connections. (They are not entirely physical connections; however, one may think of them in this way.) At any given moment data logically moves on only one of these connections. That is, programs do not receive (input) and transmit (output) data at the same time.

Two file connections in the computer system are usually given special designations. These files are called *standard input* (or simply input), and standard output (or simply output).

Standard input is most likely to be the keyboard of the computer. It is the source of numbers and characters that a user enters for program calculations. The standard output device is usually the computer monitor. This device may also be a printer in some installations. Together the standard input and output constitute the *terminal* of the computer.

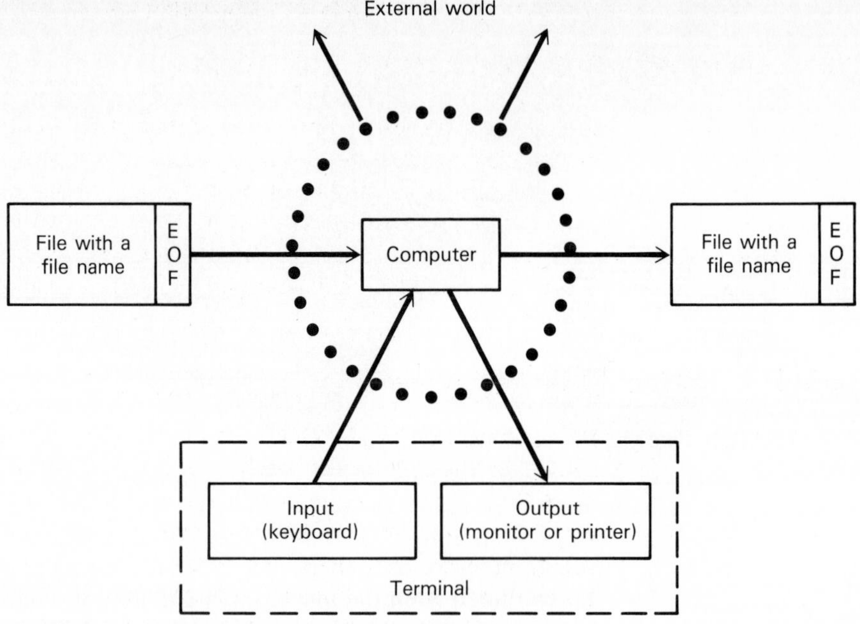

Fig. 23-1 The computer *sees* data in groups called files.

Files are terminated with a special mark which signifies the end of the file. This is useful, as the amount of information varies from one file to another. The mark is called the end-of-file (*EOF*) mark.

Files include data which is to be received by a program, or results (data) which are to be provided by the program. *All data (files) which are to be transmitted between the computer and the external world must be specified in the program heading*. This is an important rule in Pascal. The syntax for the program heading is repeated in Fig. 23-2. The list of identifiers within the parentheses, which are identified by a dagger (†), includes all the files with which the program expects to communicate. Practically all programs use standard input and output. It is therefore safe to include these in the program heading as a matter of habit. Including standard input and output files in the header and not using them will not produce any errors. A sample heading might look like:

```
PROGRAM example (INPUT, OUTPUT);
```

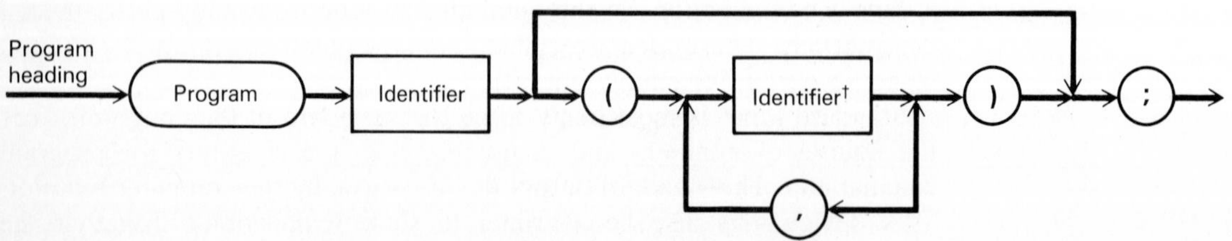

†See text

Fig. 23-2 Syntax diagram for a program heading.

If other files are needed they must also appear in the list.

23-2 COMMUNICATING WITH A USER: THE TERMINAL

Recall from the preceding chapter that procedures describe a set of operations to be performed. Pascal includes a number of procedures which relieve users of a number of programming tasks. These subprograms are called *standard procedures*.

Procedures which are useful for terminal operations include READ, READLN, WRITE, and WRITELN. These are discussed in the following sections.

23-2-1 READ and READLN Procedures

READ and READLN procedures are very similar. The syntax for both is shown in Fig. 23-3. The READ and READLN procedures accept data from the keyboard (standard input) and assigns the data it receives to variables within the computer program. When entering such data, the user separates each data item by one or more spaces. (Under some circumstances spaces are not needed—see Example 23-1—but it is best to include spaces to avoid potential problems.) The data is expected as a sequence of alphanumeric characters that are translated by the READ procedure into integer, real, character, or other data formats for storage within the computer. The sequence is contained in a *line* that is normally demarcated by special control characters; in particular, these characters may be composed of a combination of *carriage return* and *line feed* characters.

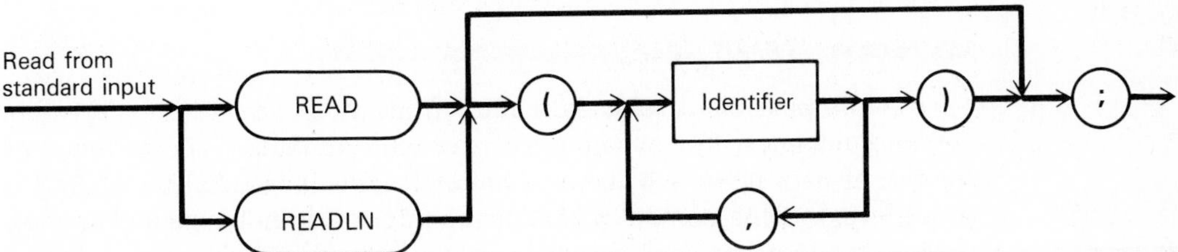

Fig. 23-3 Syntax diagram for invoking the READ and READLN procedures.

Example 23-1 Using READ and READLN

Examine the following program.

```
PROGRAM indemo(INPUT, OUTPUT);
VAR
    one, two: INTEGER;
    three, four: REAL;
    five, six: CHAR;
```

```
BEGIN
    READ(one, two);
    READ(three, four);
    READLN(five, six)
END. (* End of input demonstration program. *)
```

Table 23-1 summarizes examples of data which might be entered into the computer from the keyboard, and the values which are assigned to corresponding variables within the computer's memory.

TABLE 23-1 SUMMARY OF ENTRIES AND THEIR INTERNAL VALUES FOR EXAMPLE 29-1

	EQUIVALENT VALUES WITHIN THE COMPUTER					
Input	**one**	**two**	**three**	**four**	**five**	**six**
30, −100, 2.65, −0.81, A, B	30	−100	2.65	−0.81	'A'	'B'
−2, +5, −6.9, 2.1E+05, C, D	−2	5	−6.9	2.1E05	'C'	'D'
−8, 9, −0.002, 23, EF,	−8	9	−0.002	23.0	'E'	'F'

The sample program provides for six data items: two integers, two real numbers, and two characters. Some important possibilities include the following:

- Real numbers can be entered as decimal (fixed-point) or scientific (exponential) values
- Character values do not have to be separated by spaces in some limited cases

To avoid possible errors, data entry from the keyboard should follow certain guidelines. For example, be sure that the data is compatible with the list of data items which the computer expects (READ or READLN procedures). If the computer expects an integer, do not type a character.

Most modern terminals include editing features which can be used to cancel characters if mistakes are made during entry of the data. In addition, most terminals echo (display on the monitor) the characters being entered, even though this is not an operation included within the READ or READLN procedure. Rather, this is a *local* operation being carried out by the terminal itself. To verify values which actually reside within the computer, the computer must be instructed to write out (output) previously stored values.

When the user is satisfied with the data as it appears on the monitor, the return key (carriage return) is struck. This validates the data and initiates physical transfer between the keyboard and the computer.

Example 23-1 includes both READ and READLN procedure calls. Example 23-2 provides a second case which helps to distinguish the two procedures. In brief, after the computer accepts data with a READLN command, any remaining values on the input line are discarded. After the data for a READ procedure has been accepted, any remaining values on the input line are available for the next READ or READLN procedure.

Example 23-2 Differences between READ and READLN

In the following program fragment, the variables "one," "two," "three," and "four" are REAL data types.

```
READ(one, two);
READLN(three);
READ(four);
```

One example of data entry using these calls is given in the following list:

1. −1.35 **2.** 2.0E−03 **3.** −21.0 **4.** 2.1314

The leading numbers indicate the sequence in which the data is entered; they are *not* part of the data entry. The first READ receives items 1 and 2. The READLN accepts item 3. When READLN completes its operation, it advances the input device to a new line. Hence item 4 is accepted by the second READ command on a new line.

PROBLEMS FOR SECTION 23-2-1

1. Write out one possible set of input values which satisfies the following program fragment.

```
REPEAT
  READLN(number);
  process(number);
UNTIL number < 0.0;
```

   Assume "process" is a procedure which operates on the variable number. In this problem, the exact procedure is not important. The variable number is a REAL data type.

2. The following statement is found within a program:

```
READLN;
```

   What is the effect of this procedure call?

3. What does `READ(input);` mean?

23-2-2 WRITE and WRITELN Procedures

The procedures WRITE and WRITELN are analogous to READ and READLN with the important difference being the nature of the file connection. With WRITE and WRITELN it is understood that the standard output connection (device) will receive the data in the call. The standard output device varies from one computer installation to another. It may be a printer. However, in this text the monitor is considered to be the standard output device.

The syntax for WRITE and WRITELN is exactly the same as that shown in Fig. 23-3 with the exception of the keywords.

Example 23-3 Using a WRITELN Procedure

A manager of a company test department must keep records of all the signal generators that are tested. (Assume the company manufactures signal generators in addition to other products.) The record for one signal generator has the following format:

Model number: integer
Series number: integer
Test 1: real number
Test 2: real number
Test 3: real number
Test 4: real number

Each test consists of some measurement which is made under a different set of signal-generator operating conditions. For example, one test might be the magnitude of the output signal when the line voltage is adjusted to a specified low limit. The following program fragment will calculate the average results of test 3 for all signal generators which have been tested and display the results on the computer's monitor.

```
PROGRAM demo(INPUT, OUTPUT);
TYPE testresult =
RECORD
   modnumber: ARRAY[1..7] OF INTEGER;
   serialno: ARRAY[1..7] OF INTEGER;
   test1: REAL;
   test2: REAL;
   test3: REAL;
   test4: REAL;
END; (* testresult record *)
VAR
siggen: ARRAY[1..100] OF testresult;
index: INTEGER;
sum, average: REAL;
BEGIN
sum := 0.0;
FOR index := 1 TO 100 DO
   sum := sum + siggen[index].test3;
```

```
average := sum/100;
   WRITELN(' The average test3 result is ', average)
END. (* end of demo program. *)
```

Some facts will help to explain this program:

- A record type is defined. It is identified as "testresult" and contains six fields.
- An array is declared. It consists of 100 records of TYPE testresult.
- A FOR loop is used to sum the results of "test3" from each of the 100 records.
- The average is calculated by dividing the sum by 100.
- The average is displayed on the monitor (standard output device) using the WRITELN procedure.

In particular, study the WRITELN statement in the example. Within the parentheses which list the variables to be transmitted to the terminal notice the following:

```
' The average test3 result is ', average
```

Normally a list of data to be transmitted will be found within the parentheses, in this case, a phrase enclosed within single quotation marks, followed by a comma and then the variable "average." Whenever phrases appear (bracketed by single quotation marks), the characters will be displayed on the terminal as a message. In this case the message " The average test3 result is " will appear on the monitor. This will be followed on the same line by the value of the variable average. *Because the program uses WRITELN, the next WRITE or WRITELN statement which is executed will appear on a new line.*

PROBLEMS FOR SECTION 23-2-2

1. An array contains real numbers. It has three rows and five columns. Using FOR statements, write a program fragment which will output the values of the array on the monitor of the computer. This output should consist of three rows, and each row should contain five columns of data.

2. Repeat Prob. 1. However, in this case output the results in a column-first format. This means that the terminal should display the results with the following format:

```
row1, col1    row2, col1    row3, col1
row1, col2    row2, col2    row3, col2
                 . . .
row1, col5    row2, col5    row3, col5
```

where the row number and column number refer to the positions in the original array.

23-2-3 Data Formats

When data is to be output to the terminal, it is often desirable to have control over the way in which it is printed. For example, when real numbers are being displayed, such questions as "How many positions should the number occupy?" and "How many digits should appear after the decimal point?" are important. If relevant information is not included within the program, then the computer will make default (arbitrary) decisions regarding such matters. They could vary from one machine to another because such decisions are implementation-dependent.

Automatic formatting is the term applied to those instances when choices are left to the computer. Table 23-2 contains typical default values.

TABLE 23-2 TYPICAL IMPLEMENTATION FORMATS

When Data Is	Format Is
BOOLEAN	The word TRUE or FALSE will be printed.
REAL	Exponential (scientific) notation is used. The number of digits varies from one machine to another.
INTEGER	The number of digits varies from one machine to another. Usually, the number is right-justified. If the value to be printed is 25, and the computer provides eight printing positions for integer values, then the result will appear as bbbbbb25, where "b" signifies a blank.

There is a way for the user to specify the format of the data. The syntax for specifying the format is shown in Fig. 23-4. There are three syntactical possibilities, and each of these is explained with a simple example.

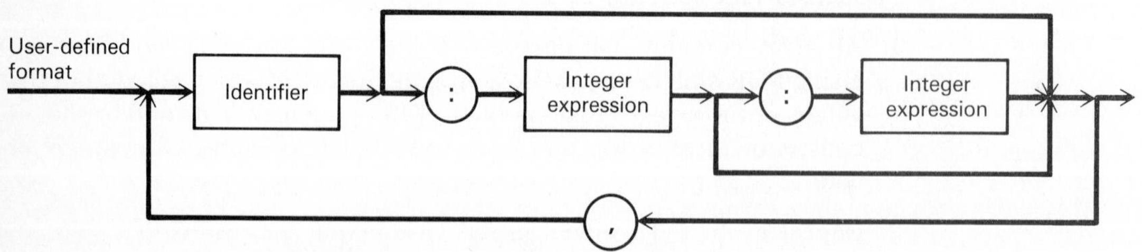

Fig. 23-4 Syntax diagram for specifying user-defined formats.

Example 23-4 Format, Case 1

This first instance is really the computer-controlled, or automatic, format. A simple example of this is

```
WRITELN(var1, var2, var3);
```

Notice, there are no colons (:) in this example. When data is *not* followed by a colon, then the computer controls the format.

Example 23-5 Format, Case 2

In this case, a series of data items will be followed by the colon, and the colon in turn followed by an integer expression. (A constant is a simple instance of an integer expression.)

```
WRITELN(cats:5, dogs:6, pigeons:7);
```

The data list specifies the following:

A minimum of 5 positions will be allocated for the variable "cats"
A minimum of 6 positions will be allocated for the variable "dogs"
A minimum of 7 positions will be allocated for the variable "pigeons"

Assuming that all the variables are INTEGER data types, there are two questions which need to be answered. What happens if the actual value of the variable contains fewer digits than the allotted number? What happens if the actual value contains more digits than the format specifies?

If the format sets aside more positions than the actual integer occupies, the data will be printed in a right-justified manner, and blanks will be inserted ahead of the number itself. Suppose that cats is −2. This will be printed as bbb−2 (where "b" stands for blank).

If the format sets aside too few positions, then the computer will automatically increase the number of printing positions. This means that the number will never be "chopped off," or truncated.

Example 23-6 Format, Case 3

In this example, assume that the variables are all REAL data types. The WRITELN procedure statement appears as follows:

```
WRITELN(one:5:3, two:7:1, three:8:2);
```

In each instance of the data list two colon-integer pairs appear. The first integer specifies the number of printing positions which are set aside. The second integer determines how many digits appear after the decimal point. In other words, this will produce a fixed-point result on the monitor. For example, if the variable "one" has a value of 1.201, when the procedure WRITELN (above) is executed, the result 1.201 will appear on the monitor. The decimal point itself is included in the count of printing positions.

A word of caution is in order. For some computers the first printing position in a WRITE or WRITELN procedure is interpreted as a control command. The interpretation of the control character varies from one machine to another. However, a number of machines use the protocol outlined in Table 23-3 to guide operations of the standard output device.

TABLE 23-3 TYPICAL STANDARD OUTPUT CONTROL CHARACTERS

If First Character Is	Action Taken Is
Blank space	Use single vertical spacing
+	Print over the same line—do not insert a line feed
0	Use double spacing (vertical)
1	Skip to the beginning of the next page

PROBLEMS FOR SECTION 23-2-3

1. Given the following program segment:

```
VAR
one: INTEGER;
two: REAL;
three: CHAR;
BEGIN
one := 100;
two := -5.6;
three := '$';
WRITE('sample':10, one:4, two:5:2, three:2)
END.
```

What appears on the monitor of the computer? Include in your answer blank character positions.

2. The manager of software documentation is an important position in an industrial organization. It is helpful to be able to include flow diagrams in such documentation. One software documentation program includes resources for drawing flow diagrams and includes a procedure to draw a rectangle using the ASCII "+" character. Write a fragment (procedure) which could be used for such a purpose. There are three parameters to consider: the column in which the rectangle is to begin, the width of the rectangle, and the height of the rectangle.

3. Good programs should prevent a user from making mistakes. What factors (possible errors) should one consider in a program like the one described in Prob. 2? Do not write any error routines; just make a list of possible errors.

23-3 I/O AND THE SECONDARY STORAGE SYSTEM

Pascal includes various ways in which to create, access, and manipulate data within the secondary storage system of a computer. To accomplish this, data is organized into files, which have been previously described in Chap. 20. In that chapter the method for declaring a FILE data type was discussed. The material in this section will describe how to access (read) data from a file, and write data into a file.

Recall an important rule:

> *All files which are to be connected with a program must appear in the program heading.*

Example 23-7 Files in the Program Heading

A computer is used to control the operation of a robot that is to move production material onto a conveyer belt in a manufacturing plant. The robot responds to a series of commands which designate three-dimensional movements of its arm. The list of movements constitutes the data for the program. It is stored in a file, and this fact must be included in the program heading. The heading might look as follows:

```
PROGRAM TEST (INPUT, OUTPUT, robot1);
```

In this case "robot1" is the name of the file which contains the list of movements and which is stored in the secondary storage system.

23-3-1 Files Revisited

A file consists of a sequence of data elements, followed by a special mark call an end-of-file (EOF) mark. These elements will all be of the same type, such as characters, numbers, or records. A file of files is *not* permitted. Initially a file is empty except for the EOF mark. File elements are added in sequence, with the most recent data element followed by the EOF.

Only one element of the file may be accessed at any one time. A *window* identifies the element in the file which is being accessed. The window can be thought of as a pointer to the element currently being addressed. The window is referred to by a *buffer variable;* a typical example is

```
filex↑
```

This consists of two parts: "filex" is the name of the file, and the symbol "↑" reminds the user that this is a pointer element.

Files must be declared as variables within the program. Values for the buffer filex are stored within the main memory of the computer. The actual or physical element being accessed is found in the secondary storage system. Thus, a copy of the element being accessed is available within the main memory of the computer. The buffer variable and pointer behave somewhat differently for the read, write, reset, and rewrite operations which can be performed on these sequential access (SA) files.

Example 23-8 What the File Pointer Does During a Write Operation

Figure 23-5 indicates what happens to the file window and its pointer during a write operation. The ↑ is used for the pointer and indicates which element is being accessed. An element is added, and the window is automatically moved to the right by one position. The buffer variable (filex ↑) will be undefined at the end of the operation. (One cannot be sure of the value which is obtained if an attempt is made to read this window location.)

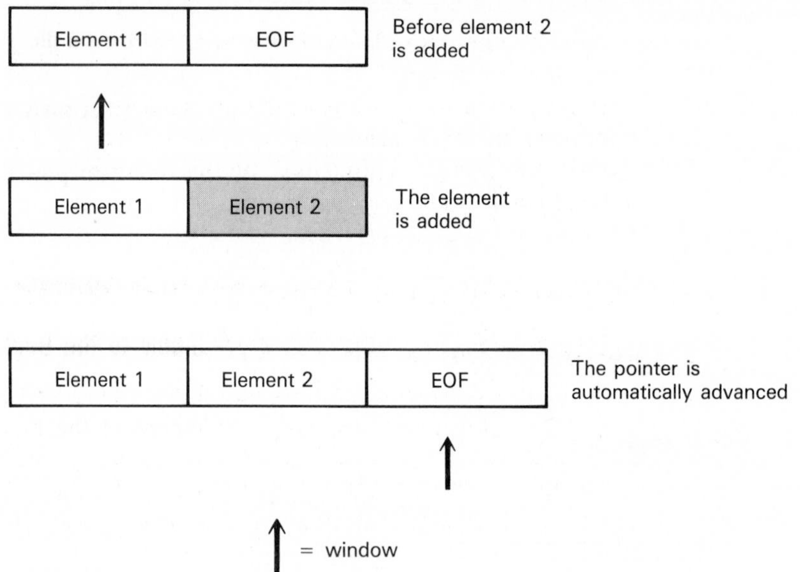

Fig. 23-5 File changes which occur when new data is added to an SA file.

Example 23-9 Actions of the Pointer During a Read Operation

Figure 23-6 describes what happens to the file window and its associated pointer during a file read operation. Data is transferred from the file to the locations associated with the buffer variable. The pointer is not automatically moved to the next data element in the file. An instruction must be provided within the program which moves the pointer to the next file element (see below).

Data elements in SA files can be examined only in strict sequence. If the window presently points to the fifth element of a file and it is necessary

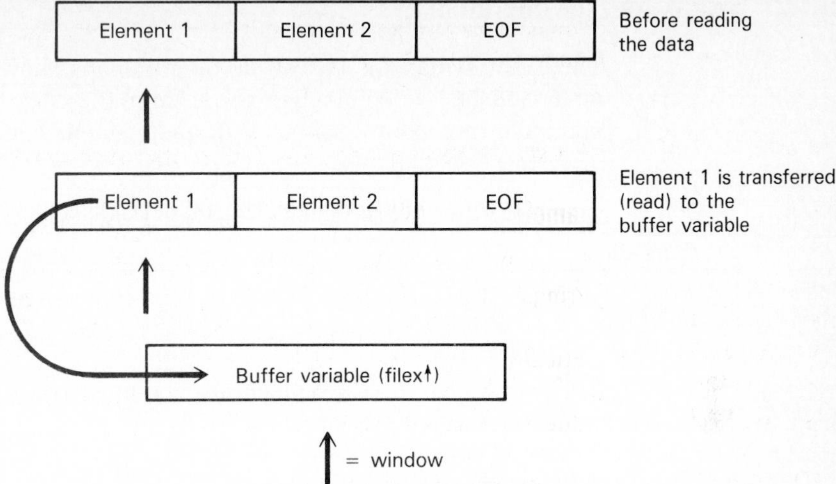

Fig. 23-6 What takes place when data is read from a file.

to access the third element, the program must instruct the computer to go back to the first element in the file and then advance the pointer to the third position. The reset operation is used to position the pointer to the beginning of the file.

Example 23-10 Positioning the Window to the Beginning of a File

When a reset operation is executed, two important things take place: the pointer is positioned to the first element of the file, and the contents of the first location are transferred to the memory associated with the buffer variable. Should the file be empty, the buffer variable would then contain undefined, useless information. Fortunately there is a way to check for this undesirable condition. In particular, it is possible to check to see if the pointer is at the EOF mark. This will be described later in the chapter when the Pascal syntax for all these operations is discussed.

Example 23-11 Starting a New File with the Rewrite Operation

The rewrite operation permits one to start a new file. The file may contain a number of elements before the rewrite procedure is invoked. These values will be erased, so caution is advised when you are invoking this procedure. When the procedure is complete, the access window is located at the first position within the file and the file is considered to be empty. It contains only the EOF indicator.

23-3-2 Syntax for File Operations

The exact syntax for Pascal file operations is shown in Table 23-4. This table includes the keywords to be used in the operation, the nature of the operation (procedure or function), and a simple example.

TABLE 23-4 SUMMARY OF PASCAL I/O OPERATIONS

Operation	Syntax	Type	Example
Append the present value of the buffer variable to the end of the file. You must be sure you are at the end of the file	PUT(filename);	PROCEDURE	PUT(myfile);
A combined operation which assigns a value to the buffer variable, and then appends the buffer variable to the end of the file. This is only applicable to text files (a text file is a FILE OF CHAR;)	WRITE(filename, element);	PROCEDURE	WRITE(myfile, value);
Empty a file and open it for writing	REWRITE (filename);	PROCEDURE	REWRITE (myfile);
Move the window to the start of the file, transfer the first element into the buffer variable; this is valid only when you want to read a file	RESET (filename);	PROCEDURE	RESET(myfile);
Move the window to the next element, transfer the value of the element into the buffer variable; EOF (see below) must be false	GET(filename);	PROCEDURE	GET(myfile);
Assign the value currently in the buffer variable to another variable, move the pointer to the next element, transfer the value of this element to the buffer variable; this is valid only for text files	READ(filename, element);	PROCEDURE	READ(myfile, value);
Test to determine if the value in the buffer variable is the EOF mark; if so, then the result is true	EOF(filename);	FUNCTION	result := EOF(myfile);
Test for the end-of-line marker. The result is true if the next character to be read is the end of the line. If true, the buffer variable will be a blank after READ or GET	EOLN(filename);	FUNCTION	result := EOLN(myfile);
Reads as many lines as needed from a text file in order to complete the variable list. The procedure then skips to the beginning of the next line in the text file	READLN(filename, list of variables);	PROCEDURE	READLN(myfile, A, B, C, D);
Writes a complete line of text (up to the end of the line), then adds carriage return and line feed characters	WRITELN (filename, list of variables);	PROCEDURE	WRITELN(myfile, A, B, C, D);

PROBLEMS FOR SECTION 23-3-2

1. The file named "myfile" is a TEXT file. Are the following two sets of statements equivalent?

   Set 1:

   ```
   location↑ := value;
   ```

   Set 2:

   ```
   WRITE(myfile, value);
   ```

2. Write a program fragment which puts the window at the start of a file, moves the window element 10 element locations into the file, and then reads the data found in that location.

3. Describe what happens when a reset (file) operation is performed, and this is followed by a write (to file) operation.

23-3-3 Exercising I/O

Two examples are included in this section. The first indicates how to make a copy of an SA file, and the second includes a program which can be useful for updating wiring lists.

Example 23-12 Making a Copy of an SA File

Arbitrary file reading and writing operations on the same SA file are not permitted in Pascal. Such interleaved reading and writing sequences would be useful in making a copy of such a file. The following program fragment shows how SA file copying could be achieved.

```
PROGRAM filecopy(INPUT, CUTPUT, oldfile, backupfile);
(* A program which reads 'oldfile' and copies its
contents into the file 'backupfile.' *)
VAR
oldfile, backupfile: TEXT;
value: CHAR;
BEGIN
(* Get ready to read from 'oldfile.' *)
RESET(oldfile);
(* Get ready to make a new copy in 'backupfile.' *)
REWRITE(backupfile);
WHILE NOT EOF(oldfile) DO
    BEGIN
        WHILE NOT EOLN(oldfile) DO
            BEGIN
```

```
            READ(oldfile, value);
            WRITE(backupfile, value)
         END; (* A line has been transferred. *)
   (* Now, add the carriage return and line feed
   characters into backupfile. *)
   WRITELN(backupfile);
   (* Get ready to read the next line of oldfile by
   using READLN to get past the carriage return and
   line feed characters to the start of the next line. *)
   READLN(oldfile);
END; (* End of while (EOF) *)
END. (* End of the program. *)
```

Example 23-13 Updating Wire Lists

One of the products produced in a factory is an electronic controller for a heating, ventilating, and air-conditioning (HVAC) system. The documentation package for the controller includes a wiring list. In part, the list is used for the automatic wiring machine that assembles the controller board. From time to time this list has to be modified. For example, there may be some engineering changes that must be incorporated into the product. The wiring list is kept in a file named "wirelist." The basic data structure for this list is a record which contains the following information for each wire:

Wire number: A decimal number which identifies the wire

Signal name: A character string which includes the logical name of the signal found on the wire in question; this is used for the logical and schematic drawings

Source: The integrated-circuit part and the pin number of that part on which the signal originates; a character string, such as "Q3-11," which means the wire comes from pin 11 of integrated-circuit element 3.

Destination: The integrated-circuit part and the pin number on which the wire terminates; a character string similar to the one found in the source field

Loading: An integer which measures the level of electrical load being carried on the wire by the signal source

A large program exists which will service the wire list. One of the servicing operations which needs to be performed is the updating of the list. The program fragment shown below describes one way in which this could be done. The program is broken down into a series of logical steps:

- Ask the user what kind of operation is needed. Several questions need to be resolved, including:

  Do you want to delete a wire?
  Do you want to modify an entry?
  Do you want to add a wire?
  Are you finished updating the list?

- To delete a wire, read the file wirelist one record at a time. Copy this list one record at a time into a temporary file called "tempfile." If the program encounters the record to be deleted, it is not copied into the temporary file. When the temporary file is complete, copy the temporary file back into the file wirelist. In this way, wirelist will always contain the correct, and most recent, version of the wiring information.
- To modify the entry for a wire, read the file wirelist one record at a time, and copy this record into the temporary file tempfile. If the entry is to be modified, do not copy its corresponding record. Instead, modify the information and then copy it. When all records have been processed in this way, recopy tempfile into wirelist.
- To add an entry for a wire, append the new information (record) onto the end of the file wirelist.
- If no more changes are to be made, simply end the program.

Only part of the entire program will be presented here. In particular, the procedure which adds a new wire to the list will be demonstrated. The procedure assumes that the user has already entered the data for the new wire, and that it includes all the information required for the five fields which comprise a record. (Information which is essential to the entire program will also be included.)

```
PROGRAM undatewirelist(INPUT,OUTPUT,wirelist,tempfile);
TYPE
(* Define the fields of the wire record. *)
wire =
   RECORD
      number : INTEGER;
      signame: ARRAY[1..16] OF CHAR;
      wiresource: ARRAY[1..10] OF CHAR;
      wiredest: ARRAY[1..10] OF CHAR;
      elecload: INTEGER
   END; (* End of definition of wire record. *)
VAR
wirelist,tempfile: FILE OF wire;
newwire: wire;
(* Other variables, constants, etc., of the main
program appear here. *)
(* Other program procedure definitions would appear
here. *)
PROCEDURE addawire(newwire: wire, VAR wirelist: FILE OF wire);
BEGIN
(* Prepare to read the file wirelist *)
RESET(wirelist);
(* Move the window of the wirelist file to the EOF mark *)
WHILE NOT EOF(wirelist) DO
   GET (wirelist);
(* The file is now positioned to the place where new
data can be appended *)
```

```
wirelist↑ := newwire;
PUT(wirelist)
END; (* End of the procedure which appends a new wire
to the file wirelist *)

(* Other procedures of the program appear here. *)
(* Other parts of the main program appear here. *)

WRITE(' Please enter the new wire number. ');
READLN(newwire.number);
WRITE(' Now I need the signal name (16-character limit) ');
READLN(newwire. signame);
WRITE(' OK, I am ready for the source of the wire. ');
READLN(newwire.wiresource);
WRITE(' Next is the destination. ');
READLN(newwire.wiredest);
WRITE(' What is the electrical load? ');
READLN(newwire.elecload);
(* The new wire information has been obtained; call
the procedure which adds a wire. *)
addawire(newwire, wirelist);
(* Other parts of the main program. *)
END. (* End of the update wirelist program. *)
```

There are many ways to solve the problem posed by this example. One alternative would be to omit the electrical load as a parameter within the procedures and to include a separate procedure which calculates the electrical load from the information known about the integrated-circuit elements.

PROBLEMS FOR SECTION 23-3-3

1. Write a procedure which asks the user the questions shown in Example 23-13 and, depending on the answers, calls the correct procedure. In the program include CALL statements to the procedure "deletewire," "changewire," and "addawire," but do not include the definitions of the procedures themselves.

2. Service managers keep records of all customers. New customers are added to a file called "newcustomers." There is one master customer list which is kept on a file called "masterlist." Write a program which can be used to periodically update the master list. That is, write a program which appends all data found in the file newcustomers to the file masterlist. Assume that both files are of type TEXT.

23-4 ADDITIONAL I/O TOPICS

The I/O statements, standard procedures, and functions described to this point are recognized and available for use on all installations. A number of computers include useful features which go beyond those available on standard versions. This section mentions two elements which greatly enhance the power of Pascal. Remember, however, that these features depend on the computer and components of the computer in use, the operating system that it uses, and the particular form of Pascal.

23-4-1 DA Files

The first useful tool to be described is related to direct-access, or DA, files.

Example 23-14 One Case of DA File Access

One of the newer versions of Pascal is called UCSD Pascal. This version was developed at the University of California at San Diego, hence the name UCSD.

In UCSD Pascal, individual records of a file can be accessed in random fashion. Random fashion includes the ability to skip over records or to go back and forth to certain records as often as needed. The procedure which supports this is called the *SEEK* procedure. It has the form

SEEK(<file identifier>,<number of the record>);

The first record in the file is numbered 0. A program fragment which includes a SEEK request follows:

```
PROGRAM seekdemo(INPUT, OUTPUT, myfile);
VAR
   myfile: FILE OF record;
BEGIN
(* Go to the start of the file. *)
RESET(myfile);
(* Get the fifth record. *)
SEEK(myfile, 4);
GET(myfile); (*The window is also advanced. *)
(* Statements here process the record *)
(* Reposition the window to the fifth record *)
SEEK(myfile, 4);
(* Restore the modified record. *)
PUT(myfile);
(* Continue with the program. *)
END.
```

Example 23-15 A Second Case of DA File Access

Another popular version of Pascal was originally developed in the research laboratory of the Oregon Museum of Science and Industry. (It is now available as a commercial product from other sources.) This version is called OMSI after the originators of the first version. This version also includes a SEEK procedure. However, there are minor differences between this version and the one described in the previous example. (It also demonstrates that many minor differences usually exist between different versions of Pascal.) The format for the OMSI SEEK procedure is

SEEK(<file identifier>,<component number>);

In this case the file *cannot* be a text file, and the computer must be connected to a device which can deal with DA files. (Such devices are often magnetic disks or other peripherals.) The file component number must be an unsigned integer expression. The first file element is numbered 1. (Recall USCD starts with 0!) Because this DA extension to standard Pascal violates the restriction of not being able to read and write to the same file simultaneously, another change is necessary when this procedure is used in a program. DA files must be identified by /SEEK calls to reset or rewrite operations. A program fragment might include:

```
(* Go to the beginning of the file. *)
RESET(myfile/SEEK);
(* Access the fifth record *)
SEEK(myfile,5);
(*Assign a new value *)
myfile↑ := . . . (* New values on right-hand side of
this statement. *)
(* Write the new value *)
PUT(myfile);
```

23-4-2 Other I/O Devices

The methods for moving data into or out of computers described thus far have some limitations. For these methods (I/O procedures such as READLN or WRITELN) to be useful on as many computers as possible, certain facts are assumed. One fact in particular is that the computer includes certain generally accepted parts, such as a standard input and output device and other *file-oriented* devices. While this computer arrangement is found on many machines, it does not provide means for dealing with special needs. A computer may also include a timer, a special device for accepting switch signals, or special output devices, such as those needed to control an oscilloscope. In such circumstances, special, non-Pascal programs may have to be included. In particular, assembly language routines or programs may be found embedded within the Pascal program which enable the computer to control these special devices. Consult the Pascal user's manual for the computer you are using to carry out such operations.

SUMMARY

Pascal commands move data into or out of the computer in groups called files. The machine or peripherals which supply or receive the data are referred to as file-oriented devices. The data is grouped together under the file name. The data in the file is terminated with a special mark, an end-of-file (EOF) mark. Two files (or file-oriented devices) within the computer are given special designations. One, a source of data, is called the standard input device and is identified in Pascal by the keyword INPUT. A second device normally receives data from the computer and is referenced as the standard output. In Pascal, the keyword OUTPUT identifies this device.

All files which a Pascal program expects to use must be referenced in the program heading. A sample program heading is

```
PROGRAM sample(INPUT, OUTPUT, file1, file2, . . .);
```

It is convenient to always include INPUT and OUTPUT in the heading file list even if such I/O files are not used within the program.

The READ and READLN procedures move data into the computer. These procedures deal in particular with TEXT files. A TEXT file has an implicit definition which is

```
TYPE
TEXT = FILE OF CHAR;
```

The general form of a request to read a text file is either

READ(<name of file>,<parameter list>);
or
READLN(<name of file>,<parameter list>);

When the name of the file is omitted, the standard INPUT file (or device) is assumed. The parameter list includes the data which is expected. If a data-terminating mark (EOF) is expected, then this must be supplied. When data is being entered from a keyboard, an EOF character must be supplied. Such marks vary from computer to computer and the user's or Pascal language manual must be consulted to determine the EOF character. One widely used character is control-Z(^Z). That is, depress the control key and the key for the letter "z" simultaneously.

To transmit text files to the standard output device, use the WRITE or WRITELN procedures which are recognized by all Pascal installations. To invoke such procedures, use call statements similar to those for accepting (reading) data into the computer:

WRITE(<name of file>,<parameter list>);
or
WRITELN(<name of file>,<parameter list>);

READLN and WRITELN procedures behave in a slightly different manner than their counterparts, READ and WRITE. In most instances TEXT files are said to be line-oriented. This means that certain special characters are embedded in the string of alphanumeric characters comprising the text. These special characters are often (the code for) a carriage return followed by (the code for) a line feed. With READLN and WRITELN procedures, the following is expected:

- READLN accepts the next text character on a new line when it detects the control sequence.
- WRITELN outputs the next text character on a new line.

Not all data will be of type TEXT, but in standard Pascal all files are assumed to be sequential-access (SA) files. That is, a file consists of data of the same type which cannot be accessed out of sequence. In order to read and write data in such cases, the program must have information about its position in the file. This position is called the access window or simply window. There are two procedures used to access data from the window. One is called GET, and it accesses data from the file and makes it available to the program. In addition, it moves the window to the next element in the file. Thus, in order to skip over 10 elements of the file, the program could contain 10 GET requests (perhaps in the form of a FOR loop). The GET procedure in this case would be used only to move the window. To actually read or accept the data from the file, a program statement must assign the data being accessed to a variable. This is accomplished by a statement of the form

<variable to be assigned> := filename ↑ ;

The object "filename" implies the data within the window.

A similar method is used to write an element to a file. The first step assigns a value to the element presently accessed. This is done with a statement of the form

filename ↑ := <value to be assigned>:

The second step makes use of the PUT procedure. Calling or invoking this procedure actually adds the element to the file. For SA files, elements can be added only at the end of the file. It is therefore important to check for the EOF before attempting to add an element. Pascal includes a boolean function which produces a true result when EOF is detected. The function is designated EOF. In practice it would appear in an expression or assignment statement and it would have a form given by

EOF(filename)

In addition to the EOF function, the reset and rewrite procedures are provided to position the window within a file. The reset procedure positions the window to the first element in the file and accesses the first element for reading purposes. The rewrite procedure effectively erases the contents of a file because it positions the window to the start of an empty file which contains only an EOF mark. For this reason, exercise caution before using the rewrite procedure because the contents of the file in question will be destroyed. These procedures are invoked using

RESET(filename);

and

REWRITE(filename);

For text-oriented devices the function EOLN can also be used; it returns a true result if the next character is the code used to represent the end of the line.

Some versions of Pascal include facilities to deal with (to read and write) direct-access (DA) or random-access files. In particular, the procedure SEEK may be found in such systems.

Finally, many versions of Pascal permit use of special I/O instructions. These are useful when the need exists to control equipment which is unique to the installation.

REVIEW PROBLEMS

1. Is there anything wrong with the following?

```
PROGRAM wrong(INPUT, OUTPUT);
VAR
myfile: FILE OF INTEGER;
.
.
.
END.
```

2. Write equivalent forms for each of the following:

```
WRITE(OUTPUT, ch);
READLN(INPUT);
EOLN(INPUT);
```

3. The file "myfile" is type TEXT. Write equivalent statements for each of the following:

```
myfile↑ := value; PUT(myfile);
value := myfile↑; GET(myfile);
```

4. Write a program which will accept two pieces of information from a user: frequency value (f) and inductance value (L). In addition, include statements in the program which calculate the reactive impedance of the inductor, using the formula

$$\text{Reactive impedance} = 2\pi fL$$

where

f = the frequency specified by the user

L = the inductance value specified by the user

π = 3.14159

Include instructions which print the values of f, L, and the inductive impedance. The program should terminate if the user enters a negative value for f.

5. One individual within a company is responsible for inventory control. The company manufactures electronic navigational subassemblies. A file of parts records called "partsfile" exists on the company's computer system. Each record has the following fields:

Number: a number which specifies where in the file the part is to be found—this is called a key
Description: An array of 50 characters which describes the part

A second file, called "newparts," contains new parts which must be periodically added to the file partsfile. Write a program that will merge the two files. That is, the program should read the elements of partsfile and the elements of newparts and create an updated version of partsfile. The records in newparts should be merged into the updated file so that the number field of the updated file is in increasing order.

REVIEW QUESTIONS

1. Define the term "file."
2. What is meant by standard input? How is this designated in Pascal?
3. What is meant by standard output? How is this designated in Pascal?
4. What is the typical standard input device? What is the typical standard output device?
5. What must be included in all Pascal program headings?
6. What is a TEXT file?
7. What two procedures are available in Pascal for accepting data from the standard input device?
8. What two procedures are available in Pascal for sending data to the standard output device?

APPENDIX

COMPLETE ASCII CODES

Decimal Code	Character	Comment†
0	NUL	Null, tape feed, shift, ^ P
1	SOH	Start of heading, start of message, ^ A
2	STX	Start of text, end of address, ^ B
3	ETX	End of text, end of message, ^ C
4	EOT	End of transmission, shuts off TWX machine, ^ D
5	ENQ	Enquiry, WRU, ^ E
6	ACK	Acknowledge, RU, ^ F
7	BEL	Bell, ^ G
8	BS	Backspace, format effector, ^ H
9	HT	Horizontal tab, ^ I
10	LF	Line feed, ^ J
11	VT	Vertical tab, ^ K
12	FF	Form feed, page, ^ L
13	CR	Carriage return, ^ M
14	SO	Shift out, ^ N
15	SI	Shift in, ^ O
16	DLE	Data link escape, ^ P
17	DC1	Device control 1, ^ Q
18	DC2	Device control 2, ^ R
19	DC3	Device control 3, ^ S
20	DC4	Device control 4, ^ T
21	NAK	Negative acknowledge, ERR, ^ U
22	SYN	Synchronous idle, ^ V
23	ETB	End of transmission block, logical end of medium, ^ W
24	CAN	Cancel, ^ X
25	EM	End of medium, ^ Y
26	SUB	Substitute, ^ Z
27	ESC	Escape, prefix, shift, ^ K
28	FS	File separator, shift, ^ L
29	GS	Group separator, shift, ^ M
30	RS	Record separator, shift, ^ N
31	US	Unit separator, shift, ^ O
32	SP	Space
33	!	
34	“	
35	#	
36	$	
37	%	
38	&	
39	’	
40	(	
41	)	
42	*	

Decimal Code	Character	Comment†
43	+	
44	,	
45	-	
46	.	
47	/	
48	0	
49	1	
50	2	
51	3	
52	4	
53	5	
54	6	
55	7	
56	8	
57	9	
58	:	
59	;	
60	<	
61	=	
62	>	
63	?	
64	@	
65	A	
66	B	
67	C	
68	D	
69	E	
70	F	
71	G	
72	H	
73	I	
74	J	
75	K	
76	L	
77	M	
78	N	
79	O	
80	P	
81	Q	
82	R	
83	S	
84	T	
85	U	
86	V	
87	W	
88	X	
89	Y	
90	Z	
91	[	

Decimal Code	Character	Comment†
92	\	
93	]	
94	^	
95	_	
96	`	
97	a	
98	b	
99	c	
100	d	
101	e	
102	f	
103	g	
104	h	
105	i	
106	j	
107	k	
108	l	
109	m	
110	n	
111	o	
112	p	
113	q	
114	r	
115	s	
116	t	
117	u	
118	v	
119	w	
120	x	
121	y	
122	z	
123	{	
124	|	
125	}	
126	~	Tilde
127	DEL	Delete, rubout

† Depress the control key together with the key which follows.

ANSWERS TO SELECTED PROBLEMS AND QUESTIONS

CHAPTER 3

SECTION 3-1

1. LET C=A-B

SECTION 3-3-3

1. Keyboard, secondary storage system, events external to the computer (an alarm).
3. Eventually, no room on the stack to store all interrupts.

SECTION 3-4-5

2. On separate lines: MOV AX,R1 ADD AX,R2 ADD AX,R3 ADD AX,R4 ADD AX, R5 ADD AX,R6 ADD AX,R7 ADD AX,R8 ADD AX,R9 ADD AX,R0 MOV C,AX

Review Questions

1. Fetch, execute instruction.
3. General registers, temporary registers, ALU, flags register, EU control, communication buses.
5. NMI, Normal.
7. data transfer, arithmetic/bit manipulation, program transfer.
9. See Table 3-2
11. Control transfers to a predefined block of instructions which are executed. When logically complete, control is returned to the instruction following the instruction where it was called.

CHAPTER 4

SECTION 4-1-1

1. Applications for special-purpose keyboards include: Household appliances—washing machines, calculators, microwave ovens, videocassette recorders, television and stereo equipment. Machinery and heavy equipment—control consoles. Alarm and security systems.

SECTION 4-1-2

1. Transmission OCR requires that the media be at least partially translucent. Thus heavier stocks or totally opaque materials cannot be read.
   Further, any dirt or smudges, or variations in the opacity of the medium itself can cause errors to be made in the reading of the text.

SECTION 4-1-3

1. MICR readers require the sensing of the magnetic ink to work. If anything interferes with the intimate contact between the reader's drum and the paper,

faulty reading will occur. Other problems include a typeface that is somewhat difficult to read normally and that normally typed or handwritten text cannot be read.

SECTION 4-1-6

1. Postal zip codes; hotel room entry (security)
2. Some alternative uses for bar-coding include:
   Inventory control during the manufacturing process
   Component identification
   Machine-readable identification for use on ID cards
   Identification and cataloging of materials in a library

SECTION 4-1-7

1. An identification card could be issued to each authorized user of a computer center indicating what computer systems that person was permitted to access, during what hours, etc. A password could be recorded on the stripe which the card holder must know and enter into a keyboard in order to enter the secure area.

SECTION 4-1-8

1. Students indicate the answers to the multiple choice questions on a mark-sense card using a pencil. The instructor completes an identical card with the correct answers (this constitutes the answer key). When all the student's answer cards have been collected, the instructor uses a mark-sense reader connected to a computer which has a program to read the answer key, then read each of the student's cards, compare the student's response with the key, and grade the test accordingly, usually printing some form of summary.

SECTION 4-1-9

1. Ultrasonic tablet: uses sound waves and a sonar system to determine the position of an object (usually a stylus, finger, or other pointing device) in two or three dimensions (depending on type).
   Light pen: a pointer device that is used in conjunction with a CRT display screen. The device determines the position of the pointer with respect to the vertical and horizontal coordinates of the screen.
   Mouse: a hand-held device, rolled on a flat surface, which controls an electronic pointer on the CRT screen. By activating a switch (some mice have multiple switches) on the mouse, further software response can be elicited.
   Joystick: a pair of potentiometers (variable resistances) are controlled by a single knob that can move in two axes. Thus as the control is moved from its center, neutral position, signals are generated indicating which quadrant the control is in.
   Touch screen: A system conceptually identical to the light pen, but that uses optical sensing or ultrasonic ranging to locate the position of a pointer with respect to the CRT screen.

SECTION 4-2-1*c*

1. Thermal printing has the following disadvantages:
   Special paper or special ribbons must be used.

The image has all the inherent problems of dot-matrix print.
The image can be obliterated (will blacken) if the finished document is subjected to heat.

SECTION 4-2-3*a*

1. 560 (80 × 7) pixels per line.
   115 nanoseconds(ns) per pixel.

REVIEW QUESTIONS

1. An input device is used to provide data that the computer is expected to process.
3. Text-type data is information in the form of words or numbers. Examples include input to: word processing, business, language translation, scientific or engineering calculations.
   Nontext data is information that is in some other form—electrical, pressure, temperature, position—that must first be converted by the use of a transducer. Examples include: machine control, process control, data acquisition.
5. The keyboard is so universal for two reasons: it is familiar to a great many people; Both numeric and alphabetic data can be entered, as well as numeric representation of nontext data. Voice recognition is the most likely replacement.
7. MICR has been made popular by the banking industry. MICR is a high-speed, reliable system; one problem is delicacy of the medium (paper tears, creases, and dirt).
9. The punched card is the medium; it carries the data, impressed upon it as a series of holes in rigidly defined patterns and locations. The card punch is the device responsible for impressing these punched holes onto the card. The card reader decodes the patterns into electrical representations of the data.
11. Both mark-sense cards and punched cards can use similarly sized and shaped paper cards, to carry the data.
    Punched cards differ from mark-sense cards in that the punched cards have holes in them, whereas the mark-sense cards have blackened marks performing the same function. Mark-sense cards are usually read by reflection methods; punch cards by transmission (if optical) or direct contact (electrical).
13. The two types of voice-recognition systems are speaker-dependent (trained to recognize the speech of one specific talker) and speaker-independent (trained to recognize speech based on its inherent characteristics).
15. A transducer is a device that converts a physical property into an electrical signal. Examples of such physical properties include: Temperature, Pressure, Electrical characteristics (voltage, current, resistance), Magnetism, Light intensity, Speed, Weight, PH (acidity or alkalinity), Rotational displacement
17. The fully formed character printer is popular because its output most closely resembles the output of a typewriter, the standard for business communications. Advantages include the ability to make multiple copies, print quality, and interchangeability of type styles. Disadvantages include relative slowness and high cost.
19. Thermal printing is accomplished using the dot-matrix approach to character formation, but instead of using the impact method, the needle is electrically heated and causes a chemical reaction in the paper to cause the paper to darken directly. Alternatively, the heated needle is placed in contact with a special plastic ribbon which transfers dye to the paper as a result of its being heated.
21. Laser printing is performed by having a laser "write" the text to be printed on an electrostatically charged drum. This drum is used to pick up carbon particles which are transferred, then fused to a paper surface. This process

provides for very high quality print, at very high speed. In addition, it readily allows the mixing of text and graphical output. The disadvantages tend to be in the area of cost and size of equipment.

23. Plotters are used primarily to produce continuous line drawings, such as blueprints and schematics. The two types of plotters are flat-bed plotters and moving-paper plotters.
25. The topmost line is erased and all lines already on the screen are moved up one line, making the bottom-most line available for the new text. Horizontal scrolling allows lines longer than the screen's width to be displayed one section at a time; reverse scrolling moves all the lines on the screen down by one line, clearing the top line for new text.
27. Three types of electronic displays are: 7-segment display, dot-matrix display, and indicator display. The 7 segment display: suitable for displaying numerals; often found on electronic calculators. Several different technologies available for producing the light required; these technologies trade off on the qualities of power consumption, clarity of display, size, weight, and controlling circuitry required.

    The dot-matrix display: allows the creation of the full alphanumeric character set, in addition to graphics. The advantages are: far smaller power consumption and weight (compared to a CRT display). The disadvantages: lack of readability; complexity of controlling circuitry required. The indicator display: may consist of a single labelled indicator lamp (conventional, fluorescent, or semiconductor) that has a single meaning when lit. This can transmit a great deal of information, rapidly, and is most frequently used as an indicator of "out of normal" conditions.
29. Digital recording results in more natural sounding speech.
31. The primary criteria for selecting a speech synthesizer would be the quality of reproduction required, the amount of computer storage available for the storage of the digitized models, the variety of the vocabulary that will be required, and the speed with which the sound must be recreated.

CHAPTER 5

SECTION 5-1

1. (a) .25E2 (b) .314159E1 (c) −.225E1 (d) .1E−3
3. −128, +127

SECTION 5-2-1

1. (a) 28200 (b) −32431 (c) −9628 (d) 2 (truncation)

SECTION 5-2-2

3. Actual ans. = −21.815, Computer ans. = −21.82, %error = .02292
5. −.4206E1

SECTION 5-2-3

1. (a) −.25E2 (b) 0.0E0 (c) .21835E5

SECTION 5-3-1

1. Store COMPLEX data as two real numbers; the real part and the imaginary part.

SECTION 5-3-1*d*

3. (a) LE MESSAGE (b) A SAMPLE MES

SECTION 5-3-1*e*

1. (a) A=65,B=66...Z=90, A<B<...<Z (b) a=97,b=98...z=122, a<b<... <z (c) 0<1<2...<9

SECTION 5-3-2

1. Address of Ith item = A+(I−LB)E
3. Address=A+(I−SR)*2+(J−SC); A=Starting add. of array, SR=Starting row index, SC=Starting column index

SECTION 5-3-3

1. Days=(Mon,Tues,Wed,Thurs,Fri,Sat,Sun)
3. Test results from QC dept.
   Record format: Component tested,test run,result,error
   Data from process control.
   Record format: sensor,date,time,reading

REVIEW QUESTIONS

1. Numbers without decimal points.
3. A real number with a decimal point in a specified position.
5. The limit of values a number can have
7. First digit after decimal point is nonzero.
9. The power of 10 by which mantissa is multiplied.
11. A number exceeding the largest number which computer can store.
13. Integer,complex,dbl.prec.,character,logical,pointer,fixed-point real,floating-point real.
15. Result: true if and only if both operands are true.
17. A pointer variable is an address.
19. A collection of data of the same type.
21. An array of records.

CHAPTER 6

SECTION 6-1-1

1. (2.75) real constant; (−3) integer constant: (array6,1) data in 6th row, 1st col. of like but untyped data: (MATRIX(I,J) data item in row I, col. J of a collection of data. I,J are determined at time item is accessed.: (2.1415) real constant: (hit)variable quantity: (miss)variable quantity.

SECTION 6-3

3. A^{x}=exp(x*ln(A))

REVIEW QUESTIONS

1. data, operations, order
3. Data which changes during program execution.
5. Real (integer) data which changes during the program.
7. / = divide real data: div = integer division (truncate results).
9. Square root, absolute value, Sin, Cos, arctan, exp. ln.
11. Sin(x)/Cos(x)
15. See Table 6-1.

CHAPTER 7

SECTION 7-1-2

1. (a)process;decision;process;decision.
   (b)process;process;decision-process;decision-process.

SECTION 7-2-4*a*

1. Data in an array is arranged from smallest to largest. If data is examined from largest to smallest then index is decremented. To calculate values for a straight line for negative values of the x axis. Decrement the index for each iteration of the loop in which the calculation is performed.
3. 1002 seconds or 16.7 minutes.

SECTION 7-4-1

3. A subprogram is slower than in-line code. It takes time to transfer control to subprogram and return. During transfer no useful work is done. Loss in speed is made up by reduction in number of instructions.

SECTION 7-4-3

1. 47
2. formal: MALE, FEMALE, UNKNOWN
   actual: JOHN, MARY, LEE

REVIEW QUESTIONS

1. Control statements
3. See Figs. 7-2, 7-3
5. Sequence; IF-THEN-ELSE; Loop (DO-WHILE, DO-UNTIL)
7. The position of the decision block.
9. Efficiency of program writing, Ease of program testing, Ease of program modification, Modularity.
11. Special words recognized by the HLL for particular purposes. They cannot be used for variable names.
12. The THEN branch includes instructions to be executed if the test condition is TRUE. The ELSE branch includes instructions to be executed if the test condition is FALSE.
14. The initial value of the index; the final (test) value of the index; the index increment (for each iteration).
16. :=

18. A combination of DO loops in which one is completely contained within the body (process block) of the other.
20. A separately identifiable group of instructions which can be executed from any point in the program.

CHAPTER 8

SECTION 8-1

1. CHAR(6),REAL(6,1),REAL(6,3)INT(2),CHAR(1)
3. (a) BLANK(5), CHARACTER STRING(11,'Part Number'), BLANK(5), CHARACTER STRING (4, 'Type'), BLANK(5), CHARACTER STRING (5,'Value'),BLANK(5), CHARACTER STRING(9,'Tolerance')
(b) In some computers a TAB instruction automatically inserts 5 spaces. In (a), BLANK(5) can be replaced with TAB.

SECTION 8-2

3. (a)1100 bits/sec. (b)80000 bits/sec.

SECTION 8-3-1

2. Logical connection is 1. To write to file use 1 to signify the connection. Physical device number is 8. Number 7 is a secondary number within the drive. The file name is MAIL; it is located on drive 1 of the dual disk system; if is sequential; it is OPENed for writing.
4. (a) 10 OPEN "MYFILE" FOR OUTPUT AS #1
(b) 10 OPEN "R",1,"B:OURFILE",256
"R" stands for random input/output mode.

SECTION 8-4

1. Open for write; read a record component; write a record component; rewind; test for end of file.
2. It is destroyed. REWRITE erases data in Pascal files.
4. PUT #2,25

REVIEW QUESTIONS

1. Input/output (i/o).
3. Disk, keyboard, cassette, card reader.
5. Format.
6. Computer reports an error.
8. Serial, parallel transmissions.
10. Half-duplex; full-duplex.
12. Establish connection, perform transactions (read,write), disconnect.
14. Pascal.
16. Transmit additional commands to the device; specify a subchannel within the device.
18. SA; Data is accessed in strictly sequential order.
DA; Data can be accessed in a random fashion or order.
19. CLOSE.
21. Review Table 8-1.

CHAPTER 9

SECTION 9-1

1. Collect data from a nuclear power plant; control airplane traffic; analyze x-rays; draw airframes, cars, machines to help in the design; simulate a circuit.

SECTION 9-3

1. Here are a few:
   BASIC: out of data, illegal function call, overflow (number too large), out of memory, undefined line number, subscript out of range, duplicate definition, string too long, missing operand, device timeout, device fault, out of paper.
   Pascal (Turbo): negative square root attempted, negative argument in log function, string concatenation more than 255 characters, array subscript out of range.

SECTION 9-4

1. Fairness: let no job suffer indefinite postponement.
   Maximize throughput: Complete the largest number of jobs per unit time.
   Minimize system overhead: Do not delay jobs because of instructions which are required by the Scheduler program itself.
   Resources: Try to keep system devices (disks, etc.) busy all the time.

SECTION 9-5

1. root/wiring/navigation/Shoran/subass1
3. DIR\TEST

SECTION 9-6-2

1. Move erases source lines. Copy repeats lines.

SECTION 9-7-1

1. SAVE "A:WIRELIST"
3. RUN 100

SECTION 9-7-2

1. LINE NUMBER SEQUENCE 10,20,30,40,20,30,40,...(the sequence 20,30,40 is repeated 11 times in total).

REVIEW QUESTIONS

1. A program which translates HLL statements into machine code.
3. Compiled languages are translated and executed in a serial manner. Interpreted languages are translated and executed concurrently.
5. Adds necessary programs from a library into the compiled code.
7. An error at the time the program is executed.

9. A mistake in thinking.
11. Schedule the work of the CPU; provide for communication between the computer and its peripherals; organize and keep track of the user's programs.
14. Minimize the time it takes to locate a given piece of information.
16. A group of files and subdirectories. Subdirectories are groupings of files.
18. Log-on, Edit, Compile, Link, Debug.
20. Programs are submitted (and executed) in a strict serial manner.
22. A system dedicated to use by one individual at a time.
24. The original statements comprising the user's program.
26. Compile but do not load; suppress warning messages; check subscripts (within bounds); put executable code in a named file; do not convert capital letters to lowercase.
28. A program which helps to locate and correct errors during execution.
30. Unconditional interrupt; resume program; display sequence of line numbers being executed; discontinue display of line numbers being executed.

CHAPTER 10

SECTION 10-2

1. O.K.; O.K., but may have too many digits for some computers; contains a decimal point; O.K.; contains letters; contains special characters (comma); contains special characters ($) and decimal point; contains special character ($); O.K.; contains a decimal point.

REVIEW QUESTIONS

1. Allow users to communicate and exchange information.
3. A feature which expands the ability of a user to communicate with the computer without misinterpretation (error).
5. Extensive documentation, modularity, clarity.
7. Use PRINT statements to check partial results and the sequence of instructions.

CHAPTER 11

REVIEW PROBLEM

1. A) PRINT ABC
   B) PRINT 6 * ONE CELL
   C) PRINT FIRSTNAME$
   D) PRINT "THE VALUE IS ";RTOT
   E) PRINT A, B, C
   F) PRINT
      PRINT "   "; X
   G) PRINT "NAME: "
   H) PRINT TOTAL CAPACITANCE=";
      PRINT C1+C2 + C3
   I) PRINT "THE CAPACITANCE REACTANCE IS: "; CAPACITANCE
   J) PRINT "THE EFFECTIVE TOTAL RESISTANCE="; ETOT/ITOT; "OHMS."

REVIEW QUESTIONS

1. BASIC is easy to learn
   A powerful language
   Easy to debug

A language that can take advantage of hardware features
Ability to utilize machine language subroutines

3. Syntax is the set of rules that define the structure, format, and contents of allowable commands in the BASIC language.
5. The SAVE command causes the program currently in the computer's memory to be written to the diskette or other storage device.

   The LIST command causes the lines of the program currently in memory to be displayed, starting with the lowest-numbered line and continuing until the highest-numbered line has been displayed.

   The CLS command causes the CRT screen to be cleared and the cursor to be positioned in the upper left-hand corner (home position).
7. A numeric quantity is what we commonly associate with a number; an algebraic value with an implied or explicit sign and an implied or explicit decimal point.

   An alphanumeric quantity is a group of characters consisting of the set of numerals, alphabetic characters (upper- and lowercase letters), and special characters (such as punctuation, symbols, and graphic characters).
9. A literal is a group of characters which do not represent a storage location, but explicitly contain the value of interest.

CHAPTER 12

REVIEW PROBLEMS

1. a. invalid—imbedded space
   b. valid
   c. invalid—contains two type specifiers ($ and %)
   d. valid
   e. invalid—variable name must begin with an alphabetic character
   f. valid
   g. valid
   h. valid
   i. invalid—contains 19 characters
   j. invalid—contains illegal character (*)
3. a. FIRSTNAME$
   b. SPEEDMM#
   c. PASSING%
   d. POWER or POWER! (Single precision) or POWER# (double precision)
   e. PARTNAME$
   f. WEIGHT (OR WEIGHT!)
   g. FAILURES = ! or FAILURES
   h. TON# (double precision) or TON or TON! (single precision)
   i. VOUT (OR VOUT!)
   j. PHONENUMBER$
5. a. (125 * 34 + 16) / (6 * 3)
   b. 12 × 42 + (16/19 ^ 2) + 9
   c. X ^ (3+2) / (2 * Z)
   d. 1 / (2 * PI * F * C)
   e. (X2 − X1) / (Y2 − Y1) (NO CHANGE)
   f. (C1 * C2) / (C1 + C2)
   g. (Q1 * Q2) / (K * D)
   h. (C ^ 2 * H) / (4 * PI)
   i. D * 1.745 * 10 ^ −2

CHAPTER 13

REVIEW PROBLEMS

1. Actual quantity on hand, cost, and selling price.

2. Desired quantity to have in stock, manufacturer, item's shipping weight.
3. Our stock number, quantity of this item appearing in a given device, our company's name.
4. The inner parentheses are not needed, but have been included to make the formula more readable.
   Eliminating unnecessary parentheses, the formula becomes:

   LET R = 1 / (1/R1 + 1/R2 +1/R3 + 1/R4)

5. The INPUT statement is suitable to be used when the data is to be entered at execution time. Specific examples might be entry of an access password, the choice of a function to be performed, or the entry of information specific to this particular iteration of the program.
   The READ/DATA statements are suitable when the data is to be included as part of the program; this implies that the data will not frequently change. Specific examples might be the names of the days of the week, a series of numeric values representing the concentrations of certain chemicals used, or initialization values for a series of variables, which is always to be used.
7. (a) 1 (VALUES FOR THE VARIABLE A ARE READ TWICE)
   (b) 9
   (c) ABCDEFG
9. (a) 1 2 6
   (b) 7 6 8
   (c) A1 = 13, A2 = 9, A3 = 10, B1 = 4, B2 = 5, B3 = 12, B4 = 11

REVIEW QUESTIONS

1. Every time we modify a program we run the risk of introducing errors.
3. Iteration refers to the number of times a program repeats a given function or operation.
6. A delimiter marks the beginning and end of a piece of data. Common delimiters in BASIC include double quotes, commas, semicolons, spaces, and carriage returns.

CHAPTER 14

REVIEW PROBLEM

1. (a) THE VALUE OF I IS 1
   THE VALUE OF I IS 2
   THE VALUE OF I IS 3
   THE VALUE OF I IS 4
   THE VALUE OF I IS 5
   (b) 6 36
   7 47
   8 64
   9 81
   (c) POINT HAS A VALUE OF 4
   POINT HAS A VALUE OF 9
   CLOSING VALUE OF POINT IS 14
   (d) 330

REVIEW QUESTIONS

1. BASIC executes statements beginning with the lowest line number, in ascending order.

2. An unconditional branch causes execution to continue with the named line number.
3. The GOTO statement causes an unconditional branch to occur.
5. A program loop is a construct in which certain statements are executed repeatedly.
6. The FOR/NEXT loop is a structure that is provided by BASIC which allows a series of statements to be executed a controlled number of times.
7. An index variable is the value which is used to keep track of how many times a loop has been executed.
9. The FOR/NEXT loop will count down if the starting value is larger than the ending value AND the increment is a negative value.
10. The term default is defined as the value or conditions that will prevail unless explicitly changed.
13. A comparison can result in only one of two conditions: the relationship is true or the relationship is false.
14. The IF statement provides the means for testing a relationship and performing alternate actions based on whether the condition is true or false.
15. The IF statement consists of the following four parts:
    The keyword IF
    The relationship to be tested
    The keyword THEN
    The operation to be performed if the condition is true.
16. The compound IF statement tests more than one condition, and evaluates the entire compound relationship as being true or false.
17. The individual relationships in a compound IF statement are joined using the keywords AND, OR, and NOT.
18. The order of evaluations is AND, then OR, then NOT.
20. You would use multiple IF statements if doing so makes the program easier to understand.

CHAPTER 15

REVIEW PROBLEMS

NOTE: Line numbers are shown only when they are the destinations of GOTO statements.

1.
```
REM SUBROUTINE TO CALCULATE POWER CONSUMPTION.
REM   EXPECTS VALUE IN VARIABLES:   I, E
REM   RETURNS WITH VALUE IN :       P
LET P = I * E
RETURN
```
4.
```
REM SUBROUTINE TO PRINT A REPORT HEADING
REM ALL VALUES ARE SELF-CONTAINED
REM RETURNS WITH VALUE OF LINECTR RESET TO ZERO
PRINT "AMERICAN ENERGY SURVEY COMPANY"
PRINT "POWER CONSUMPTION REPORT FOR THE ACME CORPORATION"
PRINT
PRINT "RESULT OF SURVEY CONDUCTED MAY 1 THROUGH MAY 15"
PRINT
LINECTR = 0
```
6.
```
REM SUBROUTINE TO CONVERT FREQUENCY TO WAVELENGTH IN
REM METERS.
REM   ASSUMES VALUES IN VARIABLE:  FREQUENCY
REM   RETURNS NO VALUE;  PRINTS RESULT OF CONVERSION
REM   C = 300000000
PRINT FREQUENCY; "HERTZ IS A WAVELENGTH OF ";C/FREQUENCY;
```

```
" METERS."
RETURN
```

8.

```
      REM SUBROUTINE TO SIMULATE THE ACTION OF AN AND GATE
      REM   ASSUMES VALUES IN VARIABLES: A%, B%
      REM   RETURNS VALUE IN VARIABLE:       Q%
      REM   RETURNS VALUE OF 9 IN Q% IF VALUE OF A% AND B%
      REM   ARE NOT
      REM   ZERO OR ONE.
      IF A% = 0 OR A% = 1 OR B% = 0 OR B% = 1 THEN 1200
      REM ERROR CONDITION
      Q% = 9
      GOTO 1400
1200  REM VALUES VALID
      Q% = 0
      IF A% = 1 AND B% = THEN Q% = 1
1400  RETURN
```

REVIEW QUESTIONS

1. A subroutine, in BASIC, is a block of code (group of statements) which performs some function, and is accessed from one or more places in a larger program.
3. The GOSUB statement is used to enter a subroutine; the RETURN statement marks the exit point.
5. Yes; in BASIC, one subroutine may call another.
8. Yes; a program may contain any number of subroutines.
9. Yes; a GOSUB is frequently made conditional:

IF TAXABLE$ = "YES" THEN GOSUB 5000

10. Yes; a RETURN may be made conditional:

IF COUNT = 0 THEN RETURN

CHAPTER 16

REVIEW PROBLEMS

1. (a) 31 members
   (b) 366 members
   (c) 9 members
   (d) 384 members
   (e) 64 members
   (f) 24 members
   (g) 315 members
   (h) 1334 members
   (i) 10 members
   (j) 2520 members
2. DIM TRANSISTORS(15) (for numeric part number.)
3. DIM STVALS(24) (there are 25 values used with a multiplier.)
4. DIM STVALS(3,48) (there are 49 standard 5% tolerance values—other tolerances have fewer values.)
5. DIM PARTNAMES$(22) (we might also declare PARTNAME$(23) and use PARTNAME$(0) to store the number of the PC board to which it applies!)
6. DIM PARTNAMES$(1,22) (or PARTNAME$(1,23), as described above.)
8. DIM PARTS$(5,1,39)

9. DIM MEASUREMENTS(1,37) (MEASUREMENTS(0,N) are voltages; MEASUREMENTS(1,N) are current readings.)

REVIEW QUESTIONS

1. The analogy to a one-dimension array is the list. The dimension is the list's length.
2. The subscript of the first member of an array is (0).
3. All members of an array must be of the same data type; all integers, single precision, double precision, or strings.
5. The purpose of the DIM statement is to inform the BASIC interpreter that it must set aside a certain amount of space to accommodate the array.
6. The two-dimension array is analogous to a table. The two dimensions represent the table's width and length.
7. The subscript of the first member of a two-dimension array is (0,0).
9. Many arrays, of different-size dimensions and of different numbers of dimensions can be used in a single BASIC program. They must all be declared in a DIM statement.

CHAPTER 17

REVIEW PROBLEMS

1. (a) 12345678901234567890ABC123DEF456ABC123
   (b) ABCDEFGHIJKLMNOPQRSTUVWXYZEND OF STRING
   (c) 5
   (d) 123456
   (e) FGHIJKLMNOPQRSTUVWXYZ
   (f) 123.4987.6
   (g) JKLM
   (h) 0
   (i) 123456
   (j) 4

REVIEW QUESTIONS

1. Numeric values represent algebraic quantities. Alphanumeric values represent alphabetic characters, punctuation, special characters, and the numerals 0 through 9, but without regard to the quantity that they represent.
3. Concatenation is the connection of the end of one string to the beginning of the next to form a new, continuous string. The operation is indicated using the addition operator (+) between two string values.
5. The first aspect taken into account when comparing two strings are the string's lengths.
7. The LEN function returns the length, or number of characters contained in a string. Spaces are counted.
9. The LEFT$ function returns N characters from the source string, beginning with the leftmost.
11. The MID$ function returns N characters from the source string, beginning with a specified character (counting from the leftmost).
12. The LEFT$, RIGHT$, and MID$ functions all return string values; the LEN function returns a numeric value.
14. Rounding can be accomplished by adding .5 to the value before the operation that causes truncation occurs.

16. The two parameters of the INSTR function are the string to be searched, and the string of characters for which we are searching.
19. It is called a binary search since the list is repeatedly divided into two parts, and half the list is eliminated from consideration with each examination.

CHAPTER 18

REVIEW PROBLEM

1. (a) OPEN "I",#1,"SOFTWARE"
   (b) OPEN "I",#4,"PARTSFILE"

REVIEW QUESTIONS

2. A file is a collection of related information in a computer-readable form.
5. The OPEN statement informs the BASIC interpreter that it is to make the preparations necessary to access a file of a given name.
6. The file number allows the file to be referenced symbolically in later references to it.
7. The WRITE # statement can be used to write data to a file.
8. The INPUT # statement can be used to read data from a file.
10. The STR$ function converts a numeric value into its corresponding string equivalent. The STR$ function will work correctly only when given a numeric value as its parameter (integer or floating point). Otherwise a TYPE MISMATCH error will occur.
15. Dynamic updating refers to the interactive process of being able to modify, delete, or insert a record at any point in the file.
16. The current record is the record that was most recently read from the original file.
17. We insist that record deletion be verified since this is a destruction of data. We simply want to make sure that the operator did not press the wrong key or make a mistake. Any such operation would be a good candidate for verification procedures.

CHAPTER 19

SECTION 19-1

1.
```
Program first(OUTPUT);
BEGIN
   Writeln('Ashley Black');
   Writeln('33 Main Street');
   Writeln('Anytownorcity');
   Writeln('Student I.D. 25-80-5104')
END.
```

REVIEW PROBLEM

1. Program wirelist(INPUT,OUTPUT,wraplist);

REVIEW QUESTIONS

1. A method for solving a problem.
3. Comments.
5. Yes.
7. BEGIN, END.

CHAPTER 20

SECTION 20-1

1. O.K.,O.K.,reserved word,O.K. but may be too long for some computers, first char. is a no., contains special chars., O.K., contains special chars.
3. IF, IN
5. Procedure, Program
7. Standard identifier, standard identifier, reserved word, user-defined, user-defined, reserved word, standard identifier, standard identifier.

SECTION 20-2-1

1. −2, +50,250,MAXINT returns an integer value.
3. *Record* is a reserved word. Using it in this way changes its meaning. ; is omitted from last case.

SECTION 20-2-2

1. 0.157E0; −0.2001E03; 0.1532E3; −0.410623E5
3. small,large,medium,gross:REAL;

SECTION 20-2-3

1. wastevalve:boolean;
   mixingmotor:boolean;
   overflowsensor:boolean;
   powerfailsignal:boolean;
   interlock:boolean;

SECTION 20-2-4

1. 'a' is not a character variable; second case has ";" omitted.

SECTION 20-3-1

1. CONST
```
    eachstep=1;
    pi=3.14159;
    poslimit=10;
    neglimit=-10;
    threshold=0.0;
```
3. CONST
```
    noofcharacters=80;
```

SECTION 20-3-2

1. VAR
```
    frequency,hipass,lowpass,bandpass:REAL;
    omega,f,leftbracket,rightbracket:CHAR;
    error, endofdata,hipassswitch,lowpassswitch,bandpassswitch:BOOLEAN;
    noofstages,n,index,power:INTEGER;
```

SECTION 20-3-3*a*

1. type
   day = (mon,tues,wed,thurs,fri,sat,sun);
3. change wire size to AWG18, AWG20, AWG22

SECTION 20-3-3*b*

1.
```
type
  weekday = (1,2,3,4,5,6,7);
  month = (1,2,3,4,5,6,7,8,9,10,11,12);
var
  birthday;weekday;
  birthmonth:month;
```

SECTION 20-3-3*c*

1.
```
const
  start = 1;
  finish = 10:
type
  currentrange = 1..10;
  frequency = 60..100;
  switch = 0..1;
  index = start..finish;
  range = -5..5;
```

SECTION 20-3-3*d*

1.
```
type
  index = 1..5;
  upper = 5..10;
  alphabet = 'A'..'Z';
  number = '0'..'9';
var
  lorange:index;
  hirange:upper;
  letter:alphabet;
  digit:number;
```
3.
```
var
  bignumber:1000..maxint;
```

SECTION 20-4-1

1. T,blank,blank,1,s,.,blank
   There is no location defined for msgbuffer[35]
3. (a)
```
CONST
  numberofints = 100
VAR
  buffer:array[1..numberofints] of integer;
```
   (b)
```
VAR
  buffer:array[1..100] of integer;
```
5.
```
VAR
  valves:array[1..37] of boolean;
```

SECTION 20-4-2

1. No. of resistors produced by different machines each day of a month; Airport landings and days of the month (several airports); Numbers of people with various diseases across several cities; population density by streets and avenues; frequency spectra with time.

```
VAR
  resistors:array[1..noofmachines,1..30] of integer;
  landings:array[1..noofairport,1..30] of integer;
  infected:array[1..disease,1..city] of integer;
  density:array[1..avenue,1..street] of integer;
  spectra:array[1..freq,1..maxtime] of real;
```

3. Add the following to const: noofdays=31;, and add a third dimension to each array definition [1..noofdays].

SECTION 20-4-3

1. If base type has n values, associated set type has 2^n values (n=3, therefore the set type can have 6 values).

SECTION 20-4-4

1. Output is a standard identifier.
3. type wirerecord=

```
  RECORD
    signalname:packed array[1..16]of char;
    source:packed array[1..10] of char;
    destination:packed array[1..10] of char;
    wiresize:integer;
    length:real;
    END;
```

SECTION 20-4-5

1. A collection of data.
3. EOF marker.
5. var

```
  products:text;
```

7. The variables mail and greeting are files, each containing a packed array of 100 characters.

SECTION 20-5

1. The identifier ^listelement has been used before it is defined. This is one case in which this is permitted. There is nothing wrong with this arrangement.

REVIEW PROBLEMS

1. freq100Hz, Final, Timeconstant, wait1, out1voltage
3. reserved words: DOWNTO,LABEL. standard identifiers: COS,BOOLEAN,ABS,[,:=. not recognized:&. user-defined: DOWNTOEARTH.
5. 0.25E-1, −0.65E01,0.2370E2, −0.1024E04,0.265E0

7. decimal point, comma.
9. Interchange order.
11. type
    guncolor=(red,green,blue);
13. (a) var
        matrix:array[1..3,1..5] of integer;
    (b) matrix[2,4]

REVIEW QUESTIONS

1. Identifiers are names.
3. integer,real,boolean,real,enumerated,subrange.
5. true,false
7. 'A'<'B'<...'Z' and '0'<'1'<...<'9'
9. Packed array: storage of several components of an array into each word of computer memory.

CHAPTER 21

SECTION 21-1-1

1. (a) int1+int2 (b) 1−x+x*x/2−x*x*x/6 (c)a*b/3 (d) a+b*c (e) (b−a)/(c+d)
3. (a)true (b) −1 (c) 2 (d) 5.0 (e)true (f)5 (g)−0.1 (h)true (i) true
5. array[1]*array[10]

SECTION 21-1-2

1. (a) x*x—a*a (b) a/4.0*x*x (c) 4.0*k−6.0*k1*k2 (d)r*r/a2*10.0 (e) x+y/(z+w)
3. (a) operator omitted (b) operator omitted (c) two adjacent operators (d) operator omitted (e) O.K.

SECTION 21-1-3

1. not(first and second) and (first or second)

SECTION 21-1-4

1. All true.

SECTION 21-1-5

1. type
    electricalpart=(res,caps,inds,tran,ic,diodes,fus,sw,relay);
   var
    part:electricalpart;
    ...
   The required expression is not(part=(res or caps or inds))

SECTION 21-1-6

1. ('a','e','i','o','u',())
3. both false.

SECTION 21-2-1

1. tananglex := sin(x)/cos(x);
3.
```
var
  m:array[1..5] of integer;
  result:integer;
begin
result:=abs(m[1]-3)+abs(m[2]-3)+abs(m[3]-3)+abs(m[4]-3)+
abs(m[5]-3)
end.
```

SECTION 21-2-2

1.
```
var
  root1,root2,a,x,b,c:real;
begin
  x:=sqrt(sqr(b)-4.0*a*c);
  root1:=(-b+x)/(2.0*a);
  root2:=(-b-x)/(2.0*a)
end.
```

SECTION 21-2-4

1.
```
var
  msg:array[1..10] of char;
begin
  msg[1]:=pred(msg[1]);
          ...
  msg[10]:=pred(msg[10])
end.
```
3. both true.

SECTION 21-2-5

1. second,third,fourth,(error),0,1

SECTION 21-3-1*b*

1. The coin may have a value of half dollar.

SECTION 21-3-1*c*

1. Illegal.

SECTION 21-3-2

1.
```
var
  sum,number:integer;
begin
  sum:=0.0;
  number:=1;
repeat
```

```
    sum: = sum + number;
    number: = number + 1;
  until number> = 500;
  end.
```

SECTION 21-3-3

1. message[index]: = chr(127-ord(message[index]));
3. ord('r') = 114;127 − 114 = 13; 'r' will be coded as carriage return; the message will include a termination character where it should not; use a termination character which cannot be confused (i.e., 255).

SECTION 21-3-4

1. Change highest = 100;
3. sum: = 0.0

```
   for index: = 1 to 50 do
     sum: = sum + sqr(2*index);
```

SECTION 21-3-5

1. for index = 2 to 99 do

```
     begin
       sum: = 0.0;
         for smooth: = (index − 1) to (index + 1) do
           begin
             sum: = sum + array(smooth);
             array[index]: = sum/3.0
           end;
     end.
```

REVIEW PROBLEMS

1. (a) a,b,c,d = identifiers = factors = terms
   (a + b) = term + term = simple expression = factor
   (c + d) = term + term = simple expression = factor
   (a + b)*(c + d) = factor*factor = term = simple expression = expression
   (b) a,b,c,d = identifiers = factors
   a and b = factor and factor = term
   c and d = factor and factor = term
   a and b or c and d = term or term = simple expression = expression
3. not(a and b) and (a or b)
5. jobb,jobc,4
7. (a)abs(x) (b)arctan(0.5) (c)chr(50) (d)cos(y) (e)exp(− x) (f)ln(100) (g)odd(number) (h)sin(z) (i)sqr(a + b) (j)sqrt(250)
9. (a)See Figs. 7-9,7-10. (b)UNTIL-test is made after process block; WHILE-test is made before process block.
13. The product of the row number and the column number.
15. sum: = 0.0;

```
    for index: = 1 to 100 do
      sum: = sum + testarray.temperature[index];
    avg: = sum/100;
```

REVIEW QUESTIONS

1. See Table 21-1.
3. See Tables 21-1 and 27-2 but remove MOD and DIV.
5. See Table 21-3.

CHAPTER 22

SECTION 22-2-1

1. while (index < 100)do
   index: = index + 1;
   for index: = 1 to 100 do
   index: = index + 1;

SECTION 22-2-2

1. Add to the program
   const
   N = 10;
   In the main section change the FOR statement
   for index: = 1 to N do

SECTION 22-2-4

1. (a) actual:a,b,x,y,p,q
   formal:h,k,l,m,w,v
   (b) By reference:h,k,l,m
   By value:w,v

SECTION 22-3

1. +9, +9,yes
3. If the answer is not real, results like 1/9 will be returned as 0. Modifications: change function type to real: in the else branch replace xpowery: = x with

```
if y<0
  then
    xpowery: = 1/x
  else
    xpowery: = x;
y: = abs(y);
```

SECTION 22-4

1. 124.7,375.3, −31325., −1.9952

SECTION 22-5

3. A = 10,B = 100

REVIEW PROBLEM

1. procedure Rtot(var RT:real;R1:real;R2:real);

```
begin
   RT: = R1*R2/(R1 + R2)
end;
```

REVIEW QUESTIONS

1. As program modules or procedures.
3. As many times as needed.

CHAPTER 23

SECTION 23-2-1

1. 100.3<CR>,25.2<CR>, −5.1 (<CR> = carriage return)
3. same as read because *input* is the standard input.

SECTION 23-2-3

1. ____sample_100 − 5.60_$
3. values for the starting column, width, or height which are out of limits (i.e., <0)

SECTION 23-3-2

1. No. Set 1 only assigns a value to the buffer. To make these equivalent (for text files only) add *put(location)* to set 1.
3. Data is written at the start of the file and the window is positioned to the next location.

REVIEW PROBLEMS

1. myfile must appear in header.
3. write(myfile,value);
   read(myfile,value);

REVIEW QUESTIONS

1. A collection of data identified by a single name.
3. The second of two normal connections. Data from the computer is normally passed to this device. Its designation is *output*.
5. All files to be used in the program including input, output.
7. read, readln.

INDEX